NEW
ENGLAND

NEW ENGLAND

A COLLECTION FROM
HARPER'S MAGAZINE

GALLERY BOOKS

Gallery Books
an imprint of W.H. Smith Publishers, Inc.
112 Madison Avenue
New York, New York 10016

This volume first published in 1990 by

The Octopus Group Limited
Michelin House, 81 Fulham Road, London SW3 6RB

This edition published in 1990 by Gallery Books
an imprint of W.H. Smith Publishers Inc.
112 Madison Avenue, New York 10016

ISBN 0 8317 4256 9

Printed in Great Britain

CONTENTS

A VACATION IN VERMONT

OF the Green Mountains one might probably say, paraphrasing Montesquieu's famous prediction about the *spirit of laws*, that they are more generally admired than visited. Poets sing without seeing them. They have furnished ready and familiar figures to orators who could hardly point them out on the map: That they stimulate the virtues of the patriot, and grow a stalwart race of men, is one of those axioms which one meets over and over again in the pages of writers who have never felt their rugged breezes, or measured the sons of Vermont in their own homes. Nor is this service which the State renders to rhetoric shared in anything like an equal degree by other States, which also have mountains, loftier perhaps and grander than its own. Even the White Mountains seem to be less frequently used, while the Alleghanies, the Rocky Mountains, and other noble chains throughout the country are almost unknown in literature and oratory. Only one thing is therefore wanting to complete the singular pre-eminence of Vermont. If her mountains and valleys were more often traversed and better known, if her children were studied through personal contact and acquaintance, the phrases of enthusiasm and admiration would not perhaps be subdued, but they would be well informed, just, rational, more serviceable to their authors, and not less complimentary to their objects.

The present article can, of course, repair this neglect only in part. To describe the whole State, or even all its leading beauties, would require a dozen volumes instead of as many pages; or if attempted on a small scale would be little more than a catalogue of natural objects, without those minute details which could alone justify them to the critical eye. We shall therefore take for description two favorite points in the Vermont landscape, and then invite the reader with their aid to complete the picture. One of these shall be the highest peak in the State; the other, one of the lowest valleys. The former is in the northeast, and stands guard over the Connecticut; the latter is in the southwest, and opens out into Champlain and the Hudson. Mount Mansfield will illustrate the grandeur and majesty of the Green Mountains themselves. Otter Creek irrigates a narrow vale between the mountains, and supplies the power for one of the leading industries of the State. Both regions, too, are somewhat frequented by tourists, and one of them is on the direct line of a railway.

Mount Mansfield is accessible either from the east or from the west. If from the west, the last railway station is Underhill, where there is a popular summer hotel, and whence carriages can ascend as far as the Half-way House. For the rest of the distance the tour is only for pedestrians, but there is a good foot-path, and a succession of views, as one ascends, affords a pleasant diversion, relieves the labor, and prepares for the final panorama which is revealed from the summit. The favorite route is, however, by way of Stowe, which lies southeast of the mountain. It is reached by stage from Morrisville, eight miles distant on the St. Johnsbury and Lake Champlain Railroad, or from the better known and more convenient station of Waterbury, ten miles distant, on the Central Vermont Railroad. This great thoroughfare furnishes the means of easy access from New York and Boston, and connects with the more important lines of communication in all directions.

The tourist who like myself chooses the last described course finds at Waterbury the final traces of a corrupt urban civilization. Beyond here all is primitive, idyllic, Arcadian; at Waterbury the contentious hackman still survives. But it is a mild form of contention, sobered apparently and rendered decorous by the clear air, or the solemn mountains, or the grave religious tone of a Vermont village. We had missed the stage, and the runners for several livery-stables offered to provide special transportation. Their rivalry, though really keen, was suppressed into a sympathetic desire to furnish the traveller the most comfortable, the swiftest, and safest conveyance; and from this desire every low, mercenary consideration was sternly banished. "Don't take that other fellow's team," said one of them, in a sad tone; "the last time he went over, a wheel run off, and he nearly killed his party." "That man," retorted the other, brushing a kindly tear out of his eye, "lost his way last week, and was five hours on the road." Then a third began, in a mild, expostulating voice: "Ladies and gentlemen, I wouldn't go with either of them men. If you *really* want to go, I have a team," etc. Thus the strife of these benevolent gentlemen went on. We finally decided to wait for the stage, and the three rivals walked off together with an air of pious resignation, humming in chorus one of Moody and Sankey's hymns. In some other parts of the world, I suppose, a writer who wished to show that the inherent friendship of these men could survive all brief professional differences would say that they repaired to the nearest bar and took a drink together. At Waterbury the evening prayer-meeting would seem to be a more fitting place for the fraternal reconciliation.

The stage is ready at last, and the two hours' drive, especially if one has an outside seat, is no unpleasant experience on a July evening. It is the very heart of the Green Mountains. The road is good; the hills are neither too prolonged nor too abrupt. Enticing trout streams shoot across the way or ripple along its side. Mount Mansfield and Camel's Hump are seen, now on one hand, now on the other, as we pursue our sinuous course. The farms are neat, orderly, and apparently prosperous, although the oats and wheat seem to have a hard battle for life with the rocks and the sand. The people are plain, but cheerful, civil, and obliging. One observes little of that outward sullenness by which in some other parts of the country

the poorer farmers take revenge on society for inequalities that are really due to their own idleness and improvidence. The Vermont farmer works, saves, keeps clear of mortgages, and—is polite.

At a little village where we stopped to water the horses a Green Mountain boy of some seventy summers, wrinkled and browned, but with flexible muscles in his gaunt frame and a smart twinkle in his eyes, entertained the passengers with some conversation.

"Goin' up to Stowe?"

"Yes."

"Ever been there?"

"No."

"Wa'al, our girls about these parts they've all gone to the White Mountains."

"Indeed! That's surprising. There's such fine scenery right here at home, why do they go to the White Mountains?"

"Why do they go to the White Mountains? Wa'al, they go there because they git three dollars a week."

"Oh!" rejoined the coach, hastily, with some embarrassment; "we had not thought of it in that light."

"Yes, sir," added the veteran, clinching his argument—"yes, sir, one of my girls gits three dollars a week, and don't have nothing to do but wash tumblers." And he bowed kindly as the stage moved away.

It seemed fitting to one of our party, a cynical person, to remark afterward that even washing tumblers day after day might become monotonous, and exclude the opportunities for that æsthetic culture now so much needed by domestic servants. "Still," he added, "if the newspapers may be trusted, they have the society of Dartmouth students in the busy season."

Let us respect honest toil. Not all Vermont girls are drawn to the White Mountains even by the liberal conditions which are there offered. Enough of them at least remain to do the service of the Mount Mansfield House, and to do it well. Neat, quick, intelligent, obliging, they lose no caste by earning their way; in winter they are the belles of "society." Brawny young farmers will find them the best of wives, and if another war should afflict the country, their sons will rush to arms not less promptly than did their fathers and brothers twenty years ago.

Stowe is a typical Vermont village of some one thousand inhabitants. The houses are nearly all white, and the white houses nearly all have green shutters,

MOUNT MANSFIELD FROM STOWE.

though slight differences in the styles of architecture and a modest discrimination in the choice of flowers and the arrangement of flower beds afford a partial satisfaction to the eye. There is a small white church, and its spire, or "steeple," as the parishioners call it, shoots ambitiously upward into the clear blue air. There is a hotel, the Mount Mansfield House, built in 1864, and for some time in charge of a veteran Boston journalist—a spacious building, with broad verandas and long halls, with vast *salons*, where the waltz may safely be attempted, and well-disposed lawns, across which the croquet balls bound from morning till night, and the harmless missiles of tennis make their abrupt flights. From "Sunset Hill," a sharp elevation back of the hotel, the village resembles a flock of geese on the wing, the two main streets diverging toward the east and the west, while the apex, where the leader may be imagined, points timidly toward Waterbury on the south. Many other things may also be seen from Sunset Hill.

In the rear is the Worcester range; south, Camel's Hump; west, Mount Mansfield itself; and in the intervals, especially toward the northwest, the green valley with its silver streams, its well-stocked farms, its neat farm-houses, with their barns and other buildings grouped in little colonies about them. This is, too, a good point from which to begin the work of seeing a man's face in the profile of Mount Mansfield. The illustration provides all the materials of the problem. The features are all there in bold relief—forehead, nose, mouth, lips, chin—and the reader who fails to catch the resemblance will never understand why the mountain was called "Mans-field." He will be reduced to the false theory that its namesake was a famous English judge.

The distance from Stowe to the summit of the mountain is about nine miles. For five miles the route follows the ordinary country road through a pleasant valley; then it breaks off into the mountain, and winds about by easy grades to the top.

The carriage road has now been open several years, and the ascent can be made in any vehicle with the greatest comfort.

The way is thickly wooded—along the lower part with beech, maple, birch, and even oak, which, however, gradually disappear, until the evergreen varieties alone remain, and these seem ill satisfied with their existence. Shade is therefore abundant, and the sun's rays are little felt. But this is at the cost of another form of enjoyment. Short of the summit itself no satisfactory view is obtained, with perhaps a partial exception in favor of the Half-way House. This seems once to have been a habitable house, at least for horses; though, thanks to the fretful porcupine, it now offers hospitality neither to quadrupeds nor to bipeds. The hedgehogs have attacked the stalls and floor with ferocity and persistence, and have created vast intervals in the most solid partitions. The little animals are abundant all over the mountain, and many wild stories are told of their exploits. A horse belonging to the hotel was attacked by one, said John, the driver, and they afterward pulled seven hundred quills out of the poor beast; and if John had been coining a story he would not have been so recklessly exact.

Half a mile before the summit is reached the woods open, and the carriage climbs a stiff rocky ledge for the rest of the way.

The Nose towers up directly above us, and the other features stretch away in the distance, massive, solemn, forbidding.

The description of the mountain and its views may properly be prefaced by a few useful facts and figures. The highest point, the Chin, is 4359 feet above sea-level, and 3670 above the village of Stowe. The Nose, the next peak, is 340 feet lower; the Forehead, 160 feet below the Nose.

THE NOSE AND SMUGGLER'S NOTCH.

THE MOUNTAIN ROAD.

From the Nose to the Chin—the extreme points of ordinary exploration—the distance is about one and a half miles. The mountain has long been accessible to adventurous tourists, but it is only within the last twenty years, or since the opening of the Mount Mansfield House, that they have come in any number or regularly. The completion of the carriage road to the summit brought, of course, a large increase of both transient and permanent guests.

We can now examine the face of the giant as calmly and fearlessly as the Lilliputians walked about over the prostrate Gulliver.

To reach the point of the Nose involves a sharp though short climb, facilitated by a flight of rude steps which have been formed by the ledges of the rock. The old Latin line must be reversed before it can be applied to the Nose. The ascent is safe and not difficult, but the descent— *hic labor, hoc opus est.* The stone is as smooth and slippery as ice; and a single false step would precipitate one two hundred feet or more to the bottom. This is

on the west. The northern side is nearly perpendicular; and although the process which shaped it began thousands of years ago, it has not yet ceased. From time to time immense masses of rock detach themselves and plunge into the abyss below, where they still lie heaped upon one another in wild disorder. One of these terrible bowlders was formerly poised on the very end of the Nose, almost without visible means of support. It was supposed that it could be pried loose by hand, but repeated attempts led only to disappointment. One day in 1859, however, it started voluntarily, and rolled down the precipice, shaking the mountain like an earthquake, and at the bottom bursting into a thousand fragments. A party of men and women had been on the rock but half an hour before it fell, and others had been strolling about the foot of the cliff where it lodged.

The Summit House is situated at the foot of the Nose, on the eastward slope of the ridge. It is a frame building of two stories, with ample balconies, comfortable rooms, and a satisfactory cuisine. Its

MOUNT WASHINGTON FROM MOUNT MANSFIELD.

manager at the time of our visit was De- mis, a French Canadian, who had been so long on the mountain that he could hardly walk on level ground. He was, of course, well stocked with stories, most of them based on personal experience. Thunder-storms on the summit are not infrequent, but Demis remembered one in particular which broke forth without any warning on a bright sunny day. He was sitting in the "parlor," when he saw a flash, and before he knew it the room was full of lightning, and he was up to his knees in the electric fluid. "I was half stunted to death," added the veteran Gaul, somewhat obscurely. And in proof of his story he showed us where the same bolt had struck the end of the Nose, leav- ing a long scar, brightly polished as by some mechanical instrument. Demis's only permanent companions on the mount- ain were five cats, a few chickens, and Dolly the cow. Dolly had lived nine years in this lofty region. Her predecessor was there seventeen years. An artificial grass- plot, built up much as the peasants on the Rhine create soil for vineyards, was her

only pasture, except such browsing as she might get among the evergreens and ferns; but she seemed happy, and in the winter, when brought down to the village, she re- turned invariably to the summit as often as she could escape.

For the walk to the Chin some little time is necessary, though the rise is grad- ual and not troublesome. The ridge of the mountain is narrow and nearly bare, a few dwarfish cedars, and a carpet of moss softer and richer than the finest tapestry of Smyrna, being the only forms of vegetable life. By a brisk walk the visitor can in fifteen minutes reach the Lips. These are mere accumulations of great bowlders, deposited there by volcan- ic or glacial movements, and not specially interesting, except, perhaps, the so-called "Rock of Terror," which, poised precari- ously on its apex, seems ready on slight provocation to roll down, and the caves, which are formed by series of overlying bowlders, though one of them is of consid- erable depth. Geologists have found evi- dence for the glacial theory in scars or scratches made on the surface of the rocks here and there in a direction pretty consistently from the northwest to the southeast. But the eye of the layman will not readily find or recognize them.

From the Chin the spectator has one of the most comprehensive, variegated, and cludes the spires and towers of Montreal, one hundred miles distant. Directly beneath, and between the first and second chins, lies the Lake of the Clouds; lower down, the dark recesses of the Smuggler's Notch; and across this, the Sterling Mountains. Moving to the east, the eye falls first upon a succession of dark and heavy ridges, thickly wooded, giving and receiving shadows in

OLD WOMAN OF THE MOUNTAINS.

ROCK OF TERROR.

beautiful views to be found in all New England. Toward the west, the eye, starting from the base of the mountain, runs over the Winooski Valley, threaded by roads and streams, and dotted with countless white villages; takes in Lake Champlain, which on a clear day can be seen for nearly its entire length; and is arrested only by the Adirondacks in the remote horizon. On the north, the outlook is even more extensive, and at rare intervals, under peculiarly favorable conditions, even includes endless variety; farther away, the valley of the Connecticut; and beyond, the White Mountains. Mount Washington itself can sometimes be seen, though indistinctly. The picture is completed by Stowe and its neighbors, nestling in the rich valley, and directly south the rival peak of Camel's Hump and the main chain of the Green Mountains. Such is, in general, the scope of the view afforded from the summit of Mount Mansfield. The countless details which give it grace, picturesqueness, and value can not even be enumerated, but must be left with the assurance that not one which the imagination could crave will be found wanting by the most exacting lover of nature.

The neighborhood of Stowe affords a multitude of other charming resorts, some of which must be at least mentioned. One of these is the Smuggler's Notch, a narrow pass between Mount Mansfield and the Sterling Mountain. It is supposed to have been used in former times by smugglers, as it is an easy and convenient connection between western and eastern Vermont, and a link in the chain of communication between Montreal and Boston, once an important thoroughfare for contraband traffic. At the summit of the pass there is a deserted inn, the Notch House. The local guide-book says it affords accommodation for man and beast; and this is true, for if the visitor brings with him sandwiches for the man and oats for the beast, they can be eaten in the ruins of the edifice. Otherwise a common famine will be the result. A good road following the course of a noble trout stream ends only at the Notch House, and the source of the stream, the "Mammoth Spring," which is not improperly named. Beyond the house a foot-path leads through a succession of mighty bowlders which have fallen from the cliffs above, under abrupt precipices which stretch up on either side to appalling heights, through damp ravines where the ferns grow in fantastic luxuriance and beauty, finally issues at the western mouth of the pass, and then descends swiftly to the valley. It is customary in visiting the Notch to include also Bingham's Falls, named after an eminent citizen of Stowe, who has done much to make the region accessible and agreeable to tourists. They are composed of a series of chasms worn in the solid rock.

Other attractions are Moss Glen Cascade, only four miles from Stowe, in Worcester Mountains; Gold Brook, a favorite drive; Morrisville Falls and Johnson Falls, somewhat more distant; and various other choice rural nooks which will well repay a visit. The roads are, for mountain roads, uniformly good, and ladies unaccompanied ride in confidence and safety all over the country.

For loftiness, grandeur, and majesty,

Mount Mansfield is, of course, inferior to Mount Washington. Its charms are of a more modest nature. But it has, nevertheless, peculiar advantages of its own, which will not escape the eye of discerning visitors, and which to a large class of persons will recommend it even above the White Mountains. One of these is the singular extent and freedom of the view which may be had from its summit. Instead of being only one of a vast army of peaks, and distinguished from its comrades merely by a slight superiority in height, it is more like an isolated structure rising out of a surrounding plain. In at least two directions, east and west, the landscape is unobstructed for a hundred miles. The country lies spread out in a vast plateau, beginning at the very base of the mountain, and enlivened by every element which belongs to a complete picture. The landscape itself is therefore an ample reward for the toil and expense of the visit. But there is a further felicity in the exemption of the real lover of nature from the intrusion of unsympathetic Philistines. Unfortunately no part of the world in these days of rapid and cheap travel is absolutely free from the shoddyite, the cockney, and the snob; but Mount Mansfield as a resort is in this respect at least comparatively favored. It is little frequented by "fashionable" people, and even less so by that still lower class who pursue and imitate fashionable people. Serious, thoughtful, and appreciative persons form the larger part of its summer patrons. They who spend there one season generally spend also the next and the next; acquaintances are renewed from year to year; and in this way Mount Mansfield is gradually enrolling a considerable band of faithful, zealous, and devout disciples.

The scene changes now abruptly to another part of Vermont, and to other elements of interest and attraction. Our route lies diagonally across the State, from the Alps to the Apennines; from Mont Blanc to Carrara; from a region newly settled and still full of a wild beauty and vigor to a region rich in colonial and Revolutionary traditions, and throbbing with a varied and active industry.

The history of southwestern Vermont goes back to a time when, strictly speaking, there was no Vermont; when there was a New Hampshire and a New York, but when it was uncertain to which of

SMUGGLER'S NOTCH.

the two the valley of Otter Creek belonged. The settlers in the disputed tract hated, indeed, the "Yorkers." The bailiffs
of the western tyrant found no little difficulty in performing their duties; and if
the local chronicles are veracious, the
sturdy villagers now and then tied one of
them to a tree and, whip in hand, taught
him the error of his ways. Incidents in
this border warfare are given in Miss Hemenway's excellent *Vermont Gazetteer*,
and in various productions, poetical and
unpoetical, of home talent. Not even the
outbreak of the Revolution wholly allay-
ed this fierce hostility. There exists, for
instance, the record of a meeting of delegates from "the towns on the west side of
the Green Mountains," held September 25,

1776, in Dorset, at the house of Deacon Cephas Kent, a leading patriot, and ancestor of many eminent men, Chancellor Kent being one. There were present Colonel Seth Warner, the Revolutionary hero, several Allens, and representatives of the Chittendens, Morgans, Fays, Saffords, Robinsons, and Marshes, all historic families of Vermont. The tone of the assembly may be learned from the resolutions which were adopted. They affirm that the people of that section were tired of the "tyranny of New York toward the New Hampshire Grants"; that, for geographical reasons, they could not well co-operate with New York in the war of Independence; and that they were determined, in their participation in the common cause, to recognize only the superiority of the Continental Congress. In virtue of this, and a still higher authority, Ethan Allen demanded and obtained the surrender of Fort Ticonderoga. On this basis the Vermonters fought the battle of Bennington, and thus prepared the way for the surrender of Burgoyne himself. Every town and hamlet throughout the region has its own proud Revolutionary legends, its own noble list of martyrs, its own heroes. Take Dorset again. The champion of Revolutionary Dorset is a valiant citizen who, aided by one ally, captured at Bennington seven prisoners, one of them a colonel, and brought them safely off the field. It is evident that such a people would not submit to the authority even of New York if it were unjust and distasteful. By their efforts they won, in fact, a double independence—first their independence, with the other colonies, from England, and then their independence as a State in the Union of States.

In the neighborhood of Dorset arise two streams, which, after this single early meeting, turn their backs rudely upon each other, and thenceforth flow in opposite directions. The Battenkill bears southward for twenty miles or more, then strikes westward through the mountains, and onward to the Hudson. Otter Creek is true throughout to its Vermont allegiance. Its course is north, and it finally empties into Lake Champlain, at Vergennes. The valley through which the two flow is narrowest about the point where the Battenkill leaves it; obtains its most striking natural characteristics near Manchester and Dorset, and then, pro-

ceeding northward, gradually widens out into a spacious and fertile plain, lying between the main line of the Green Mountains and Lake Champlain.

The first of the towns just named, Manchester, is, in respect to outward beauty and to popularity as a summer resort, easily superior to all the others. It lies on a high plateau formed by a long, low spur of Mount Equinox; has one broad street, luxuriantly shaded; is calm, decorous, and soothing; and being well provided with hotels, is favorably known to the annual fugitives from New York and Boston. The ascent of Equinox is easily made, and the vicinity affords an abundance of delightful excursions.

One of these is, for example, to Dorset Mountain. It should first be explained, however, that the term Green Mountains is applied only to the range east of the valley, that on the west being known as the Taconic Mountains. Between the two chains there are also some striking differences. The Taconic Mountains are higher, bolder, and more imposing. The water which flows down from them is much harder than that from the east. They are also much richer in natural deposits, yielding marble, slate, and a superior quality of the ordinary building limestone. Mount Equinox is one of the peaks in the Taconic range. Dorset Mountain, five miles farther north, is another, and the one at which Otter Valley properly begins.

I have adhered to the older name, Dorset Mountain, although an attempt has been made to provide another, more ambitious, more sonorous, but not more honorable or dignified. This upstart term is Mount Æolus, and the author of the unhappy innovation is Professor Charles H. Hitchcock, who in 1861 visited the region with a class of students from Amherst College. Dr. Hitchcock gave the following explanation of the phenomenal absence of snow in Dorset Valley: "Æolus, the god of the winds, fled from fallen Greece, and took up his abode in the caves and marble halls of this mountain. When this god calls home Boreas, driving before him snow and hail, there comes also Auster, with warm breath and weeping showers, and the frost-work volute and scroll soon disappear." The ceremony of christening was performed. Standing on a natural platform near the mouth of the cave, the party broke a bottle of water over the mountain, the chorus of the winds furnished music, and when this had subsided a poem was read, of which the following stanza is a sample:

> "Then blow, ye winds, ye breezes all,
> Obey your king's command;
> He sits in this grand marble hall;
> Ye are his servant band."

six wide, and it is said that explorers have penetrated forty or fifty rods without finding any end.

If Dorset Mountain is little favored by snow, it has plenty of snowy marble. Viewed from the east, the whole hill-side seems to be ridged and furrowed with quarries, and the vast accumu-

SKETCHES NEAR STOWE.

Thus Dorset Mountain became Mount Æolus; for the new term has obtained some little currency, and has the authority even of print.

The cave to which allusion has been made is no insignificant affair. It is composed of a succession of rooms, one of which is eighty-six feet long and thirty-

lations of débris tell the tale of years of industrious burrowing in the earth.

The Dorset quarries were the earliest to be discovered and worked in Vermont, and their products are still, in respect to quality, among the best. The first quarry was opened in 1785, six years before the State was admitted into the Union, and it is still owned by the descendants of the original proprietors. This discovery was the great sensation of the day. People came hundreds of miles to get the crude slabs for fire-place stones and other domestic uses, and a brisk traffic in the new commodity soon sprang up. In 1808 a second quarry was opened, and subsequently many others, following in rapid succession. All but two of these are still in operation. The channelling process, now familiar to mining engineers, was introduced in 1841; the first derrick for hoisting the blocks in 1848; the first tunnelling in 1859. In 1818 the first attempt at sawing marble was made, but it was many years before the experiment proved successful. For a long time after these works were opened they had little competition, and the demand for their products far exceeded the supply; but the trade was subsequently injured by the introduction of Italian marbles, and the discovery of other Vermont quarries, especially those near Rutland.

Of this town, Rutland, some patriarch who should die now might say that he found it brick or frame and left it marble. The chaste, cold, glossy stone is almost oppressively plenty in this smart and thriving village, and meets the eye in a multitude of forms and uses—buildings, pavements, walls, besides interior decoration and finishing. Rutland is in fact the best advertisement of its own leading industry. To use the language of the exchange, its principal capitalists are already "in marble" before their death, and without the aid of the sculptor. Concerns like the Vermont Marble Company, Sheldon and Slason, Flint Brothers, Ripley and Sons, Gilson and Woodfin, and others, with their fifteen or twenty quarries, give an idea of the extent to which the marble interest engrosses the capacity and the resources of this neighborhood.

The more important quarries and works are situated north and west of the town itself, at Centre Rutland, West Rutland, Sutherland Falls, and lesser points in the vicinity. The Vermont Marble Company is, in fact, domiciled at all three of these places. It has finishing-works at Centre Rutland, quarries at West Rutland, and both quarries and mills at Sutherland Falls. At the first-named point no marble is excavated, but there is a splendid water-power, which naturally is not neglected,

and here one can observe every stage in the process except the quarrying itself. The marble is brought to the mills in massive cubes, is sawed, turned, chiselled, polished, mounted, and emerges as tombstones, capitals, cornices, columns, mantelpieces, and table-tops. Much of this work, especially the hand-work, can, of course, be studied in every place where people die and have monuments set up by the local stone-cutter over their graves, but the heavier preliminary labor is best to be seen near the quarries themselves.

The marble is delivered at the mills in elongated cubes—parallelopipeds, I suppose Euclid would say—from ten to fifteen feet long and three to five feet square, and placed on the frames for sawing. An expert will then decide as to the manner of reduction, that is, the thickness and number of the slabs, according to the quality, the shape and size of the block, or the special nature of the orders to be filled. In outward appearance a "gang," as a set of saws is called, resembles the old-fashioned upright saw-mill, except that the vertical frame contains not one but many saws, arranged at different intervals, corresponding to the desired thickness of the cuts. One process, therefore, divides an entire block into slabs. The saw has, it should be added, no teeth. The cutting is the joint effect of the hard edge of the steel blade and the wet sand which is fed into the opening, and thus produces an incisive friction. The ordinary progress is about two and a half inches an hour, and the gangs work night and day. The polishing of small pieces is done on a revolving iron disk some twelve feet in diameter. The marble is thrown upon this, and caught by fixed wooden strips like the radii of a circle, while the motion of the wheel, which is supplied with sand and water, furnishes the attrition. It takes two or three hours to polish a surface down one inch. Heavy pieces are smoothed by hand, with the aid of pumice-stone. Marble is turned into circular shapes in a lathe, exactly like iron, and is bored with an ordinary dry drill.

The West Rutland quarries are not, like those of Dorset, in the side of a great mountain, but seem to form the bed of a low hill or ridge rising very little above a level. The excavations follow, therefore, nearly vertical lines directly into the earth; and the cuts themselves, which are shaped to the seams of the stone, have at the sur-

A MARBLE QUARRY.

.face an eastward inclination of about forty degrees, then of sixty, and again of twenty, until in some places they are almost perpendicular. The cuts are marked off from fifty to seventy feet long, twelve to sixteen feet wide, and about four feet deep, and are afterward subdivided into desired or convenient sizes. Some of this work, under ledges and in close quarters, is still necessarily done by hand; but the substitution of machinery for manual labor is nowhere more strikingly illustrated than in a Vermont marble quarry. Three of the machines thus used may be described. For the diamond borer or drill the power is steam, and the work is done by two drills terminating in diamond points about one foot apart. By going frequently over the course a close line of holes is formed, not unlike the perforated division between postage stamps, and as the instrument works with great rapidity, it makes a cut one foot deep and seventy-five feet long in one day. It can be adjusted to any angle near the perpendicular, and is used for upright drilling. Another machine, the Wardwell, for vertical work, is a spe-

cies of locomotive on a track, along which it moves backward and forward, and makes complete cuts by means of systems of chisels acting on the trip-hammer principle. There are two of these, four or five feet apart, and both sides of a block are therefore cut at once. The horizontal cut is made by the Ingersoll drill. It is a small instrument hanging and movable on a fixed cylinder, and adjustable there to an angle either above or below the horizontal. The power is supplied in the form of steam in rubber pipes. Besides

SUTHERLAND FALLS.

these three leading varieties there are other machines, differing in slight details, all of use for special kinds of work, but difficult to describe in the language of a layman.

The final rupture between a block and its ancient bed is an interesting process. Let us suppose the two cuts to be made, one nearly vertical, and the other, or horizontal one, at right angles to it, and both one or two feet deep. A series of wedges is then inserted into the openings, and a man with a heavy hammer goes along tapping them lightly one after another.

As they are driven in, the men listen sharply for the effect, the crack gradually widens, the great mass of stone begins to heave and swell under the strain, the quick ear of the experts detects the critical moment, and a simultaneous blow on all the wedges throws the monster loose. Now and then, of course, a failure is made, and a block splits in two. But the judgment of the workmen is singularly correct, and the block is generally thrown out in its full integrity.

At West Rutland there are half a dozen or more quarries belonging to as many different firms; and others are strewn along the hill-sides throughout the region, especially between Rutland and Sutherland Falls, and north as far as Brandon. One of the finest quarries in respect to quality, connected with one of the most extensive mills, is that at Sutherland Falls. The common laborers are nearly all foreigners — French Canadians, Irish, and Swedes—but they are temperate and orderly; strikes are rare; and here, as in the other marble districts, the proprietors have shown themselves the friends of their employés by building neat little cottages, founding libraries and reading-rooms, and endowing churches. For the Green Mountain State likes to boast of its men as well as of its mountains.

THE DUTCH INFLUENCE IN NEW ENGLAND

FOUR years ago it was proposed by a cosmopolitan New-Englander, the Hon. S. R. Thayer, American Minister at the Hague, to erect at Delfshaven some durable memorial in recognition of Dutch hospitality to the Pilgrims while in Holland. In the ungracious criticism of a denominational newspaper it was intimated that the sons of the Pilgrims had no call to erect such a memorial anywhere in Holland. Such "hospitality" was unsuspected at the time, and it "has taken near two centuries and three-quarters to discover it."

The *condition* of a majority of the English refugees for conscience' sake in the Dutch land of liberty was one of poverty and obscurity. In England most of them had been farm laborers or mechanics. In Leyden the rank and file of John Robinson's congregation probably had little or nothing to do socially with the hundreds of other Englishmen—university students, merchants, military men —then dwelling also in "ye goodly and pleasante citie." Their settlement and church in Robinson's house along Clock Alley were modest enough, but one hundred and thirty-five English families were gathered in the other English church, Rev. Robert Durie pastor, whose house of worship was next door to their own. We have read well the records in the city archives of Leyden, and along with the names in Dutch spelling of these future beginners of New England there is a pathetic monotony of *saaiwerker, baeywerker, brouwersknect, handschoenmaker, bombasijnwerker, wolcammer, hoedenmaker*, etc. That is, they were workers in or makers of serge, baize, gloves, hats, clocks, kegs, stockings, pumps; or they were dyers, coopers, brewers, servants, etc., with whom the richer folks belonging to the English and Scottish church in the great city of Leyden had little in common. The Separatists were therefore thrown all the more closely with their Dutch fellow-Calvinists of like social rank. Not only were their leaders facile in speaking and reading the Dutch vernacular, but probably one-half of the Plymouth settlers were born in Leyden, and picked up Dutch just as the offspring of aliens among us imbibe American English.

Despite their occasional poverty from lack of employment, the Separatists were treated well, and richly enjoyed the vital freedom they lacked in England. It is to their *condition* that every one of the plaintive references to their life in the republic, and found in the writings of Winslow, Bradford, and others, refer. Always in speaking of "ye Low-Cuntries in which they had lived," their words are those of praise. Hear what Bradford, in the name of the Governor and Council, says in his letter (dated in old style) of March 19, 1627, to the Dutch at New Amsterdam:

"Now, forasmuch as this [alliance between England and Holland against Spain, their common foe] is sufficient to unite us together in love and good neighborhood in all our dealings; yet are many of us tied by the good and courteous entreaty [treatment] which we have found in your country, having lived there many years with freedom and good content, as many of our friends do to this day; for which we are bound to be thankful and our children after us, and shall never forget the same, but shall heartily desire your good and prosperity as our own forever." Still again Bradford wrote from Plymouth, October 1, 1627: "Acknowledging ourselves tied in a strict obligation unto your country and state for the good entertainment and free liberty which we had, and our brethren and countrymen yet there have and do enjoy, under your most honorable Lords and States."

The unmistakable feelings of the Pilgrims themselves are here expressed at a time when Plymouth had many reminders of the land and the city, "which had been," as Bradford still later wrote, "their resting place near 12 years," "fair and bewtifull," "of a sweete situation." Nowhere on the map of the United States does one find the name of Scrooby, Bawtry, or Austerfield, but at Plymouth the oldest thoroughfare in New England is appropriately named Leyden Street. Here in 1630, when the Pilgrim rill of immigration--almost wholly from Leyden—had ceased, while the Puritan flood had begun, were many proofs that the first settlers of New England, like those of New Netherland, had come directly, not from Great Britain, but from Holland. Some of the tangible evidences were Dutch seeds, books. provisions—food for body and mind —Dutch ovens, cradles, furniture, tools, and hardware of all sorts, especially of the Delft sort (such as saved the *Mayflower* from going to pieces during a storm at sea, as Bradford tells), military gear and equipment, clothing, books printed on Dutch presses, spinning-wheels, and kitchen implements. These were things seen and temporal, capable of preservation in a museum. In addition there were realities not tangible, but as traceable as water-marks in paper. Distinctively Dutch influences in the primal basic life of New England are clear to the unprejudiced student.

In this paper we shall pass over the political influences, of which we have elsewhere written,* and glance at the procedure of these men of "distinctive America" in things social.

There are good reasons, other than religious, why these Englishmen who had lived or had been born in the Dutch Republic departed at so many points from ancestral precedents, and followed lines of development distinct from those of their countrymen in every part of the world, not excepting those south of Delaware Bay.

Coming from the land of feudal holdings, manors, primogeniture, and entail, they at once abolished these and other features and relics of feudal society, and distributed property, when no will had been made, equally among the intestate owner's children. In this radical procedure were they acting, as Bradford in his history, quoting a Dutch law-book, says they did in their marriage customs, "according to ye laudable custome of ye Low-Cuntries"? Or were they "reverting," like academic students, to the primitive Germanic system of towns (*tuin, ton*) and common lands? Bradford, who was the chief statesman of the Plymouth men, as Brewster was the theological and ecclesiastical guide, remarks with practical wisdom on marriage as being that upon which "many questions aboute inheritances doe depende." Whom did they follow, the ancient farmers in the "mark" of Tacitus' time, or those of the seventeenth century whom they saw before their eyes in the various United

States of Netherland? If the founders of New England were acquainted with the primitive Teutonic social order, they have most skilfully concealed their erudition.

Rather, is it not more reasonable to suppose that they followed the precedent they had seen in "ye Low-Cuntries," in which were the common acres, pastures, forests, to which daily issued, out of the town or dorp, boers or farmers, shepherds, swine and cattle, for work and food? These things in the late sixteenth and early seventeenth centuries were not matters of antiquity or archæology. They were right before the eyes of the tens of thousands of English folk dwelling in the Dutch Republic.

Wherever the Dutch farmers in America who refused to live under the semi-feudal patroons made their settlements they discarded the artificial un-Netherlandish system of patroons and manors, and followed their ancestral and familiar methods of commonage in land, representation in government, and democratic ideas and instincts of freedom inherited for ages. What they would not allow kings or clerics at home to do, they refused to patroon or West India Company. In New Netherland the history of the monopolies of the West India Company and the patroons is one thing; the history of the Dutch people is something wholly different. The first has been written; the second has not. Washington Irving's caricature still stands among the "authorities" in too many histories, so called. What the two hundred thousand Englishmen or their descendants east of the Hudson River in 1675 accomplished has been celebrated in song, story, poem, history, painting, and statue, and Forefathers' day was instituted as early as 1769. What the fewer than ten thousand people of Netherlandish blood in the Middle States achieved awaits the competent narrator.

There was published in Leyden in 1616, the composition and press-work having possibly been partly done by some of the Pilgrim printers, Ubbo Emmius' *History of Friesland*, in which the details of local organization and government of the town of this ultra-democratic Dutch province are given at length. Page after page of this book, with its account of the elections after prayer, and with written ballots, of magistrates and select-men, reads

---

* *The Influence of the Netherlands in the making of the English Commonwealth and the American Republic.* Boston: 1891.

like descriptions of early New England town meetings.

Not only did Massachusetts Pilgrims and Puritans and the Connecticut settlers—whose leaders, Davenport and Hooker, had been living several years in Holland—lay out the land in the old Teutonic manner prevalent in Friesland, but they also built their houses with stockades, gates, "a trench of six foote long and two foote broad," with common forest, pasture, and arable land, with "common fence," common herd or swine, daily assembled and led out at sound of horn, tended by day and led back by night.

After houses, land, food, and social order, the colonists' first necessity for prosperous continuance was a medium of exchange in trade. It was from the Dutch that the New-Englanders learned how to get wealthy by trading with the Indians. As they had seen their Dutch hosts excel in statesmanship, combining states in a federal republic with a written constitution under the red, white, and blue flag, with the toleration of religion, free speech, a free press, with judiciary independent of the executive, public schools, freedom of the press and of commerce, so they knew the financial abilities of the Hollanders.

In America these Dutchmen discovered Indian money, and at once turned the shell heaps of Long Island into mints. The Dutch Midas was slow but sure in making four blue and eight white beads equal to a penny. Fort Orange and Manhattan became bustling marts of trade, whence were despatched fleets of fur-laden ships to Europe; and later shingles, sawed lumber, and ginseng were exported. The Pilgrims first secured a supply of strings of wampum, blue and white, made of drilled shells, and then borrowed the process of manufacture. At first the circulation was slow, but when the red men found at Plymouth and in Connecticut a sufficient volume of currency for business, the demand was great and constant. The Pilgrims were soon able to send home cargoes more valuable than sassafras. They paid off their debts contracted in England on hard terms and undertook commendable ventures of trade. The maiden voyage of the first ship built in New England, by Winthrop in 1630, and named the *Blessing of the Bay*, was to the Dutch on Long Island to obtain a stock of Indian money. Later on, the

English settlers in the whole "Region of the Savages," Woesten-hoek or Housatonic (the aborigines talking good ordinary Dutch when they uttered this "Indian" name), got food and clothing in times of need and made money in selling ginseng to the Dutch, who opened the market in Corea, Japan, and China (after the Jesuit had discovered it in Vermont) for this once abundant American plant. It was with this ginseng, first exported to Chinese Asia and sold there by the Dutch, that the first American ships that sailed from Boston and Salem, and which carried the American flag round the world, were loaded, to be exchanged for tea, silk, and the fire-crackers without which the Fourth of July cannot be celebrated by Young America.

The Hollanders were the first to knock in the head the "bullion theory," by which Spain ruined herself in America, becoming poor and losing her colonies. The Spanish political economists taught that all wealth lay in the precious metals —gold and silver. Hence her slavery of the Indians, her greed and cruelty, and her silver fleets on the Atlantic—so often the prey of English buccaneer and Dutch *vrijbuiter*, or, as the Spaniards corrupted the term, filibuster. The Old and New Netherlanders taught both Spaniards and Englishmen that the true mines were, as Lord Bacon said, "aboveground." In soil and sea were the true lodes, and farmers, traders, fishermen, were the best miners. One never reads in American colonial history of the Dutch seeking gold like the Spaniards or Englishmen. His head was too level, and his eye too clear. Excelling as farmers, yet even more as traders, the Dutch laid the foundations of the commercial supremacy of New York by inherited instincts re-enforced by wise policy and large ideas. They gave points not only as to fish, fur, and wampum to their neighbors down East. Quickest to catch customers, they sent out their agents among the Indians, forestalling the fur and other crops. Incomparable as is the modern Boston "drummer," he is but the evolution of the Dutch *bos-loper*, or wood-ranger, who scoured the forests for trade. With perfection of dress and manners, irresistible in tongue, brainy and resourceful always, as is our commercial tourist in this Columbian year, he probably does not proportionately excel the skilful *bos-loper* who in the seventeenth century scoured the Indian villages along the Mohawk, and even to Duluth.

It was Captain John Smith—who, like all the military men in the early colonies —Gorgas, Dudley, Miles Standish, Lyon Gardiner, Leisler, Argall, Wingfield, Raleigh, had served in the Dutch armies—who first pointed out the gold mines in the ocean. Smith, who had first discovered and named both Plymouth and New England, prophesied that their main staple of wealth would be fish. So it proved. For over a century a golden codfish has hung in the legislative halls of Massachusetts as the symbol of her wealth drawn from the sea. It was Smith's prophecy that has gilded the flashing dome on Beacon Hill. He saw how the Dutch had "built Amsterdam on herring bones," had become the best fed, clothed, housed, and educated people in Europe, and handled easily the Spaniard on land and sea because of their skill in boats, hooks, and nets. "Never would Spaniard pay his debts, his friends, and his army half so truly as the Hollanders still have done by this contemptible trade in fish." The Dutch had not only taught the British the science of hunting in the deeps, how to catch whales and herring, but also how to cure food-fish, and to transmute the poorer sorts into manure for agriculture. The immigrants to America were quick to imitate, and also to improve. Those who gave the promise and potency of the later "codfish aristocracy" had qualities of mind and body equal to those of any race on earth, and a rich civilization was possible. At first, as Bradford complained and explained, their fishing did not pay, but in due time the Yankee made the "contemptible trade of fish" not only a lucrative business, but a school of heroes. They enriched their own inventive brains, furnished Friday food for all southern Europe, traded at the ends of the earth, and maintained what proved to be a permanent nursery of the United States navy. As some of them have declared, the chief motive of the settlers of the Massachusetts Bay Colony was not only the worship and glory of God, but also the catching of fish and the making of money. In both their aims they finally succeeded. The vocabulary of the deep-sea fisherman, with, for example, its "dipsy," its Dutch pronunciation of a shoal (school) of fish, bears witness to these first teachers.

It was because the English of the seventeenth century were far inferior in the knowledge and methods of agriculture to the Dutch that the first-comers to Massachusetts took so largely to the sea. In farming, gardening, floriculture, stock-raising, and breeding, the Dutch of the seventeenth century were without superiors. They were the first to introduce and acclimate the Oriental fruits, flowers, grains, and plants that are now commonplace in our parks and gardens. They invented the enclosed and covered forcing-bed, the hot-house, the winnowing fan, and the plough in its modern form. Most of the early books in English on scientific husbandry are by Dutch authors, or are translations from the land of bulbs. The Dutch first acclimated and then introduced most of the garden vegetables into England and into Atlantic colonies. They taught the use of artificial grasses and the rotation of crops. The fen country and the eastern counties of England, from which five-eighths of the settlers of New England came, were for the most part drained, reclaimed, and converted into a garden, and the chief seat of English manufacturing industry. And as in Holland and eastern England the Dutchmen changed swamps and morasses breathing malaria and fevers into dry land rich in mutton, turnips, and healthy men and women, so in America they excelled with grain, flowers, cattle, spade, and hoe. The best dikes, drainage, reclamation of land, gardens, and farms in colonial days were along the Hudson River and in the Mohawk Valley. From the first the Dutchman, though selecting the best land, at once manured the soil, and had little of that propensity to waste the resources of nature which is so characteristic of the hurried Yankee. The Dutch farmer in New York used the best tools. From these slow but sure folks the Eastern settlers learned to improve their land (having usually taken up the worst first), beautify their gardens, enrich their tables with vegetables, salads, and grains; plant the best white and carnation roses, tulips, gillyflowers, white lilies, violets, and marigolds, and those flowers that now seem so old-fashioned to us. Some of the best fruits domesticated among us came directly from the agricultural experiment stations and botanical gardens in Leyden and Amsterdam. During the century or more in which all kinds of airily fanciful and economically impossible schemes for raising silk, coffee, tea, madder, quinine, were being insisted on by the English government and proprietors, the Dutchman kept quietly improving his acres and live-stock. From the first he understood the climate and economic conditions of his new home, and relied upon the reports and experiences of the Vaderland. In this way he saved himself many a disaster and bitter disappointment, while continually improving both ground and animals. Of the latter he was almost as careful as of his children.

The Dutchman's farming tools and methods, as well as his amusements and luxuries, were later borrowed by the folks living east of the Hudson. The Yankee, though slow to imitate the painstaking of the boer, in due time learned that his root crops, vegetables, buckwheat cakes, flowers, sleds, sleighs, skates, light ploughs, winnowing-fans, axes, saw-mills, and hot-houses were better than his own. As Dr. Eggleston says, "New England cattle in early times survived the long winters rather as outlines than as oxen." The Easterners were slower than the Dutch in learning how different the climate of their new home was from that of the old country. While the Dutch thought little of travelling all the way from Albany to New York on sleighs, and of doing their hauling in midwinter, making of snow and ice a highway, while their milk, butter, and juicy steaks were plentiful even in February, their neighbors eastward had to cut and haul their firewood in clumsy carts in autumn, live on salt meat, make long journeys only with the greatest difficulty, and invent various ways of sustaining the life of man and beast during the prolonged and tedious winters. From the opening of the eighteenth century the adoption of the New York farmers' ways of farming and quick transportation and stock-raising made life more agreeable, and aided powerfully in the evolution of that most agreeable of all persons, the modern New-Englander. It was on a Dutch sleigh that the Rhode-Islander of English Quaker and Scotch-Irish descent, Oliver H. Perry, made rapid transit to Lake Erie. It was by means of the Dutch invention called a "camel" that he floated his green-timber ships over the bar and out to victory, under the same red and white stripes that floated from the masts of Piet Hein, Von Tromp, and De Ruyter. In the mastery of the great forests, in the interest of agriculture, house-erection, and that ship-building in which the Massachusetts men ultimately led the world, they made slow progress with axe and old-fashioned saw-pit. After they had borrowed the Dutch saw-mill they were able to make such progress that at the opening of the Revolution probably one-half of British ships were colony-built. The saw-mill operated by water was a new thing in England even in 1635, was not common until after 1700, and its introduction caused strikes, a riot, and the smashing of the machinery by the angry and jealous saw-pit men. In Holland, the lumber market of Europe, wherever there was water-power, or, failing this, wind-power, there was a saw-mill, and in Germany these saws moved by power other than human had been known for many centuries. The Dutch in the Hudson River region introduced them on their first coming, and before the end of the seventeenth century had nearly forty in operation. New Amsterdam was built with sawed lumber. They even exported boards and shingles to Europe. The hardy men of Massachusetts soon imitated the Dutch, and utilized the abundant power all around them, and in due time New England was dotted over with these promoters of civilization.

That the New-Englander, landed by Providence on a soil mostly barren and consisting chiefly of glacial drift, and later kept off the sea by embargoes laid chiefly by Southern politicians, was driven to invention so as to surpass the world, is an old story. At first, however, both he and his kinsmen of like speech and blood beyond sea borrowed long and often from the brainy men behind the dikes. The Hollanders in their heroic age were foremost in mental initiative, and their name and fame as quick-witted inventors, handicraftsmen, and makers of comforts lie embedded in many an English phrase, nickname, and proverb. The sixteenth and seventeenth century literature and folk-speech is especially full of compliments to the refugees who laid the foundations of England's manufacturing and commercial supremacy. None the less, even in Connecticut, was the skill of the Knickerbockers admired. A new invention or improvement was said to "beat the Dutch." The sure proof that the Yankees, even more than the British, were impressed, and that they acknowledged the fact, is that Bartlett, the authority on Americanisms, finds this phrase first in a song composed at the siege of Boston. The things in the kitchen, bedroom, parlor, and woman's apparel reveal by their telltale etymology their Dutch origin as surely as does buckwheat. The Delft tiles on the hearth, the crockery on the dresser, the blue tiles lining the front of the fireplaces in the best houses, show how the Dutch had a part in the evolution of the New England house. It is wholly proper that at the World's Fair in Chicago, in the "John Hancock house"—itself a proof of how the Haarlem architectural decoration was copied in America—there should be one room generously walled with Delft tiles. This is not only the tribute paid to the potent Dutch influence in the Housatonic Valley, but to the important domestic influence of the blue and white crockery of Delft. Hundreds of open fireplaces in New England were decorated with these tiles after the Dutch fashion, and contained not only "proverbs in porcelain," but abundant Biblical illustration. From the evidences of relics, nearly as much of the imported fine furniture in the northern colonies came from Holland as from England. Not a few of the old teapots and other table service, which followed upon the introduction of those Oriental hot drinks which drove out the beer and tankards, did indeed come over from Holland, though not on the *Mayflower*, as so often anachronistically alleged. When, too, the open fireplace gradually gave way to supposed improvement, it was to a Dutch thing with a Dutch name—the stove. Not only in Plymouth, but elsewhere, numerous houses had what can be occasionally seen throughout New England to-day (nor by this do we mean the later substitute of tin)—a Dutch oven. It was under this spacious dome of brick and clay that those famous articles of Yankee diet, the pumpkin pie, brown bread, baked beans, and fishballs, had their evolution. No smoker of tobacco in the snow-white meerschaum rejoiced more in his coloring of the seafoam clay than did the rosy housewives of Massachusetts Bay in the rich hues of bean, bread, and fish. The *browning* clubs of early days met in the kitchen rather than in the parlor or vendôme. The doughnut may have been too cosmopolitan an article to claim invention at the hands of any one people; yet what Yankee

"fried cake" or doughnut ever equalled an *olekoek*? Was not cruller, whose derivation confounds the dictionary-makers, who call it "a kind of" doughnut, first brought to perfection by Captain Kroll (pronounced and sometimes spelled crull), the whilom commander and Dutch church elder at Fort Orange? To this day the "cookey" (koekje), noodles, hodgepodge, smearcase, rullichies, cold-slaw, and other dishes that survive in New England farmhouses, are, despite their changed pronunciation and spelling, proofs that the Yankees enriched their monotonous menu of early colonial days by borrowing the more varied fare of their Dutch neighbors in the West and South. As for the popular American winter breakfast luxury, the buckwheat cake, it was introduced from Central Asia by the Hollanders, acclimated, cultivated, named "beech-mast" (*boekweit*), and in the form associated with heat, sweets, aroma, and good cheer is a Dutch invention.

The Dutch, like the Puritans, were Calvinists, and Calvinism always breeds cleanliness and democracy, as surely as it never breeds poverty or arbitrary government. The Dutch invented linen underclothing, besides starch and its application to ornamental dress. They believed in plenty of soap, starch, and linen for bed and body, and they knew how to make both cheap. In the making of soap from wood-ashes they led the way. In the evolution of the post and frame, enclosed and canopied bed, bolster, the modern pillow covered with removable case, and the bolster cased and not merely tucked under the sheet, in the invention of the thimble, in the perfection and multiplication of spinning-wheels for the domestic treatment of yarn, and of home machinery for the preparation of flax into linen, and of the blending of the two into linsey-woolsey, the Dutch were the inventors, and the English, on either side of the Atlantic, the borrowers. The parlor with picture ornaments and bric-à-brac, and the "best room" kept ever ready for hospitality, were institutions among New-Netherlanders from the first.

Need we pursue the subject further, and show how American speech betrays our indebtedness to the Dutchmen? Whenever we utter the anglicized words anchor, caboose, ballast, school (of fishes), sloop, stoker, stove, doily, brandy, duffel, cambric, easel, landscape, boss, stoop, forlorn hope, body-guard, boodle, scow, Santa Claus, blickey (tin), and a host of words in art, music, seamanship, handicraft, war, exploration, and the lines of human achievement most followed in the seventeenth century, we are but mispronouncing, more or less fluently, Dutch words. These words are the labels of things borrowed from the little country which, after England, had most to do with the making of the American republic.

From the first fight and flight of the Indians before the prowess of Miles Standish to this day of ours the military spirit has never waned among the brave New-Englanders. Yet, apart from the ancestral fighting spirit of these English colonists, it must not be forgotten that the school in which they were trained was the Dutch army and the republican War of Independence in the Low Countries. In the development of legal science we have heard some of the brilliant lawyers of Massachusetts confess the great indebtedness of the law that rules us to Grotius and the great Dutch jurists whose names are more famous than familiar. The ancestral drops of "Nederlandsche bloet" in Oliver Wendell Holmes, Washington Allston, and a host of the bluest-blooded New-Englanders, whose names, as the records in the Nederlands show, *were Dutch before they were English*, hint at a force in letters and art still unspent.

Thanksgiving day in its original and precedents was a Dutch institution. Our national "Sunday in the middle of the week" began with the Pilgrims, who, whether consciously imitating or not, were following out what they had previously often enjoyed in their home of freedom behind the dikes. A day of thanksgiving and prayer was frequent after victory or good harvests in the Dutch states. The severe Sabbath laws of both Pilgrim and Puritan in style and verbal form are curiously like those of Zealand. Within the "meeting-house" (neither Pilgrim nor Puritan, any more than the Anabaptist, would ever call brick or stone walls a "church," though they might figuratively think of Christians as "living stones") the close imitation of Dutch ways was not confined to foot-stoves, plain or whitewashed walls, baptismal quilts, collection-bags like scoop-nets on fishing-poles, and "tithing-men" who rapped or tickled sleepy male or female, and kept the boys in order. The likeness in more serious things was even closer. The majority of university-bred clergymen from Europe (as well as physicians and lawyers) who immigrated to the American colonies after the English universities had closed to non-conformists were educated at Leyden or Utrecht, the rolls of the former still showing over four thousand seven hundred names of English-speaking students between 1573 and 1873, the majority living in the seventeenth and eighteenth centuries. Not only was the first "printery" at Cambridge from Amsterdam, but Harvard even invited to her presidency from the same city the Bohemian bishop Comenius, who had found a home in the republic of seven states. Dutch theology fed not only John Robinson and Elder Brewster as they testify, but the Puritan writers and thinkers of old and New England were mightily moulded by the federal theology of the Dutch professor Coccejus. There are some also who declare Coccejus to be the true founder of Biblical theology, before which the old dogmatic or systematic theology is trembling, and out of which "New England theology" has so largely grown.

All know and gladly recognize the moral earnestness and insistence on reform which characterize the children of the American Puritans. The abolition of slavery is probably by a majority credited to the agitation alleged to have begun north of Long Island Sound. Yet the first ecclesiastical protest in America against human slavery was raised, not, as internal evidence shows, by Quakers, but by the Dutch Mennonites, successors to the Anabaptists, at Germantown, Pennsylvania, April 18, 1688. Wendell Phillips gladly acknowledged the fact, and hung a photograph of the original document in the Boston Public Library. The first book against slavery came from the same sect and quarter in Pennsylvania. It was later that the Quakers of English descent roused themselves and circulated their own writings and those of the Pennsylvania Dutchmen—we use the term correctly—in New England. The influence of these writings was powerful in the land where manacles for the slavers, sent to Africa from New England ports, were made by the deacons and church members down to the Revolution, and where West India molasses produced by slave labor was turned into New England rum.

As the English Bible and the first English sacred poetry of the Reformation, hymns and psalms, reflect the color and rhythm of the richer German models of Luther, so in the development of popular music in New England there is a distinctively Dutch influence. In Holland, where for fifty years the British army had its chief history and the Puritans found their base of supplies, the voorzanger and the singing-school, in which the children were taught hymns and patriotic songs, were commonplace. In New Netherland and western Massachusetts this old custom of the Vaderland was immediately instituted and tenaciously held. Every Dutch church of any importance in New Netherland had its precentor, who taught the young folks and led the congregation's singing. The voorzanger was as active as the catechist or the *krank-bezoeker*, or visitor of the sick — religious men who performed their functions before Plymouth Rock was stepped upon — and he continued in vigorous life long after New Netherland became New York. This Dutch idea, borrowed and improved upon in New England, early in the eighteenth century became a powerful factor in the evolution of Yankee civilization. Those singing-schools which on winter evenings gathered the rosy youth of New England together softened the rigor of a harsh climate, and made Lowell Mason and Thomas Hastings possible. Yet long before the monotony of the night life of the young folks of New England was broken by the sleigh-ride and the singing-school, the jingle of the merry bells, the swift glide of the runners on the frosty starry nights, and the singing-school were the commonplace enjoyments of the Dutch youth on Long Island and in the Raritan, Hudson, and Mohawk regions. It is probable that the singing-school, when once established in Yankee land, accompanied by the Dutch sleighing and skating, did more to drive out the custom of "bundling," against which so many of the parsons fulminated, of which the old records are rather full, than all the sermons or legal devices, real or alleged. Beyond the names of native instrument players or makers of eminence in Massachusetts is that of the Van Hagens, mother and son, who brought from the Netherlands both voice and instruments, and for a half-century prepared the way of musical Boston.

The beginnings and development of the free public-school system which is now the glory of our country, and which New England, without originating, did so much to develop, have not yet been fully told by the special historical student. The archives of Leyden and other Dutch cities and the history of the Brethren of the Common Life—out of whose schools came forth Thomas à Kempis and Erasmus—show that there were in Holland from the fourteenth century onwards three sorts of schools. Besides the monastery or church and private educational enterprises there were public schools sustained by taxation, absolutely free to the children of the poor, and open, with only a small charge, to all those of the burghers or citizens able to pay. In England, as we know, the "public" school is a private school, only in recent days the "board" schools being public in the American sense. In Holland the revenues from the confiscation of abbey lands were applied to the foundation of five universities and public schools. The first founders of Massachusetts and Connecticut certainly saw the free public schools of Holland in operation, and in them not a few were educated. As Mr. Motley suggests, the impulses to popular education were from the republic, and not from England. "Distinctive America" would not be what she has been without the public schools. However much in this, as in other lines of enterprise, the New-Englanders improved upon their models, we must not forget the original impulses and influences.

Just as where one American studies critically Dutch history and civilization there are a thousand who devote themselves to French or German, and ten thousand to English historic literature, so where one private person reads Bradford or Winslow there are a thousand who depend on poets or romancers for their facts about early New England. Whether or not Miles Standish was a Roman Catholic and John Alden an Irishman, as experts insist, we all know how Priscilla was married by the magistrate, after "the laudable custom of Holland." Mr. Longfellow bases his poetry on Bradford, who quotes by chapter and verse from the Dutch laws. Happily it is no longer true, what Bradford's editor declared forty years ago, that "no copy of this work [quoted from] exists in any of the public libraries in this neighborhood." Few marriages were solemnized in Massachusetts by clergymen until near the end of the seventeenth century, the Dutch influence in this respect persisting in some slight degree even to-day.

Indeed, "ye laudable custome of ye Low-Cuntries" was followed not only in marriage, but also by confederacy of states, by revolutionary war, by declaration of independence, written constitution, and red, white, and blue flag. The fifty or more Dutch books or pamphlets published in Holland between 1775 and 1783, and now in the Athenæum Library in Boston, show that the Dutchman understood then, as he to-day more clearly than any other European does, the American spirit and procedure. Hence the first foreign salute ever fired to the American flag, even before it had stars on its field, but was still a copy of that of the United States of the Netherlands, was by the Dutch Governor at St. Eustatius, November 16, 1776. In a word, the procedure not only of the men of Plymouth, but of Lexington and Concord, was a wonderful close copy of that of the Dutch. The latter technically founded their union and declared that they took up arms in the name of Philip II. of Spain; and this because they were good lawyers. The Parliamentarians in 1664, who issued their commissions in the name of King Charles I.,

and the Lexington men who fired their guns at British redcoats for abridging and interfering with their "right to proceed unmolested along the King's highway," did but imitate those Dutch lawyers, without whose writings neither the laws of New England nor of the United States would be what they are to-day.

In the evolution of that noble type of man and very agreeable person, the modern New-Englander, there have been many potent influences. Not the least of the factors moulding him has been the influence of Dutch precedent, contact, and example. This influence has been exerted on both sides of the Atlantic, politically, socially, and religiously. Though "without observation," it has been real. The counter influence of the New-Englanders upon the New-Netherlanders may have been vastly greater. Nevertheless, of the energies which have made and are making the typical composite American, those contributed by the Dutch were among the first and most lasting. Arising at Holland's heroic age, they acted upon a people in their formative period. If Faith, Morality, Freedom, Law, and Education, as symbolized in the granite statues of the national monument at Plymouth, be the leading characteristics of New England civilization, then there is equal debt to their exemplars on both sides of the North Sea.

WHITTIER COUNTRY

A MESBURY FERRY commences at the Powow River bridge—a rude stone structure with two arches, under which the water runs with great velocity at the turn of the tide. Over the bridge the road sweeps to the right and left, on one hand to the little village of Amesbury Mills, and on the other to the banks of the Merrimac, which it follows along its length to Haverhill. The first portion of this left-hand road was in Revolutionary days the terminus of a chain ferry from the opposite bank, and the old house is still standing which at that time was used as a tavern and hostelry for those who travelled on what was then the main road through the Eastern States. It was here that Washington halted for a short time on his journey through New England, and from the foot of the old garden, terminated by a grass-grown wharf, you can see the break in the opposite bank of the river where the road once descended to the water's edge. The only landmark of the ferry on the farther bank is a mound of grass-grown stones nearly destroyed by the ice of the spring freshets. It is very likely, as you stand gazing at this ruin of a former time, that the tall thin figure of an elderly man will come down upon the wharf, and noticing through his huge round blue spectacles the direction of your gaze, will say: "Well, looking at the old ferry, are you? That's where George Washington crossed when he made the tour of the New England States in 1789." And if you enter into conversation with genial Uncle Nathan Nutter, who, by-the-way, has a treasure-trove of ancient lore, he will give you all the particulars of that great event. One of these stories, still handed down at the ferry, relates that when Washington crossed the river a French vessel lay at one of the wharves, a short distance below the landing, with the American colors flying under the French flag. Washington noticed it, and with a wave of his hand called attention to the fact, when a crowd immediately started on the run for the vessel, and made the captain haul down his colors, and hoist them again below the Stars and Stripes. "Oh!" said Uncle Nathan, "they'd have torn his vessel all to pieces if he hadn't." In connection with this treasured legend of the people, I am reminded of a good-humored thrust from the British Minister in regard to it, when I was encamped on the bank of the river just below his summer residence. He had come down to the water with his daughter, and was busily engaged in bailing out a dilapidated and leaky boat, when I offered him my dory, which was in a better condition. After accepting the offer he entered into conversation, and spoke of this portion of the country as reminding him very strongly of Devonshire, where he was born, and of the names all through Essex County recalling to him memories of England. "Yes," said I, "but we have not the old historical recollections which England possesses; our country is too

THE LAURELS.

young." "And yet," replied he, with a quizzical smile, "the carpenter at the 'castle' tells me that the *great George Washington crossed here!*" and stepping into the dory, Sir Edward pulled off with a fair, even stroke, as though he had not passed all his life in diplomacy.

Among the people of Amesbury that portion of the road at the ferry is known as Mudnock, and this euphonious name descends from the first settlement of the town in 1639. There are still remaining traces of ancient roads and cellars in the surrounding fields; and one day I came across, in the middle of a wood, a long deep trench overgrown with brush, and with a large pine standing in the centre, which had evidently grown there since the trench was excavated. There are no traditions connected with these old remains; and I have heard since of an ancient burial-ground in the middle of thick woods, where the head and foot stones to the graves are rough blocks of granite without inscriptions of any kind, and all records and traditions are utterly wanting to indicate who sleeps in this mysterious Golgotha. One mild warm day in the Indian summer I visited, with an eccentric bachelor friend, an old weather-beaten house almost fallen in decay; back of it were growing a few willow-trees, and in front the ground sloped away across the road to the river, over which we could see the wooded hills of "The Laurels," which Whittier has so often sung about. At the end of this ancient house there are traces of a still older foundation, with part of a

cellar, together with warped fragments of hard-burned bricks nearly overgrown with turf. "Here," said Huntington, stopping and indicating the ground at his feet, "is the place where stood the house of Mabel Martin, 'the witch's daughter.' The early records make no mention of the fact, and, indeed, locate the original homestead at some distance back from the stream, and out of sight of the water, but Whittier in his poem has described this identical spot. Notice in his verses how closely the description agrees with the landscape. There were willows once on the banks of the river, though they have since been cut away; and here by this old mound can you not see traces of the 'door-yard tree,' though a lilac-bush now grows from its ancient root-hold?

"'Poor Mabel, in her lonely home,
    Sat by the window's narrow pane,
    White in the moonlight's silver rain.

"'The river, on its pebbled rim,
    Made music such as childhood knew;
    The door-yard tree was whispered through

"'By voices such as childhood's ear
    Had heard in moonlights long ago;
    And through the willow boughs below

"'She saw the rippled waters shine;
    Beyond, in waves of shade and light,
    The hills rolled off into the night.'"

The hills are "The Laurels," sweeping back from the river in waves of evergreen verdure, not so dense and thickly wooded as in the days of Mabel Martin, for much of the forest has been cleared away, leaving exposed the gray lichen-covered rocks.

The river-shore on this side is covered with small rounded pebbles.

The ruinous cottage, at the time we visited it, was occupied by an old woman whom all the neighborhood knew as Marm Mitchell. Her appearance would have condemned her, had she lived at an earlier period, to follow in the long line of victims to Gallows Hill, and even the present generation looked upon her with no favoring glance.

In her pumpkin hood, wearing a short brown cape, and carrying a long staff in her hand, she led her solitary cow beside the roads, and at night slept among her hens and chickens, which occupied her rooms with the same freedom as herself. Her lips were never opened with reference to her past history, and it was only vague rumors that associated this poor wreck of a once handsome woman with a station far above her present circumstances.

After her death letters were found hinting darkly at some terrible crime committed in her youth, but so guarded were the allusions that nothing definite was ascertained. For aught to the contrary, she may have been the translation of Goody Martin's soul haunting the scenes of her former incantations.

From a hill back of this old house can be had a distant view of Amesbury, once the home of Whittier. He visits it but seldom now, coming sometimes in the early spring-time, and again in late autumn to vote in town-meeting with his old friends and neighbors.

"Home of my heart! to me more fair
    Than gay Versailles or Windsor's halls,
The painted, shingly town-house where
    The freeman's vote for Freedom falls!
The simple roof where prayer is made,
    Than Gothic groin and colonnade;
The living temple of the heart of man,
Than Rome's sky-mocking vault, or many-spired
    Milan!"

It was on one of these town-meeting days that Huntington called for me, and together we entered "the painted, shingly town-house," which stands not far from the poet's residence. The assembled voters were discussing the question of a police force in the village, and farmers in from the country, tradesmen from their stores, manufacturers and mechanics, were collected in little groups over the floor of the hall, or wandering from place to place greeting acquaintances or friends. Among these townsmen there was pointed out to me the tall, thin figure of an old man wrapped in a long brown coat, with a high fur collar and woollen mantle around his neck, almost coming up to the brim of his tall black hat. He was talking with the various groups around him, and soon afterward coming our way, Huntington introduced him as Mr. Whittier. The poet is much above the average height of men, and few of his pictures that I have seen resemble him. His hair and beard are quite white, he wears no mustache, and his lips are set with an expression of much decision and energy, which is emphasized by a short, quick utterance.

Soon after the introduction he invited us to his house, Mr. Currier, of Amesbury, an intimate friend of the poet, going with us. On reaching the cottage and entering the study, we found a cheerful wood fire burning in an open fire-place stove, Mr. Whittier remarking, as we spoke of the cheerful glow, that this was one luxury he always indulged himself in, and then piling on some solid sticks of hickory, he divested himself of his overcoat, bringing into view a black undercoat somewhat "seedy," and worn white on the back seams. Putting on his glasses, he turned up the leaf of a small table standing between the two windows of his study, drew up a chair, and prepared to look over a volume of sketches that I had brought with me. His questions were short and sharp.

"What's that?" "Moss Glen Falls." "Where?" "Stowe, Vermont." Then he turned rapidly to another, pointing with his long forefinger to the sketch, and sometimes dashing his finger over it as he noticed some particular thing in the drawing; every few moments he would stoop over the sketch, and scrutinize it more closely. After looking the book through once, he went over it again with a magnifying-glass, and read the names written on the margins of the sketches. On seeing a sketch of some palmettoes among the Florida studies, he said, "They are not very picturesque, not as good as some of our rock-maples"; and then he made a number of inquiries about that portion of the country, and laughed very heartily at an account I gave him in regard to my sleeping on a snake at one time in camp. Whittier seemed to think that there were not many snakes, except the black-snake, in Florida. After closing the book, he brought out a sketch of the Rocks Bridge and the Newbury shore, by

Harry Fenn, drawn on gray paper, and then searching in his writing-table, he found a large envelope, and produced some curious drawings from tablets found in the mounds of the West, putting on his glasses again, and looking with evident interest over my shoulder at them. At this time Mr. Currier left, and the conversation

under the lee of a large log, or made a shelter of pine boughs:

"Sat down again to moose and samp
In trapper's hut and Indian camp;
Lived o'er the old idyllic ease
Beneath St. François' hemlock-trees;
Again for him the moonlight shone
On Norman cap and boddced zone."

ROCKS VILLAGE.

turned upon my yacht, and I mentioned the time when lying at Bordentown, New Jersey, one of the canal officers came on board evenings, and repeated, when the moon rose over the heights of Point Breeze, the poem commencing

"Yon mountain's side is black with night."

As I quoted the first line, Whittier took it up, and with a smile repeated the first verse:

"Yon mountain's side is black with night,
While broad-orbed o'er its gleaming crown
The moon, slow rounding into sight,
On the hushed inland sea looks down."

As he finished the verse, he said that it was Lake Winnipiseogee. Then he continued speaking about camp life, and mentioned the stories related by his father of his camp life in Canada, when they slept

In the course of this rambling conversation about a life of adventure we spoke of the Northmen, and Mr. Whittier gave a minute description of the old stone tower at Newport, which he had seen. He said that it was constructed of small stones such as could be gathered on the beach, cemented together with lime made from shells, which was as hard as the stone itself. It is raised on eight columns about eight or nine feet high, also composed of small stones and cement. It is a very beautiful and picturesque piece of work. "But," said I, "it is stated that this tower is nothing but an old mill." "Yes," said Whittier, "it is mentioned in an old deed as the old stone mill, but a professor who came over here from Norway to make researches and see if he could find traces of the Northmen here on these shores said, on seeing the mill, that he could show just such ruins on the coast of Iceland, and he believed it to be built by the Northmen." Mr. Whittier also mentioned a peculiar sculptured rock to be found somewhere in West Newbury, but he did not know the location, and had never seen it, though he had alluded to it in his poem of "The Double-headed Snake of Newbury" as the "Northman's Written Rock"; "but," he continued, "there is a historical society started at Newburyport, and perhaps they will hunt it up." While we were talking about camp life and the Northmen, Huntington came in with news of the State election, and for a time the conversation took a political turn, until Huntington gave a certain prominence to his own peculiar views, which started a discussion on the prohibition question. In the course of this new topic the old-fashioned New England beverage cider was mentioned, and Mr. Whittier stated that he had once derived much benefit when unwell, "when nothing tasted good," from the use of cider. Huntington suggested that without cider we should not have vinegar. "Well," said Whittier, "vinegar is not of much use, after all." "Except," replied Huntington, "to eat on cabbage and cucumbers." "Neither of which are fit to be eaten," remarked the poet; "I think it would be a good idea to start a prohibition party on those two articles. As for cabbage, it is not fit to be eaten; if you cook it in the house, you have got to burn your house down afterward to get rid of the smell; it is certainly the most diabolical smell that was ever invented;" and Whittier, who was sitting near the open stove grate, upon the top of which he had deposited his tall hat, folded his hands and laughed a hearty silent laugh. "What do you think of onions, Mr. Whittier?" asked I. "Well," he replied, "onions are not quite so bad, for you *can* get rid of the smell of those in three or four days." "Then," said Huntington, "you would not approve of the old-fashioned 'boiled dinner'?" "*No.* I think that is a detestable dish. I remember that my father used to have it, in which cabbage, onions, beets, potatoes, turnips, and carrots were all boiled up together, and turned out into a great dish all in a heap, with a great greasy piece of meat in the middle. I think that is

the reason why the present generation is not so strong as the former. It is owing to the way the parents lived, eating so much pork and potatoes. Our last war showed that. The farmers were not nearly as strong as the men recruited in the cities — Portland, Portsmouth, and Boston." "But the people in the cities do not have the free air we get in the country," said Huntington. "I know that," replied Whittier; "but they live better, and that makes a great difference."

Finally, we returned from boiled dinner to poetry again, and I asked Whittier about the story of Evangeline. He said that it had once occurred to him to write it, but he did not suggest it to Hawthorne, though he possibly talked with Longfellow about it; but he did not remember. Hawthorne suggested it to Longfellow.

We then spoke of the poem "In School Days," and Whittier expressed great regret at the destruction of the old schoolhouse.

I then questioned him about Ramoth hill, in the poem of "My Playmate," and he said that it had no existence—it was merely fancy.

Huntington then asked the poet's opinion of a singular occurrence which took place many years ago on the Rocks Bridge, in East Haverhill, where the draw-tender, Mr. Davis, saw repeated visions of his death, which was to take place on the bridge, and which did actually occur as he had predicted, and under the same conditions.

Whittier remembered the circumstance, and had seen the place, when a boy, where he died. He did not doubt the story, and spoke of Mr. Davis as being a man of strong religious feeling. It was mysterious, but everything in life is mysterious, and that it was impossible to explain how tables were lifted bodily up into the air, as they were in these days. He considered the Salem witchcraft as a manifestation of what we call spiritualism nowadays. He remembered when a boy of going with his parents to quarterly meeting in Salem, and of seeing a tree standing on Gallows Hill, dead and leafless, but with the heart still apparently alive, or left sound, and they told him that was the tree the witches were hung upon.

"You wrote a poem," said I, "about the witch times—'The Witch of Wenham.'" "Yes," said Whittier; "that was suggested by an old house near where I stopped

BIRTH-PLACE OF "THE COUNTESS."

that she was not a witch, for she was tired of hearing it, but the justice could not think of any form of oath to suit her case. At last, however, he fixed up something, and Aunt Mose swore to it, and so relieved her mind."

This was in Whittier's boyhood, and even at a later day this belief in witches still prevailed among the older people; for Huntington well remembered that when his grandfather was kicked by his old gray horse he insisted that the accident was caused by an old woman who lived near him, and whom he devoutly believed to be a witch.

Rocks Village, where lived Aunt Mose,

"The muttering witch-wife of the gossip's tale,"

is a charming little nook on the Merrimac River, away from the busy lines of traffic—

"A place for idle eyes and ears,
    A cobwebbed nook of dreams;
Left by the stream whose waves are years
    The stranded village seems."

And it is here that Whittier also found, amid

"Old customs, habits, superstitions, fears,
    All that lies buried under fifty years,"

the incidents for his sweet poem of "The Countess." "The countess" was a young girl of scarcely twenty years when the Count Francis Vipart came to Rocks Village with a friend, both exiles from the island of Guadeloupe. He saw Mary Ingalls, a beautiful, golden-haired, blue-eyed girl, the belle of the little village; and her beauty, together with a gentle and sweet disposition, attracted him at once. He walked with her along "the straggling road" which comes down "over the wooded northern ridge," to her church, standing near the burial-ground on the land "that slopes against the west." The church is now removed; but later in the afternoon of the day on which we visited the place we met an old gentleman of eighty who remembered the church, and the time when only two slept in the grave-yard, which is now full. He also informed us that the worshippers were called together by the sound of a horn.

"The countess" was the daughter of a laboring man, and an L of the house where

in Danvers, at Oak Knoll, where it was said that a young girl was brought, and confined in the garret; but in the night she escaped, assisted by some friend on the outside. The house is still standing there, quite near, on the farm of Mr. Spring." Whittier then related an amusing anecdote about an old woman who lived, I think, at the Rocks Village. She was called Aunt Mose.

"One night," said Whittier, "there was a husking at the village, and about the middle of the evening a big black bug came flying in, buzzing about the room, and flying into the faces of the company. At last it was knocked down with a stick, and at the same time Aunt Mose, who was at home, fell down-stairs, and the next day was all covered with bruises, and the huskers always insisted afterward that the black bug was Aunt Mose, and the bruises were where the stick struck her. Old Captain Peaslee, who lived near her, and had a house and a number of barns, covered them all over with horseshoes to keep Aunt Mose out, for he was dreadfully afraid of her. At last this state of affairs became so unbearable that poor Aunt Mose went to a justice of the peace for him to swear her

she was born is still standing, said to contain the room where the event took place, and which has since been shown to me by the present occupants of the place.

It is a quaint low-studded room, lighted with large many-paned windows. The L once formed a main portion of the original house, but has since been removed to the rear, and a more modern structure built in front. In the best front room stands the first stove used in Haverhill—an heirloom from the old doctor, Elias Weld,

> "Whose ancient sulky down the village lanes
> Dragged, like a war-car, captive ills and pains."

It is an open fire-place stove, with a huge hollow iron vase on top serving the purpose of a heater. The kitchen of the homestead still remains in its original condition, an antique wainscoted room, very suggestive of comfort for long winter evenings. And it was here in these ancient rooms that the little love romance of Rocks Village was lived out.

> "Her simple daily life he saw
> By homeliest duties tried,
> In all things by an untaught law
> Of fitness justified.
>
> "For her his rank aside he laid;
> He took the hue and tone
> Of lowly life and toil, and made
> Her simple ways his own."

There is still living in a neighboring town a white-haired old lady of eighty who treasures up with pious care a set of knives and forks which were a bridal gift from the count to his young wife; and she will relate to the curious listener how the Count Francis Vipart established evening dances in the village for the young people, and how devoted he was to his beautiful wife. "My mother," said she, "knew her well, and often used to say that she was the most beautiful girl she had ever seen, so gentle and kind."

Late in the afternoon of that autumn day we stood by the grave of the countess, marked by slate head and foot stones. On the head-stone is the inscription:

MARY,
Wife of FRANCIS VIPART,
of Guadeloupe,
died Jan. 5, 1807,
æt. 21,

the last *u* in Guadeloupe being omitted, and placed over the other letters afterward. The head-stone is quite elaborately ornamented with a funeral urn and weeping-willows at the top, like an ancient sampler, and elaborate though rudely carved columns at the sides. On the foot-stone are simply the words,

MARY VIPART, 1807.

Before leaving I made a sketch of the spot, with its sere dead ferns, its tangle of wild-brier vines, crimson-leaved by frost, and the short brown spires of withered grass growing in tufts over the moundless grave.

> "Ah! life is brief, though love be long;"

and short indeed it was to the lovely Mary Ingalls, who lived out her love romance in one brief year, and came to her long rest in the grave-yard near the village church. Naturally delicate and frail, she sacrificed herself by unremitting exertions at the bedside of her sick mother, and a quick consumption ended all too soon her beautiful and loving life.

The count was inconsolable after her death; he parted with everything that could remind him of his gentle wife, and finding the scenes of his married life too painful after his short year of happiness, he left the village never to return.

I almost wish to pass over the sequel of Count Francis Vipart in silence. As related to us by Miss R. I. Davis, who wrote to Guadeloupe and obtained his subsequent history, the count returned after the death of his beautiful Mary, was married again, and left many descendants on the island, where he is buried.

And this was in 1807, an era of great events in France. Eylau and Friedland were fought; Napoleon was at the zenith of his power. Glory called the French-

GRAVE OF "THE COUNTESS."

man to the victorious eagles of his great Emperor. Vipart should have been inconsolable, and drowned his sorrow in the excitement of the battle-field. He should have gloriously closed his romance by falling in the disastrous retreat from Moscow, the last of his regiment, or in doing some heroic deed for the memory of his lost darling. But what a prosaic end!—he marries, and is the father of a family.

It was twelve months after my first visit before I again found myself standing in the pleasant study of the Quaker poet, and by a singular coincidence we resumed our conversation where we had left it a year ago. In some way a reference was made to the poem of "The Witch of Wenham," and the poet said the old house, which stands near Oak Knoll, had been painted white, and green blinds placed upon it, which he thought was a great pity. I then mentioned Hawthorne's story of the *House of the Seven Gables*, and asked him if the writer had ever mentioned the story to him, or indicated in any way what house he referred to in the romance. "No," said the poet, "he never mentioned it but once, and then he said the story was about half finished, and, to use his own words," continued Whittier, with a peculiar smile, "'it darkens damnably.'"

Continuing to speak of other witch houses in Danvers, Whittier mentioned the old Rebecca Nourse house, and stated that the old sounding-board that used to hang over Rev. Mr. Jarvis's pulpit, and on which the devil, in the form of a yellow bird, used to perch, was now owned by a lady living near the church. Talking so much about witches led us into other inquiries on the subject, and we discussed the phenomenon of clairvoyance, as to whether it was mind-reading, Whittier taking the ground that it was not, and relating a curious incident that occurred to him when a young man living in Haverhill.

He was out walking one day, late in the afternoon, and on his return home was accosted by a neighbor with the remark, "Why did you not speak to me this afternoon when you passed me on the hill?" "Why," said Whittier, "I have not been on the hill this afternoon." "But certainly you passed me there, with a light-colored bundle under your arm, and you went by without speaking."

"At that time," said Whittier, "I was distant from the hill about a mile, in a direct line from it, and under my arm I had some books wrapped up in a newspaper. Now how did that man see me on the hill? It is something we can not account for."

I then gave a curious circumstance which once happened to myself, where a mental picture formed itself of a transaction which did not occur until some hours after I first saw it in my mind. Whittier remarked that he never *saw* anything, though he was sometimes enabled to read the *thoughts* of persons in the room with him.

We then spoke of the legends and traditions of Amesbury as suited for illustration, the poet mentioning the birth-place of Josiah Bartlett, on the road to the ferry, which had been torn down a few days before—the very day after I had made a sketch of it. On showing the drawing to Whittier, he recognized another sketch on the same page, and indicated it as the scene of his poem "The Witch's Daughter," pointing out a pile of stones behind the willow-trees in the drawing as marking the site of the old house he wrote about, saying, "The house thee has in thy sketch was probably contemporary with the one I referred to; but can thee not show more of the river?"

Indeed, "the river," the beautiful Merrimac, is always first in the mind of the poet:

"Sing soft, sing low, our lowland river,
    Under thy banks of laurel bloom;
Softly and sweet, as the hour beseemeth,
    Sing us the songs of peace and home.

"Bring us the airs of hills and forests,
    The sweet aroma of birch and pine,
Give us a waft of the north wind laden
    With sweet-brier odors and breath of kine.

"Sing on! bring down, O lowland river,
    The joy of the hills to the waiting sea;
The wealth of the vales, the pomp of mountains,
    The breath of the woodlands, bear with thee."

On one of my last visits to the poet he said, "There was a man drowned in our river lately," and spoke as though it was an unusual and strange freak for the river to use any one in such a shabby way, and then went on to speak of its scenery, and lament the destruction of the woods along its banks, regretting as a true lover of nature any inroads made upon its picturesque character. While looking at the drawing of the old house by the river, Whittier mentioned that during the witchcraft delusion an old woman was carried across the ferry to be tried in Salem, and it was

SCENE OF POEM "THE WITCH'S DAUGHTER."

at this same place that Governor Andros, of charter fame, came down to the water to cross over on his way to Pemaquid; a plot was laid to shoot him as he landed on the Amesbury side, but a young girl at the ferry loved an officer on Andros's staff; she betrayed the secret, and Andros crossed at another place. As the poet closed the book, I asked him if he could tell me where the old block-house used to stand in Amesbury, but owing to his deafness he misunderstood me, and replied that there was no block-house now standing in Amesbury, but he remembered the one which used to stand in Haverhill, near his father's.

"There were two block-houses, but this one I remember perfectly. It was a massive structure, built of solid oak logs, with the walls double, and filled in with bricks between. There was a double thick plank door made bullet-proof, and studded with iron nails. Over the door, and projecting from the second story, was a species of balcony, also of thick planks, with a bullet-proof breastwork around it, through which were cut loop-holes, so that the defenders could creep from the interior of the house and fire down upon those who might be about the door. The windows were narrow, and with small diamond-shaped panes set in lead;" and here Whit-

tier made motions with his fingers to indicate more clearly the shape and mode of setting. "A paved road led into the block-house, and formed a passageway across the room below, the floor of which was paved with large flat slabs of a slate-like stone such as they could get anywhere in the pastures about the place. A huge fire-place occupied one end of the large apartment, and from the beams above were hung hams, onions, squashes, and all the various family stores."

When Whittier was a boy the old block-house was in excellent repair, but was removed to make way for modern improvements. "It was a great pity," said Whittier, "to have destroyed it; it ought never to have been done, for it would have lasted another hundred years. It showed not the slightest sign of decay." "If some one had only been there to make a sketch of it!" said I. "Yes," replied the poet, "but no one ever thought of such things in those days. It was an unheard-of thing that any one should go out to look at nature just for love of nature; he would have been thought crazy or foolish. Why, to show how little people understood those things at that time, when Wilson, the ornithologist, was here in America, he visited Haverhill, and the people noticed this man looking about in the woods with a gun, and gazing into all the bushes and up into the trees in a manner which to them gave serious doubts of his sanity. They watched him for some time, and at last the report spread that he was a British spy sent by the English, as it was about the time of the war of 1812. So, considering this suspicion a sufficient ground for action, he was arrested, and brought before the judge as a very suspicious character seen hanging about the town, with no visible means of support, and apparently spying out all that he could. The judge examined him, and found that his sole business was shooting birds. 'Well,' said the judge, 'what do you do with them—eat them?' 'No,' said Wilson. 'Sell them?' 'No; I study them.' Here was a strange statement; neither judge nor people could make it out. That a man should devote all his time to studying birds was a thing before unheard of, and entirely unworthy of credit; and as during the investigation it had come out that Wilson was an Englishman, the case looked very suspicious indeed. Every one imagined that he was a spy sent by the English to find out the best way of taking Haverhill;" and here Whittier stopped and laughed heartily at the ludicrous conceit. "Wilson finally showed a letter from a Boston gentleman who happened to be quite well known, and after consideration the judge concluded that as some one in Boston indorsed him, he could venture to let him go without much danger."

In reverting to places of interest around Amesbury, Whittier mentioned a legend connected with an old mill on the Salisbury road, near the Salisbury Point depot, though he could not remember where the story originated, or how he came by it. The miller would stop his mill at sundown and leave all secure, but it would start up again at twelve o'clock midnight, and grind away until sunrise, stopping all at once on the approach of the miller in the morning. There are no traces left of the mill except a portion of the dam.

There is also another legend, dating back over a hundred years, connected with this same solitary road, where the headless spectre of a man is sometimes seen in the twilight walking beneath the shade of the willows, and carrying his head in a tin pail hung upon his arm. The poet had never heard of this second ghostly story, and laughed as it was related to him.

The valley of the Merrimac abounds with these curious stories, handed down from past generations, and still to be gathered from old wives' tales; not so pleasing, perhaps, as Hugh Tallant's simple stories

"Of the brown dwarfs and the fairies
  Dancing in their moorland rings,"

but sufficient to have given the poet suggestions for many of his songs.

It was while walking under Hugh Tallant's sycamores, which formed a leafy archway over the river road not far from the Haverhill Academy, that the story of Floyd Ireson was thought over by the poet, then a young student. It had been related to him by a Marblehead girl, whose relatives perhaps had taken part in that scene of retribution, when old "Flud Oirson" was,

"fur his horrd horrt,
Torr'd an' futherr'd an' corr'd in a corrt
By the women o' Morble'ead!"

Several months after Whittier mentioned this origin of the poem, I met in Salem an old man who related some anecdotes of Ireson, having received them fresh from the lips of one of the actors in the drama, one of the avengers who "torr'd an' futherr'd" him.

It appears, from his account, that the Freemasons held secret meetings on the subject, and when all was arranged they carried their tar and bags of feathers down among the rocks by night. At twelve o'clock Floyd Ireson was summoned, and went through the ordeal. He was then kept in a warehouse under guard until daylight, when he was put in a dory and dragged about the town, and then carried in a cart to Salem, though the Salem authorities stopped him at what is now the Mill Street railroad crossing; and here it was that my grandfather remembers seeing him standing in the cart, with huge lumps of tar on each temple, wherein were stuck two long goose feathers like horns. The old man who gave my informer the details said that he helped daub the "torr" on, and he rubbed it in pretty effectually. After his punishment Ireson still remained in Marblehead, though he appeared to become reckless of his life. On one occasion he landed on the property of the old man referred to before as one of his persecutors, and deliberately proceeded to carry off a large log lying on the shore; the proprietor started to prevent him, but Ireson worked slowly, and made a noose fast

THE OLD BLOCK-HOUSE.

round the end of the log, which he towed away into deep water. The owner called for him to stop, but Ireson replied with opprobrious epithets. Again the hail came, "Stop, Ireson, or I shall fire at you!" "Fire away, old man; you can't hit me!" and Ireson sailed away with the log in tow.

Incidents like these went to show the towns-people that Floyd Ireson wished to provoke them to take his life, and according to this narrator, who perhaps was prejudiced by his own share in the transaction, the skipper never denied the charge made when he was tarred and feathered.

Again, on Cape Ann, I came across an "ancient mariner" who had a friend in Gloucester named John Tucker, the said Tucker having once picked up Floyd Ireson far out at sea, where he had been driven in his dory from Marblehead, and brought him into Gloucester, not knowing who he was. When the old man landed there he had not a cent to take him back to Marblehead or to buy him a supper. He was taken in charge by Alfonso Mason, who fed him and kept him overnight, and the next day, with the aid of contributions from his friends, sent him on his way to Marblehead; then, after he was safely away, Mason informed the contributors who the man was that they had helped, whereat they were exceeding wroth, and

swore that if they had known it before, he would never have received a penny from them. Whittier himself, as he once related to a friend, came very near the same experience of tar and feathers, in the old abolition days, in New Hampshire, saving himself with his companions by a hasty retreat.

After Whittier related his story of the haunted mill, the conversation turned on the simplicity and credulity of some of the country people. "And that reminds me," said the poet, "of an incident that once occurred at South Hampton in slavery days. It seems there was a runaway negro hid in the great swamp there, and the people of the place, who were all Democrats, were dreadfully frightened, for they thought he had come there to cut all their throats; so they collected together, and after much trouble ran down the negro, and led him a captive to the country store. In some way I received information of what was going on, and with a friend went up there to look after matters. When we arrived they had the negro penned up in one corner of the room; his mouth was wide open and his eyes rolling vacantly; in fact, he was so thoroughly frightened that he could not speak. In the mean time the store was crowded with citizens very much excited, some of whom were for hanging the negro at once, while others were for having a trial first. Presently, and soon after our arrival, the meeting was addressed by the principal man of the village, who was very drunk, and who, I believe, had been in some of the West India islands. He was strongly in favor of letting the negro go; 'for,' said he" (and here Whittier imitated his gestures), "'I've lived, gentlemen, where they kept nigger servants, and I tell you that nigger's all right; he knows what he's about; he's a sensible nigger. I know, because I've seen 'em.' Then there was an excited discussion, and we managed to intercede for the runaway, so that finally they agreed to let him go."

What became of him afterward the poet did not say, but it is probable that this poor passenger on the "under-ground railroad" was well provided for by the quiet Quaker and his friends.

In a drawer of his writing-table the poet still keeps the large iron key of the slave pen at Richmond, which was sent to him when the city was captured by the Union troops. The key is made of wrought iron, is about five inches long, and has

KEY OF THE RICHMOND SLAVE PEN.

been broken and welded together again. It was as appropriate a gift to the poet as the key of the Bastile to Washington, both marking a new era in the liberties of man.

The earliest of Whittier's associations are found in the poems of "Snow-Bound" and "In School Days." The little schoolhouse no longer "sits beside the road," having been sold and removed a number of years ago. It had hardly started on its journey, when one of the wheels on which it was placed broke down, and the building was left in the middle of the road until burned by the boys.

There are still left faint traces of the foundations, a stone wall having been built directly across the site of the fireplace. On digging into the ground at the end of and near the western embankment, I found the remains of the chimney where it had fallen to the ground; the sod had

grown over the bricks, and mingled with them were fragments of plaster from the walls, and pieces of broken window-glass turned iridescent with age, as though these fragments of "the western window-panes" still reflected back a few last rays of the "winter sun" which long years ago "shone over it at setting."

The blackberry vines clambered around my feet, the sumacs still grew thickly about the place, and even a faint depression in the greensward showed where

" The feet that creeping slow to school
Went storming out to playing."

It required not much effort for the imagination to see once more the sweet brown-eyed heroine of the country school and her bashful boy hero of half a century ago:

" Still memory to a gray-haired man
That sweet child-face is showing.
Dear girl! the grasses on her grave
Have forty years been growing!"

But only the poet knows by what name his little heroine was called.

Mr. Ayer, living in the next house to the Whittier homestead, was a playmate of the poet, and went with him to the same road-side school. At the sale of the schoolhouse he came into possession of the "master's desk, deep scarred by raps official," afterward disposing of it, and it was carried away to parts unknown. A few of the benches were also saved, to be afterward destroyed, and some boards left after the burning of the building were worked up into various little objects.

"Can you tell us, Mr. Ayer," said we, "who was the little girl in 'In School Days'?" "Well," he replied, "there were several girls who attended the school in Whittier's time, all nearly of the same age; but I am inclined to think it was my little sister Lydia. She died when she was fourteen, and lies buried in the family lot just over the hill."

With this early playmate of the poet we walked down the road to visit the Whittier burial-place on the old farm. Turning to the right, we entered a rough pasture-land, and after climbing a hill, came to a level space on top, inclosed on three sides by a rude stone wall. Here are the sunken graves marking the place of their former tenants, removed by the poet to a more suitable resting-place. There are five of them, I think. Mr. Ayer pointed out the grave of the "uncle, innocent of books," who is mentioned in "Snow-Bound," and who was killed by the falling of a tree. He had gone out in the morning with his axe, and turned into a path which is still visible on the right of the Haverhill road. At noontime the family missed him at dinner, and soon afterward his dog came up to the house barking wildly, and starting off again toward the woods. At this some of the family followed the dog, accompanied by Mr. Ayer's father, and on reaching the woods they found the unfortunate uncle crushed under a fallen tree. Mr. Ayer cut away the limb which held him down, and the dying man was carried in a sleigh to the old homestead, living but a short time after reaching it.

After leaving the place, we walked along the road to the farm-house. Here, beside the gate, built into the wall, is the horse-block, with rude steps to climb upon it. Noticing some deep semicircular depressions in its surface, we called the attention of Mr. Ayer to them, when he laughed, and said: "Oh, that is where the children used to crack the hickory and butter nuts; they would sit upon the big old stone and hammer away for hours."

Passing up the pathway, which in Whittier's boyhood was swept twice a day, we entered the end door, walking through the pantry into the east front room. This was Whittier's study. Here he would have his little table in the centre of the room, a cheerful fire burning in the great old fire-place, and sit for hours and hours reading.

"He was a great reader," said Mr. Ayer. "I have often been in here and seen him sitting in that spot, absorbed in his book. He used to load me down with papers for my father to read; he was as good as a library."

The room remains in the same condition as in Whittier's boyhood — the old fire-place, the warped floor and antique window-panes, rough uneven ceiling, and protruding beams. On the other side of the front door, across the entry, is the room where the poet was born, Mr. Ayer's mother being with Mrs. Whittier when the event took place. This room remains in its original state, with the exception of the papering.

The great kitchen, famous as the scene of the winter's evening in "Snow-Bound," has been altered slightly by a partition

WHITTIER'S SCHOOL-HOUSE.

placed across one end, near the door of the east front room, and a portion of the great open fire-place has been bricked up. When we entered the kitchen there was a stout, buxom woman frying doughnuts, and heaping a huge platter up with them. She made no objections when Mr. Ayer removed her dish-towel from its nail over the fire-place, and exhibited to us the large broad-headed wrought-iron nail as the identical one on which hung "the bull's-eye watch"—

"The bull's-eye watch that hung in view,
 Ticking its weary circuit through,
 Pointed with mutely warning sign
 Its black hand to the hour of nine."

And here in the corner of the fire-place to the left sat the "uncle, innocent of books,"

"A simple, guileless, child-like man....
 Next, the dear aunt, whose smile of cheer
 And voice in dreams I see and hear,"

was Mercy Hussey, well remembered by the people of the place. The "elder sister" was Mary, afterward Mrs. Caldwell. It is Elizabeth who was the poet's favorite, and whose epitaph he has written in the beautiful lines commencing:

> " As one who held herself a part
> Of all she saw, and let her heart
> Against the household bosom lean,
> Upon the motley-braided mat
> Our youngest and our dearest sat."

In the portrait that I saw of Elizabeth Whittier at the poet's residence there was the same pure face and "large sweet ask-dimmed by her hasty and ungovernable temper. She at last loved a young surgeon, Moses Eliot, who afterward was in the war of 1812. He returned her passion, but his reason told him that he could never be happy with a woman of so violent a temper, and who loved as fiercely as she hated; so he went South to escape from the unhappy attachment, and died a victim of yellow fever in Florida.

HOME OF WHITTIER AT AMESBURY.

ing eyes" that mirrored the gentle soul of his loved sister. The school-master was Joshua Coffin.

> "Brisk wielder of the birch and rule,"

who taught school in that place in Whittier's boyhood. After the publication of "Snow-Bound" an old gray-haired man visited the scenes of the poem, and inquired for Whittier.

> "A careless boy that night he seemed;"

but long years had rolled over him since that night of the past when he

> "Held at the fire his favored place."

That rival of "Petruchio's Kate" was Harriet Livermore, another young teacher in the neighborhood, who often called upon the Whittiers.

> "She sat among us, at the best,
> A not unfeared, half-welcome guest."

She was by "nature passionate and bold," and possessed of great talents, which were After the death of her lover, Miss Livermore turned devotee, and travelled through the Holy Land and Egypt, dying at last in her old age at Germantown, Pennsylvania.

"The wise old doctor" was Elias Weld, to whom in after-years Whittier dedicated his poem of "The Countess," under the initials E. W.

And so as we stood there, the whole home circle clasped us round, and we recalled and repeopled that "Snow-Bound" evening of so long ago, when the kitchen held so many dear to the poet, and now guests of the larger circle of the world.

After leaving the house we crossed over to the barn, which has been raised several feet from the ground, repaired and repainted, but kept with the same internal arrangements as in Whittier's boyhood. The farm-house has also been repainted in Quaker drab or gray, the same tint used in the lifetime of the elder Whittier. As I caught a glimpse of the homestead doorway it reminded me of the

"Sweet doorway pictures of the curls,
And curious eyes of merry girls,
Lifting their hands in mock defense
Against the snow-ball's compliments,"

and led me to speak of breaking out the road after a snow-storm. "Oh, yes," said Mr. Ayer, "it was different then from what it is now. In those days every farmer owned two pair or more of oxen. The Whittiers owned two pair, my father owned a pair, and the next neighbor owned a pair or two, and so on. On the morning after a storm they would come along to our house, collect our oxen, and keep on to the next house, and so on until they had six or seven yoke. Then all the men and boys would pile on to the great ox-sled, and away we would go over and through the drifts. Oh, it was great fun!"

And so we followed Mr. Ayer over the farm, visiting the brook and the stepping-stones, and climbing the hill to see the "gap in the old wall," which still remains as when Whittier wrote his poem of "Tell-ing the Bees," every step calling up associations of the early life of the poet,

"Kindred in soul of him who found
In simple flower and leaf and stone
The impulse of the sweetest lays
Our Saxon tongue has known."

As we stepped into the road once more, Mr. Ayer pointed out the walnut-trees mentioned in the poem of "My Playmate," and indicated the hill beyond as the one pictured in "Maud Muller." There was a white-covered butcher's cart coming down the hill at the time, and as we went away over

"the spring that flowed
Through the meadow across the road,"

we looked back, and saw Whittier's early playmate bargaining for a fore-quarter of lamb, and he was still standing there as we turned a sudden curve, shutting out all view of the old homestead, and leaving us alone with those pictures

"Which Fancy's self, in reverent awe, is seen
To paint, forgetful of the tricks of art,
With pencil dipped alone in colors of the heart."

THE HARVARD AND YALE BOAT-RACE

"THEM'S the Harvards!" is the way many a crew are greeted by the New London urchin, as, with bags in hand, they step from the New York train and group themselves together, waiting for the train to pull out from the station and allow them to cross to the wharf and board the cranky launch which, with steam up, is waiting to convey them to their quarters, four miles up the Thames. Some of them perchance have been there before, and to them the scenes are not new; but, nevertheless, they gaze about them, and over their faces comes a pained expression as they remember how Eli's band led them down the course a little less than a year ago.

When all are on board, the needle-shaped launch backs away out into the stream, and then turns her bow up river towards the massive piers which support that triumph of human ingenuity over

GOING TO THE RACE.

space, the iron bridge, the connecting link between the Groton and New London shores.

In a few moments the launch reaches the bridge, and as she pokes her nose by the piers, all those on board instinctively turn their eyes to the little point of land on the left shore, and tell each other that "there is the finish." And then all eyes are turned up the river, and as they rest upon a gravel bank, 'way off in the distance, it hardly seems possible that the man who measured that course was accurate. Certainly there are no four miles in the country that are longer, or look longer. Soon the Navy-yard, one of the decaying relics of warlike times, is reached, and with a wide sweep to the left the launch makes for deeper water near the New London shore. The banks of the river are now rocky and wild. Occasionally a white painted cottage stands out from its green background of trees, but were it not for the railroad tracks which

mark and mar the left shore, one would almost imagine that he was about to steam into an unexplored channel.

While beauty of nature is appreciated, it does not appeal, however, to those half-browned boys, who are looking but for one object, "Red Top," their home for the next two weeks. In a short space of time the launch takes a swing to the right, and there, straight ahead, with its red roof flashing crimson rays against the blue sky, is Harvard's boating home. Even in its loneliness there is a home-like air about the place. Closely snuggled against a rugged cliff, whose sides have been cruelly gnawed by the avaricious bridge-builder, it nevertheless has the dignity of being perched on a small bluff, and though it shares the limited space with a four-stoned cemetery, its broad welcoming piazza and wide open door completely take away the chilly sensation which the graveyard gives.

With a bell to stop and two bells to

back her, the embryo pilot of the Harvard launch brings her within a few feet of the wide float—near enough to throw a rope to the "heeler" who stands ready to catch it. Scarcely does she touch the float when, one after the other, the crew pile out and greet the "subs," who have been sent down earlier to make things ready. Then each one makes for the quarters, eager to have his section of the common bedroom allotted. The captain, of course, takes the captain's room in the corner. Then the "veterans," if there are any, take their old rooms if they want them, and the remainder are distributed as the captain thinks best, the subs, of course, being looked out for last, and generally getting the two cots near the chimney.

But scarcely have all had a chance to unpack their flannel suits and arrange their belongings before the order is given to get ready for their first practice row on the Thames. So down the little pathway which leads to the boat-house they go, and almost in less time than it takes to tell it they have gotten into their rowing-togs and taken their places by the shell. Together they lift it gently and carry it out on the float. Then, all together, they drop it into the water. When each man is in his place the cockswain gives his orders to push off and get under way.

With a long, steady swing they fall to their work, and having taken a dozen strokes or so, they "let her run," and rest on their oars.

Half a mile up the river, on the same side as Red Top, they see a small cluster of houses with a flag-staff in front. But, as the Yale crew have not arrived, no large blue flag with a white "Y" in the centre graces the top of the staff. They know, however, that they will be there in a day or two, and it is with reluctance that they obey the order, "Eyes in the boat!" And now the launch comes up with the coach perched in the bow. As soon as he is within hearing distance he speaks to the crew, calls upon them for their best efforts from now on until the race, and then sends them off down the river.

Somehow the sweeps feel differently than they did in the sluggish water of the Charles, and as the crew feel the shell shoot along, they gather renewed interest and enthusiasm from the change, and buckle down to their work with renewed

zeal. But the coach is merciless. Fault after fault he brings to their notice. Stretch after stretch he makes them row, and not until the shadows have crept from the banks and almost covered the entire river in darkness does he give the signal to return to the boat-house. With weary backs they lift their shell and carry it up the float. But a bucket of cold water and a brisk rub bring back their spirits, and the crew appetite asserts itself in loud cries for supper. What a supper they eat! Chops, steak, toast, and milk disappear as if by magic, and not until their tired stomachs refuse to be more heavily laden do they rise from the table.

Once fed, like animals, they long for sleep, and in spite of songs, banjo-playing, and rowing incidents, they wait impatiently for ten o'clock to come, and the order, "All to bed!" Then for a few moments pandemonium is let loose. Because they can sleep, they do not want to. The mystic initiation of the new members is gone through, pillows and water are thrown, and the commotion increases until all are in such a state of hysterical excitement that it requires sharp words on the part of the captain to restore order. When all is quiet, the captain blows out the last candle, and tells the crew that not a man shall rise until called in the morning.

Thus it is generally with a crew the first night at New London. Afterwards, as the day of the race approaches, and the men become more nervous and irritable, they allow no one to deprive them of even a second's rest. They are too much worried, and are glad of the chance to think the race over quietly to themselves.

They rise the following morning at seven, take a short walk, and then are ready for breakfast. From eight until eleven their time is their own, and they pass it in reading, playing quoits, lounging on the piazza, or taking rambling walks through the woods back of the quarters.

At eleven, or thereabouts, just as the morning breeze, which generally springs up about that time, is beginning to roughen the surface of the river, they get into the shell and begin their day's work. The hot June sun reddens and blisters their shoulders, and causes them to long for the morning row to end. But they are kept at their work, and after a series of short rows they gradually become ac-

customed to the heat and more contented. After an hour or so they return to
the float, and in a few moments dinner
is served. After dinner they loaf about,
some doing one thing, some another.
Perhaps one or two of them will jump
into the skiff, and spend an hour fishing
in the shade of the old wharf which projects into the river from the point below
the boat-house. At four o'clock they
again assemble, and from four to six, or
even later, they are sent for long stretches
down the course. When they return they
are tired and hungry, and it requires a
good supper to bring up their spirits.
The evening, as usual, is passed in singing
and chaffing one another, but all are glad
when bedtime comes.

The first excitement in their daily routine is the arrival of the Yale crew. They
have been there but a day or two when
one afternoon they see coming up the
river the Yale launch, loaded well down
to her water-line with a living freight of
Yale men and coaches. As they pass
the quarters they cheer their rivals, and
in return the Harvard men dip the faded
crimson flag, which in a listless way has
been floating over the roof of Red Top,
and give three times three for Yale. From
now on the blue flag with the white "Y"
in its centre waves from its staff, and the
work of the substitutes begins. For it is
the duty of the substitutes of each crew to
keep an eye on their opponents.

Let a man get into a shell from either
float, and the fact is immediately noted at
the other. Let a crew start out, and there
is work for the substitutes immediately.
Off they are sent in the pair oar or sin-
gles, and are not allowed to return until
they have followed and observed the crew
from the beginning until the end of their
row. Perhaps, instead of taking to the
water, they run up or down the banks,
and from some elevated point closely observe the crews, and count the number of
strokes they are rowing to the minute.
Often it happens that the substitutes of
both crews meet at the same point of observation, and talk and chat with each
other, exchanging all sorts of useless information. When they return to the
quarters they are besieged with questions,
and given to understand that if they cannot see any better they had better pack
up and go home.

Upon them is ventilated all the irrita-
bleness of the crew. If they come back
bringing the report that the other crew are
rowing well, they are told that they do
not know what good rowing is. If they
report faults, they are told that they must
have been cross-eyed: "they were not
rowing that way when they started." After a time they learn how to properly
construct their reports, and interweave
facts and fancies in a manner more acceptable to the crew, so their life becomes
easier.

It is the incidents of the life at New
London which in after-years come back
to one, and the enjoyment of race-week is
not limited to the chosen few who represent the blue and the crimson.

With a room at the Pequot, Fort Gris-
wold, or Crocker House, the last week in
June can be pleasantly passed listening
to crew gossip, following the crews, and
watching the yachts sail swiftly in and
drop anchors in the wide harbor which
forms the outlet for the beautiful river
which is to be the scene of the great
struggle to come.

It is great fun to follow the crews.
You seldom see them together, for when
one go up the river the other go down,
and *vice versa*. Occasionally, however,
by accident they meet, and then you are
confronted by a cat-and-dog situation.
Both crews cease rowing and rest on
their oars. Neither will make the first
move, and so they sit and glare at each
other. In vain the safety-valves on the
launches give warning of too much pressure. Neither crew propose to give
points on their rowing, and so they do
not row. When, however, patience is almost exhausted, by the aid of the tide, or
by rowing by pairs and fours, they become sufficiently separated, and are once
more off in opposite directions.

It is a beautiful sight to see one of the
crack crews dip their oars in the water,
carry them home with a swing, and shoot
them out quickly for a fresh hold and
stroke. Scarcely a splash can be seen,
and the shell travels as steadily as though
driven by some unseen power entirely
independent of the eight men. The Ga-
briel voice of the cockswain, however, reminds you that, beautiful as is the sight,
there is tyranny in the government of
those grand specimens of muscular development, and that they are but human,
after all. "Watch your time, six!"
"What's the matter with you, five?"
"Eyes in the boat, four!" "Up!"

"Shoot!" And long after you cannot make out the faces of the men you hear the exasperating cry which gives the beat to the stroke: "Up!" "Shoot!"

Having seen the crews row, you compare their good points, and try to settle in your mind which one will surely win. And in the evening, at the hotel, you compare notes with others, and discuss the pros and cons until your judgment is so disturbed that you give up trying to reach a conclusion, and confine your statements to guessing.

As the day of the race approaches, there slowly gather at the different hotels a crowd of enthusiasts, many of whom have come miles to see the race. At the Crocker House you find a small army of newspaper men, quick on the scent of every item of interest in regard to the crew, and with them is always a small contingent of graduates, who love to talk over the races of other years, and compare this year's crews with last.

The evening before the race, in their quarters up the river, the well-trained oarsmen gather together after supper and talk over the coming race. Anxiety is betrayed in faces and actions, and only frequent changes in position enable them to endure the suspense between supper and bedtime. Perhaps they try to sing or joke, but the songs lack enthusiasm as they ring out in the night air, and the jokes fall flat. They realize fully for the first time how much depends on their twenty-odd minutes of work on the morrow, and how horrible it will be if they should lose the race. All day long they have noted the preparations. Old graduates have visited them, wished them luck, and tried to cheer them up. The passing yachts have saluted them, and the gay parties on board have awakened their enthusiasm by cheers. There was excitement in every breath of wind, and instinctively they have partaken of the excitement, until every nerve in their bodies tingles. When finally bedtime comes, with one last look at the heavens to try in vain to determine the weather for the morning, they turn to their cots and try to sleep. But to many of them sleep comes slowly. Over and over again they mentally row the race, win it, lose it, get ahead, break something and fall behind, until exhausted nature rebels, and they fall into a troubled sleep, to awaken in the morning feeling tired and exhausted.

But while they try to sleep, and all about them is silent and still, at the boat-house all is activity and life. The last touches are being given to the preparation of the shell, which, resting upon its wooden horses, and vibrating slightly with each touch of the polisher's hand, has a personality which only an old oarsman can appreciate. Note how the polish glistens with each flash of the lantern's rays. It has taken hours of work to get it, and the faithful attendant goes over it and over it, until from stem to stern it shines like a mirror, and feels to the hand like the surface of glass. When finished it is perfect, and stands silently ready to do its share of the work.

At New London, things are different; the town is one blaze of light, crowds throng the streets, venders and hawkers fill the square, and eager hackmen beseech each passer-by with, "Ride to the Pequot House?" In the harbor, lights twinkle from the mast-heads of many crafts, and ever and anon comes the cry from some owner to his men telling them to come this way or that.

At the Crocker House, a crowd surges in and out. Rooms are in demand. Everybody is excited. Bets are made. Drinks are taken. Chaos reigns. Until, late in the evening, the crowds thin out, and only here and there can be seen small knots of men who discuss, argue, and reason over the chances. It is early in the morning before the electric lights fall sadly and reflectively upon the weary clerk at the desk as he gazes at the empty lobby, and tells the sleepy bell-boy to rearrange the chairs and pick up the loose papers. It has been a wild evening, yet fun and good frolic have predominated, and only occasionally has some misguided youth made notable exhibition of his animal nature by drunken speech and incoherent language.

If one goes to the Pequot House, a barrack-shaped building with rickety walls and several annexes, situated just where the New London shore turns its front to the Sound, one finds a wharf, and from the wharf up the bank a poorly cared-for driveway, which joins the New London road at an acute angle. From the road to the hotel stretch beautiful green lawns. The whole scene is one of great natural beauty mingled with traces of the interference and neglect of man. But everything is full of life there.

The broad piazza is alive with people. Pretty maidens, lovely women, jolly matrons, sit, walk, and chatter with men in full dress or yachting suits. Through the open windows come the strains of music, and the lights thrown out on the lawns show groups of fellows whose gay laughing conversation plainly tells of the good time they are having. The anchorage-ground off the wharf is well illuminated with myriads of lights from the yachts, and small boats are continually passing to and fro, bringing parties to the shore. Every once in a while the scene about the hotel is enlivened by the arrival of parties from New London. With a song or a cheer they announce their coming in the distance, and as they greet old friends almost the first question is, "Who'll win?" and then they say, "Let's adjourn."

Bright and early the next morning everybody is up and on the move. Carriages are engaged, tickets are bought, and arrangements made to see the race. Either crimson or blue is in every buttonhole, and the wearers are eager for the fun to begin. The yachts in front of the Pequot House weigh anchor, and either steam up themselves toward the bridge, or else are towed up by some friendly tug. They have got to get their positions in the lines. Every one is hurrying towards New London as a centre. At the wharves launches are continually coming in and backing out, some for pleasure, some on business connected with the race. Above the bridge the yachts are being anchored in two long lines, forming a lane through which in a few hours the two crews will pass. From the bowsprits to mast-heads, and from mast-heads to sterns, flags of gay colors fly, and pretty women walk the decks and level glasses at every passing boat. Once in a while a cheer is heard, and horns and whistles give evidence of the excitement and noise to come. Every ripple on the water is noticed and scowled at, for every one dreads a postponement.

Four miles up the river, at the quarters, it is as still and quiet as a village Sunday. A few men in bright-colored blazers and white duck trousers are scattered about, some looking at books, some talking with each other, but all keeping one eye on the weather and the condition of the water. In the boat-house the last finishing touches are being given to the rigging of the shells. Straps are tested, nuts are tightened, and lastly the round leather buttons on the sweeps are given a coating of lard to make them turn easily. In front of the boat-house the captain and coaches are having a final understanding, and as they see the referee's boat approach and hear the whistle's signal they call to their men, and then all disappear. While they dress, through the window and cracks in the side of the boat-house they see a small fleet of steam-craft of all sizes and shapes come slowly up the river, and restlessly change their positions in the deep water to the eastward of the start. Then the breeze brings to their ears the sound of faint cheering, and coming up the railroad track on the other side of the river they see the observation train, with its tiers of seats crowded with people, all framed in by canopies of crimson or blue. Cold chills creep up and down their spines as they realize that the long-expected hour has at last arrived. They are glad when the orders are given to pick up the shell, carry her out, and put her into the water. Then, when they find themselves in their places, and feel the rough handle of the sweep in their grasp, the greater part of their nervousness vanishes, and with a last tug at their toe-straps they are ready to be off. In short stretches and with frequent stops they worry their way across the river, stealing occasionally a glance at their opponents, who are slowly rowing down. Then an order is given to keep their eyes in the boat, and they know that they are dangerously near the start. They drift by the starting-boat, and feel the hands of the boatman as he grasps the stern and holds it in position. Above and about them they hear an indistinct buzz of cheers and shouts, but their hearts beat so quickly that their eyes are half blurred, and they can with difficulty hold their gaze on the back of the man in front.

At the word they quickly peel off their jerseys and pass them to the boatman. Then comes a time which tries the patience of all. They back her up a little, pull the bow round, then go out to the full reach. A second; it is a year to each man in the shells. There is a horrible silence, then the "Are you ready? Go!" from the referee sends them off with a rush.

If the reader has ever handled a sweep in a 'varsity race he will know how each man feels while he waits for the start.

There he is with his feet firmly pressed against the stretcher, his knees slightly bent, and the blade of his sweep just covered with water. At the "Go!" like a spring he uncoils, gives a short swing with his shoulders, a shove with his legs, tears his blade from the water, rushes forward, and digs the water again. Three strokes and there is headway; a fourth, and he can feel the need of slower work and longer pulls. He hears nothing; he sees nothing. His mind is a blank. There are a great throbbing in his head, an uncomfortable feeling about his stomach. His breath does not seem to come right. "Oh dear!" he thinks to himself, "I can never stand this." But as the stroke lengthens, and the recover becomes slower, the mist slowly clears away from before his eyes, the uncomfortable feeling vanishes, and the true work of the race begins. He now sees the man in front of him, and gathering all his wits about him, he watches his time, tries to move with him, thinks of a thousand things in a second, but principally he is interested in as to where the other crew is. He knows soon enough. As he comes forward for a stroke he catches a glimpse out of the corner of his eye of a moving mass beside him on the water. They are there. "But we're holding them," he says to himself, and he shuts his teeth hard and puts more drive into his legs. "Half a mile," shouts the cockswain. "Only half a mile!" It seems as though he had been rowing for hours. "Why don't we gain?" These thoughts flash through his mind. But he pulls with his might. If he gains there comes to him slowly the knowledge that his crew are ahead, the moving mass beside him has gradually dropped astern, and now as he comes forward he can see his opponents as they struggle to regain the space they have lost. The sight gives him courage, and he feels as strong as an ox. The race becomes interesting. He never rowed so well in his life. Not a muscle becomes tired. "One mile!" shouts the cockswain. "Only three more," he thinks to himself, and the time passes quickly until the next mile flag is reached. Then something happens which brings his heart into his mouth. His oar, as he shoots it out on the recover, strikes a wave, the handle twists in his grasp, and before he can control it the blade is the wrong way. He stops rowing, and wrenches his oar out of the water. The delay has enabled his opponents to catch up, and as he sees them his spirits fall. But quickly getting into the stroke, he makes up for what he has lost by pulling all the harder, and soon he feels more at ease, for he knows he is gaining. Another mile, and he hears about him the cheers of the spectators on the decks of the yachts. A half-mile farther and he feels sure of the race. "Now, boys," shouts the cockswain, "only a half-mile more."

Jove! how he pulls! and as nearer and nearer he gets to the finish, the more he sees and the more he hears. Cannon crash in his ear. Whistles and yells of delight are heard on all sides. Pulling a strong steady stroke, his crew swing along, and just before they cross the line they spurt to show what they can do. "Let her run!" shouts the cockswain, and the race is over.

Perhaps there are artists who can picture on canvas a face expressive of perfect happiness, but they cannot give to a face an expression of perfect delight unless they have seen how a man looks who has won a university race.

Let us go back, however, to the first half-mile. Suppose, instead of gaining, he loses. He no longer catches a glimpse of the moving mass beside him. There is a strange silence all about him. Spurt after spurt is called for. His arms and legs begin to grow heavy. The mist is coming back before his eyes. His breath feels hot and his mouth gets dry. "One mile!" shouts the cockswain. "Only one!" he thinks to himself. "Now pick it up!" He tries for a few strokes, pushes a little harder on his stretcher, and then he falls back into the weary way he was going.

Now a pain comes in his side, and he has hard work to breathe. He has to row easier for a stroke or two. "Two miles!" "You're gaining!" He rouses again, and makes another gallant effort, but it's useless. "Will the race never end?" "Three miles!" "Is that all?" He now begins to hear the cannon and whistles as they greet the crew ahead, and looming up over the cockswain's head he sees the referee's boat, closely followed by a small fleet of steamers. Everything appears to haul him back. He has the sensation as though he was rowing up hill. A buzzing commences in his ears, his arms grow heavier, and when at length the finish-line is crossed he drops his sweep, and slipping back against the knees of the man behind him, he rests his weary body, while sob after sob shakes his frame.

In a few moments, however, severe as has been his struggle, he finds his strength coming back, and he wonders why he did not pull harder.

But how does the race appear to the spectator? Perhaps he is fortunate enough to have a chance to watch it from a launch. If he is, he finds himself at the start on the other side of the river from the crews, for the water is too shallow the first half-mile of the course to allow a launch to follow closely, so he has to content himself with watching from a distance. He sees the Yale crew coming slowly down the river, then the Harvard crew leave the float and paddle across. Now the two crews are together near the bank. The referee's boat gets as close as possible. After a little manœuvring he notices that the two crews are opposite each other, man for man. Then he sees their arms wave as they strip off the jerseys. There is a moment or two of delay. Then a shout is heard from the observation train, clouds of spray rise on both sides of the crews, and he knows they have started. How quickly the men move! The shells fairly jump. In a few seconds, however, the splashing has stopped, and the blades begin to linger in the water. Long powerful strokes have taken the place of the short drives which were used at the start. As one crew come forward the other go back. The crews seesaw with each other, but the cockswains travel steadily along. Now one sharp bow is ahead; now the other. Exciting? Just a trifle. The spectator feels as though he were rowing himself, and he inwardly wishes he was. Bow and bow the two crews pass the first half-mile flag. The launch approaches nearer, and crossing behind the crews, it follows the race a little in the rear, but just enough to one side to give a good view of the crews. Both crews have settled down to their best rowing. How grandly the men pull! The brown backs rise and fall with clocklike precision. Even at a distance the straining muscles can be seen to contract as the blades take the water.

And when the drive with the legs puts still more of a strain upon those broad backs and strong arms, their muscles stand out like tightened whip-cords.

Now slowly but surely one crew creep ahead. Gradually the cockswain in one shell gets opposite the stroke oar in the other. There he balances for a time, first a little ahead, then a little behind, then by a series of steady advances he is placed on the line with the next man—number seven. Here the same scene is repeated, and so on up the shell, until by good rowing his crew pull him clean ahead, and the observer can see the space between the crews grow wider and wider. But from the Navy-yard the launch has to take a position more directly behind, and no longer can he see by just how much one crew lead. He gets a stern view of the crews, and can only observe the blades rise, skim the water, then disappear from sight.

Now the men in the losing crew begin to get tired. The pace is too hot for them, and they slowly lose their form and move raggedly. The blades no longer take the water together; they tumble in one after the other, and splashing commences. There are generally one or two men in the crew who stand out from the others, and call attention to themselves by their pallor, by the wabbly way in which they row. Every moment it seems as though they must stop and give up; but they keep on, and your heart goes out to them as you see them make effort after effort to sit up and pull harder. The losing shell is driven slower and slower. The referee's boat and the steamers and launches find it difficult to keep from running it down. They slow up a little, and become so crowded together that collisions seem inevitable. Their occupants become alarmed, and to the excitement of the race is added the excitement of the actual danger. But the skilled pilots keep clear of each other, and steer on down the river.

The two crews are now in the lane between the yachts. As they pass them, from the deck of each one a puff of smoke rises, a report is heard, and soon the smoky haze settles down over the struggling men, and the banks echo and re-echo with cheers, whistles, and explosions.

Under cover of the friendly smoke the last crew crosses the line and the race is finished.

ROUNDABOUT TO BOSTON

I.

DURING the four years of my life in Venice the literary intention was present with me at all times and in all places. I wrote many things in verse, which I sent to the magazines in every part of the English-speaking world, but they came unerringly back to me, except in three instances only, when they were kept by the editors who finally printed them. One of these pieces was published in the Atlantic Monthly; another in Harper's Magazine; the third was got into the New York Ledger through the kindness of Dr. Edward Everett Hale, who used I know not what mighty magic to that end. I had not yet met him; but he interested himself in my ballad as if it had been his own. His brother, Charles Hale, later Consul - General for Egypt, whom I saw almost every moment of the two visits he paid Venice in my time, had sent it to him, after copying it in his own large, fair hand, so that it could be read. He was not quite of that literary Boston which I so fondly remembered my glimpses of; he was rather of a journalistic and literary Boston which I had never known; but he was of Boston, after all. He had been in Lowell's classes at Harvard; he had often met Longfellow in Cambridge; he knew Doctor Holmes, of course; and he let me talk of my idols to my heart's content. I think he must have been amused by my raptures; most people would have been; but he was kind and patient, and he listened to me with a sweet intelligence which I shall always gratefully remember. He died too young, with his life's possibilities mainly unfulfilled; but none who knew him could fail to imagine them, or to love him for what he was.

II.

Besides those few pitiful successes, I had nothing but defeats in the sort of literature which I supposed was to be my calling, and the defeats threw me upon prose; for some sort of literary thing, if not one, then another, I must do if I lived; and I began to write those studies of Venetian life which afterwards became a book, and which I contributed as letters to the Boston Advertiser, after vainly offering them to more æsthetic periodicals. However, I do not imagine that it was a very smiling time for any literary endeavorer at home in the life-and-death civil war then waging. Some few young men arose who made themselves heard amid the din of arms even as far as Venice, but most of these were hushed long ago. I fancy Theodore Winthrop, who began to speak, as it were, from his soldier's grave, so soon did his death follow the earliest recognition by the public, and so many were his posthumous works, was chief of these; but there were others whom the present readers must make greater effort to remember. Forceythe Willson, who wrote The Old Sergeant, became known for the rare quality of his poetry; and now and then there came a poem from Aldrich, or Stedman, or Stoddard. The great new series of the Biglow Papers gathered volume with the force they had from the beginning. The Autocrat was often in the pages of the Atlantic, where one often found Whittier and Emerson, with many a fresh name now faded. In Washington the Piatts were writing some of the most beautiful verse of the war, and Brownell was sounding his battle lyrics like so many trumpet blasts. The fiction which followed the war, with an increasing tendency to the realism that now prevails, was yet all to come. Whatever was done in any kind had some hint of the war in it, inevitably; though in the very heart of it Longfellow was setting about his great version of Dante, peacefully, prayerfully, as he has told in the noble sonnets which register the mood of his undertaking.

At Venice, if I was beyond the range of literary recognition I was in direct relations with one of our greatest literary men, who was again of that literary Boston which mainly represented American literature to me. The official chief of the consul at Venice was the United States Minister at Vienna, and in my time this minister was John Lothrop Motley, the historian. He was removed, later, by that Johnson administration which followed Lincoln's so forgottenly that I name it with a sense of something almost prehistoric. Among its worst errors was the attempted discredit of a man who had given lustre to our name by his work, and who was a devoted patriot as well as accomplished scholar. He visited Venice during my first year, which was the darkest period of the civil war, and I remember with what instant security, not to say severity, he rebuked my scarcely whispered misgivings of the end, when I ventured to ask him what he thought it would be. Austria had never recognized the Secessionists as belligerents, and in the complications with France and England there was little for our minister but to share the home indignation at the sympathy of those powers with the South. In Motley this was heightened by that feeling of astonishment, of wounded faith, which all Americans with English friendships experienced in those days, and which he, whose English friendships were many, experienced in peculiar degree.

I drifted about with him in his gondola, and refreshed myself, long a-hungered for such talk, with his talk of literary life in London. Through some acquaintance I had made in Venice I was able to be of use to him in getting documents copied for him in the Venetian Archives, especially the Relations of the Venetian Ambassadors at different courts during the period and events he was studying. All such papers passed through my hands in transmission to the historian, though now I do not quite know why they need have done so; but perhaps he was willing to give me the pleasure of being a partner, however humble, in the enterprise. My recollection of him is of courtesy to a far younger man unqualified by patronage, and of a presence of singular dignity and grace. He was one of the handsomest men I ever saw, with beautiful eyes, a fine blond beard of modish cut, and a sensitive nose, straight and fine. He was altogether a figure of worldly splendor; and I had reason to know that he did not let the credit of our nation suffer at the most aristocratic court in Europe for want of a fit diplomatic costume, when some of our ministers were trying to make their office do its full effect upon all occasions in "the dress of an American gentleman." The morning after his arrival Mr. Motley came to me with a

JOHN LOTHROP MOTLEY.

handful of newspapers which, according to the Austrian custom at that day, had been opened in the Venetian post-office. He wished me to protest against this on his behalf as an infringement of his diplomatic extra-territoriality, and I proposed to go at once to the director of the post: I had myself suffered in the same way, and though I knew that a mere consul was helpless, I was willing to see the double-headed eagle trodden under foot by a Minister Plenipotentiary. Mr. Motley said that he would go with me, and we put off in his gondola to the post-office. The director received us with the utmost deference. He admitted the irregularity which the minister complained of, and declared that he had no choice but to open every foreign newspaper, to whomsoever addressed. He suggested, however, that if the minister made his appeal to the Liéutenant-Governor of Venice, Count Toggenburg would no doubt instantly order the exemption of his newspapers from the general rule.

Mr. Motley said he would give himself the pleasure of calling upon the Lieutenant-Governor, and "How fortunate," he added, when we were got back into the gondola, "that I should have happened to bring my court dress with me!" I did not see the encounter of the high contending powers, but I know that it ended in a complete victory for our minister.

I had no farther active relations of an official kind with him, except in the case of a naturalized American citizen, whose

CHARLES HALE.

worshipper's own showing, scarcely level with the popular movement which he did not so much direct as follow; but it is a good deal for a prince to be able even to follow his people; and it cannot be said that Motley does not fully recognize the greatness of the Dutch people, though he may see the Prince of Orange too large. The study of their character made at least a theoretical democrat of a scholar whose instincts were not perhaps democratic, and his sympathy with that brave little republic between the dikes strengthened him in his fealty to the great commonwealth between the oceans. I believe that so far as he was of any political tradition, he was of the old Boston Whig tradition; but when I met him at Venice he was in the glow of a generous pride in our war as a war against slavery. He spoke of the negroes and their simple-hearted, single-minded devotion to the Union cause in terms that an original abolitionist might have used, at a time when original abolitionists were not so many as they have since become.

For the rest, I fancy it was very well for us to be represented at Vienna in those days by an ideal democrat who was also a real swell, and who was not likely to discredit us socially when we so much needed to be well thought of in every

property was slowly but surely wasting away in the keeping of the Venetian courts. An order had at last been given for the surrender of the remnant to the owner; but the Lombardo-Venetian authorities insisted that this should be done through the United States Minister at Vienna, and Mr. Motley held as firmly that it must be done through the United States Consul at Venice. I could only report to him from time to time the unyielding attitude of the Civil Tribunal, and at last he consented, as he wrote, "to act officiously, not officially, in the matter," and the hapless claimant got what was left of his estate.

I had a glimpse of the historian afterwards in Boston, but it was only for a moment, just before his appointment to England, where he was made to suffer for Sumner in his quarrel with Grant. That injustice crowned the injuries his country had done a most faithful patriot and high-spirited gentleman, whose fame as a historian once filled the ear of the English-speaking world. His books seemed to have been written in a spirit already no longer modern; and I did not find the greatest of them so moving as I expected when I came to it with all the ardor of my admiration for the historian. William the Silent seemed to me, by his

THEODORE WINTHROP.

way. At a court where the family of Count Schmerling, the Prime Minister, could not be received for want of the requisite descents, it was well to have a minister who would not commit the mistake of inviting the First Society to meet the Second Society, as a former Envoy Extraordinary had done, with the effect of finding himself left entirely to the Second Society during the rest of his stay in Vienna.

III.

One of my consular colleagues under Motley was another historian, of no such popularity, indeed, nor even of such success, but perhaps not of inferior powers. This was Richard Hildreth, at Trieste, the author of one of the sincerest if not the truest histories of the United States, according to the testimony both of his liking and his misliking critics. I have never read his history, and I speak of it only at second hand; but I had read, before I met him, his novel of Archie More, or The White Slave, which left an indelible impression of his imaginative verity upon me. The impression is still so deep that after the lapse of nearly forty years since I saw the book, I have no misgiving in speaking of it as a most powerful piece of realism. It treated passionately, intensely, though with a superficial coldness, of wrongs now so remote from us in the abolition of slavery that it is useless to hope it will ever be generally read hereafter, but it can safely be praised to any one who wishes to study that bygone condition, and the literature which grew out of it. I fancy it did not lack recognition in its time, altogether, for I used to see it in Italian and French translations on the bookstalls. I believe neither his history nor his novel brought the author more gain than fame. He had worn himself out on a newspaper when he got his appointment at Trieste, and I saw him in the shadow of the cloud that was wholly to darken him before he died. He was a tall thin man, absent, silent: already a phantom of himself, but with a scholarly serenity and dignity amidst the ruin, when the worst came.

I first saw him at the pretty villa where he lived in the suburbs of Trieste, and where I passed several days, and I remember him always reading, reading, reading. He could with difficulty be roused from his book by some strenuous appeal from his family to his conscience as a host. The last night he sat with Paradise Lost in his hand, and nothing could win him from it till he had finished it. Then he rose to go to bed. Would not he bid his parting guest good-by? The idea of farewell perhaps dimly penetrated to him. He responded, without looking round,

"They, hand in hand, with wandering steps and slow,
Through Eden took their solitary way,"

and so left the room.

RICHARD HILDRETH.
By permission of William Rutter & Co.

I had earlier had some dealings with him as a fellow-consul concerning a deserter from an American ship whom I inherited from my predecessor at Venice. The man had already been four or five months in prison, and he was in a fair way to end his life there; for it is our law that a deserting sailor must be kept in the consul's custody till some vessel of our flag arrives, when the consul can oblige the master to take the deserter and let him work his passage home. Such a vessel rarely came to Venice even in times of peace, and in times of war there

BRATTLE STREET, CAMBRIDGE.

was no hope of any. So I got leave of the consul at Trieste to transfer my captive to that port, where now and then an American ship did trade. The flag determines the nationality of the sailor, and this unhappy wretch was theoretically our fellow-citizen; but when he got to Trieste he made a clean breast of it to the consul. He confessed that when he shipped under our flag he was a deserter from a British regiment at Malta; and he begged piteously not to be sent home to America, where he had never been in his life, nor ever wished to be. He wished to be sent back to his regiment at Malta, and to whatever fate awaited him there. The case certainly had its embarrassments; but the American consul contrived to let our presumptive compatriot slip into the keeping of the British consul, who promptly shipped him to Malta. In view of the strained relations between England and America at that time this was a piece of masterly diplomacy.

Besides my old Ohio-time friend Moncure D. Conway, who paid us a visit, and in his immediate relations with literary Boston seemed to bring the mountain to Mahomet, I saw no one else more literary than Henry Ward Beecher. He was passing through Venice on his way to those efforts in England in behalf of the Union which had a certain great effect at the time; and in the tiny parlor of our apartment on the Grand Canal, I can still see him sitting athletic, almost pugilistic, of presence, with his strong face, but kind, framed in long hair that swept above his massed forehead, and fell to the level of his humorously smiling mouth. His eyes quaintly gleamed at the things we told him of our life in the strange place; but he only partly relaxed from his strenuous pose, and the hands that lay upon his knees were clinched. Afterwards, as he passed our balcony in a gondola, he lifted the brave red fez he was wearing (people wore the fez for one caprice or another) and saluted our eagle and us: we were often on the balcony behind the shield to attest the authenticity of the American eagle.

IV.

Before I left Venice, however, there came a turn in my literary luck, and from the hand I could most have wished to reverse the adverse wheel of fortune. I had labored out with great pains a paper on recent Italian comedy, which I sent to Lowell, then with his friend Professor Norton jointly editor of the North American Review; and he took it and wrote me one of his loveliest letters about it, consoling me in an instant for all the defeat I had undergone, and making it sweet and worthy to have lived through that misery. It is one of the hard conditions of this state that while we can mostly make out to let people taste the last drop of bitterness and ill-will that is in us, our love and gratitude are only semi-articulate at the best, or altogether tongue-tied. As often as I tried afterwards to tell Lowell of the benediction, the salvation, his letter was to me, I failed. But perhaps he would not have understood, if I had spoken out all that was

cle, in his letter, and asked me where he should send it, and I answered, to my father-in-law, who put it in his savings-bank, where he lived, in Brattleboro. There it remained, and I forgot all about it, so that when his affairs were settled some years later and I was notified that there was a sum to my credit in the bank, I said, with the confidence I have nearly always felt when wrong, that I had no money there. The proof of my error was

ENGLISH ELMS AT LOWELL'S GATE.

in me with the fulness I could have given a resentment. His message came after years of thwarted endeavor, and reinstated me in the belief that I could still do something in literature. To be sure, the letters in the Advertiser had begun to make their impression; among the first great pleasures they brought me was a recognition from my diplomatic chief at Vienna; but I valued my admission to the North American peculiarly because it was Lowell let me in, and because I felt that in his charge it must be the place of highest honor. He spoke of the pay for my arti-

sent me in a check, and then I bethought me of the pay for Recent Italian Comedy.

It was not a day when I could really afford to forget money due me, but then it was not a great deal of money. The Review was as poor as it was proud, and I had two dollars a printed page for my paper. But this was more than I got from the Advertiser, which gave me five dollars a column for my letters, printed in a type so fine that the money, when translated from greenbacks into gold at a discount of 2.80, must have been about a dollar a thousand words. However, I was richly content with that, and would gladly have let them have the letters for nothing.

Before I left Venice I had made my sketches into a book, which I sent on to Messrs. Trübner & Co., in London. They had consented to look at it to oblige my friend Conway, who during his sojourn with us in Venice, before his settlement in London, had been forced to listen to some of it. They answered me in due time that they would publish an edition of a thousand, at half profits, if I could get some American house to take five hundred copies. When I stopped in London I had so little hope of being able to do this that I asked the Trübners if I might, without losing their offer, try to get some other London house to publish my book. They said Yes, almost joyously; and I began to take my manuscript about. At most places they would not look at me or it, and they nowhere consented to read it. The house promptest in refusing to consider it afterwards pirated one of my novels, and with some expressions of good intention in that direction, never

paid me anything for it; though I believe the English still think that this sort of behavior was peculiar to the American publisher in the old buccaneering times. I was glad to go back to the Trübners with my book, and on my way across the Atlantic I met a publisher who finally agreed to take those five hundred copies. This was Mr. M. M. Hurd, of Hurd & Houghton, a house then newly established in New York and Cambridge. We played ring-toss and shuffleboard together, and became of a friendship which lasts to this day. But it was not till some months later, when I saw him in New York, that he consented to publish my book. I remember how he said, with an air of vague misgiving, and an effect of trying to justify himself in an imprudence, that it was not a great matter anyway. I perceived that he had no faith in it, and to tell the truth I had not much myself. But the book had an instant success, and it has gone on from edition to edition ever since. There was just then the interest of a not wholly generous surprise at American things

SYRINGA THICKET, LOWELL'S GARDEN.

LOWELL'S WILLOWS.

among the English. Our success in putting down the great Confederate rebellion
had caught the fancy of our cousins, and
I think it was to this mood of theirs that
I owed largely the kindness they showed
my book. There were long and cordial
reviews in all the great London journals,
which I used to carry about with me like
love-letters; and when I tried to show
them to other people, I could not understand their coldness concerning them.

At Boston, where we landed on our return home, there was a moment when it
seemed as if my small destiny might be
linked at once with that of the city which
later became my home. I ran into the
office of the Advertiser to ask what had
become of some sketches of Italian travel
I had sent the paper, and the managing
editor made me promise not to take a
place anywhere before I had heard from
him. I gladly promised, but I did not
hear from him, and when I returned to
Boston a fortnight later, I found that a
fatal partner had refused to agree with
him in engaging me upon the paper.
They even gave me back half a dozen
unprinted letters of mine, and I published
them in the Nation, of New York, and
afterwards in the book called Italian
Journeys.

But after I had encountered fortune in
this frowning disguise, I had a most joy-
ful little visit with Lowell, which made
me forget there was anything in the
world but the delight and glory of sitting
with him in his study at Elmwood and
hearing him talk. It must have been
my freshness from Italy which made him
talk chiefly of his own happy days in the
land which so sympathetically brevets all
her lovers fellow-citizens. At any rate he
would talk of hardly anything else, and
he talked late into the night, and early
into the morning. About two o'clock,
when all the house was still, he lighted a
candle, and went down into the cellar,
and came back with certain bottles under
his arms. I had not a very learned pal-
ate in those days (or in these, for that
matter), but I knew enough of wine to
understand that these bottles had been
chosen upon that principle which Longfellow put in verse, and used to repeat
with a humorous lifting of the eyebrows
and hollowing of the voice:

> "If you have a friend to dine,
>   Give him your best wine;
> If you have two,
>   The second-best will do."

As we sat in their mellow after-glow, Lowell spoke to me of my own life and pros-

pects, wisely and truly, as he always spoke. He said that it was enough for a man who had stuff in him to be known to two or three people, for they would not suffer him to be forgotten, and it would rest with himself to get on. I told him that though I had not given up my place at Venice, I was not going back, if I could find anything to do at home, and I was now on my way to Ohio, where I should try my best to find something; at the worst, I could turn to my trade of printer. He did not think it need ever come to that; and he said that he believed I should have an advantage with readers, if not with editors, in hailing from the West; I should be more of a novelty. I knew very well that even in my own West I should not have this advantage unless I appeared there with an Eastern imprint, but I could not wish to urge my misgiving against his faith. Was I not already richly successful? What better thing personally could befall me, if I lived forever after on milk and honey, than to be sitting there with my hero, my master, and having him talk to me as if we were equal in deed and in fame?

The cat-bird called in the syringa thicket at his door, before we said the good-night which was good-morning, using the sweet Italian words, and bidding each other the *Dorma bene* which has the quality of a benediction. He held my hand, and looked into my eyes with the sunny kindness which never failed me, worthy or unworthy; and I went away to bed. But not to sleep; only to dream such dreams as fill the heart of youth when the recognition of its endeavor has come from the achievement it holds highest and best.

V

I found nothing to do in Ohio; some places that I heard of proved impossible one way or another, in Columbus and Cleveland, and Cincinnati; there was always the fatal partner; and after three weeks I was again in the East. I came to New York, resolved to fight my way in, somewhere, and I did not rest a moment before I began the fight.

My notion was that which afterwards became Bartley Hubbard's. "Get a basis," said the softening cynic of the Saturday Press, when I advised with him, among other acquaintances. "Get a salaried place, something regular on some paper, and then you can easily make up the rest." But it was a month before I achieved this vantage, and then I got it in a quarter where I had not looked for it. I wrote editorials on European and literary topics for different papers, but mostly for the Times, and they paid me well and more than well; but I was nowhere offered a basis, though once I got so far towards it as to secure a personal interview with the editor-in-chief, who made me feel that I had seldom met so busy a man. He praised some work of mine that he had read in his paper, but I was never recalled to his presence; and now I think he judged rightly that I should not be a lastingly good journalist. My point of view was artistic; I wanted time to prepare my effects.

There was another and clearer prospect opened to me on a literary paper, then newly come to the light, but long since gone out in the dark. Here again my work was taken, and liked so much that I was offered the basis (at twenty dollars a week) that I desired; I was even assigned to a desk where I should write in the office; and the next morning I came gleefully down to Spruce Street to occupy it. But I was met at the door by one of the editors, who said lightly, as if it were a trifling affair, "Well, we've concluded to *waive* the idea of an engagement," and once more my bright hopes of a basis dispersed themselves. I said, with what calm I could put on, that they must do what they thought best, and I went on skirmishing baselessly about for this and the other papers which had been buying my material.

I had begun printing in the Nation those letters about my Italian journeys left over from the Boston Advertiser; they had been liked in the office, and one day the editor astonished and delighted me by asking how I would fancy giving up outside work to come there and write only for the Nation. We averaged my gains from all sources at forty dollars a week, and I had my basis as unexpectedly as if I had dropped upon it from the skies.

This must have been some time in November, and the next three or four months were as happy a time for me as I have ever known. I kept on printing my Italian material in the Nation; I wrote criticisms for it (not very good criticisms, I think now), and I amused myself very

much with the treatment of social phases
and events in a department which grew
up under my hand. My associations personally were of the most agreeable kind.
I worked with joy, with ardor, and I
liked so much to be there, in that place
and in that company, that I hated to have
each day come to an end.

I believed that my lines were cast in
New York for good and all; and I renewed my relations with the literary
friends I had made before going abroad.
I often stopped, on my way up town, at
an apartment the Stoddards had in Lafayette Place, or near it; I saw Stedman,
and reasoned high, to my heart's content,
of literary things with them and him.

With the winter Bayard Taylor came
on from his home in Kennett and took
an apartment in East Twelfth Street, and
once a week Mrs. Taylor and he received
all their friends there, with a simple and
charming hospitality. There was another
house which we much resorted to—the
house of James Lorrimer Graham, afterwards Consul-General at Florence, where
he died. I had made his acquaintance at
Venice three years before, and I came in
for my share of that love for literary men
which all their perversities could not extinguish in him. It was a veritable passion, which I used to think he could not
have felt so deeply if he had been a literary man himself. There were delightful
dinners at his house, where the wit of the
Stoddards shone, and Taylor beamed with
joyous good-fellowship and overflowed
with invention; and Huntington, long
Paris correspondent of the Tribune, humorously tried to talk himself into the
resolution of spending the rest of his life
in his own country. There was one evening when C. P. Cranch, always of a most
pensive presence and aspect, sang the
most killingly comic songs; and there
was another evening when, after we all
went into the library, something tragical
happened. Edwin Booth was of our number, a gentle, rather silent person in company, or with at least little social initiative, who, as his fate would, went up to
the cast of a huge hand that lay upon one
of the shelves. "Whose hand is this, Lor-
ry?" he asked our host, as he took it up
and turned it over in both his own hands.
Graham feigned not to hear, and Booth
asked again, "Whose hand is this?" Then
there was nothing for Graham but to say,
"It's Lincoln's hand," and the man for

whom it meant such unspeakable things
put it softly down without a word.

VI.

Of the evenings at the Taylors' I can
recall best the one which was most significant for me, and even fatefully significant. Mr. and Mrs. Fields were there
from Boston, and I renewed all the pleasure of my earlier meetings with them.
At the end Fields said, mockingly, "Don't
despise Boston!" and I answered, as we
shook hands, "Few are worthy to live in
Boston." It was New-Year's, and that
night it came on to snow so heavily that
my horse-car could hardly plough its way
up to Forty-seventh Street through the
drifts. The next day and the next, I
wrote at home, because it was so hard to
get down town. The third day I reached
the office and found a letter on my desk
from Fields, asking how I should like to
come to Boston and be his assistant on
the Atlantic Monthly. I submitted the
matter at once to my chief on the Nation, and with his frank good-will I talked it over with Mr. Osgood, of Ticknor &
Fields, who was to see me further about
it if I wished, when he came to New York;
and then I went to Boston to see Mr.
Fields concerning details. I was to sift
all the manuscripts and correspond with
contributors; I was to do the literary
proof-reading of the magazine; and I was
to write the four or five pages of book-
notices, which were then printed at the
end of the periodical in finer type; and I
was to have forty dollars a week. I said
that I was getting that already for less
work, and then Mr. Fields offered me ten
dollars more. Upon these terms we closed,
and on the first of March, which was my
twenty-ninth birthday, I went to Boston
and began my work. I had not decided
to accept the place without advising with
Lowell; he counselled the step, and gave
me some shrewd and useful suggestions.
The whole affair was conducted by Fields
with his unfailing tact and kindness, but
it could not be kept from me that the
qualification I had as practical printer for
the work was most valued, if not the most
valued, and that as proof-reader I was expected to make it avail on the side of economy. Somewhere in life's feast the course
of humble-pie must always come in; and
if I did not wholly relish this bit of it, I
dare say it was good for me, and I digested it perfectly.

CONCORD

GEORGE WILLIAM CURTIS was born in Providence, February 24, 1824. From the age of six to ten he attended school at Jamaica Plain, near Boston; then was in school in Providence until he was fifteen, when his father moved to New York. He did not go to college, but he studied and read largely at home. About 1838 he came under the influence of Emerson, and he heard him lecture often. He eagerly accepted Emerson's thought, and made it his own with a boy's ardor and devotion. A spirit of genuine hero-worship took possession of him, and it became a dominating influence in shaping his life. This interest led him and his brother Burrill to Brook Farm, where they spent two years, in 1842-3. They went as boarders, and did not join the community or commit themselves to its principles. Joining eagerly in the amusements of the place, they assisted somewhat in the work. Their chief object, however, was educational, and George studied German, music, and agricultural chemistry.

One of the friendships which Curtis formed at Brook Farm was with John S. Dwight, who afterwards became well known as an interpreter of music. Dwight taught music at the farm, Curtis studied with him, and they became intimate friends. They were drawn very close to each other, frequently exchanged letters after Curtis left Brook Farm, and the friendship continued throughout life. After he left the farm, in the autumn of

1843, Curtis spent the winter at his father's house in New York. In the spring of 1844 he went with Burrill to Concord, Massachusetts, and lived there on a farm for the next year and a half. His object was to become acquainted with country life, and to obtain a practical knowledge of agriculture. It was in the spirit of the teachings of Emerson that he should thus seek to combine study with out-door living. He frequently wrote to Dwight, and he visited Brook Farm from time to time.

The letters which Curtis wrote at this time to his friend at Brook Farm show the influence of Emerson, and some of them are little more than echoes. Yet it is interesting to note how clear and sound was his thought about the reforms of the day. He could not accept the teachings of the Brook-Farmers, though he had lived with them and seen them on their best side. His letters, however, indicate many of the characteristics of the man we admired and loved so much, for they show his charming command of language, a deep interest in poetry, music, and every form of art, a graceful and polished manner, and a profound concern for the good of his fellow-men. He was, even then, an independent in politics and religion, capable of speaking his own thought firmly, and wise to see the higher ethics which should rule in the lives of men.

The first letter was written in New York, and refers to the change made at Brook Farm, early in 1844, in the adoption

of the teachings of Fourier. He dis-
cusses at great length his own attitude
towards Brook Farm and association,
neither of which he finds himself able to
accept. He shows himself a pronounced
individualist, and distinctly rejects the
cardinal doctrines of communism. The
letter is too long to give in full; but some
parts of it will help to explain his reasons
for seeking the quiet of a Concord farm:

New York, *March* 3, 1844.

Your letter was very grateful to me. I had
supposed the silence would be broken by some
music-burst of devotion, and that all friends
would be nearer to you the more imperative
the call upon your strength to battle for the
Ideal. . . . I do not think (and what a heresy!)
that your life has formed more than an object,
not yet a centre. The new order will systema-
tize your course, but I do not see that it aids
your journey. Is it not the deeper insight you
constantly gain into music which explains the
social economy you adopt, and not the economy the music? One fine symphony or song
leads all reforms captive, as the grand old
paintings in St. Peter's completely ignore all
sects. . . .

With respect to association as a means of
reform, I have seen no reason to change my
view. Though, like the monastic, a life of devotion, to severe criticism it offers a selfish and
an unheroic aspect. When your letter first
spoke of your personal interest in the movement, I had written you a long statement of
my thought, which I did not send. It was
only a strong statement of Individualism,
which would not be new to you, perhaps, and
the essential reason of which could not be
readily treated. What we call union seems to
me only a name for a phase of individual action. I live only for myself; and in proportion to my own growth, so I benefit others. As
Fourier seems to me to have postponed his
life in finding out how to live, so I often felt
it was with Mr. Ripley. Besides, I feel that
our evils are entirely individual, not social.
What is society but the shadow of the single
men behind it? . . . .

The effect of a residence at the Farm, I imagine, was not greater willingness to serve in
the kitchen, and so practically assert that labor
was divine, but discontent that there was such
a place as a kitchen. And, however aimless
life there seemed to be, it was an aimlessness
of the general, not of the individual life. Its
beauty faded suddenly if I remembered that it
was a society for special ends, though those
ends were very noble. In the midst of busy
trades and bustling commerce, it was a congregation of calm scholars and poets, cherishing
the ideal and the true in each other's hearts,
dedicated to a healthy and vigorous life. As an
association it needed a stricter system to en-
sure success; and since it had not the means to

justify its mild life, it necessarily grew to this.
As reformers you are now certainly more active, and may promise yourselves heaven's reward for that. That impossibility of severance from the world, of which you speak, I
liked, though I did not like that there should
be such a protest against the world by those
who were somewhat subject to it. This was
not my first feeling. When I first went it
seemed as if all hope had died from the race,
as if the return to simplicity and beauty lay
through the woods and fields, and was to be a
march of men whose very habits and personal
appearance should wear a sign of the coming
grace. The longer I stayed, the more surely
that thought vanished. I had unconsciously
been devoted to the circumstance, while I had
earnestly denied its value. Gradually I perceived that only as a man grew deeper and
broader could he wear the coat and submit to
the etiquette and obey the laws which society
[association] demands. Now I feel that no
new order is demanded, but that the universe
is plastic to the pious hand.

Besides, it seems to me that reform becomes
atheistic the moment it is organized, for it
aims, really, at that which conservatism represents. The merit of the reformer is his sincerity, not his busy effort to emancipate the
slave or to save the drunkard. And the deeper
his sincerity, the more deeply grounded seems
to him the order he holds to be so corrupt.
God always weighs down the Devil. Therefore the church is not a collection of puzzling
priests and deceived people, but the representative, now as much as ever, of the religious
sentiment. . . . There is indeed a latent movement badly represented by these reforms—and
that is the constant perception of the supremacy of the individual. But the stronger the
feet become, the more delicate may be the
movements. The more strictly individual I
am, the more certainly I am bound to all others. I can reach other men only through myself. So far as you have need of association,
you are injured by it.

You will gather what I think from such
hints as these. I recognize the worth of the
movement, as I do of all sincere action. Other
reasons must bind me peculiarly to the particular one at Brook Farm. "Think not of any
severance of our loves," though we should not
meet immediately. Burrill will see if there is
any such place as we wish about you. I have
not much hope of his success. The scent of
the roses will not depart, though the many are
scattered. I hardly hope to say directly how
very beautiful it lies in my memory. What a
heart-fresco it has become. All the dignity,
the strength, the devotion, will be preserved
by you. That graceful aimlessness comes no
more, and yet that was necessary. Long before I knew of the changes, I perceived that
the growth of the place would overshadow the
spots where the sunlight had lain so softly and
long. . . .

I wish this was me instead of my letter, for a warm grasp of the hand might say more than all these words.

Yr friend,　　　　　　　G. W. C.

NEW YORK, *March* 27, 1844.

At last I imagine our summer destiny is fixed. This morning Burrill received a reply from Emerson, informing us of a promising place near Concord. The farmer's name is Capt. Nathaniel Barrett, of pleasant family and situation, and a farm on which more farm-work than usual is done. Altogether the prospect is very alluring and satisfactory, and I have little doubt of our acceptance of the situation. We shall not then be very far removed from you; and at some æsthetic tea, or transcendental club, or poets' assembly meet you, perhaps, and other Brook-Farmers. At all events we shall breathe pretty much the same atmosphere as before, and I understand more fully the complete privacy of the country life.

Burrill brought pleasant accounts of your appearance at Brook Farm. The summer shall not pass without my looking in upon you, though only for an hour. That time will suffice to show me the unaltered beauty of aspect, though days would not be enough to express all that they suggested. Emerson writes that there is a piano and music at the farm mentioned. I have no faith in pianos under such circumstances, but it shows a taste, a hope, a capability; possibly it is equal to all spiritual significance except music. . . .

Let me hear from you before I leave New York, which will be in two or three weeks. I shall not leave all my good friends, and all the fine music here, without a pang. But if we stop for pangs!　　　Yr friend,

G. W. CURTIS.

NEW YORK, MONDAY MORNING, *April* 8, 1844.

The few last days have been like glimpses of Brook Farm, seeing so constantly Mr. Ripley, and Charles, and List, and Isaac, and Georgiana, and M. Fuller. The three last days of the past week were occupied by the sessions of the Convention, about which there was no enthusiasm, but an air of great resolution, which always precedes success. To be sure, the success to me is the constant hope in humanity that inspires them, the sure glowing prophecies of paradise and heaven being individual not general prophecies, and announcing the advent in their own hearts and lives of the feet beautiful of old upon the mountains. In comparison with this, what was done and what was doing lost much of its greatness. Leave to Albert Brisbane, and *id omne genus*, these practical etchings and phalansteries; but let us serve the Gods without bell and candle. Have these men, with all their faith and love, not yet full confidence in love? Is that not strong enough to sway all institutions that are, and cause them to overflow with life? Does that ask houses and lands to

express its power; does it not ride supreme over the abounding selfishness of the world, and so raise men from their sorrow and degradation, or so inspire them that their hovels are good enough for them?

But all difference of thought vanished before the profound, sincere eloquence of these men. Last night, at William Channing's church, the room was full, and the risen Lord Jesus might have smiled upon a worthy worship. From all sections were gathered in that small room men led by the same high thought; and in the light of that thought joining hands and hearts, unknown to each other, never to be seen again, and in the early dawn setting forth with hard hands and stout hearts, to hew down the trees which shall be wrought into stately dwellings for those who come after in the day. . . .

The meetings of the Convention were made interesting by some speeches of W. H. Channing. His fervor kindles the sympathy of all who listen. I do not think he is a man of great intellect; his views of society are not always correct. He speaks very often as an infidel in the capability of men might speak. He is fanatical, as all who perceive by the heart and not the head are, as deeply pious men are apt to be. But I never heard so eloquent a man, one who commanded attention and sympathy not by his words or thoughts, but the religion that lay far below them. It is a warm, fragrant, southern wind, at which the heart leaps; not the pure, cold ocean air, which braces the frame. Between him and some whom I have heard is the same difference as between Goethe and Novalis. The one a June meadow, with flower scents and cloud shadows, and the soft sultry music of humming bees and singing birds, with clear skies bending over; a deep sea the other, whereon sail stately ships, wafted by health-bearing breezes, in whose waters the sick gain strength, in whose soundless depths the coral and precious stones repose forever, which supplies the clouds whose shadow makes the meadow beautiful. . . .

The *Dial* stops. Is it not like the going out of a star? Its place was so unique in our literature. All who wrote and sang for it were clothed in white garments, and the work itself so calm and collected, though springing from the same undismayed hope which fathers all our best reforms. But the intellectual worth of the time will be told in other ways, though the *Dial* no longer reports the progress of the day.

On Friday we leave for Boston. I do not know precisely if we shall go immediately to Concord. We may possibly be detained in Boston until the following Monday, in which case I shall not fail to come out and see you. So endeth my New York correspondence.

Yours truly and ever,

G. W. CURTIS.

Curtis and his brother went to live on a Concord farm, one mile north of the

THE EASY CHAIR ANTICIPATED.

village, near the Concord River, and over-looking its meadows. Here a small cottage, adjoining the farm-house, was fitted up for the brothers, but they had their meals with the farmer and his family. The place was one in every way adapted to the purposes they had in view in seeking the retirement of a farm.

CONCORD, FRIDAY EV'G, *May* 10*th*, 1844.

Since our arrival here I have been busy enough. From breakfast at 6 to dinner at 12½ hard at hard work, and all the afternoon roaming over the country far and near. When we came the Spring was just waking. Now it is opening like a rose-bud with continually deepening beauty. The apple-trees in full bloom, making the landscape so white, seem to present a synopsis of the future Summer glory of the flower-world.

Our farm lies on one of the three hills of Concord. They call it Punkatassett. Before us, at the foot of the hill, is the river; and the

slope between holds a large part of the Captain's orchard. Among the hills at one side we see the town, about a mile away; and a wide horizon all around, which Elizabeth Hoar tells me she has learned is the charm of Concord scenery. The summit of the hill on which we are is crowned with woods, and from a clearing commands a grand prospect. Wachusett rises alone upon the distance, and takes the place of the ocean in the landscape. The Blue Hill, in a measure, supplied that want at West Roxbury. Otherwise the landscape is a garden, which only pleases.

We are much pleased with our host and his family. He is that Capt. Nathan Barrett to whom Messrs. Pratt and Brown came for seed, and who raises a great deal of seed for Ruggles, Nourse, and Mason. We go into all work. The Captain turns us out with the oxen and plough, and we do our best. Already I have learned a good deal. The men are very courteous and generous.

Indeed, I am disposed to think it just the place we wanted. As yet I see no reason to doubt it. It is so still a life, after the city and after the family at Brook Farm. I am glad to be thrown so directly and almost alone into Nature, and more ready than ever to pay my debt in a human way, by learning the names of her beautiful flowers, and the places where they blossom. We study Botany daily, and have thus far kept pace with the season. I have found here the yellow violet, which I do not remember at West Roxbury. Already we have the rhodora and the columbine, which you have probably found. And with our afternoons surrendered to the meadows and hills, and our mornings to the fields, we find no heavy hours; but every Sunday surprises us. I am to bed at 9 and rise at 4½ or 5. I practise the orphic which says, "Baptize thyself in pure water every morning when thou leavest thy couch," which I more concisely render, Wash betimes.

For the last three evenings I have been in the village hearing Belinda Randall play and sing. With the smallest voice, she sings so delicately, and understands her power so well, that I have been charmed. It was a beautiful crown to my day, not regal and majestic like Frances O.'s in the ripe Summer, but woven of Spring flowers and buds. Last night I saw her at Mr. Hoar's, only herself and Miss E. Hoar, G. P. Bradford, Mr. and Mrs. Emerson, and myself and Mr. Hoar. She played Beethoven, sang the "Adelaide" serenade, "Fischer Mädchen," "Amid this Green Wood." I walked home under the low, heavy gray clouds, but the echo lingered about me like starlight.

We have a piano in the house, and a very good one. It was made by Currier, and is but a few years old. The evenings do not all pass without reminding me of the flute music of the last Summer, and making me half long to hear it again. Yet I am too contented to wish to be back at the Farm. The country about us is wilder than there, but I need now this tender severity of Nature and of friendship. With John Hosmer, Isaac, Geo. Bradford, and Burrill, I am not without some actual features of the Farm as I knew it. When I shall see you, I cannot say. I shall not willingly break the circle of life here, though occasion will make me willing enough.

Let me not remain unmentioned to my friends at Brook Farm and in the village; and when you can ungroup yourself for an hour, paint me a portrait of the life you lead.

Yr friend,   G. W. C.

CONCORD, May 24th, '44.

MY DEAR FRIEND,—I heard of you at Ole Bull's concert, and have sympathized with you in your delight. I was in Worcester that evening, and had hoped to have come down to Boston and heard him once more. . . . But who of all heard? Was it not as if he walked above the earth, and of his sublime conversation you heard now and then the notes? Did not the

singular beauty of the man unite with his performance to make the completest musical festival you have heard? Indeed, I owe more to him than one can know except as he feels the same debt—are you not that one? . . . Since I had been here I had heard no music, and felt that I needed to hear some, as an adequate expression of all that I felt. When Belinda Randall came, that demand was satisfied. Ole Bull satisfies the claim of the same nature which our whole life makes, and of itself creates, rather reveals, newer and ' leeper demands, and will, I suppose, until the celestial harmonies are heard by us. . . . To lovers of music a bare description is as an outline to a painter which he can readily fill up, and supply with shadows and sunlight. Yet not he, so magnificently as sunlight and shadows sweep over this landscape. It seems to me that a century of splendor has been rushing by since I have been here. The persons who make Concord famous I have hardly seen. The consciousness of their presence is like the feeling of lofty mountains whom the night and thick forests hide. . . .

The next letter describes a visit to Hawthorne, who was then living in the "Old Manse." The address by Emerson which is mentioned is the one he delivered in Concord, August 1, 1844, on the anniversary of the emancipation of the negroes in the British West Indies. It was soon after printed in a pamphlet, and was included in the "Miscellanies" of 1884.

CONCORD, August 7th, 1844.

My regret at not seeing you was only lessened by the beautiful day I passed with Mr. Hawthorne. His life is so harmonious with the antique repose of his house, and so redeemed into the present by his infant, that it is much better to sit an hour with him than hear the Rev. Barzillai Frost! His baby is the most serenely happy I ever saw. It is very beautiful, and lies amid such placid influences that it too may have a milk-white lamb as emblem; and Mrs. Hawthorne is so tenderly respectful toward her husband that all the romance which we picture in a cottage of lovers dwells, subdued and dignified, with them. I see them very seldom. The people here who are worth knowing, I find, live very quietly and retired. In the country friendship seems not to be of that consuming, absorbing character that city circumstances give it, but to be quite content to feel rather than hear or see. And that very independence, which withdraws them into the privacy of their homes, is the charm which draws thither.

Mr. Emerson read an address before the antislavery friends last Thursday. It was very fine. Not of that cold, clear, intellectual character which so many dislike, but ardent and strong. His recent reading of the history of the cause has given him new light and warmed a fine enthusiasm. It commenced with allusions to the day "which gives the immense fortification of a fact to a great principle"; and then drew in strong, bold outline the progress of British emancipation. Thence to slavery in its influence upon the holders, to the remark that this event hushed the old slander about inferior natures in the negro; thence to the philosophy of slavery, and so through many detached thoughts to the end. It was nearly two hours long, but was very commanding. He looked genial and benevolent, as who should smilingly defy the world, the flesh, and the devil to enslave him. The address will be published by the Society; and he will probably write it more fully, and chisel it into a fitter grace for the public criticism. He spoke of your unfortunate calls, but said you bore the sulkiness very well. George Bradford also was very sorry; and it was hard that you should come so far, with the faces of friends as a hospitable city before you, and find a mirage only, or (begging Burrill's pardon) one house.

For the last six weeks I have been learning what hard work is. Afternoon leisure is now remembered with the holiday which Saturday brought to the schoolboy. During the haying we have devoted all our time and faculty to the making of hay, leaving the body at night fit only to be devoted to sheets and pillows, and not to grave or even friendly epistolary intercourse. Oh, friends, live upon faith, say I, as I pitch into bed, with the ghosts of sundry morning resolutions of letters kicking my sides or thumping my back; and then sink into dreams, where every day seems a day in the valley of Ajalon, and innumerable Joshuas command the sun and moon to stay, and universal leisure spreads over the universe like a great wind. Then comes morning and wakefulness and boots and breakfast and scythes and heat and fatigue, and all my venerable Joshuas endeavor in vain to make oxen stand still, and I heartily wish them and I back in our valley ruling the heavens. In attending scythes over unseen hassocks which do sometimes bend the words of our mouths into shapes resembling oaths—those most crooked of all speech, but therefore fitted for the occasional crooks of life, particularly mowing. Yet I now and then sweat and get tired very heartily, for I want to drink this art of farming to the bottom, and taste not only the morning froth, but the afternoon and evening strength, dregs, and bitterness, if there be any.

When haying is over, which event will take place on Saturday night of this week, fair weather being vouchsafed, I shall return to my moderation. Toward the latter part of the month I shall stray away toward Providence and Newport, and sit down by the sea, and in it too, probably. So I shall pass until harvest. Where the snows will fall upon me, I cannot yet say.

Say to Charles that I was sorry not to have

seen him; but if persons of consequence will travel without previous annunciation, they may chance to find even the humblest of their servants not at home. I know you will write when the time comes, so I say nothing but that I am your friend ever.   G. W. C.

CONCORD, *Sept.* 23, 1844.

Shall we not see you on the day of the cattle show? Certainly Brook Farm will be represented, and I think you may by this time be farmer enough to enjoy the cattle and the ploughing. Besides, as I remember a similar excursion last year at which I assisted, the splendor of the early morning, which was not yet awake when we came away from the Farm, will amply repay any extraordinary effort. And still another *besides:* I do not want the winter to build its white impenetrable walls between us before I have heard your voice once more. I should hope to come and look at you for one day at least in West Roxbury, but our Captain has work, autumnal work, the end whereof is not comprehended by the unassisted human vision. Potato-digging, apple-picking, threshing, the gathering of innumerable seeds, must be done before winter; and yet to-day is like a despatch from December to announce to us that snow and ice and wind are to be just as cold this winter as they were the last.

And I have had a long vacation too. I think on the very day I wrote my last letter to you, as I was whetting my scythe for the last swath of the season, my hat half fell off, and suddenly raising my hand to catch it, I thrust it against the scythe, and cut my thumb just upon the point. It has healed, but I never shall find it quite so agile as formerly. I could not use the hand, my right hand, for more than a fortnight. It was like losing a sense to lose its use. After a week of inaction in Concord, I went to Rhode Island, and remained three weeks, and am now at home a fortnight. I came back more charmed than ever with Concord, which hides under a quiet surface most precious scenes. I suppose we see more deeply into the spirit of a landscape where we have been happy. There we behold the summer bloom where it is spring or autumn or winter with men generally.

We shall remain with Capt. Barrett through the winter. The spring will bring its own arrangements, or, rather, the conclusion of those which are formed during the winter. I suspect that our affections, like our bodies, have been transplanted to Massachusetts, and that our lives will grow in the new soil. Not at all ambitious of settling and becoming a citizen, I am very well content with the nomadic life until obedience to the law of things shall plant me in some home.

And are you still at home in the Farm? Rumors, whose faces I cannot fairly see, pass by me sometimes breathing your name and others but I have long ago turned rumor out of door as an impostor and impertinent person, who apes the manners and appearance of its betters. I shall receive none as from you, however loudly they may shout your name, except they show your hand and seal.

Autumn has already begun to leave the traces of her golden fingers upon the brakes, and occasionally upon some tall nut trees. It seems as if she were trying her skill before she comes like a wind over the landscape. She warbles a few glittering notes before her wonderful majestic Death-song.

Dear friend, why should I send you this chip of ore out of the mine of regard which is yours in my heart? Come and dig in it.

Your friend,   G. W. CURTIS.

The winter was spent at Concord, with visits to Providence, Brook Farm, and elsewhere. The next letter was written January 12, 1845, and speaks of his reading Elizabeth Barrett and Ben Jonson. The following paragraph shows how he enjoyed his winter in the country:

Burrill has not yet returned, and leaves me still a hermit. I am well pleased with my solitude, nor do I care much to go out of the country during the winter; but domestic circumstances make it advisable to go to Providence. There I shall have a good library at hand, which I miss a good deal here. Indeed, I think it likely that every year, while my home is in the country, I may perform a pilgrimage to the city for two or three months, for purposes of art and literature and affection. This idea implies a very free life, but there seems now to be no hinderance to it.

The next summer Curtis and his brother removed to the neighborhood of Emerson, secured a room in a farm-house, cared for their own beds, lived in the simplest and most economical manner, hired a small piece of ground, on which they labored half the day, and roamed the woods or read the other half. This farm was that of Edmund Hosmer, who was afterward described by Curtis as Emerson's "sturdy farmer neighbor." He lived one-half mile east of Emerson, on a cross-road which led directly to Walden Pond through the woods. It was during this summer Thoreau built his hut at the pond; and he was aided in the erection of its frame-work by Alcott, Edmund Hosmer, and Curtis. A few years later Curtis wrote of this event: "One pleasant afternoon a small party of us helped him raise it—a bit of life as Arcadian as any at Brook Farm."

As will be seen by the following letters, the Curtises were not bound closely to the tasks of their "garden-plot":

CONCORD, *March* 13, 1845.

MY DEAR FRIEND,—The cold gray days at Brook Farm were the sunniest of the month. I wish I could step into the parlor when my heart is ready for music and surrender to Beethoven and Mozart, or, indeed, when I find men very selfish and mean, look in upon your kindliness and general sympathy. But while your intercourse at the Farm is so gentle and sweet, you will not forget that it springs from the characters whose companions are still in outer darkness and civilization. I meet every day men of very tender characters under the roughest mien. Even in the midst of the world, I constantly balance my ledger in favor of actual virtue, and enjoy intercourse, not so familiar, but as sweet as that I saw at Brook Farm. Is it not the tendency of a decided institution of reform to be unjust to the barbarians? I do assure you the warm, tender south winds blow over us here in the unsocial state, no less than the chilly east.

The snow on the ground belies the season. It is warm to-day, and the birds sing. I should have enjoyed more my ride in the soft snow on Tuesday, if conscience had not arrayed me against Mr. Billings; but I am most glad to see that I am recovering from the argumentative. I am beginning to enjoy more than ever the pure, still characters which I meet. Intellect is not quite satisfying, though so alluring. It is a scentless flower. But there is a purer summer pleasure in the sweetbrier than the dahlia, though one would have each in his garden. It is because Shakespeare is not solely intellectual, but equally developed, that his fame is universal. The old philosophers, the sheer intellects, lack as much fitness to life as a man without a hand or an eye. And because life is interpreted by sentiment, the higher the flight of the intellect, the colder and sadder is the man. Plato and Emerson are called poets; but if they were so, their audience would be as wide as the world. Milton's fame is limited because he lacked a subtlety and delicacy corresponding with his healthiness and strength. Milton fused in Keats would have formed a greater than Shakespeare. If Milton's piety had been Catholic and not Puritanical, I do not see why he should not have been a greater poet.

I shall not have much work to do before we undertake our garden-plot. We take care of the cattle daily, and that is about all. Yesterday, in the sunlight, I walked to the woods. It was a spectacle finer than the sleet. . . .

CONCORD, *April* 5, 1845.

Judge, my unitary friend, how grateful was your letter, perfumed with the flowers and moonlight, to an unfortunate up to his ears in manure and dish-water! For no happier is my plight at this moment. I snatch a moment out of the week, wherein the significance of that fearful word business has been revealed to me, to send an echo, a reply, to your letter. Since

Monday we have been moving and manuring and fretting and fuming, and rushing desperately up and down turnpikes with bundles and baskets, and have arrived at the end of the week barely in order. Yesterday, in the midst, while I was escorting a huge wagon of that invaluable farming wealth, I encountered Mrs. Pratt and family making their reappearance in civilization. All Brook Farm, in the golden age, seemed to be strapped on the rear of their wagon as baggage, for Mrs. Pratt was the first lady I saw at Brook Farm, where ladyhood blossomed so fairly. Ah! my minute is over, and I must leave you, to lie in wait for another.

Evening.—I have captured an evening instead, my first tolerably quiet evening in this new life, this new system of ours for a summer sojourn. The waves of my nomadic life drift me on strange shores. . . .

CONCORD, *April* 17, 1845.

As a good friend, am I not bound to advise you how my new household works, here in the very bosom of terrible civilization, which yet keeps me very warm? A long wet day like this, when I have been gloriously imprisoned by dropping diamonds, tries well the power of my new solitary life to charm me. It has not failed. It is going away now through the still dank midnight, but it bears the image of my smile. A long wet day with my books and fire, and Burrill for external and my thoughts for internal company. After a morning service prolonged far beyond the hour of matins, led by the sweet and solemn Milton, I read Miss Martineau's last tale, founded upon the history of Toussaint l'Ouverture, in whom I have been interested. I have just read Victor Hugo's *Bug-Jargal*, his first novel, and also based upon the insurrection of St. Domingo. I feel that Miss Martineau's picture is highly colored, but the features must be correct. . . .

Let history and great men fade from our sight. Lately I have grown to be a sad rhymer, and shall end my letter with hints of a life sweeter than these records of mine. More and more I feel that my wine of letters is poured by the poets, not handed as cold sherbet by the philosophers. Some day I may speak more fully upon these things. Meanwhile, secretly and constantly, I turn over pebble after pebble upon the shore, not uncheered by the hope that one day a pearl may glitter in my hands. . . .

CONCORD, *May* 3, '45.

I am weary of these winds, which have blown so constantly through the spring, and would so gladly exchange their long wail, tonight, for some of your music. And yet they are musical; and when I feel vexed at their persistency, they seem to fade and breathe against my face with a low sigh, like one who shouts a secret which I cannot understand, and then mourns softly that I cannot. In spite of the wind, we went to a new pond near to us this afternoon. There we separated, and

Burrill went roaming over the hills and along the shore, and I sat down with *Bettine* upon the margin. That is the best wood-book I know. I read it for the first time in the Brook Farm pine woods on a still Sunday; but today, as I followed her vanishing steps through fairyland, the wind that rustled and raged around was like the tone of her nature interpreting to my heart, rather than to my mind, what I read. . . .

The year has piloted us into the flowery haven of May; but I lay so languidly charmed with the beauty, and looking to see if I cannot this time see the goddess whose smiles I feel, that it will be June and summer before I know it. I treat the seasons as I do poetry. Sometimes I dissect a line which has fascinated me or a poem to expose the secret. But it folds and fades and changes under my glance, as a cloud at twilight; and the beauty of the spring is as elusive as the foam upon a wave. In the midst of summer, the summer that we anticipated in January seems farther off. It sinks constantly into itself. The deep solitude of rest, the murmurous silence of woods at noon —these are as real in winter as when we are melting in July. The senses will have their share. . . .

CONCORD, *June* 24, 1845.

MY DEAR FRIEND,— . . . It was pleasant just after reading it [*Consuelo*] to make a trip to Wachusett with Mr. Hawthorne and Mr. Bradford. We had soft, warm weather, and a beautiful country to pass. From the mountain the prospect was very grand. It is not too high to make the landscape indistinct, but enough so to throw the line of the level country on the east back into the misty horizon and so leave a sealike impression. To the north was Monadnock, lonely and grim and cold. A solitary lover he seemed, of the rough Berserker sort, of the round and virgin-delicate Wachusett. Toward the northwest the lower part of the Green Mountain range built a misty wall, beyond which we could not have seen had it been away. Nearer were smaller hills and ponds and woods. On the mountain we found the pink azalea and the white potentilla tridenta. It was a fine episode in the summer. About the 12th of July Burrill and I mean to go into Berkshire, and if possible to reach the White Mountains before the autumn catches us. This last is doubtful; but I felt when I came down from Wachusett as if I should love to go on from mountain to mountain until winter stopped us.

Last Sunday Father Taylor preached here. All the heretics went to church. In the evening he preached temperance. After the afternoon service we teaed with him at Mr. Emerson's. He is a noble man; truly the Christian apostle of this time. It is impossible to pin him anywhere. He is like the horizon, wide around, but impossible to seize. I know no man who thrills so with life to the very tips, nor is there any one whose eloquence is so thrilling to me. I have found that one of the best things of living in Concord is that we have here the types of classes of men in society generally. The types are magnetic to each other, and draw each other into their vicinity.

The lonely life pleases as much as ever. If I sometimes say inwardly that such is not the natural state of man, I contrive to quiet myself by the assurance that such is the best state for bachelors. What disembodied comforter of Job suggests such things?

Yr friend,   G. W. C.

CONCORD, Sept. 14, 1845.

MY DEAR FRIEND,—I returned last week from a long and beautiful visit to the mountains, among which I had never been before. I went in the middle of July to Berkshire, and returned home for two or three days to set off for the White Hills, and back again through the length of Berkshire. In all about seven weeks. The garden served us very well. We had weeded so faithfully that weeds did not trouble us, and Burrill staid in Concord a part of the time I was in New Hampshire. . . .

I have so many things to say about my wanderings that I cannot write any more, for I mean to come to Brook Farm and see you some day during the autumn. In the late autumn we are going to New York to pass the winter. Give my love to Mrs. Ripley and the Archon, and to the two Charleses, and believe me, as always, your friend,   G. W. C.

CONCORD, October 25, 1845.

MY DEAR FRIEND,—My Concord days are numbered, but before I go I like to write you again, although it is not impossible that I may come here again next year. The autumn, since I saw you, has fulfilled the promise of the day I left Brook Farm—bright, clear, and cool. On Wednesday the day was so remarkably beautiful that, having nothing especial to do, and seeing that Ole Bull was to give another concert, we walked to Boston and heard him once more (I fear for the last time), and walked back the next morning. The air was very still and bright, and cold enough to spur us on, without an unpleasant chill.

I was very glad to part with Ole Bull having my first impressions deepened and strengthened. The wonder with which I heard him in New York had subsided; and I gave myself, or rather he drew me, wholly to his music. It seems as if he improvised with the orchestra, as a Beethoven would at the piano. The music is full of every sort of movement and variety, but has great unity of character, and constantly suggests beautiful and distinct images rather than pictures. I thought of glorious young gladiators leaping into the lists, of fleecy clouds sweeping over starlight skies, and the beach-line of the sea. Every image was of the graceful, vigorous, and entirely healthy character of his person, which I suppose is only a fair expression of his soul. The music

should not be criticised as a work of art, but only as the articulate reverie of Genius, for it is such as only he should play, because it is so entirely individual. It is full of delicate tenderness, and each piece is much like a gentle strong child wandering in fairyland, melted now by the sweetest child-deep piety in the adagio-religioso, now leaping down the Polacca Guerriera like a young angel down a ladder from heaven, and roaming wistful and silent and amazed in the solitude of the prairie, at times running and leaping and shouting, and then sighing and weeping and losing its voice in aerial cadences, until the smiles make rainbows through the tears again.

All these things whirled through my mind as I sat listening to him, with my eyes closed to preserve the realm of vision unspoiled, last Saturday evening. But there is no end to such stuff. Music is so fully suggestive; and, after all, if you abandon yourself to that, you are very apt to find yourself only among corresponding images. The adagio of the Fifth Symphony reminds me, in one part, of majestic waves, black and crowned with creamy foam; and they swell as if the whole sound of the ocean thundered in each; and when they have almost gained a height through which the sun may shine and reveal the long-haired mermaids and the splendid colors which hide so much, then they pale upon themselves and stream backward into the sea, the foam uppermost like a shroud. But when I considered this, one evening, I found it was only the image of the sound transferred to a visible object. It is like watching the clouds, and seeing their palaces and mountains. It is easy to sport with the symbol, and it shows the greatness of the composer when he arouses the thought of the sea and sky for an echo; but that is only the sensuous influence of his music, and farther we cannot go in words, for good music is so because it is inexpressible in words. There is always correspondence, but not identity. And the impression of the same object in a poem, painting, or statue should be as different as the different necessities which constitute those arts, and the differing direction of the various genius which so expresses itself.

Ole Bull's last concert (that I heard) was a cheap one, and the audience was very cheap. I felt at once the want of sympathy between that and him, and that destroyed the unity of the impression, which is so pleasant. The music which he played was of the best and played in the best way, but was played apart from the sympathy of the hearers to the soul of his art. When he was encored, he came and showed his mastery of the violin as a juggler his power over cards. I should have been sorry to have seen it in any one but a true artist; but while he satisfied every just claim in the style and selection of the music of the concert, he permitted the rabble to hear what they had paid fifty cents to hear. He could not be accused of lowering or pampering the popular taste, for the music that he played was elevating, and the gymnastics not music at all.

I was glad to see Mrs. Ripley last Monday, and to hear from her the result of your Sunday meeting. I was a little sceptical, because I think that permanent forms of worship spring from a very deep piety, and the pious persons whom I know I could count on my hands. Such themes are too good for heel-taps to a letter, and I shall wait the issue of your movement with a great deal of interest. Give my love to Mrs. Ripley, and tell her I hope the whole winter will not pass without my hearing from her. I feel sorry to go from Concord, which we shall do in about a fortnight, for it is a quiet place, full of good people and pleasant spots. But I have found the same everywhere, so

"To-morrow to fresh woods and pastures new."

Your friend,   G. W. C.

The concluding part of the above letter refers to the religious society which was organized at Brook Farm by William Ellery Channing. He preached in a grove on the farm one Sunday afternoon, and those present were very much stirred by his eloquence and his truly apostolic gift of interpreting the religious life. At the conclusion of his sermon those present joined hands, and he recited a brief pledge, which all repeated. It was very impressive, and helped to consolidate and give direction to the religious convictions of the community. This society finally grew into the Religious Union of Associationists, which was organized in Boston in January, 1847, and of which Channing was the minister.

After spending the winter at his father's house in New York, Curtis returned to Concord in May. He went to the house of Minot Pratt, whom he had known at Brook Farm, which was situated at the foot of the hill on which he had spent his first summer in Concord. Here also he worked on the farm in the morning, and read or walked in the afternoon. During the summer he went to Saratoga with a sick friend; he also made a trip to Monadnock, making a visit to a Brook Farm friend at the same time. He left Concord in the middle of July, and in August he sailed for Europe.

In reading these letters one is surprised to find so little about Emerson, Hawthorne, Thoreau, and Alcott; but the explanation seems to be that Dwight was familiar with these persons and their habits of life. There was not the incentive, therefore, to describe them that there would have been had he been quite unacquainted with them. One episode of the last weeks of his stay in Concord Curtis described eight years later, in his article on Emerson contributed to *The Homes of American Authors*, which was published by the Putnams in 1853. He there says:

It was in the year 1845 that a circle of persons of various ages, and differing very much in everything but sympathy, found themselves in Concord. Toward the end of the autumn Mr. Emerson suggested that they should meet every Monday evening through the winter in his library. "Monsieur Aubépine," "Miles Coverdale," and other phantoms, since generally known as Nathaniel Hawthorne, who then occupied the old Manse—the inflexible Henry Thoreau, a scholastic and pastoral Orson, then living among the blackberry pastures of Walden Pond—Plato Skimpole [Margaret Fuller's name for Alcott], then sublimely meditating impossible summer-houses in a little house upon the Boston road—the enthusiastic agriculturist and Brook-Farmer [Minot Pratt], then an inmate of Mr. Emerson's house, who added the genial cultivation of a scholar to the amenities of the natural gentleman—a sturdy farmer neighbor [Edmund Hosmer], who had bravely fought his weary way through inherited embarrassments to the small success of a New England husbandman, and whose faithful wife had seven times merited well of her country—two city youths, ready for the fragments from the feast of wit and wisdom—and the host himself, composed the club. Ellery Channing, who had that winter harnessed his Pegasus to the New York *Tribune*, was a kind of corresponding member. The news of this world was to be transmitted through his eminently practical genius, as the club deemed itself competent to take charge of tickings from all other spheres.

I went, the first Monday evening, very much as Ixion may have gone to his banquet. The philosophers sat dignified and erect. There was a constrained but very amiable silence, which had the impertinence of a tacit inquiry, seeming to ask, "Who will now proceed to say the finest thing that has ever been said?" It was quite involuntary and unavoidable, for the members lacked the fluent social genius without which a club is impossible. It was a congress of oracles on the one hand, and of curious listeners upon the other. I vaguely remember that the Orphic Alcott invaded the Sahara of silence with a solemn "saying," to which, after due pause, the honorable member for blueberry pastures responded by some keen and graphic observation, while the Olympian host, anxious that so much good material should be spun into something, beamed smiling encouragement upon all parties. Miles Coverdale, a statue of night and silence,-sat a little removed, under a portrait of Dante, gazing imperturbably upon the group; and as he sat in the shadow his dark hair and eyes and suit of sables made him, in the society, the black thread of mystery which he weaves into his stories; while the shifting presence of the Brook-Farmer played like heat-lightning around the room.

I remember little else but a grave eating of russet apples by the erect philosophers, and a solemn disappearance into night. The club struggled through three Monday evenings. Plato was perpetually putting apples of gold in pictures of silver; for such was the rich ore of his thoughts, coined by the deep melody of his voice. Orson charmed us with the secrets won from his interviews with Pan in the Walden woods; while Emerson, with the zeal of an engineer trying to dam wild waters, sought to bind the wide-flying embroidery of discourse into a whole of clear sweet sense. But still in vain. The oracular sayings were the unalloyed saccharine element; and every chemist knows how much else goes to practical food—how much coarse, rough, woody fibre is essential. The club struggled on valiantly, discoursing celestially, eating apples, and disappearing in the dark, until the third evening it vanished altogether. But I have since known clubs of fifty times the number, whose collective genius was not more than that of either one of the Dii Majores of our Concord coterie. The fault was its too great concentration. It was not relaxation, as a club should be, but tension. Society is a play, a game, a tournament; not a battle. It is the easy grace of undress; not an intellectual, full-dress parade.

In its way this experience was almost as unique as that of Thoreau at Walden Pond, which it antedated by more than a year. Here were two city-bred youths, with every opportunity of wealth and culture about them, lovers of books and music, and able to attend college if they chose, leaving all these things behind and seeking the retreat of a farm. This action was taken in part for purposes of health and physical development, and in part for the sake of the wider and more human culture they would thus secure. It was because these young men were in close touch with the spirit of the time, especially as it had been voiced by Emerson, that they went so far out of the conventional way of securing the necessary training for the business of life.

The effect of this episode upon the life of George William Curtis was one of decided importance. It gave him that love of nature which marked all his writing, and it developed that sympathy with man which was so distinct a feature of his career. His independent spirit was early trained by his connection with Brook Farm, into sympathy with which he seemed likely to be drawn by his contact with its communistic teachings at the most susceptible period of youth. Yet his critical mind led him to see its limitations, and that it could not cure the evils of society. His banter of Dwight about the way in which the Brook-Farmers regarded the people who did not join them is indicative of the satire he in later years directed against the foibles of fashionable society. His insistence upon the value of individual initiative showed the vigor of his independent mind and his strong love of personal liberty. When it is remembered that these letters were written by a youth of twenty, it will be seen that, though they do not show any great merit, they indicate a mind of wide sympathies, a genuine love of culture in the largest sense, and an active spirit of individual freedom.

The kind of training which Curtis secured at Brook Farm and Concord better fitted him for such a career as his than he could have obtained at any college of his day. It brought him into actual contact with life, made him self-reliant, and increased his knowledge of men and the world. It brought him into sympathy with some of the ablest men of our century, so that he learned of them what no book could give. He received from them the enthusiasms which youth needs, and which are the manure of all its after-crop of ideas and achievements. He fertilized his mind at the very sources of culture; and the whole of his mind, instead of some part of it, was affected by the process of enrichment. He became strong in body, mind, conscience, and imagination by his first-hand study of life and men, by his open-air sympathy with nature, and by his daily intercourse with men of toil and of affairs. His whole after-career found its incentive and its meaning in these years of unique preparation.

THE WHITE MR. LONGFELLOW

W E had expected to stay in Boston only until we could find a house in Old Cambridge. This was not so simple a matter as it might seem; for the ancient town had not yet quickened its scholarly pace to the modern step. Indeed, in the spring of 1866 the impulse of expansion was not yet visibly felt anywhere; the enormous material growth that followed the war had not yet begun. In Cambridge the houses to be let were few, and such as there were, fell either below our pride, or rose above our purse. I wish I might tell how at last we bought a house; we had no money, but we were rich in friends, who are still alive to shrink from the story of their constant faith in a financial future which we sometimes doubted, and who backed their credulity with their credit. It is sufficient for the present record, which professes to be strictly literary, to notify the fact that on the first day of May, 1866, we went out to Cambridge and began to live in a house which we owned in fee if not in deed, and which was none the less valuable for being covered with mortgages. Physically, it was a carpenter's box, of a sort which is readily imagined by the Anglo-American genius for ugliness, but which it is not so easy to impart a just conception of. A trim hedge of arbor-vitæ tried to hide it from the world in front, and a tall board fence behind; the little lot was well planted (perhaps too well planted) with pears, grapes, and currants, and there was a small open space which I lost no time in digging up for a kitchen-garden. On one side of us were the open fields; on the other a brief line of neighbor-houses; across the street before us was a grove of stately oaks, which I never could persuade Aldrich had painted leaves on them in the fall. We were really in a poor suburb of a suburb; but such is the fascination of ownership, even the ownership of a fully mortgaged property, that we calculated the latitude and longitude of the whole earth from the spot we called ours. In our walks about Cambridge we saw other places where we might have been willing to live; only, we said, they were too far off. We even prized the architecture of our little box, though we had but so lately lived in a Gothic palace on the Grand Canal in Venice, and were not uncritical of beauty in the possessions of others. Positive beauty we could not have honestly said we thought our cottage had as a whole, though we might have held out for something of the kind in the brackets of turned wood under its eaves. But we were richly content with it; and with life in Cambridge, as it began to open itself to us, we were infinitely more than content. This life, so refined, so intelligent, so gracefully simple, I do not suppose has had anywhere else its parallel. It was the moment before the old American customs had been changed by European influences among people of easier circumstances; and in Cambridge society kept what was best of its village traditions, and chose to keep them in the full knowledge of different things. Nearly every one had been abroad; and nearly every one had acquired the taste for olives without losing a relish for native sauces; through the intellectual life there was an entire democracy, and I do not believe that since the capitalistic era began there was ever a community in which money counted for less. There was little show of what money could buy; I remember but one private carriage (naturally, a publisher's); and there was not one livery, except a livery in the larger sense kept by the stableman Pike, who made us pay now a quarter and now a half dollar for a seat in his carriages, according as he lost or gathered courage for the charge. We thought him extortionate, and we mostly walked through snow and mud of amazing depth and thickness.

The reader will imagine how acceptable this circumstance was to a young literary man beginning life with a fully mortgaged house and a salary of untried elasticity. If there were distinctions made in Cambridge they were not against literature, and we found ourselves in the midst of a charming society, indifferent, apparently, to all questions but those of the higher education which comes so largely by nature. That is to say, in the Cambridge of that day (and, I dare say, of this) a mind cultivated in some sort was essential, and after that came civil manners, and the willingness and ability to be agreeable and interesting; but the question of riches or poverty did not enter. Even the question of family, which is of so great concern in New England, was in abeyance. Perhaps it was taken for granted that every one in Old Cambridge society must be of good family, or he could not be there; perhaps his mere residence tacitly ennobled him; certainly his acceptance was an informal patent of gentility. To my mind, the structure of society was almost ideal, and until we have a perfectly socialized condition of things I do not believe we shall ever have a more perfect society. The instincts which governed it were not such as can arise from the sordid competition of interests; they flowed from a devotion to letters, and from a self-sacrifice in material things which I can give no better notion of than by saying that the outlay of the richest college magnate seemed to be graduated to the income of the poorest.

In those days, the men whose names have given splendor to Cambridge were still living there. I shall forget some of them in the alphabetical enumeration of Louis Agassiz, Francis J. Child, Richard Henry Dana, Jun., John Fiske, Dr. Asa Gray, the family of the Jameses, father and sons, Lowell, Longfellow, Charles Eliot Norton, Dr. John G. Palfrey, James Pierce, Dr. Peabody, Professor Parsons, Professor Sophocles. The variety of talents and of achievements was indeed so great that Mr. Bret Harte, when fresh from his Pacific slope, justly said, after listening to a partial rehearsal of them, "Why, you couldn't fire a revolver from your front porch anywhere without bringing down a two-volumer!" Everybody had written a book, or an article, or a poem; or was in the process or expectation of doing it, and doubtless those whose names escape me will have greater difficulty in eluding fame. These kindly, these gifted folk each came to see us and to make us at home among them; and my home is still among them, on this side and on that side of the line between the living and the dead, which invisibly passes through all the streets of the cities of men.

II.

We had the whole summer for the exploration of Cambridge before society returned from the mountains and the seashore, and it was not till October that I saw Longfellow. I heard again, as I heard when I first came to Boston, that he was at Nahant, and though Nahant was no longer so far away, now, as it was then, I did not think of seeking him out even when we went for a day to explore that coast during the summer. It seems strange that I cannot recall just when and where I saw him, but early after his return to Cambridge I had a message from him asking me to come to a meeting of the Dante Club at Craigie House.

Longfellow was that winter (1866-7) revising his translation of the Paradiso, and the Dante Club was the circle of Italianate friends and scholars whom he invited to follow him and criticise his work from the original, while he read his version aloud. Those who were most constantly present were Lowell and Professor Norton, but from time to time others came in, and we seldom sat down at the nine-o'clock supper that followed the reading of the canto in less number than ten or twelve.

The criticism, especially from the accomplished Danteists I have named, was frank and frequent. I believe they neither of them quite agreed with Longfellow as to the form of version he had chosen, but waiving that, the question was how perfectly he had done his work upon the given lines. I myself, with whatever right, great or little, I may have to an opinion, believe thoroughly in Longfellow's plan. When I read his version my sense aches for the rhyme which he rejected, but my admiration for his fidelity to Dante otherwise is immeasurable. I remember with equal admiration the subtle and sympathetic

LONGFELLOW'S HOUSE AT CAMBRIDGE.

scholarship of his critics, who scrutinized
every shade of meaning in a word or
phrase that gave them pause, and did
not let it pass till all the reasons and
facts had been considered. Sometimes,
and even often, Longfellow yielded to
their censure, but for the most part, when
he was of another mind, he held to his
mind, and the passage had to go as he
said. I make a little haste to say that
in all the meetings of the Club, during a
whole winter of Wednesday evenings, I
myself, though I faithfully followed in
an Italian Dante with the rest, ventured
upon one suggestion only. This was
kindly, even seriously, considered by the
poet, and gently rejected. He could not
do anything otherwise than gently, and
I was not suffered to feel that I had done
a presumptuous thing. I can see him
now, as he looked up from the proof-
sheets on the round table before him, and
over at me, growing consciously smaller
and smaller, like something through a reversed opera-glass. He had a shaded
drop-light in front of him, and in its
glow his beautiful and benignly noble
head had a dignity peculiar to him.

All the portraits of Longfellow are
likenesses more or less bad and good,
for there was something as simple in the

physiognomy as in the nature of the man.
His head, after he allowed his beard to
grow and wore his hair long in the manner of elderly men, was leonine, but mildly leonine, as the old painters conceived
the lion of St. Mark. Once Sophocles,
the ex-monk of Mount Athos, so long a
Greek professor at Harvard, came in for
supper, after the reading was over, and
he was leonine too, but of a fierceness
that contrasted finely with Longfellow's
mildness. I remember the poet's asking
him something about the punishment of
impaling, in Turkey, and his answering,
with an ironical gleam of his fiery eyes,
"Unhappily, it is obsolete." I dare say
he was not so leonine, either, as he looked.

When Longfellow read verse, it was
with a hollow, with a mellow resonant
murmur, like the note of some deep-throat-
ed horn. His voice was very lulling in
quality, and at the Dante Club it used
to have early effect with an old scholar
who sat in a cavernous arm-chair at the
corner of the fire, and who drowsed audi-
bly in the soft tone and the gentle heat.
The poet had a fat terrier who wished always to be present at the meetings of the
Club, and he commonly fell asleep at the
same moment with that dear old scholar,
so that when they began to make them-

selves heard in concert, one could not tell which it was that most took our thoughts from the text of the Paradiso. When the duet opened, Longfellow would look up with an arch recognition of the fact, and then go gravely on to the end of the canto. At the close he would speak to his friend and lead him out to supper as if he had not seen or heard anything amiss.

III.

In that elect company I was silent, partly because I was conscious of my youthful inadequacy, and partly because I preferred to listen. But Longfellow always behaved as if I were saying a succession of edifying and delightful things, and from time to time he addressed him-

EVANGELINUS SOPHOCLES.

self to me, so that I should not feel left out. He did not talk much himself, and I recall nothing that he said. But he always spoke both wisely and simply, without the least touch of pose, and with no intention of effect, but with something that I must call quality for want of a better word; so that at a table where Holmes sparkled, and Lowell glowed, and Agassiz beamed, he cast the light of a

gentle gayety, which seemed to dim all those vivider luminaries. While he spoke you did not miss Fields's story or Tom Appleton's wit, or even the gracious amity of Mr. Norton, with his unequalled intuitions.

The supper was very plain: a cold turkey, which the host carved, or a haunch of venison, or some braces of grouse, or a platter of quails, with a deep bowl of salad, and the sympathetic companionship of those elect vintages which Longfellow loved, and which he chose with the inspiration of affection. We usually began with oysters, and when some one who was expected did not come promptly, Longfellow invited us to raid his plate, as a just punishment for his delay. One evening Lowell remarked, with the cayenne poised above his blue-points, "It's astonishing how fond these fellows are of pepper."

The old friend of the cavernous arm-chair was perhaps not wide enough awake to repress an "Ah?" of deep interest in this fact of natural history, and Lowell was provoked to go on. "Yes, I've dropped a red pepper pod into a barrel of them, before now, and then taken them out in a solid mass, clinging to it like a swarm of bees to their queen."

"Is it possible?" cried the old friend; and then Longfellow intervened to save him from worse, and turned the talk.

I reproach myself that I made no record of the talk, for I find that only a few fragments of it have caught in my memory, and that the sieve which should have kept the gold has let it wash away with the gravel. I remember once Dr. Holmes's talking of the physician as the true seer, whose awful gift it was to behold with the fatal second sight of science the shroud gathering to the throat of many a doomed man apparently in perfect health, and happy in the promise of unnumbered days. The thought may have been suggested by some of the toys of superstition which intellectual people like to play with.

I never could be quite sure at first that Longfellow's brother-in-law, Appleton, was seriously a spiritualist, even when he disputed the most strenuously with the unbelieving Autocrat. But he really was in earnest about it, though he relished a

THE WHITE MR. LONGFELLOW.

joke at the expense of his doctrine, like some clerics when they are in the safe company of other clerics. He told me once of having recounted to Agassiz the facts of a very remarkable séance, where the souls of the departed outdid themselves in the athletics and acrobatics they seem so fond of over there, throwing large stones across the room, moving pianos, and lifting dinner tables and setting them atwirl under the chandelier. "And now," he demanded, "what do you say to that?" "Well, Mr. Appleton," Agassiz answered, to Appleton's infinite delight, "*I say that it did not happen.*"

One night they began to speak at the Dante supper of the unhappy man whose crime is a red stain in the Cambridge annals, and one and another recalled their impressions of Professor Webster. It was possibly with a retroactive sense that they had all felt something uncanny in him, but, apropos of the deep salad-bowl in the centre of the table, Longfellow remembered a supper Webster was at, where he lighted some chemical in such a dish and held his head over it, with a handkerchief noosed about his throat and lifted above it with one hand, while his face, in the pale light, took on the livid ghastliness of a man hanged by the neck.

Another night the talk wandered to the visit which an English author (now with God) paid America at the height of a popularity long since toppled to the ground, with many another. He was in very good humor with our whole continent, and at Longfellow's table he found the champagne even surprisingly fine. "But," he said to his host, who now told the story, "it cawn't be *genuine*, you know!"

Many years afterwards this author revisited our shores, and I dined with him at Longfellow's, where he was anxious to constitute himself a guest during his sojourn in our neighborhood. Longfellow was equally anxious that he should not do so, and he took a harmless pleasure in outmanœuvring him. He seized a chance to speak with me alone, and plotted to deliver him over to me without apparent unkindness, when the latest horse-car should be going in to Boston, and begged me to walk him to Harvard Square and put him aboard. "Put him aboard, and don't leave him till the car starts, and then watch that he doesn't get off."

These instructions he accompanied with a lifting of the eyebrows, and a pursing of the mouth, in an anxiety not altogether burlesque. He knew himself the prey of any one who chose to batten on him, and his hospitality was subject to frightful abuse. Perhaps Mr. Norton has somewhere told how, when he asked if a certain person who had been outstaying his time was not a dreadful bore, Longfellow answered, with angelic patience, "Yes; but then you know I have been bored so often!"

There was one fatal Englishman whom I shared with him during the great part of a season: a poor soul, not without gifts, but always ready for more, especially if they took the form of meat and drink. He had brought letters from one of the best Englishmen alive, who withdrew them too late to save his American friends from the sad consequences of welcoming him. So he established himself impregnably in a Boston club, and came out every day to dine with Longfellow in Cambridge, beginning with his return from Nahant in October and continuing far into December. That was the year of the great horse-distemper, when the plague disabled the transportation in Boston, and cut off all intercourse between the suburb and the city on the street railways. "I did think," Longfellow pathetically lamented, "that when the horse-cars stopped running, I should have a little respite from L., *but he walks out.*"

In the midst of his own suffering he was willing to advise with me concerning some poems L. had offered to the Atlantic Monthly, and after we had desperately read them together he said, with inspiration, "I think these things are more adapted to music than the magazine," and this seemed so good a notion that when L. came to know their fate from me, I answered, confidently, "I think they are rather more adapted to music."

He calmly asked me, "Why?" and as this was an exigency which Longfellow had not forecast for me, I was caught in it without hope of escape. I really do not know what I said, but I know that I did not take the poems, such was my literary conscience in those days; I am afraid I should be weaker now.

IV.

The suppers of the Dante Club were a relaxation from the severity of their toils on criticism, and I will not pretend that their table-talk was of that seriousness which duller wits might have given themselves up to. The passing stranger,

LONGFELLOW'S DINING-ROOM.

HARVARD SQUARE, CAMBRIDGE.

especially if a light or jovial person, was always welcome, and I never knew of the enforcement of the rule I heard of, that if you came in without question on the Club nights, you were a guest; but if you rang or knocked, you could not get in.

Any sort of diversion was hailed, and once Appleton proposed that Longfellow should show us his wine-cellar. He took up the candle burning on the table for the cigars, and led the way into the basement of the beautiful old Colonial mansion, doubly memorable as Washington's headquarters while he was in Cambridge, and as the home of Longfellow for so many years. The taper cast just the right gleams on the darkness, bringing into relief the massive piers of brick, and the solid walls of stone, which gave the cellar the effect of a casemate in some fortress, and leaving the corners and distances to a romantic gloom. This basement was a work of the days when men built more heavily if not more substantially than now, but I forget, if I·ever knew, what date the wine-cellar was of. It was well stored with precious vintages, aptly cobwebbed and dusty; but I could not find that it had any more charm than the shelves of a library: it is the inside of bottles and of books that makes its appeal. The whole place witnessed a bygone state and luxury, which otherwise

lingered in a dim legend or two. Longfellow once spoke of some old love-letters which were dropped down on the basement stairs from some place overhead; and there was the fable or the fact of a subterranean passage under the street from Craigie House to the old Batchelder House, which I relate to these letters with no authority I can allege. But in Craigie House dwelt the proud fair lady who was buried in the Cambridge churchyard with a slave at her head and a slave at her feet.

"Dust is in her beautiful eyes,"

and whether it was they that smiled or wept in their time over those love-letters, I will leave the reader to say. The fortunes of her Tory family fell with those of their party, and the last Vassal ended his days a prisoner from his creditors in his own house, with a weekly enlargement on Sundays, when the law could not reach him. It is known how the place took Longfellow's fancy when he first came to be professor in Harvard, and how he was a lodger of the last Mistress Craigie there, long before he became its owner. The house is square, with Longfellow's study where he read and wrote on the right of the door, and a statelier library behind it; on the left is the drawing-room, with the dining-room in its rear; from its square hall climbs a beautiful stairway with twisted banisters, and a tall clock in their angle.

The study where the Dante Club met, and where I mostly saw Longfellow, was a plain, pleasant room, with broad panelling in white painted pine; in the centre before the fireplace stood his round table, laden with books, papers, and proofs; in the furthest corner by the window was a high desk which he sometimes stood at to write. In this room Washington held his councils and transacted his business with all comers; in the chamber overhead he slept. I do not think Longfellow associated the place much with him, and I never heard him speak of Washington in relation to it except once, when he told me with peculiar relish what he called the true version of a pious story concerning the aide-de-camp who blundered in upon him while he knelt in prayer. The father of his country rose and rebuked the young man severely, and then resumed his devotions. "He rebuked him," said Longfellow, lifting his brows and making rings round the pupils of his eyes, "by throwing his scabbard at his head."

All the front windows of Craigie House look out over the open fields across the Charles, which is now the Longfellow Memorial Garden. The poet used to be amused with the popular superstition that he was holding this vacant ground with a view to a rise in the price of lots, while all he wanted was to keep a feature of his beloved landscape unchanged. Lofty elms drooped at the corners of the house; on the lawn billowed clumps of the lilac, which formed a thick hedge along the fence. There was a terrace part way down this lawn, and where a white-painted balustrade was set some fifteen years ago upon its brink, it seemed always to have been there. Long verandas stretched on either side of the mansion; and behind was an old-fashioned garden with beds primly edged with box after a design of his own. Longfellow had a ghost story of this quaint plaisance, which he used to tell with an artful reserve of the catastrophe. He was coming home one winter night, and as he crossed the garden he was startled by a white figure swaying before him. But he knew that the only way was to advance upon it. He pushed boldly forward, and was suddenly caught under the throat—by the clothes-line with a long night-gown on it.

Perhaps it was at the end of a long night of the Dante Club that I heard him tell this story. The evenings were sometimes mornings before the reluctant break-up came, but they were never half long enough for me. I have given no idea of the high reasoning of vital things which I must often have heard at that table, and that I have forgotten it is no proof that I did not hear it. The memory will not be ruled as to what it shall bind and what it shall loose, and I should entreat mine in vain for record of those meetings other than what I have given. Perhaps it would be well, in the interest of some popular conceptions of what the social intercourse of great wits must be, for me to invent some ennobling and elevating passages of conversation at Longfellow's; perhaps I ought to do it for the sake of my own repute as a serious and adequate witness. But I am rather helpless in the matter; I must set down what I remember, and surely if I can remember no phrase from the Autocrat that a reader could live or die by, it is something to recall how, when a certain potent cheese was passing, he leaned over to gaze at it, and asked: "Does it kick? Does it kick?" No strain of high poetic thinking remains to me from Lowell, but he made me laugh unforgettably with his passive adventure one night going home late, when a man suddenly leaped from the top of a high fence upon the sidewalk at his feet, and after giving him the worst fright of his life, disappeared peaceably into the darkness. To be sure, there was one most memorable supper, when he read the Biglow Paper he had finished that day, and enriched the meaning of his verse with the beauty of his voice. There lingers yet in my sense his very tone in giving the last line of the passage lamenting the waste of the heroic lives which in those dark hours of Johnson's time seemed to have been

"Butchered to make a blind man's holiday."

The hush that followed upon his ceasing was of that finest quality which spoken praise always lacks; and I suppose that I could not give a just notion of these Dante Club evenings without imparting the effect of such silences. This I could not hopefully undertake to do; but I am tempted to some effort of the kind by my remembrance of Longfellow's old friend George Washington Greene, who often came up from his home in Rhode

Island, to be at those sessions, and who was a most interesting and amiable fact of those delicate silences. A full half of his earlier life had been passed in Italy, these times he brought out a faded Italian anecdote, faintly smelling of civet, and threadbare in its ancient texture. He liked to speak of Goldoni and of Nota,

LONGFELLOW'S STUDY.

where he and Longfellow met and loved each other in their youth with an affection which the poet was constant to in his age, after many vicissitudes, with the beautiful fidelity of his nature. Greene was like an old Italian house-priest in manner, gentle, suave, very suave, sooth as creamy curds, cultivated in the elegancies of literary taste, and with a certain meek abeyance. I think I never heard him speak, in all those evenings, except when Longfellow addressed him, though he must have had the Dante scholarship for an occasional criticism. It was at more recent dinners, where I met him with the Longfellow family alone, that he broke now and then into a quotation from some of the modern Italian poets he knew by heart (preferably Giusti), and syllabled their verse with an exquisite Roman accent and a bewitching Florentine rhythm. Now and then at

of Niccolini and Manzoni, of Monti and Leopardi; and if you came to America, of the Revolution and his grandfather, the Quaker General Nathanael Greene, whose life he wrote (and I read) in three volumes. He worshipped Longfellow, and their friendship continued while they lived, but toward the last of his visits at Craigie House it had a pathos for the witness which I should grieve to wrong. Greene was then a quivering paralytic, and he clung tremulously to Longfellow's arm in going out to dinner, where even the modern Italian poets were silent upon his lips. When we rose from table, Longfellow lifted him out of his chair, and took him upon his arm again for their return to the study.

He was of lighter metal than most other members of the Dante Club, and he was not of their immediate intimacy, living away from Cambridge, as he did, and

I shared his silence in their presence with full intelligence. I was by far the youngest of their number, and I cannot yet quite make out why I was of it at all. But at every moment I was as sensible of my good fortune as of my ill desert. They were the men whom of all men living I most honored, and it seemed to be impossible that I at my age should be so perfectly fulfilling the dream of my life in their company. Often the nights were very cold, and as I returned home from Craigie House to the carpenter's box on Sacramento Street, a mile or two away, I was as if soul-borne through the air by my pride and joy, while the frozen blocks of snow clinked and tinkled before my feet stumbling along the middle of the road. I still think that was the richest moment of my life, and I look back at it as the moment, in a life not unblessed by chance, which I would most like to live over again—if I must live any.

The next winter the sessions of the Dante Club were transferred to the house of Mr. Norton, who was then completing his version of the Vita Nuova. This has always seemed to me a work of not less graceful art than Longfellow's translation of the Commedia. In fact, it joins the effect of a sympathy almost mounting to divination to a patient scholarship and a delicate skill unknown to me elsewhere in such work. I do not know whether Mr. Norton has satisfied himself better in his prose version of the Commedia than in this of the Vita Nuova, but I do not believe he could have satisfied Dante better, unless he had rhymed his sonnets and canzonets. I am sure he might have done this if he had chosen. He has always pretended that it was impossible, but miracles are never impossible in the right hands.

V.

After three or four years we sold the carpenter's box on Sacramento Street, and removed to a larger house near Harvard Square, and in the immediate neighborhood of Longfellow. He gave me an easement across that old garden behind his house, through an opening in the high board fence which enclosed it, and I saw him oftener than ever, though the meetings of the Dante Club had come to an end. At the last of them, Lowell had asked him, with fond regret in his jest, "Longfellow, why don't you do that Indian poem in forty thousand verses?" The demand but feebly expressed the reluctance in us all, though I suspect the Indian poem existed only by the challenger's invention. Before I leave my faint and unworthy record of these great times I am tempted to mention an incident poignant with tragical associations. The first night after Christmas the holly and the pine wreathed about the chandelier above the supper table took fire from the gas, just as we came out from the reading, and Longfellow ran forward and caught the burning garlands down and bore them out. No one could speak for thinking what he must be thinking of when the ineffable calamity of his home befell it. Curtis once told me that a little while before Mrs. Longfellow's death he was driving by Craigie House with Holmes, who said he trembled to look at it, for those who lived there had their happiness so perfect that no change, of all the changes which must come to them, could fail to be for the worse.

I did not know Longfellow before that fatal time, and I shall not say that his presence bore record of it except in my fancy. He may always have had that look of one who had experienced the utmost harm that fate can do, and henceforth could possess himself of what was left of life in peace. He could never have been a man of the flowing ease that makes all comers at home; some people complained of a certain gêne in him; and he had a reserve with strangers, which never quite lost itself in the abandon of friendship, as Lowell's did. He was the most perfectly modest man I ever saw, ever imagined, but he had a gentle dignity which I do not believe any one, the coarsest, the obtusest, could trespass upon. In the years when I began to know him, his long hair and the beautiful beard which mixed with it were of one iron-gray, which I saw blanch to a perfect silver, while that pearly tone of his complexion, which Appleton so admired, lost itself in the wanness of age and pain. When he walked, he had a kind of spring in his gait, as if now and again a buoyant thought lifted him from the ground. It was fine to meet him coming down a Cambridge street; you felt that the encounter made you a part of literary history, and set you apart with him for the moment from the poor and mean. When he appeared in Harvard Square, he beatified if not beautified the ugliest and vulgarest looking spot on the planet outside of New York.. You could meet him sometimes at the market, if you were of the same provision-man as he, for Longfellow remained as constant to his tradespeople as to any other friends. He rather liked to bring his proofs back to the printer's himself, and we often found ourselves together at the University Press, where the Atlantic Monthly used to be printed. But outside of his own house Longfellow seemed to want a fit atmosphere, and I love best to think of him in his study, where he wrought at his lovely art with a serenity expressed in his smooth, regular, and scrupulously perfect handwriting. It was quite vertical, and rounded, with a slope neither to the right nor left, and at the time I knew him first, he was fond of using a soft pencil on printing paper, though commonly he wrote with a quill. Each letter was distinct in shape, and between the verses was always the exact space of half an inch. I have a good many of his poems written in this fashion, but whether they were the first drafts or not I cannot say; very likely not. Towards the last he no longer sent his poems to the magazines in his own hand, but they were always signed in autograph.

I once asked him if he were not a great deal interrupted, and he said, with a faint sigh, Not more than was good for him, he fancied; if it were not for the interruptions, he might overwork. He was not a friend to stated exercise, I believe, nor fond of walking, as Lowell was; he had not, indeed, the childish associations of the younger poet with the Cambridge neighborhoods;

and I never saw him walking for pleasure except on the east veranda of his house, though I was told he loved walking in his youth. In this and in some other things Longfellow was more European than American, more Latin than Saxon. He once said quaintly that one got a great deal of exercise in putting on and off one's overcoat and overshoes.

I suppose no one who asked decently at his door was denied access to him, and there must have been times when he was overrun with volunteer visitors; but I never heard him complain of them. He was very charitable in the immediate sort which Christ seems to have meant; but he had his preferences, humorously own-

THE OLD CLOCK ON THE STAIRS.

GEORGE WASHINGTON GREENE.

ed, among beggars. He liked the German beggars least, and the Italian beggars most, as having most savoir-faire; in fact, we all loved the Italians in Cambridge. He was pleased with the accounts I could give him of the love and honor I had known for him in Italy, and one day there came a letter from an Italian admirer, addressed to "Mr. Greatest Poet Longfellow," which he said was the very most amusing superscription he had ever seen.

It is known that the King of Italy offered Longfellow the cross of San Lazzaro, which is the Italian literary decoration. It came through the good offices of my old acquaintance Professor Messadaglia, then a deputy in the Italian Parliament, whom, for some reason I cannot remember, I had put in correspondence with Longfellow. The honor was wholly unexpected, and it brought Longfellow a distress which was chiefly for the gentleman who had procured him the impossible distinction. He showed me the pretty collar and cross, not, I think, without a natural pleasure in it. No man was ever less a bigot in things civil or religious than he, but he said, firmly, "Of course, as a republican and a Protestant, I can't accept a decoration from a Catholic prince." His decision was from his conscience, and I think that all Americans who think duly about it will approve his decision.

VI.

Such honors as he could fitly permit himself he did not refuse, and I recall what zest he had in his election to the Arcadian Academy, which had made him a shepherd of its Roman Fold, with the title, as he said, of "Olimipico something." But I fancy his sweetest pleasure in his vast renown came from his popular recognition everywhere. Few were the lands, few the languages he was unknown to: he showed me a version of the Psalm of Life in Chinese. Apparently even the poor lost autograph-seeker was not denied by his universal kindness; I know that he kept a store of autographs ready written on small squares of paper for all who applied by letter or in person; he said it was no trouble; but perhaps he was to be excused for refusing the request of a lady for fifty autographs, which she wished to offer as a novel attraction to her guests at a lunch party.

Foreigners of all kinds thronged upon him at their pleasure, apparently, and with perfect impunity. Sometimes he got a little fun, very, very kindly, out of their excuses and reasons; and the Englishman who came to see him because there were no ruins to visit in America was no fable, as I can testify from the poet himself. But he had no prejudice against Englishmen, and even at a certain time when the coarse-handed British criticism began to blame his delicate art for the universal acceptance of his verse, and to try to sneer him into the rank of inferior poets, he was without rancor for the clumsy misliking that he felt. He could not understand rudeness; he was too finely framed for that; he could know it only as Swedenborg's most celestial angels perceived evil, as something distressful, angular. The ill-will that seemed nearly always to go with adverse criticism made him distrust criticism, and the discomfort which mistaken or blundering praise gives probably made him shy of all criticism. He said that in his early life as an author he used to seek out and save all the notices of his poems, but in his latter days he read only those that happened to fall in his way; these he cut out and amused his leisure by putting together in scrap-books. He was reluctant to make any criticism of other poets; I do not remember ever to have heard him make one; and his writings show no trace of the literary dislikes or contempts which we so often mistake in ourselves for righteous judgments. No doubt he had his resentments, but he hushed them in his heart, which he did not suffer them to embitter. While Poe was writing of "Longfellow and other Plagiarists," Longfellow was helping to keep Poe alive by the loans which always made themselves gifts in Poe's case. He very, very rarely spoke of himself at all, and almost never of the grievances which he did not fail to share with all who live.

He was patient, as I said, of all things, and gentle beyond all mere gentlemanliness. But it would have been a great mistake to mistake his mildness for softness. It was most manly and firm; and of course it was braced with the New England conscience he was born to. If he did not find it well to assert himself, he was prompt in behalf of his friends, and one of the fine things told of him was his resenting some things said of Sumner at a dinner in Boston during the old pro-slavery times : he said to the gentlemen present that Sumner was his friend, and he must leave their company if they continued to assail him.

But he spoke almost as rarely of his friends as of himself. He liked the large, impersonal topics which could be dealt with on their human side, and involved characters rather than individuals. This was rather strange in Cambridge, where we were apt to take our instances from the environment. It was not the only thing he was strange in there; he was not to that manner born; he lacked the final intimacies which can come only of birth and lifelong association, and which make the men of the Boston breed seem exclusive when they least feel so; he was Longfellow to the friends who were James, and Charles, and Wendell to one another. He and Hawthorne were classmates at college, but I never heard him mention Hawthorne; I never heard him mention Whittier or Emerson. I think his reticence about his contemporaries was largely due to his reluctance from criticism: he was the finest artist of them all, and if he praised he must have praised with the reservations of an honest man. Of younger writers he was willing enough to speak. No new contributor made his mark in the magazine unnoted by him, and sometimes I showed him verse in manuscript which gave me peculiar pleasure. I remember his liking for the first piece that Mr. Maurice Thompson sent me, and how he tasted the fresh flavor of it, and inhaled its wild new fragrance. He admired the skill of some of the young story-tellers; he praised the subtlety of one in working out an intricate character, and said modestly that he could never have done that sort of thing himself. It was entirely safe to invite his judgment when in doubt, for he never suffered it to become aggressive, or used it to urge upon me the manuscripts that must often have been urged upon him.

Longfellow had a house at Nahant where he went every summer for more than quarter of a century. He found the slight transition change enough from Cambridge, and liked it perhaps because it did not take him beyond the range of the friends and strangers whose company he liked. Agassiz was there, and Appleton; Sumner came to sojourn with him; and the tourists of all nations found him there in half an hour after they reached Boston. His cottage was very plain and simple, but was rich in the sight of the illimitable sea, and it had a luxury of rocks at the foot of its garden, draped with sea-weed, and washed with the indefatigable tides. As he grew older and feebler he ceased to go to Nahant; he remained the whole year round at Cambridge; he professed to like the summer which he said warmed him through there, better than the cold spectacle of summer which had no such effect at Nahant.

The hospitality which was constant at either house was not merely of the worldly sort. Longfellow loved good cheer; he tasted history and poetry in a precious wine; and he liked people who were acquainted with manners and men, and brought the air of capitals with them. But often the man who dined with Longfellow was the man who needed a dinner; and from what I have seen of the sweet courtesy that governed at that board, I am sure that such a man could never have felt himself the least honored guest. The poet's heart was open to all the homelessness of the world; and I remember how once when we sat at his table and I spoke of his poem of The Challenge, then a new poem, and said how I had been touched by the fancy of

"The poverty-stricken millions
   Who challenge our wine and bread,
And impeach us all as traitors,
   Both the living and the dead,"

his voice sank in grave humility as he answered, "Yes, I often think of those things." He had thought of them in the days of the slave, when he had taken his place with the friends of the hopeless and hapless, and as long as he lived he continued of the party which had freed the slave. He did not often speak of politics, but when the movement of some of the best Republicans away from their party began, he said that he could not see the wisdom of their course. But this was said without censure or criticism of them, and so far as I know he never permitted himself anything like denunciation of those who in any wise differed from him. On a matter of yet deeper interest, I do not feel authorized to speak for him, but I think that as he grew older, his hold upon anything like a creed weakened, though he remained of the Unitarian philosophy concerning Christ. He did not latterly go to church, I believe; but then, very few of his circle were church-goers. Once he said something very vague and uncertain concerning the doctrine of another life when I affirmed my hope of it, to the effect that he wished he could be sure, with the sigh that so often clothed the expression of a misgiving with him.

VII.

When my acquaintance with Longfellow began he had written the things that made his fame, and that it will probably rest upon: Evangeline, Hiawatha, and the Courtship of Miles Standish were by that time old stories. But during the eighteen years that I knew him he produced the best of his minor poems, the greatest of his sonnets, the sweetest of his lyrics. His art ripened to the last, it grew richer and finer, and it never knew decay. He rarely read anything of his own aloud, but in three or four cases he read to me poems he had just finished, as if to give himself the pleasure of hearing them with the sympathetic sense of another. The hexameter piece, Elizabeth, in the third part of Tales of a Wayside

Inn, was one of these, and he liked my liking its rhythmical form, which I believed one of the measures best adapted to the English speech, and which he had used himself with so much pleasure and success.

About this time he was greatly interested in the slight experiments I was beginning to make in dramatic form, and he said that if he were himself a young man he should write altogether for the stage; he thought the drama had a greater future with us. He was pleased when a popular singer wished to produce his Masque of Pandora, with music, and he was patient when it failed of the effect hoped for it as an opera. When the late Lawrence Barrett, in the enthusiasm which was one of the fine traits of his generous character, had taken my play of A Counterfeit Presentment, and came to the Boston Museum with it, Longfellow could not apparently have been more zealous for its popular acceptance if it had been his own work. He invited himself to one of the rehearsals with me, and he sat with me on the stage through the four acts with a fortitude which I still wonder at, and with the keenest zest for all the details of the performance. No finer testimony to the love and honor which all kinds of people had for him could have been given than that shown by the actors and employees of the theatre, high and low. They thronged the scenery, those who were not upon the stage, and at the edge of every wing were faces peering round at the poet, who sat unconscious of their adoration, intent upon the play. He was intercepted at every step in going out, and made to put his name to the photographs of himself which his worshippers produced from their persons.

He came to the first night of the piece, and when it seemed to be finding favor with the public, he leaned forward out of his line to nod and smile at the author; and when they had the author up, it was the sweetest flattery of the applause which abused his fondness that Longfellow clapped first and loudest.

Where once he had given his kindness he could not again withhold it, and he was anxious no act should be interpreted as withdrawal. When the Emperor Dom Pedro of Brazil, who was so great a lover of Longfellow, came to Boston, he asked himself out to dine with the poet, who had expected to offer him some such hospitality. Soon after, Longfellow met me, and as if eager to forestall a possible feeling in me, said, "I wanted to ask *you* to dinner with the Emperor, but he not only sent word he was coming, he named his fellow-guests!" I answered that though I should probably never come so near dining with an emperor again, I prized his wish to ask me much more than the chance I had missed; and with this my great and good friend seemed a little consoled. I believe that I do not speak too confidently of our relation. He was truly the friend of all men, but I had certainly the advantage of my propinquity. We were near neighbors, as the pleonasm has it, both when I lived on Berkeley Street and after I had built my own house on Concord Avenue; and I suppose he found my youthful informality convenient. He always asked me to dinner when his old friend Greene came to visit him, and then we had an Italian time together, with more or less repetition in our talk, of what we had said before of Italian poetry and Italian character. One day there came a note from him saying, in effect, "Salvini is coming out to dine with me to-morrow night, and I want you to come too. There will be no one else but Greene and myself, and we will have an Italian dinner."

Unhappily I had accepted a dinner in Boston for that night, and this invitation put me in great misery. I must keep my engagement, but how could I bear to miss meeting Salvini at Longfellow's table on terms like these? We consulted at home together and questioned whether I might not rush into Boston, seek out my host there, possess him of the facts, and frankly throw myself on his mercy. Then a sudden thought struck us: Go to Longfellow, and submit the case to him! I went, and he entered with delicate sympathy into the affair. But he decided that, taking the large view of it, I must keep my engagement, lest I should run even a remote risk of wounding my friend's susceptibilities. I obeyed, and I had a very good time, but I still feel that I missed the best time of my life, and that I ought to be rewarded for my sacrifice, somewhere.

Longfellow so rarely spoke of himself in any way that one heard from him few of those experiences of the distinguished man in contact with the undistinguished, which he must have had so abundantly.

But he told, while it was fresh in his mind, an incident that happened to him one day in Boston at a tobacconist's, where a certain brand of cigars was recommended to him as the kind Longfellow smoked. "Ah, then I must have some of them; and I will ask you to send me a box," said Longfellow, and he wrote down his name and address. The cigar-dealer read it with the smile of a worsted champion, and said, "Well, I guess you *had* me, *that* time." At a funeral a mourner wished to open conversation, and by way of suggesting a theme of common interest, began, "*You've* buried, I believe?"

Sometimes people were shown by the poet through Craigie House who had no knowledge of it except that it had been Washington's headquarters. Of course Longfellow was known by sight to every one in Cambridge. He was daily in the streets, while his health endured, and as he kept no carriage, he was often to be met in the horse-cars, which were such common ground in Cambridge that they were often like small invited parties of friends when they left Harvard Square, so that you expected the gentlemen to jump up and ask the ladies whether they would have chicken salad. In civic and political matters he mingled so far as to vote regularly, and he voted with his party, trusting it for a general regard to the public welfare.

I fancy he was somewhat shy of his fellow-men, as the scholar seems always to be, from the sequestered habit of his life; but I think Longfellow was incapable of marking any difference between himself and them. I never heard from him anything that was *de haut en bas*, when he spoke of people, and in Cambridge, where there was a good deal of contempt for the less lettered, and we liked to smile though we did not like to sneer, and to analyze if we did not censure, Longfellow and Longfellow's house were free of all that. Whatever his feeling may have been towards other sorts and conditions of men, his effect was of an entire democracy. He was always the most unassuming person in any company, and at some large public dinners where I saw him I found him patient of the greater attention that more public men paid themselves and one another. He was not a speaker, and I never saw him on his feet at dinner, except once, when he read a poem for Whittier, who was absent. He disliked after - dinner speaking, and made conditions for his own exemption from it.

VIII.

Once your friend, Longfellow was always your friend; he would not think evil of you, and if he knew evil of you, he would be the last of all that knew it to judge you for it. This may have been from the impersonal habit of his mind, but I believe it was also the effect of principle, for he would do what he could to arrest the delivery of judgment from others, and would soften the sentences passed in his presence. Naturally this brought him under some condemnation with those of a severer cast; and I have heard him criticised for his benevolence towards all, and his constancy to some who were not quite so true to themselves, perhaps. But this leniency of Longfellow's was what constituted him great as well as good, for it is not our wisdom that censures others. As for his goodness, I never saw a fault in him. I do not mean to say that he had no faults, or that there were not better men, but only to give the witness of my knowledge concerning him. I claim in no wise to have been his intimate; such a thing was not possible in my case for quite apparent reasons; and I doubt if Longfellow was capable of intimacy in the sense we mostly attach to the word. Something more of egotism than I ever found in him must go to the making of any intimacy which did not come from the tenderest affections of his heart. But as a man shows himself to those often with him, and in his noted relations with other men, he showed himself without blame. All men that I have known, besides, have had some foible (it often endeared them the more), or some meanness, or pettiness, or bitterness; but Longfellow had none, nor the suggestion of any. No breath of evil ever touched his name; he went in and out among his fellow-men without the reproach that follows wrong; the worst thing I ever heard said of him was that he had *gêne*, and this was said by one of those difficult Cambridge men who would have found *gêne* in a celestial angel. Something that Björnstjerne Björnson wrote to me when he was leaving America after a winter in Cambridge, comes nearer suggesting Longfellow than all my talk. The Norsemen, in the days of their stormy and reluctant conversion,

used always to speak of Christ as the White Christ, and Björnson said in his letter, "Give my love to the White Mr. Longfellow."

A good many years before Longfellow's death he began to be sleepless, and he suffered greatly. He said to me once that he felt as if he were going about with his head in a kind of mist. The whole night through he would not be aware of having slept. "But," he would add, with his heavenly patience, "I always get a good deal of rest from lying down so long." I cannot say whether these conditions persisted, or how much his insomnia had to do with his breaking health; three or four years before the end came, we left Cambridge for a house farther in the country, and I saw him less frequently than before. He did not allow our meetings to cease; he asked me to dinner from time to time, as if to keep them up, but it could not be with the old frequency. Once he made a point of coming to see us in our cottage on the hill west of Cambridge, but it was with an effort not visible in the days when he could end one of his brief walks at our house on Concord Avenue; he never came but he left our house more luminous for his having been there. Once he came to supper there to meet Garfield (an old family friend of mine in Ohio), and though he was suffering from a heavy cold, he would not scant us in his stay. I had some very bad sherry which he drank with the serenity of a martyr, and I shudder to this day to think what his kindness must have cost him. He told his story of the clothes-line ghost, and Garfield matched it with the story of an umbrella ghost who sheltered a friend of his through a midnight storm, but was not cheerful company to his beneficiary, who passed his hand through him at one point in the effort to take his arm.

After the end of four years I came to Cambridge to be treated for a long sickness, which had nearly been my last, and when I could get about I returned the visit Longfellow had not failed to pay me. But I did not find him, and I never saw him again in life. I went into Boston to finish the winter of 1881–2, and from time to time I heard that the poet was failing in health. As soon as I felt able to bear the horse-car journey I went out to Cambridge to see him. I had knocked once at his door, the friendly door that had so often opened to his welcome, and stood with the knocker in my hand when the door was suddenly set ajar, and a maid showed her face wet with tears. "How is Mr. Longfellow?" I palpitated, and with a burst of grief she answered, "Oh, the poor gentleman has just departed!" I turned away as if from a helpless intrusion at a death-bed.

At the services held at the house before the obsequies at the cemetery, I saw the poet for the last time, where

"Dead he lay among his books,"

in the library behind his study. Death seldom fails to bring serenity to all, and I will not pretend that there was a peculiar peacefulness in Longfellow's noble mask, as I saw it then. It was calm and benign as it had been in life; he could not have worn a gentler aspect in going out of the world than he had always worn in it; he had not to wait for death to dignify it with "the peace of God." All who were left of his old Cambridge were present, and among those who had come farther was Emerson. He went up to the bier, and with his arms crossed on his breast, and his elbows held in either hand, stood with his head pathetically fallen forward, looking down at the dead face. Those who knew how his memory was a mere blank, with faint gleams of recognition capriciously coming and going in it, must have felt that he was struggling to remember who it was lay there before him; and for me the electly simple words confessing

his failure will always be pathetic with his remembered aspect: "The gentleman we have just been burying," he said, to the friend who had come with him, "was a sweet and beautiful soul; but I forget his name."

I had the privilege and honor of looking over the unprinted poems Longfellow left behind him, and of helping to decide which of them should be published. There were not many of them, and some of these few were quite fragmentary. I gave my voice for the publication of all that had any sort of completeness, for in every one there was a touch of his exquisite art, the grace of his most lovely spirit. We have so far had two men only who felt the claim of their gift of the very best that the most patient skill could give their utterance: one was Hawthorne and the other was Longfellow. I shall not undertake to say which was the greater artist of these two; but I am sure that every one who has studied it must feel with me that the art of Longfellow held out to the end with no touch of decay in it, and that it equalled the art of any other poet of his time. It knew when to give itself, and more and more it knew when to withhold itself.

What Longfellow's place in literature will be, I shall not offer to say; that is Time's affair, not mine; but I am sure that with Tennyson and Browning he fully shared in the expression of an age which more completely than any former age got itself said by its poets.

FRENCH CANADIANS IN NEW ENGLAND

THE emigration of the French Canadians from the province of Quebec into the United States has become of great importance to two countries. On one side of the border it is regretted and belittled by the party which it threatens with loss of power, while it is utilized by the party that is out of power as evidence that the Conservative government is hostile to the true interests of the Dominion. On the other side of the border the movement is becoming of importance by reason of its present and prospective effects on the industrial and political conditions of the United States. In the Dominion there is felt to be a loss of population whose characteristics are thoroughly known and appreciated. In the United States there is an accession of population with traditions and training that are not in harmony with the institutions under which the new-comers are seeking a home, and with habits and faith at variance with New England life and teachings. It is largely a question of aptitude whether the French Canadians will ever be assimilated to the political and social conditions of that part of the United States into which most of the immigrants have come. The country has received many foreigners, and apparently has absorbed the men of strange races who have landed on our shores utterly untaught in all the methods of self-government, and unconscious of the obligations imposed upon the citizens of a free republic. The Slavs, the Russians, and even the Italians who have recently been flocking to the country are certainly not at first additions to the political intelligence and virtue of our population. Their idea of government is of a power which controls and directs them, but over which they have no influence, and the suggestion that a single vote is of importance to themselves, and effective for improving their own condition, does not appeal to them with any force until they learn that it can be sold. As far as the French Canadian is concerned, it is still a question whether in politics he is not possessed of just that little knowledge which is a dangerous thing. Living all his life under British institutions, which, however, have been but half applied and not at all appreciated in the province dominated by the people of his race, he has come to know how valuable his vote may be in a close contest to one or the other of the candidates, but he has not learned the real importance of conscientious and intelligent action, especially in local affairs.

The French Canadians have been coming to the United States in great numbers, and for many years. The first who came in sufficiently important numbers to attract attention left their native land in consequence of the results of their rebellion of 1837. They found homes on the borders of Lake Champlain, in northern New York, and in the agricultural regions about the city of Burlington. It was at Burlington that the French Canadians established their first parish in New England, and it was there that they first learned the impossibility of maintaining, in association with Irish Roman Catholics, their church and priesthood as they had been taught to maintain them at home.

It was not, however, until after the civil war that the great popular movement began which has resulted in what many distinguished Canadians, chiefly those opposed to the existing government, delight in calling "the exodus."

The war had so stimulated manufacturing enterprises in New England, and prices were so enormously inflated by reason not only of a debased currency, but of an artificial demand, that the temptation was strong to emigrate from the worn and gradually narrowing farms of Quebec to the busy hives of industry in the republic. It was partly the accident of location, and partly the contrast between the strenuous circumstances of Canada and the forced prosperity of the neighboring States, that led the *habitants* to New England. The New-Englanders were the nearest neighbors of the Québecois, but the stony farms of Vermont and New Hampshire and the forests of Maine did not attract the French yeomanry. Those who fled from the wrath of the English after their defeat in 1837 found homes just across the border, but those who came later looked further south, to the smoking factory stacks of Lowell, Fall River, Providence, and the other busy cotton towns of Massachusetts and Rhode Island.

Some of the reasons of the large emigration from French Canada have been pointed out in former articles. It is not necessary, therefore, to state them in this paper. Generally it may be said, by way of summing up, that under existing conditions Quebec could not support the population that it would have had to-day if there had not been considerable emigration. It is not that the province does not

possess the natural capacity to sustain a population many times its present number, but, with a race of farmers unwilling to open new lands, untaught in scientific methods of agriculture, and with laws and a priestly domination that prevent the sturdiest and most energetic of Europeans from settling in the province, the opportunities for prosperity are now fully utilized.

In a directory of French Canadians published at Lowell, in Massachusetts, a number of interesting facts and statistics are given. The work is known as the *Guide Français*, and is sufficiently well thought of by Father Hamon and other French-Canadian writers to be quoted by them as an authority. According to the *Guide*, the number of French Canadians in the United States in 1891 was 997,596. In New England the enumeration and distribution of French-Canadian population, according to this authority, are as follows:

Maine	52,986
New Hampshire	47,682
Vermont	31,467
Massachusetts	165,325
Rhode Island	37,338
Connecticut	27,598
Total	362,396

This differs somewhat from the total given by Father Hamon, who, in this particular, depends upon the enumeration made by the *curés* of the New England parishes. The compilers of our own census have prepared a statement in answer to a private letter, which shows that the total number of French persons born in Canada, and who were in New England in 1890, was 205,761. While it is true that the statistics of our census are not comparable with the results obtained by the compilers of the *Guide Français*, or by Father Hamon, they tend to verify these results. The totals of the directory and of the reports of the *curés* of the parishes include not only the native French Canadians, but those who are of French-Canadian parentage. Consequently the difference is very slight, and it may be assumed that there are in New England at least 300,000 French Canadians, some of them born in Canada of French-Canadian parents, and some born in the United States. In a work entitled *Les Canadiens-Français de la Nouvelle Angleterre*, Father Hamon gives the number of French-Canadian Catholics in New England in 1891 as 302,659—about one-third of the total Catholic population of the six States. As these statistics are collected by the Church for its own purposes, they are probably nearly accurate. The book, it should be stated, was written for the purpose of enforcing upon the people who had quitted their native parishes the duty of remaining faithful to their Church, and of preserving their language, and their loyal love at least for the country of their ancestors.

In addition to the French Canadians who had settled in New England, Father Hamon says that there are about 100,000 other French Canadians in the northern part of the State of New York and the dioceses of Syracuse and Albany. An interesting and important fact is also mentioned by the reverend writer in connection with the French Canadians who are in New England. He points out that most of the English-speaking Roman Catholics "are concentrated in certain great cities of the East, like Boston, where alone there are 250,000 Catholics; while the Canadians, on the contrary, for the most part establish themselves in the small manufacturing towns, and they already form a majority in several of them." It is not quite clear whether Father Hamon intends to assert that they form a majority of the whole population of these several towns or only of the Catholics.

Continuing, he says, "Finally, these new-comers have built in twenty years one hundred and twenty churches or chapels served by Canadian priests, fifty great convents where the *religieuses* from Canada give to 30,000 children an education that is Catholic and French."

The immigration is important in number and in character. It is worthy of a much closer and more thorough study than has yet been bestowed upon it by the officials whose duty it is to compile the industrial and social statistics of the Federal government and the States. From the vague reports that have been published, it is not possible to reach definite conclusions. It is clear, however, that the mass of the Canadians who are settled in New England are not rapidly becoming proprietors of the soil, their holdings, according to their own reports, being very much below the average per capita assessed valuations in the six States, as appears from the census of 1890. They remain operatives in the mills and factories.

A few of them are storekeepers; fewer still are physicians and lawyers. Recently the French-Canadian press in the United States, and especially in New England, has rapidly developed. This is a pretty sure sign that the active politicians are taking a decided interest in the French-Canadian vote, and are prepared to avail themselves of the customary electioneering methods for the purpose of securing it.

In 1887 there were in New England 16,806 French-Canadian voters; in 1889 the number had increased to 28,465; in 1891 it had grown to be 33,663. In every one of the six States, except Vermont, votes equal in number to the solid French-Canadian vote would suffice to reverse the political supremacy if they should be transferred from the prevailing party to the minority. In the Presidential election just held this vote played an important part, especially in Massachusetts. It is said that most of the French Canadians voted for the Democratic candidate because of the injuries inflicted on the farmers of Quebec by the McKinley tariff. However that may be, it is the fact that the French-Canadian vote was a matter of much solicitude to the politicians of both parties, and it is its growing importance in American politics that makes the immigration of interest in this country.

It is perfectly evident that these people are coming with the intention of remaining in this country. At first they came for a season's work in the brickyards, on the farms, or in the lumber camps. When they began to find employment in the factories, their stay was necessarily longer. Even then, however, they hoped to return in a few years, and many of them realized their expectations. Most of these had come for the purpose of earning enough money to pay off encumbrances on their farms, to get even with the world. There were very few of them in the earlier days of the immigration who did not expect to return to their old home in the course of time. The love of the French Canadian for his home is intense. It is the characteristic of his race. He and his kind across the sea cling to barren ancestral acres, although they know no art by which they can be made fruitful. They love the land on which they and their ancestors were born, and they love their relations, and the neighbors among whom they were reared. Their religion, customs, manners, language, are all dearer to them than are similar ties to the men and women of Teutonic blood. The French Canadian loves Quebec because it is French. When the colony was founded, his attachment to the new land was the more quickly formed because his neighbors also came from the pleasant orchards, farms, and towns of Normandy and Brittany. Their parishes and their lakes and rivers were named from their patron saints. In time the love of the transplanted Frenchman for Quebec came to be as passionate as that which animated the hearts of those who remained at home for the land from which Louis had sent forth his colonists.

It was with great reluctance that any of the French Canadians contemplated the permanent abandonment of their old homes. They came to New England to repair the ravages that time and hard conditions had wrought in their patrimonies. They confidently expected to be able to return in a few years to dwell in plenty in the land from which they had been expelled by the strenuous compulsions of poverty. But time and prosperity have wrought changes. The French Canadian is more content with New England than he was. Many thousands of his compatriots have joined him. He has them for his neighbors. They work by his side in the factory. He buys his food and drink of men of his own race. His parish priest is French. He hears and speaks his native tongue. He is no longer dependent on what seemed to him the cold hospitality of the native New-Englanders. He is no longer exposed to the jealousies of the people of his own faith and of other tongues. The French Canadian in New England is happy. Instead of thinking of returning to Quebec, he is inviting his relatives and neighbors to come to him.

Father Hamon's description of the arrival of a French-Canadian family in America illustrates both the cause and the effect of the movement from the old home to this country.

"A *habitant*," writes the priest, "poor in earthly goods but rich in children, decides to emigrate to the States. The family arrives in a manufacturing centre, say either Lowell, Holyoke, or Worcester. With the father and mother there are eight children of different ages. Every one is clad in homespun made by the housewife. The friends and relatives of the family await them at the station to welcome them. They exchange vigorous hand-shakes and embraces, and then the immigrants are conducted to the quarters which have been prepared for them in advance. Visit the family a year afterwards. You will be surprised by the change which has taken place. The young men, with their woollen clothes, have taken on the *air monsieur*. The girls are well clad, and, most assuredly, ribbons are not lacking in their toilets. Even the grandparents have yielded a little, and accommodate themselves in a measure to the American fashion. Every one appears to be content with his lot. 'One lives very well here,' say they. 'One is well lodged, well warmed, well clad. We have fresh meat every day of the week, and more money at the end of the month than we had in Canada at the end of the whole year.'"

This is a truthful picture of the French Canadian in New England, and a faithful portrayal of the change which, in recent years, has come over the spirit of the immigrant, whose sole purpose in the earlier day was to make what money he needed and return home.

It cannot be said, however, that he is yet assimilated. He remains a distinct being in the community. He tries to preserve his language, his faith, and his social and domestic characteristics. He is struggling against absorption by the mighty mass of strange humanity, of which, notwithstanding the importance of his movement to his own race at home, he remains an inconsiderable part. His priest is with him. Sometimes he comes from Canada, but often he comes from old France. He teaches his parishioners the necessity of preserving their faith and their tongue, and urges them to rear their children in parish schools like those in which they themselves were taught in New France.

"The best method by which the Canadians may preserve their faith," said the Bishop of Springfield, in bestowing his blessing on the parish school at Holyoke, "is to conserve their language, to remain attached to their customs, and to instruct their children in the maternal tongue."

The whole influence of the Church is directed towards the accomplishment of these objects. The zealous heads of the establishment in Quebec see to it that their old communicants shall not live in their new homes without the spiritual nourishment with which they were provided in their native country from the day of their birth to the day of their departure from the dwellings of their fathers. Cardinal Taschereau speaks of the "means that must be adopted to preserve their faith, in preserving their language and their nationality." Throughout the periodical and more permanent literature of the Church, so far as it relates to the French Canadians, the injunction is inculcated to preserve among the enemies of their religion their manners, national traditions, and language as the most "powerful ramparts of the Catholic faith." How intense, how all-absorbing, is the passion that the Church would implant, may be best illustrated by an extract from Father Hamon's chapter on Nationality. I give the passage in the original, for to translate it would seriously detract from its dignity. The reverend priest, in speaking of the pride of other races in their material prosperity, declares that it is to the pride of nationality that he pays willing homage, and continues:

" *Mais partout sur terre on a droit de porter haut à la tête et le cœur quand on peut dire: 'Moi, j'appartiens à la race qui la première courba le front sous la main du Christ, et qui, pendant quatorze siècles, écrivit avec la plume et l'épée les actes de Dieu en ce monde. Ma patrie c'est la France.'* "

In order to keep the French Canadians firm in their religion and national principles, dioceses have been established in every State in New England. Other dioceses have been founded in other States, and especially in New York, but we are now concerned only with those members of the race who have found homes in New England, because there they constitute the most important percentage of the total population. In the diocese of Burlington (Vermont) there were eight French - Canadian parishes in 1891, and eighteen mixed (French and English-speaking Catholics) parishes. In the diocese of Springfield there were twenty-two French-Canadian parishes and ten mixed; in the diocese of Providence there were fourteen of the one and four of the other; in the diocese of Connecticut there were five French Canadian and twenty-six mixed; in the archdiocese of Boston there were nine of the one and six of the other; in the diocese of Portland there were seventeen of the one and eight of the other. Some of the parish churches are costly edifices; and in addition there are the schools and convents. In coming to the United States the priest has been obliged to surrender the power of compelling his parishioners to pay their contributions towards the building of churches, presbyteries, schools, and convents, but the French Canadians have not yet entirely outgrown the habit of responding to the demands of the priest for voluntary contributions for the purposes of his church.

Besides being devout and loyal to his native language, the French Canadian in New England is thrifty, generally peaceable, and fairly honest. He works for small wages. He is deft and quick to learn. He is an admirable mechanic. If he is inclined to vice, it is to deception, trickery, and petty larceny. Graver crimes are rare among the French Canadians.

The objections to him are, first, that he is a competitor in the labor field (this is of such small moment that it is not worthy of much consideration); second, that he is Catholic and foreign, and that he not only declines to become a political and social entity in the community in which he takes up his residence, but that he threatens to overturn New England institutions, and even to revolutionize its common-school system. This certainly is a more serious accusation against him than the first, and yet the danger threatened cannot be said to be imminent. Not only has he not yet overturned New England institutions, he has not even unsettled them.

The native New - Englander calls the French Canadian "queer" or "curious." This because he speaks French and is docile. The Irish American, also a Roman Catholic, does not like him because he is willing to work for lower wages than were paid before he came here with his family and his friends. Soon enough, however, he recovers from his modesty, and learns to exact the market rates. Nor does this English-speaking son of the Church quite comprehend the reverent obedience yielded by the Canadian to the authority of the *curé*. As for himself, he is more or less emancipated, and is often inclined to treat the priest with the familiarity of equality. There are signs that the Canadian himself is being influenced by his surroundings, and is questioning the authority which demands implicit obedience for his soul's sake. He sees that the most prosperous members of the community are those free from interference, priestly or other, with their domestic, industrial, and social lives. The Protestant missionaries may not obtain very much more encouragement from their labors among the French Canadians in the United States than they obtain in Canada, but there is no doubt that there is a loosening of the ties in this country.

The French Canadian in New England is feeling the influence of the institutions of the republic. Politically he remains a difficult factor. He brings with him, from his home in Quebec, a careless indifference to communal affairs. He does not want to spend his evenings in talking politics, nor his days in voting, unless he can make something. At home his enthusiasms are aroused when his creed or his race is threatened. There, too, election day is turned into a festivity for him; and he likes festivities, with their color, their gayety, their social comminglings. Here it is different. In national affairs he has shown intelligence by deciding to vote against the perpetuation of a tariff system which he believed was impoverishing his people at home by the taxes which it imposed on barley, hay, eggs, and horses. In town affairs he is at sea. It is said that the French Canadians are bought up in town politics, and it may be that their votes are purchased in municipal elections.

It may be that the French Canadian may eventually change the political aspect of New England; but if he does he has become, by mere translation over a purely artificial border, more puissant than his race has ever yet shown itself to be in the long centuries of its history. Sometimes people fear that he will "capture" the common-school system and transform the secular schools into parochial schools; that the limited education permitted by the Church will take the place of what is esteemed by the friends of the present system a broad and liberal teaching. It may be that some of these fears will be realized. The problem is just presenting itself, and the results cannot be foretold; but he who believes that the common schools can be permanently transformed into Roman Catholic institutions must forget the history of the country, the elevating and liberalizing influences of republican institutions upon all sects and all conditions of men. He must shut his eyes to the movement now going on in the Church itself, under the guidance of Leo XIII., looking to the harmonizing of its practices and its teachings with the basic principles of our free institutions. In a country in which every decade has been a long forward step in civilization, where the energies and capabilities of the people have been so encouraged by their political institutions that prosperity and progress have overcome the most cunningly devised obstacles, where there is every stimulant to confidence and hope—in such a country to be distrustful of the future is to be not only a pessimist, but a pessimist without reason.

It may be that trouble will result from the increasing immigration of the French Canadians. It is the fact that they stand in need of a great moral and intellectual elevation before they will attain the public virtues and the political sense that are essential not only to the highest achievements, but to the proper conduct of a popular form of government. It is in the local government that evil foreign influences are first felt. It will be in the town meeting that the French Canadian will first give evidence of incurable incompatibility. As I said at the outset of this article, however, the question is one of aptitude for his new surroundings. In all his social and industrial relations he has been found to be tractable and teachable. If it be true that he has few political virtues; if his comprehension of his power in the town meeting is dull or narrow; if, when he grows more enlightened, his first impulse is to use that power for the aggrandizement of his Church; if the political knowledge that he has brought from Canada is of the commercial value of his vote—there is still little reason to believe that he will always remain unworthy of American citizenship, and no reason whatever to fear that he will ever be a serious menace to American institutions. He may be an annoyance or an inconvenience; he may, for a time, increase the expensiveness of politics; but he will not materially damage the stalwart growth of the American democracy. It is far more reasonable to believe, whatever difficulties he may add to our present problem, that in the end we shall greatly prize his American-born descendants.

NEW ENGLAND FISHERFOLK

OF all those relationships between man and elemental nature which alternate so singularly in character between strife and alliance, there is none which in its various phases is more humanly appealing than the bond, or battle, as momentary circumstances may have it, between the fisher and the sea. Between aeronaut and atmosphere, chemist and his elements, miner and his ore, the relationship, if intimate, is still strictly severe, often hostile, never imbued with anything akin to this other singular sympathy.

The fisher's life, overhung as it is with the shadow of potential unexplainable death, and invested with a myriad, as if reflected, moods of the great element with which he must be in daily, almost in hourly, touch, has provided much of the poetry, and perhaps more of the pathos, in the stories of many lands, but in none more than in that of coastwise New England.

There is a singular lack of poetry, and almost of picturesqueness, in the history of the original States, founded and fostered by sectarians of a bigotry so extreme as to seem nearly akin to fanaticism, and the mark of his stern forebears is writ large in the character of the New-Englander of to-day.

Even where, as a fisher, he is brought into close contact with the element which in all time has been the most potent spur to human imagination, the trammels of ascetic ancestry are so strong upon him that we find in his conception barely a trace of the intensely vivid imagery, half superstition, half religion, with which association with the sea has imbued the fisher of other lands—notably the Breton and the Sicilian. He is eminently shrewd, keenly observant, almost clairvoyant in his estimate of character, and surpassingly deft in every detail of his craft, but, beyond and above all, a Yankee—that quintessence of practicality which may reasonably be regarded as the antithesis of romance in its any and every form.

From your fisher of Gloucester or

Cape Cod the realistic poetry which impregnates the Breton stories of Pierre Loti is as much a thing apart as the plaints of a Romeo or the imaginings of a Shahrazad. And yet that selfsame atmosphere of romance is as truly a part of the fisher of Finistère as his technical knowledge of sails and tides.

Yet—so pervasive is that subtle sea-charm which permeates all that is brought within its influence—a romance as unmistakable as that which surrounds Plougastel or Capri, though of a different quality, lies about these little fishing-towns of New England, which contrasts them strangely with the bustling commercialism of the great mercantile and manufacturing centres, so near in actual measurement of miles, so infinitely distant in every other sense.

Stranger though he be in thought and speech to aught that smacks of ideality, an influence beyond his control, as beyond his perception, has clothed every detail of the fisher's life, every most trifling accessory of his occupation, with a poetical significance unspeakably appealing to the imagination.

"They that go down to the sea in ships"—what an inheritance is theirs, what a birthright of marvel and mystery! The association, as new to-day as it was old in David's time, is inevitable. No mere insensibility to romanticism is sufficient to lessen the permanency of its influence. The sea will infallibly mark its own, and is not to be eluded or denied.

In such a village as those of which we have been speaking the sea is, in a material sense, the source of all good, and of all evil as well. It enriches or impoverishes, saves or destroys, robs or restores. Its will is the pivot on which existence revolves. So it is but natural, and far from being a fanciful supposition, that the life of the people should reflect faithfully certain broad, general qualities which may be said to be strictly characteristic of the element whereupon they are so intimately dependent. Pre-eminent among these we distinguish a vast and highly admirable simplicity, a freedom from conventionality, wherein much that is unworthily petty, suspicious, and unjust in human thought has given

place to a kindly and tolerant, while in no sense a credulous, view of men and things.

It is a supremely sane attitude of mind —sane with the clean, wholesome sanity of the sea—when contrasted with the veritable labyrinth of prejudice wherein we, whose lives are necessarily more complicated, move and have our being. One rarely hears a New England fisherman indulging in petty disparagement of a neighbor. This is not to say that his tolerance is fatuously invariable, but only that his judgment, whether favorable or the reverse, is expressed simply and broadly, without a suggestion of either favor or fear, above all, without a hint of malice. "Them Harrises be'n't no good!" said one such philosopher, and that was the expression of a simple conviction.

Disapproval is as generous and as elemental as commendation. One is inevitably tempted to a reflection upon the pains which a less simple society would be at to adduce a multitude of trivial slurs in support of this amply self-sufficient statement.

In the well-ordered regularity of life in a fishing-town the sea once more supplies the cue. Monotony, that chiefest bugbear of more elaborate conditions of existence, is less accepted as inevitable than totally disregarded in the sense of an objection.

In dependence on the sun and the wind and the tide events move forward day by day, and men rise and retire, labor and take their ease, with machinelike orderliness. And this, their submission to the requirements of routine, is parent, no doubt, to the serene repose which is so noticeable in the older men. Long before it is possible for individual preference to point out an independent line of activity, the daily round of duty has been, almost imperceptibly, laid out, and the boy finds himself pledged to the performance of certain well-defined labors, the which he accepts without argument, if not without reflection.

There are exceptions, as in all conditions of society—lads who rebel and strike out for themselves. Every battle-ship in our navy has its tale of these. But for the most part, to an

WHARVES WHEREUNDER THE TIDE MURMURS MYSTERY

extent undreampt of in our larger cities, where the ebb and flow of life is so ceaseless and so erratic, it is a case in the fishing-town of "like father, like son." The latter takes up the work where the former drops it, sails the same boat, cleans fish with the same knife, mends and re-mends the same nets, and spins the same yarns in his hours of leisure.

But where the fisher's life is most appealingly in sympathy with the sea is in a respect which he of all men is probably the furthest from perceiving — its profound melancholy. In this regard, if in no other, coastwise New England is nearly akin to that coastwise Finistère of which we have spoken, and which inspired *Mon Frère Yves* and *Pêcheur d'Islande*. There is lacking the fanciful imagination of the Breton, which has peopled every mood of the ocean with the personalities of saints and demons, and thereby achieved so great a degree of picturesqueness; there is lacking, too, the extremity of devoutness which associates the woe or weal of the fishing-fleet with the direct intent of the Virgin. There are no pageants, no *pardons*, no

invocations to the sea, no little porcelain *Notre Dame de la Recouvrance*, before which, when the fleet is out, the women of the village watch and pray, and tapers continually burn.

But all these, indescribably pathetic though they be, are not, it must be remembered, intrinsically so, but only in such sense as they are the manifestations, the outward signs, of a great elemental undercurrent of tragedy—the ominous, indescribably alluring relation between the fisher and the sea.

Apart from the peculiar phenomena wherein this emotion finds expression under varying conditions lies the emotion itself, vast, majestic, large with infinity of suggestion, and identical, we may imagine, the sea-coasts of the world around. Here in New England the very severity of earlier conditions seems to have bequeathed an added force to the tragedy.

It is, perhaps, not too much to say that these fisher families are exemplifications, as perfect as may be, of absolute adherence to a very high, if simple, code of ethics. One can barely conceive of social relations more

To and from the Wharves the Schooners come and go

essentially righteous, of religious convictions more consistently followed, of a more rational or saner observance of hygienic and physiological principles.

And, withal, from cradle to grave it is always the tragic aspect of the fisher's life which is seen to be most heavily underscored, most unmistakably emphasized. Those most familiar in a sympathetic sense with the sea will realize that even in its gayest moods it is inseparable from this hint of melancholy. It is too old, too cruel, with all its kindness, and the custodian of too many terrible memories and awful secrets to be ever less than ominous. And it may almost be said that as the land approaches the sea it comes under this influence, and shows, even in its conformation, a reflection of the lurking grimness before it.

The long swelling sand dunes of Cape Cod, rolling away in majestic emptiness, mile on mile, and the gaunt, grim rocks of Maine, wrinkled, as are the faces of the fisher-folk, with much gazing across the sea — are they not equally suggestive of infinite loneliness, ageless endurance, stupendous power,

and, more than all, the pitiable littleness of man?

The fancy could be carried further, down to the blackened and mussel-covered piles of the wharves, where-under the tide rises and murmurs mystery, and retires as if to seek yet other stories from the informing deeps beyond. Above, the weather-beaten planking is strewn with an infinity of discarded rubbish—spars, anchors, chains, sail-cloth, blocks, and cordage. Where they have been, whence they come, there is no knowing now. Only in two respects are all alike. In their time they have been new, strong, well fitted to their appointed uses. Now they are but mute additional proofs of the impotency of man's device. The omnipotent and everlasting sea has laid hand on one and all, as upon those who made them, and they are as if they had never been. The sea! the sea! the sea! To and from the wharves the schooners come and go. They too are blackened, and bear witness to the eternal struggle and the inevitable end.

So, little by little, is born in the observer not merely a realization of the pervading melancholy inseparable from this environment, but an appreciation of the primary cause, the emotion which lies below. Every most trivial detail of this people's life is instinct with the thought of facing an unknowable and invincible force, wherewith they may struggle for a little, may even seem to master or cajole, but which must inevitably stand victor in the end. Each year the sea claims its tithe, and this comes as no unexpected calamity, but as a duly calculated nemesis.

One catches a trace of its abiding presence, now and again, in the eyes of a mother or a wife or a sweetheart as she watches him who is to her the fisher of all fishers, on his way toward the shore—oftener, even, in a strange, unconscious glance of apprehension toward the sea itself, which, perhaps, has already smitten, and holds yet other blows in store.

All this tends directly, one cannot but think, to the formation and preservation of a very strong, albeit unobtrusive, nobility of character, as it so apparently induces an admirable simplicity of life. Beneath the evidence of these immaculately kept houses, these scrupulously tended nets and boats, these trim gardens, and severe places of worship, and clear-eyed, sturdy children; back of this spirit of fair dealing and clean living, and earnest, consistent endeavor: there lies a marvellous strength of conviction and an appreciation of duty which is not far from being the chief of our national moral sinews.

The fisher-folk are, to a great extent, a people set apart, barred off by the peculiar conditions which surround them from participation in much of what we are wont to say makes life worth living. More than any other class of Americans they are forced into that close intimacy with elemental nature from which it is the tendency of civilization to wean us. They are part and parcel of the great universal system, and so are impelled and controlled, as is nature's self, by magnificently broad and yet singularly simple laws. As a result, we find them unconsciously imbued in thought, word, and deed with nature's own dignity and sanity and force.

From conditions so elemental it would be strange did there not result the poetry and the picturesqueness which invest whatever is supremely natural, and that are lacking in all that smacks of artificiality or design.

Just as there is no trace of intention in the attitude of the fisher himself, so is there nothing resembling studied effect in what, as the logical result of his needs, has come to be in his surroundings. Even the most sequestered inland villages of New England are not free, in these progressive days, from the reproach of atrocious architecture, made worse by glaring combinations of the unspeakable commodity known as enamel paint. Nature is foully wronged in the presence of grottos and rockeries which have not even the redeeming grace of utility, far less that of ornament, and incongruous iron stags profane the even velvet of the lawns.

But of these and kindred crimes the fisher's environment is guiltless before nature and nature's God. The tints of his shingles and sails and wharves are those lent by the fingers of the salt wind and water. Even where the work is that of his own hands it runs on broad unoffending lines of architecture, and in simple blacks and whites and greens and maroons unspeakably grateful to the eye long weary of gaudier hues. His flowers are the simplest, and while trained away from disorderly riot, yet grow naturally and freely, untrammelled by the intention of ornamental borders.

And if he err in angularity of line or blatancy of hue, his omnipresent mentor, the sea, is at hand to correct, gnawing and rounding and moulding with busy teeth and fingers, till the sharp corners are made smooth and the gaudy tints softened and the sea's great aim is once more attained—the reduction of all with which it comes in contact to a gray in color and to a curve in form.

Let us leave it as we found it, this modest little cluster of gray and white cottages nestling in a curve of wooded shore, and staring ingenuously from square, green-shuttered windows at the blackened wharves, eloquent of the comings and goings of the simple, brave men who go down to the sea in ships.

Your Fisher of Gloucester or Cape Cod

Let us leave it with twilight settling down upon the gables, for this is of all hours the best. The schooners are in; the daily work is done; smoke from a score of chimneys spires skyward;—and there, beyond the laughter of the ripples on the peaceful shore, beyond the smooth gray stretch of harbor water, beyond the white foam of surf on the bar—there lies a wide, unruffled calm. There is peace, and there is a truce declared between the fisher and the sea.

THE GREEN MOUNTAINS IN SUGAR-TIME

WHEN we think of Vermont, it is as we think of Labrador or Alaska—as something within the boundaries of the continent, but aloof from the attributes and intimacy of the commonwealth; and it is only by poring over a map and a guide that we are made to understand how near it is to the city, and that its population is not isolated from us by an arctic environment. Every reputable person with a proper respect for himself knows that the State has the same characteristics, the same homely virtues, and the same, pervasive common-school intelligence as the rest of New England; but the unrevised, intuitive idea of it is that it is bleak and distant, that its surface is broken by many mountain ranges, and that maple sugar is an ameliorating staple.

A proposition to investigate it in March elicits some domestic opposition; but March is the time for the maples, and acquiescing in preparations which suggest a polar expedition, we leave the city in the warm and idealizing haze of a premature spring.

All the forenoon we reach northward by the banks of the Hudson, which are clear of snow even up to the heights of Cro'nest and the Storm King; the slopes are brown with the budding foliage, and the water traffic shows that the river men have finally dismissed the winter. But in the afternoon the scene changes; we have passed Troy, and still bearing northward, we look out of the car windows on a landscape with a communicative chilliness of color and feeling. The skies are overcast by heavy clouds, and the air has a moist penetrativeness; the dépôts are small and uncomfortable; the soil is scrubby and fallow; the homesteads are seriously unbeautiful; and we detect a dialect in the murmured conversation of the car which convinces us that we are in Vermont.

We come nearer to the hills that at first are distant, and wind through narrow valleys, where there are clumps of silvery birches, elders, and maples. We sometimes discover a rugged hut, from which a column of smoke is ascending amidst the maples, from each of which a pail is suspended. The hours are long, the frostless cold increases, and the dullness of the day ends in rain. We alight in a precise and well-conditioned town among the hills, where marble is so common that it is used for fences and for the door-steps of frame houses. The life is placid, and the business is invisible, though the blocks of stores indicate no small measure of prosperity and ambition. But the littleness of purpose and achievement, in contrast with the vigorous metropolis that we left in the morning, is soon dismissed in the glow and crackle of a birch-wood fire, which seems to lubricate the whole being. The outer weather is nothing to us until morning, and in the morning our discontent is revived in finding that all the hills have disappeared in what Emerson graphically describes as "the tumultuous privacy of the storm." The fast-flying flakes, whirled by a biting wind, muffle the distance, and when in moments of respite the nearer hills shape themselves again, it is as in a mirage— dubious and vanishing. What consolation there is comes to us in the intimation that it is a sugar snow, which with the relaxation of a thaw will leave the maples in a soft, yielding condition; and

as it is to study the maples that we have ventured into this northern latitude, we take courage with the afternoon train for Shrewsbury, where the maple orchards are famous.

There are many groves on the way, bordered by sentinel evergreens, whose branches are overlaid by snow, and have the crisp whiteness of ostrich feathers. All down the slopes the maples have preponderance, and, like those we have already seen, are tapped, though beads of ice seal the incisions. In half an hour the train leaves us at one of the villages which Shrewsbury embraces, and we watch it disappear up the heavy grade in the confusion of the storm before we comprehend that we are standing alone on the platform of the dépôt, which is terraced in one mountain and confronted by another, with little more than a gully between. The snow is mystifying, and no tavern is visible among the cluster of houses in the hollow; but while we are debating as to our proper course, a young man opens the door of the station and invites us to come in. He is a small, wiry fellow, with sharp features; and over the Morse instrument, through which he has been exchanging civilities with the operator at Rutland, is a silver cornet.

"Do you play?" we inquire, as we linger before the stove, which is snapping with heat.

"Occasionally, at dances," he answers; and as he closes the door of the ticket office we notice that it is secured by a peculiar lock, which excites our interest.

"It's an invention of mine; I have a patent issued on it," he explains; and he then unfastens another door opening into a smaller apartment, strung before the window of which is a lot of watches, with various tools spread on the bench below for adjusting and repairing them. He applies himself to these with easy familiarity, and speaks of a fertilizer and Bible dictionary for which he is agent. At least six violins are hung against the wall; and as we pick at the strings of one of them he tells us, without any boastfulness, that this instrument also was made by him.

We do not wait to hear of his other occupations, as his versatility seems limitless, and we once more face the storm, following his directions down the hill to a little tavern in a street of less than a dozen houses, which, for all the life that can

GATHERING SAP IN A SNOW-STORM.

be seen, might be tenantless. Not a soul is afoot or discoverable through the windows, and our only greeting is from a half-bred bull-dog, whose growls give urgency to our raps at the tavern door, which, with some delay, is opened for us by a man who has been asleep, and is not yet fully awake.

"Boston or New York?" he inquires, after a superficial survey of us, which apparently convinces him that one of those two cities has cast us forth; and when we have answered him by registering, and have drawn chairs around the stove, he communicates the singular fact to us that he himself has been in the metropolis.

"I went daown with my daughter, and put up at a haouse somewhere near Madison Square—a new haouse of polished red brick. There's a heap of nonsense abaout them taverns o' yours. We sat daown at a table, and a fellow comes skipping up with a silver tray and a pencil and a piece of paper. That's all tomfoolery, that sort of thing is. What a man wants is good clean victuals with a flavor to 'em; but this fellow kept skipping araound with his silver tray, and when we got through I didn't kneow what we'd had to eat. I'd a sight liefer have a bit of boiled pork with milk gravy, or a cup of tea and a doughnut, than all the stuff they had on their bill of fare. And what do ye suppose they charged us?"

Supposing that he had blundered into Delmonico's, perhaps, we ironically suggested twenty-five cents.

"No, sir," he said, with emphasis, "though it wa'n't worth any more than that. They stuck us for two seventy-five;

and they charged us two dollars for one room, and two fifty for the other!" He wabbled with laughter at the delicious absurdity of the reminiscence, but a minute after his view of the exorbitance struck him querulously. "Yes," he added, "that's all confounded nonsense!"

"I guess you'll find it pretty wild up here," he went on. "We're a wild country and a wild people—it 'll seem as strange for you to be up here as for us to be daown to New York." But we were not dismayed by the prospect; we were willing to sacrifice personal comfort to the picturesque, and if we could find human nature simple and unmodernized among the mountains, we should be more than satisfied.

Our host himself was a local celebrity, who, in addition to the business of the tavern, officiated as auctioneer at all sales in the neighborhood. He was loquacious, and sometimes grandiose in a blundering way. His vocabulary was florid and various, and he was fond of displaying it, though the effect was often Malapropian. "There is a throne," he said, "set with diamonds, sardonics, and amaranthes, with vacillating waters shining araound it, and palms waving their coruscating branches over it." What throne he referred to we do not know, but his description of it was amply pleasing and graphic to the villagers who happened to hear it. Once he had been the driver of a stage-coach, then a dealer in dry-goods, and then a peddler. "I surveyed all the professions," he said, modestly, "and concluded to be a Jack of all trades." While he was a peddler he had a popular article

A SUGAR TOWN IN THE GREEN MOUNTAINS.

of soap for sale, which was guaranteed to remove all blemishes from the skin and moral character of the person using it; it would curl the hair, and a poodle-dog's tail to which it was applied had become as curvilinear as a watch spring, and could not be unwound for several years. The demand for it was so great at Whitehall one day that an assistant salesman became necessary, and the peddler engaged a young man who had just graduated from some country college. "A *ne plus ultra* critter, who couldn't add up an account without 'plussing' this and 'plussing' that— a fellow with a good deal of Latin in him, and not a bit of sense." At the end of the day it was found that he had taken in a large amount of counterfeit coin and a spurious ten-dollar note.

"Look here, you should be careful; that's bad," said the disgusted peddler, showing him the note, which was a common wood-engraving. "Bad? why, bless me," responded the innocent, in amazement, "I didn't know that a bank would issue counterfeit money!"

Not all of his anecdotes are repeatable; but one more is worth telling for the light it throws upon his versatility. He wished to purchase a team of horses from one Deacon Woodbury at S——, and a friend who was with him introduced him as Elder Dawley, to which he was about to object, when his companion whispered to him, "Be quiet, you'll get the team for twenty dollars less as a parson than as a layman"; and, indeed, the deacon was so devoutly considerate of the church that the purchase was effected on very easy terms. At dinner, however, the elder was called upon for grace before meat, and though unfamiliar with devotions of any kind, he was unwilling to expose the fraud to which he had lent himself, and he returned thanks with an unction that put him high in the deacon's esteem. It became known that a minister was in the village, and he was invited to console a sick old man, which he did, as he says, to the entire satisfaction of all the relatives. On the following day, a lawyer having failed to appear for him, he conducted a case of his own in court, and in the afternoon wielded the hammer at an auction. Later in the evening the fiddler was missing from a dance, and he offered himself as a substitute. While he was poring over the music with great attentiveness, though he could not read a note, a child of yesterday's invalid happened to look in, and was struck aghast by the sight she saw. "Why, ma," she cried, as soon as she reached home, "would you believe it?—that old minister who was here yesterday is a-fiddling away like all possessed at the dance!"

. If Mr. Dawley was unscrupulous, it is to be said in his favor that he was obliging, and that he possessed plenty of that Yankee adaptativeness which we had already observed in the station-master, who, as we found out while our host was un-

burdening himself of his experiences with garrulous suavity, had made the chairs in which we were sitting.

All the afternoon the snow continued to fall, and no one ventured out of the houses; but in the evening a few who could not content themselves at home came into the tavern, and deposited themselves around the stove with the apparent object of cooling it by a phenomenal frequency of expectoration. The village store over the way had a similar circle, and the silence and vacuity sent us early to bed.

The brilliant light that forced itself through our shutters next morning told us that the skies were clear. They were such a blue as we had never seen before in sunlight: a deep, luminous, midnight blue, and the mercury in the thermometer

on the porch had shrunk to zero. All yesterday's snow was crisp and glazed, and creaked beneath the feet, and the wind was full of stings. The sugar-makers reflected the hue of the sky. But we were not to be confined, and set out up the whited mountains along a zigzag path and between the straight-laced pines, which, next to the maples, were the most abundant. The way followed the curvatures and undulations of the mountain, and every moment more and more of the vast forms were unfolded to us, with every notch defined as by a black edge against that intensely blue vault, which was unfeathered by a single

A SUGAR SHANTY AT NIGHT.

cloud. In contrast with its surroundings, the noisy brook that held to the road like a dear companion was utterly black as it broke through the clotted snow and ice, which imprisoned it for a reach, and then let it burst forth with a contentious and vehement murmur. A chickadee that made a poor breast against the wind was the only visitant of the bird world that had come out on this piercing morning; and every branch snapped against the

THE SUGAR-MAKER'S DAUGHTER.

frosty seizure, while the loose dry leaves of the past autumn were borne shrieking along the compact and crusted snow. There were ghostly birches with dark scars on their bark, and heavily branched beeches; the austere firs were crested with downy white, and fringed, where the sun had struck them, with pendent icicles: and here was a wild cherry on a little knoll, with a bark of so rich and glistening a copper bronze that it looked like some warm artery veined against the sky. But outnumbering all the others were the maples, that stood inside the fences and out along the roadway, in scattered groups and single file, and in swarms on the slopes, where the distance between each was so narrow that the lower growths of the branches had been prevented, and it was only high above the ground that they could spread themselves. Hanging from each—scarcely one had not been tapped—was a red bucket or a tin pail; and the tin pails in the distance caught the sunshine, and were so emblazoned by it that they seemed like the shields of some advancing army. But not a drop of sap was flowing, and when the buckets contained any it was concealed under ice and frozen snow, which also formed a solid bow from the mouth of the spout.

There is a human and poetic quality in maples, which is easily felt, and though the land would be worth more for its lumber than for its sugar, many farmers would no more part with their maple bush or orchard than with any precious heirloom. There are careless and avaricious growers who bore their trees in several places at once, or before the proper season, and then the trees, like overdriven creatures, fail and die of exhaustion. The gentle method succeeds best, by prolonging the life, and to this end those whom we first mentioned devote something like affectionate care.

At the top of the mountain we met one of the largest sugar producers of the neighborhood, a gentleman who has an orchard of two thousand trees, and who lives in a long, low, old-fashioned house, out of every window of which the beautiful hills are seen undulating in such close lines that there seems to be little or no space between them—hills so profusely wooded that we could understand how applicable their name might be in summer, though they were now white and leafless in the wintry inthrallment.

The glowing stove was an unspeakable blessing, for the wind had not abated nor lost its penetrativeness: and as we thawed ourselves the host placed a dish of apples before us, with an invitation to eat, which is an almost invariable part of an introduction in Vermont. "Two days ago," he said, "I went to Rutland, and before leaving told the boys to tap as many trees as they could; but though the morning was soft and clear, I felt the approach of a storm in

A GREEN MOUNTAIN COUNTRY DANCE.

the afternoon, and as soon as I got home again I stopped the work—none too soon, either." A centre table was strewn with books, magazines, and newspapers, agricultural, religious, and secular. There were more books in the capacious window-seats, and though it seemed as far from the top of this hill to the city as from the top of a Sierra Nevada, the world and its immediate doings were scarcely less familiar up here than in Roxbury or Harlem.

One can venture among these mountains into spots which the whistle of the locomotive has never pierced, and where the mail is left in very small quantities by a dilapidated coach, without finding much that is genuinely primitive. The unenlightened but shrewd settlers of earlier days, who knew more of nature than of cities, are in their last generation, and the children have lost the simplicity and individuality of their progenitors. It is said that elementary education is more general in Vermont than in any other State, and with the little learning the irreverent spirit of the age has crept in. Those whose fathers wore homespun and were vigorously distinct in character, ape the ways of town, and are drifting into vulgar and uninteresting "cockneyism."

As Mr. Dawley said, "the ideas of the country are 'advanced.'" One afternoon

A COUNTRY AUCTION IN VERMONT.

we approached a queer old house, which
had been a tavern in coaching days, and
which now stood back from the highway,
in great need of a coat of paint. The
earth was piled around its tottering frame
to a height of three or four feet, and the
refuse of the barn-yard was scattered before it with unpromising thriftlessness.
There flashed upon us a picture of what
we should find within—a slovenly woman
and children, the children dirty and crying, and the woman scolding. We tapped
at the door—perhaps we might find a bit
of old furniture, or a "character," something picturesque, though neither clean
nor comfortable. What we saw took our
breath away. A young and pretty girl
opened the door—a girl with all the un-
blemished purity and sweetness of maid-
enhood shining in her face; dressed neatly and in excellent taste, and wearing
her hair plaited into a braid, from which
not one vagrant hair escaped. Her father
was away, but she ushered us into a small
parlor, with a piano among its other furniture, wherein sat a smooth and dignified
woman, her mother, who, when we blundered out some remark indicating our surprise at the comfort of the interior, said
with some severity that city folks supposed the people living in the mountains to

be wild, but that there was as much intelligence and culture among them as among
others. She uttered "culture" with the
sibillant Bostonian twang, and that she
possessed some of it herself was more than
a matter of surmise, from the well-worn
copies of Tennyson, Pope, and other poets
on a side table. The exterior dilapidation
was accounted for by their intention to
build a new house in the spring, and the
earth was piled up around the old one for
greater warmth. As there was no place
of public entertainment within six or sev-
en miles, and as the first train was not
due until late at night, we were glad of
the tea she prepared for us—served in a
brilliant silver urn of recent design, with
sugar bowl and milk jug to match—and
we spent a very pleasant evening before a
crackling fire of birch.

While waiting for the weather to moderate, we were not without diversions.
One day we listened to the florid eloquence of Mr. Dawley at an auction in
"the flats," where many curious characters were gathered; and another day was
relieved by a country dance, which was
attended by the young men and women
from neighboring farms. The dance and
the auction are almost the only dissipa-
tions the people know, and one yields

them about as much amusement as the other.

But at last the inimical wind fell, and what was left of it veered round toward the south. A radiant vapor now hung upon the hills; the creek fiercely repulsed

The sap was collected then in troughs, each about three feet long, hollowed out of sections of poplars, and was conveyed to the kettles in barrels, from which it was transferred by scoops. There were five or more kettles, from ten to thirty

OLD-FASHIONED SUGAR CAMP.

the ice, and hurried it away to dissolution, and the woods were full of a moisture which softened every sound. Quick to feel the genial change, the maples relaxed, and in all the groves sleds were moving and smoke was rising from the sugarhouses, while the sap dripped abundantly into the buckets, and the sound of its fall mingled with the patter of the snow melting on the feathered evergreens.

Sugar-making now and sugar-making as it was are very different things, and what it has gained in facility it has lost in picturesqueness. The old camp with its primitive appliances is no more; the "kettle" has been superseded by the "pan," and the trough is become a mass of crumbling decay. The women and children are kept at home, and no longer know the old-time delights of "sugaring off," though in the Arcadia of the past their services were not despised, and the whole household set up its abode in the woods.

gallons in capacity, and each was filled with sap, which was kept boiling, the larger kettles being refilled from the smaller ones as evaporation reduced the quantity. When the contents were reduced to a desired consistency, the hot syrup was dipped out and passed through a flannel strainer into covered tubs, from which again it was poured into a large, thick-bottomed kettle for the process of "stirring off," some milk and the whites of several eggs being added to it. Thus prepared, it was placed over a slow fire, and kept just below boiling-point until the sediment and all foreign matters in it floated to the top and were removed, when it became deliciously translucent. It was now exposed to a greater heat and gently boiled, the evaporation continuing, and bringing it nearer to the point of granulation. Now the sugar-maker was all watchfulness, and it fared ill with those who distracted him, for if the golden liquid seething in the kettle boiled the least bit too much, it would become dry in quality, while if it boiled too little, it would become "soggy." He tested it constantly, plucking threads of it from his stirring stick, and trailing them round in cups of cold water. While the threads yielded waxily to the touch, the sugar was not yet done, but as soon as one broke crisp between his fingers, the moment had come to take the kettle off the fire. As the sugar began to cool, it crystallized round the sides, and gradually the whole mass, under a vigorous stirring, became granular.

In that way sugar was made years ago, and when the sap flowed profusely the operations were continued through the night, and the fires cast strange shadows in the woods. But instead of a hut of logs a permanent sugar-house is now built, and furnished with many elaborate devices to prevent waste and deterioration. Formerly, when the maples were tapped with an auger, an "elder quill" was inserted in the incision to conduct the sap into the trough below; that is, a small piece of elder wood about three inches long with the pith bored out of it, which formed a tube; but in most orchards to-day a galvanized iron spout is used, which has the advantage of not souring the sap nor choking many pores. Everything is "improved." The collections are made with the unvarying order of collections from letter-boxes, and if the grove is on a hill, and the sugar-house is in a hollow, the sap, as it is gathered, is emptied into a "flume," which quickly conducts it to a large reservoir within the building, wherein it is strained through cloth. A scoop or a ladle is as anachronistic as a javelin. From the reservoir the sap is conducted, as required, through tin pipes into a "heater," whence it passes through a series of iron tubes to be delivered, after straining, in a condition for "sugaring off."

Maple sugar as it reaches the market is of a clearer color for all these improvements; but there are some who actually say that the flavor has fallen off, and that the new patent evaporators are a snare. One change has certainly not been for the better, and that is the abandonment of the social life of the old camps, which made sugar-time in the Green Mountains enduring memories with those who are now ebbing away.

BOSTON AT THE CENTURY'S END

I.

A PECULIAR circumstance accentuates the landscape at a certain point on the New England coast. The mountains and the sea there part company. This happens for the traveller southward bound along the continent's shore. Having passed in succession the heights of Mount Desert and Camden with feet in the salt waves, the grand tumultuous masses of the White Mountains rising far inland, and the lone peak of Agamenticus, finally from the Cape Ann headlands there appears to the southwestward a billowy blue range across the wide waters. Though their greatest elevation lacks the thousand by a foot for each of the year's days, these heights have all the character and dignity of true mountains, and they are the last outposts of the continent's titanic rock ribs that may greet the eye along all the rest of the eastern coast of our great republic. These hills have a truly alpine history, for geology says that they were once many thousands of feet high and perpetually snow-crowned. In political history, too, they have played an alpine part, for they gave their name to Massachusetts Bay and its famous colony, cradle of modern democracy. Massachusetts meant "the place of the great hills," the Indians explained. But having imparted their name, the hills re-

signed it to the waters and the nascent commonwealth, and thenceforth were called the Blue Hills of Milton.

Nature stamped the landscape at the head of Massachusetts Bay, where one of the world's renowned cities grew up, with the gracious individuality of the mid-New England seaboard in its most pleasing aspects. The region with its mountain landmark was geographically a point of departure, and politically it became a point of arrival; in natural scenery it was a sort of meeting-place, an assemblage of divers very attractive elements. The rocks and the glacial débris, the meadows and the marshes, the sparkling streams and the placid lakes, the bays and the meandering inlets, the crescent beaches and the rough headlands pounded by the surging sea, all combined to produce delightful scenery of well-nigh kaleidoscopic variety.

When the great navigator John Smith sailed into the island-studded expanse now known as Boston Bay, there spread indefinitely before him what seemed to be a most royal river with vast inland-reaching potencies, and in honor of England's future King the splendid-seeming stream was named the Charles; but less than a score of miles from the narrows the fresh waters of three rivers of only moderate size poured into their salty estuaries, and nothing further was seen of the expected great stream.

These three rivers broke through the barrier of the wild rock hills that encircle the Boston basin and made leisurely way

to the sea, meandering around gracefully
modelled drumlins that give peculiar
character to the landscape—hills of glacial drift in gently rounded wave forms,
contrasting markedly with the rugged
rocky heights near by. In shape like a
half-watermelon cut lengthwise, these
hills rose first from the meadows of river
valleys, then from the far-spreading salt
marshes, and lastly from the salt waters
direct, in peninsulas and islands about
and within the bay. Here and there were
also rocky promontories jutting out, as if
in final reminder of the mountains.

Much of this was changed as time went
on. But it is important to note the
physical environment whose features did
much to shape the great city which has
spread all around this bay, whose many
liquid fingers reach up through the varied landscape. Had this urban growth
been a conscious one, had such a momentous future been suspected, the process would naturally have adapted itself
to topographical requirements, and many
enormous costs might have been avoided.
We are told that the rambling streets of the
towns that clustered on the slopes of the
drumlin peninsulas—islands moored to
the main only by slender necks of land—
were largely engineered by cows. We
know how the chief of these drumlin
half-islands, Shawmut, was called Tremont and Trimountain for a while before
it became Boston, "the Metropolis of
North America," as the maps of the eighteenth century had it. Though that
rank passed to Philadelphia, and thence to
New York, the steady growth of the port
kept on. But the town meeting served
the community's purposes in self-government almost to the end of the present
century's first quarter. It is worth remembering that, in the period of Boston's first corporate cityhood, in the third
decade of the nineteenth century, when
Salem and Nantucket ranked next in importance among Massachusetts towns, the
United States was a land of rural communities, and the greatest city of North
America was not on the continent at all.
It was Havana, on the island of Cuba.

II.

Certain things must be held in mind
for an understanding of Boston at the
century's end. The community was
founded as the concrete expression of a
mental and spiritual ferment, a striving

for a life of greater freedom than that
left behind. This striving had a very
practical material basis, for the city's
physical growth was that of an empori-
um. The dual nature of this beginning
has persistently marked the community's
development. These factors have inter-
acted—there has always been a decidedly
practical side to Boston's ideality, while
the material conditions have very largely advanced along ideal lines. In other
words, the shaping of ideals has strongly
tended towards definite ends to be attained by practical methods, and material
growth has, to a notable extent, been exerted towards certain ideals. From the
simplest beginnings, in both these aspects there has been an ever-increasing
complexity.

The primary ideal of the community,
though for a life of greater freedom, had
in view only the freedom of its own members from certain restrictions upon worship,
and in some respects there was actually
less freedom than in the life left behind.
But the leaven had been set to work; the
realization of even this very limited ideal
involved the introduction of new factors of growth in mind and spirit, and a
consequent weakening of old limitations.
Hence originated for America the free
public-school system with its fruitage of
popular freedom of thought, and the New
England town meeting with its fruitage
of popular free speech, also the higher
education fostering the pursuit of the
ideal.

With such instrumentalities made active, it was inevitable that, with the
achievement and maintenance of freedom for themselves, the members of this
community should have been imbued
with a love of freedom for all men. It is
natural that, in a community based upon
religious aspirations, the first outcome of
these tendencies should have been religious freedom—not only in equal toleration of other creeds, but revolutionizing
the primal faith in the great liberalizing
movement that not only made the Puritan capital the home of Unitarianism,
but, in its native-born element, the least
Puritanical of all the cities in the country.

Logically continuing these lines came
the great impulse towards social freedom,
first manifest in the anti-slavery movement, which for a half-century overshad-
owed the complementary agitation for

industrial emancipation that was almost contemporary with the dawn of the anti-slavery movement, finding its earlier expression in communal experimentation, as at Brook Farm.

Turning to the material evolution of the New England metropolis, there may first be noted, as concomitant of its rich commerce, the great ship-building industry of which it was so long the seat—an industry which, in the meetings of its very numerous caulkers for political action, originated the word "caucus." Then the great shoemaking and leather industries, of which Boston has always been the mart; and the "merchant princes," with their elegance and their culture, the scope of their foreign adventurings firing the imagination and broadening the mind, while building up the superb East India trade of the port, so full of romance and splendor. Next the era of industrial and financial corporations, beginning with the mill-owning period early in this century—the development of the great water-powers of the Merrimac. Successive main steps in this era have been the period of railway-building and investment that, from Boston out, has woven over the continent a large proportion of its giant web of steel; the huge copper-mining enterprises, which, together with other notable mining investments, are said in certain years—lean and hungry for other financial harvests—to have yielded returns surpassing those from the combined railway and banking properties owned in the city; and the organization of the great telephone monopoly, with its creation of a wonderful new industry for the world. With each of these new steps, together with the enormous advances of real-estate values from period to period, as in various sections "acre land" became "foot land," there have been deposited successive layers of tremendous wealth, creating strata upon strata of rich families—their social eminence dated back by the knowing ones to this or that period when were acquired the ample means that made possible the leisurely culture of the fortune-favored.

There are not a few fairylike, though strictly veracious, tales of the happy turns of fortune's wheel that conferred good luck upon various individuals in these select companies, suddenly lifted above the vicissitudes of the common lot. But there is perhaps nothing more interesting than the story of the little group that originally shared the ownership of the great telephone patent; how, ever confident of the big future of the invention, they met with rebuff after rebuff from men corpulent of purse but lean in faith, and therefore holding it but a "scientific toy"; how bitterly they were disappointed by the decision of the Western Union Telegraph Company not to take up its option to acquire the patent outright for a half-million dollars in cash; and how the next thing, they found themselves millionaires overnight, as it were!

III.

The beginning of this century saw Boston a world-famous town, but it was only the chief of several old and detached communities grouped about the bay whose commercial advantages gave the port its standing. The ending of the century sees Boston increased multifold in population and area; a genuine metropolis, a *millionenstadt*, as the Germans say—a million-peopled city—practically enclosing the bay, which then laved the shores of the huddled and hilly peninsula of Shawmut. While the municipality itself now has but little more than a half-million inhabitants, the metropolitan title to double that figure rests not only on the natural geographical expansion of a dense population whose coalescence has effaced all but political demarcations between a large number of local communities, but on the fact that it has become a great civic entity in itself. At present the metropolitan organization is in a nascent state. What is now commonly called Greater Boston is for various purposes organized as the metropolitan districts. In this respect there is a strong resemblance to the organization of the metropolitan population of London, where the administrative County of London comprises an aggregation of parishes and districts, while the Metropolitan Police District, called Greater London, has a much wider extent.

In Greater Boston, likewise, the several metropolitan districts are not coextensive. The Metropolitan Sewerage District comprises a certain number of municipalities, some of which are not included in the Metropolitan Water District, and a still larger group constitutes the Metropolitan Parks District. Each of these districts is administered by a commission appointed by the Governor of the Commonwealth. The Metropolitan Postal District is organized by the national government, and comprises yet another group of municipalities served from the Boston Post-Office. Probably in the near future a metropolitan county will be organized to administer various functions of mutual concern to the various municipalities of the Greater Boston group.

This Greater Boston development is one aspect of the very notable process of more efficient organization that characterizes the Boston of to-day—a systematization and co-ordination of functions, public and quasi-public; a general and very extensive unification of utilities that is telling immensely in economizing the working capacity for collective and individual activities, as well as in accelerating the metropolitan growth of the community.

The local transit system furnishes the first great example of this tendency. For fully a generation Boston had been suffering from an extraordinary congestion of street traffic, due to the concentration of trade in the ancient section of the city, where all the street-railway lines converged. Among the rival companies there was infinite contention, and their cars, all aiming for one point, seemed fairly to stumble over each other in their tortuous progress, wasting in the aggregate centuries of precious time for the community. Various remedies were tried in vain—including very costly street-widenings—but the congestion more than kept pace with the improvements. Finally, just on the verge of the electric-railway era, a sagacious and far-seeing capitalist saw golden opportunities in the work of bettering these unbearable conditions. He boldly undertook the colossal task. By quick and masterly steps he gained control of the several corporations and consolidated them into one great company, the first to monopolize the entire street-railway traffic of a great American city. The result was not only the development of a financial bonanza of the first magnitude, but a tremendous increase in public efficiency through the unification of the various antagonistic services in one coherent system. The gain in traffic, however, that naturally followed the systematization and cheapening of transit facilities was so sudden and enormous that the congestion soon became intensified.

With the beginning of the tenth decade there chanced to be elected a young Mayor of a daring and pertinacious temperament vigorously aggressive in character, and of an originative mind. For some years the city charter had embodied the distinctive American principle of concentrating great powers in the hands of the chief executive. The young Mayor was the first to take full advantage of this authority. He made his mark as no predecessor has done. His first act was to propose a series of reforms and improvements, largely of a radical and transforming character that involved an entrance upon certain colossal undertakings. His predecessor, a shrewd old merchant, smiled grimly. Those things were all very well, he said, but it would take at least twenty-five years to carry that programme into effect. But the public "caught on." All the things suggested were desirable. Why should they not be realized? was asked on all sides. And before the year was over every recommendation that the Mayor had made was adopted!

This marked for Boston the entrance upon a period of conscious and intentional evolution along scientifically systematic lines—a process that appears destined more and more to characterize the world's social and political development, in place of the groping and painful growth heretofore known throughout history. In fact, it seems inevitable that the methods of evolutionary science, having been discovered, must be consciously applied to these as to all other indicated ends.

IV.

Among the recommendations made by the Mayor at that time was one for the comprehensive organization of the local transit service for the metropolitan community upon the most efficient basis possible. The question was therefore elaborately investigated by a special commission, and the great possibilities of the situation were shown. A few years passed before the work of realizing these possibilities could be undertaken. The most difficult phase of the problem was how to overcome the barrier of the congested district. A threatened invasion of the historic Common to this end aroused a public protest so strong that to avert it it was proposed to go beneath rather than through the congested district, building a subway system around the Common and

A TRANSFER STATION.

beneath the streets, across the entire section. At a "referendum" election the citizens determined that the proposed subway should be undertaken as a municipal enterprise, and at the same time a private corporation was authorized to construct a system of elevated railway lines. In three years and a half the great subway was finished. Meanwhile the elevated railway company had gained control of the surface and underground systems, making it possible to follow in their entirety the general lines laid down in the programme recommended by the original transit commission.

The main features of the great unified transit system are:

1. A net-work of surface electric lines for more strictly local transit, extending throughout the city and far out into the suburban districts, reaching the latter very largely through broad avenues with reserved central spaces that permit swift and relatively unimpeded movement.

2. Trunk lines of elevated electric railway across the more densely populated metropolitan area, and also connecting the two great steam-railway terminals. These elevated lines, with relatively infrequent stations, are for rapid transit in the true sense, assuring quick movement between all parts of Greater Boston by means of connections and free transfers between the elevated and surface cars. At the elevated terminals the surface cars reach the elevated level by inclined tracks, transferring passengers to and from the remoter suburbs, many surface lines converging at these terminals. By the elevated circuit connections between the steam-railway terminals the suburban services of those lines are brought into touch with the local transit system. This elevated connection is also designed with reference to use by regular steam-line trains, with possibilities for unbroken express trains across the city between eastern and northern New England and Canada on one side, and New York and beyond on the other.

3. The carrying of both the surface cars and the elevated trains quickly across the

THE DESCENT TO THE SUBWAY, PUBLIC GARDENS.

congested district through the subway—which is adapted to use by both features of the great co-ordinated system—and likewise underneath the harbor by tunnel to and from East Boston and the northeasterly sections of Greater Boston.

The completed subway is a marvel of convenience and public comfort, with its white enamelled walls, its brilliant electric illumination, its sweet and wholesome air, its commodious stations where people await their cars sheltered from wind and rain, from summer heat and winter cold—everything as cleanly as the traditional Dutch housewife's kitchen. Moreover, it gives certainty of prompt transit in place of vexatious, halting progress. There is no more congestion in the streets above. This costly work does not cost the municipality a cent, for it has been leased to the street-railway company at a rental that not only covers all interest and sinking-fund charges, but eventually yields a profit to the city. Its construction with businesslike promptness and thoroughness by public officials, the Transit Com-

mission, at a cost much within the original estimate, suggests the very pertinent question: Why could not the same board of eminent citizens, who have thus given to their charge the same conscientious attention that they would to the affairs of a railway corporation of which they might be directors, with equal success operate as a public enterprise the entire transit service of the metropolitan community? Perhaps this will come in due time, for there is nothing to prevent the taking over of the whole system by right of eminent domain whenever public sentiment may demand it.

With the approaching completion of the elevated lines the entire rapid-transit system will be perfected. The consequent acceleration of public movement will immensely promote intercourse between all sections of Greater Boston, with a corresponding impetus to metropolitan development.

The terminal facilities of the steam-railway lines have also undergone a remarkable improvement. All the trunk lines entering the city have been concentrated in two great passenger terminals on opposite sides of the business district, on the water-front, and within less than a mile of each other. On the north side there is a great union station which, though provisional in character, is of substantial construction. It accommodates five main lines controlled by two corporations. The new South Terminal Station, accommodating the four trunk lines of the two other principal railway companies of New England, is the largest in the world. It has a unique feature in the special sub-terminal division that occupies the entire space underneath the regular trackage area of the vast triple-roofed train-house. This is designed for suburban traffic exclusively, and has great loops for the speedy despatch of trains at short intervals. Its design anticipates the ultimate application of electric motive power to all suburban trains, for the en-

THE SUBWAY ENTRANCE, ADAMS SQUARE.

trance of smoking locomotives would be out of the question in the comparatively low and vaulted space which, with its finish of white enamelled brick, looks like an expanded subway.

The transit system of Greater Boston is capped by these two big terminals. In the thoroughness with which the various local and general features of this system complement each other, and thus facilitate traffic across and about the metropolitan area, as well as between the city and other parts of the country, it stands unrivalled on this side of the Atlantic.

A further systematization of traffic occurs in the concentration of the great railway freight terminals at various convenient points on deep-water frontage, and thence communicating by marginal lines with all the principal wharves. Railway and ocean freights are thus brought together, and handling charges reduced to a minimum. The Commonwealth, alive to the importance of advancing the commercial prestige of its capital, has lately adopted the policy of a public dock and freight terminals system. It has therefore begun the construction of magnificent deep-water terminals with the most modern facilities for accommodating the largest steamships. With these advantages, existing and prospective, the time-honored rank of Boston as a seaport is assured indefinite perpetuation. The stranger looking about the harbor might hardly credit the statement that Boston is the second port of the Union both for imports and exports, for he would see little of the old-time bustle of commerce, the traditional "forest of shipping" that once fringed the water-front. So well organized are present methods of handling shipping that, as a rule, the big ocean steamships lie neatly stowed away like packages on shelves, nearly hidden in pocketlike slips behind huge bulks of pier sheds, warehouses, and grain-elevators.

It is not so very long, however, since the commercial outlook for Boston seemed rather dubious. Local capital had looked so far afield that it had ignored the possibilities of the magnificent harbor as one of the great portals of the continent. The rich East India trade had been driven to New York by injudicious taxation. Shortly after the civil war the Cunard Line, whose original American terminal was at Boston, had almost abandoned the port, re-

IN THE SUBWAY—THE PARK STREET STATION.

ducing its service to small fortnightly freight-boats that went around to New York for their outward cargoes. Then matters began to mend; new transatlantic lines were attracted to the port, larger and larger steamships were put on, and now the commerce with Liverpool exceeds that of any other American port, while a big ocean traffic has grown up with other British and Continental ports and other parts of the world. A fine transatlantic passenger business has also developed, and the old standard line suddenly found itself put to its mettle by rival companies with superior accommodations. In certain staple trades Boston stands far at the head among American cities. It is the great American centre of the wool business, the boot-and-shoe and leather industries, and stands very high in various lines of manufacturing.

In financial resources Boston has always ranked second only to New York.

V.

The three great metropolitan departments of Greater Boston demonstrate that co-operation has its advantages for municipalities as well as for individuals. Both convenience and necessity demanded that certain public activities be undertaken for the joint account of the group of Greater Boston municipalities. Various considerations prevented the consolidation of these communities in one great municipality. The State therefore made itself the agent for administering the needed functions. To this end the Commonwealth advanced its credit and issued bonds to obtain the funds for the several purposes. More favorable terms were thus secured than would have been possible on purely municipal account. Interest and sinking-fund charges on these bonds are met from the regular municipal tax levies, the proportions severally fixed according to population, valuation, and estimated benefits. This policy of municipal co-operation began with the establishment of a metropolitan sewerage system. A net-work of trunk-line sewers was constructed throughout the metropolitan district to receive from the various local systems the sewage which is now discharged into deep water on the north and the south sides of Boston Bay.

The magnificent metropolitan water system has lately been established on similar lines, and has afforded another convincing example of the benefits from municipal co-operation. The history of the water-works in the several municipalities of Greater Boston makes a splendid argument for the public administration of monopolies of public service. In the various municipal water-works, for the ten years ending 1893, the average daily consumption of water had doubled; the total cost of the works had increased from $26,883,000 to $40,505,000, and the net debt had increased only from $16,537,000 to $18,655,000. The increase in total cost of works was therefore $13,622,000, and in the net debt $2,118,000. Of the total increased cost $11,504,000 was paid for from revenue. Of this amount, however, only $1,469,000 came from the general tax levy. The balance, $10,035,000, was paid from water-works revenue, and represented profits on operation. An eminent civil engineer remarked that any great private corporation, such as a railway or manufacturing undertaking, might well be proud of an exhibit like that. But

each of these municipalities, as a rule, had its own independent source of supply, with separate pumping plants, etc. The demand has equalled the maximum capacities of these supplies, and new sources were remote. Only by co-operation could the proper new sources be secured. The State, therefore, again came forward as agent for the associated municipalities. With extraordinary celerity an abundant supply of exceptionally pure and soft water was introduced from the Nashua River, where, on the site of one of the largest impounding reservoirs in the world, a large manufacturing village had to be wiped out of existence. The new system is so planned as to admit of indefinite extension, to include river after river when needed, and answer every demand of a population of many millions. The metropolitan supply is delivered to the mains of each municipality, which continues to operate its own distributing system. Under the new system the municipalities are getting water of far better quality at much cheaper rates than before.

The operation of the same tendency toward the unification of public utilities is illustrated, under private ownership, by the gas service. The gas business in Boston has in recent years had a scandalous history. It has been a football for speculators, and a source of corruption both legislative and municipal. Very lately, however, the same sagacious capi-

THE ELEVATED RAILWAY.

talist who unified the street-railway system saw another golden opportunity in the gas-supply. He obtained control of the several companies, and instituted elaborate new central works on a novel basis. Coal is brought direct to these works from the great Nova Scotia fields by a fleet of large steamers. By an improved process this coal is converted into the best form of manufacturing - coke, and into various chemical products, so that the gas itself becomes, in fact, a by-product, supplied to other companies and to consumers at extraordinarily low rates — so low, in fact, as to be available for fuel on a general scale. Indeed, both the chief products, the gas and the coke,

POINTING OUT BACK BAY RESIDENCES TO A STRANGER.

are available for manufacturing-fuel with far greater economy than is the original coal when consumed direct, and the neighborhood of the central plant is designed to become a centre for manufacturing operations on a great scale, having the advantages of cheap fuel combined with the best railway and deep-water transportation facilities. At every step in the process of conversion—mining, shipping, delivery, handling, coking, etc. — the most improved methods, largely automatic, are used, reducing labor cost to a minimum. This undertaking is looked to as an instrumentality for the restoration of New England's once great iron industries on terms of production equal to those enjoyed by Pennsylvania and favored sections of the West and South.

VI.

In late years notable tendencies in municipal Boston have been towards a specialization of administrative functions. At the same time public activities have been extended, both industrially and as the result of a higher conception of the proper sphere of municipal activities. In-

dustrially, for example, the city is doing more and more work directly instead of by contract, with a notable increase in public efficiency, as in the repair and construction of public buildings, the watering of streets, and in the establishment of a municipal printing plant.

The manifest disposition is more and more to administer, through public instrumentalities, to wants of a higher plane than those of mere public necessities. The latter are likewise looked after with greater elaboration as the new conceptions gain place in the public consciousness. These new conceptions are not paternalistic, are not derived from an indolent looking to public authority to make things easy for the individual, but rather from a wholesome disposition to municipal self-help, towards utilizing the "hand of the people," as Edward Bellamy called the government, for doing what can be better done collectively than individually.

With an extension of municipal functions the interests of larger numbers of citizens are enlisted, and the inclination to participate in the work becomes more general. In Berlin, for example, more than ten thousand persons, acting in advisory and administrative capacities, voluntarily take part in the government of the city. In Boston there is a similar tendency, though participation is hardly on so broad a scale. But a large and increasing part of the administrative work of the municipality is carried on by many public-spirited citizens, who freely give valuable time to the tasks. In later developments of these activities women serve on administrative boards and advisory committees side by side with men, to excellent advantage. There are now one hundred and one citizens who, without remuneration, thus participate in the government of the city. The specially incorporated bodies, the Trustees of the Public Library, the Trustees of the City Hospital, and the Board of Overseers of the Poor, are thus constituted. The Park Commission is also similarly composed, and has carried out its great work with striking efficiency, the most eminent citizens deeming it a privilege to serve as members. Very lately the same principle has been applied to the public institutions of the city, and separate boards of trustees have been substituted for a single governing body that was necessarily inflexible in its administration of widely diverse responsibilities. The institutions for paupers, for children, and for the insane are therefore now governed by boards composed of philanthropic men and women who serve without pay.

There are three other notable unpaid commissions. The Board of Municipal Statistics does a valuable work in collecting, co-ordinating, and interpreting facts that relate to municipal government in all parts of the world. The knowledge thus made available is of much service in guiding the enlightened conduct of a modern municipality. This board directs the editing of an attractive municipal newspaper called the *City Record*, a weekly official gazette of the city.

The second of these boards is the Baths Commission. Boston was the first American city to establish a system of free public baths. For nearly a generation numerous floating baths, and several open beach baths for nude bathing, have been enjoyed by many thousands throughout the summer season. Besides these, the new Baths Commission has charge of free indoor-cleanliness baths and all-the-year-round swimming-pools. The same board

THE FLOATING BATH.

NORTH END BEACH, THE SCENE OF THE PUBLIC SWIMMING EXHIBITION.

has charge of the public-convenience stations, and also of free in-door gymnasia for winter exercise. For some time the Park Department has made a feature of finely equipped out-door gymnasia. Not only do the departments of public parks and of baths supplement the educational work of the public schools in physical culture by athletic training in the gymnasia, but the latter gives to the school-children free instruction in swimming. A unique civic festival is that of the public swimming exhibition by the boys and girls thus trained, held at North End Beach towards the end of the summer. At that fine maritime pleasure-ground crowds of delighted spectators cover the shore and the recreation piers to witness this charming exhibition. Under skilled instructors children rapidly acquire the art, and lighten the tasks of their teachers by teaching others. Lads who could not swim very commonly become proficient inside of three weeks, and acquire the freedom and grace of experts. They learn all the fancy strokes, and, with the boldness of Newfoundlands, dash out into deep water for half a mile and back.

The third new board has a purely recreative function. This is the Music Commission, having charge of the out-door concerts in the parks and other public places by a municipal band organized for the purpose. Free in-door chamber concerts for the winter are also given in school-rooms throughout the city, and the commission, acting as individual citizens, conducts a series of cheap high-class orchestral concerts, whose deficit, if any, is made up from a guarantee fund subscribed by private beneficence.

Courses of municipal lectures are also given under an advisory committee constituted by the Mayor.

Two other advisory committees, appointed in like manner, have charge of the Raudidge fund for free excursions for children, and of the municipal camp for boys, where hundreds of deserving school-

THE MASSACHUSETTS INSTITUTE OF TECHNOLOGY.

boys enjoy, in turn, a week's camping-out on an island in the bay at the city's expense.

A voluntary board of great importance is a creation by the Mayor, and is without official sanction or authority. This is the Merchants' Municipal Commission, sometimes familiarly called "the Mayor's cabinet." Its members represent the several mercantile trade organizations, and are appointed, at the request of the Mayor, by the Associated Board of Trade. The function of this committee is to advise the Mayor on all matters relating to the public welfare, and particularly concerning the great mercantile, commercial, and financial interests of the city. Being a non-partisan body of representative business men, its judgment commands the highest respect. It has proved itself of extraordinary utility, and has been of much service in influencing legislation relating to the city.

VII.

A noteworthy series of civic activities has to do with the attractiveness of Boston as a residential community, and as a point of interest for strangers. Its remarkable historical associations, its great educational facilities, and the charm of a beautiful environment have made the city's equipment especially rich for these purposes. But of late years the public consciousness has been aroused to the value of these things as working capital for the community, and whereas heretofore such elements were left to develop as they might, there has been awakened a lively sense of the value of cultivating and exploiting these advantages to their best possibilities. The result is seen in a striking gain in those things that give rational zest to life, and make a city worth living in because it has so much that makes life worth the living.

A most conspicuous example is the growth of the wonderful system of public parks. It is no vainglorious spirit of local pride that claims this as the most comprehensive, scientifically devised, artistically planned, and well-executed series of public pleasure grounds and ways possessed by any of the world's great cities. As a system its origin dates back less than a quarter of a century. From first to last it is the creation of the greatest modern master of landscape design and of his most eminent disciple. In determining the sites for this remarkable group of public open spaces, and in their improvement, the aim has been to meet the various recreative needs of a metropolitan population as completely as possible. The aim has likewise been to follow the lines of Nature, and to carry to ideal conclusions the suggestions of the peculiarly gracious landscape with which the region is favored. To this end there has been a restoration of Nature, with a reverent assistance of her processes through the art that simulates her most delicate handiwork.

In contemporary civilization two great complementary tendencies are in operation ; one is bringing the country into the town, and the other is carrying the town into the country. This Boston park - work has been of the former kind. The urban population, with its life at high-tension, nervous, stressful, overwrought, therefore finds great relief and pleasant relaxation in the series of noble pleasure-grounds in its .midst and round about—magnificent stretches of wholesome woodland wilderness, ranging from several hundred to several thousand acres each, and crowned by the mountainlike range that gave the Commonwealth its name, converted to a public domain in its whole length and breadth; little gems of precious scenery rescued forever from spoliation; idyllic expanses of pastoral country - side ; fenland levels with bosky

banks and meshed by meandering creeks; river reaches devoted to summer and winter pleasurings for miles and miles in length, their borders reclaimed for health and beauty; other miles of ocean shore and of harbor - side dedicated in perpetuity to public enjoyment — and all these multiform aspects of Nature at her best connected by parkways and boulevards that cover the metropolitan

THE GATEWAY OF THE PAUL REVERE SCHOOL.

area with a net - work of over a hundred miles of pleasure-courses that are determining the future distribution of population along rational lines of growth, while furnishing arteries of intercommunication for the swift and noiseless vehicle of the future, the automobile. Moreover, this same metropolitan area is well dotted with play-grounds for children and youth. For Boston was a pioneer in the modern play-ground movement, and has assured to coming generations the great boon that means room to develop freely the bodily activities, and at the same time give a safeguard against vicious and criminal tendencies.

This superb work of park development has had two main phases—the municipal and the metropolitan. The latter exemplifies the striking responsiveness of an intelligent modern community to suggestions for which experience has prepared them. In the year 1891 a student of municipal science, in an essay on the metropolitan organization of Greater Boston, emphasized the need of a comprehensive system of park development for the whole metropolitan group of communities. This struck a popular chord. In two years the State had decreed the undertaking. The metropolitan park system has thus furnished the third great demonstration of the value of municipal co-operation, and in five years' work it has largely transformed the face of Greater Boston with enduring beauty.

The heightening ideals for "a more beautiful public life" have also found expression in better standards for civic architecture. The more recent public buildings, as a rule, exhibit a refinement and a quiet dignity quite in contrast with the ostentatious crudeness so common in work of the kind. Not only at central points is this tendency manifest; in all sections the pleasing appearance of school-houses and fire-stations, and of service buildings, bridges, terraces, etc., in the public parks, gives a distinctive civic character and sets better standards for private work.

The same tendency appears in the existence of an official Art Commission, composed of members nominated by five public and quasi-public organizations, artistic and educational. This board exerts a most desirable censorship in the choice of sites and designs for public monuments, statues, fountains, mural decorations, etc., in public places and buildings. It also, when so requested by Mayor or City Council, acts in a like capacity as to the design of any municipal building or other structure or adornment. A general regard for the good looks of the city is likewise manifest in the statutes that limit the height of buildings and forbid the erection of the "sky-scraping" edifices that now characterize almost all other large American cities. When

THE DOME OF THE STATE HOUSE FROM MOUNT VERNON STREET.

THE OLD STATE HOUSE AND ITS MODERN SURROUNDINGS.

the erection of structures even within these limitations threatened to overtop the famous public buildings, that in late years had made Copley Square a great centre for monumental architecture, there was a formidable manifestation of the same civic spirit that had repeatedly prevented the spoliation of the Common, had saved historic buildings, had forbidden the demolition of the beautiful and time-honored State House, and had kept vandal hands from the public parks. In consequence the desired moderate heights were prescribed for all new structures on or near the square.

VIII.

In educational equipment, taken all in all, Boston still stands unrivalled among American cities. A cumbersome and not entirely reputable or competent school board, it is true, hampers the public schools, and in some respects keeps the standard below what it should be. In many things, however, the Boston schools have set the pace for general advancement throughout the country. As everywhere else in Massachusetts, the scholars are supplied with free text-books, paper, pencils, drawing implements, etc.

At the other end of the scale stand the academic institutions of Greater Boston: the foremost American university, the greatest technical school in America, and five other institutions of university or collegiate rank—two of them for women; also three celebrated schools of the fine arts, and a great conservatory of music.

Altogether the student population comprises many thousands of youth of both sexes. These, with their young hopes and their buoyant outlook upon life, give color to the community such as is imparted to no other American city in like degree. Besides these institutions the public has the advantage of practically a great free university in the shape of the remarkable series of lecture courses given

dinated as the basis for a free university, similar to the University of London, with some examining board authorized to give degrees and diplomas.

As a centre for general research, and as a working-place for scholars in all lines of investigation, the great libraries give Boston unrivalled rank in America. Three of these have collections of hundreds of thousands of volumes each, while many special libraries, with doors hospitable to investigators, severally possess many thousands of volumes. The Boston Public Library is the pioneer of its kind in the world. With its foundation, less than a half-century ago, began for mankind an educational movement of unspeakable worth for civilization. From a beginning of less than ten thousand volumes in 1852

THE MALDEN PUBLIC LIBRARY.

every season. It has been said that more free lectures of this kind, devoted to various fields of learning—literary, scientific, technical, artistic, etc.—are given in Boston in the course of a month than in all other great American cities put together in the course of a year. Several institutions are engaged in this work. At the head stands the Lowell Institute, a unique foundation with an enormous fund, whose income must be used solely for providing free courses of lectures, and for like educational purposes. The administration is hereditary in the family of the founder; the trustee and the curator are the two sole officials. Every year foremost scholars and scientists are called from all parts of the world to lecture for the institute. These courses, together with the Old South lectures in history and good citizenship, those of the Dowse Institute in Cambridge, and those given under various other auspices, might easily be co-or-

the library has grown to more than seven hundred thousand volumes in 1899. The splendid people's palace of learning that houses its central collections is famed as one of the great architectural achievements of the century. The manifold activities concentrated within this magnificent building make it in itself a veritable city of books. The stranger marvels at the work here done for public enlightenment — free access, as in the most exclusive club, to many thousands of volumes on the reference shelves; the special libraries open for use by classes, with lectures on various topics of interest; frequent exhibitions of rare books, objects of historical importance, and works of art; the reader assisted in many thoughtful ways; and the stranger from any part of the world finding the latest newspaper from the chief city of his nation or State. The Public Library has fifty-seven outlying agencies, including ten branches with large permanent collections. Some of these branches are specially endowed, and several have fine buildings of their own. For the West End branch there was recently purchased, and adapted to library purposes, the beautiful old West Church, a model of refined Colonial architecture. Facing a charming garden space, with a noble and cheerful interior, the structure is ideally suited to its new use. Besides the branches, the Public Library maintains five reading-rooms, twelve delivery stations, and twenty-nine places for the deposit of books. A map of Boston issued by the Library shows the various branches and delivery stations, with the percentage of card-holders in each ward. These percentages range from thirty-four down to four—highest in districts with native-born and

THE CAMBRIDGE PUBLIC LIBRARY.

well-to-do populations, and lowest in the foreign-born and tenement-house sections.

There are more than thirty public libraries in the other municipalities of the metropolitan districts. Many of these have beautiful and costly buildings, some with art-galleries attached. Together with those of the Boston Library their collections represent a total of over one million and three hundred thousand volumes free for public use in Greater Boston, while the other great and valuable libraries available to scholars carry the number to the neighborhood of three million volumes. It is not improbable that the various public libraries of Greater Boston will eventually furnish another example of the benefits of municipal co-operation, through some form of union for mutual economy and utility.

A feature of immense value in Boston's equipment is its musical life, which, in its variety and richness, in the

THE BRIGHTON BRANCH OF THE BOSTON PUBLIC LIBRARY.

number and character of concerts, and in the opportunities for instruction, makes the city the second musical centre in America. In some respects it stands first—as in its possession of one of the world's finest orchestras, giving sixty symphony concerts every season, and in the number and excellence of choral performances. In theatrical entertainments Boston has long ranked among managers as "the best show town in the United States"—an indication of the high average of prosperity in the community, as well as of a strong love of amusement.

IX.

It has taken hardly more than a half-century to change the character of the Boston population from one substantially homogeneous to one with considerably more than fifty per cent. of foreign birth or parentage. Moreover, to the old native-born Boston element there has been added a great native-born accretion from

From a photograph.—Copyright, 1899, by H. W. Weller, Boston.

A WINTER-NIGHT VIEW ON BOSTON COMMON.

all parts of New England, together with a cognate Canadian immigration. The latter has come chiefly from the maritime provinces, for which Boston is an extra-territorial metropolis. To the cradle of the Revolution they have thus returned,

with interest, the old-time Tory migration of Revolutionary days, which carried to New Brunswick and Nova Scotia much of the best blood of the Puritans. The ancient wrongs of expatriation and confiscation have been thereby avenged by bringing back, with various sturdy and admirable traits, a sort of atavistic Puritanism that finds expression in bigoted agitations, like that of the "A. P. A."

By far the largest foreign element is furnished by the Irish, and other large elements are the Scandinavians, the Germans, the Italians, the Polish and Russian Jews, the Portuguese, and the Armenians. The ethnic basis of the population has been radically affected by these changes. But the Boston spirit remains the same in all essentials. It has impressed itself strongly upon the new elements. Observers agree that the Boston Irishman, the Boston Italian, the Boston Jew, the Boston negro, all have something of the distinctive bearing that marks the Bostonian to the manner born. The late John Boyle O'Reilly, himself an eminent example of the Bostonized Irishman, used to enjoy telling about a talented office-boy of his, born in the old country, who came to him one day with a poem which a visit to Bunker Hill Monument had inspired him to write. It began: "Here where our fathers stood—!"

Certain visitors from the West were impressed by the typical Boston hackman whom they engaged to drive them about and show them the sights. Passing through a fashionable Back Bay street, he indicated a certain stately dwelling: "Home of Dr. S——. Married a Burgess."

There is a peculiar Boston wit, epigram-

THE ITALIAN QUARTER.

matic and delighting in odd comparisons, as locally typical in its flavor as that of Paris or Berlin. A classic exponent of this was the late Thomas G. Appleton, who called Nahant "cold roast Boston." A recent example is that which said of the new subway stations on the Tremont Street mall, "They look as if the Public Library had littered on the Common." It was a club wit who gave the name of "Folding Bed-ouins" to a class of urban nomads, the residents of apartment-houses.

The Boston temperament has always been marked by an extraordinary mental alertness — a keen intellectual appetite almost fierce in its eagerness. This has made the New England metropolis a sociological storm-centre—the focus of reforms, religious, political, social, and industrial. The working of the leaven has so permeated the lump that in a marked degree what still passes for orthodoxy at home would be heterodoxy abroad. The results are manifest in a general social liberalization. There is a growing mutual tolerance and an agreement among diverse creeds as to essentials in faith. And in the fine arts—exactly contrary to a mistaken impression that obtains abroad as to the Boston attitude—there is a wholesome acceptance by the community of standards which, until very recently, have been tabooed by the prudishness dominant in the conventions of most other American centres. A modified "Continental Sunday" is the rule in Boston. For nearly all classes it is a day for recreation in the truer sense of the word. For almost a generation the Public Library has been open on Sundays, and with the Museum of Fine Arts the same has been the case from the beginning.

This progressive tendency has made Boston peculiarly a city of "isms." The fundamental Puritanism passed into political revolutionism, and the same im-

A CHARACTERISTIC NARROW STREET.

generation has passed since a coachman in livery would have been hooted at by urchins on the street. When the British consul drove out in a dog-cart for the first time with a lackey at his side, a prominent merchant remarked to a resident Englishman, "I suppose that was some lord or other I saw driving with your consul this morning."

In general social conventions there is now little to distinguish between Boston and other great centres. With the great growth of wealth—a good authority has reckoned over two hundred millionaires in the city—there has been a corresponding growth in social formality, elaboration, and elegance. But extravagance is not good form, and there is probably less ostentation than in any other great American city.

pulses further found expression in Unitarianism, Transcendentalism, and Abolitionism. These have made their mark upon the world. Precisely what forms these tendencies have taken of late it might be difficult to define. The current having become more diffused, its force has naturally diminished in intensity. Now that the less serious terms "cult" and "fad" are in vogue, it might seem that there has likewise been a lapse in earnestness. The more profound movements, however, have ever been accompanied by expressions of what might be called the waste energy of radicalism, finding vent in much that is merely extreme, eccentric, or morbid. Now, as ever, the typical Boston mind is singularly responsive to genuinely progressive ideas, giving hospitable reception to all true reform movements.

X.

Socially, Boston long retained the old-fashioned New England habits, largely compounded of democratic simplicity and a traditional English formality. With an abundance of substantial comfort, there was little social display. Less than a

There is no one phase of society that can be called representatively Boston. Literary Boston, artistic Boston, scientific Boston, musical Boston, fashionable Boston — each constitutes a little social world in itself, each merges with the others more or less, and each has something typical of the whole. These social elements are severally represented in the many and varied clubs that enrich the life of the city. There are certain clubs, however, that are collectively representative, epitomizing what may properly be called "Boston." Dining clubs, social and political, without domicile other than some favorite hotel or restaurant, are an institution as perhaps nowhere else. There is one organization, unique in its way, which, though a supper club, is superbly domiciled, for it is blessed with a score or more of the richest habitations. It never has had an election of officers or of members, and not even members know if there are any officers beyond the chairman at the meetings. One awakens to find himself famous — that is, a member—perhaps grown such by some evolutionary process. It is an honor to be coveted, for of a Thursday evening this club draws together an assemblage which in brilliant character could hardly be paralleled elsewhere on this side of the Atlantic. Here may be met men of the highest distinction in all the superior walks of life—in letters, science, art, music, and all the learned vocations. The programme for an evening is made up of two or three brief papers or addresses by members or guests, followed by a fine supper. The purpose of the club is to provide a common meeting-ground for men of intellectual distinction and leading citizens of wealth and culture, largely with a view to interesting the latter in the activities of the former. Not a few of the community's most valued institutions and undertakings may trace their origin or their prosperity to the expositions of such needs made at these meetings. The wealthy members take turns in furnishing the entertainments at their homes, and the others do the rest.

At gatherings like these it would seem that Boston is still the intellectual capital of the United States. Yet the primacy has passed, probably forever, in certain things where the city once was undisputed leader. Throughout the world the word Boston stands for much, and for great things many and various. But the

THE JEWISH QUARTER.

city is pre-eminently known as the seat of the golden age in American literature. That age necessarily went by. Some of its great names now gleam more brightly than ever, and others are already filmed with the dimness that oblivion must some time bring to all. The great market for literature and art in America has been developed in the greatest city. Around the great market the activity in these things has been mainly concentrated, although at the same time a decentralizing process has been going on in such regards. There is much in "atmosphere," and with the spread of culture over the land, every section is finding its special interpreters. Boston, however, is still the centre for a vast amount of literary activity, as it is still the centre for a deal of first-class publishing—a good second in these, as in so many other important regards—while, taking all the phases of mental activity together, with its great institutions and instruments of learning, it yet holds rank as the intellectual, though not the literary, capital of the country.

In certain respects the rank of Boston among American cities is much like that of Edinburgh and Dublin in Great Britain, or Dresden, Munich, and Hamburg in Germany—a place where life is rich, and where it is a delight to live, but which no longer stands first. There is, however, but little of civic jealousy about the Boston of to-day. For example, Boston sentiment favored holding the World's Fair of 1893 in New York, and then it cordially and unreservedly applauded the magnificent achievements of Chicago. Intimacy between cities, as between individuals, begets friendship. And the intimacy be-

tween the metropolis of New England and the metropolis of America is expressed in the enormous daily intercourse between one and the other—far greater than between any other great cities in the country—until Boston has been said to have become an eastern annex of Greater New York. There is strong competition, of course, and in business rivalry one often succeeds in gaining at the expense of the other—as the commerce of Massachusetts Bay has lately been gaining at the cost of that of New York Bay.

Boston is still very far short of the ideal. As almost everywhere in the United States, politics plays a pernicious part in civic affairs, though its evils have never been so rampant as in other great cities, and of late years have been checked by wise civil-service regulations. But even the recent young chief executives, who, in setting the standard for "the new Mayor," have done so much for municipal advancement, have too often felt constrained to adopt courses and to seek the aid of both measures and men that have kept their achievements all too short of their possibilities. But the tendency is strongly towards the ideal, and, as the record shows, the recent advance has been highly gratifying.

The Boston spirit perhaps shows its cosmopolitanism best in its growing indifference to relative urban rank. It is content to see the city steadily waxing in beauty and in greatness, more habitable in the ways of health, comfort, and the higher enjoyments of life, satisfied in the expression of its always strong individuality along the lines that carry it steadily onward and upward.

THE WATER-FRONT OF BOSTON.

ADMIRAL GEORGE DEWEY

ADMIRAL GEORGE DEWEY will occupy a unique place in history. He will stand out clearly as the first figure among the commanders and generals of the Spanish-American war. But his fame will not rest merely on the victory of May 1, 1898, in Manila Bay, for he is not only a distinguished naval hero; he is a great man in the true significance of the term.

His thorough preparation for the battle before leaving Hong-kong, his courage and confidence in attacking the Spanish ships in their home waters under their own land-batteries, his rare tact, diplomacy, and executive capacity during the year following the victory, his marvellous devotion to duty under trying conditions of war and climate, and also his unselfish, modest demeanor in the face of the unlimited praise and love of the American people, support conclusively his right not only to primary position among the leaders of the war, but to be classed among the truly great Americans of the closing days of this century. These inferences are drawn from the best of

premises, and I hope that I tell the truth in attempting to discuss Admiral Dewey only as I saw him and knew him from May, 1898, to March, 1899.

The beginning and development of this acquaintance with the great Admiral can be attributed to a series of most interesting experiences. Although I had exchanged official letters with him while United States Minister at Bangkok, it was reserved for me to know him well first at Manila after his triumph, which had set the Asiatic world agog at the same time that it roused the enthusiasm of America. It was my intention, on leaving Siam, to return with all speed to the United States and volunteer for the army. In fact I did proffer my services to the government by special letter through the State Department, but either I was not needed or I did not bring the necessary influence to bear.

When I reached Hong-kong in early May, 1898, I was asked, to my surprise, but pleasure, to go to Manila as the correspondent of a prominent New York daily, acting in connection with other representative papers of leading cities. I took up this task with some misgivings as to my capabilities after four years of diplomatic service, but did my best until the fall of Manila in August, when I resigned, to devote my entire time to study of the general situation. By special permission and courtesy of the Admiral I proceeded to Manila in May, 1898, on the United States auxiliary despatch - boat *Zafiro*, and was practically his guest aboard different vessels of the squadron for nearly three months. During this period I saw him frequently, and even every day in times of special excitement. After the fall of Manila I did not see so much of him, but still enough to feel his remarkable influence and note the principal traits of his character and their practical workings.

I should not fail to mention that the first directing agency that brought me into more than usual acquaintance with him was the fact that I was a fellow-Vermonter; the second was my experience in the diplomatic service, which he held should have taught me to be cautious and discriminating, and hence worthy of his confidence and trust.

To those who were associated with the Admiral during the days that Hong-kong was the rendezvous of the squadron, before the descent on Manila, his preparedness for the battle was in no sense a surprise, but well known. His captains and staff had absolute confidence in him and his mastery of the situation. This remarkable trust in their commander was shared not only by the ward-room officers, but by the petty officers and sailormen of every ship. When the signal was run up to weigh anchor in Mirs Bay and make the course for the coast of Luzon, there was not a faint heart at muster. The *Olympia* was leading and the Admiral was aboard. That was ample inspiration for all.

The people of the United States may not have realized until May 1 what a strong character Dewey possessed, but the officers who were to execute his commands and the men behind the guns knew. This must be remembered as a most helpful influence in the successful consummation of his plans. If you would arouse the indignation of any of the officers or men under Dewey's command who came to Manila with him, suggest by even mild intimation that the complete-

ness of the victory, or the Admiral's skilful management of affairs that followed, was unexpected or in a measure surprising.

Standing one day on the superstructure of the *Olympia*, I said to the gunner who had charge of one of the big eight-inch rifles of the forward turret,

"Where did you think you were going and what did you expect to do when you sailed away from Mirs Bay?"

" Go and do?" he replied, with a scornful expression and tone that made me feel quite insignificant and ashamed for asking such a foolish question.

"Damn little did I or any one else on this ship care, as long as the old man was ordering it. We knew we were going to a hot place, and meant to make it hotter still for the Spaniards. But, man, we would have sailed straight into hell after him!"

In my note-book, where this incident is recorded, are several other sentences and phrases of the answer to my question, which, on account of the strong sailor language used, I will, for obvious reasons, omit. But they all served in their way to demonstrate the full trust of this gunner and his gun's crew in the Admiral.

Possibly no better evidence of Admiral Dewey's capability of inspiring confidence among those who came in contact with him can be found than the influence he exerted over the British captains of the two auxiliary vessels, the *Nanshan* and the *Zafiro*, purchased at Hong-kong to accompany the squadron to Manila and carry coal and supplies. Both of them told me that while they fully realized the great risk they were running and the certainty of being put to death if captured, they left their first conference with the Admiral supremely impressed with the idea that such a man knew what he was about, and could not be beaten. Therefore they would be safe in continuing commanders of their steamers. They were paid double what they received in times of peace, but even that inducement would not have sufficed if they had not been moved by reliance on the Admiral's judgment and courage. These remarks were not merely post-bellum comment swelling the tide of popular adulation. It so happened that skippers of ships coming to Bangkok before the battle used to me almost the same words as these captains, in explanation of their willingness to remain with the Americans, which the latter employed in discussing the matter with me soon after the great combat.

I would lay special stress on these actual ante-bellum conceptions of Dewey in order to show that his qualities of successful leadership and true greatness were demonstrated before the fight—while, however, they were not appreciated at home—as much even as in the long, trying period that ensued until and after the fall of Manila. In several letters which I received from British army and naval friends at Hong-kong, and from Americans stopping or living there, written in March and April, 1898, some of which I now have before me, I find without exception this expression of the same sentiment: Dewey is the right man for the peculiar and difficult situation; no American need have any fear of the outcome of a fight in Philippine waters with him in command. General Wilsone Black, military commander-in-chief and acting Governor of Hong-kong, who has all the keenness of perception and judgment of men which characterize typical Scotchmen of his kind, was an ardent admirer of Dewey, and yet the only time he saw and knew him was during the exacting period when the American squadron was anchored in sight of Government House preparing to fight.

Possibly this regard for Dewey may have had its influence in persuading the Governor that it was not against the neutrality laws that several hundred tons of "delicacies" for the Admiral should be shipped every few weeks from Hong-kong to Manila! By careful comparison of what one man could consume with the total export of "delicacies" on United States despatch-boats during the time of war, every man in Dewey's squadron must have been an admiral! This, assisted by some other notable incidents which are a part of history, certainly had the effect to make every Jackie at Manila an advocate of an Anglo-American alliance.

It is often said that the way to get at an Asiatic is through his stomach; from what I saw at Manila I think that rule applies even to Americans and Europeans. To go further and still continue telling the truth: When Admiral Dewey wanted to make Admiral von Diederichs, the German commander, penitent, he sent him over a leg of frozen mutton, and straightway there was a temporary lull in German activity; when he wanted to show his appreciation of the hearty sympathy of Captain Chichester, he sent him over a leg of mutton, and forthwith Sir Edward strode from his cabin and took his bearings to see if the *Immortalité* lay between the *Kaiser Wilhelm* and the *Olympia!* All of which at the same time goes to prove that Dewey was an eminently practical as well as theoretical diplomatist.

Photograph by Blanchard, Montpelier, Vermont.

DR. JULIUS Y. DEWEY, FATHER OF THE ADMIRAL.

"This battle was won in Hong-kong Harbor," said Admiral Dewey to me when I first saw him in May, 1898, and heard him describe the great fight. Many times since then have I heard him repeat the same sentiment, and the more the truth of it is considered the more light it sheds on his character. While he was brave, strong, prompt, and decisive in action, he was thoughtful, cautious, deliberate, and sure in preparation. Day after day he summoned his captains to

THE FIRST PAGE OF DEWEY'S LOG ON THE "WABASH."

discuss all the possibilities and eventualities of a conflict with the enemy. He gave them an opportunity to say when, where, and how the battle should be fought. From junior to senior he called upon them to express their opinions freely. If any man had a novel idea, it was given careful consideration. If it was an old one with improvements, it was viewed in all phases. After the Admiral had patiently heard his captains and duly interrogated them, he quietly told them his own exact plan of battle and just what he expected of each man. Whether this was made up originally out of his own ideas, or from such in union with the best points advanced by his captains, it was reached only after thorough deliberation, and was final.

His details of preparedness also included obtaining all data and information possible, not only of the Spanish fleet, forts, mines, the depths and location of channels and entrances to Manila and Subig bays, the state of tides, currents, and winds, but the constant training of his men at target practice, in preparing for action, in landing, in fire drill, and in all other possible conditions of actual battle, until every officer and man could imagine himself a veteran in advance, and knew his precise station and rank, as well as his own and his neighbors' capability of doing their duty. Admiral Dewey's squadron, when it sailed out of Mirs Bay, may be compared to a thoroughbred horse trained to the hour by an expert who knew not only his animal, but its competitors and the conditions of the race.

I am often vexed when I hear critics who do not understand the situation as it then existed endeavor to belittle Dewey's victory by emphasizing the weakness of the enemy; but while I do not admit that they were weak—considering the strong land-batteries at Cavite, Manila, and those at Corregidor, which had first to be passed or silenced, and the number of their vessels, having the advantage of location, home waters, and land support—I claim that under the leadership of Admiral Dewey, and the perfect condition for fighting which characterized both ships and men, a much larger, stronger force would likewise have been defeated—not without loss of lives and possibly of a ship or more, but with absolute, unquestioned triumph for the Americans. With everybody and everything in that squadron working as a unit for one purpose under the guidance of one hand, with no bickerings and no jealousies in its living energy, and with no engines and no guns untested in its inanimate power, it formed within its limits an irresistible force that would have gained victory with any foe, or left no ship nor man to mark its defeat.

The supreme incident in the train of events, beginning with his first coming to Hong-kong up to the hour of the battle, which showed this remarkable deliberation and readiness, was the giving of the situation that faced him will support the correctness of my argument.

In Hong-kong, although the sympathy of the British naval and army men was with us, there was a strong tendency to exaggerate unintentionally the dangers of an isolated movement on Manila, to describe and picture the Spanish fleet as

A PAGE OF DEWEY'S LOG ON THE "WABASH" RECORDING HIS FIRST SALUTE TO A SPANISH SHIP.
Written just after graduating from Annapolis, when the Admiral was on his practice cruise in the Mediterranean.

famous command. "You may fire when you are ready, Gridley." There you have the man. What composure and yet what strength, what confidence and yet what decision of character, are shown in those words, which must be as immortal as the memory of the man who uttered them.

But with all this deliberation, care, and masterly perfection of force there were mingled the influences of profound courage supported by intensity and tenacity of purpose. Otherwise even with his excellence of arrangement he might have quailed at the outlook. Here, again, in estimating the greatness of the Admiral and of his victory, much must be taken into consideration. A brief review of some of the depressing features of the overmatching the American, and generally to impress on the Admiral, his officers, and his men the extremely hazardous undertaking before them. Spanish agents were hard at work spreading open and mysterious reports about channels mined and forests of torpedoes laid in both the Boca Chica and the Boca Grande, respectively between Corregidor and Marivales on the north and Corregidor and El Fraile on the south, and in those portions of Manila Bay where it would be necessary for an invading fleet to manœuvre. Among all the marvellous stories that were told and retold, it was exceedingly difficult to obtain exact and reliable information. There seemed to be nothing definite. And yet the Admiral discriminated so carefully in sifting out what was reliable that, later, he found conditions to be approximately as he finally concluded when making his ultimate plans.

Another discouraging feature of the problem before him was the knowledge that not only no re-enforcements nor assistance of any kind had been despatched by the government to support him in case of need, but that probably none would come for nearly two months, either naval or military. In this connection it is well to remember that Dewey had long before this advised the government to send him more and stronger ships and be ready for developments in the Far East. Finally there was the desperate necessity before him of being obliged to retire, if the battle was not decisive, to some point for repairs — but where? Neutrality laws were against him in all the ports of Asia, and America was 8000 miles away!

To use a land phrase in treating a naval subject. Dewey, in going to Manila, was burning all his bridges behind him, and he had to succeed. If he failed, his alternatives were defeat ending in hopeless retreat, or the utter annihilation of his squadron. If there ever was in history a situation requiring more courage in a commander than this, it certainly has not been recorded. If Dewey had lost in-

stead of won under such discouragements, history would have ultimately done him justice even if the people had been temporarily ungrateful. In the light of what actually happened, he is personally deserving of exclusive credit for the success of the descent on Manila. All that the government did was to tell him that he might go—to loosen the leash, as it were, and to release him from the immediate control of the Navy Department.

Then, when he sailed down the coast of the Philippines, nothing daunted him and his brave captains. He was ready to fight in open sea, in Subig, or before Manila under the land-batteries. He made a bold reconnoissance of Subig Bay with the *Boston* and *Concord* as if it were San Francisco Harbor; but when he reached the entrance to Manila Bay, and knew that the enemy must be awaiting him there, he took the lead himself with the *Olympia*, despite the hazard of first contact with mines and the fact that her high freeboard and superstructure formed a shining mark even for Spanish gunners. Some commanders would not have sailed in; others would have at least tarried while a reconnoissance was made.

In concluding my observations on these conditions before the battle I must cite the crowning proof of his prepared-

DEWEY AS A LIEUTENANT.
About 1863, age twenty-six.

ness and accuracy of judgment. I will
quote his own words from my note-
book, but preface them with the statement that they were well corroborated
by what from time to time I was told
by his able captains—Wildes, Gridley,
Dyer, Coghlan, Lamberton, Walker,
Wood—as well as Flag-Lieutenant
Brumby and Secretary Ensign Caldwell. He said:

"I told you that this battle was won
in Hong-kong Harbor. To show you
more plainly what I mean I will say
that we—that is, my captains and staff-
officers working with me—so planned
out this fight with reference to all possible contingencies that we were fully
prepared for exactly what happened.
Although I recognized the alternative,
from reports that reached me, that the
Spanish Admiral Montojo might meet
me at Subig, or possibly near Corregidor, I had finally made up my mind
that the battle would be fought right
here that very morning at the same
hour with nearly the same position of
opposing ships. That is why and how,
at break of day, we formed in perfect
line, opened fire, and kept our position
without mistake or interruption until
the enemy's ships were practically destroyed and the order was given to cease
firing and retire from action."

These are essentially the words of
a conversation which took place with-

DEWEY AS A LIEUTENANT-COMMANDER.
About 1865—age twenty-eight.

in a few weeks after the battle. They
were modestly told in ordinary discussion, but disclosed a marvellous precision of plan and judgment, which alone
would enable him to rank with the
great naval commanders of history.

If there was any criticism of the
Admiral and his movements implied
in what was written and said in America which annoyed him and those under him, it was the repetition of the
observation, If Dewey had only sailed
away! or, Why did not Dewey sail
away? The best answer that can be
given, in the opinion not only of those
at Manila, but of naval experts everywhere, is that it was so nearly impracticable and impossible for him to
sail away that under the conditions it
amounted to a prohibition. In the first
place, he had not sufficient coal or coal
capacity to undertake the long voyage
across the Pacific, nor could he venture

DEWEY AT THE AGE OF THIRTY.

the hazard of coaling in the open sea; he could not have coaled at any Japanese port, and it is doubtful if at that critical period in the early part of the war he would have been allowed to coal at Hong-kong, even with the favoring feature of British friendliness, for only shortly before he had been ordered away from there to Mirs Bay; the fastest speed of his squadron would have been that of the slowest vessel, the collier *Nanshan*, as a result of which it would have taken him nearly two months to reach America, if he could have gone, and in the mean time another Spanish squadron might have been fitted out, come to the Philippines, and completely controlled the Asiatic situation, and even prepared to descend on our Pacific coast cities. If he had sailed away and met disaster, the whole world would have condemned him as a naval commander and strategist, for there was no other neighboring haven whatever that he could seek, and he would have abandoned one where he was safe and in control. If he had departed and left not only the Spanish non-combatants, but foreigners, to the mercy of conditions which would arise with all naval protection gone, he would have been likewise censured; or, if by going away he had allowed the Spaniards to recoup and thereby have prolonged the war, everybody would have said now, Why did not Dewey stay? Finally, if it be true that by a canon of international law a dependency—after the overthrow of the power that held it—cannot be abandoned and left a prey to some other ambitious power, or to the unrestrained influences of native control, but is entitled at least to the temporary protection of the conqueror, what would the world have said if Admiral Dewey had violated this sacred duty and responsibility by sailing away?

Possibly in no way did Admiral Dewey's traits of character show to better advantage than in his treatment of newspaper men. Never seeking their attention or suggesting any references to himself, he was invariably courteous and firm, but often more considerate of them and their wishes than they had a right to expect. I never heard any newspaper man at Manila—and I knew them all well—speak otherwise, even in private, than in most respectful terms of the Admiral. They agreed that he personally was the fairest and best press censor of all those who held sway over their telegrams from the opening of hostilities to the present. I would cast no reflection on Lieutenant Brumby, to whom the Admiral soon turned over the responsibilities of censorship, but neither he nor any one else in navy or army could rival the Admiral in quick perception of what was permissible news and what was not, together with the rare faculty of showing to the correspondent with unfailing urbanity why this or that sentence should be changed or omitted. But he did not stop there. If he saw that an important item was missing, either from lack of information or fear of its being cut out, he would suggest that it be inserted, thus saving many correspondents the unhappy experience of being "scooped." He was not harsh in his restrictions; in fact, he was inclined to be more liberal than Brumby, and certainly far more tolerant than Colonel Thompson of the army.

The best evidence of the success of his method is that during the long period from May 1 to August 13, when the censorship was controlled on the *Olympia*, not one correspondent took unfair advantage of the simple rules that governed despatches. It would have been possible at any time to send different telegrams from those which were inspected, for two reasons — first, the despatches were never viséd by any mark or stamp, but merely read; second, they were all sent under personal cover to Hong-kong, there to be forwarded.

The Admiral's code for newspaper men was brief, but comprehensive and expressive. He said: "Gentlemen, you are left largely to your own good and experienced judgment not only as correspondents, but as American citizens; but you will always bear in mind that you must not send what will give actual aid and comfort to the enemy, or that which will unduly excite and disturb the people at home."

If he made up his mind that certain statements should not be sent, there was nothing to be gained by arguing the question; but if he entertained the slightest doubt, he would listen carefully to the correspondent's prayer, and, if convinced, pass the despatch. In the Admiral's dealings with the newspaper correspondents the traits of character that emphasized themselves were tact and urbanity, mingled with due dignity and firmness.

These supreme qualities of diplomacy, which were brought out so fully later not only in his dealings with the German admiral, but with Aguinaldo and his leaders, were first plainly evinced in his treatment of newspaper men.

One incident, which I particularly remember, will illustrate his methods, and his high motives as well. There had been an occurrence which was fairly pregnant with sensational possibilities. It was assuredly teeming with news. It concerned, as such items usually did for a considerable period, the German squadron's movements. All the correspondents prepared vivid but even then accurate descriptions. Brumby referred so important a subject to the Admiral. Quoting again from notes made at the moment, I find that the Admiral said, in substance:

"If you gentlemen wish, you can send these telegrams just as you have written them, but I hope you will not. If you forward your despatches at this time, when our people are excited to the fever-point, your news may be the influence that will inspire them to demand action on the part of the government that would not only seriously embarrass it at Washington, but me right here, and might lead to further serious complications or war. Now if you will let the matter all alone and leave it to me, I will settle it all right, we will save great excitement at home, and avoid all chances of war. Do just as you think best."

It is needless to add that there was no further argument, and even to-day that affair has not been fully described. In some further treatment of the subject I may call on my note-book to tell the story

of one of the most exciting little incidents of the war, unless in the mean time it is told by others who remember it.

The Admiral's forbearance under most trying circumstances aroused the respect

THE HOUSE IN WHICH DEWEY WAS BORN, MONTPELIER, VERMONT.

of all who witnessed his self-control where any man would have been forgiven for losing his temper. I would not imply that the Admiral did not ever give way to the impulses of righteous wrath. He did, as he himself often acknowledged, and as those with and under him were now and then aware. He had the quality of "getting mad," but the same temperament which fostered at times such a spirit made him, in the supreme hour of battle, a most dangerous and powerful enemy. On the other hand, if he ever was actuated by anger he never allowed his expression of it to interfere in any way with the individual discipline of the squadron or with its general interests in connection with other forces either of our army or those of foreign navies at Manila. There is no denying the fact that he employed, on certain occasions, vigorous language in referring to the tactics of those whose methods were irritating, but at the moment when firmness of purpose had to accomplish its chief end and nothing must interfere with suc-

THE STATE-HOUSE, MONTPELIER, VERMONT.

The House in which Dewey was born stands opposite the State-House. The Statue in the Portico is of Ethan Allen, and a Statue of Dewey is to face it.

cessful achievement, his calmness and forbearance were extraordinary. These qualities were manifested at the critical hour without weakening his strength as a great commander or lessening the respect of those who tried his patience the most.

At this point I must relate a historical fact which may have been told, but which I have not seen in print. It is conclusive illustration of the unselfishness and self - restraint of the Admiral which those who witnessed what I describe will never forget. Before the fall of Manila, on August 13, 1898, the navy, under the Admiral, and the army, under General Merritt, made elaborate preparations for the capture of the city. Negotiations followed with General Jaudenes for the surrender, but an informal compromise was finally arranged, with the understanding that the American land and sea forces should make a mild attack on the southern defences of Manila " to satisfy Spanish honor" before the white flag was raised. Due notice was given of the proposed engagement so that there need be no loss of life among non-combatants. At the same time Admiral Dewey sent

formal notice to the commanders of the British, German, French, and Japanese squadrons in the bay that he was about to attack the defences of Manila, and requested them to withdraw to such distance as would leave the water in front of Manila free for the movements of his ships. They weighed anchor and complied with his wishes.

It was understood that in the advance on Manila the army and navy were to move together at a given signal — the army from trenches at Pasay and Malate, and the navy along the entire waterfront. Everything being apparently in readiness, and the required time of waiting having passed, the Admiral ran up the signal on the *Olympia* for all ships to prepare for action. In a short time these fighting-machines were in perfect shape for battle, with guns shotted, decks stripped, and battle-flags flying. Every man was keyed to the point of action. The foreign ships looked on with expectant interest, and even the Spaniards crowded the old walls of Manila to see the approach of the American vessels. Suddenly, as we all waited for the signal to start, Lieutenant Brumby came from the Admiral's cabin and ordered young Scott to run up the signal to bank fires and await further orders. Imagine the chagrin not only of every officer and Jackie in the squadron, but of the Admiral, who was compelled to withdraw his order. What was the matter? All we knew was that General Merritt had been alongside a few minutes before the last order was given. It did not take long to ascertain the truth—the army was not ready.

Had this occurred only once, it might not have made a lasting impression upon us who saw it, but the feelings of the officers and men of the navy, from Admiral down, can be appreciated when it is known that the next day this remarkable experience was in the main repeated, and not until a day later was the army formally announced as ready. Then, after the unfortunate delays of the past few days, the Admiral, in supreme patience and forbearance, ordered his ships to prepare for action, weighed anchor, and steamed over opposite the defences of Manila.

It is not my purpose to reflect on the army in general, or upon General Merritt and General Greene in particular. Their records as skilful commanders speak for themselves. Nor would I wish to do other than give well-deserved credit to such able officers as Generals Anderson and MacArthur, whom everybody trusted. The army may have had the best reasons in the world for being unprepared when they first thought they would be ready, and when the Admiral had been led to suppose they would be prepared. The fact is, however, they were not, and the Admiral and his men suffered the great annoyance of delay.

In the presence of the commanders of the foreign squadrons and of the officers of the Spanish army, looking respectively from the decks of their ships and the walls of their town, he had been forced twice to revoke his own orders, and haul down his own battle-flags without a battle! Can anything more trying to a man's spirit be imagined than this, especially when the fault was in no way his?

When in a fortunate moment I was discussing the general situation with the Admiral, not more than half an hour after he had revoked a second time his order to prepare for action, I asked him directly what was the cause of the extraordinary delay. Without the slightest sign of passion or displeasure, but with extreme composure, he replied at once,

"Because the army, after doing its best, is not quite ready, and of course we must act together."

"Is it not," I continued, "rather disappointing, in the sight of all these foreign vessels, to prepare for action and then take no further steps?"

"That does not matter. We are not making war for them. If they care to watch us, they must take things as they find them."

By this conversation it can be seen that he completely forgot himself and blamed no one. He would not even admit that the army officers whose business it was to do such things should have at least informed him a few hours earlier that they would not be ready, and so have saved him the necessity of recalling his orders on two separate occasions.

Although every other officer on the *Olympia*, as well as on the *Baltimore*, *Raleigh*, *Boston*, *Concord*, *Charleston*, *Monterey*, *Petrel*, and even little *Callao*, was indignant at the delay, and so expressed himself without reserve, the Admiral never uttered one word of complaint, unless he may have given voice to his feelings in private to Captain Lamberton, Lieutenant Brumby, or Ensign Caldwell.

The American people cannot be too grateful to Admiral Dewey for his successful direction of relations with the German Admiral von Diederichs at Manila. Those of us who were there will never forget his mingled diplomacy and courage in dealing with a troublesome situation that might have led to war with a less brave and tactful man in charge. There were times when his patience was sorely taxed, and to those whom he could trust he made observations that cannot be published. It may cover the ground if I say that I know that he was vexed by the movements of the ships of the German squadron and the attitude of the German admiral; but I must add that he was invariably confident as to the outcome, and believed that if left to himself and hampered by no instructions from Washington, he could settle the little unpleasantness to the complete satisfaction of all concerned. From the beginning to the end of the German episode he endeavored in every dignified way to avoid a collision, and would seek in his consideration of the activity of the German ships some other motive than intentional hostility to himself and the United States. While he deplored their seeming disregard of the courtesies due a blockading squadron, he never, to my knowledge, said that he believed that they were really planning and hoping for trouble with him. When any discussion arose in a gathering of persons or officers where he was present, over the conduct of the German ships, he strove to minimize the matter and allay any excitement. There was a certain limit beyond which the German admiral could not have gone. Up to that limit Dewey chose to use diplomatic methods to check his restless visitor, rather than foster a feeling of resentment at home towards the Germans which might develop into a wave of popular remonstrance and bring unfortunate complications.

Judging from notes which I made at the time, Admiral Dewey apparently reasoned as follows:

"The United States does not want war with Germany, and Germany does not want war with the United States. War might result from conditions here in the Philippines, but it can be avoided. War will not come on our part except on my initiative. It is therefore my duty to do all in my power to prevent complications which might help to bring on war, even if I must submit to some irregularities of action on the part of the German admiral."

Dewey moreover appreciated, up to the time when the *Monterey* arrived, that the German squadron was stronger in ships, equipment, and armored protection than his own squadron, and that it would be folly to think of fighting until he was reenforced.

Instead, then, of assuming a belligerent attitude, he took a firm stand for his rights without bullying or boastfulness, which had the desired effect. When the Germans realized that he objected to their activity in and around Manila Bay, and that he intended to check it, not by war or threats of war, but by forceful diplomatic insistence on his undoubted rights, they began to mend their course, and finally ceased to be a source of irritation.

Hale and hearty Captain Sir Edward Chichester, of the *Immortalité*, said to me last November in Hong-kong:

"Your Admiral accomplished by tact, firmness, and good judgment in Manila Bay what many naval men would have thought only possible by war. Dewey is a natural fighter, but true fighter that he is, he prefers to win a peaceful victory. He is a great man."

That is the testimony of one of Britain's noblest old sea-dogs, and no man is a better authority. When the accurate history of the long period of waiting at Manila is fully known to our people, they will not only find that all their praise and love of Dewey are deserved, but that their thanks are due Captain Chichester for the tangible moral support that his unique personality gave Dewey during the most discouraging days of the summer, when nobody knew what the next week or month had in store.

My conclusion in regard to Dewey's experience with von Diederichs is this: It proved beyond quibble or doubt that he is a great diplomatist and statesman as well as naval commander. He accomplished what is a desideratum of true diplomacy—the achievement of the object or purpose without entailing counter-responsibilities or developing conditions more serious than those originally involved.

Admiral Dewey was undoubtedly moved more than once to speak in plain terms to representatives of Admiral von Diederichs, but there was so much moral force and logic of position in what he said that the German commander could not possibly take offence.

Then finally the Admiral knew, as others about him did, that the Germans in the Far East, and probably a good part of the German people, did not really appreciate what was going on at Manila, and were not in sympathy with this naval demonstration.

Physically the Admiral is not an impressive man in the sense that some of our noted military men are, but he has a poise of body and head when standing or sitting that attracts the eye of the stranger. He has dignity with absolute ease. He carries himself gracefully for a man whose legs are trained to the sea, and he is not affected in manner or movement. His step is usually light, but not especially quick. He is not tall, and is rather under the average height of naval men; but, in good condition, he has the appearance of being fairly well rounded. His bones are small and his fingers long and slight. His hands are often employed in nervous gestures—not in the French, but in the New England style — emphatic and serious, but not gymnastic. He has an interesting habit of drawing his fingers over his eyes when about to express some thought or consider a new suggestion. When a little agitated or disturbed he will pull and roll the ends of his long white mustache.

As he talks he shakes his head to give emphasis to what he is saying. If he is specially interested his eyes move quickly about, watching your own expression and possibly that of others, looking bright and cheerful one moment and severe the next, according to your answers or comment. Still, his eyes are not what would be called shifting. He has a firm, earnest, controlling look in them when he has orders to give or hears reports on important matters.

He could not be called handsome, because he is not sufficiently tall, but he has a prepossessing, clear-cut, interesting, almost classical face that seems equal to the responsibility of giving expression to the thoughts that have birth in his active brain. He is much better looking than the average photograph or sketch. None of his pictures brings out the best that is in his face, nor the lines which one notices in his actual presence. The ordinary portrait that is seen all over the land gives no conception of the real force and strength that he possesses, and is therefore disappointing to the man who has been accustomed to seeing him in person. His hair is an iron-gray tending towards whiteness, which becomes his composed but earnest visage. The nose is large, but it indicates his force of character, and does not mar the general·effect of his physiognomy. There are resolution and persistency in the lines of his mouth, and when his lips are moving in stating an order or giving an opinion where he has made up his mind, there is no difficulty in determining whether he is in earnest. His complexion has naturally been sallow much of the time at Manila, for that condition is superinduced by the climate, but after his long voyage home it is quite probable that he will have considerable color. He

always looks clean and neat, but is not over-particular, and gracefully accepts the conditions of war and sailor life even if they do not give him all the privileges, comforts, and pleasures of the club. His wonderful adaptability has made him as much at home in the stripped cabin of the *Olympia* as he would have been in a hotel or club in New York or Washington. In fact, he gave no signs on the flag-ship of desiring luxurious surroundings, and the simplicity of furniture dating back to the days of fighting, compared with his simplicity of dress and manner, seemed to present a harmonious situation in line with his habits and wishes. There was no "fuss and feathers" about him or his environment at Manila.

Admiral Dewey is a remarkable illustration of the adaptability of men of our race to the conditions and circumstances that unexpectedly surround and meet them. He shows the ability of our leaders to cope successfully with new and broad responsibilities. But with this natural tendency of his American blood and training, and the inspiration which he received from birth and early childhood in Vermont, there are certain indispensable latent qualities such as consummate leadership, executive capacity, indomitable courage, strength of conviction, which were only fully brought out by the battle of Manila, and the cares that preceded and followed that engagement. Long before, to his large circle of friends in naval, political, and business circles, he had shown qualities of diplomacy, urbanity, discrimination, and self-possession which, put to their full test in the Manila campaign, proved equal to the emergency.

In meeting Admiral Dewey the stranger might not from first impressions consider him a great man in the true meaning of the term, but he would go away invariably prepossessed in his favor. I never knew a naval or military officer, a newspaper correspondent, traveller, or business man who did not leave his presence, after being introduced for the first time, charmed with his personality, his affability, his *savoir-faire*, and his unaffected bearing. They say first impressions are lasting, but experience teaches me that in the case of the Admiral later and final impressions correct and enlarge the first. A few further instances of his rare qualities of leadership, diplomacy, courage, judgment, and urbanity, supplementing what has gone before, must suffice for this imperfect sketch of some phases of the Admiral's character and of his career at Manila.

His relations with Aguinaldo before the arrival of the army were conducted with singular tact. I can say here authoritatively that the Admiral not only never earnestly favored the return of Aguinaldo to the Philippines, but he never formally recognized him as an ally, or promised him and his followers any degree of independence. The Admiral permitted Aguinaldo to come back to Cavite, but he never urged him. There was no American name that carried so much weight in Filipino councils as that of Admiral Dewey, and I wish to add that I honestly believe that if plenipotentiary powers and orders had been given Admiral Dewey after the fall of Manila, such as England gave Kitchener in the Upper Nile Basin, he would have successfully solved the problem of our relations with the natives, and avoided those conditions which have resulted in the present warfare—unless the development of sentiment against accepting responsibility, and the failure to ratify the treaty until after prolonged delay, should have proved disastrous even to his masterful control of the situation.

The profound patience with which he awaited the arrival of troops two months after the battle of Manila Bay was only surpassed by the greater resignation with which he looked for the arrival of re-enforcements in the form of the *Monterey* and *Monadnock*. The former did not put in an appearance until three months after the battle, and the latter four months. Had these monitors come when they were most needed, it is probable that the German demonstration would never have been known to history.

One of the best proofs of his courage and devotion to duty is the fact that during the entire length of his stay of over a year, he was never absent from Manila Bay for more than part of a day, and then only to run out to Subig.

To make this self-abnegation the more prominent, it can be remembered that every other officer and man in his squadron, including his own staff-officers, had made trips to Hong-kong, by which they were much benefited and refreshed. When the *Olympia* went to Hong-kong,

he transferred his flag to another ship and remained.

He planned for all contingencies. He never was taken by surprise, and he never intended to be. When it was understood that Camara was coming to the Philippines he was not in the least disturbed, but said he was ready, and would do to him what he had to Montojo. He provided against all probability of torpedo attack from the Spaniards at Manila by unremitting night surveillance until they gave up all hope of doing his ships harm. He guarded so carefully the health of his men that in the hottest season the per-centage of sick was incredibly small. He made frequent visits to the different ships of his command, and to the navy-yard at Cavite, taking peculiar pleasure in the latter as his own special prize and pet.

To briefly allude to other characteristics and qualities I might mention his unselfish thought of others, especially of his army colleagues, first General Merritt and later General Otis; his avoidance of act or word that suggested the importance of his own unique position; his never-failing politeness towards all that called upon him; his love for his native town of Montpelier and State of Vermont; his finesse of manner and speech, and man-of-the-world nature mingled with a directness and force of speech and rugged sailor spirit which respectively showed themselves as conditions demanded; and finally his every-day, matter-of-fact method of living, acting, and talking, which kept him far from being a saint or perfect man, and made him seem at times exactly like scores of other average men, who have all in their way their foibles, weaknesses, and petty vices, as well as their strong points and virtues.

As he now returns to his home land the American people will not only be able to confirm all here portrayed of his character, but to show to him that love which has been waiting long months for its actual expression. If I were asked, in conclusion, what has been the most marked effect on the Admiral of his great victory, followed by an appreciation of the imperishable fame and glory that are his reward, and by a supreme realization of the deep, all-prevalent love of his fellow-countrymen for him, I would say that he has become gentler in spirit, touched to his innermost nature by such sincere affection.

FROM A WINTER NOTE-BOOK

WE had walked abreast of the year from the very beginning, and that was when the first blood-root came up between the patches of April snow, while yet the big drift at the bottom of the meadow held fast. In the shadow of the woods and under the blown pine-needles clots of snow lay till far into May, but neither the season nor the flowers took any note of them, and, before we were well sure Winter had gone, the lackeys of my Lord Baltimore in their new liveries came to tell us that Summer was in the valley, and please might they nest at the bottom of the garden?

Followed Summer, angry, fidgety, and nervous, with the corn and tobacco to ripen in five short months, the pastures to reclothe, and the fallen leaves to hide away under new carpets. Suddenly, in the middle of her work, on a stuffy-still July day, she called a wind out of the Northwest, a wind blown under an arch of steel-bellied clouds, a wicked, bitter wind with a lacing of hail to it, a wind that came and was gone in less than ten minutes, but blocked the roads with fallen trees, toppled over a barn, and—blew potatoes out of the ground. When that was done, a white cloud shaped like a dumbbell whirled down the valley across the evening blue, roaring and twisting and twisting and roaring all alone by itself. A West-Indian hurricane could not have been quicker on its feet than our little cyclone, and when the house rose atiptoe, like a cockerel in act to crow, and a sixty-foot elm went by the board, and that which had been a dusty road became a roaring torrent all in three minutes, we felt that the New England Summer had creole blood in her veins. She went away, red-faced and angry to the last, slamming all the doors of the hills behind her, and Autumn, who is a lady, took charge.

No pen can describe the turning of the leaves—the insurrection of the tree-people against the waning year. A little maple began it, flaming blood-red of a sudden where' he stood against the dark

NOTE.—The photographs illustrating this article were made by Arthur R. Dugmore, who visited Brattleboro, Vermont (the home of Rudyard Kipling), and remained there to witness the climatic changes that are described in this article. All of his photographs were made directly from nature, and upon the scenes described.

THE ROAD-SIDE GROWTH ALL DEAD FROM FROST.

When these go the curtain comes down, and whatever powers shift the scenery behind work without noise. In tropic lands you can hear the play of growth and decay at the back of the night silences. Even in England the tides of the winter air have a set and a purpose; but here they are dumb altogether. The very last piece of bench-work this season was the trailed end of a blackberry-vine, most daringly conventionalized in hammered iron, flung down on the frosty grass an instant before people came to look. The blue bloom of the furnace was still dying along the central rib, and the side sprays were cherry red, even as they had been lifted from the charcoal. It was a detail, evidently, of some invisible gate in the woods; but we never found that workman,

green of a pine belt. Next morning there was an answering signal from the swamp where the sumacs grow. Three days later the hill-sides as far as the eye could range were afire, and the roads paved, with crimson and gold. Then a wet wind blew, and ruined all the uniforms of that gorgeous army; and the oaks, who had held themselves in reserve, buckled on their dull and bronzed cuirasses and stood it out stiffly to the last blown leaf, till nothing remained but pencil shading of bare boughs, and one could see into the most private heart of the woods.

Frost may be looked for till the middle of May and after the middle of September, so Summer has little time for enamel-work or leaf-embroidery. Her sisters bring the gifts. Spring, wind-flowers, Solomon's-seal, Dutchman's-breeches, Quaker-ladies, and trailing arbutus, that smells as divinely as the true May. Autumn has golden-rod and all the tribe of the asters, pink, lilac, and creamy white, by the double armful.

though he had left the mark of his big cloven feet as plainly as any strayed deer. In a week the heavy frosts with scythes and hammers had slashed and knocked down all the road-side growth and the kindly bushes that veil the drop off the unfenced track.

There the seasons stopped awhile. Autumn was gone, Winter was not. We had Time dealt out to us—more, clear, fresh Time—grace-days to enjoy. The white wooden farm-houses were banked round two feet deep with dried leaves or earth, and the choppers went out to get ready next year's stores of wood. Now chopping is an art, and the chopper in all respects an artist. He makes his own axe-helve, and for each man there is but one perfect piece of wood in all the world. This he never finds, but the likest substitute is trimmed and balanced and poised to that ideal. One man that I know has evolved very nearly the weapon of Umslopogaas. It is almost straight, lapped at the butt with leather, amazingly springy, and carries a two-edged blade

THE WHITE FARM-HOUSES BANKED WITH LEAVES.

for splitting and chopping. If his Demon be with him—and what artist can answer for all his moods?—he will cause a tree to fall upon any stick or stone that you choose, uphill or down, to the right or to the left. Artistlike, however, he explains that that is nothing. Any fool can play with a tree in the open, but it needs the craftsman to bring a tree down in thick timber and do no harm. To see an eighty-foot maple, four feet in the butt, dropped, deftly as a fly is cast, in the only place where it will not outrage the feelings and swipe off the tops of fifty juniors, is a revelation. White pine, hemlock, and spruce share this country with maples, black and white birches, and beech. Maple seems to have few preferences, and the white birches straggle and shiver on the outskirts of every camp; but the pines hold together in solid regiments, sending out skirmishers to invade a neglected pasture on the first opportunity. There is no overcoat warmer than the pines in a gale when the woods for miles round are singing like cathedral organs, and the first snow of the year powders the rock ledges.

The mosses and lichens, green, sulphur, and amber, stud the copper floor of needles, where the feathery ground-pine runs aimlessly to and fro along the ground, spelling out broken words of half-forgot-

ten charms. There are checkerberries on the outskirts of the wood, where the partridge (he is a ruffed grouse really) dines, and by the deserted logging-roads toadstools of all colors sprout on the decayed stumps. Wherever a green or blue rock lifts from the hill-side, the needles have been packed and matted round its base, till, when the sunshine catches them, stone and setting together look no meaner than turquoise in dead gold. The woods are full of color, belts and blotches of it, the colors of the savage—red, yellow, and blue. Yet in their lodges there is very little life, for the wood-people do not readily go into the shadows. The squirrels have their business among the beeches and hickories by the road-side, where they can watch the traffic and talk. We have no gray ones hereabouts (they are good to eat, and suffer for it), but five reds live in a hickory hard by, and no weather puts them to sleep. The woodchuck, a marmot and a strategist, makes his burrow in the middle of a field, where he must see you ere you see him. Now and again a dog manages to cut him off his base, and the battle is worth crossing fields to watch. But the woodchuck turned in long ago, and will not be out till April. The coon lives—well, no one seems to know particularly where Brer Coon lives; but when the Hunter's Moon is large and full he descends into the corn-lands, and men chase him with dogs for his fur, which makes the finest kind of overcoat, and his flesh, which tastes like chicken. He cries at night sorrowfully, as though a child were lost.

They seem to kill, for one reason or another, everything that moves in this land. Hawks, of course; eagles for their rarity; foxes for their pelts; red-shouldered blackbirds and Baltimore orioles because they are pretty, and the other small things for sport—French fashion. You can get a rifle of a kind for twelve shillings, and if your neighbor be fool enough to post notices forbidding "hunting" and fishing, you naturally seek his woods. So the country is very silent and unalive.

There are, however, bears within a few miles, as you will see from this notice, picked up at the local tobacconist's:

THE PINES HOLD TOGETHER IN SOLID REGIMENTS.

JOHNNY GET YOUR GUN! BEAR HUNT.

As bears are too numerous in the town of Peltyville Corners Vt. the hunters of the surrounding towns are invited to participate in a grand hunt to be held on Blue Mountain in the town of Peltyville Corners Vt. Wednesday, Nov. 8th, if pleasant. If not, the first fine day. Come one, come all!

They went, but it was the bear that would not participate. The notice was printed at somebody's Electric Print Establishment. Queer mixture, isn't it?

The bear does not run large as a rule, but he has a weakness for swine and calves which brings punishment. Twelve hours rail and a little marching take you up to the moose-country; and twenty-odd miles from here as the crow flies you come to virgin timber, where trappers live, and where there is a Lost Pond that many have found once but can never find again.

Men, who are of one blood with sheep, have followed their friends and the railway along the river valleys where the towns are. Across the hills the inhabitants are few, and, outside their State, little known. They withdraw from society in November if they live on the uplands, coming down in May as the snow gives leave. Not much more than a generation ago these farms made their own clothes, soap, and candles, killed their own meat thrice a year, beef, veal, and pig, and sat still between-times. Now they buy shop-made clothes, patent soaps, and kerosene; and it is among their tents that the huge red and gilt Biographies of the Presidents, and the twenty-pound family Bibles, with illuminated marriage-registers, mourning-cards, baptismal certificates, and hundreds of genuine steel-engravings, sell best. Here, too, off the main travelled roads, the wandering

THE CHOPPER MAKES HIS OWN AXE-HELVE.

quack — Patent Electric Pills, nerve cures, etc. — divides the field with the seed and fruit man and the seller of cattle-boluses. They dose themselves a good deal, I fancy, for it is a poor family that does not know all about nervous prostration. So the quack drives a pair of horses and a gayly painted wagon with a hood, and sometimes takes his wife with him. Once only have I met a peddler afoot. He was an old man, shaken with palsy, and he pushed a thing exactly like a pauper's burial-cart, selling pins, tape, scents, and flavorings. You helped yourself, for his hands had no direction, and he told a long tale, in which the deeding away of a farm to one of his family was mixed up with pride at the distances he still could cover daily. As much as six miles sometimes. He was no Lear, as the gift of the farm might suggest, but sealed of the tribe of the Wandering Jew — a tremulous old giddy-gaddy. There are many such rovers, gelders of colts and the like, who work a long beat, south to Virginia almost, and north to the frontier, paying with talk and gossip for their entertainment.

Yet tramps are few, and that is well, for the American article answers almost

THE MAN WITH THE PLOUGHSHARE.

exactly to the vagrant and criminal tribes of India, being a predatory ruffian who knows too much to work. Bad place to beg in after dark—on a farm—very—is Vermont. Gypsies pitch their camp by the river in the spring, and *cooper* horses in the manner of their tribe. They have the gypsy look and some of the old gypsy names, but say that they are largely mixed with Gentile blood.

Winter has chased all these really interesting people south, and in a few weeks, if we have anything of a snow, the back farms will be unvisited save by the doctor's hooded sleigh. It is no child's play to hold a practice here through the winter months, when the drifts are really formed, and a pair can drop in up to their saddle-pads. But the doctors come and go. Four horses a day some of them use, and use up—for they are good men.

Now in the big silence of the snow is born, perhaps, not a little of New England conscience which her children write about. There is much time to think, and thinking is a highly dangerous business. Conscience, fear, undigested reading, and, it may be, not too well cooked food

have full swing. A man, and more particularly a woman, can easily hear strange voices—the Word of the Lord rolling between the dead hills; may see visions and dream dreams; get revelations and an outpouring of the spirit, and end (such things have been) lamentably enough in those big houses by the Connecticut River which have been tenderly rechristened The Retreat. Hate breeds as well as religion—the deep, instriking hate between neighbors, that is born of a hundred little things added up, brooded over, and hatched by the stove when two or three talk together in the long evenings. It would be very interesting to get the statistics of revivals and murders, and find how many of them have been committed in the spring. But for undistracted people winter is one long delight of the eye. In other lands one knows the snow as a nuisance that comes and goes, and is sorely man-handled and messed at the last. Here it lies longer on the ground than any crop—from November to April sometimes—and for three months life goes to the tune of sleigh-bells, which are not, as a Southern visitor once hinted, ostentation, but safeguards. The man who drives without them is not loved.

The snow is a faithful barometer, fore-telling good sleighing or stark confine-ment to barracks. It is all the manure the stony pastures receive; it cloaks the ground and prevents the frost bursting pipes; it is the best—I had almost writ-ten the only—road-maker in the States. On the other side, it can rise up in the night and bid the people sit still as the Egyptians. It can stop the mails; wipe out all time-tables; extinguish the lamps of twenty towns, and kill man within sight of his own door-step or hearing of his cattle unfed. No one who has been through even so modified a blizzard as New England can produce talks lightly of the snow. Imagine eight-and-forty hours of roaring wind, the thermometer well down towards zero, scooping and gouging across a hundred miles of newly fallen snow. The air is full of stinging shot, and at ten yards the trees are invis-ible. The foot slides on a reef, polished and black as obsidian, where the wind has skinned an exposed corner of road down to the dirt ice of early win-ter. The next step ends hip-deep and over, for here an unseen wall is banking back the rush of the singing drifts. A scarped slope rises sheer across the road. The wind shifts a point or two, and all sinks down, as sand in the hour-glass, leaving a pot-hole of whirling whiteness. There is a lull, and you can see the surface of the fields setting furious-ly in one direction—a tide that spurts foam be-tween the tree-boles. The hollows of the pas-ture fill while you watch; empty, fill, and discharge anew. The rock ledges show the bare flank of a storm-chased liner for a moment, and whitening, duck under. Irresponsi-ble snow devils dance by the lee of a barn where three gusts meet, or stag-ger out into the open till they are cut down by the main wind. At the worst

of the storm there is neither Heaven nor Earth, but only swizzle into which a man may be brewed. Distances grow to night-mare scale, and that which in the summer was no more than a minute's bareheaded run, is half an hour's gasping struggle, each foot won between the lulls. Then do the heavy-timbered barns talk like ships in a cross-sea, beam working against beam. The winter's hay is ribbed over with long lines of snow dust blown be-tween the boards, and far below in the byre the oxen clash their horns and moan uneasily.

The next day is blue, breathless, and most utterly still. The farmers shovel a way to their beasts, bind with chains their large ploughshare to their heaviest wood-sled, and take of oxen as many as Allah has given them. These they drive, and the dragging share makes a furrow in which a horse can walk, and the oxen, by force of repeatedly going in up to their bellies, presently find foothold. The

THE DESERTED LOGGING-ROAD.

WHERE THE TRAPPERS LIVE.

finished road is a deep double gutter between three-foot walls of snow, where, by custom, the heavier vehicle has the right of way. The lighter man when he turns out must drop waist-deep and haul his unwilling beast into the drift, leaving Providence to steady the sleigh.

In the towns, where they choke and sputter and gasp, the big snow turns to horsepondine. With us it stays still; the wind, sun, and rain get to work upon it, lest the texture and color should not change daily. Rain makes a granulated crust over all, in which white shagreen the trees are faintly reflected. Heavy mists go up and down, and create a sort of mirage, till they settle and pack round the iron-tipped hills, and then you know how the moon must look to an inhabitant. At twilight again the beaten-down ridges and laps and folds of the uplands take on the likeness of wet sand—some huge and melancholy beach at the world's end—and when day meets night it is all goblin country. To westward, the last of the spent day—rust-red and pearl, illimitable levels of shore waiting for the tide to turn again. To eastward, black night among the valleys, and on the rounded hill slopes a hard glare that is not so much light as snail-slime from the moon. Once or twice perhaps in the winter the Northern Lights come out between the moon and the sun, so that to the two unearthly lights is added the leap and flare of the Aurora Borealis.

In January or February come the great ice-storms, when every branch, blade, and trunk is coated with frozen rain, so that you can touch nothing truly. The spikes of the pines are sunk into pear-shaped crystals, and each fence-post is miraculously hilted with diamonds. If you bend a twig, the icing cracks like varnish, and a half-inch branch snaps off at the lightest tap. If wind and sun open the day together, the eye cannot look steadily at the splendor of this jewelry. The woods are full of the clatter of arms; the ringing of bucks' horns in fight; the stampede of mailed feet up and down the glades; and a great dust of battle is puffed out into the open, till the last of the ice is beaten away and the cleared branches take up their regular chant.

Again the mercury drops twenty and more below zero, and the very trees swoon. The snow turns to French chalk, squeaking under the heel, and their breath cloaks the oxen in rime. At night a tree's heart will break in him with a groan. According to the books, the frost has split something, but it is a fearful sound—this grunt as of a man stunned.

Winter that is winter in earnest does not allow cattle and horses to play about the fields, so everything comes home; and since no share can break ground to any profit for some five months, there would seem to be very little to do. As a matter of fact, country interests at all seasons are extensive and peculiar, and the day is not long enough for them when you take out that time which a self-respecting man needs to turn himself round in. Consider. The solid undisturbed hours stand about one like ramparts. At a certain time the sun will rise. At another hour, equally certain, he will set. This much we know. Why in the name of Reason, therefore, should we vex ourselves with vain exertions? An occasional visitor from the Cities of the Plains comes up panting to do things. He is set down to listen to the normal beat of his own heart—a sound that very few men have heard. In a few days, when the lather of impatience has dried off, he ceases to talk of "getting there" or of "being left." He does not desire to accomplish matters "right away," nor does he look at his watch from force of habit, but keeps it where it should be—in his stomach. At the last he goes back to his beleaguered city, unwillingly, partially civilized, soon to be resavaged by the clash of a thousand wars whose echo does not reach here.

The air which kills germs dries out the very newspapers. They might be of tomorrow or a hundred years ago. They have nothing to do with to-day — the long, full, sunlit to-day. Our interests are not on the same scale as theirs, perhaps, but much more complex. The movement of a foreign power, an alien sleigh on this Pontic shore, must be explained and accounted for, or this public's heart will burst with unsatisfied curiosity. If it be Buck Davis, with the white mare that he traded his colt for, and the practically new black sleigh-robe that he bought at the Sewell auction, *why* does Buck Davis, who lives on the river flats, cross our hills, unless Murder Hollow be blockaded with snow, or unless he has turkeys for sale? *But* Buck Davis with turkeys would surely have stopped here, unless he were selling a large stock in town. A wail from the sacking at the back of the sleigh tells the tale. It is a winter calf, and Buck Davis is going to sell it for one dollar to the Boston Market, where it will be turned into potted chicken. This leaves the mystery of his change of route unexplained. After two days' sitting on tenter-horns it is discovered, obliquely, that Buck went to pay a door-yard call on Orson Butler, who lives on the saeter where the wind and the bald granite scaurs fight it out together. Kirk Demming has brought Orson news of a fox at the back of Black Mountain, and Or-

THE FARMERS SHOVEL A WAY TO THEIR BEASTS.

son's eldest son, going to Murder Hollow with wood for the new barn floor that the widow Amidon is laying down, told Buck that he might as well come round to talk to his father about the pig. *But* old man Butler meant fox-hunting from the first, and what he wanted to do was to borrow Buck's dog, who had been duly brought over with the calf, and left on the mountain. No, old man Butler did *not* go hunting alone, but waited till Buck came back from town. Buck sold the calf for a dollar and a quarter, and not for seventy-five cents, as was falsely asserted by interested parties. *Then* the two went after the fox together. This much learned, everybody breathes freely, if life has not been complicated in the mean time by more strange counter-marchings.

Five or six sleighs a day we can understand, if we know why they are abroad; but a metropolitan rush of traffic disturbs and excites.

GOING OUT FOX-HUNTING.

HAWTHORNE AMONG HIS FRIENDS

IN the Salem *Gazette* of Tuesday, August 29, 1876, occurs the following brief obituary:

"Mr. William B. Pike, a former Collector of this port, who has been in failing health for some years past, died on Saturday afternoon in the sixty-sixth year of his age. He was in early life a mechanic, working for several years as a carpenter with his father, the late Jacob Pike. He was a Democrat in politics, and his opinions and judgment upon political matters were generally deferred to by his party associates, by whom he was regarded as a man of more than average discernment and sagacity. He was intimate with Hawthorne, Pierce, Wright, and other well-known gentlemen of his party; was a man of warm friendship, and was even too ready to render assistance to those who asked aid at his hands. Mr. Pike was appointed to office in the Boston Custom-house, and also held official position here for about eighteen years. He was weigher and gauger under Polk, Taylor, and Fillmore, and was appointed Collector under Pierce, retaining his office through the administration of Buchanan."

For several years I knew Pike well, and saw him nearly every day till within a few months of his death. He had a full and ready mind, an unfailing fund of common-sense and shrewd observation, a sunny and cheerful temper, and a child-like purity of heart. And these rare qualities, together with the fact that Pike had been for many years intimate with Hawthorne, contributed to make him always extremely interesting to me. To an unusual degree he had evidently been taken into the confidence of Hawthorne, who to him was indeed sacrosanct. That Pike was not unworthy of this privilege is indicated by the fact that he was not prone to talk about it; and although on other matters communicative enough, and a lavish giver from his exhaustless stores of anecdote and reminiscence, a fine reserve seemed to fetter his tongue whenever, as frequently befell, he was approached by strangers and questioned upon the subject of his friend. It was a reticence caught unconsciously, as it seemed to me, from the mysterious shyness of Hawthorne himself.

We were conversing one day upon the topic of so-called spiritual manifestations, and I found that Pike had once been profoundly interested in these matters. He had long ago, however, come to the conclusion that the very singular phenomena which he had witnessed were a delusion and a snare to those who imagined them to be of any practical value. I referred to the fact that Hawthorne's intuitions, as revealed by several passages in his Note-Books and elsewhere, were so true that he seems never for a moment to have had any faith in that vital article of the spiritualistic faith, namely, that we may actually communicate with departed friends. In this connection Pike spoke of having once written to Hawthorne detailing his experiences and ideas regarding the rappers, and he remembered having received a reply which he thought would interest me; and in a few days he gave me the following letter, with a few other mementos of his friend:

"Lenox, *July* 24, 1851.

"Dear Pike,—I should have written to you long since, acknowledging the receipt of your gin, and in answer to your letter, but I have been very busy with my pen. As to the gin, I can not speak of its quality; for the bottle has not yet been opened, and will probably remain corked till cold weather, when I mean to take an occasional sip. I really thank you for it, however; nor could I help shedding a few quiet tears over that which was so uselessly spilt by the expressman.

"The most important news I have to tell you (if you have not already heard it) is that we have another daughter, now about two months old. She is a very bright and healthy child, and neither more nor less handsome than babies generally are. I think I feel more interest in her than I did in the other children at the same age, from the consideration that she is to be the daughter of my age—the comfort (at least so it is to be hoped) of my declining years.

"What a sad account you give of your solitude in your letter! I am not likely ever to have that feeling of loneliness which you express; and I most heartily wish that you would take measures to remedy it in your own case, by marrying Miss B—— or somebody else as soon as possible. If I were at all in the habit of shedding tears, I should have felt inclined to do so at your description of your present situation—without family, and estranged from your former friends. Whenever you find it quite intolerable (and I can hardly help wishing that it may become so soon), do come to me. By-the-way, if I continue to prosper as heretofore in the literary line, I shall soon be in a condition to buy a place; and if you should hear of one, say worth from $1500 to $2000, I wish you would keep your eye on it for me. I should wish it to be on the sea-coast, or, at all events, with easy access to the sea. Very little land would suit my purpose; but I want a good house, with space enough inside, and which will not need any considerable repairs. I find that I do not feel at home among these hills, and should not like to consider myself permanently settled here. I do not get acclimated to the peculiar state of the atmosphere; and, except in midwinter, I am continually catching cold, and am never so vigorous as I used to be on the sea-coast. The same is the case with my wife; and though the children seem perfectly well, yet I rather think they would flourish better near the sea. Say nothing about my wishes; but if you see a place likely to suit me, let me know. I shall be in Salem probably as soon as October, and possibly you will have something in view by that time.

"Why did you not express your opinion of *The House of the Seven Gables*, which I sent you? I suppose you were afraid of hurting my feelings by disapproval; but you need not have been. I should receive friendly censure with just as much equanimity as if it were praise; though, certainly, I had rather you would like the book than not. At any rate, it has sold finely, and seems to have pleased a good many people better than the other; and I must confess that I myself am among the number. It is more characteristic of the author, and a more natural book for me to write, than the *Scarlet Letter* was. When I write another romance, I shall take the Community for a subject, and shall give some of my experiences and observations at Brook Farm. Since the publication of the *Seven Gables* I have written a book for children, which is to be put to press immediately.

"My wife, with the baby and Una, is going eastward in two or three weeks to see her mother, who, I think, will not survive another winter. I shall remain here with Julian. If you can be spared from that miserable Custom-house, I wish you would pay me a visit, although my wife would hardly forgive you for coming while she was away. But I do long to see you, and to talk about a thousand things, relating to this world and the next. I am very glad of your testimony in favor of spiritual intercourse. I have heard and read much on the subject, and it appears to me to be the strangest and most bewildering affair I ever heard of. I should be very glad to believe that these rappers are, in any one instance, the spirits of the persons whom they profess themselves to be; but, though I have talked with those who have had the freest communication, there has always been something that made me doubt. So you must allow me to withhold my full and entire belief, until I have heard some of the details of your own spiritual intercourse.

"On receiving your letter, I wrote to Longfellow, requesting him to forward you any books that might facilitate your progress in the Swedish language. He has not told me whether or no he did so. I asked him to send them to the Mansion House in Salem. I wish you had rather undertaken Latin, or French, or German, or indeed almost any other language, in which there would have been a more extensive and attainable literature than in the Swedish. But if it turns out to be a pleasure and improvement to yourself, the end is attained. You will never, I fear (you see that I take a friend's privilege to speak plainly), make the impression on the world that, in years gone by, I used to hope you would. It will not be your fault, however, but the fault of circumstances. Your flower was not destined to bloom in this world. I hope to see its glory in the next.

"I had much more to say, but it has escaped my memory just now, and it is of no use trying to say any real thing in a letter. Hoping to see you sooner or later, your friend ever,
                    "NATH⸳ HAWTHORNE.
"Excuse this illegible scrawl; but I have contracted such a habit of scrawling that I can not possibly help it."

Let it be noted regarding this letter that it is given here just as it ran from Hawthorne's pen, driven at hot epistolary speed. It is by no means, however, the "illegible scrawl" which he calls it. The handwriting is not in the least difficult to decipher, and not only is every word spelled in full, even to the ands, but the punctuation itself is as perfect as in any printed page of his works. It is quite amusing, however, to notice that amid an accuracy which may be regarded as singular in an unpremeditated epistle, dashed off at a rate which, had the hand been less steady, might well have been illegible, there is one lapse—the word withhold is spelled with one h.

There is something very charming in Hawthorne's reference to the *Seven Gables*, and in his apprehension that it might have been disappointing to his friend. And the fine prophecy, so frank and tender, as to the flower "not destined to bloom in this world," shows the relations of intimate friendship and confidence in which these men stood to each other.

Lenox, where this letter was written, has gone into our annals not merely as a delightful summer resort, but, dating back to the days of Miss Sedgwick, it has ever been with artist and author a chosen place of sojourn. What drew Hawthorne thither has not been revealed. If he sought seclusion, it was surely to be found in the humble abode which he secured among the hills of Berkshire. He called it "the ugliest little red cottage you ever saw." It is situated on the outskirts of the charming village of Lenox, being, in fact, over the line and within the limits of Stockbridge; and it is so embosomed in foliage that to a passing stranger it might easily escape observation. Within, however, it is cozy and not inconvenient, and the rear windows furnish an unobstructed view of a wide and varied landscape. Shouldering groups of mountains cluster about a delightful little lake called Stockbridge Bowl. Conspicuous among these hills is Bald Head of the *Wonder-Book;* and beyond the water, looking in the blue distance,

so Hawthorne thought, "like a headless sphinx," is visible the vast bulk of Monument Mountain, whose legend has been sung by Bryant. Hawthorne lived in great retirement at Lenox, and is to this day referred to by the villagers as "the silent man." Often, too, he was strangely shy, so much so that he has been known to leave the highway for the fields rather than encounter a group of approaching villagers. And still he had wonderful nerve, and possessed a poise and readiness equal to any emergency, and comporting well with that stalwart and manly form, Websterian brow, and eyes which seemed to possess the strange power of exploring the twilight recesses of the heart and mind. Higginson, in one of his admirable papers in the *Literary World*, entitled "Short Studies of American Authors," reveals the impression which Hawthorne made upon him:

"The self-contained purpose of Hawthorne, the large resources, the waiting power—these seem to the imagination to imply an ample basis of physical life; and certainly his stately and noble port is inseparable, in my memory, from these characteristics. Vivid as this impression is, I yet saw him but twice, and never spoke to him. I first met him on a summer morning, in Concord, as he was walking along the road near the Old Manse, with his wife by his side, and a noble-looking baby-boy in a little wagon which the father was pushing. I remember him as tall, firm, and strong in bearing;......when I passed, Hawthorne lifted upon me his great gray eyes, with a look too keen to seem indifferent, too shy to be sympathetic—and that was all......Again I met Hawthorne at one of the sessions of a short-lived literary club; and I recall the imperturbable dignity and patience with which he sat through a vexatious discussion, whose details seemed as much dwarfed by his presence as if he had been a statue of Olympian Zeus."

Once, while Hawthorne was Surveyor at the port of Salem, two Shakers, leaders in their community, visited the Customhouse, and were conducted through its various departments. With what keen scrutiny the broad-hatted strangers were regarded by Hawthorne, as they passed through his room, we may well imagine from the fact that no sooner was the door shut as they passed out, than the elder of the celibates asked, with great interest, who that man was; and remarking upon his strong face and those eyes, the most wonderful he had ever beheld, he said: "Mark my words, that man will make in some way a deep impression upon the world."

An accomplished scholar and essayist, one of whose noblest productions—"Olympus and Asgard"—fills the place of honor in the *Atlantic* for January, 1859, tells me that Hawthorne, when he first dwelt at the Old Manse, and was comparatively little known, had made a singular impression upon the villagers, among whom a report was current that this man Hawthorne was somewhat uncanny—in point of fact, not altogether sane. My friend, the son of a Concord farmer, and at that time a raw college youth, had heard these bucolic whisperings as to the sanity of the recluse dweller at the ancient parsonage, but he knew nothing of the man, had read at that time none of his productions, and, of course, took no interest in what was said or surmised in the village gossip about him. And one day casting his eye toward the Manse as he was passing, he saw Hawthorne up the pathway, standing with folded arms, in motionless attitude, and with eyes fixed upon the ground. "Poor fellow," was his unspoken comment; "he does look as if he might be daft." And when, on his return, a full hour afterward, Hawthorne was seen standing in the same place and attitude, the lad's very natural conclusion was, "The man is daft, sure enough." My friend, who has now these many years worshipped at the shrine of Hawthorne, is inclined to believe that there was a latent insanity in him. But in this connection he expresses an opinion which others entertain as well, namely, that everybody is a monomaniac on some point or other. "Indeed," said he, "whole communities are delivered over to lunacy sometimes, as Bishop Butler says." Except, however, in the sense that

"True wit to madness nearly is allied,
And thin partitions do their bounds divide,"

no one knew Hawthorne, so Pike has assured me, who was not strongly impressed with the evident vigor and sanity of the man in mind and body; and with the fact, as Hawthorne himself says, that he had a system "naturally well balanced, and lacking no essential part of a thorough organization."

When Hawthorne decided to leave Lenox and move to West Newton, he sold at auction various household goods which he did not care to transport thither.

Among these was a plain mahogany desk, upon which he wrote *The House of the Seven Gables*, *The Wonder-Book*, *The Snow-Image*, and nearly the whole of *The Blithedale Romance*—the final chapters of the latter having been composed after his departure from Lenox. A short time since, certain young men, lovers of Hawthorne and members of the Berkshire Athenæum, secured this homely yet convenient arrangement of drawers, shelves, and writing-desk, and it may be seen now in the museum of that institution, bearing an appropriate placard, and surmounted by a framed document, sworn to and subscribed before a notary, authenticating the above facts for the benefit of future generations.

I would advise no man, unless his faith in the greatness and purity of Hawthorne is established beyond the possibility of disturbance, to investigate too closely into the muck-heaps of local prejudice which even to this day are found to exist among certain cliques and coteries of his native town. Persons of intelligence and respectability are met who actually regard their illustrious townsman with feelings of strong personal aversion. I have endeavored honestly and patiently to look into this strange matter for the purpose of discovering, if I could, the cause of an animosity so pronounced that were I to repeat here the sentiments of rancor and bitterness toward Hawthorne which I have heard spoken, the record would be read with astonishment and incredulity. I rejoice to say, however, that these people are in a very small minority, and that to most Hawthorne is a bright particular star, dwelling aloft beyond the reach of detraction. Hawthorne was a Democrat in politics at a time when, by these unfriendly people, themselves of Whiggish proclivities, grave doubts were entertained whether a Democrat might by any possibility be admitted to heaven; and he was considered not overselect in his associates. It is true that, with a few rare exceptions, Hawthorne held himself aloof from what was regarded as the best society of his native town. Flattering invitations from the wealthiest families were not accepted, nor acknowledged even, and the very existence of the writers was ignored. This was discouraging and of course not wholly agreeable to an aristocracy which, finding this stalwart and handsome young man stranded on their shores like some wonderful marine monster, would fain capture him for the entertainment and distinction which might accrue to them thereby. It is thought that this was boorish and rude, and indicative of a soul hopelessly Democratic and depraved. It once befell that he was appointed, without his knowledge or consent, secretary of the Salem Lyceum, an honorable association which for more than half a century has given annual courses of lectures. He quietly ignored the association, performing none of the duties of secretary, declining to introduce the speakers, and not even attending the lectures. On one occasion, however, Thoreau being the lecturer, Hawthorne had ventured, it seems, into the anteroom; and it being whispered among the audience that he was without, there was some eagerness at the close of the lecture to see him. Do you remember Thackeray's sketch of himself in one of the Roundabout Papers? A rear view like that was all the dispersing crowd could get of Hawthorne, for he had promptly planted his nose in a corner, and as the audience passed by into the street nothing was visible save the broad of his back. And this ludicrous incident is to this day cited as indisputable evidence of the man's innate boorishness. It is claimed, too, that the associates whom Hawthorne seemed to prefer while he was Surveyor of the port of Salem were for the most part stipendiaries of the Customhouse and dubious hangers-on, who were not only Democrats, but quaffers of strong waters, tellers of stories unfit for ears refined, and men whose walk and conversation were not improving. And with such as these Hawthorne was wont to go down the harbor now and then on the government tug, with convivial intent. Undoubtedly all this may be to some extent true. And Hawthorne, who in his earlier days is known to have delighted in sitting, himself unknown, a silent observer in bar-rooms and country taverns, listening to the talk of hangers-on at such resorts, admits freely, in the prologue to the *Scarlet Letter*, how great a change, following his appointment as Surveyor, had occurred in his associates and surroundings: "Such," he says, "were some of the people with whom I now found myself connected. *I took it in good part, at the hands of Providence, that I was thrown into a position so little akin to my past habits, and set myself seriously to gath-

er *whatever profit was at hand.* After my fellowship of toil and impracticable schemes with the dreamy brethren at Brook Farm; after living for three years within the subtle influence of an intellect like Emerson's; after those wild, free days on the Assabeth, indulging fantastic speculations, beside our fire of fallen boughs, with Ellery Channing; after talking with Thoreau about pine-trees and Indian relics, in his hermitage at Walden; after growing fastidious by sympathy with the classic refinement of Hillard's culture; after becoming imbued with poetic sentiment at Longfellow's hearth-stone—it was time, at length, that I should exercise other functions of my nature, *and nourish myself with food for which I had hitherto had little appetite.* Even the old Inspector was desirable, as a change of diet, to a man who had known Alcott. I looked upon it as an evidence, in some measure, of a system naturally well balanced, and lacking no essential part of a thorough organization, that, with such associates to remember, I could mingle at once with men of altogether different qualities, and never murmur at the change."

Let it be said in passing, that the portraiture of the old Inspector here referred to was regarded by many of Hawthorne's warmest friends as a sketch which, in spite of its merit as a bit of inimitable character painting, should not have been published while the original was living; for he had reached a patriarchal age, and was surrounded by children and grandchildren, who must needs boil with pious wrath and indignation at seeing their revered progenitor thus portrayed. And the local haters of Hawthorne now living can not forget nor forgive this act, which, it must be admitted, was as injudicious as it surely was utterly free from any touch of malice or personal aversion.

A man like Hawthorne, or Goethe, or Shakspeare, endowed by the Creator with exceptional genius, lives an ideal life, a life of thought, and may not be gauged by common standards. In a manner they are in the world, but not of it, nor do their souls readily contract taint or blemish. They refuse to be fed on conventionalities and commonplaces.

" Bring me wine, but wine which never grew
    In the belly of the grape,
  Or grew on vine whose tap-roots, reaching through
    Under the Andes to the Cape,
    Suffered no savor of the earth to 'scape."

James finely says: "Hawthorne had a democratic strain in his composition, and a relish for the common stuff of human nature. He liked to fraternize with plain people, to take them on their own terms, and put himself, if possible, into their shoes. His Note-Books, and even his tales, are full of evidence of this easy and natural feeling about all his unconventional fellow-mortals, this imaginative interest and contemplative curiosity, and it sometimes takes the most charming and graceful forms. Commingled as it is with his own subtlety and delicacy, *his complete exemption from vulgarity*, it is one of the points in his character which his reader comes most to appreciate—*that reader, I mean, for whom he is not, as for some few, a dusky and malarious genius.*" And James elsewhere remarks: "In fact, Hawthorne appears to have ignored the good society of his native place almost completely; no echo of its conversation was to be found in his tales or his journals."

A few particulars further regarding Hawthorne's friend and correspondent may not be uninteresting. William B. Pike was born at Salem, October, 1810. He received a public-school education, but stopped short of the High School, and practiced carpentry with his father. His parents were Methodists, and at an early age he became interested in religious matters. He joined the Sewall Street Methodist Church, under the pastorate of Rev. Jesse Fillmore, and became a devoted and successful class-leader. He contemplated entering the ministry, and prepared and preached several sermons. Applying for a position as chaplain in the navy, he was strongly recommended by certain influential gentlemen of Essex County, who respected him for his talents and piety, and under the impression that he had been regularly ordained, represented that as the case in their letters of recommendation. It is said that Pike knew of this error, and that, in his eagerness to secure the appointment, he failed to correct it. However this may be, these gentlemen, happening to learn from his pastor that Pike had not been ordained, recalled their letters, and the chaplain project fell through. This was a great disappointment to Pike, and the failure occurred in a manner so mortifying that in the revulsion he withdrew forever from the Methodist fold, and betook himself for some

years to the Episcopal communion of old St. Peter's. He afterward became profoundly interested in the works of Swedenborg, and was one of the pioneer members of the New Jerusalem Society, which for some years has had a house of worship on Essex Street, and is quite respectable in numbers and intelligence.

About the time of Jackson's election, in 1832, Pike adopted strong Democratic principles, which he held ever after with unswerving fidelity. And he became remarkably well informed in current politics, as well as in general political history, for he had a tenacious memory, and was an insatiable reader. Among his Democratic friends he was regarded as an oracle, and being vigorously aggressive, he became an acknowledged leader of that party in Essex County. In the second year of Van Buren's administration, under the Collectorship of Bancroft the historian, Pike and Hawthorne both secured places at the Boston Custom-house, Pike as assistant measurer, and Hawthorne as weigher and gauger, and both, after a brief service, were rotated out of office. Hawthorne returned to his lonely chamber on Union Street, and to his literary labors, and Pike worked off and on at his trade, but was ever alert as a politician, and wrote frequently for the press. His papers were mostly of a political character, and were contributed chiefly to the Salem *Advertiser* and the *People's Advocate*. These articles appeared generally as editorial, but the authorship was easily recognized, for they were strongly marked with his well-known peculiarities of thought and style.

During the administration of Polk, Pike was commissioned weigher and gauger at the Salem Custom-house, and thereafter, in one capacity or another, remained continuously in the customs service till the end of Buchanan's administration. During the closing hours of the administration of his personal friend Frank Pierce, he was promoted to the Collectorship, then a very lucrative berth. Soon after, he built a residence at Groveland, in a region hallowed by the genius of Whittier. It is opposite the city of Haverhill; and here the valley of the Merrimac, everywhere abundantly beautiful, puts on its loveliest aspects, and will live forever in radiant verse as the scene of Cobbler Keezar's Vision. The period of Pike's residence at Groveland was the sunniest and most fruitful in happy memories of his life. The spot was, indeed,

"A place of nestling green for poets made."

Here he was wont to entertain his friends with generous hospitality. Here, also, he was induced, contrary to the advice of his friends, to put money into a shoe factory; but the venture was not a success, for he had no knowledge of the business, and, besides, he was lacking in the peculiar intelligence and shrewdness, and that instinct for the main chance, which go to make up a successful and enterprising business man. For men like him, savings-banks are the only snug harbor for spare cash.

It was about this time, I think, that Hawthorne, while consul at Liverpool, wrote Pike strongly urging him to throw up his Custom-house berth, and join him there in the capacity of vice-consul; but Pike, it seems, could not be persuaded to go abroad.

Pike had a strongly marked, benignant face, indicative of intelligence and individuality. He was gray at twenty, and always looked older than his years, and his white hairs "thatched an intellectual tenement," capacious and in good repair. His countenance, except when engaged in animated conversation, was grave and kindly. He had a keen sense of the ludicrous, a vivid recollection of localities and incidents, a quick apprehension of personal peculiarities and traits, and he was a most graphic and entertaining narrator. He had, also, a unique way of receiving good things, which was so characteristic and appreciative that if you chanced upon a nux postcoenatica of real genuine old particular flavor, you would surely go with it to Pike. No matter how side-splitting the story might be, he would look you in the eye through it all, with a face perfectly impassive, until the conclusion, and then breaking into a brief volcanic laugh, the grave look would immediately return, as if he were engaged in digesting a matter profoundly serious.

Pike was exceptionally sympathetic and free-handed, especially to his kins-people. He had several sisters, all of whom he survived. Some were married, but not advantageously, and all were at times in straitened circumstances. Generous brother that he was, he kept them ever in mind, looking after and helping them promptly in their straits, even to the

extent, upon occasion, of parting with his last dollar.

For some maiden aunts he hired a small house, where they lived with him in great contentment. It was a sorry apology for a house, to be sure, but the inmates had conceived for it a strong attachment, and the sly owner endeavored to persuade Pike to buy it, offering the house and lot for $1300. So it befell one day that our tender-hearted friend conferred with a fellow-stipendiary of Uncle Sam who happened to know the property well, and asked his advice. "The cellar is damp, I think." Pike admitted this to be the fact, and confessed that a slender stream of water gurgled through the middle of the cellar almost continually. "And there is no cellar wall, I believe. It is merely boarded up, is it not?" Pike gravely, and with child-like innocence, admitted that this also was true. "And is not the house itself a flimsy, ramshackle old rookery? You are a carpenter, Pike, and you dwell in the house, and must be competent to judge of its value." Pike did know all about the house, and then and there told its strange, eventful history. The owner, a house-painter, who has these many years been gathered to his fathers, had managed in some sort of dicker, or in settlement of a debt, to secure a little lot of land on Crombie Street. Upon this lot, it seems, he had hauled first a porch, which was fit for nothing better than fuel, and might have served a useful end in tempering the local baker's oven with reference to its daily yield of brick-loaf, bun, and ginger-bread, or in helping Deacon Safford to brew his famous julep—that horrible decoction, the memory of which to this day hath power to distort the face as if one were quaffing verjuice. But the owner had other aims. By-and-by, watching his chances, he had secured portions of two other dismantled houses, which also were hauled on to the lot. "Hitching these sorry wrecks together somehow," said Pike, "he finally put in a few windows, and *called it a house.*"

Here the colloquy ended. And yet, to the vast amazement of his interlocutor, it transpired not long afterward that Pike had actually bought this thing of shreds and patches. His excuse was that the inmates had become attached to the dwelling (doubtless because their guileless and devoted kinsman had made it a very paradise to their hearts), and the mere fact of this attachment weighed so strongly with Pike that, out of sheer kindliness, the snug little sum of $1300, which he happened to be able to spare at the time, was foolishly flung away upon this insalubrious rattletrap. And shortly after, poor fellow, he fell sick of a slow fever, which Dr. Floto attributed to the dampness of the cellar, and was laid by for many weeks.

The close of every life is a tragedy more or less pathetic. The prophecy of his friend Hawthorne was fulfilled. "*You will never, I fear, make the impression on the world that, in years gone by, I used to hope you would. It will not be your fault, however, but the fault of circumstances. Your flower was not destined to bloom in this world. I hope to see its glory in the next.*" While Pike held the Collectorship, the emoluments of that office had rendered him comforta-

bly well off. Temperate, upright, honorable, singularly pure in heart and life, but generous and free-handed to a fault, when he lost his place and his income, his means dwindled, and he became abjectly poor and dependent; blindness and other infirmities overtook him; but through all these thronging misfortunes his mind was unclouded, and his soul kindly and serene. And so the end drew nigh, and bidding his friends and the world goodnight,

> " He hath crossed the languid river,
>   He hath paid the last obole,
> Day for him hath set forever,
>   He hath won the mystic goal."

Twelve years earlier, Hawthorne had preceded him into the Silent Land; and now his friend of many years has also "sailed beyond the sunset, and touched the Happy Isles."

A NEW ENGLAND GARDEN

WE are apt to have a confused notion regarding our love of nature. To the average man and woman it is not so much nature in its most frankly natural guise that appeals, as nature humanized and made intimate to our lives. "Que belle la solitude," said the Frenchman,

"quand il y a quelqu'un à qui on peut dire que la solitude est belle!" It is just the same with the instinct that impels the city man to make for himself a home in the country, or which leads the man whose lot is cast continually in the country to delight therein. In neither case is there a desire to lose one's self in nature, but rather to impress on it one's personality, and to establish an intimacy with it that will allow one's own individuality to flourish more unrestrictedly.

* The illustrations accompanying this article are of a garden which has just been completed for the Hon. Charles F. Sprague at Brookline, Massachusetts, by Mr. Charles A. Platt, the leading exponent of the formal garden in this country.

THE GARDEN AND CASINO FROM THE TOP OF THE HOUSE.

In his country home, if anywhere, a man should be able to be himself. That "an Englishman's house is his castle" may be a survival of days when the hand of every man was against his fellow, but the enduring fact is that in the home the human unit has its fullest possibility of individual expression, and, above all, in the country home.

The feverish complexity of American city life, in which men are necessarily restricted by so many conventions, has led to a reaction in favor of country residences to which at least a temporary escape may be made. They are being built in all parts of the country, and more and more with the intention that they shall be veritably homes. As a result, the laying out of grounds and gardens is a subject of very present interest.

There are two distinct methods—the formal and the landscape—differing both in principle and in outward manifestations. The adherents of the formal method would make the garden an integral part of the house, the two forming a unified scheme—a "villa," as the Romans called it. (How that poor word has been abused in modern England! Signifying originally a country retreat upon which the owner impressed his individuality, it is now applied to the "suburban residence," that smug contrivance for shaping to one general pattern the home life of so many thousands, and swamping individuality in a colorless mediocrity.) The unity of feeling is obtained by prolonging the architectural character into the immediate surroundings of the house; by preserving in them something of the orderliness, the lines, masses, and balance of the structure itself, and by imparting to them a sense of human occupancy through the repetition of some of the human artifices which are concentrated in the house; in one word, by adopting an arrangement that is architectonic. The supporters of the landscape theory, on the other hand, profess to take their cue from nature. Nature, they say, is the ultimate inspiration, and the highest art is in conforming to its methods. Nature "abhors straight lines," therefore the aim of the landscape gardener should be to eliminate straight lines, to reproduce an ordered disorder, and, in fact, make the demarcation between the house and its surroundings as complete as possible. It is just on this point that it may fairly be said the two schools join clear issues. The object of the landscapist is to suggest that the garden is a part of the landscape; that of the formalist to separate the two and make the garden belong to the house. The former is called the English method, because it has been prac-

tised in England since the beginning of the eighteenth century. It might also be called the American method, for, until recently, the same ideas have prevailed here. In both countries, however, there is a reaction towards the formal garden. This not only has the sanction of universal practice before the eighteenth century, as we shall show presently, but is more in accordance with the purposes and possibilities of a garden.

Let us frankly admit that the latter is largely a sentimental reason. Why not? Surely sentiment should cling to a man's home; a simple and unaffected one, growing out of the conditions, and colored by the individual's idiosyncrasies and means of gratifying them. Now a country house is not complete without some appurtenances. These will ordinarily be the stables and offices, flower and kitchen gardens, approaches to the house, and walks from which the flowers may be enjoyed and the practical needs of the kitchen-garden attended to. One may seek to make these accessories as free as possible from sign of man's handiwork, but it is impossible to separate them in theory or practice from the house. They are all integral parts of one scheme, of which the house is the nucleus and emphatic feature. Then should there not be a uniformity of feeling preserved throughout?

Architecture and nature represent antagonistic principles. Nature is to a great

extent imitated in painting and sculpture, but architecture is an independent creation of man's. In certain details he has taken a hint from natural objects, but still in its main characteristics a building is an excrescence upon nature, in sharp contrast to its surroundings. Perhaps a

DETAIL OF THE STAIRWAY FROM THE HOUSE TO THE GARDEN.

turf-covered hut can be said to grow out of nature; and to a certain extent a woodman's timbered cottage may seem to accord with the surrounding forest, but more by association of ideas than in actual fact. What makes the latter interesting, however, is the evidence of human habitation in the clearing of the trees, the accompanying out-houses, and the scattering around of implements and various paraphernalia which lessen the abrupt contrast between the natural forest and

THE CASINO AND THE PERGOLA.

garden and keep out the rabbits, and the place begins to take on a human, living interest, and has put forth formal roots, as it were, which enable it to hold its own in the contrast with nature.

If this be granted, two conclusions seem to follow: firstly, that the chief artificial feature, the house, does need some subsidiary ones; and, secondly, that they and it are mutually related. Then surely it results that the relationship should be frankly admitted and logically expressed. Logic in this case requires that, as the house is entirely formal, as different as possible from nature, some degree of formality should embrace the arrangement of the subsidiary features. The formality of the house is the consequence of architecture, and it is by a prolongation of architectural devices into the immediate surroundings that they will be made in a measure formal. In a measure only, because the flowers, trees, and vegetables will soften the rigidity. Need one add that the architectural features do not necessarily include all the appurtenances which were mentioned above by way of illustration? They will vary according to the size and character of the house. The first characteristic of a house is that it forms a mass, so the garden should be compact rather than amorphous. The second characteristic is straight lines

the artificial structure. But, substitute for the timbered cottage a residence of larger dimensions and greater degree of formality, deliberately refrain from surrounding it with any signs of method and orderliness, leave it in complete contrast with the picturesque disorder of the forest, and it would look strangely incongruous, even uncanny, in its solitariness. It would be equally so if placed in a more open site—upon the side of a hill, for example. Group near it, however, a stable and barn, a gardener's and coachman's cottage, laundry, cow-house, and the other offices of a country residence, add only a fence to enclose the kitchen-

vertical and horizontal; therefore the principal paths, terraces, and bounding lines should be straight rather than rambling. The third characteristic is balance, so that the several parts into which the immediate surroundings are divided should preserve a due relation to one another and to the central mass. Lastly, that which completes the charm of any residence is the evidence of human habitation, of its being a home. In the same way, the most delightful thing about a garden is the fact that it is artificial, that it has been contrived by man, and in some *one* way more than another, because the men and women who used it and loved it delighted to have it so. M. Brunetière, in his recent lecture on "Art and Morality," said, "We have become men, and can become more so each day only by detaching ourselves from nature, and by trying to institute in the midst of it 'an empire within an empire.'" The context of his argument was different, but this thought contains the germ-principle of the formal garden. We fly from the restrictions of the city not that we may lose ourselves in the impersonality of nature, but for detachment; that in the soothing and unexacting companionship of nature we may find ourselves. This is our end, and the means we employ are human artifices rather than imitations of nature.

We shall feel this individual human influence pervading the home as soon as

we turn aside from the country road. And, by-the-way, what a beautiful feature of the landscape a road is! For example, that white serpentine road which creeps from the head of Lake Lucerne up into the fastnesses of the St. Gothard Pass— appearing, disappearing, and reappearing, gliding over stone arches above the torrent, making a turn at times to avoid some obstacle, but gaining vantage farther

THE CASINO.

on, steadily mounting—a testimony to the patient, indomitable effort of man. We may admire the unrestrained grandeur of the Alpine scenery none the less for loving that road; and as long as we were neither cynics nor hermits, and had to make a home in those mountains, we should choose it to be within sight of that road. And why? Simply because it sets a human impress upon nature, and pre-

THE GARDEN WALK, FROM THE PERGOLA TO THE TERRACE STAIRWAY.

al welcome to the mansion. We have no concern here with the house itself, but, imagining ourselves guests, we find the gardens open to us and contributing to the hospitality. Step out on to the broad terrace, which invites promenade and offers a view of the garden, very likely of the landscape beyond. Its sides may be bevelled slopes of grass, or formed of masonry with balustrades; in either case it will testify to human contrivance and care. It is an open-air continuation of the social possibilities of the house. Below it and approached by steps is the flower-garden, symmetrically

vents one's own individuality from being absolutely swallowed up.

But to resume our approach to the country house. The formal entrance to the grounds, be it only a gate within two well-defined posts, marks the transition from outside. The drive with its carefully kept surface, trim borders and shrubs on either hand, most dignified if it runs beneath an avenue of trees, leads up to a fore-court—an open space in front of the hall door. Ranged around this used to be, and often still are, the stables and offices. Anyhow, its characteristics are spacious and orderly, suggesting a form-

shaped and bounded by walls, balustrades, or clipped hedges. The side which gets the sun will probably have its wall brilliant with climbing roses. All round the garden is a border filled with annuals and perennials, whose variety and free growth pleasantly assuage the stiffness of the lines and boundaries. The interior space is geometrically divided up into beds, edged with trim box borders and separated by smooth gravel paths. The flatness of the effect is relieved by trees in pots, trimmed to shape, or "pleached," to use the old English word for a practice derived at least from Pliny's time. The beds in their summer bravery of color are contrasted with their green borders, and with the light hue of the gravel walks; and the geometrical pattern which all three combine to make exhibits the planning of a human mind and the infinite care and detailed skill of human husbandry. Special objects of interest are disposed about the garden, varying, according to the fancy and means of the owner, from a simple seat commanding some choice view or inviting to quiet and shade, up to fountains, statuary, and a formal summer-house. The old English word for the last was "gazebo"; "casino" the Italians called it, adding often a "pergola," or colonnade, topped with transverse beams at intervals for the support of vines. Should your eye tire for a moment of these human artifices, it can roam across the low boundary on the shady side to the rolling uplands beyond, sprinkled with trees or plumaged in straggling patches with the thick foliage of the woods. You can still enjoy the spontaneity of nature and the freedom of wide expanse of earth and sky, and then come back with a renewed sense of intimacy to the ordered details of the garden, which, whether modest or sumptuous, are such as man has made them, because he loved to have them so, and wished to make this little spot of earth, called home, an individual personal possession.

This, too, was the traditional idea of a garden. Pliny the younger, as mentioned above, wrote of his Tuscan villa, describing the architectural features in which the garden abounded. Here was the text which the architects of the Italian Renaissance expanded in their treatment of

country houses. Le Nôtre followed them in laying out the gardens of Versailles. In old England the formal garden flourished, independent at first alike of Italian and French influence; a tradition of Pliny filtered down through mediævalism. No example of the mediæval gardens survives in England, but an idea of them may be formed from illuminated manuscripts. "The Romance of the Rose," for example,

THE STAIRWAY FROM THE GARDEN TO THE TERRACE.

in the British Museum (Harleian MS. 4425), contains an illumination showing a formal garden walled in and entered by a gateway, with fountain, rectangular grass-plots separated by walks, a fence of flowers on a wooden trellis, and amongst other trees a "pleached" orange-tree. From the chapter-house accounts given in the *History of Hampton Court Pal-*

ON THE TERRACE, LOOKING TOWARD THE STAIRWAY AND THE CASINO.

ace it is clear that Wolsey laid out the gardens with enclosing walls, "knottes" or figured flower-beds, arbors, and alleys. When, after Wolsey's death, the palace came into the hands of Henry VIII., he introduced statues and various devices, probably borrowed from Italy. At any rate it is certain that in building his palace of Nonsuch, near Cheam in Surrey, he employed Italian workmen, and there is little doubt that Italian examples were freely copied in the gardens. Hentzner, a German who travelled through England in the sixteenth century, published an account in Latin of many gardens, amongst others Lord Burleigh's, which were clearly inspired by those of Italy. From this time on it is easy to trace the history of the formal garden in England, for numerous treatises were written on the subject. The point to notice is that the advisability of adhering to the tradition of the formal garden is never questioned by these writers, who only concern themselves with its development. By degrees these refinements resulted in extravagant conceits, spontaneity was lost in a pedantic system, and a revolt ensued.

Addison began the attack in *The Spectator;* Pope followed it up in *The Guardian*, and made much fun of the ridiculous lengths to which the practice of "pleaching" had been carried. He gives a catalogue of some of the objects represented, including "a St. George in box, his arm scarce long enough, but will be in a condition to stab the Dragon by next April"; and "a quickset hog shot up into a porcupine through being forgot a week in rainy weather." He laid out his own grounds at Twickenham, down by Thames' side, in what was now called the "natural" manner, and the vogue spread all over England. Kent, the architect, devoted himself to laying out grounds in imitation of Claude and Poussin. Walpole, the master of Strawberry Hill Gothic, goes into nicely modulated raptures over Kent's achievements. "Selecting favorite objects, and veiling deformities by screens of plantations, he realized the compositions of the greatest masters in painting. The living landscape was chastened and polished, not transformed." Then, as now, it should be noticed, the "natural" method consisted in playing pranks with nature, disguising or improving it at will. The formal garden still had its champions.

One of them, Sir William Chambers, writes: "Our virtuosi have scarcely left an acre of shade, or three trees growing in a line, from the Land's End to the Tweed." Under the wave of naturalism, however, nearly all the old gardens of England were obliterated.

The landscape gardener, as Mr. Reginald Blomfield says in his book *The Formal Garden in England*, "turns his back upon architecture at the earliest opportunity, and devotes his energies to making the garden suggest natural scenery, to giving a false impression as to its size by sedulously concealing all boundary lines, and to modifying the scenery by planting or cutting down trees, as may be necessary to what he calls a picture." Again, "Deception is a primary object of the landscape gardener, and thus to get variety and to deceive the eye into supposing that the garden is larger than it is, the paths are made to wind about in all directions, and the lawns are not to be left in broad expanse, but dotted about with pampas grasses, foreign shrubs, or anything else that will break up the surface." As was said by a witty Frenchman, "Rien n'est plus facile que de dessiner un parc anglais; on n'a qu'à enivrer son jardinier et à suivre sa trace."

For nearly two centuries the incoherent affectation of the "natural" garden has been perpetuated, but a reaction has at last set in. Both in America and in England we are discovering that the house and garden are logically, sentimentally, and practically one. Instead of employing an architect to design the one and a gardener to fumble over the other, we are intrusting both to the architect. In seeking inspiration, it is only reasonable that

he should turn to Italy, where the tradition of the formal garden has been maintained and treated with such refinement. The problem is to adapt these methods to the different climatic and social conditions

THE GROTTO AND THE TERRACE.

of America. The subject is an important one, even to those who cannot have country homes, for it includes also the laying out of parks and public squares in a city— of any grounds, in fact, which are associated with architecture. It is beginning to be realized that the rambling haphazard of our New York squares, for instance, will not compare in dignity and reposefulness with the formal arrangements adopted on the continent of Europe. The subject will therefore take its place in the movement that is astir for municipal embellishment.

JOHN GREENLEAF WHITTIER

WHITTIER, the poet and the man, has been personally described quite as often as any of the New England authors. His private life has been searched out in every detail, until, grateful and pleased as he became in later years with all friendly recognition, he was led even in his verse to deprecate the publicity which exposed the simple manners of his homely existence.

> "O living friends who love me,
> O dear ones gone above me,
> Careless of other fame,
> I leave to you my name.
> Hide it from idle praises,
> Save it from evil phrases.
> Why, when dear lips that spake it
> Are dumb, should strangers wake it?"

The testimony of Whittier's "living friends" will be gathered together from many and various hands, because he has filled a large place in the life of our republic. Remote from the field of battle, he has nevertheless been present in spirit and by his influence at many a national conflict, and has comprehended the situation of affairs from his own retired standpoint with remarkable clearness and common-sense.

The picture of his poetic figure will never be absent from the gallery of men beloved by the people of the United States. He stands holding the double crown of patriot and poet, and will be remembered in war-time with Garrison and Phillips, and in all time with Emerson and Lowell, Longfellow and Holmes. The solitary

JOHN GREENLEAF WHITTIER AT FORTY-FIVE.

people of the world have always turned to Whittier as one whose personal experience made him peculiarly their friend.

A life of invalidism made consecutive labor of any kind an impossibility. For years he was only able to write for half an hour or less, without stopping to rest, and these precious moments were devoted to some poem or other work for the press which was almost his only source of income. His letters suffered, looked at from a literary point of view; they were brief and unstudied, and often filled to him the place of "personal talk," but they were none the less delightful to his friends; to the world of literature they are perhaps less important than those of most men who have achieved a high place. With the advance of years, and the death of his unmarried sister, his friends became all in all to him. They were his mother, his sister, and his brother; but in a certain sense they were always friends of the imagination. He saw some of them only at rare intervals, and sustained his relations with them chiefly in his hurried correspondence.

Whittier was between twenty and thirty years of age when his family left the little farm near Haverhill, where he was born, and moved into the town of Amesbury, eight miles distant. Meanwhile he had identified himself with the antislavery cause, and had visited, in the course of his ceaseless labors for the slaves, New York, Philadelphia, and Washington. These brief journeys bounded his travels in this world.

In the year 1843 he wrote anxiously to his publisher, Mr. Fields, "I send with this 'The Exiles,' a kind of John Gilpin legend. I am in doubt about it. Read it and decide for thyself whether it is worth printing."

He began at this rather late period (he was then thirty-six years old) to feel a touch of satisfaction in his comparatively new occupation of writing poetry, and to speak of it without reserve to his chosen friends. His poems were then beginning to bring him into personal relation with the reading world. Many years later, when speaking of the newspaper writing which absorbed his earlier life, he said that he had written a vast amount for the press; he thought that his work would fill nearly ten octavo volumes; but he had grown utterly weary of throwing so much out into space from which no response ever came back to him. At length he decided to put it all aside, discovering that a power lay in him for more congenial labors.

From the moment of the publication of his second volume of poems, Whittier felt himself fairly launched upon a new career, and seemed to stand with a responsive audience before him. The poems "Toussaint L'Ouverture," "The Slave-Ships," and others belonging to the same period followed in quick succession.

. A homely native wit pointed Whittier's familiar correspondence. Writing in 1849, while revising his volume for publication, he speaks of one of his poems as "that rascally old ballad 'Kathleen,'" and adds that it "wants something, though it is already too long." He adds: "The weather this morning is cold enough for an Esquimaux purgatory—terrible. What did the old Pilgrims mean by coming here?"

With the years, his friendship with his publisher became more intimate. In writing him he often indulged his humor for fun and banter: "Bachelor as I am, I congratulate thee on thy escape from single (misery!) blessedness. It is the very wisest thing thee ever did. Were I autocrat, I would see to it that every young man over twenty-five and every young woman over twenty was married without delay. Perhaps, on second thought, it might be well to keep one old maid and one old bachelor in each town, by way of warning, just as the Spartans did their drunken helots."

Discussing the question of some of his "bad rhymes," and what to do about them, he wrote once: "I heartily thank thee for thy suggestions. Let me have more of them. I had a hearty laugh at thy hint of the 'carnal' bearing of one of my lines. It is now simply *rural*. I might have made some other needful changes had I not been suffering with headache all day."

Occasionally the fire which burned in him would flame out, as when he writes in 1851: "So your Union-tinkers have really caught a 'nigger' at last! A very pretty and refreshing sight it must have been to Sabbath-going Christians yesterday—that *chained* court-house of yours. And Bunker Hill Monument looking down upon all! But the matter is too sad for irony. God forgive the miserable politicians who gamble for office with dice *loaded* with human hearts!"

From time to time, also, we find him expressing his literary opinions, eagerly and simply as friend may talk with friend, and without aspiring to literary judgment. "Thoreau's *Walden* is capital reading, but very wicked and heathenish. The practical moral of it seems to be that if a man is willing to sink himself into a woodchuck he can live as cheaply as that quadruped; but, after all, for me, I prefer walking on two legs."

It would be unjust to Whittier to quote this talk on paper as his final opinion upon Thoreau, for he afterward read everything he wrote, and was a warm appreciator of his work.

His enthusiasm for books and for the writers of books never faded. "What do we not all owe you," he writes Mr. Fields, "for your edition of De Tocqueville! It is one of the best books of the century. Thanks, too, for Allingham's poems. After Tennyson, he is my favorite among modern British poets."

Again: "I have just read Longfellow's introduction to his 'Tales of the Inn'—a splendid piece of painting! Neither Boccaccio nor Chaucer has done better. Who wrote 'A

HOME AT AMESBURY.

Loyal Woman's No?' Was it Lucy Larcom? I thought it might be."

In 1866 he says: "I am glad to see 'Hosea Biglow' in book form. It is a grand book; the best of its kind for the last half-century or more. It has wit enough to make the reputation of a dozen English satirists."

This appreciation of his contemporaries was a strong feature of his character. His sympathy with the difficulties of a literary life, particularly for women, was very keen. There seem to be few women writers of his time who have failed to receive from his pen some token of recognition. Of Edith Thomas he once said in one of his notelets, "She has a divine gift, and her first book is more than a promise—an assurance." Of Sarah Orne Jewett he was fond as of a daughter, and from their earliest acquaintance his letters are filled with appreciation of her stories. "I do not wonder," he wrote one day, that *The Luck of the Bogans* is attractive to the Irish folks, and to everybody else. It is a very successful departure from New England life and scenery, and shows that Sarah is as much at home in Ireland and on the Carolina Sea Islands as in Maine or Massachusetts. I am very proud that I was one of the first to discover her." This predisposition to think well of the work of others gave him the happy opportunity in more than one instance of bringing authors of real talent before the public who might otherwise have waited long for general recognition.

This was especially the case with one of our best beloved New England writers, Lucy Larcom. As early as 1853 he wrote a letter to his publisher introducing her work to his notice. "I enclose," he says, "what I regard as a very unique and beautiful little book in MS. I don't wish thee to take my opinion, but the first leisure hour thee have, read it, and I am sure thee will decide that it is exactly the thing for publication. . . . The little prose poems are unlike anything in our literature, and remind me of the German writer Lessing. They are equally adapted to young and old. . . . The author, Lucy Larcom, of Beverly, is a novice in writing and book-making, and with no ambition to appear in print, and were I not perfectly certain that her little collection is worthy of type, I would be the last to encourage her to take even this small step to publicity. Read 'The Impression of Rain-drops,' 'The Steamboat and Niagara,' 'The Laughing Water,' 'My Father's House,' etc."

He thus early became the foster-father of Lucy Larcom's children of the brain, and, what was far more to her, a life-long friend, adviser, and supporter.

One of his most intimate personal friends for many years was Lydia Maria Child. Beginning in the earliest days of the antislavery struggle, their friendship lasted into the late and peaceful sunset

PORTRAIT FROM PHOTOGRAPH TAKEN AT THE ASQUAM HOUSE, JULY, 1885.

tivals indeed. They would sit side by side, while memories crowded up and filled their faces with a tenderness they could not express in words. As they told their tales and made merry, they would sit with their hands on each other's knees, and with glances in which tears and laughter were closely intermingled.

"It was good to see Mrs. Child," some one remarked after one of those interviews.

"Yes," said Whittier, "Liddy's bunnets aren't always in the fashion" (with a quaint look, as much as to say, I wonder what you think of anything so bad), "but we don't like her any the worse for that."

Shortly after Mrs. Child's death he wrote from Amesbury: "My heart has been heavy ever since I heard of dear Maria Child's death. The true, noble, loving soul! *Where* is she? *What* is she?

How is she? The moral and spiritual economy of God will not suffer such light and love to be lost in blank annihilation. She was herself an evidence of immortality. In a letter written to me at seventy years of age she said: 'The older I grow the more I am awestruck (not frightened, but awed) by the great mystery of an existence here and hereafter. No thinking can solve the problem. Infinite wisdom has purposely sealed it from our eyes.'"

In 1862 and '63 Whittier was in frequent correspondence with Mr. Fields. Poems suggested by the stirring times were crowding thick upon his mind.

of their days. As Mrs. Child advanced in years, it was her custom in the winter to leave her cottage at Wayland for a few months and to take lodgings in Boston. The dignity and independence of Mrs. Child's character were so great that she knew her friends would find her wherever she might live, and her desire to help on the good work of the world led her to practise the most austere economies.

Mrs. Child's chief pleasure in coming to town was the opportunity she found of seeing her friends. Whittier always sought her out, and their meetings at the houses of their mutual cronies were fes-

"It is a great thing to live in these days. I am thankful for what I have lived to see and hear," he says. "There is nothing for us but the old Methodist ejaculation, 'Glory to God!'"

The volume entitled *In War-time* appeared at this period, though, as usual, he seems to have had little strength and spirit for the revision of his poems. For this, however unwillingly, he would often throw himself upon the kindness of his friend and publisher.

In writing to ask some consideration for the manuscript of an unknown lady during this year, he adds: "I ought to have sent to you about this lady's MS. long ago, but the fact is, I *hate* to bother you with such matters. I am more and more impressed with the Christian tolerance and patience of publishers, beset as you are with legions of clamorous authors, male and female. I should think you would hate the very sight of one of these *importunates*. After all, Fields, let us own the truth: *writing folks are bores*. How few of us (let them say what they will of our genius) have any common-sense! I take it that it is the Providential business of authors and publishers to torment each other."

These little friendly touches in his correspondence show us the man far more distinctly than many pages of writing about him. Some one has said that Whittier's epistolary style was perfect. Doubtless he could write as good a letter on occasion as any man who ever lived, but he sustained no such correspondence. His notes and letters were homely and affectionate, with the delightful carelessness possible in the talk of intimate friends. They present no ordinary picture of human tenderness, devotion, and charity, and these qualities gain a wonderful beauty when we remember that they come from the same spirit which cried out with Ezekiel:

"The burden of a prophet's power
Fell on me in that fearful hour;
From off unutterable woes
The curtain of the future rose;
I saw far down the coming time
The fiery chastisement of crime;
With noise of mingling hosts, and jar
Of falling towers and shouts of war,
I saw the nations rise and fall
Like fire-gleams on my tent's white wall."

"The fire and fury of the brain" were his indeed; a spirit was in him to redeem the land; he was one of God's interpreters; but there was also the tenderness of divine humanity, the love and patience of those who dwell in the courts of the Lord.

Whittier's sister Elizabeth was a sensitive woman, whose delicate health was a constant source of anxiety to her brother, especially after the death of their mother, when they were left alone together in the home at Amesbury. As one of their intimate friends said, no one could tell which would die first, but they were each so anxious about the other's health that it was a question which would wear away into the grave first, for the other's sake.

It was Whittier's sad experience to be deprived of the companionship of all those most dear to him, and for over twenty years to live without that intimate household communion for the loss of which the world holds no recompense. For several years, before and after his sister Elizabeth's death, Whittier wore the look of one who was very ill. His large dark eyes burned with peculiar fire, and contrasted with his pale brow and attenuated figure. He had a sorrowful, stricken look, and found it hard enough to reconstruct his life, missing the companionship and care of his sister, and her great sympathy with his own literary work. There was a likeness between the two; the same speaking eyes marked the line from which they sprang, and their kinship and inheritance. Old New England people were quick to recognize "the Batchelder eyes," not only in the Whittiers, but in Daniel Webster, Caleb Cushing, Nathaniel Hawthorne, and William Batchelder Greene, a man less widely known than these distinguished compatriots. Mr. Greene was, however, a man of mark in his own time, a daring thinker, and one who was possessed of much brave originality, whose own deep thoughtfulness was always planting seeds of thought in others, and who can certainly never be forgotten by those who were fortunate enough to be his friends.

These men of the grand eyes were all descended from a gifted old preacher of great fame in early colonial days, a man of true distinction and devoted service, in spite of the dishonor with which he let his name be shadowed in his latest years. It would be most interesting to trace the line still farther back into the past, but when the Batchelder eyes were by any chance referred to in Whittier's presence, he would look shyly askance, and sometimes speak, half with pride, half with a sort of humorous compassion, of his Hampton ancestor. The connection of the Whittiers of Haverhill with the Greenes was somewhat closer than with other branches of the Batchelder line. One of the poet's most entertaining reminiscences of his boyhood was the story of his first visit to Boston. Mr. William Greene's mother was an interesting woman of strong, independent character and wide interests, wonted to the life of cities, and one of the first, in spite of his boyish shyness, to appreciate her young relative. Her kind eagerness, during one of her occasional visits to the Whittiers, that Greenleaf should come to see her when he came to Boston, fell in with his own dreams, and a high desire to see the sights of the great town.

One can easily imagine how his imagination must have glorified the natural expectations of a country boy, and when the time arrived, how the whole household lent itself to furthering so great an expedition. He was not only to have a new suit of clothes, but they were, for the first time, to be trimmed with "boughten buttons," to the lad's complete satisfaction, his mind being fixed upon those as marking the difference between town and country fashions. When the preparations were made, his fresh homespun costume, cut after the best usage of the Society of Friends, seemed to him all that heart could desire, and he started away bravely by the coach to pass a week in Boston. His mother had not forgotten to warn him of possible dangers and snares; it was then that he made her a promise which, at first from principle and later from sentiment, he always most sacredly kept—that he would not enter a playhouse. As he told the story, it was easy for a listener to comprehend how many good wishes flew after the adventurer, and how much wild beating of the heart he himself experienced as the coach rolled away; how bewildering the city streets appeared when he found himself at the brief journey's end. After he had reported himself to Mrs. Greene, and been received with most affectionate hospitality, and had promised to reappear at tea-time, he sallied forth to the great business of sight-seeing.

"I wandered up and down the streets," he used to say. "Somehow it wasn't just what I expected, and the crowd was worse and worse after I got into Washington Street; and when I got tired of being jostled, it seemed to me as if the folks might get by if I waited a little while. Some of them looked at me, and so I stepped into an alleyway and waited and looked out. Sometimes there didn't seem to be so many passing, and I thought of starting, and then they'd begin again. 'Twas a terrible stream of people to me. I began to think my new clothes and the buttons were all thrown away. I staid there a good while." (This was said with great amusement.) "I began to be homesick. I thought it made no difference at all about my having those boughten buttons."

How long he waited, or what great thoughts may have come from this first glimpse at the ceaseless procession of humanity, who can say? But there was a sequel to the tale. He was invited to return to Mrs. Greene's to drink tea and meet a company of her guests. Among them were some ladies who were very gay and friendly; we can imagine that they were attracted by the handsome eyes and quaint garb of the young Friend, and by his quick wit and homely turns of speech, all the more amusing for a rustic flavor. They tried to tease him a little, but they must have quickly found their match in drollery, while the lad was already a citizen of the commonwealth of books. No doubt the stimulus of such a social occasion brought him, as well as the strangers, into new acquaintance with his growing gifts. But presently one of the ladies, evidently the favorite until this shocking moment, began to speak of the theatre, and asked for the pleasure of his presence at the play that very night, she herself being the leading player. At this disclosure, and the frank talk of the rest of the company, their evident interest in the stage, and regard for a young person who had chosen such a profession, the young Quaker lad was stricken with horror. In after-years he could only remember it with amusement, but that night his mother's anxious warnings rang in his ears, and he hastened to escape from such a snare. Somehow this pleasant young companion of the tea party hardly represented the wickedness of playhouses as Puritan New England loved to picture them; but between a sense of disappointment and homesickness and general insecurity, he could not sleep, and next morning when the early stage-coach started forth, it carried him as passenger. He said nothing to his amazed family of the alarming episode of the playing-woman, nor of his deep consciousness of the home-made clothes, but he no doubt reflected much upon this Boston visit in the leisure of the silent fields and hills.

It is impossible to convey to those who never saw Mr. Whittier, the charm of his gift of story-telling; the exactness and simplicity of his reminiscences were flavored by his poetical insight and dramatic representation. It was a wonderful thing to hear him talk in the twilight of the scenes of his youth, and the figures that came and went in that small world; the pathos and humor of his speech can never be exceeded; and there can never be again so complete a linking of the ancient provincial lore and the new life and thought of New England as there was in him. While he was with us, his poems seemed hardly to give sufficient witness of that rich store of thought and knowledge; he was always making his horizon wider, at the same time that he came into closer sympathy with things near at hand. For him the ancient customs of a country neighborhood, the simple characters, the loves and hates and losses of a rural household, stood for a type of human life in every age, and were never trivial or narrow. As he grew older, they became less and less personal. He sometimes appeared to think of death rather than the person who had died, and of love and grief rather than of those who felt their influence. His was the life of the poet first of all, and yet the tale of his sympathetic friendliness, and his generosities and care-taking for others will never be fully told. The dark eyes had great powers of insight; they could flash scorn as well as shine with the soft light of encouragement.

He accustomed himself, of course, to more frequent visits to Boston after his sister's death, but he was seldom, if ever, persuaded to go to the Saturday Club, to which so many of his friends belonged. Sometimes he would bring a new poem for a private first reading, and for that purpose would stay to breakfast or luncheon, but late dinners were contrary to the habit of his life, and he seldom sat down to one.

In the spring of 1865 he came to Campton, on the Pemigewasset River, in New Hampshire, a very beautiful place for those who love green hills and the mystery of rivers.

We were passing a few weeks there by ourselves, and it was a great surprise and pleasure to see our friend. He drove up to the door one afternoon just as the sun was slanting to the west, too late to drive away again that day. In our desire to show him all the glories of the spot, we carried him out at once, up the hill-side, leaping across the brook, gathering pennyroyal and Indian posy as we went, past the sheep, and on and up, until he, laughing, said: "Look here, I can't follow thee; besides, I think I've seen more of this life than thee have, and it isn't all so new to me! Come and sit down here; I'm tired." We sat awhile overlooking the wonderful panorama, the winding river, the hills, and fields all green and radiant, listening at times to a mountain stream which came with wild and solitary roar from its solemn home among the farther heights. Presently we returned to supper; and afterward, sitting in the little parlor which looked toward the sunset on the high hills far away, his mind seemed to rise also into a higher atmosphere. He began by quoting the last verse of Emerson's "Sphinx":

"Uprose the merry Sphinx,
    And couched no more in stone;
She melted into purple cloud,
    She silvered in the moon;
She spired into a yellow flame;
    She flowered in blossoms red;
She flowed into a foaming wave;
    She stood Monadnock's head."

He talked long and earnestly upon the subject of our spiritual existence independent of the body. I have often heard him dwell upon this subject since; but the awful glory of the hills, the dark and silence of our little parlor, the assured speech touching the unseen, of one who had thought much and suffered much, and found a refuge in the tabernacle not made with hands, were very impressive. We felt "it was good for us to be there." Speaking of his faith in the visions of others—though he did not have these visions himself, and believed they were not vouchsafed to all—he told us of a prophecy that was written down twenty-five years before by an old man in Sandwich (a village among the hills, about fifteen miles from Campton), predicting the terrible civil war which had just been raging between the North and the South.

This man was in the fields at noonday, when a darkness fell upon his vision and covered the earth. He beheld the divided nation and the freed people and the final deliverance from the terrors of war. The whole series of events was clearly detailed, and Whittier had stored them away in his memory. He said that only one was wrong. He foretold foreign intervention, from which we were happily spared. The daughter of this prophet was living; he knew her well—an excellent woman and a Friend who was often impressed to speak in meeting. "She is good," said Whittier, "and speaks from her experience, and for that reason I like to hear her; but, not knowing how to present her thoughts, she says all she has to say in fifteen minutes, but talks an hour; so I listen fifteen minutes. The rest I do not hear."

Spiritualism, as it is called in our day, was a subject which earnestly and steadily held his attention. Having lived very near to the Salem witchcraft experience in early times, the topic was one that came more closely home to his mind than to almost any one else in our century. There are many passages in his letters on this question which state his own mental position very clearly.

"I have had as good a chance to see a ghost," he once said, "as anybody ever had, but not the slightest sign ever came to me. I do not doubt what others tell me, but I sometimes wonder over my own incapacity. I should like to see some dear ghost walk in and sit down by me when I am here alone. The doings of the old witch days have never been explained, and, as we are so soon to be transferred to another state, how natural it appears that some of us should have glimpses of it here! We all feel the help we receive from the Divine Spirit. Why deny, then, that some men have it more directly and more visibly than others?"

In Robert Dale Owen he always took a strong and friendly interest; and when, late in life, reverses fell upon him in the shape of humiliating revelations of his own credulity, Whittier's relations to him were unchanged. "I have read with renewed interest," he wrote, "the paper of R. D. Owen. I had a long talk with him years ago on the subject. He was a very noble and good man, and I was terribly indignant when he was so deceived by the pretended materialized 'Katie King.' I could never quite believe in 'materialization,' as I had reason to know that much of it was fraudulent. It surely argues a fathomless depth of depravity to trifle with the yearning love of those who have lost dear ones, and 'long for the touch of a vanished hand.'

In the year 1866 a very fine portrait of Abraham Lincoln was engraved by Marshall. A copy of it was presented to Whittier, who wrote concerning it: "It was never my privilege to know Abraham Lincoln personally, and the various pictures have more or less failed to satisfy my conception of him. They might be, and probably were, what are called 'good likenesses,' so far as outline and detail were concerned; but to me they always seemed to lack one great essential of a true portrait—the informing spirit of the man within. This I find in Marshall's portrait. The old harsh lines and unmistakable mouth are there, without flattery or compromise; but over all and through all the pathetic sadness, the wise simplicity and tender humanity of the man are visible. It is the face of the speaker at Gettysburg, and the writer of the second inaugural."

It was during this year, also, that the "Tent on the Beach" was written. He had said again and again in his notes that he had this work in hand, but always declared he was far too ill to finish it during the year. Nevertheless, in the last days of December the package was forwarded to his publisher. "Tell me," he wrote, "if thee object to the personal character of it. I have represented thee and Bayard Taylor and myself living a wild tent life for a few summer days on the beach, where, for lack of something better, I read my stories to the others. My original plan was the old 'Decameron' one, each personage to read his own poems; but the thing has been so hackneyed by repetition that I abandoned it in disgust, and began anew. The result is before thee. Put it in type or the fire. I am content—like Eugene Aram, 'prepared for either fortune.'"

He had intended also to accomplish some work in prose at this period, but the painful condition of his health forbade it. "I am forbidden to use my poor head," he said, "so I have to get along as I can without it. The Catholic St. Leon, thee knows, walked alert as usual after his head was cut off."

I am tempted to quote still further from a letter of this period: "I enclose a poem of mine which has never seen the light, although it was partly in print from my first draft to spare me the trouble of copying. It presents my view of Christ as the special manifestation of the love of God to humanity.... Let me thank the publisher of Milton's prose for the compliment of the dedication. Milton's prose has long been my favorite reading. My whole life has felt the influence of his writings."

There is a delightful note on the subject of the popularity of the "Tent on the Beach," which shows his natural pleasure in success. "Think," he says, "of bagging in this tent of ours an unsuspecting public at the rate of a thousand a day! This will never do. The swindle is awful. Barnum is a saint to us. I am bowed with a sense of guilt, ashamed to look an honest man in the face. But Nemesis is on our track; somebody will puncture our tent yet, and it will collapse like a torn balloon. I know I shall have to catch it; my back tingles in anticipation."

It was perhaps in this same year, 1866, that we made an autumn visit to Whittier, which is still a well-remembered pleasure. The weather was warm and the fruit was ripening in the little Amesbury garden. We loitered about for a while, I remember, in the afternoon, among the falling pear leaves and in the sweet air, but he soon led the way into his garden-room, and fell into talk. He was an adept in the art of conversation, having trained himself in the difficult school of a New England farm-house, fit ground for such athletics, being typically bare of suggestion and of relief from outside sources. The unbroken afternoons and the long evenings, when the only hope of entertainment is in such fire as one brain can strike from another, produce a situation as difficult to the unskilled as that of an untaught swimmer when first cast into the sea. Persons long habituated to these contests could face the position calmly, and see the early "tea things" disappear and the contestants draw their chairs around the fire with a kind of zeal; but to one new to such experience there was room for heart-sinkings when preparations were made, by putting fresh sticks on the fire, for sitting from gloaming to vespers, and sometimes on again unwearied till midnight.

Mrs. Stowe and Whittier were the invincible Lancelots of these tourneys, and any one who has had the privilege of sitting by the New England hearth-stone with either of them, will be ready to confess that no playhouse, or game, or any of the distractions the city may afford, can compare with the satisfaction of such an experience. Upon the visit in question, Whittier talked of the days of his antislavery life in 1835 or '36, when the English agitator, George Thompson, first came to this country. The latter was suffering from the attack of many a mob, and was fatigued by frequent speaking and as frequent abuse. Whittier invited him to his home in the neighborhood of Haverhill, where he could find quiet and rest during the warm weather. Thompson accepted the invitation, and remained with him a fortnight. They used to rake hay together, and go about the farm unmolested. At length, however, a pressing invitation came for Thompson to go to Concord, New Hampshire, to speak in the cause of freedom, and afterward to continue on to the village of Plymouth and visit a friend in that place. Whittier was included in the invitation, and it was settled that they should accept the call. They travelled peaceably enough, in their own chaise, as far as Concord, where the speech was delivered without interruption; but when they attempted to leave the hall after the address was ended, they found it almost impossible. A crowd followed them with the apparent intention of stoning and killing them. "I understood how St. Paul felt when he was thrice stoned," said Whittier. The missiles fell around them and upon them like hail, not touching their heads, providentially, although he could still remember the sound the stones made when they missed their aim and struck the wooden fence behind them. They were made very lame by the blows, but they managed to reach their friend's house, where they sprang up the steps three at a time, before the crowd knew where they were going. Their host was certainly a brave man, for he met them at the door, and throwing it open, exclaimed, "Whoever comes in here must come over my dead body." The door was then barricaded, and the crowd rushed round to the back of the house, thinking that their victims intended to go out that way; but they waited until it was dark, when Whittier exchanged his friend's hat for that of his host, and anything else peculiar about his dress being well disguised, the two managed to pass out unperceived by the crowd, and go on their way to Plymouth. They stopped one night on their journey at a small inn, where the landlord asked if they had heard anything of the riot in Concord. Two men had been there, he said, one an Englishman by the name of Thompson, who had been making abominable and seditious speeches, stirring up people about "the niggers"; the other was a young Quaker by the name of Whittier, who was always making speeches. He heard him lecture once himself, he said (a base lie, Whittier told us, because he had never "lectured" in his life), and it was well that active measures had been taken against them. "We heard him all through," said Whittier, "and then, just as I had my foot on the step of the chaise, ready to drive away from the door, I remarked to him, 'Wouldn't you like to see that Thompson of whom you have been speaking?' I took good care not to use 'plain' language, that is, the Quaker form. 'I rather think I should,' said the man. 'Well, this is Mr. Thompson,' I said, as I jumped into the chaise. 'And this is the Quaker, Whittier,' said Thompson, driving away as fast as he could. I looked back, and saw him standing, mouth wide open, gazing after us in the greatest astonishment."

The two kept on to Plymouth, where they were nearly mobbed a second time. Years after, Whittier said, when he was passing through Portland once, a man, seeing him go by, stepped out of his shop and asked if his name was Whittier, and if he were not the man who was stoned, years before, by a mob at Concord. The answer being in the affirmative, he said he believed a devil possessed him that night; for he had no reason to wish evil either to Whittier or Thompson, yet he was filled with a desire to kill them, and he thought he should have done so if they had not escaped. He added that the mob was like a crowd of demons, and he knew one man who had mixed a black dye to dip them in, which would be almost impossible to get off. He could not explain to himself or to another the state of mind he was in.

The next morning we walked with Whittier again in his little garden, and saw his grapes, which were a source of pride and pleasure. One vine, he told us, came up from a tiny rootlet sent to him by Charles Sumner, in a letter from Washington.

Later we strolled forth into the village street as far as the Friends' meeting-house, and sat down upon the steps while he told us something of his neighbors. He himself, he said, planted the trees around the church: they were then good-sized trees. He spoke very earnestly about the worship of the Friends. All the associations of his youth and all the canons of his education and development were grounded on the Friends' faith and doctrine, and he was anxious that they should show a growth commensurate with the age. He disliked many of the innovations, but his affectionate spirit clung to his people, and he longed to see them drawing to themselves a larger measure of spiritual life, day by day. He loved the old custom of sitting in silence, and hoped they would not stray away into habits of much speaking. The old customs of the meeting-house were very dear to him.

One cold, clear morning in January I heard his early ring. He had been ill, but was so much better that he was absolutely gay. He insisted upon blowing the fire, which, as sometimes happens, will struggle to do its worst on the coldest days; and as the flames at last began to roar, his spirits rose with them. He was rejoicing over Garibaldi's victory. The sufferings of Italy had been so terrible that even one small victory in their behalf seemed a great gain. He said that he had been trying to arouse the interest of the Friends, but it usually took about two years to thoroughly awaken them on any great topic.

He remained several hours that morning talking over his hopes for the country — of politics, of Charles Sumner, of whom he said, "Sumner is always fundamentally right"; and of John Bright, for whose great gifts he had sincere admiration. Soon afterward, at the time of this great man's death, Whittier wrote to us: "Spring is here to-day, warm, birdfull. . . . It seems strange that I am alive to welcome her when so many have passed away with the winter, and among them that stalwartest of Englishmen, John Bright, sleeping now in the daisied grounds of Rochdale, never more to move the world with his surpassing eloquence. How I regret that I have never seen him! We had much in common in our religious faith, our hatred of war and oppression. His great genius seemed to me to be always held firmly in hand by a sense of duty, and by the practical common-sense of a shrewd man of business. He fought through life like an old knight-errant, but without enthusiasm. He had no personal ideals. I remember once how he remonstrated with me for my admiration for General Gordon. He looked upon that wonderful personality as a wild fighter, a rash adventurer, doing evil that good might come. He could not see him as I saw him, giving his life for humanity, alone and unfriended, in that dreadful Soudan. He did not like the idea of fighting Satan with Satan's weapons. Lord Salisbury said truly that John Bright was the greatest orator England had produced, and his eloquence was only called out by what he regarded as the voice of God in his soul."

When at length Whittier rose to go that winter morning, with the feeling that he had already taken too large a piece out of the day, we pressed him to stay longer, since it was already late. "Why can't you stay?" urged his host. "Because, I tell you, I don't want to," which set us all laughing, and settled the question.

Our first knowledge of his arrival in town was usually that early and punctual ring to which I have referred. He would come in looking pale and thin, but full of fire, and, as we would soon find, of a certain vigor. He became interested one morning in a plan proposed to him for making a collection of poems for young people, one which he finally completed with the aid of Miss Lucy Larcom. We got down from the shelf Longfellow's *Poets and Poetry of Europe*, and looked it over together. "Annie of Tharaw" was a great favorite of his, and the poem by Dirk Smit, on "The Death of an Infant" found his ready appreciation. He easily fell thus into talk of Burns, who was Whittier's master and ideal. "He lives, next to Shakespeare," he said, "in the heart of humanity."

In speaking of Rossetti and of his ballad of "Sister Helen," he confessed to being strangely attracted to this poem, because he could remember seeing his mother, "who was as good a woman as

ever lived," and his aunt, performing the same strange act of melting a waxen figure of a clergyman of their time.

The solemnity of the affair made a deep impression on his mind, as a child, for the death of the clergyman in question was confidently expected. His "heresies" had led him to experience this cabalistic treatment.

There was some talk, also, of the advantages, in these restless days, accruing to those who "stay put" in this world, instead of to those who are forever beating about, searching for greater opportunities from position or circumstance. He laughed heartily over the tale, which had just then reached us, of Carlyle going to hunt up a new residence in London with a map of the world in his pocket.

We asked Whittier if he never felt tempted to go to Quebec from his well-beloved haunts in the White Mountains. "Oh no," he replied. "I know it all by books and pictures just as well as if I had seen it."

This talk of travelling reminded him of a circus which came one season to Amesbury. "I was in my garden," he said, "when I saw an Arab wander down the street, and by-and-by stop and lean against my gate. He held a small book in his hand, which he was reading from time to time when he was not occupied with gazing about him. Presently I went to talk with him, and found he had lived all his life on the edge of the Desert until he had started for America. He was very homesick, and longed for the time of his return. He had hired himself for a term of years to the master of the circus. He held the Koran in his hand, and was delighted to find a friend who had also read his sacred book. He opened his heart still further then, and said how he longed for his old, wild life in the Desert, for a sight of the palms, and the sands, but, above all, for its freedom." This interview made a deep impression, naturally, upon Whittier's mind, he, who was no traveller himself, having thus sung:

"He who wanders widest, lifts
  No more of beauty's jealous veil
  Than he who from his doorway sees
  The miracle of flowers and trees."

The memory of a visit to Amesbury, made once in September, vividly remains with me. It was early in the month, when the lingering heat of summer seems sometimes to gather fresh intensity from the fact that we are so soon to hear the winds of autumn. Amesbury had greatly altered of late years: "large enough to be a city," our friend declared; "but I am not fat enough to be an alderman." To us it was still a small village, though somewhat dustier and less attractive than when we first knew it.

As we approached the house, we saw him from a distance characteristically gazing down the road for us, from his front yard, and then at the first glimpse suddenly disappearing, to come forth again to meet us, quite fresh and quiet, from his front door. It had been a very hot, dry summer, and everything about that place, as about every other, was parched and covered with dust. There had been no rain for weeks, and the village street was then quite innocent of watering-carts. The fruit hung heavily from the nearly leafless trees, and the soft thud of the pears and apples as they fell to the ground could be heard on every side in the quiet house-yards. The sun struggled feebly through the mists during the noontide hours, when a still heat pervaded rather than struck the earth; and then in the early afternoon, and late into the next morning, a stirless cloud seemed to cover the face of the world. These mists were much increased by the burning of peat and brush, and, alas! of the very woods themselves, in every direction. Altogether, as Whittier said, quaintly, "it was very encouraging weather for the Millerites."

His niece, who bears the name of his beloved sister, was then the mistress of his home, and we were soon made heartily welcome inside the house, where everything was plain and neat as became a Friend's household; but as the village had grown to be a stirring place, and the house stood close upon the dusty road, such charming neatness must sometimes have been a difficult achievement. The noonday meal was soon served and soon ended, and then we sat down behind the half-closed blinds, looking out upon the garden, the faded vines, and almost leafless trees. It was a cozy room, with its Franklin-stove, at this season surmounted by a bouquet, and a table between the windows, where was a larger bouquet, which Whittier himself had gathered that morning in anticipation of our arrival. He seemed brighter and better than we

had dared to hope, and was in excellent mood for talking. Referring again to the Millerites, who had been so reanimated by the mists, he said he had been deeply impressed lately with their deplorable doctrines. "Continually disappointed because we don't all burn up on a sudden, they forget to be thankful for their preservation from the dire fate they predict with so much complacency."

He had just received a proof of his poem "Miriam," with the introduction, and he could not be content until they had both been read aloud to him. After the reading they were duly commented upon, and revised until he thought he could do no more; yet twice before our departure the proofs were taken out of the hand-bag where they were safely stowed away, and again more or less altered.

Whittier's ever-growing fame was not taken by him as a matter of course. "I cannot think very well of my own things," he used to say; "and what is mere fame worth when thee is at home, alone, and sick with headaches, unable either to read or to write?" Nevertheless he derived very great pleasure and consolation from the letters and tributes which poured in upon him from hearts he had touched or lives he had quickened. "That I like," he would say; "that is worth having." But he must often have known the deeps of trouble in winter evenings when he was too ill to touch book or pen, and when he could do nothing during the long hours but sit and think over the fire.

We slept in Elizabeth's chamber. The portrait of their mother, framed in autumn leaves gathered in the last autumn of her life, hung upon the wall. Here, too, as in our bedroom at Dickens's, the diary of Pepys lay on the table. Dickens had read his copy faithfully, and written notes therein. Of this copy the leaves had not been cut; but with it lay the *Prayers of the Ages*, and volumes of poems, which had all been well read, and *Pickwick* upon the top.

In the year 1867 Charles Dickens came to America to give his famous Readings. Whittier, as we have seen, was seldom tempted out of his country home and habitual ways, but Dickens was for one moment too much for him. To our surprise, he wrote to ask if he could possibly get a seat to hear him. "I see there is a crazy rush for tickets." A favorable answer was despatched to him as soon as

WHITTIER IN HIS STUDY.
After a photograph by J. H. Thurston, Boston.

practicable, but he had already repented of the indiscretion. "My dear Fields," he wrote, "up to the last moment I have hoped to occupy the seat so kindly promised me for this evening. But I find I must give it up. Gladden with it the heart of some poor wretch who dangled and shivered all in vain in your long *queue* the other morning. I must read my *Pickwick* alone, as the Marchioness played cribbage. I would so like, nevertheless, to see Dickens, and shake that creative hand of his. It is as well, doubtless, so far as he is concerned, that I cannot do it; he will have enough and too much of that, I fear. I dreamed last night I saw him surrounded by a mob of ladies, each with her scissors snipping at his hair, and he seemed in a fair way to be 'shaven and shorn,' like the Priest in 'The House that Jack built.'"

The large events of humanity were to Whittier a portion of his own experience, his personal life being, in the ordinary sense, devoid of incident. The death of Charles Dickens, in 1871, was a personal loss, just as his life had been a living gain to this remote and invalid man. One long quiet summer afternoon shortly after, Whittier joined us for the sake of talking about Dickens. He told us what sunshine came from him into his own solemn and silent country life, and what grateful love he must ever bear to him. He wished to hear all that could be told of him as a man. Tea came, and the sun went down, and still he talked and questioned, and then, after a long silence, he said, suddenly, "What's he doing now? Sometimes I say, in Shakespeare's phrase, O for some 'courteous ghost,' but nothing ever comes to me. He was so human I should think thee must *see* him sometimes. It seems as if he were the very person to manifest himself and give us a glimpse beyond. I believe I have faith; I sometimes think I have; but this desire to see just a little way is terribly strong in me. I have expressed something of it in my verses to Mrs. Child about Loring."

He spoke also of the significance of our prayers; of their deep value to our spirit in constantly renewing the sense of dependence; and farther, since we "surely find that our prayers are answered, what blindness and fatuity there is in neglect or abuse of our privilege!"

He was thinking of editing a new edition of John Woolman. He hoped to induce certain people who would read his own books, to read that, by writing a preface for it.

The death of Henry Ward Beecher was also a loss and a sadness to him in his solitary life. "I am saddened by the death of Beecher," he wrote; "he was so strong, so generous, so warm-hearted, and so brave and stalwart in so many good causes. It is a mighty loss. He had faults, like all of us, and needed forgiveness; and I think he could say, with David of old, that he would rather fall into the Lord's hands than into the hands of man."

It is anticipating the years and interrupting the narrative to mention here a few of the men who gladdened his later life, by their friendship, but the subject demands a brief space before we return to the current story of his days.

Matthew Arnold went to see him on his arrival, and it is needless to say that Whittier derived sincere pleasure from the visit; but Arnold's delightful recognition of Whittier's "In School Days" as one of the perfect poems which must live, gave him fresh assurance of fulfilled purpose in existence. He had followed Arnold with appreciation from his earliest appearance in the world of letters, and knew him, as it were, "by heart" long before a personal interview was possible. In a letter written after Arnold's return to England, he says: "I share thy indignation at the way our people have spoken of him—one of the foremost men of our time, a true poet, a wise critic, and a brave, upright man, to whom all English-speaking people owe a debt of gratitude. I am sorry I could not see him again."

When the end came, a few years later, he was among the first to say, "What a loss English literature has sustained in the death of Matthew Arnold!"

As I have already suggested, he kept the run of all the noteworthy people who came to Boston, quite as surely as they kept in pursuit of him.

"I hope thee will see the wonderful prophet of the Bramo Somaj, Mozoom-dar, before he leaves the country. I should have seen him in Boston but for illness last week. That movement in India is the greatest event in the history of Christianity since the days of Paul.

"So the author of *Christie Johnston* is dead. I have read and re-read that charming little story with ever-increasing admiration. I am sorry for the coarseness of some of his later writings; but he was, after all, a great novelist, second only in our times to George Eliot, Dickens, and Thackeray.... I shall be glad to hear more about Mr. Wood's and Mrs. ——'s talks. Any hint or sign or token from the unseen and spiritual world is full of solemn interest, standing as I do on the shore of 'that vast ocean I must sail so soon.'....

"You will soon have Amelia Edwards with you. I am sorry that I have not been able to call on her. Pray assure her of my sincere respect and admiration."

And again: "Have thee seen and heard the Hindoo Mohini? He seems to have really converted some people. I hear that one of them has got a Bible!"

The phrase that he is "beset by pilgrims" occurs frequently in his letters, contrasted with pleased expressions, and descriptions of visits from Phillips Brooks, Canon Farrar, Governor and Mrs. Claflin, and other friends whose faces were always a joy to him.

I have turned aside from the narrative of every-day life to mention these friends; but it is interesting to return and recall the earlier years, when he came one day to dine in Charles Street with Mr. Emerson. As usual, his coming had been very uncertain. He was never to be counted on as a visitor, but at length the moment came when he was in better health than ordinary, and the stars were in conjunction. I can recall his saying to Emerson: "I had to choose between hearing thee at thy lecture and coming here to see thee. I chose to see thee. I could not do both." Emerson was heard to say to him, solicitously, "I hope you are pretty well, sir! I believe you formerly bragged of bad health."

It was Whittier's custom, however, to make quite sure that all "lions" and other disturbing elements were well out of the way before he turned his steps to the library in Charles Street. I recall his coming one Sunday morning when we were at church, and waiting until our return. He thought that would be a safe moment! He was full, as Madame de Sévigné says, "*de conversations infinies*," being especially interested just then in the question of schools for the freedmen, and eagerly discussed ways and means for starting and supporting them.

We were much amused by his ingenuity in getting contributions from his home town. It appears that he had taken it into consideration that there were a number of carriage-makers in Amesbury. He suggested that each one of these men should give some part of a carriage — one the wheels, one the body, one the furnishings, etc., dividing it in all among twenty workmen. When it was put together, he had a carriage which was sold for two hundred dollars, which was exactly the sum requisite for Amesbury to give.

LAWN AT OAK KNOLL, DANVERS.
After a photograph by J. H. Thurston, Boston.

His benefactions were ceaseless, and they were one of the chief joys of his later life. The subject of what may be done for this or that person or cause is continually recurring in his letters. Once I find this plea in verse after the manner of Burns:

> "O well-paid author, fat-fed scholar,
> Whose pockets jingle with the dollar,
> No sheriff's hand upon your collar,
> No duns to bother,
> Think on't, a tithe of what ye swallow
> Would save your brother!"

And again and again there are passages in his letters like the following: "I hope the Industrial Home may be saved, and wish I was a rich man just long enough to help save it. As it is, if the subscription needs $30 to fill it up, I shall be glad to give the mite." "I have long followed Maurice," he says again, "in his work as a religious and social reformer—a true apostle of the gospel of humanity. He

saw clearly, and in advance of his clerical brethren, the necessity of wise and righteous dealing with the momentous and appalling questions of labor and poverty."

He wrote one day: "If you go to Richmond, why don't you visit Hampton and Old Point Comfort, where that Christian knight and latter-day Galahad, General Armstrong, is making his holy experiment? I think it would be worth your while."

General Armstrong and his brave work in founding and maintaining the Hampton School for the education, at first, of the colored people alone, and finally for the Indians also, was one of the near and living interests of Whittier's life. Often and often in his letters do we find references to the subject; either he regrets having to miss seeing the general, upon one of his Northern trips, or he rejoices in falling in with some of the teachers at Asquam Lake or elsewhere, or his note is jubilant over some new gift which will make the general's work for the year less difficult.

Once he writes: "I am grieved to hear of General Armstrong's illness. I am not surprised at it. He has been working in his noble cause beyond any mortal man's strength. He must have a rest if it is possible for him, and his friends must now keep up the school by redoubled efforts. Ah me! There is so much to be done in this world! I wish I were younger or a millionaire."

And yet again: "I had the pleasure of sending General Armstrong at Christmas, with my annual subscription, one thousand dollars which a friend placed in my hand. I wish our friend could be relieved from the task of raising money by a hundred such donations."

The choice of the early breakfast hour for his visits was his own idea. He was glad to hit upon a moment which was not subject to interruptions, one when he could talk at his ease of books and men. These visits were always a surprise. He liked to be abroad in good season, and had rarely missed seeing the sun rise in forty years. He knew, too, that we were not late people, and that his visits could never be untimely. Occasionally, with the various evening engagements of a city, we were not altogether fit to receive him, but it was a pleasure to hear his punctual ring, and to know that we should find him in the library by the fire. He was himself a bad sleeper, seldom, as he said, putting a solid bar of sleep between day and day, and therefore often early abroad to question the secrets of the dawn. We owe much of the intimate friendship of our life to these morning hours spent in private, uninterrupted talk.

"I have lately felt great sympathy with ——," he said one morning, "for I have been kept awake one hundred and twenty hours—an experience I should not care to try again."

One of Whittier's summer pleasures, in which he occasionally indulged himself, was a visit to the Isles of Shoals. He loved to see his friend Celia Thaxter in her island home, and he loved the freedom of a large hotel. He liked to make arrangements with a group of his more particular friends to meet him there; and when he was well enough to leave his room, he might be seen in some carefully chosen corner of the great piazzas, shady or sunny, as the day invited him, enjoying the keenest happiness in the voluntary society and conversation of those dear to him. Occasionally he would pass whole days in Celia Thaxter's parlor, watching her at her painting in the window, and listening to the conversation around him. He wished to hear and know what interested others. He liked nothing better, he once said, than going into the "store" in the old days at Amesbury, when it was a common centre, almost serving the purpose of what a club may be in these later days, and sitting upon a barrel to hear "folks talk." The men there did not know much about his poetry, but they understood his politics, and he was able to put in many a word to turn the vote of the town. In Celia Thaxter's parlor he found a different company, but his relations to the people who frequented that delightful place were practically the same. He wished to understand their point of view, if possible, and then, if he could find opportunity, he would help them to a higher stand-point.

I remember one season in particular, when the idle talk of idle people had been drifting in and out during the day, while he sat patiently on in the corner of the pretty room. Mrs. Thaxter was steadily at work at her table, yet always hospitable, losing sight of no cloud or shadow or sudden gleam of glory in the landscape, and pointing the talk often with keen wit. Nevertheless, the idleness of it all palled upon him. It was Sunday, too, and he longed for something which would move us to "higher levels." Suddenly, as if the idea had struck him like an inspiration, he rose, and taking a volume of Emerson from the little library, he opened to one of the discourses, and handing it to Celia Thaxter, said:

"Read that aloud, will thee? I think we should all like to hear it."

After she ended he took up the thread of the discourse, and talked long and earnestly upon the beauty and necessity of worship—a necessity consequent upon the nature of man, upon his own weakness, and his consciousness of the Divine Spirit within him. His whole heart was stirred, and he poured himself out toward us as if he longed, like the prophet of old, to breathe a new life into us. I could see that he reproached himself for not having spoken out in this way before, but his enfranchised spirit took only a stronger flight for the delay.

We heard from him again, shortly after, under the shadow of the great hills where he always passed a part of every year. He loved them, and wrote eloquently of the loveliness of nature at Ossipee: "the Bear Camp winding down" the long green valley close by the

THE HOUSE AT HAMPTON FALLS—WHITTIER ON THE BALCONY.

door, the long Sandwich and Waterville ranges, and Chocorua filling up the horizon from west to northeast.

The frequent loneliness of his life often found expression. Once he says:

"I wish I could feel that I deserved a tithe even of the kind things said of me by my personal friends. If one could but *be* as easily as preach! The confession of poor Burns might, I fear, be made of the best of us:

'God knows I'm no the thing I would be,
Nor am I even the thing I could be.'

And yet I am thankful every day of my life that God has put it into the hearts of so many whom I love and honor and reverence to send me so many messages of good-will and kindness. It is an unspeakable comfort in the lonely and darkening afternoon of life. Indeed, I can never feel quite alone so long as I know that all about me are those who turn to me with friendly interest, and, strange to say, with gratitude. A sense of lack of desert on my part is a drawback, of course;

but then, I say to myself, if my friends judge me by my aim and desire, and not by my poor performance, it may be all right and just."

The painful solitude of his life after his dear niece's marriage was softened when he went to live with his cousins at Oak Knoll, in Danvers, a beautiful country-seat, sheltered and suited to his needs.

At Danvers he was able to enjoy the free open air. He loved to sit under the fine trees which distinguished the lawn, to play with the dogs, and wander about unmolested until he was tired. The ladies of the house exerted themselves to give him perfect freedom and the tenderest care. The daughter became his playmate, and she never quite grew up, in his estimation. She was his lively and loving companion. Writing from Danvers, one December, he says, "What with the child, and the dogs, and Rip Van Winkle, the cat, and a tame gray squirrel who hunts our pockets for nuts, we contrive to get through the short dark days."

He showed more physical vitality after

he went to Danvers, and his notes evince a wide interest in matters private and public outside his own library life. He still went to Portland to see his niece and her husband whenever he was able, and now and then to Boston also. But Philadelphia and the Centennial was not to be thought of. "I sent my hymn," he wrote from Amesbury in 1876, "with many misgivings, and am glad it was so well received. I think I should like to have heard the music, but probably I should not have understood. The gods have made me most unmusical."

"I have just got J. T. F.'s charming little book of *Barry Cornwall and his Friends*. It is a most *companionable* volume, and will give rare pleasure to thousands.... I write in the midst of our Quaker quarterly meeting, and our house has been overrun for three days. We had twelve to dine to-day; they have now gone to meeting, but I am too tired for preaching.

"I don't expect to visit Philadelphia. The very thought of that Ezekiel's vision of machinery and the nightmare confusion of the world's curiosity shop appalls me. I shall not venture."

He was full of excellent resolutions about going often to Boston, but he never could make a home there. "I see a great many more things in the city than thee does," he would say, "because I go to town so seldom. The shop windows are a delight to me, and everything and everybody is novel and interesting. I don't need to go to the theatre. I have more theatre than I can take in, every time I walk out."

No sketch of Whittier, however slight, should omit mention of his friendship for Bayard Taylor. Their Quaker parentage helped to bring the two poets into communion; and although Taylor was so much the younger and more vigorous man, Whittier was to see him also pass, and to mourn his loss. He took a deep interest in his literary advancement, and considered "Lars" his finest poem. Certainly no one knew Taylor's work better, or brought a deeper sympathy into his reading of it. "I love him too well to be a critic of his verse," he says, in one of his letters. "But what a brave worker he was!"

The reading of good books was, very late in life, as it had been very early, his chief pleasure. His travels, his romance,

his friendships, were indulged chiefly by proxy of the printed page. "I felt very near Dr. Mulford through his writings," he said. "He was the strongest thinker of our time, and he thought in the right direction. *The Republic of God* is intellectually greater than St. Augustine's *City of God*, and infinitely nearer the Christian ideal."

"That must be a shrewd zephyr," Charles Lamb used to say, speaking of his Gentle Giantess, "that can escape her." And so we may say of Whittier and a book. "Has thee seen the new book by the author of *Mr. Isaacs*?" he asked (having sent me *Mr. Isaacs* as soon as it appeared, lest I should miss reading so novel and good a story). In the same breath he adds: "I have been reading *The Freedom of Faith*, by the author of *On the Threshold*, just published by Houghton and Co. It is refreshing and tonic as the northwest wind. The writer is one of the leaders of the new departure from ultra-Calvinism. Thank thee just here for the pleasure of reading Annie Keary's biography. What a white, beautiful soul! Her views of the mission of Spiritualism seem very much like ——'s. I do not know when I have read a more restful, helpful book.

"How good Longfellow's poem is! A little sad, but full of 'sweetness and light.' Emerson, Longfellow, Holmes, and myself are all getting to be old fellows, and that swan-song might serve for us all. 'We who are about to die.' God help us all! I don't care for fame, and have no solicitude about the verdicts of posterity.

"When the grass is green above us,
   And they who know us and who love us
      Are sleeping by our side,
   Will it avail us aught that men
   Tell the world with lip and pen
      That we have lived and died?

"What we *are*, will then be more important than what we have done or said in prose or rhyme, or what folks that we never saw or heard of think of us."

Later he describes himself as listening to the *Life of Mrs. Stowe*. "It is a satisfying book, a model biography, or, rather, autobiography, for dear Mrs. Stowe speaks all through it. Dr. Holmes's letters reveal him as he is, wise, generous, chivalrous. Witness the kindliness and delicate sympathy of his letters during the Lord Byron trouble.... Miss W. has read us some of Howells's *Hazard of New Fortunes*. It strikes me that it is a strong book. That indomitable old German, Linden—that saint of the rather godless sect of dynamiters and anarchists—is a grand figure; one can't help loving him."

Whittier never relinquished his house at Amesbury, where his kind friends Judge Cate and his wife always made him feel at home. As the end of his life drew near, it was easy to see that the village home where his mother and his sister lived and died was the place he chiefly loved; but he was more inaccessible to his friends in Amesbury, and the interruptions of a fast-growing factory town were sometimes less agreeable to him than the country life at Oak Knoll. He was a great disbeliever in too much solitude, however, and used to say, "The necessary solitude of the human soul is enough; it is surprising how great that is."

Once only he expresses this preference for the dear old village home in his letters. "I have been at Amesbury for a fortnight. Somehow I seem nearer to my mother and sister; the very walls of the rooms seem to have become sensitive to the photographs of unseen presences."

Toward the end of his days, however, he spent more and more time with his beloved cousins Gertrude and Joseph Cartland, whose interests and aims in life were so close to his own.

The habit of going to the White Mountains in their company for a few weeks during the heat of summer was a fixed one. He grew to love Asquam, with its hills and lakes, almost better than any other place for this sojourn. It was there he loved to beckon his friends to join him. "Do come, if possible," he would write. "The years speed on; it will soon be too late. I long to look on your dear faces once more."

His deafness began to preclude general conversation; but he delighted in getting off under the pine-trees in the warm afternoons, or into a quiet room upstairs at twilight and talking until bedtime. He described to us, during one visit, his first vision of the hills. His parents took him where he could see the great wooded slope of Agamenticus. As he looked up and gazed with awe at the solemn sight, a cloud drooped, and hung suspended as it were from one point, and filled his soul with astonishment. He had never forgotten it. He said nothing at the time, but this cloud hanging from the breast of the hill filled his boyish mind with a mighty wonder, which had never faded away.

Notwithstanding his strong feeling for Amesbury, and his presence there always at "quarterly meeting," he found himself increasingly comfortable at Danvers and happy in the companionship of his devoted relatives. Something nearer "picturesqueness" and "the beautiful" came to please the sense and to soothe the spirit at Oak Knoll. He did not often make record in his letters of these things; but once he speaks charmingly of the young girl in a red cloak, on horseback, with the dog at her side, scampering over the lawn and brushing under the sloping branches of the trees. The sunset of his life burned slowly down, but in spite of illness and loss of power, he possessed his soul in patience. After a period when he felt unable to write, he revived and sent a letter, in which he spoke as follows of a poem which had been sent for his revision: "The poem is solemn and tender; it is as if a wind from the Unseen World blew over it, in which the voice of sorrow is sweeter than that of gladness—a holy fear mingled with holier hope. For myself, my hope is always associated with dread, like the shining of a star through mist. I feel, indeed, that Love is the victorious, that there is no dark it cannot light, no depth it cannot reach; but I imagine that between the Seen and the Unseen there is a sort of neutral ground, a land of shadow and mystery, of strange voices and undistinguished forms. There are some, as Charles Lamb says, 'who stalk into futurity on stilts,' without awe or self-distrust. But I can only repeat the words of the poem before me. . . ."

One of the last, perhaps the very last visit he made to his friends in Boston was in the beautiful autumn weather. The familiar faces he hoped to find were absent. He arrived without warning, and the very loveliness of the atmosphere which made it possible for him to travel had tempted younger people out among the falling leaves. He was disappointed, and soon after sent these verses to rehearse his experience:

"I stood within the vestibule
    Whose granite steps I knew so well,
    While through the empty rooms the bell
Responded to my eager pull.

VIEW FROM WHITTIER'S WINDOW, HAMPTON FALLS.

"I listened while the bell once more
  Rang through the void, deserted hall;
  I heard no voice, nor light footfall,
And turned me sadly from the door.

"Though fair was Autumn's dreamy day,
  And fair the wood-paths carpeted
  With fallen leaves of gold and red,
I missed a dearer sight than they.

"I missed the love-transfigured face,
  The glad, sweet smile so dear to me,
  The clasp of greeting warm and free:
What had the round world in their place?

"O friend, whose generous love has made
  My last days best, my good intent
  Accept, and let the call I meant
Be with your coming doubly paid."

But even this journey was beyond his strength. He wrote: "Coming back from Boston in a crowded car, a window was opened just behind me and another directly opposite, and, in consequence, I took a bad cold, and am losing much of this goodly autumnal spectacle. But Oak Knoll woods were never, I think, so beautiful before."

In future his friends were to seek him; he could go no more to them; the autumn had indeed set in.

Now began a series of birthday celebrations, which were blessings not unmixed in his cup of life. He was in the habit of writing a brief note of remembrance on these anniversaries; in one of which, after confessing to "a feeling of sadness and loneliness," he turns to the Emerson Calendar, and says, "I found for the day some lines from his 'World Soul'—

'Love wakes anew this throbbing heart,
  And we are never old;
  Over the winter glaciers
    I see the summer glow,
  And through the wild piled snowdrift
    The warm rose-buds blow.'

Reading them, I took heart."

On another occasion he says: "In the intervals of visitation on that day my thoughts were with dear friends who have passed from us; among whom, I need not say, was thy dearest friend. How vividly the beautiful mornings with you were recalled! Then I wondered at my age, and if it was possible that I was the little boy on the old Haverhill farm, unknown, and knowing nobody beyond my home horizon. I could not quite make the connection of the white-haired man with the black-locked boy. I could not help a feeling of loneliness, thinking of having outlived many of my life-companions; but I was still grateful to God that I had not outlived my love for them and for those still living. Among the many tokens of good-will from all parts of the country and beyond the sea, there were some curious and amazing missives. One Southern woman took the occasion to include me in her curse of the 'mean, hateful Yankees.' To offset this, I had a telegram from the Southern Forestry Congress assembled in Florida, signed by president and secretary, informing me that 'In remembrance of your birthday, we have planted a live-oak tree to your memory, which, like the leaves of the tree, will be forever green.'"

The lines of Whittier's life stretched "between heaven and home" during the long period of eighty-four years.

It was not, however, until 1890 that we could really feel he had left the years of active service and of intellectual achievement as things of the past. He was shut out from much that gave him pleasure, but the spirit which animated the still breathing frame, though waiting and at times longing for larger opportunity, seemed to us like a loving sentinel, covering his dear ones as with a shield, and watching over the needs of humanity.

The end came, the door opened, while he was staying with the daughter of an old friend at Hampton Falls, in New Hampshire—that saintly woman whom we associate with one of the most spiritual and beautiful of his poems, "A Friend's Burial." After a serious illness in the winter of 1892 he was almost too frail for any summer journeying, but with his usual wisdom and instinctive turning of the heart toward old familiar places, he thought of the hospitable house where he seemed to gain much strength, and where he found much happiness and the quietness that he loved. His last illness was brief; he was ministered to by those who stood nearest him. And thus the waves of time passed over him and swept him from our sight.

Old age appears to every other stage of human existence as a most undesirable state. We look upon its approaches and its ravages with alarm. Death itself is far less dreadful, and "the low door," if it will only open quickly, brings little fear to the thoughtful mind. But the mystery of decadence, the long sunsetting, the loss of power—what do they mean? The Latin word *saga*, from which the French get *la sagesse*, and we "the sage," gives us a hint of what we do not always understand—the spiritual beauty and the significance even of loss, in age.

Whittier, wearing his silver crown, brought the antique word into use again, and filled it with fresh meaning for modern men.

THE NEW ENGLAND NEGRO

NEAR the lower edge of one of those hills that billow the surface of western Connecticut stands a small house, old, rough, and unpainted, whose youth was passed ere the first page of this century had been turned. In fact, it has been so long a part of Nature that it is like Nature herself, and she has set her seal upon it in the clusters of silvery lichens that overlap each other on the old shingles, while a great maple-tree tenderly shadows it with wide arms as if in benediction.

The front of the house shows but one story, but the foundations, following a dip of the land, gain another in the rear, where the kitchen door opens on a large broad door-stone.

Just off the kitchen, by the southern window of her little bedroom, is the favorite seat of Nancy, widow of Roswell Freeman, now, according to her reckoning, in her ninety-first year—a remnant of the days when New England, with her imperfect human conscience, was as eager as the transatlantic nations for a share of profit in the slave trade.

In the history of the world conquest of territory has usually meant a conquest of people—dwellers within walls—and in a general sense "captive" was but another name for slave. When the *Mayflower* and the first few of the fleet following in her wake brought to the New England coast the groups of colonists, a rare condition awaited them. An epidemic among the Indians had almost depopulated the seaboard, and they had but to enter and possess land already prepared for cultivation.

But rapidly increasing numbers required an enlargement of borders, so purchases and treaties followed, with that occasional gain by warfare that proves the power of might. However, an enemy whose fortress was generally the quickly shifted wigwam, and whose ramparts the trees of the interminable forest, was more easily routed than captured; yet there were occasional seizures of persons, and Indian captives as slaves became members of many households. Labor was a scarcity. The majority of the colonists were not of the laboring class, and there

was work to be done in house and field that lacked the needed hand. In 1637 Hugh Peters wrote to John Winthrop, Jun., that he "hears of a dividend of Indian women and children from the Pequot captives, and he would like a share." But these local tribes were soon pushed into the wilderness, leaving here and there their representatives in the white man's home.

In the sixteenth century the system of slavery was fast disappearing from western Europe, as being inconsistent with their duty for Christians to hold Christians as slaves. But this charity did not extend to heathens and infidels! In the latter part of the seventeenth century the African slave trade was considered the most profitable part of British commerce. New England naturally followed the lead of older countries, and her exchange, for humanity, of rum, molasses, and other commodities acceptable on the Guinea and Gold coasts began. In 1638 Samuel Maverack, of Massachusetts, bought African slaves, and in 1650 "a neager mayde 25£" appears in an inventory in Hartford. Erelong every well-to-do family had its quota of negroes for necessary domestic service and labor on the "plantation" of the Northern agriculturist, not in large numbers, as later on the cotton plantations of the South, but one or two, or even seven or eight, in a family.

The slaves imported were of various colors, tribes, and physiognomies. Some were jet-black, with features approaching those of the European; some were of a tawny yellow, with flat noses and projecting jaws. These latter, coming from the delta of the Niger, were noted for an indomitable capacity for endurance, and therefore esteemed the best slaves. A few were Mohammedans, among whom were occasionally found persons of some education, who knew Arabic, and could read the Koran. But the great mass were pagans, in a condition of gross barbarism.

Their African superstitions and languages soon died out, and it was found that the race increased in strength in this climate with its long winter of rest. Values varied with the individual's age and capacity. In 1707 a house and lot on the main street of Stratford, Connecticut, with twenty-four acres of land, were given for a negro man. An inventory of 1728—showing that some Indian slaves remained even after the great African importation—gives:

One Indian slave called	Dick	....	£45
" negro woman	"	Libb	....	50
" " man	"	Abel	....	40
" " "	"	Aaron	....	90
" mulatto boy	"	Ned	....	35
" negro	"	Tim	....	12
" "	" "	Cuffee	....	55
		Sharper	....	40

In 1747 Abel and Libb were valued, "boath," at £240,

One negro girl named Darciss	....	£170
" " " in the 6th year of her age	....	100
" " boy "L 3d " his "	....	60

which seems a startling advance, until it is realized that colonial paper money had depreciated to about one-tenth of its face value. In the "setting out" of each of four sisters, married between 1750 and 1760, after all the items of furniture, linen, silver, "chaney," pewter, etc., a horse and side-saddle, and a cow, comes:

One negro girl, in lawful money .... 33£

And in a manuscript "Book of Inventory of Damages Committed by the British in Middlesex County, New Jersey, during the Revolutionary War," among a long list of slaves enticed or carried away by the British, are recorded:

1 Negro fellow named Oliver	£ 90
A Young Negro Man and Wench	180
1 Negro Boy, aged 14 years, to serve until 21 years old. Press'd and Taken away by the Hessian Troops	40
1 Negro man aged ab't 20 years, a cooper	90

The names of the slaves present an interesting question. "The Hebrew Invasion in nomenclature" was of Puritan sympathies, and that colored children, as well as white, born into that atmosphere should be named from the Old Testament needs no explanation. But what was the law of selection that made only heroes of Roman history honored in remembrance? Why did not a Pharaoh or Xerxes appeal to doting parents as well as Cato and Hannibal, Cæsar and Pompey and Scipio? From an early day the law—of Connecticut, at least—obliged the owners to teach their slaves to read, and that they were made to attend religious services, following at a respectful distance behind their masters, and sitting in "the niggers' pew" in the gallery of the meeting-house, goes without saying. The masters as-

sumed the responsibility of the negro souls, and for generations they clung habitually to such forms of worship as their first owners followed.

Slaves were regarded as possessing the same rights as apprentices—food, shelter, clothing, and instruction in some line of work—and manumission was not allowed except upon security that the freed slave should not become a burden on the parish.

In the Northern colonies the slaves were a part of the family, living under the roof or close to it. One may see now occasionally in New England, where the gracefully sloping roof-lines speak of the long ago in our history, certain long two-story buildings, generally at right angles to the houses, and of greatly inferior style and construction. These were the slave quarters, and it was not uncommon for the most intelligent of the number to have the others in charge. Our modern home-makers would stand aghast at the prospect of taking into so close a home-relation this very combustible raw material in the form of humanity. But the early colonist was a marked man in more than one respect. His high courage never wavered before the swinging gleam of a tomahawk or the message conveyed by a snake-skin filled with arrows, and his energy and perseverance were tireless and persistent in the separation of rocks from the soil of the hill-side fields, that the land might yield her increase. Nor was he daunted by the savage instincts of the African, but sought to implant in that desert nature the higher principles of right, of mine and thine, and to lead him through fear to love, from self-seeking to self-sacrifice.

Several generations of New England training told to his benefit. Faithful, truthful, honest, thrifty, respectable, and self-respecting the Northern negro became. All that was best in his impressible nature was developed and steadied, and he bore a good part in the domestic life and economy. But the rigor of the New England climate never put a sharp note in the mellow voices of these children of the sun, and the reserve of New England had no following among them. No environment of repression could hedge in that expansive nature; he was then as now, and now as then, sun-loving, fun-loving, pleasure-loving, sympathetic, friendly at the first touch, childlike; as an old darky travelling by rail said, under remonstrance for buying everything the perpetual train - boy offered, " We niggers is allers childrin."

Conscience is sometimes the development of mixed motives. It is easy to see what is right when it is for one's advantage. In the first generations of American slavery it was considered, if not a godly act, at least one for which thanks might be returned in divine service. Deacons, elders, and parsons all owned slaves, not only with a clear conscience, but received them within the pale of Christianity with rejoicing. The pendulum swung far out. But as years passed, sentiment changed. To buy for a small sum a slave, half or full grown, with a prospect of from twenty to forty years' service rendered, seemed a prudential investment, but after a few generations it was realized that the years of infancy and infirmity made little return for the care and comforts they required, and it was a question if the period of work much overvalued that of necessities. Moreover, the masters were feeling keenly the weight of the hand of oppression. It was to them unkind, unjust, unbearable. There was a longing for the clear air of liberty and independence, and the signs of the gathering storm were welcomed. And was slavery compatible with "the inalienable rights of man"? Connecticut forbade the importation of slaves in 1771. Benjamin Franklin was president of the first abolition society in 1775. Vermont freed all her slaves in 1777, before she joined the Union. At least one New England town petitioned for a committee "to pray the Colonial Assembly that the negroes might be released from their slavery and bondage."

The negroes themselves were intensely interested in the struggle for independence. Every suggestion of freedom appealed to them strongly. They were allowed to make up the quota drafted for the army, an enlistment for one year securing a man's freedom. Some did valiant service, notably Peter Salem, who shot Major Pitcairn at the battle of Bunker Hill.

When independence was assured for the nation, the Northern States freed their slaves with more or less promptitude. Massachusetts proclaimed hers free at once; but most of the States provided for a gradual emancipation. Individuals, however, freed theirs as they were

disposed, without reference to law, often with the result that the negroes preferred remaining with the masters exactly in the old relation, being sure of kindness, support, and provision for all needs. In all cases the sick and aged were cared for at the expense of the owners.

Connecticut's charter was a very liberal one; not suffering from crown appointments, she had the power to elect her own Governor. Like the Israelites of old making their yearly pilgrimages to Jerusalem, in the very early days of the colony each "freeman" went up to Hartford to cast his vote. Although this custom could not continue with increased settlements, "election week" became a time when no one willingly failed of presence at the capital. People of distinction from all parts of the State were assembled, many colored men naturally in attendance on their masters, and those of all grades made it the pivot of the year.

Election day — not the day of votecasting, but of the inauguration of the Governor — was one of great festivity. The Governor, being met outside the town by the militia, was escorted to the State-house, where he stood on the porch while the military paraded and saluted. Later the gay procession attended divine service, the "election sermon" being preached by some eminent divine. Afterward came the feasting and the election ball.

The colored people, peculiarly alive to this effect of pomp and ceremony, not only made every effort to be present, but the imitative instinct stirred them to elect a Governor for themselves. It is not easy to say when the custom began, but the following notice shows that more than ten years before the Declaration of Independence it was well established:

HARTFORD, *May* 11, 1766.

I, Governor Cuff of the Niegro's in the province of Connecticut, do resign my Governmentship to John Anderson Niegor man to Governor Skene. And I hope that you will obey him as you have Done me for this ten years' past when Colonel Willis' niegor Dayed I was the next. But being weak and unfit for that office do Resine the said Governmentshipe to John Anderson.

I John Anderson having the Honour to be appointed Governor over you I will do my utmost endevere to serve you in Every Respect and I hope you will obey me accordingly.

JOHN ANDERSON
Governor over the niegors in Connecticut.

Witnesses present:

The late Governor Cuff, Hartford.

Quackow.

Peter Wadsworth.

Titows.

Pomp Willis.

John Jones.

Fraday.

The colored Governor having no legislative power, and no public records having been kept of the meetings and elections, it is difficult to determine how long Hartford held sway as the centre of the colored government, but before 1800 the high office and attendant festivities had drifted to the old town of Derby.

Derby, in the old days when settlements were few in number and far in distance, took a long reach. Twelve miles of the Naugatuck River, that had not then learned to sing in tune with the hum of factories, lay within her eastern border, and she stretched out and away northward and westward, fanlike, following the Housatonic's windings for her more distant limit. But as numbers multiplied and the resources of the land were developed, section after section broke away from the original holding, like icebergs from the border of an arctic glacier, and put out to sea on its own account. Oxford and Seymour, with their various dependencies, were parts of Derby in those old days, and families reached over from hill to hill.

The first Governor from Derby was Quosh, a native African, stolen when a boy and sold to the slave-traders. He was a man of immense size and herculean strength. His first purchaser probably had this knowledge of the slave-dealers—a boy was measured from ankle to knee, the proportionate length indicating his final height. Quosh was the slave of Mr. Agar Tomlinson at Derby Neck, the owner of a large estate and a number of slaves. These latter were quartered in a small house in touch with that of their master, and under the immediate control of Quosh. When he was called to assume the high office of Governor, his dignity and self-importance were so sensibly affected that it was commonly said that "Uncle Agar [Mr. Tomlinson] lived with the Governor"! Quosh held the office many years, and was a decided power over his following. His ability and faithfulness to his master are vouched for by the will of the latter, pro-

bated in 1800, by which Quosh and his wife, Rose (formerly the slave of Rev. Mr. Yale), were given their freedom, their little house, the use of a certain tract of land, a barn was to be built, he was to have a yoke of oxen, a good cow, and necessary farming implements. Quosh then took the name of Freeman, but as "Governor Quosh" is best remembered.

Little Roman (his wife's name was Venus), who was so short that his sword dragged on the ground, was Lieutenant-Governor under Quosh, and Eben Tobias in turn held the higher office. His son, Hon. Eben D. Bassett, was well educated, and during the civil war exerted himself successfully in enlisting colored soldiers. Through President Grant's administration of eight years he served creditably as our minister to Haiti. He said of himself, "My success in life I owe greatly to that American sense of fairness which was tendered me in old Derby, and which exacts that every man, whether black or white, shall have a fair chance to run his race in life, and make the most of himself."

Seymour, originally called Chusetown, and later Humphreysville, had a noted Governor in Juba Weston; he, having been owned by the family of General Humphreys, was "quality" among the colored people. Juba served a number of years, and his sons Nelson and Wilson were likewise honored, Wilson Weston being the last Governor, a few years before our late civil war.

Fully a century, therefore, the custom existed, the pride in it yet remaining with those who were old enough during its sway to remember its significance; and the pleasure of the attendant festivity has but to be spoken of to bring over the dark faces an expression that tells of unforgotten draughts "of joy's delicious springs."

The formalities of the election have not come down to us, save in one instance, when it was by test of wind and muscle, the successful candidate being he who first climbed a steep and almost unscalable sand bank. Eben Tobias, decked with feathers and flying ribbons, won that day, and it was in his drilling of the escort that the command "Fire and fall off!" was literally interpreted by some of the men throwing themselves from their horses.

The white customs were carefully followed. The people assembled at Derby, Oxford, Waterbury, or Humphreysville, as was ordered, the Governor and his escort in uniforms—anything but uniform—that were hired or borrowed or improvised for the occasion, according to fancy or ability. Mounted on such steeds as could be impressed into the service—remnants of their former selves—they mustered outside the village, and with all the majesty and glitter of feathers and streaming ribbons and uniforms, with fife and drum, made their way by the main thoroughfares, sometimes stopping to fire a salute before a squire's house, to the tavern which was to be the centre of festivity. Then the Governor, dismounting, delivered his speech from the porch, and the troops "trained." Then the clans gathered with more and more enthusiasm for the election ball. Families went entire, a babe in arms being no drawback, as the tavern-keeper set apart a room and provided a caretaker for them. Sometimes more than a dozen little woolly-heads would be under surveillance, while the light-hearted mothers shuffled and tripped to the sound of the fiddle. New Haven and Hartford, as well as intervening towns, were represented. Supper was served for fifty cents each, and they danced and feasted with a delight the more sedate white man can hardly appreciate, spinning out the night and often far into the next day. To their credit it must be recorded that although they were not strict prohibitionists, their indulgence was limited. The influence of the Governors was for moderation, which was generally observed.

A newspaper notice of more than fifty years ago strikes the key-note of the great day:

ATTENTION, FREEMEN!

There will be a general election of the colored gentlemen of Connecticut, October first, twelve o'clock, noon. The day will be celebrated in the evening by a dance at Warner's tavern, when it will be shown that there is some power left in muscle, catgut, and rosin.

By order of the Governor,
From Headquarters.

Quosh Freeman's only son, Roswell, often called "Roswell Quosh," was also one of the Governors. He was very tall, very thin, and very dark, by profession a fox-hunter, therefore called "the farmers' benefactor," and the board on which he dressed the fox-skins shows a record of 331 foxes killed. Perhaps it is because the negro is not as far removed from primitive life as the white man that he seems to have more comprehension of the animal creation. He has by instinct what the white man has by training—the power to secure whatever game he seeks. And he can give to the effort a peculiarly patient, cautious, cunning, long-sustained watchfulness, intensely animate as to his senses, and as entirely inanimate as to his physique, that seem never to fail; be it fox or partridge, "'possum up a gumtree" or domesticated Brahma, the right second is seized, and the aim is unerring.

As a sportsman, Roswell was always a welcome companion to the gentry of similar tastes. He was a man of principle, living quietly and soberly, and, it is said, was never in a quarrel with any one. He and his wife Nancy may well be considered marked figures in the colored ranks. No one had a higher standard of right, better principles, kinder instincts as friend and neighbor, was more respected in his position, or more worthy the good esteem of his contemporaries. Nancy, a devoted churchwoman, is still before the mind's eye of many as she and her little flock of children rose to view in the gallery, like a row of blackbirds, so dark were the little ones; and the vision shows her also in her shiny black silk dress and mantilla, her neat bonnet with a black lace veil hanging at the side, as she made her way to the chancel-rail on communion Sundays, the only one of her color, and the last of the congregation, but with unconscious dignity and reverence. One of the disabilities keenly felt by the old who live at a distance is being debarred the service of the sanctuary. Tears come to her eyes when she speaks of those old days, and her big Bible is her friend in her little home, as she has what she calls her "church" every morning.

There came a time to the good housewives when, the young colored people having grown up to freedom, and the older ones become unable for many duties, the problem of domestic service asserted itself, and the lack of the quick feet and nimble fingers of even the very young slaves was felt. Children of all grades were trained to be helpful, not helpless, and though play was not ignored, occupation must be useful in the main. As one busy mother expressed it, "every kit must catch her own mouse." So the custom became common of taking colored children for a term of years, thereby securing a service trained according to one's own mind. The agreement made with a child's parents might vary somewhat with circumstances, but the unwritten law was, if a boy remained until he was twenty-one he was to receive one hundred dollars; if a girl remained till she was eighteen, she was to have a cow. The children were also to have their clothing, and a certain—or uncertain—amount of "schoolin'"—the three R's, or at least sufficient to enable them to read the Bible. They were usually from eight to ten years old when thus bound out; but cases are known of children being taken as young as three or four, in order to set their feet in the right path early. This custom, supplementing the slave system, prevented for a couple of generations the retrogression which is apt to follow when the race is left to its own system of development.

In many cases relations thus established existed through life, and devoted service was rendered; but then, as now, the marriage of a well-trained servant necessitated a readjustment of household lines.

Nancy Freeman enjoys telling her own tale. Her speech, like that of all the negroes who have belonged to the North for generations, is simply that of the uneducated white person in the same section; but it is not possible for the pen to give her soft voice or her expressive face and gesture.

"How long have you lived in this house, Nancy?"

"Ever since I come here a bride, sixty-seven year ago."

"Were you born in slavery?"

With dignity: "No, I never was a slave; my parents were, but not in my memory."

"Where were you born?"

"Why, up in Chusetown, Humphreysville, yer know. My father's name was Daniel Thompson, and my mother's name was Tamar Steele; yer know, they took the names of the people that owned 'em. When I was nine years old I went to live with Mr. Truman Coe, up in Coe's Lane, on Derby Hill, yer know, an' if I staid till I was eighteen I was to have a cow, an' if I staid till I was nineteen I was to have a cow an' a feather bed."

"And you staid?"

"Yes; but, yer see, the way of it was, when I was sixteen Roswell come an' asked if I would accept of his company, *an' I accepted of it!* But I staid till I was eighteen, an' I got my cow, an' then I staid another year, an' I got my feather bed. I don' think you'll find many girls now, white or colored, that 'll wait two year, let alone three, as I did."

"Were you married at Mr. Coe's?"

"*To be sure!* I tol' Miss Mabel—that's Mr. Coe's sister, that lived there—that she'd better git that dress o' mine she was a-makin' finished by Monday—it was May-day; trainin'-day, that was—by two o'clock, for I guessed I should need it, an' I thought they'd better git a couple o' loaves o' cake made, for there might be some folks a-comin', an' they'd like to have some to give 'em."

"Didn't they expect you to be married then?"

"Oh, I guess they thought somethin' about it, but when they see Priest Swift a-comin', *then* I guess they begun to think."

"Were you married in the parlor?"

"*Of* course! an' my folks was there, an' Roswell's, an' we had some cake and currant wine. I'd helped pick the currants, an' squeezed 'em, an' I'd stirred the cake, an' I was awful proud to marry the Gov'nor's son."

"What did you wear?"

"A white muslin dress all worked over with little dots, low neck an' short sleeves, an' white silk gloves, an' white stockin's, an' low blue prunell' shoes, an' a white silk handkercher roun' my neck."

As her guest stepped out on the doorstone, scattering the young turkeys gathered there for the meal Oliver was preparing for them in the kitchen, Nancy's bent figure stood in the doorway, and putting one hand on the casing to steady herself, she reached out the other to the new clapboards on the outside of the building. "See what my Heavenly Father has given me!" patting them tenderly.

"That looks very nice, Nancy. But how did He give them to you?"

"*My turkeys!* Every day last summer I prayed—O my Heavenly Father, don' let anything happen to my turkeys—an' they grew bigger an' bigger, an' I sol' them, an' put the money *here*," with another succession of pats; "an' if I have good luck with these, I'll put new boards on the end this fall."

YALE UNIVERSITY

IT is hard to give a systematic account of Yale University, past or present, because Yale itself is not systematically arranged, and never has been. At no time in its history have its methods and traditions borne the impress of a consistent plan. It is the result of a growth, often quite unforeseen by those in authority, through which the collegiate school of 1700 developed with slow steps into the college of 1800 and the university of 1900.

Yale College was founded, after a fashion, at the beginning of the last century, along the north shore of Long Island Sound. For many years it was difficult to say what it was or where it belonged. It was not called a college, but a collegiate school, because the General Assembly of Connecticut was afraid to attract the notice of England to any undertaking of this kind. Such notice would certainly have cost the college its charter, and might readily have produced the same result to the colony itself. Its teaching force did not at first receive the names of president and professors, but was obliged to content itself with the less-honorable titles of "rector" and "tutors." Even the location of the school was very uncertain, and it was oftentimes a house divided against itself. The poet's description of Harvard's earliest beginnings,

> "Two nephews of the President
> And *the* Professor's son—
> Lord! how the Seniors ordered round
> That Freshman class of one!"

could not be applied to Yale; for if the rector lived at Milford and the tutors at Saybrook, the Senior class was located at the former place and the Freshman class at the latter. It was not until the removal of the school to New Haven in 1716, and the amendment of its charter in 1745, that it successively attained a local habitation and a name.

The teaching in those early days was meagre enough. Even after the institution had assumed the name of a college, the president was often the only man competent to give anything like professorial instruction. A professorship of divinity was founded in 1746, and one of mathematics and natural philosophy in 1770. But it was not until the administration of Timothy Dwight, the grandfather of the present incumbent, that a group of professorships was established which gave a standard of scholarship to the institution, and an element of permanence to the academic body. With rare discernment, President Dwight secured the services of three young men of first-rate talent—Kingsley in the classics, Day in mathematics, and Silliman in natural science—who remained in the service of the college for nearly half a century, and who made it a college in fact as well as in name.

It was hardly a Congregational college to the extent which is often assumed. Undoubtedly its foundation was stimulated by the distrust which the more conservative element in Massachusetts and Connecticut felt toward the liberal tendencies of Harvard at the end of the seventeenth century. The hopes and interests of men like the Mathers were centred in Yale for this reason. But it is none the less true that Yale was a Connecticut college rather than a Congregational one, and was put in the hands of Congregational ministers as being the chief educational authorities of the colony. A large part of the money given to the college in its early days came from Episcopalians. Elihu Yale was as much an Episcopalian as he was anything; and Dean Berkeley was a prominent though somewhat erratic member of the English Establishment. The college itself was once, at least, near going over to Episcopacy—so near that poor old Increase Mather, in Boston, died of fright. In the middle of the last century we not infrequently find Episcopal ministers preaching in the college chapel as guests of the college authorities. The *odium theologicum* was not so constant a force in those days in Connecticut as it perhaps was in Massachusetts. Connecticut Congregationalism was often a political and social matter rather than a religious one; and in its capacity as an "established" Church it had enough affinity with Episcopalianism to cause the members of these two Churches to be banded together in the closing years of the last century in defence alike against the Quaker, the Methodist, the infidel, or the democrat, as necessity might demand.

The differences between the Congregationalism of Connecticut and of Massachusetts had much to do with the different lines of development taken by Yale and Harvard respectively. The fierce schism between orthodox and Unitarian in Massachusetts found little response in Connecticut, where the lines of conflict were social and political rather than intellectual. There was in Connecticut almost none of the awakening and ferment which filled eastern Massachusetts for at least two generations. As we look back upon Yale life or Connecticut life in the early years of the nineteenth century, we may admit that it was less varied and less active than the life of Harvard or of Massachusetts. But this difference was not without its benefits to Yale. The very absence of intellectual controversy gave it broader political sympathies and affiliations. Those matters which formed the starting-point of much of the life of Boston and of Harvard tended to withdraw Boston and Harvard from contact with the nation as a whole. People who did not understand the Unitarian controversy were frightened and repelled by the name of Unitarianism. The fact that Massachusetts was always ready to take an advanced position carried her too far for the rest of the United States to follow. It was so in the Constitutional Convention of 1788; it was so in the antislavery movement; it was so in many essential matters which affected the development of Harvard College. By contrast with Harvard, Yale had a national character. It did not move too fast for the people of the United States as a whole. In 1800, as in 1894, it was a national college. It drew its students from all parts of the country, to a far greater degree than Harvard. It was then, as now, pre-eminently the mother of colleges. Columbia and Princeton, in the eighteenth century, like Johns Hopkins and Cornell and a hundred other colleges in the nineteenth, have had Yale graduates as their first presidents.

Another characteristic of Yale which has brought her closer to the national life than Harvard has been her relative poverty. Professors and students have both had to work for a living. There has been, unfortunately, no opportunity to cultivate, as Harvard has done, the literary tastes and graces. Yale has not been able to number among her professors names like those of Lowell, Longfellow, and Holmes. The Yale professors have been men engaged in actual teaching-

work, and unfortunately too often overworked in their teaching. It would have been a great thing for Yale could she have strengthened the literary side of her life. Yet there were advantages in the universal necessity of hard work without the graces. It created an *esprit de corps* which would otherwise have been unattainable. It fostered a democratic spirit among the students. Poor and rich were associated together in their work and in their play. Men were judged by their strength and efficiency as men rather than by their social or pecuniary standing in the outside world. This democratic standard of judgment was an important element both in bringing Yale into closer contact and fuller sympathy with the nation as a whole, and in educating the students themselves in moral standards. At Yale, to a greater extent than at Harvard, the value of the education is due to the college life even more than the college instruction. In this respect, as in many others, the history of Yale has been like that of some of the English public schools. Even where the course and the methods of teaching have been most open to criticism, there has been an influence in college life that could not be weighed or measured, and that sometimes could hardly be understood by those who felt it, which made men of those who came under its influence, and which caused graduates to look back upon their years of Yale life with an almost unreasoning affection.

The comparative poverty, the strength of college feelings and traditions, and the absence of contact with a great intellectual centre like Boston, made the development of the university idea slower at Yale than at Harvard. As early as 1813 professional schools began to group themselves about Yale College, but they were loosely attached to it, and formed no organic part of the whole. They depended upon the eminence of individual instructors for their success, and with the death of those instructors they sank into comparative insignificance. The counter-attractions of similar schools in large cities, with their superior facilities for attending courts or hospitals, put Yale at a disadvantage in these matters, as compared with Harvard, Columbia, or the University of Pennsylvania — a disadvantage which, in many of the more practical lines of study, is still felt to-day. Nevertheless, the medical school attained great eminence under the leadership of Nathan Smith, the law school had the benefit of an instructor of extraordinary ability in Samuel J. Hitchcock, while the early history of the divinity school is associated with the still more celebrated name of Nathaniel W. Taylor. But the connection of these schools with Yale College scarcely consisted in anything more than the fact that the names of their professors and students appeared in the same catalogue. It was not until 1843, nearly twenty years after its first foundation, that the law school was authorized to give degrees, nor were such degrees given by the theological school until 1867.

A most important forward step was taken in 1846 by the establishment of courses of graduate instruction. Little was expected from this project at the time. It received but scant support from the college authorities. Had it not been for the disinterestedness of its leaders, it would have been in constant danger of abandonment. But it met a real need in giving advanced instruction to those who were pursuing science for its own sake, independent of the promise of diplomas on the one hand, or the restrictions of college life on the other. The first courses were in chemistry. Instruction in engineering was soon added. The school received the warm support of a group of men engaged in the publication of the *American Journal of Science*, with James D. Dana at their head. The scope of instruction was gradually widened until its courses included not merely physical science, but philology and politics. Degrees were first given in 1852. It was not until nearly ten years later that the liberal gifts of Mr. Sheffield gave the means of establishing systematic courses of undergraduate instruction in the school, which from that time forth bore his name.

Both in its origin and in its subsequent development the Sheffield Scientific School has been what its name implies—a *scientific* school as distinct from a technical one. It has attempted to teach principles rather than details. It has not attempted, as so many other schools have done, to teach a man things he would otherwise learn in the shop or the mine, but to teach him what he would *not* learn in the shop or the mine. Its leaders have had no sympathy with the idea that college instruction could take the place of practical experience. They have tried so to shape their instruction as to enable the Sheffield graduate to get the fullest benefit from practical experience. They do not try to teach mechanical details, which change from year to year or from shop to shop, but scientific principles which shall enable a man to turn all details to the best advantage. They use a great deal of laboratory work, but the laboratory work is treated as a means of study rather than as an end of study. It is one of the advantages of the Yale man in starting life that he knows how much he has to learn. He does not conceive himself equal to the master-mechanic on his own ground. He readily concedes to the master-mechanic the superiority in some points of professional skill; and the mechanic is, for that very reason, all the more ready to recognize the college man's superiority in others.

It has cost Professor Brush and his associates some hard battles to enforce this view of the matter. At this very day the Sheffield School is in danger of losing grants from the national government amounting to $25,000 a year because of its attitude on these points. The school has for more than thirty years enjoyed the appropriations made to the State of Connecticut for the endowment of colleges in agriculture and the mechanic arts. Before the acceptance of the grant the college stated exactly what it proposed to do. It furnished instruction in theoretical principles underlying mechanics and agriculture, and gave free tuition to a large number of Connecticut students. The scientific study of agriculture in America may almost be said to have arisen from the work of Professor Johnson and his co-laborers at Yale. It was here that the impulse started which led to the founding of agricultural experiment stations all over the country. But the agricultural interests are dissatisfied because instruction is not given in the practical operations of farming. With some honorable exceptions, the farmers do not appreciate scientific work as the mechanics appreciate it. They want a college to teach the things which farmers know, rather than those which farmers do not know. The mechanical interests, on the other hand, are eager for new knowledge, and have given the warmest recognition to the college for its services in developing it.

In its present condition the Sheffield Scientific School offers the student a choice of some seven courses, according to the line of work for which the student would prepare himself—one for the chemist, one for the biologist, one for the civil engineer, one for the mechanical engineer, one for the mining engineer, one for the agriculturist, one for the general business man. But each of these is a college course rather than a purely professional one. The Sheffield students have had in times past and present the benefit of instruction from men whose eminence was far removed from the ordinary courses of applied science—men like William D. Whitney or Thomas R. Lounsbury, Daniel C. Gilman or Francis A. Walker. The scientific course has led men to their professions by a shorter road than the academic, and without the study of Greek, but it has been, in its underlying principles, a collegiate course rather than a technical one.

The separate existence of two collegiate departments side by side has constituted a distinguishing feature of Yale development. The Lawrence Scientific School at Harvard has never been of anything like co-ordinate importance with the college proper. The schools of mines at Columbia and of science at Cornell have made the element of technical training more prominent than it has been at Yale. Not a few of Yale's friends have looked at this double collegiate development with regret, and have believed that each department suffered from the lack of those elements for which the other was distinguished. The Sheffield Scientific School, with its independent character and freer methods, attracted the progressive elements, and left the academic department in constant danger of over-conservatism; the monopoly by the academic department of traditions, of religious influences, and of many of the things that did so much to characterize college life, made the course in the scientific school seem somewhat imperfect by contrast; while Harvard, with its fuller elective course and more progressive, not to say destructive, spirit, was combining the freedom of a scientific school with the traditions of a college. The two things at Yale seemed to be drifting farther and farther apart. But within the last twenty years a great change has taken place for the better. It began in 1872, when six representatives of the alumni were admitted to a place in the corporation of the college. In itself

this change amounted to little, for the clerical element in the corporation was left in a majority, and could do anything it chose without let or hinderance; but it was significant and fruitful in giving a degree of publicity to the management of the college which it had never before possessed, and in bringing the alumni into fuller co-operation and sympathy with the college government.

Meantime a change was going on in the faculty as well as in the corporation. The administration of President Woolsey, which terminated in 1871, had borne the impress of his personality in every detail. A man of tremendous force, first-class scholarship, and high ideals, he had secured fellow-workers of the same sort, and had infused the whole college with a spirit of thorough work and lofty aims which has been worth more to it than anything else in its whole history. But President Woolsey was born before the days of modern science; and though he acquainted himself with its results, he scarcely sympathized with its fundamental spirit. His attitude toward science was not unlike that of Sir George Cornewall Lewis or Professor Jowett; and his force of character and purpose was so great as to hold the whole college to his own lines of thought. His successor was a man of less intensity of purpose, and though conservative himself, did not keep the work of the college from broadening.

In 1876 the progressive element in the academic faculty became strong enough to begin the introduction of the elective system in Junior and Senior years. In 1884 it was carried still further—not to the extent which prevailed at Harvard, but sufficiently far to stimulate the intellectual life of the college and increase the opportunity for active work in new lines. In 1886, with the accession of President Dwight, the scientific school obtained its due recognition as a co-ordinate department of the university, and the way was paved for greater co-operation between the different parts than had previously been possible. Meantime the life of the students in the two schools had become assimilated much more rapidly than the courses of study. This was chiefly due to the increasing development of athletics as a factor in Yale life. When the students of the two departments worked side by side in the boat, on the diamond, and in the still fiercer character school of the football field, no narrow traditions of college life or college association could prevent the recognition of prowess, the formation of friendships, and the mutual influence on character of the men in the two departments.

Thus a separation, which seemed at one time to involve some danger to the intellectual and social development of Yale, and to force the students to a choice between science without tradition on the one hand, or tradition without science on the other, has proved in the end a benefit. It has enabled the university to meet at once the needs of those who must shorten their period of professional study and those who must lengthen it. To the former, the Sheffield School offers a combination of college life and professional study in a three years' course. To the latter, the college offers a full four years' course, which is but a preparation for subsequent professional training. The separation further allows a freedom in the choice of courses of study, without that danger of random election of easy optionals against which the Harvard authorities have so constantly been compelled to fight. It enables the system of prescribed courses of study and examination to be carried out to a very considerable degree without involving the attempt to force all types of intellect into one mould.

There is reason to hope that the closer co-operation between the college and the scientific school is but the beginning of a similar tendency with respect to other departments. In his championship of the university idea, President Dwight has done away with much of the spirit of isolation which once prevailed. He has a number of difficulties to overcome, but the spirit of the age is on his side. We know more about the connection between different branches of knowledge than we did thirty years ago. The process of specialization has been accomplished by an increase of mutual dependence, and the different departments of the university have come to recognize this. The scientific school has long had the co-operation of the art school in parts of its instruction. The academic department has now begun to seek the same co-operation. In the courses of graduate instruction, students of every department, undergraduate and professional alike, meet side by side with mutual advantage. In all the special schools there have been men—like

Baldwin in Law, Fisher in Church History, or Weir in Art—whose work is as indispensable to the non-professional student as to the professional. The various collections, chiefly in the Peabody Museum, have a usefulness not bounded by the lines of any department. The work of a paleontologist like Marsh, or of geologists and mineralogists like the Danas, is not for any one class alone, but for the whole scientific world. The increase of laboratory work, whether in chemistry, or physics, or mineralogy, or biology, or psychology, has tended to bring students of different departments more and more together; and a similar result is accomplished by gatherings like the mathematical club, the classical club, the modern-language club, the philosophical club, or the political science club, where undergraduates, graduates, professional students, and instructors meet on an equal footing to read and discuss papers on subjects of common interest.

With university extension — that is, with the effort to lecture to classes outside of the membership of the university itself—Yale has had little to do. This is not so much from lack of sympathy with the movement as from lack of time on the part of the instructors. Their strength is so fully occupied with the regular students that they have little left to devote to extra ones. For the same reason Yale has discouraged the attendance of "special" students who are not graduates of any college nor pursuing any of the recognized courses for a degree. It may be occasionally a hardship to exclude a zealous man from special privileges, but in the majority of cases it is a worse hardship to allow a man who has more zeal than training to take the time of an already overworked instructor from the teaching of his regular students. If a man (or woman) is a college graduate, Yale will offer him whatever facilities she has available. If a man is not a college graduate, the rule is that he must study in one of the regular courses provided for the attainment of a degree.

To the graduate of any college Yale offers the choice of more than two hundred courses of instruction. Twenty-four of these are in psychology, ethics, and pedagogics; twenty-nine in political science and history; twenty-six in Oriental languages and biblical literature; thirty-two in classical philology; thirty-three in modern languages and literature; forty in natural and physical science; twenty-five in mathematics, pure and applied. Besides these, there are courses in drawing, painting, and art history, in music, and in physical culture. It is a question whether the philosophical department of any university in Germany offers as wide a range of teaching. Among all these courses the graduate has absolute freedom of choice. It is assumed he knows what he wants, and is able with the advice of his instructors to select that which best fits his individual case. He can study for a degree or not, exactly as he pleases. The Yale degree of Ph.D. is not given for any defined course or specified amount of work, but for high scientific attainment, of which evidence is given by theses embodying original research.

Side by side with the courses of graduate instruction, and partly coincident with them, we have the work of the professional schools—in theology, law, medicine, and art. In each of these there is a prescribed course of instruction, usually occupying three years, and leading to a degree or diploma at the end. In the law school, however, the degree of LL.B. is given at the end of two years; and for those who are able to study longer, courses are offered leading to the degrees of M.L. and D.C.L. In the theological school nearly all the students are college graduates; in the other professional schools the non-graduates are in the majority. In this last respect Yale is at a disadvantage as compared with Harvard or Columbia. The effort, which the Columbia authorities have so successfully carried out, of making the fourth year of the college course serve at the same time for the first year of professional study, has not found its counterpart in Yale. There are several reasons for this. In the first place, the professional schools have grown up on an independent basis, and are reluctant to sacrifice any part of the separate jurisdiction which they have acquired. In the second place, the university has no large disposable endowments whose income can be used in smoothing the way for a combination. Every part has to work for a living, and therefore has to be left free to get it in the best way it can. Finally, in spite of all that has been done to broaden the courses of instruction, the undergraduate departments have a sep-

arate life of their own, and an *esprit de corps* of their own, which make the problem of fusion at Yale much harder than at Columbia, or even at Harvard. For though the instruction of undergraduate, graduate, and professional students is losing its separate character, though they meet in the same laboratories and the same lecture-rooms, nevertheless there remains much in the social and intellectual life of the several parts which continues absolutely separate. The college remains a college, even though it has become part of a university. A striking instance of this separateness of undergraduate life is seen in the very slight effect produced by the admission of women as graduate students in 1892. It scarcely affected the college life in any definable way. For years past, indeed, women had been attending some of the graduate classes by individual arrangement with the instructor, and no one had even been troubled by it. It was thought better to recognize the position and work of such students, and give them the degree of Ph.D. if they deserved it. Since this recognition there are naturally a good many more women in the graduate classes than there were before; and where graduate and undergraduate instruction are coincident it has resulted in their admission to undergraduate class-rooms. But it has not in any sense encroached upon the privacy of college life, or affected the traditions connected with it. To a man who knows what college life really means, the recent action in the graduate department at Yale does not involve the admission of women to Yale College any more than it involves the admission of men to Vassar College. It rather involves an emphasis on the essential distinction between the college life which has been developed by men and women separately and the university work of training specialists, where there need be no distinction of sex.

The two undergraduate departments at Yale have certain obvious points of difference from one another; they have certain less obvious but more fundamental points of similarity which distinguish them from the professional schools, and even from the undergraduate department of a university like Harvard. They differ from one another in that the required studies of the "academic" department are largely classical, while those of the

Sheffield School are predominantly scientific; in the fact that one gives the degree of B.A. after four years' study, while the other gives the degree of B.S. after three years; and in the fact that one has two years of prescribed work and afterwards a direct choice of electives, while the other has one year of prescribed work and afterwards a choice of courses or groups of study, instead of individual studies. They also differ in the fact that the academic department has the dormitory system developed in a high degree, while the scientific school does not; so that the faculty of the former is obliged to take greater oversight over the conduct of its students than is the case with the latter. But both departments are alike in requiring from their students a high degree of regularity as to attendance and continuous study. The constant pressure to work is not only much stricter than in the graduate or professional schools, but stricter than in the undergraduate department of Harvard or Princeton or almost any American college. Harvard is strict about her degrees and lax about the previous course of her students. If a man has been idle for four years he will lose his degree. Yale, on the other hand, has no room for idlers in her elective halls. Her facilities are so far over-crowded that every bad man elbows a good man out of place. She has no room for the vast number of "special" students—a few of them deserving, the majority incompetent —who clamor for entrance at every large university. A man must pass certain examinations or he cannot enter Yale. He must be regular in his attendance or he will be sent home. He must maintain a certain standard of scholarship or he will be "dropped." This stringency of requirement is the heritage which Yale has received from President Woolsey and the group of men who worked under him. However much the undergraduate may chafe under it or rebel against it, it is this which makes college life and college reputation what it is. No body of young men, left to go their several ways, good or bad, will work out the mass of college traditions and college sentiments which help to mould and make a man in a way that mere book study can never do.

There is no room in an article like this to describe these college traditions and customs in detail; nor are the associations that gather round the Fence, or "Mory's,"

or the Old Brick Row, of a kind which can readily be reproduced in black and white. Every college graduate must fill the picture out for himself. It is enough to say that the special characteristic of Yale life which has distinguished it from other colleges has been a keener intensity of competition than exists almost anywhere else. It shows itself in every form of effort—literary and athletic, political and social. For a few coveted positions on the college journals there are dozens of men toiling months or years to offer the best essays or stories or reports of current events. For a few positions of honor on the athletic teams there are hundreds of men running their regular courses of exercise, and filling the sidewalks of New Haven with costumes calculated to strike the stranger aghast. And so in every department of college life. The contest takes its keenest and perhaps most questionable form in connection with the secret-society system. The societies of the academic department at Yale differ from those of most other colleges in not running through the course, but changing in successive years of study. No man who is ambitious for college success can afford to rest on his laurels in the earlier years of his course. An election to one of the societies of Sophomore or Junior year is chiefly thought of as a stepping-stone toward the higher honor of election into the narrower circle of "Skull and Bones," "Scroll and Key," or "Wolf's Head." As the time for Senior society elections draws nigh, the suspense on the part of the candidates becomes really terrible. When the afternoon of election finally arrives, the scene is perhaps the most dramatic in college life. There is a crowd gathered on the campus—all interested, and some fearfully so. One Senior after another appears from the different society halls, and silently seeks his man amid the throng. At last he finds him; a tap on the shoulder sends a Junior to his room on what is probably the happiest walk he has ever taken; there is a moment's burst of applause from the crowd, varying in intensity according to the popularity of the man chosen, but always given with good-will, and then every one relapses into anxious expectation, until the whole series of elections has been given out. On the whole, the Senior society choices are given with conscientious fairness. There are mistakes made, sometimes bad ones, especially mistakes of omission; but they are as a rule *bona fide* mistakes of judgment, and not the results of personal unfriendliness or chicane. There is a good deal of wire-pulling among those who hope to receive the honor, but surprisingly little among those who are to award it. Opinions differ as to the merits of the Yale society system; but there can be no question that it is a characteristic product of Yale life, with its intensity of effort, its high valuation of college judgments and college successes, and its constant tension, which will allow no one to rest within himself, but makes him a part of the community in which he dwells.

Can Yale keep these characteristics unimpaired amid increasing numbers of students and increasing complexity of outside demands? Can it preserve its distinctive features as a *college* in the midst of its widening work as a university? Can it meet the varying intellectual necessities of modern life without sacrificing the democratic traditions which have had so strong an influence upon character? Can it give the special education which the community asks without endangering the broader education which has produced generations of "all round" men, trained morally as well as intellectually? These are questions which every large college has to face. They are not peculiar to Yale. If Yale feels their difficulty most, it is because she is the largest representative of the traditional American college idea, which Harvard has, to all intents and purposes, abandoned.

The difficulty is enhanced by several factors outside of the educational sphere. In the first place, the demands of modern life make teaching more expensive. There are more things to teach, and therefore there is need of more men, while in each line there is more competition for the services of first-rate men, both inside and outside the teaching profession. The day has passed when college professors formed a class by themselves, who would not or could not engage in work elsewhere. With the increasing study of science in its various forms there has come increased contact between university life and business life. The scientific man can often, if not generally, make more money by expert work than by teaching; and under such circumstances it is not always easy for the university to retain his services. The social demands upon the professors

have taken a different shape from what they had forty years ago. Plain living and high thinking is no longer the ideal of professional success in any line. Under these circumstances a college with limited funds finds it hard to secure enough men of the right kind. The increase in the number of students enhances rather than lessens the difficulty. Additional students are often a source of expense rather than of profit. Teaching is not a work which can be performed by wholesale. No teacher, not even the most talented, can do for a class of one hundred what he would do for a class of ten. Each increase of numbers makes it all the more difficult to avoid the danger of having the class too large, or the instructor too small; nor is an increase of tuition fees to be thought of except as a last resort.

Side by side with this difficulty comes a still greater danger, in the effect of modern life on the students themselves. While the standard of life throughout the community was simple, there was every chance for the democratic spirit of equality to assert itself. The difference between what the rich student and the poor student could command was comparatively slight. It was at most a difference in rooms and in food, in dress and in comforts—differences which the healthy public sentiment of a college could afford to disregard. But to-day there are differences between rich and poor which no one can wholly despise, even though he may respect the poor man more than his rich companion. Each complication of social life inside and outside of the college creates a reason for legitimate expenditure of money, which prevents the poor man from feeling an absolute equality with the rich. The problem of lessening college expenses is one of vital importance for the future of American college life, and is perhaps the most serious difficulty with which the members of the Yale faculty have to contend.

But in meeting these difficulties Yale has certain marked and strong advantages. To begin with, all the traditions of Yale's social life work in the direction of valuing men for their character rather than their money or their antecedents. Though the college standard of character may be imperfect, and though college sentiment may tolerate wrong methods of study, and evasions in dealing with the authorities, the general fact remains that, such as the standards are, they are applied vigorously and impartially; that there is a respect for work and a respect for unselfishness—a respect for all that constitutes a gentle-man in the best sense—that renders futile any attempt to make money take the place of character, or social antecedents take the place of social qualities.

Those who thought that the democratic spirit of Yale was bound up with the Spartan simplicity of the Old Brick Row have been happily disappointed. The gifts of Farnam and Durfee, of Lawrence and White, of Welch and Vanderbilt, have provided the students with larger comforts without distorting their moral standards. There are parts of the secret society system which are in more or less constant danger of becoming rich men's cliques and undermining the democratic spirit; but there is every reason to hope that this danger will be successfully resisted in the future, as it has been in the past.

The development of college athletics has been of great service in counteracting some of the dangerous tendencies of the day. Open to criticism as athletics may be for their unnecessary expense, for the betting which goes on in connection with them, and for the distorted views which they encourage as to the relative importance of different things in life, they yet have a place in education which is of overwhelming importance. The physical training which they involve, good as it may be, is but a small part of the benefit achieved. The moral training is greater. Where scores of men are working hard for athletic honor, and hundreds more are infected by their spirit, the moral force of such an emulation is not to be despised. Critics may object, and do object, that athletic prowess is unduly exalted, and that it involves distortion of facts to rate the best football-player or best oarsman higher than the best scholar or best debater. But the critic is not wholly right in this. There is a disposition in the college world to recognize in the highest degree anything which redounds to the credit of the college. Let a student write something which brings honor to his college, whether in science or literature, and there is no limit to the recognition he receives from his fellows. Let a football-player strive to win glory for himself instead of for his college, and his fellows have no use for him. What the critic deems to be preference for the body over the mind

is in no small measure preference for collective aims over individual ones. It may be a short-sighted view of the matter to think of the high-stand man as working for himself, and the athlete as working for his college. Yet it is one which contains a large element of truth; and the honor paid to college athletes is based on a healthful recognition of this half-truth which the critic so often overlooks.

Athletics, if properly managed, have still another moral advantage in training the students to honor a non-commercial standard of success. In these days, when the almighty dollar counts for so much, this training is of first-rate importance. Of course athletics may be so managed as to be worse than useless in this respect. The least taint of professionalism, however slight, destroys the whole good; the growth of betting endangers it. Yale has by constant effort kept clear of professionalism, and much of her success in athletics has been due to this fact. Betting is harder to deal with, and constitutes a real evil, but not one for which athletics is so directly responsible as many people assume. On the whole, as athletics have been managed at Yale under the constant advice of the alumni, and without either fear or favor from the faculty, they have done great good and little harm, both physically and morally.

If there is danger of distorted sense of proportion among the students, it is to be remedied not by less encouragement to athletics, but by more encouragement to study. Yale emphatically needs more money for teaching purposes. Gifts of dormitories have done good; gifts like those for the Peabody Museum, for the Kent and Sloane laboratories, for lecture-halls like Osborn and Winchester, have done still more good; but they are wholly inadequate to meet the public demands. So fast have the numbers grown that there is to-day not a lecture-hall in Yale College which will accommodate all the students who want to take a single course of instruction, much less a laboratory which will give the room needed for the study of chemistry to all who ask it. Whatever can be done in the way of educational development without money or with limited money, Yale is trying to do. Her success is attested by her growth in numbers and public recognition, and yet more by the unswerving loyalty of her members in every capacity.

COLONIAL NEW ENGLAND

THE romantic career of John Smith did not end with his departure from the infant colony of Virginia. By a curious destiny the fame of this gallant though garrulous hero is associated with the beginnings of both the southern and the northern portions of the United States. To Virginia Smith gave its very existence as a colony; to New England he gave a name. In 1614 he came over with two ships to what was then sometimes known as "North Virginia," explored its coast minutely from the mouth of the Penobscot to Cape Cod, and thinking it a sufficiently extensive country to be worthy of a name of its own, rechristened it New England. On his return home he engaged in the service of the Plymouth Company, and again set sail for the New World in 1615, but was taken prisoner by a French fleet, and carried about on a long cruise, and finally set on shore at Rochelle, whence, without a penny in his pocket, he contrived to make his way back to England. Perhaps Smith's life of extreme excitement and hardship may have made him prematurely old. After all his varied experience he was now only in his thirty-seventh year, but he does not seem to have gone on any more voyages. The remaining sixteen years of his life were spent quietly in England in writing books, publishing maps, and otherwise stimulating the public in-terest in the colonization of the New World. But as for the rocky coast of New England, which he had explored and named, he tells us that he is not "so simple as to think that any other motive than wealth will ever erect there a common-wealth, or draw company from their ease and humors at home, to stay in New Eng-land."

But in this opinion the bold explorer was altogether mistaken. There were forces at work in the English world the value of which a man of Smith's peculiar character and training could in no wise properly estimate. During the first two decades of the seventeenth century several trading parties undertook to make a settle-ment in New England, but all failed disas-trously. Of all migrations of peoples, the settlement of New England is pre-eminent-ly the one in which the almighty dollar played the smallest part, however impor-tant it may since have become as a motive power. It was left for religious enthusi-asm to achieve what commercial enter-prise had failed to accomplish. The dem-ocratic civilization of New England is the greatest legacy which Puritanism has left to the world. In the general movement toward Puritanism which characterized the reign of Elizabeth there had sprung up a peculiar sect of Christians, which, along with the theology of Calvin and the adoption of many quaint notions of Jewish coloring, had come nearer than any other sect had yet done toward carrying Protestant principles consistently into practice. In ecclesiastical polity they had carried the English plan of local self-government so far as to give each congregation full control of its own affairs, leaving the unity of the Church to be maintained only through common allegiance to Christ and common acceptance of the Bible as the rule of faith. The persecution of these so-called Independents was begun in Elizabeth's time, and under James was carried on so vigorously as to drive many of them to Holland, the classic land of religious liberty. In 1608 an Independent congregation from Scrooby, in Nottinghamshire, fled to Leyden, and staid there ten years, growing steadily through fresh accessions, until it occurred to them that if they could be allowed to settle on the lands of the Virginia Company in America they might make the beginnings of a great Christian community. The king refused them a charter, but made no objections to their going, herein showing himself less of a bigot than Louis XIV., who would not suffer a Huguenot to set foot in Canada, though the land was teeming with Huguenots who would have been only too glad to go. The first detachment of these Independents came over in 1620 in the *Mayflower*, and founded the colony of Plymouth. They aimed at the coast of New Jersey, but by fortunate accidents reached a point where they were much less likely to be molested, either by the natives or by rival colonists. Their grant from the old Virginia Company was useless, as they settled beyond its limits; but they got a new grant the following year from the North Virginia, or Plymouth Company. This grant was not made to them directly, but to a small corporation of London merchants, to which the Plymouth Company gave up all its rights in the territory settled by the new colonists. For a few years this London corporation took charge of the colonization of the new Plymouth; but in 1627 the settlers, wishing to be entirely independent, bought up all the stock of the London corporation, and paid for it by installments from the fruits of their own labor. By 1633 they had paid everything up, and become the undisputed owners of the country they had occupied, so that there was nothing now to hinder their prosperity. For many years their

history was entirely peaceful. If they had landed in New Jersey, they would probably have been molested on the one hand by the Dutch settlers of New Netherlands, and on the other hand by the Delaware Indians, who had not yet been tamed by the terrible Iroquois. But in the land of the Massachusetts they were far removed from all white rivals, and the Indian population about them was very scanty, having been nearly extirpated a few years before by a frightful pestilence. Under these favorable circumstances— freed alike from all neighboring hostility, from the joint-stock company which they had paid up, and from the king who ignored their existence—the Plymouth colony throve apace, until by 1643 it numbered more than three thousand inhabitants.

Fortunate as these colonists were, however, their progress was in no way able to compete with that of the neighboring settlement of Massachusetts. In 1627, encouraged by the success of the Plymouth settlers, the project of colonizing New England was taken up afresh by a remarkable body of men of wealth, culture, and high social position, including many leaders of the Puritan party. They purchased a large tract of land of the Plymouth Company, and got a charter from Charles I., incorporating them as the Company of Massachusetts Bay. The affairs of this new company were to be managed by a governor, deputy-governor, and eighteen assistants, to be elected annually by the company. They could make any laws they liked for their settlers, provided they did not contravene the laws of England. But the place where the company was to hold its meetings was not mentioned in the charter. Accordingly, in 1630, the company decided to take its charter over to New England and hold its meetings there. This was a step of the very greatest importance, because the men who founded Massachusetts were highly educated and wealthy men, bent upon putting into practice a grand political idea; and it was a great thing for them to have obtained a charter which (albeit through negligence) enabled them to come away to New England, and found a colony in accordance with their own enlightened views, making such political and ecclesiastical arrangements as they liked, without fear of let or hinderance from the home government. As a recent English historian observes: "By looking at the

colony of Massachusetts, we can see what
sort of a commonwealth was constructed
by the best men of the Puritan party, and
to some extent what they would have
made the government of England if they
could have had their way unchecked."[*]

Some twenty years ago we used to hear
a great deal about "mudsills" and "F. F.
V.'s"—slang terms implying that the people of Virginia, or of the Southern States
in general, were of more aristocratic origin than the people of New England, and
were accordingly entitled to look down
upon them. "We are the gentlemen of
this country," said Robert Toombs in 1860.
This assumption was thoroughly baseless.
In point of fact the English ancestors of
the Washingtons, the Randolphs, the Fair-
faxes, and the Talbots were no higher in
social position than the families of the
Winthrops, the Dudleys, the Eatons, and
the Saltonstalls. The foremost families
which came to New England were of precisely the same rank with the foremost
families which came to Virginia, and in
many instances there was relationship between the former and the latter. So far
as mere names go, this is well illustrated
in Bishop Meade's list of old Virginia families, in which occur such names as Allen,
Baldwin, Bradley, Bowdoin, Carrington,
Cooper, Dabney, Davenport, Farley, Gib-
bon, Holmes, Hubbard, Lee, Morton,
Meade, Nelson, Newton, Parker, Russell,
Selden, Spencer, Talbot, Tyler, Vaughan,
Walton, Ward, Wilcox, and Wythe—every one of which is a name of frequent
occurrence in New England. Two-thirds
of the names in Bishop Meade's list occur
also in Savage's *Dictionary of the Settlers
of New England.* Most of the leaders of
the Massachusetts colonists were country
gentlemen of good fortune; several of
them were either related or connected by
marriage with the nobility; the greater
part of them had taken degrees at Cambridge, and accordingly one of the first
things that naturally occurred to them
was to found a new Cambridge in the
New World. If they had remained in
England, many of them would have gone
into Parliament with Hampden and Cromwell, and would have risen to distinction
under the Commonwealth.

So much for the leaders. On the other
hand, if we compare the mass of the settlers in Massachusetts and Connecticut

with the mass of the settlers in Virginia,
the advantage is altogether on the side of
the northern colonies. The settlement of
Virginia, like that of most colonies at all
times, was determined mainly by straitened circumstances at home. While the
leaders were thinking of molesting the
Spaniards, or opening new avenues of
trade, their followers were thinking of getting something to put into their mouths.
The settlement of Virginia, especially, was
determined by the prospects of sudden
wealth which attended the cultivation of
tobacco. For economical reasons the beginning of the seventeenth century in
England was a time that was ripe for
emigration. During the fourteenth and
fifteenth centuries the Black Death and
other epidemics had kept down the population of England; but during the Tudor
period the population had increased very
rapidly, until at the death of Elizabeth it
numbered nearly five millions. At the
present day that little island can find employment and food for thirty millions of
people, because of its great manufactures
and its bountiful mines, and because
through its policy of free trade it commands the markets of the whole world.
But in the sixteenth century England for
the most part fed itself, and just at that
time, when population was increasing so
rapidly, the supply of food and the supply of work were both diminishing. The
wool trade at that time began to be found
so profitable that great tracts of land
which had formerly been subject to till-
age were year by year turned into pastures for sheep. This process not only
raised the price of food, but it deprived
many people of employment, as sheep-
farming requires fewer hands than tilling
the soil. Hence pauperism increased rapidly during the latter half of the sixteenth
century; and as Henry VIII. had destroyed all the monasteries and confiscated
their revenues, the poor people could no
longer find a refuge there, and get a
scanty support out of the vast wealth of
the Church; so that, naturally enough,
we find the English poor-laws beginning
in the reign of Elizabeth. Consequently
at the beginning of the seventeenth century there were a great many men in
England who were quite disheartened by
poverty and demoralized by idleness.
Under such circumstances men who remain struggling with the conditions of
life in a complex community that has

---

[*] Doyle, *History of the United States*, p. 73.

ceased to have any need of their labor usually descend to recruit the ranks of the criminal class. Their best chance of salvation lies in migration to a new colony, where there is a great demand for labor, and where past circumstances are forgotten, so that life may be in a measure begun anew. The immense development of the English commercial and naval marine during the seventeenth century, due principally to intercourse with the thriving American colonies, greatly increased the opportunities of employment, and went far toward diminishing the numbers of the needy and idle class. Many of the sons of the men who had been driven from their farms by the wool trade made their home upon the ocean, and helped secure for their nation the dominion over the watery pathways. Many of them, all through the seventeenth century, found new homes in America, and as landed proprietors became even more independent and thrifty than they could have been as tenant-farmers in England.

While search for the physical means of subsistence is thus in most cases the principal motive for emigration, and was a principal motive in the case of most of the American colonies, the settlement of Massachusetts does not seem to have been determined to any appreciable extent by such a cause. Neither would it be quite correct to describe the founders of Massachusetts as driven from England by persecution, like the men who settled Plymouth. The men who came over in 1630 with Winthrop were mostly well-to-do farmers from Lincolnshire, Norfolk, and Suffolk—men who were making a good living at home; and they came at a time when Puritanism was waxing strong and militant, when it was nearly ready to try conclusions with the king and the bishops, when, if they had remained at home, they might indeed have been persecuted, but not with impunity. They came for the purpose of realizing a noble though incomplete ideal of society; and hence the exclusiveness which for some time characterized them—an exclusiveness which had both its good and its bad side. They attached such great importance to regular industry and sedate and decorous behavior that for a long time the needy and shiftless people who usually make trouble in new colonies were not tolerated among them. Hence the early history of Massachusetts is remarkably

free from those scenes of violence and disorder which have so often made hideous the first years of new communities. On the other hand, the strictness with which the Puritan colonists sought to realize their theocratic ideal of society resulted sometimes in reprehensible intolerance. In their restriction of the rights of citizenship to church members, in their prohibition of episcopal forms of worship, and in their rough treatment of the Quakers, the Puritans of Massachusetts showed that they had not yet fully comprehended the principles of Protestantism—just as in their prosecution of the Salem witches they showed how long it takes for civilized Christians to divest themselves of the mental habits of pagans and savages.

All things considered, then, the character of the emigration to New England appears to have been pre-eminent for its respectability. Like the best part of the emigration to Virginia, it consisted of country squires and yeomen, but with this difference in its favor, that a principle of selection had been at work whereby the squires and yeomen who followed Winthrop had approved themselves men of exceptionally serious and lofty characters, with minds that had been purified through steadfast devotion to a noble and unselfish ideal. On the other hand, the lower orders of society that we have contemplated in Virginia never had any existence in the New England colonies. Of negro slaves there were very few, and these were employed wholly in domestic service; there were not enough of them to be worth mentioning as a class in New England society. Neither were there any convicted felons, such as were shipped in such abundance to the southern colonies, to become the progenitors of the "white trash." Massachusetts and Connecticut would not admit such people on any terms. There were a few indented white servants, usually of the class known as "redemptioners," that is to say, immigrants who voluntarily bound themselves to service for a stated time in order to defray the cost of their voyage from Europe. There were many of these "redemptioners" in the middle colonies, but very few in New England; and as they had come to a land where no sort of disgrace was attached to manual labor, they usually became thrifty farmers as soon as their terms of service had expired, and thus ceased to be recognizable as a distinct class of society. Thus, as regards their social derivation, the people of New England were homogeneous in character to an unparalleled degree, and they were drawn from the very sturdiest part of the English stock. In all history there has been no other instance of a colony so exclusively peopled by picked and chosen men. The colonists knew this, and were proud of it, as well they might be. It was the simple truth that was spoken by William Stoughton when he said, in his election sermon in 1688: "God sifted a whole nation that He might send choice grain into the wilderness."

The population of New England was as homogeneous in blood as it was in social condition. The Puritan migration we are here considering was purely and exclusively English; there was nothing in it at first that was either Irish, Scotch, or Welsh, nothing that came from the continent of Europe. It began in 1620 with the founding of Plymouth. It reached its maximum between 1630 and 1640, when the first settlements were made in Massachusetts, Connecticut, Rhode Island, and New Hampshire. After the meeting of the Long Parliament in 1640, the Puritans found so much work cut out for them at home that the emigration to New England suddenly ceased. By this time 21,000 Englishmen had settled in New England, and this population "thenceforward multiplied on its own soil in remarkable seclusion from other communities for nearly a century and a half."* During the whole of this period New England received but few immigrants, and "it was not till the last quarter of the eighteenth century that those swarms began to depart [from New England] which have since occupied so large a portion of the territory of the United States." Three times between the meeting of the Long Parliament and the meeting of the First Continental Congress did the New England colonies receive a slight infusion of non-English blood. In 1652, after his victories at Dunbar and Worcester, Cromwell sent 270 of his Scottish prisoners to Boston, where the descendants of some of them still dwell. After the revocation of the Edict of Nantes in 1685, 150 families of Huguenots came to Massachusetts. And finally, in 1719, 120 families of Scotch Presbyterians came over from the north of Ireland, and settled in Londonderry in New Hampshire, and elsewhere. In view of these facts it may be said that there is not a county in England of which the population is more thoroughly English than was the population of New England at the end of the eighteenth century. From long and careful research, Mr. Savage, the highest authority on this subject, concludes that more than ninety-eight in one hundred of the New England people at that time could trace their origin to England in the strictest sense, excluding even Wales. Every English county from Northumberland to Cornwall, from Cumberland to Kent, contributed to the emigration; but the great majority came from Lincolnshire, Norfolk, Suffolk, and Essex in the east, and from Devonshire and Dorset in the southwest. The counties first settled in Massachusetts were named Norfolk, Suffolk, Essex, and Middlesex, while Boston, or "St. Botolph's town," in Lincolnshire, gave its name to the greatest of the Puritan cities.

I have dwelt somewhat explicitly upon this question of the origin of the men of New England, because it is really a matter of great interest for us, both as citizens of the United States and as students of history. These 21,000 English Puritans, who came over to New England before the meeting of the Long Parliament, have now increased to nearly 13,000,000. According to the most careful estimates, at least one-fourth of the whole population of the United States at the present moment is descended from these men. Striking as this fact may seem, it is perhaps less striking than the fact of the original migration when we stop to contemplate it in its full meaning. In these times, when great steamers are sailing every day from European ports, bringing hundreds of emigrants to a country which is at least as far advanced in material civilization as the country which they leave, the arrival of a thousand new citizens each day has come to be a commonplace event. But in the seventeenth century the transfer of 21,000 well-to-do people within twenty years from their comfortable homes in England to the American wilderness was by no means a commonplace event. It assumed somewhat the character of the migration of a whole people. In the quaint thought of some of our forefathers themselves it was aptly likened to the exodus of Israel from the Egyptian house of bondage.

I have said that in this great exodus a

---

* Palfrey, *New England*, Introduction.

principle of selection was at work which insured an extraordinary uniformity of character and of purpose among the settlers. To this uniformity of purpose, combined with complete homogeneity of race, is due the preponderance early acquired and ever since maintained by New England in the history of the American people. In view of this, it is worth while to inquire what were the real aims of the settlers of New England. What was the common purpose which brought these men together in their resolve to create for themselves new homes in the wilderness?

This is a point concerning which there has been a great deal of popular misapprehension, and there has been a great deal of nonsense talked about it. It has been customary first to assume that the Puritan migration was undertaken in the interests of religious liberty, and then to upbraid the Puritans for forgetting all about religious liberty as soon as people came among them who disagreed with their opinions. But this view of the case is not supported by history. It is quite true that the Puritans were to a certain extent chargeable with intolerance; but it is not true that in this they were guilty of any inconsistency. The notion that they came to New England for the purpose of establishing religious liberty, in any sense in which we should understand such a phrase, is entirely incorrect. It is neither more nor less than a bit of popular legend. If we mean by the phrase "religious liberty" a state of things in which opposite or contradictory opinions on questions of religion shall exist side by side in the same community, and in which everybody shall decide for himself how far he will conform to the customary religious observances, nothing could have been further from their thoughts. There is nothing they would have regarded with more genuine abhorrence. If they could have been forewarned by a prophetic voice of the general freedom—or, as they would have termed it, license—of thought and behavior which prevails in this country to-day, I think it not unlikely that they would have abandoned their enterprise in despair, and would have remained in England. The philosophic student of history often has occasion to see how God is wiser than man. In other words, he is often brought to realize how fortunate it is that the leaders in great historic events can not foresee the remote results of the labors to which they have zealously consecrated their lives. It is part of the irony of human destiny that the end we really accomplish by striving with might and main is apt to be something quite different from the end we dreamed of as we started on our arduous labor. So it was with the Puritan settlers of New England. The religious liberty that we enjoy to-day is largely the consequence of their work; but it is a consequence that was unforeseen, while the direct and conscious aim of their labors was something that has never been realized, and probably never will be.

There is no better way of finding out what Winthrop and his friends had in mind when they came to Massachusetts than to consult their own written words. And when we do this we see at once that their aim was the construction of a theocratic state which should be to Christians, under the New Testament dispensation, all that the theocracy of Moses and Joshua and Samuel had been to the Jews in Old Testament days. They should be to all intents and purposes freed from the jurisdiction of the Stuart king, and so far as possible the text of the Holy Scriptures should be their guide both in weighty matters of general legislation and in the shaping of the smallest details of daily life. In such a scheme there was no room for religious liberty as we understand it. No doubt the text of the Scriptures may be interpreted in many ways, but among all these men there was a substantial agreement as to all important points, and nothing could have been further from their thoughts than to found a colony which should afford a field for new experiments in the art of right living. The state they were to found was to consist of a united body of believers; citizenship itself was to be co-extensive with church membership; and in such a state there was apparently no more room for heretics than there was in Rome or Madrid. This was the idea which drew Winthrop and his followers from England at a time when they might have staid there and defied persecution with less trouble than it cost them to cross the ocean and found a new state.

Such an ideal as this, considered by itself and apart from the concrete acts in which it was historically manifested, may seem like the merest fanaticism. But we can not dismiss in this summary way a movement which has been at the source of all that is greatest in American history: mere fanaticism has never produced such substantial results. Mere fanaticism is sure to aim at changing the constitution of human society in some essential point, to undo the work of evolution, and offer in some indistinctly apprehended fashion to remake human life. But in these respects the Puritans were intensely conservative. The impulse by which they were animated was a profoundly ethical impulse—the desire to lead godly lives, and to drive out sin from the community—the same ethical impulse which animates the glowing pages of Hebrew poets and prophets, and which has given to the history and literature of Israel their commanding influence in the world. The Greek, says Matthew Arnold, held that the perfection of happiness was to have one's thoughts hit the mark; but the Hebrew held that it was to serve the Lord day and night. It was a touch of this inspiration that the Puritan caught from his earnest and reverent study of the sacred text, and that served to justify and intensify his yearning for a better life, and to give it the character of a grand and holy ideal. Yet, with all this religious enthusiasm, the Puritan was in every fibre a practical Englishman, with his full share of plain common-sense. He avoided the error of mediæval anchorites and mystics in setting an exaggerated value upon otherworldliness. In his desire to win a crown of glory hereafter he did not forget that the present life has its simple duties, in the exact performance of which the welfare of society mainly consists. He equally avoided the error of modern radical reformers who would remodel the fundamental institutions of property and of the family, and would thus disturb the very groundwork of our ethical ideals. The Puritan's ethical conception of society was simply that which has grown up in the natural course of historical evolution, and which in its essential points is therefore intelligible to all men, and approved by the common-sense of men, however various may be the terminology — whether theological, metaphysical, or scientific—in which it is expounded. For these reasons there was nothing essentially fanatical or impracticable in the Puritan scheme: in substance it was something that great bodies of men could at once put into practice, while its quaint and peculiar form was something that could be easily and naturally outgrown and set aside.

Yet another point in which the Puritan scheme of a theocratic society was rational and not fanatical was its method of interpreting the Scriptures. That method was essentially rationalistic in two ways. First, the Puritan laid no claim to the possession of any peculiar inspiration or divine light whereby he might be aided in ascertaining the meaning of the sacred text; but he used his reason just as he would in any matter of business, and he sought to convince, and expected to be convinced, by rational argument, and by nothing else. Secondly, it followed from this denial of any peculiar inspiration that there was no room in the Puritan commonwealth for anything like a priestly class, and that every individual must hold his own opinions at his own personal risk. The consequences of this rationalistic spirit have been very far-reaching, and in order to understand the work of the Puritans we must point out some of these consequences.

In the first place, we can now see what it was that made the Puritans so intolerant of the Quakers. The followers of George Fox did lay claim to the possession of some sort of peculiar or personal inspiration. They claimed the right to speak and act as "the spirit moved them," and they sometimes sought to exercise this alleged right to an extent that, in the eyes of the Puritans, threatened the dissolution of all human society. Nor were these obnoxious claims confined to the decorum of written or spoken discussion. The Quakers who so roused the wrath of Boston in the seventeenth century were not at all like the quiet and respectable Quakers whom one meets to-day in Rhode Island or in Pennsylvania. Many of them were very turbulent and ill-mannered, to say the least. They were in the habit of denouncing all earthly magistrates and princes, and would hoot at the governor as he passed along the street. They would allude to the Bible as the "Word of the Devil," and would rush into church on Sundays and interrupt the sermon with untimely and unseemly remarks. A certain Thomas Newhouse once came into one of the meeting-houses in Boston with a glass bottle in each hand, and, holding them up before the congregation, knocked them together and smashed them, with the discourteous remark, "Thus will the Lord break you all in pieces!" At another time a woman named Brewster came to church with her face smeared with lamp-black. And Hutchinson and Cotton Mather relate several instances of Quaker women running about the streets and coming into town-meeting in the primitive costume of Eve before the fall. Such proceedings were called "testifying before the Lord"; but one can well imagine how they must have been regarded by our grave and dignified ancestors, who could not have forgotten, moreover, the odious scenes enacted at Münster by the German Anabaptists of the preceeding century. It is not strange that the Puritans of Boston should have made up their minds that such things should not be permitted in the new community which they had endured so much to establish. Several of the Quakers were publicly whipped, or stood in the pillory. They were forbidden to enter the colony under penalty of death; and at last three of their number, who had twice been dismissed from the colony with words of warning, and had twice been "moved by the spirit" to return and "testify," were hanged on Boston Common.

What might have been the treatment of these singular agitators, if they had confined themselves to preaching the doctrine of private inspiration without shocking the general sense of decorum, may best be seen from the case of Roger Williams. Within five years from the settlement of Massachusetts this young preacher had announced the true principles of religious liberty with a clearness of insight quite remarkable in that age. Roger Williams had been aided in securing an education by the great lawyer Sir Edward Coke, and had lately taken his degree at Oxford; but the boldness with which he declared his opinions had aroused the implacable hostility of Archbishop Laud, and in 1631 he had come over to Plymouth, whence he removed two years later to Salem, and became pastor of a church there. The views of Williams, if logically carried out, involved the entire separation of church from state, the equal protection of all forms of religious faith, the repeal of all laws compelling attendance on public worship, the abolition of tithes and of all forced contributions to the support of religion. Such views are to-day quite generally adopted by the more civilized portions of the Protestant world; but it is needless to say that they were not the

views of the seventeenth century, in Massachusetts or elsewhere. For declaring such opinions as these on the continent of Europe, anywhere except in Holland, a man like Williams would in that age have run great risk of being burned at the stake. In England, under the energetic misgovernment of Laud, he would very likely have had to stand in the pillory with his ears cropped, or perhaps, like Bunyan and Baxter, would have been sent to jail. In Massachusetts it is not clear that he would have been subjected to any kind of persecution had he not written a pamphlet in which he denied the right of the colonists to the lands which they held in New England under the king's grant. This, it was thought, would have a tendency to weaken the confidence of the settlers "in the validity of the charter in which all their legal rights as a plantation were bound up,"* and therefore "tended directly and inevitably toward anarchy." Accordingly, in January, 1636, Williams was ordered by the General Court to come to Boston and embark in a ship that was about to set sail for England. But he escaped into the forest, and made his way through the snow to the wigwam of Massasoit. He was a rare linguist, and had learned to talk fluently in the language of the Indians, and now he passed a pleasant winter in trying to instill into their ferocious hearts something of the gentleness of Christianity. In the spring he was privately notified by Winthrop that if he were to steer his course to Narragansett Bay he would be secure from molestation. Though the Puritans of Massachusetts were determined that Williams should not preach in the midst of their own community, they made no objection to his moving a few miles away and founding a new community of such people as might approve of his views; and such was the first beginning of Rhode Island. It was a curious and noteworthy consequence of the circumstances under which this little colony was founded that for a long time it became the refuge of all the fanatical and turbulent people who could not submit to the strict and orderly governments of Massachusetts and Connecticut. People of extreme views, for whom the theocracy of the great majority of the Puritans was not theocratic enough; people who fancied themselves favored with di-

---

* Dexter, *As to Roger Williams*, p. 28.

rect revelations from Heaven; people who thought it right to keep the seventh day of the week as a Sabbath instead of the first day; people who cherished a special predilection for the Apocalypse and the Book of Daniel; people with queer views about property and government; people who advocated either too little marriage or too much marriage—all the eccentric people, in short, such as are apt to come into the foreground in periods of religious excitement, found in Rhode Island a favored spot where they could prophesy without let or hinderance. But the result of so much discordance in opinion was the impossibility of founding a strong and well-ordered government. Throughout the colonial period political affairs in Rhode Island were much more turbulent than in Connecticut and Massachusetts, and the general progress was slower. Rhode Island took no part in the old confederacy of the New England colonies, and after the war of independence it was the last of all the thirteen States to adopt the Federal Constitution.

In view of all these facts, I think we can see that at the bottom of the Puritan's refusal to recognize the doctrine of private inspiration, or to tolerate indiscriminately all sorts of theological opinions, there lay a grain of shrewd political sense which was not ill adapted to the social condition of the seventeenth century. But in his further conviction that religious opinion must be consonant with reason, and that religious truth must be brought home to each individual by rational argument, we may find one of the chief causes of that peculiarly conservative yet flexible intelligence which has enabled the Puritan countries to take the lead in the civilized world of to-day. Free discussion of theological questions, when conducted with earnestness and reverence, and within certain generally acknowledged limits, was never discountenanced in New England. On the contrary, there has never been a society in the world in which theological problems have been so seriously and persistently discussed as in New England in the colonial period. The long sermons of the clergymen were usually learned and elaborate arguments of doctrinal points, bristling with quotations from the Bible, or from famous books of controversial divinity, and in the long winter evenings the questions thus raised afforded the occasion for lively debate in every household. The clergy were, as a rule, men of great learning, able to read both Old and New Testaments in the original languages, and familiar with the best that had been talked and written, among Protestants at least, on theological subjects. They were also, for the most part, men of lofty character, and they were held in high social esteem on account of their character and scholarship, as well as on account of their clerical position. But in spite of the reverence in which they were commonly held, it would have been a thing absolutely unheard-of for one of these pastors to urge an opinion from the pulpit on the sole ground of his personal authority or his superior knowledge of Scriptural exegesis. The hearers, too, were quick to detect novelties or variations in doctrine; and while there was perhaps no more than the ordinary human unwillingness to listen to a new thought merely because of its newness, it was above all things needful that the orthodox soundness of every new suggestion should be thoroughly and severely tested. This intense interest in doctrinal theology was part and parcel of the whole theory of New England life; because, as I have said, it was taken for granted that each individual must hold his opinions at his own personal risk in the world to come.

Such perpetual discussion, conducted under such a stimulus, afforded in itself no mean school of intellectual training. Viewed in relation to the subsequent mental activity of New England, it may be said to have occupied a position somewhat similar to that which the polemics of the mediæval schoolmen occupied in relation to the European thought of the Renaissance, and of the age of Hobbes and Descartes. At the same time the Puritan theory of life lay at the bottom of the whole system of popular education in New England. According to that theory, it was absolutely essential that every one should be taught from early childhood how to read and understand the Bible. So much instruction as this was assumed to be a sacred duty which the community owed to every child born within its jurisdiction. In ignorance, the Puritans maintained, lay the principal strength of popery in religion as well as of despotism in politics; and so, to the best of their lights, they cultivated knowledge with might and main. But in this energetic diffusion of knowledge they were unwittingly preparing the complete and irreparable destruction of the theocratic ideal of society which they had sought to realize by crossing the ocean and settling in New England. This universal education, and this perpetual discussion of theological questions, were no more compatible with rigid adherence to the Calvinistic system than with submission to the tyranny of Rome. The inevitable result was the liberal and enlightened Protestantism which is characteristic of American society at the present day, and which is continually growing more liberal as it grows more enlightened—a Protestantism which, in the natural course of development, is coming to realize the noble ideal of Roger Williams, but from the very thought of which such men as Winthrop and Cotton and Endicott would have shrunk with dismay.

In this connection it is interesting to note the similarity between the experience of the Puritans in New England and in Scotland with respect to the influence of their religious theory of life upon general education. Nowhere has Puritanism, with its keen intelligence and its iron tenacity of purpose, played a greater part than it has played in the history of Scotland. And it is a perfectly patent fact that no other people in modern times, in proportion to their numbers, have achieved so much in all departments of human activity as the people of Scotland have achieved. It would be superfluous to mention the pre-eminence of Scotland in the industrial arts since the days of James Watt, or to recount the glorious names in philosophy, in history, in poetry and romance, and in every department of science, which since the middle of the eighteenth century have made the country of Burns and Scott, of Hume and Adam Smith, of Black and Hunter and Hutton and Lyell, illustrious for all future time. Now this period of magnificent intellectual fruition in Scotland was preceded by a period of Calvinistic orthodoxy as rigorous as that of New England at the same time—perhaps even more rigorous. The ministers of the Scotch Kirk in the seventeenth century cherished a theocratic ideal of society very like that which the colonists of New England aimed at realizing, and the outward aspect of society in the two countries was in these respects very similar. There was the same austerity, the same intolerance, the same narrowness of interests, in Scotland

that there was in New England. Mr. Buckle gave us a very graphic picture of this state of society, and the only thing which he could find to say about it, as the result of his elaborate survey, was that the spirit of the Scotch Kirk was as thoroughly hostile to human progress as the spirit of the Spanish Inquisition! If this were really so, it would be difficult indeed to account for the period of brilliant mental activity which immediately followed. But in reality the Puritan theory of life led at once to universal education in Scotland as it did in New England, and for precisely the same reasons. Popular education was begun in Scotland earlier than anywhere else in Europe, and it has ever since been maintained at a very high level, while the effects of theological discussion in breaking down the old Calvinistic exclusiveness have been illustrated in the history of Edinburgh as well as in the history of Boston.

In no respect has the vital energy of New England ideas shown itself more strikingly than in the unquestioning readiness with which the New England common-school system has been adopted as one of the fundamental institutions of society throughout the greater part of the American Union. This is not the place to discuss the question whether that system is really the best adapted to a complex society in which the greatest and most insidious of dangers lies in the tendency of the government to usurp functions that should properly be discharged by private enterprise. We have now only to observe what were the actual effects wrought in the simple society of colonial New England by the spirit that founded the common schools. By the year 1649 education had been made compulsory throughout Massachusetts and Connecticut. The school-house and the meeting-house were among the first buildings to be raised in each newly founded village; and as fast as the towns grew to a moderate size these rudimentary schools were supplemented by high schools, and in some instances by Latin schools. More remarkable still was the foundation of a university at Cambridge in 1636, before the colony of Massachusetts was seven years old. Founded as it was in a spirit of genuine popular enthusiasm, Harvard College soon attained an eminent position, with able professors, an excellent library and apparatus for those times, and solid and comfortable buildings withal. In the eighteenth century the education that could be obtained there in Latin, Greek, and Hebrew, and in theology and metaphysics, was probably as good in quality as the English universities could furnish. In 1700 Connecticut followed the example of the older colony in establishing Yale College, which soon became the worthy rival of Harvard; in 1765 Brown was founded in Rhode Island; and five years later Dartmouth began its career amid the wilds of New Hampshire, with a humble log-house for its first college hall. Under such circumstances as these, illiteracy had been quite banished from New England before the time of the Revolution. It was almost impossible to find anybody, young or old, rich or poor, who could not read, write, and cipher; in the most sequestered nooks of the mountains newspapers were regularly taken; and no small proportion of the people was in the habit of reading Bunyan and Milton and books of controversial theology, while in the larger towns the best contemporary English literature found eager purchasers. From the beginning, too, New England had a literature of its own, always characterized by erudition, sometimes by elegance of expression. The first printing-press on the American continent began its work in 1639 in Cambridge; the first newspaper was issued in Boston after the overthrow of Andros in 1690; and almanacs, the forerunners of the modern magazine, were published from the outset. Medicine and the physical sciences received no special encouragement at first, though Winthrop of Connecticut was a fellow of the Royal Society. Poetry was attempted by the clergy, though with indifferent success, but history and philosophy as well as politics were dealt with in a way that challenges admiration. It is enough to mention the works of Samuel Willard, of Increase and Cotton Mather, of Jeremiah Dummer, and Jonathan Mayhew. But far above all these towers the name of Jonathan Edwards, the greatest thinker that America has ever produced—a man who for subtlety and force, though not for breadth of intelligence, was the equal of Locke or Hume, and whose contributions to psychology, in his masterly treatise on the Freedom of the Will, can not soon be superseded, and will never be forgotten.

In surveying the society of Virginia in the colonial period we had occasion to observe how the development of schools and printing-presses was hindered by the absence of towns and the extreme diffusion of the people over the face of the country. And we saw how this diffusion of the people was a direct result of the cultivation of tobacco in enormous quantities by the employment of servile labor, which favored the growth of large isolated estates. In New England, on the other hand, a totally different set of circumstances wrought totally different results. The farmers, who made up the great body of the population, continued, as they had done in England, to raise the articles necessary for their own immediate support. They raised wheat, rye, and Indian corn, garden vegetables, cows, pigs, and poultry; and this kind of agriculture was not favorable to the employment of slave labor or to the production of very large crops. The soil and climate of New England, indeed, did not admit of any other kind of agriculture than this. Moreover, the Puritan theory of life made it absolutely necessary that the people should meet together every Sunday for religious worship; and this necessity co-operated in keeping them from getting very widely scattered. Accordingly one of the most prominent features of New England life, from the very outset, has been its concentration. In Massachusetts and Connecticut, and still more in New Hampshire, there were great stretches of unbroken forest, just as there were in Virginia. But in Virginia the cultivated spot in the midst of the wilderness was a vast tobacco plantation, with a lordly manor-house surrounded by hovels in which dwelt an ignorant and servile class. The master and his family lived in isolation, with the nearest white neighbors perhaps miles removed. In New England the cultivated spot in the midst of the wilderness was a village, with its church, town-house, school-house, inn, blacksmith shop, and variety store in the centre, surrounded by from fifty to a hundred neat and comfortable farm-houses, each one the dwelling of an independent landed proprietor. It is obvious at once that this compactness of life must have been highly favorable both to the education of the people and to their general social and political progress. All New England, so far as it was then settled at all, was dotted over with these little towns, sometimes perched on bleak hilltops with the outline of the white church spire gleaming against the sky, sometimes cozily nestled in beautiful valleys. When a village was felt to have become too populous, a portion of the inhabitants—perhaps twenty or thirty families—would move away in a body, and lay out and build another village, with a new meeting-house and a new school-house. From this method of settling the country followed the necessity of making good roads. In Massachusetts and Connecticut the roads were more numerous and in better condition than in any of the other colonies, though until after the middle of the eighteenth century there were few wheeled vehicles drawn by horses, except in the neighborhood of the large towns. In the interior of the country there were the ox-cart for summer and the ox-sled for winter, while men, women, and children all rode about on horseback. After the cessation of Indian attacks the roads were perfectly safe, as the colonies contained no unthrifty or criminal class: there were neither tramps, beggars, nor highwaymen, and crimes of violence were very much more rare than in any other part of the world. More mails from Europe were received in New England than in the middle and southern colonies, partly because of its comparative nearness to England, partly because of its greater number of sea-port towns. The middle colonies had only New York and Philadelphia, whereas in New England there were Falmouth (now Portland), Portsmouth, Newburyport, Salem, Boston, Plymouth, New Bedford, Newport, New London, Saybrook, and New Haven, at all of which points English vessels frequently touched. Through these busy coast towns, and as far south as Philadelphia, the mails ran regularly, whereas they were only sent south of Delaware Bay at irregular intervals, whenever enough letters and papers had accumulated to make it worth while to send them.

The rapid growth of these coast towns illustrates another point of difference between the northern and southern colonies which was of great importance. The settlers of New England were a maritime race, and early began to amass wealth from the whale and cod fisheries. This led to extensive ship-building, and to a steady export of dried fish, whale-oil, and cut timber, in return for which the New-Englanders received wine and sugar and manufactured goods, brought from Europe or from the West Indies in their own

vessels. In this way they came almost to monopolize the carrying trade of all the colonies, besides obtaining a considerable share in that which went on between England and the West Indies. Before the time of the Revolution this carrying trade had reached great dimensions, and had wrought very remarkable effects upon British commerce, as I shall show hereafter. It had not, indeed, begun to diminish in importance until within the memory of men now living; and in the early years of the present century it furnished that hardy and skillful race of seamen who won a dozen or more astounding victories over England at the very moment when England's naval power had touched its greatest height. But what we have now to note is the early effect of this carrying trade in stimulating the growth of town life in New England, and saving the country from the barbarizing influences of isolation. Rhode Island so throve upon this trade that, in spite of the untoward circumstances of its early history, it at last caught up with the neighboring colonies, and since the Revolution has exerted an influence in the country quite out of proportion to its size. Through this trade Boston became and remained the most populous of American cities until, shortly before the Revolution, it was passed by Philadelphia. Through the closer connection thus kept up between Boston and the mother country came the pre-eminent importance of the part played by the Puritan capital in the beginnings of the struggle against the usurpations of Parliament.

As the New England villages along the coast and on the navigable rivers increased in population, they did not wholly throw off their rural character, but developed into pleasant towns, with wide and shady streets running between handsome villa-houses with flower gardens or well-kept lawns. Such cities as New Haven and Portland, both famous for their beauty, have succeeded in preserving something of this appearance to the present day. These houses were usually built of wood, but with timbers so stout and hard as to endure almost like stone. In the coast towns of Massachusetts especially they were often very spacious and elegant, with broad staircases and twisted oak balusters, with carved chimney-pieces, on which was wrought the coat of arms of the family, and with the principal rooms wainscoted in panels and hung with tapestry. The best houses were commonly built with hipped or gambrel roofs. In the villages of the interior the houses, though solidly built, were usually smaller in size and simpler in design, a favorite style of roof being what was known as the "lean-to," from the shingled surface of which the snow could easily slide off. The inner wood-work was of pine rather than oak, and the floors were often bare, but everything was scrupulously neat. There were no cottages of one or two rooms, such as are found in English villages: the poorer houses had four or five rooms on the ground-floor, with an attic overhead; the better houses had a second story with chambers. In front of the house stood a row of maple-trees, or one or two enormous elms, while in the rear stretched an endless succession of sheds and wood-houses, leading at last to the ample barn, from the wide back door of which one could look out over miles of undulating pasture and woodland to the horizon of blue mountains which, in the Algonquin language, gave to the country the name of Massachusetts. I have often been struck with the general resemblance between some of the best of these New England farm-houses and some of the manor-houses still to be seen in the East Anglian counties, if not in other parts of England. The style of dress was rude, and the manner of living in these houses was plain and frugal. Dishes were of wood or pewter, though most families possessed a service of china and a few pieces of silver plate, which were treasured as heirlooms, and only used on occasion of a wedding or a funeral. But in the coast towns, and especially in Boston, the dress and the general style of living were the same as among country gentlemen or prosperous merchants in England. Contrary to what we have observed in Virginia, the conditions of life were such as to favor economy and insure financial solvency. From first to last, grave as some of the political errors of New England may have been, financial heresies have never found a congenial soil there. The rural Yankee, like the Scotchman, had the reputation of looking sharply after the pennies, and of being canny and shrewd at a bargain; but the liberality and generous public spirit displayed in the large towns were always as conspicuous as the strict commerial integrity.

In this New England society the chil-dren of rich and poor alike were brought up to work and support themselves, and no sort of stigma was attached to useful labor of any kind. But distinctions of birth were clearly recognized, and with absolute political equality there was an aristocracy of personal consideration, the traces of which have not even yet been obliterated. The possession of land carried with it no title to distinction or power in a community where every one was a landed proprietor. Yet good birth, high intellectual power, or distinguished services to the state formed the basis of an aristocracy which was not the less influential and respected because it was not labelled with grand titles. Every village had its "squire," who was very likely to serve year after year in some local magistracy, and to serve with honor. Only men and women of aristocratic birth were addressed as "Mr." and "Mrs." For other people, including the majority of the farmers and tradesmen, the style of address was simply the Christian name, or else "Goodwife Smith" or "Neighbor Brown." Seats were graded according to rank in the churches, and the same distinctions were preserved in the catalogues of students at Yale and Harvard until just before the Revolution, when the alphabetical arrangement was first adopted.

But in spite of this well-marked social aristocracy, the political structure of the community was absolutely democratic. It was the most complete democracy that has ever been seen in the world. All local government was conducted by the town-meeting, or primary assembly, at which every adult male was expected to be present, to speak if he liked, and to vote. Even in the largest towns, until after the beginning of the nineteenth century, the government was not representative by mayors and councils, but primary by the town-meeting. Even Boston had its municipal concerns regulated in town-meeting until the population had come to exceed forty thousand. The only representative government was that of the General Assembly of the colony. In Connecticut and Rhode Island the governor was elected by the people, and it was so in Massachusetts until 1684, when the old charter was annulled, and, in view of the haughty and rebellious spirit of the province, the crown took it upon itself to appoint the governor. So strong was the popular government resting upon these town-meetings, that whether the state had any head or not, all the wants of practical administration could be supplied by the towns. It is needless to point out how admirable was the political training which was furnished by this system. But it may not be superfluous to observe how strongly the principle of federation was suggested by this union of independent towns under the general direction of a representative Assembly at the provincial capital. It afforded in miniature a prophetic model of the federal system of the United States. From step to step the ascent was easy and logical. First, the formation of a State government by a representative federation of towns; then an attempted union of States in the short-lived New England Confederacy of the seventeenth century; and finally, when the minds of men had become ripe for so bold an undertaking, the successful union of all the liberated States under the glorious Constitution of 1789. *Tandem fit surculus arbor:* from these small beginnings and through these stages of natural development has come at last the nation which more completely than any other has solved the difficult problem of political civilization, in securing permanent co-operation among vast bodies of men without curtailing their individual and local liberties—the strongest, the freest, the most pacific nation the world has ever seen.

MY FIRST VISIT TO NEW ENGLAND

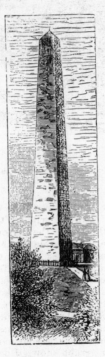

VI.

I DO not know how I first arrived in Boston, or whether it was before or after I had passed a day or two in Salem. As Salem is on the way from Portland, I will suppose that I stopped there first, and explored the quaint old town (quainter then than now, but still quaint enough) for the memorials of Hawthorne and of the witches which united to form the Salem I cared for. I went and looked up the House of Seven Gables, and suffered an unreasonable disappointment that it had not a great many more of them; but there was no loss in the death-warrant of Bridget Bishop, with the sheriff's return of execution upon it, which I found at the Court-house; if anything, the pathos of that witness of one of the cruelest delusions in the world was rather in excess of my needs; I could have got on with less. I saw the pins which the witches were sworn to have thrust into the afflicted children, and I saw Gallows Hill, where the hapless victims of the perjury were hanged. But that death-warrant remained the most vivid color of my experience of the tragedy; I had no need to invite myself to a sense of it, and it is still like a stain of red in my memory.

The kind old ship's captain whose guest I was, and who was transfigured to poetry

HOUSE OF SEVEN GABLES.

in my sense by the fact that he used to voyage to the African coast for palm-oil in former days, led me all about the town, and showed me the Custom-house, which I desired to see because it was in the preface to the Scarlet Letter. But I perceived that he did not share my enthusiasm for the author, and I became more and more sensible that in Salem air there was a cool undercurrent of feeling about him. No doubt the place was not altogether grateful for the celebrity his romance had given it, and would have valued more the uninterrupted quiet of its own flattering thoughts of itself; but when it came to hearing a young lady say she knew a girl who said she would like to poison Hawthorne, it seemed to the devout young pilgrim from the West that something more of love for the great romancer would not have been too much honor for him in his own country. Hawthorne had already had his say, however, and he had not used his native town with too great tenderness. Indeed, the advantages to any place of having a great genius born and reared in its midst are so doubtful that it might be well for localities designing to become the birthplaces of distinguished authors to think twice about it. Perhaps only the largest capitals, like London and Paris, and New York and Chicago, ought to risk it. But the authors have an unaccountable perversity, and will seldom come into the world in the large cities, which are alone without the sense of neighborhood, and the personal susceptibilities so unfavorable to the practice of the literary art.

I dare say that it was owing to the local indifference to her greatest name, or her reluctance from it, that I got a clearer impression of Salem in some other respects than I should have had if I had been invited there to devote myself solely to the associations of Hawthorne. For the first time I saw an old New England town, I do not know but the most characteristic, and took into my young Western consciousness the fact of a more complex civilization than I had yet known. My whole life had been passed in a region where men were just beginning ancestors, and the conception of family was very imperfect. Literature of course was full of it, and it was not for a devotee of Thackeray to be theoretically ignorant of its manifestations; but I had hitherto carelessly supposed that family was nowhere regarded seriously in America except in Virginia, where it furnished a joke for the rest of the nation. But now I found myself confronted with it in its ancient houses, and heard its names pronounced with a certain consideration, which I dare say was as much their due in Salem as it could be anywhere. The names were all strange, and all indifferent to me, but those fine square wooden mansions, of a tasteful architecture, and a pale buff-color, withdrawing themselves in quiet reserve from the quiet street, gave me an impression of family as an actuality and a force which I had never had before, but which no Westerner can yet understand the East without taking into account. I do not suppose that I conceived of family as a fact of vital import then: I think I rather regarded it as a color to be used in any æsthetic study of the local conditions. I am not sure that I valued it more even for literary purposes, than the steeple

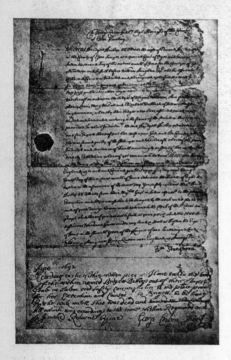

RETURN WARRANT OF SHERIFF GEORGE CORWIN FOR HANGING BRIDGET BISHOP.

which the captain pointed out as the first and last thing he saw when he came and went on his long voyages, or than the great palm-oil casks, which he showed me, and which I related to the tree that stood

"Auf brennender Felsenwand."

Whether that was the kind of palm that gives the oil, or was a sort only suitable to be the dream of a lonely fir-tree in the North on a cold height, I am in doubt to this day.

I heard, not without concern, that the neighboring industry of Lynn was penetrating Salem, and that the ancient haunt of the witches and the birthplace of our subtlest and somberest wizard was becoming a great shoe-town; but my concern was less for its memories and sensibilities than for an odious duty which I owed that industry, together with all the others in New England. Before I left home I had promised my earliest publisher that I would undertake to edit, or compile, or do something literary to, a work on the operation of the more distinctive mechanical inventions of our country, which he had conceived the notion of publishing by subscription. He had furnished me, the most immechanical of humankind, with a letter addressed generally to the great mills and factories of the East, entreating their managers to unfold their mysteries to me for the purposes of this volume. His letter had the effect of shutting up some of them like clams, and others it put upon their guard against my researches, lest I should seize the secret of their special inventions and publish it to the world. I could not tell the managers that I was both morally and mentally incapable of this; that they might have explained and demonstrated the properties and functions of their most recondite machinery, and upon examination afterwards found me guiltless of having anything but a few verses of Heine or Tennyson or Longfellow in my head. So I had to suffer in several places from their unjust anxieties, and from my own weariness of their ingenious engines, or else endure the pangs of a bad conscience from ignoring them. As long as I was in Canada I was happy, for there was no industry in Canada that I saw, except that of the peasant girls, in their Evangeline hats and kirtles, tossing the hay in the way-side fields; but when I reached Portland my troubles began. I went with that young minister of whom I have spoken to a large foundry, where they were casting some sort of ironmongery, and inspected the process from a distance beyond any chance spurt of the molten metal, and came away sadly uncertain of putting the rather fine spectacle to any practical use. A manufactory where they did something with coal-

A TYPICAL STREET IN OLD SALEM.

oil (which I now heard for the first time called kerosene) refused itself to me, and I said to myself that probably all the other industries of Portland were as reserved, and I would not seek to explore them; but when I got to Salem, my conscience stirred again. If I knew that there were shoe-shops in Salem, ought not I to go and inspect their processes? This was a question which would not answer itself to my satisfaction, and I had no peace till I learned that I could see shoe-making much better at Lynn, and that Lynn was such a little way from Boston that I could readily run up there, if I did not wish to examine the shoe machinery at once. I promised myself that I would run up from Boston, but in order to do this I must first go to Boston.

VII.

I am supposing still that I saw Salem before I saw Boston, but however the fact may be, I am sure that I decided it would be better to see shoe-making in Lynn, where I really did see it, thirty years later. For the purposes of the present visit, I contented myself with looking at a machine in Haverhill, which chewed a

shoe sole full of pegs, and dropped it out of its iron jaws with an indifference as great as my own, and probably as little sense of how it had done its work. I may be unjust to that machine; heaven knows I would not wrong it; and I must confess that my head had no room in it for the conception of any machinery but the mythological, which also I despised, in my revulsion from the eighteenth-century poets to those of my own day.

I cannot quite make out after the lapse of so many years just how or when I got to Haverhill, or whether it was before or after I had been in Boston. There is an apparitional quality in my presences, at this point or that, in the dim past; but I hope that, for the credit of their order, ghosts are not commonly taken with such trivial things as I was. For instance, in Haverhill I was much interested by the sight of a young man, coming gayly down the steps of the hotel where I lodged, in peg-top trousers so much more peg-top than my own that I seemed to be wearing mere spring-bottoms in comparison; and in a day when every one who respected himself had a necktie as narrow as he could get, this youth had one no wider than a shoestring, and red at that, while mine measured almost an inch, and was black. To be sure, he was one of a band of negro minstrels, who were to give a concert that night, and he had a right to excel in fashion.

dustries which it would have been well for me to celebrate, but I either made believe there were none, or else I honestly forgot all about them. In either case I released myself altogether to the literary and historical associations of the place. I

"GIRLS IN EVANGELINE HATS AND KIRTLES TOSSING HAY."

I will suppose, for convenience' sake, that I visited Haverhill, too, before I reached Boston: somehow that shoe-pegging machine must come in, and it may as well come in here. When I actually found myself in Boston, there were perhaps in-

need not say that I gave myself first to the first, and it rather surprised me to find that the literary associations of Boston referred so largely to Cambridge. I did not know much about Cambridge, except that it was the seat of the university where Lowell was, and Longfellow had been, professor; and somehow I had not realized it as the home of these poets. That was rather stupid of me, but it is best to own the truth, and afterward I came to know the place so well that I may safely confess my earlier ignorance.

I had stopped in Boston at the Tremont House, which was still one of the first hostelries of the country, and I must have inquired my way to Cambridge there; but I was sceptical of the direction the Cambridge horse-car took when I found it, and I hinted to the driver my anxieties as to why he should be starting east when I had been told that Cambridge was west of Boston. He reassured me in the laconic and even sarcastic manner of his kind, and we really reached Cambridge by the route he had taken.

The beautiful elms that shaded great part of the way massed themselves in the "groves of academe" at the Square, and showed pleasant glimpses of "Old Harvard's scholar factories red," then far fewer than now. It must have been in vacation, for I met no one as I wandered through the college yard, trying to make up my mind as to how I should learn where Lowell lived; for it was he whom I had come to find. He had not only taken the poems I sent him, but he had printed two of them in a single number of the Atlantic, and had even written me a little note about them, which I wore next my heart in my breast pocket till I almost wore it out; and so I thought I might fitly report myself to him. But I have always been helpless in finding my way, and I was still depressed

JAMES RUSSELL LOWELL AT FORTY.

by my failure to convince the horse-car driver that he had taken the wrong road. I let several people go by without questioning them, and those I did ask abashed me farther by not knowing what I wanted to know. When I had remitted my search for the moment, an ancient man, with an open mouth and an inquiring eye, whom I never afterwards made out in Cambridge, addressed me with a hospitable offer to show me the Washington Elm. I thought this would give me time to embolden myself for the meeting with the editor of the Atlantic if I should ever find him, and I went with that kind old man, who when he had shown me the tree, and the spot where Washington stood when he took command of the continental forces, said that he had a branch of it, and that if I would come to his house with him he would give me a piece. In the end, I meant merely to flatter him

THE WASHINGTON ELM, CAMBRIDGE.

into telling me where I could find Lowell, but I dissembled a passion for a piece of the historic elm, and the old man led me not only to his house but his wood-house, where he sawed me off a block so generous that I could not get it into my pocket. I feigned the gratitude which I could see that he expected, and then I took courage to put my question to him. Perhaps that patriarch lived only in the past, and cared for history and not literature. He confessed that he could not tell me where to find Lowell; but he did not forsake me; he set forth with me upon the street again, and let no man pass without asking him. In the end we met one who was able to say where Mr. Lowell was, and I found him at last in a little study at the rear of a pleasant, old-fashioned house near the Delta.

Lowell was not then at the height of his fame; he had just reached this thirty years after, when he died; but I doubt if he was ever after a greater power in his own country, or more completely embodied the literary aspiration which would not and could not part itself from the love of freedom and the hope of justice. For the sake of these he had been willing to suffer the reproach which followed their friends in the earlier days of the anti-slavery struggle. He had outlived the reproach long before; but the fear of his strength remained with those who had felt it, and he had not made himself more generally loved by the Fable for Critics than by the Biglow Papers, probably. But in the Vision of Sir Launfal and the Legend of Brittany he had won a liking if not a listening far wider than his humor and his wit had got him; and in his lectures on the English poets, given not many years before he came to the charge of the Atlantic, he had proved himself easily the wisest and finest critic in our language. He was already, more than any American poet,

"Dowered with the hate of hate, the scorn of scorn,
 The love of love,"

and he held a place in the public sense which no other author among us has held. I had myself never been a great reader of his poetry, when I met him, though when I was a boy of ten years I had heard my father repeat passages from the Biglow Papers against war and slavery and the war for slavery upon Mexico, and later I had read those criticisms of English poetry, and I knew Sir Launfal must be Lowell in some sort; but my love for him as a poet was chiefly centred in my love for his tender and lofty rhyme, Auf Wiedersehen, which I cannot yet read without something of the young pathos it first stirred in me. I knew and felt his greatness somehow apart from the literary proofs of it; he ruled my fancy and held my allegiance as a character, as a man; and I am neither sorry nor ashamed that I was abashed when I first came into his presence; and that in spite of his words of welcome I sat inwardly quaking before him. He was then forty-one years old, and nineteen my senior, and if there had been nothing else to awe me, I might well have been quelled by the disparity of our ages. But I have always been willing and even eager to do homage to men who have done something, and notably to men who have done something in the sort I wished to do something in, myself. I could never recognize any other sort of superiority; but that I am proud to recognize; and I had before Lowell some such feeling as an obscure sub-

altern might have before his general. He was by nature a bit of a disciplinarian, and the effect was from him as well as in me; I dare say he let me feel whatever difference there was, as helplessly as I felt it. At the first encounter with people he always was apt to have a certain frosty shyness, a smiling cold, as from the long, high-sunned winters of his Puritan race; he was not quite himself till he had made you aware of his quality: then no one could be sweeter, tenderer, warmer than he; then he made you free of his whole heart; but you must be his captive before he could do that. His whole personality had now an instant charm for me; I could not keep my eyes from those beautiful eyes of his, which had a certain starry serenity, and looked out so purely from under his white forehead, shadowed by auburn hair untouched with age; or from the smile that shaped the auburn beard, and gave the face in its form and color the Christ-look which Page's portrait has flattered in it.

His voice had as great a fascination for me as his face. The vibrant tenderness and the crisp clearness of the tones, the perfect modulation, the clear enunciation, the exquisite accent, the elect diction—I

GROVES OF ACADEME, HARVARD.

did not know enough then to know that these were the gifts, these were the graces, of one from whose tongue our rough English came music such as I should never hear from any other. In his speech there was nothing of our slipshod American slovenliness, but a truly Italian conscience and an artistic sense of beauty in the instrument.

I saw, before he sat down across his writing-table from me, that he was not far from the medium height; but his erect carriage made the most of his five feet and odd inches. He had been smoking the pipe he loved, and he put it back in his mouth, presently, as if he found himself at greater ease with it, when he began to chat, or rather to let me show what manner of young man I was by giving me the first word. I told him of the trouble I had in finding him, and I could not help dragging in something about Heine's search for Börne, when he went to see him in Frankfort; but I felt at once this was a false start, for Lowell was such an impassioned lover of Cambridge, which was truly his *patria*, in the Italian sense, that it must have hurt him to be unknown to any one in it; he said,

a little dryly, that he should not have thought I would have so much difficulty; but he added, forgivingly, that this was not his own house, which he was out of for the time. Then he spoke to me of Heine, and when I showed my ardor for him, he sought to temper it with some judicious criticisms, and told me that he had kept the first poem I sent him, for the long time it had been unacknowledged, to make sure that it was not a translation. He asked me about myself, and my name, and its Welsh origin, and seemed to find the vanity I had in this harmless enough. When I said I had tried hard to believe that I was at least the literary descendant of Sir James Howels, he corrected me gently with "James Howel," and took down a volume of the Familiar Letters from the shelves behind him to prove me wrong. This was always his habit, as I found afterwards: when he quoted anything from a book he liked to get it and read the passage over, as if he tasted a kind of hoarded sweetness in the words. It visibly vexed him if they showed him in the least mistaken; but

"The love he bore to learning was at fault"

"A PLEASANT OLD-FASHIONED HOUSE NEAR THE DELTA."

LONGFELLOW'S HOUSE, BRATTLE STREET, CAMBRIDGE.

for this foible, and that other of setting people right if he thought them wrong. I could not assert myself against his version of Howel's name, for my edition of his letters was far away in Ohio, and I was obliged to own that the name was spelt in several different ways in it. He perceived, no doubt, why I had chosen the form likest my own, with the title which the pleasant old turncoat ought to have had from the many masters he served according to their many minds, but never had except from that erring edition. He did not afflict me for it, though; probably it amused him too much; he asked me about the West, and when he found that I was as proud of the West as I was of Wales, he seemed even better pleased, and said he had always fancied that human nature was laid out on rather a larger scale there than in the East, but he had seen very little of the West. In my heart I did not think this then, and I do not think it now; human nature has had more ground to spread over in the West; that is all; but "it was not for me to bandy words with my sovereign." He said he liked to hear of the differences between the different sections, for what we had most to fear in our country was a wearisome sameness of type.

He did not say now, or at any other time during the many years I knew him, any of those slighting things of the West which I had so often to resent from Eastern people, but suffered me to praise it all I would. He asked me what way I had taken in coming to New England, and when I told him, and began to rave of the beauty and quaintness of French Canada, and to pour out my joy in Quebec, he said, with a smile that had now lost all its frost, Yes, Quebec was a bit of the seventeenth century; it was in many ways more French than France, and its people spoke the language of Voltaire, with the accent of Voltaire's time.

I do not remember what else he talked of, though once I remembered it with what I believed an ineffaceable distinctness. I set nothing of it down at the time; I was too busy with the letters I was writing for a Cincinnati paper; and I was severely bent upon keeping all personalities out of them. This was very well, but I could wish now that I had transgressed at least so far as to report some of the things that Lowell said; for the paper did not print my letters, and it would have been perfectly safe, and very useful for the present purpose. But perhaps he did not say anything very mem-

"THE ELMY QUIET OF THE CAMBRIDGE STREETS."

orable; to do that you must have something positive in your listener; and I was the mere response, the hollow echo, that youth must be in like circumstances. I was all the time afraid of wearing my welcome out, and I hurried to go when I would so gladly have staid. I do not remember where I meant to go, or why he should have undertaken to show me the way across-lots, but this was what he did; and when we came to a fence, which I clambered gracelessly over, he put his hands on the top, and tried to take it at a bound. He tried twice, and then laughed at his failure, but not with any great pleasure, and he was not content till a third trial carried him across. Then he said, "I commonly do that the first time," as if it were a frequent habit with him, while I remained discreetly silent, and for that moment at least felt myself the elder of the man who had so much of the boy in him. He had, indeed, much of the boy in him to the last, and he parted with each hour of his youth reluctantly, pathetically.

VIII.

We walked across what must have been Jarvis Field to what must have been North Avenue, and there he left me.

But before he let me go he held my hand while he could say that he wished me to dine with him; only, he was not in his own house, and he would ask me to dine with him at the Parker House in Boston, and would send me word of the time later.

I suppose I may have spent part of the intervening time in viewing the wonders of Boston, and visiting the historic scenes and places in it and about it. I certainly went over to Charlestown, and ascended Bunker Hill Monument, and explored the navy-yard, where the immemorial man-of-war begun in Jackson's time was then silently stretching itself under its long shed in a poetic arrest, as if the failure of the appropriation for its completion had been some kind of enchantment. In Boston, I early presented my letter of credit to the publisher it was drawn upon, not that I needed money at the moment, but from a young eagerness to see if it would be honored; and a literary attaché of the house kindly went about with me, and showed me the life of the city. A great city it seemed to me then, and a seething vortex of business as well as a whirl of gayety, as I saw it in Washington Street, and in a promenade concert at Copeland's restaurant in Tremont Row. Probably

I brought some idealizing force to bear upon it, for I was not all so strange to the world as I must seem; perhaps I accounted for quality as well as quantity in my impressions of the New England metropolis, and aggrandized it in the ratio of its literary importance. It seemed to me old, even after Quebec, and very likely I credited the actual town with all the dead and gone Bostonians in my sentimental census. If I did not it was no fault of my cicerone, who thought even more of the city he showed me than I did. I do not know who he was now, and I never saw him after I came to live there, with any certainty that it was he, though I was often tormented with the vision of a spectacled face like his, but not like enough to warrant me in addressing him.

He became part of that ghostly Boston of my first visit, which would sometimes return and possess again the city I came to know so familiarly in later years, and to be so passionately interested in. Some color of my prime impressions has tinged the fictitious experiences of people in my books, but I find very little of it in my memory. This is like a web of frayed old lace, which I have to take carefully into my hold for fear of its fragility, and make out as best I can the figure once so distinct in it. There are the narrow streets, stretching saltwards to the docks, which I haunted for their quaintness, and there is Faneuil Hall, which I cared to see so much more because Wendell Phillips had spoken in it than because Otis and Adams had. There is the old Colonial House, and there is the State House, which I dare say I explored, with the Common sloping before it. There is Beacon Street, with the Hancock House where it is incredibly no more, and there are the beginnings of Commonwealth Avenue, and the other streets of the Back Bay, laid out with their basements left hollowed in the made land, which the gravel trains were yet making out of the westward hills. There is the Public Garden, newly planned and planted, but without the massive bridge destined to make so ungratefully little of the lake that occasioned it. But it is all very vague, and I could easily believe now that it was some one else who saw it then in my place.

I think that I did not try to see Cambridge the same day that I saw Lowell, but wisely came back to my hotel in Boston, and tried to realize the fact. I

went out another day, with an acquaintance from Ohio, whom I ran upon in the street. We went to Mount Auburn together, and I viewed its monuments with a reverence which I dare say their artistic quality did not merit. But I am not sorry for this, for perhaps they are not quite so bad as some people pretend. The gothic chapel of the cemetery, unstoried as it was, gave me, with its half-dozen statues standing or sitting about, an emotion of such quality as I am afraid I could not receive now from the Acropolis, Westminster Abbey, and Santa Croce in one. I tried hard for some æsthetic sense of it, and I made believe that I thought this thing and that thing in the place moved me with its fitness or beauty; but the truth is that I had no taste in anything but literature, and did not feel the effect I would so willingly have experienced.

I did genuinely love the elmy quiet of the dear old Cambridge streets, though, and I had a real and instant pleasure in the yellow colonial houses, with their white corners and casements and their green blinds, that lurked behind the shrubbery of the avenue I passed through to Mount Auburn. The most beautiful among them was the most interesting for me, for it was the house of Longfellow; my companion, who had seen it before, pointed it out to me with an air of custom, and I would not let him see that I valued the first sight of it as I did. I had hoped that somehow I might be so favored as to see Longfellow himself, but when I asked about him of those who knew, they said, "Oh, he is at Nahant," and I thought that Nahant must be a great way off, and at any rate I did not feel authorized to go to him there. Neither did I go to see the author of the Amber Gods, who lived at Newburyport, I was told, as if I should know where Newburyport was; I did not know, and I hated to ask. Besides, it did not seem so simple as it had seemed in Ohio, to go and see a young lady simply because I was infatuated with her literature; even as the envoy of all the infatuated young people of Columbus, I could not quite do this; and when I got home, I had to account for my failure as best I could. Another failure of mine was the sight of Whittier, which I then very much longed to have. They said, "Oh, Whittier lives at Amesbury," but that put him at an indefinite distance, and without the introduction I

never would ask for, I found it impossible
to set out in quest of him.   In the end, I
saw no one in New England whom I was
not presented to in the regular way, except Lowell, whom I thought I had a
right to call upon in my quality of contributor, and from the acquaintance I had
with him by letter.   I neither praise nor
blame myself for this; it was my shyness that withheld me rather than my
merit.   There is really no harm in seeking the presence of a famous man, and I
doubt if the famous man resents the wish
of people to look upon him without some
measure, great or little, of affectation.
There are bores everywhere, but he is
likelier to find them in the wonted figures
of society than in those young people, or
old people, who come to him in the love
of what he has done.   I am well aware
how furiously Tennyson sometimes met
his worshippers, and how insolently Carlyle, but I think these facts are little
specks in their sincerity. Our own gentler
and honester celebrities did not forbid approach, and I have known some of them
caress adorers who seemed hardly worthy
of their kindness; but that was better
than to have hurt any sensitive spirit
who had ventured too far, by the rules
that govern us with common men.

.   [TO BE CONTINUED.]

MY FIRST VISIT TO NEW ENGLAND.

BY WILLIAM DEAN HOWELLS.

Third Part.

IX.

MY business relations were with the house that so promptly honored my letter of credit. This house had published in the East the campaign life of Lincoln which I had lately written, and I dare say would have published the volume of poems I had written earlier with my friend Piatt, if there had been any public for it; at least, I saw large numbers of the book on the counters. But all my literary affiliations were with Ticknor & Fields, and it was the Old Corner Book-Store on Washington Street that drew my heart as soon as I had replenished my pocket in Cornhill. After verifying the editor of the Atlantic Monthly I wished to verify its publishers, and it very fitly happened that when I was shown into Mr. Fields's little room at the back of the store, with its window looking upon School Street, and its scholarly keeping in books and prints, he had just got the magazine sheets of a poem of mine from the Cambridge printers. He was then lately from abroad, and he had the zest for American things which a foreign sojourn is apt to renew in us, though I did not know this then, and could not account for it in the kindness he expressed for my poem. He introduced me to Mr. Ticknor, who I fancied had not read my poem; but he seemed to know what it was from the junior partner, and he asked me whether I had been paid for it. I confessed that I had not, and then he got out a chamois-leather bag, and took from it five half-eagles in gold and laid them on the green cloth top of the desk, in much the shape and of much the size of the Great Bear. I have never since felt myself paid so lavishly for any literary work, though I have had more for a single piece than the twenty-five dollars

THE OLD CORNER BOOK-STORE.

that dazzled me in this constellation. The publisher seemed aware of the poetic quality of the transaction; he let the pieces lie a moment, before he gathered them up and put them into my hand, and said, "I always think it is pleasant to have it in gold."

But a terrible experience with the poem awaited me, and quenched for the moment all my pleasure and pride. It was The Pilot's Story, which I suppose has had as much acceptance as anything of mine in verse (I do not boast of a vast acceptance for it), and I had attempted to treat in it a phase of the national tragedy of slavery, as I had imagined it on a Mississippi steamboat. A young planter has gambled away the slave-girl who is the mother of his child, and when he tells her, she breaks out upon him with the demand:

"What will you say to our boy when he cries for
    me, there in Saint Louis?"

I had thought this very well, and natural and simple, but a fatal proof-reader had not thought it well enough, or simple and natural enough, and he had made the line read:

"What will you say to our boy when he cries for
    '*Ma*,' there in Saint Louis?"

He had even had the inspiration to quote the word he preferred to the one I had written, so that there was no merciful possibility of mistaking it for a misprint, and my blood froze in my veins at sight of it. Mr. Fields had given me the sheets to read while he looked over some letters, and he either felt the chill of my horror, or I made some sign or sound of dismay that caught his notice, for he looked round at me. I could only show him the passage with a gasp. I dare say he might have liked to laugh, for it was cruelly funny, but he did not; he was concerned for the magazine as well as for me. He declared that when he first read the line he had thought I could not have written it so, and he agreed with me that it would kill the poem if it came out in that shape. He instantly set about repairing the mischief, so far as could be. He found that the whole edition of that sheet had been printed, and the air blackened round me again, lighted up here and there with baleful flashes of the newspaper wit at my cost, which I previsioned in my misery; I knew what I should have said of such a thing myself, if it had been another's. But the publisher at once decided that the sheet must be reprinted, and I went away weak as if in the escape from some deadly peril. Afterwards it appeared that the line had passed the first proof-reader as I wrote it, but that the

OLIVER WENDELL HOLMES IN 1860.

final reader had entered so sympathetically into the realistic intention of my
poem as to contribute the modification
which had nearly been my end.

X.

As it fell out, I lived without farther
difficulty to the day and hour of the dinner Lowell made for me; and I really
think, looking at myself impersonally,
and remembering the sort of young fellow I was, that it would have been a
great pity if I had not. The dinner was
at the old-fashioned Boston hour of two,
and the table was laid for four people in
some little upper room at Parker's, which
I was never afterwards able to make
sure of. Lowell was already there when
I came, and he presented me, to my inexpressible delight and surprise, to Dr.
Holmes, who was there with him.

The Autocrat is with us still, and I
shall have to ask his sufferance in saying that I felt myself then, as always
when I met him, in the vividest intellectual presence I have ever known.
He was in the most brilliant hour of
that wonderful second youth which his
fame flowered into long after the world
thought he had completed the cycle of
his literary life. He had already received
full recognition as a poet of delicate wit,
nimble humor, airy imagination, and exquisite grace, when the Autocrat papers
advanced his name indefinitely beyond
the bounds which most immortals would
have found range enough. His renown
has since steadily grown, but that, I

fancy, may have been its most charming
moment for him, when the marvel of his
invention was still fresh in the minds of
men, and time had not dulled in any
measure the sense of its novelty. His
readers all fondly identified him with his
work; and I fully expected to find myself
in the Autocrat's presence when I met Dr.
Holmes. But the fascination was none
the less for that reason; and the winning
smile, the wise and humorous glance,
the whole genial manner was as important to me as if I had foreboded something altogether different. I found him
physically of the Napoleonic height which
spiritually overtops the Alps, and I could
look into his face without that unpleasant
effort which giants of inferior mind so
often cost the man of five feet four.

A little while after, Fields came in, and
then our number and my pleasure were
complete.

Nothing else so richly satisfactory, indeed, as the whole affair could have happened to a like youth at such a point in
his career; and when I sat down with
Dr. Holmes and Mr. Fields, on Lowell's
right, I felt through and through the dramatic perfection of the event. The kindly Autocrat recognized some such quality
of it in terms which were not the less
precious and gracious for their humorous
excess. I have no reason to think that
he had yet read any of my poor verses, or
had me otherwise than wholly on trust
from Lowell; but he leaned over toward

JAMES T. FIELDS, ABOUT 1870.

his host, and said, with a laughing look at me. "Well, James, this is something like the apostolic succession; this is the laying on of hands." I took his sweet and caressing irony as he meant it; but the charm of it went to my head long before

to time Fields came in with one of his delightful stories (sketches of character they were, which he sometimes did not mind caricaturing), or with some criticism of the literary situation from his stand-point of both lover and publisher

DINING-ROOM IN JAMES T. FIELDS'S HOUSE.

any drop of wine, together with the charm of hearing him and Lowell calling each other James and Wendell, and of finding them still cordially boys together.

I would gladly have shone before those great lights in the talk that followed, if I could have thought of anything brilliant to say, but I could not, and so I let them shine without a ray of reflected splendor from me. It was such talk as I had, of course, never heard before, and it is not saying enough to say that I have never heard such talk since except from these two men. It was as light and kind as it was deep and true, and it ranged over a hundred things, with a perpetual sparkle of Dr. Holmes's wit, and the constant glow of Lowell's incandescent sense. From time

of books. I heard fames that I had accepted as proofs of power treated as factitious, and witnessed a frankness concerning authorship, far and near, that I had not dreamed of authors using. When Dr. Holmes understood that I wrote for the Saturday Press, which was running amuck among some Bostonian immortalities of the day, he seemed willing that I should know they were not thought so very undying in Boston, and that I should not take the notion of a Mutual Admiration Society too seriously, or accept the New York bohemian view of Boston as true. For the most part the talk did not address itself to me, but became an exchange of thoughts and fancies between himself and Lowell. They touched, I remember, on certain matters of technique,

THE CHARLES, FROM THE DRAWING-ROOM OF THE FIELDS HOUSE.

and the doctor confessed that he had a prejudice against some words that he could not overcome; for instance, he said, nothing could induce him to use *'neath* for *beneath*, no exigency of versification or stress of rhyme. Lowell contended that he would use any word that carried his meaning; and I think he did this to the hurt of some of his earlier things. He was then probably in the revolt against too much literature in literature, which every one is destined sooner or later to share; there was a certain roughness, very like crudeness, which he indulged before his thought and phrase mellowed to one music in his later work. I tacitly agreed rather with the doctor, though I did not swerve from my allegiance to Lowell, and if I had spoken I should have sided with him: I would have given that or any other proof of my devotion. Fields casually mentioned that he thought The Dandelion was the most popularly liked of Lowell's briefer poems, and I made haste to say that I thought so too, though I did not really think anything about it; and then I was sorry, for I could see that the poet did not like it, quite; and I felt that I was duly punished for my dishonesty.

Hawthorne was named among other authors, probably by Fields, whose house

had just published his Marble Faun, and who had recently come home on the same steamer with him. Dr. Holmes asked if I had met Hawthorne yet, and when I confessed that I had hardly yet even hoped for such a thing, he smiled his winning smile, and said: "Ah, well! I don't know that you will ever feel you have really met him. He is like a dim room with a little taper of personality burning on the corner of the mantel."

They all spoke of Hawthorne, and with the same affection, but the same sense of something mystical and remote in him; and every word was priceless to me. But these masters of the craft I was prentice to probably could not have said anything that I should not have found wise and well, and I am sure now I should have been the loser if the talk had shunned any of the phases of human nature which it touched. It is best to find that all men are of the same make, and that there are certain universal things which interest them as much as the supernal things, and amuse them even more. There was a saying of Lowell's which he was fond of repeating at the menace of any form of the transcendental, and he liked to warn himself and others with his homely, "Remember the dinner-bell." What I recall of the whole effect of a time so happy for me is that in all that was said, however high, however fine, we were never out of hearing of the dinner-bell; and perhaps this is the best effect I can leave with the reader. It was the first dinner served in courses that I had sat down to, and I felt that this service gave it a romantic importance which the older fashion of the West still wanted. Even at Governor Chase's table in Columbus the Governor carved; I knew of the dinner à la Russe, as it was then called, only from books; and it was a sort of literary quality that I tasted in the successive dishes. When it came to the black coffee, and then to the *petits verres* of cognac, with lumps of sugar set fire to atop, it was something that so far transcended my home-kept experience that it began to seem altogether visionary.

Neither Fields nor Dr. Holmes smoked, and I had to confess that I did not; but Lowell smoked enough for all three, and the spark of his cigar began to show in the waning light before we rose from the table. The time that never had, nor can ever have, its fellow for me, had to come to an end, as all times must, and when I shook hands with Lowell in parting, he overwhelmed me by saying that if I thought of going to Concord he would send me a letter to Hawthorne. I was not to see Lowell again during my stay in Boston; but Dr. Holmes asked me to tea for the next evening, and Fields said I must come to breakfast with him in the morning.

XI.

I recall with the affection due to his friendly nature, and to the kindness afterwards to pass between us for many years, the whole aspect of the publisher when I first saw him. His abundant hair, and his full "beard as broad as ony spade," that flowed from his throat in Homeric curls, were touched with the first frost. He had a fine color, and his eyes, as keen as they were kind, twinkled restlessly above the wholesome russet-red of his cheeks. His portly frame was clad in those Scotch tweeds which had not yet displaced the traditional broadcloth with us in the West, though I had sent to New York for a rough suit, and so felt myself not quite unworthy to meet a man fresh from the hands of the London tailor.

Otherwise I stood as much in awe of him as his jovial soul would let me; and if I might I should like to give the literary youth of this day some notion of the importance of his name to the literary youth of my day. He gave æsthetic character to the house of Ticknor & Fields, but he was by no means a silent partner on the economic side. No one can forecast the fortune of a new book, but he knew as well as any publisher can know not only whether a book was good, but whether the reader would think so; and I suppose that his house made as few bad guesses, along with their good ones, as any house that ever tried the uncertain temper of the public with its ventures. In the minds of all who loved the plain brown cloth and tasteful print of its issues he was more or less intimately associated with their literature; and those who were not mistaken in thinking De Quincey one of the delightfulest authors in the world, were especially grateful to the man who first edited his writings in book form, and proud that this edition was the effect of American sympathy with them. At that day, I believed authorship the noblest calling in the world, and I should still be at a loss to name any nobler. The great authors I had met were to me the sum of greatness, and if I could not rank their publisher with them by virtue of equal achievement, I handsomely brevetted him worthy of their friendship, and honored him in the visible measure of it.

In his house beside the Charles, and in the close neighborhood of Dr. Holmes, I found an odor and an air of books such as I fancied might belong to the famous literary houses of London. It is still there, that friendly home of lettered refinement, and the gracious spirit which knew how to welcome me, and make the least of my shyness and strangeness, and the most of the little else there was in me, illumines it still, though my host of that rapturous moment has many years been of those who are only with us unseen and unheard. I remember his burlesque pretence that morning of an inextinguishable grief when I owned that I had never eaten blueberry cake before, and how he kept returning to the pathos of the fact that there should be a region of the earth where blueberry cake was unknown. We breakfasted in the pretty room whose windows look out through leaves and flowers upon the river's coming and going tides, and whose walls were covered with the faces and the autographs of all the contemporary poets and novelists. The Fieldses had spent some days with Tennyson in their recent English sojourn, and Mrs. Fields had much to tell of him, how he looked, how he smoked, how he read aloud, and how he said, when he asked her to go with him to the tower of his house, "Come up and see the sad English sunset!" which had an instant value to me such as some rich verse of his might have had. I was very new to it all, how new I could not very well say, but I flattered myself that I breathed in that atmosphere as if in the return from life-long exile. Still I patriotically bragged of the West a little, and I told them proudly that in Columbus no book since Uncle Tom's Cabin had sold so well as The Marble Faun. This made the effect that I wished, but whether it was true or not, heaven knows; I only know that I heard it from our leading bookseller, and I made no question of it myself.

After breakfast, Fields went away to the office, and I lingered, while Mrs. Fields showed me from shelf to shelf in the library, and dazzled me with the sight of authors' copies, and volumes invaluable with the autographs and the pencilled notes of the men whose names were dear to me from my love of their work. Everywhere was some souvenir of the living celebrities my hosts had met; and whom had they not met in that English sojourn in days before England embittered herself to us? Not Tennyson only, but Thackeray, but Dickens, but Charles Reade, but Carlyle, but many another minor fame was in my ears from converse so recent with them that it was as if I heard their voices in their echoed words.

I do not remember how long I staid; I remember I was afraid of staying too long, and so I am sure I did not stay as long as I should have liked. But I have not the least notion how I got away, and I am not certain where I spent the rest of a day that began in the clouds, but had to be ended on the common earth. I suppose I gave it mostly to wandering about the city, and partly to recording my impressions of it for that newspaper which never published them. The summer weather in Boston, with its sunny heat struck through and through with the coolness of the sea, and its clear air untainted with a breath of smoke, I have always loved, but

it had then a zest unknown before; and I should have thought it enough simply to be alive in it. But everywhere I came upon something that fed my famine for the old, the quaint, the picturesque, and however the day passed it was a banquet, a festival. I can only recall my breathless first sight of the Public Library and of the Athenæum Gallery: great sights then, which the Vatican and the Pitti hardly afterwards eclipsed for mere emotion. In fact I did not see these elder treasuries of literature and art between breakfasting with the Autocrat's publisher in the morning, and taking tea with the Autocrat himself in the evening, and that made a whole world's difference.

XII.

The tea of that simpler time is wholly inconceivable to this generation, which knows the thing only as a mild form of afternoon reception; but I suppose that in 1860 very few dined late in our whole pastoral republic. Tea was the meal people asked people to when they wished to sit at long leisure and large ease; it came at the end of the day, at six o'clock, or seven; and one went to it in morning dress. It had an unceremonied domesticity in the abundance of its light dishes, and I fancy these did not vary much from East to West, except that we had a Southern touch in our fried chicken and corn bread; but at the Autocrat's tea table the cheering cup had a flavor unknown to me before that day. He asked me if I knew it, and I said it was English breakfast tea; for I had drunk it at the publisher's in the morning, and was willing not to seem strange to it. "Ah, yes," he said; "but this is the flower of the souchong; it is the blossom, the poetry of tea," and then he told me how it had been given him by a friend, a merchant in the China trade, which used to flourish in Boston, and was the poetry of commerce, as this delicate beverage was of tea. That commerce is long past, and I fancy that the plant ceased to bloom when the traffic fell into decay.

The Autocrat's windows had the same outlook upon the Charles as the publisher's, and after tea we went up into a back parlor of the same orientation, and saw the sunset die over the water, and the westering flats and hills. Nowhere else in the world has the day a lovelier close, and our talk took something of the mystic coloring that the heavens gave those mantling expanses. It was chiefly his talk, but I have always found the best talkers are willing that you should talk if you like, and a quick sympathy and a subtle sense met all that I had to say from him and from the unbroken circle of kindred intelligences about him. I saw him then in the midst of his family, and perhaps never afterwards to better advantage, or in a finer mood. We spoke of the things that people perhaps once liked to deal with more than they do now; of the intimations of immortality, of the experiences of morbid youth, and of all those messages from the tremulous nerves which we mistake for prophecies. I was not ashamed, before his tolerant wisdom, to acknowledge the effects that had lingered so long with me in fancy and even in conduct, from a time of broken health and troubled spirit; and I remember the exquisite tact in him which recognized them as things common to all, however peculiar in each, which left them mine for whatever obscure vanity I might have in them, and yet gave me the companionship of the whole race in their experience. We spoke of forebodings and presentiments; we approached the mystic confines of the world from which no traveller has yet returned with a passport *en règle* and properly *visé;* and he held his light course through these filmy impalpabilities with a charming sincerity, with the scientific conscience that refuses either to deny the substance of things unseen, or to affirm it. In the gathering dusk, so weird did my fortune of being there and listening to him seem, that I might well have been a blessed ghost, for all the reality I felt in myself.

I tried to tell him how much I had read him from my boyhood, and with what joy and gain; and he was patient of these futilities, and I have no doubt imagined the love that inspired them, and accepted that instead of the poor praise. When the sunset passed, and the lamps were lighted, and we all came back to our dear little firm-set earth, he began to question me about my native region of it. From many forgotten inquiries I recall his asking me what was the fashionable religion in Columbus, or the Church that socially corresponded to the Unitarian Church in Boston. He had first to clarify my intelligence as to what Unitarianism was; we had Universalists but not Unitarians; but when I understood, I answered from such vantage as my own wholly outside Swedenborgianism gave me, that I thought most of the most respectable people with us were of the Presbyterian Church; some were certainly Episcopalians, but upon the whole the largest number were Presbyterians. He found that very strange indeed; and said that he did not believe there was a Presbyterian Church in Boston; that the New England Calvinists were all of the Orthodox Church. He had to explain Orthodoxy to me, and then I could confess to one Congregational Church in Columbus.

Probably I failed to give the Autocrat any very clear image of our social frame in the West, but the fault was altogether mine, if I did. Such lecturing tours as he had made had not taken him among us, as those of Emerson and other New-Englanders had, and my report was positive rather than comparative. I was full of pride in journalism at that day, and I dare say that I vaunted the brilliancy and power of our newspapers more than they merited; I should not have been likely to wrong them otherwise. It is strange that in all the talk I had with him and Lowell, or rather heard from them, I can recall nothing said of political affairs, though Lincoln had then been nominated by the Republicans, and the Civil War had practically begun. But we did not imagine such a thing in the North; we rested secure in the belief that if Lincoln were elected the South would eat all its fiery words, perhaps from the mere love and inveterate habit of fire-eating.

I rent myself away from the Autocrat's presence as early as I could, and as my evening had been too full of happiness to sleep upon at once, I spent the rest of the night till two in the morning wandering about the streets and in the Common with a Harvard Senior whom I had met. He was a youth of like literary passions with myself, but of such different traditions in every possible way that his deeply schooled and definitely regulated life seemed as anomalous to me as my own desultory and self-found way must have seemed to him. We passed the time in the delight of trying to make ourselves known to each other, and in a promise to continue by letter the effort, which duly lapsed into silent patience with the necessarily insoluble problem.

[TO BE CONTINUED.]

MY FIRST VISIT TO NEW ENGLAND.

BY WILLIAM DEAN HOWELLS.

Fourth Part.

XIII.

I MUST have lingered in Boston for the introduction to Hawthorne which Lowell had offered me, for when it came, with a little note of kindness and counsel for myself such as only Lowell had the gift of writing, it was already so near Sunday that I staid over till Monday before I started. I do not recall what I did with the time, except keep myself from making it a burden to the people I knew, and wandering about the city alone. Nothing of it remains to me except the fortune that favored me that Sunday night with a view of the old Granary Burying-ground on Tremont Street. I found the gates open, and I explored every path in the place, wreaking myself in such meagre emotion as I could get from the tomb of the Franklin family, and rejoicing with the whole soul of my Western modernity in the evidence of a remote antiquity which so many of the dim inscriptions afforded. I do not think that I have ever known anything practically older than these monuments, though I have since supped so full of classic and mediæval ruin. I am sure that I was more deeply touched by the epitaph of a poor little Puritan maiden who died at sixteen in the early sixteen-thirties than by the tomb of Cæcilia Metella, and that the heartache which I tried to put into verse when I got back to my room in the hotel was none the less genuine because it would not lend itself to my literary purpose, and remains nothing but pathos to this day.

I am not able to say how I reached the town of Lowell, where I went before going to Concord, that I might ease the unhappy conscience I had about those factories which I hated so much to see, and have it clean for the pleasure of meeting the fabricator of visions whom I was authorized to molest in any air-castle where I might find him. I only know that I went to Lowell, and visited one of the great mills, which with their whirring spools, the ceaseless flight of their shuttles, and the bewildering sight and sound of all their mechanism have since seemed to me the death of the joy that ought to come from work, if not the captivity of those who tended them. But then I thought it right and well for me to be standing by,

"With sick and scornful looks averse,"

while these others toiled; I did not see the tragedy in it, and I got my pitiful literary antipathy away as soon as I could, no wiser for the sight of the ingenious contrivances I inspected, and I am sorry to say no sadder. In the cool of the evening I sat at the door of my hotel, and watched the long files of the work-worn factory-girls stream by, with no concern for them but to see which was pretty and which was plain, and with no dream of a truer order than that which gave them ten hours' work a day in those hideous mills and lodged them in the barracks where they rested from their toil.

XIV.

I wonder if there is a stage that still runs between Lowell and Concord, past meadow walls, and under the caressing boughs of way-side elms, and through the bird-haunted gloom of woodland roads, in the freshness of the summer morning? By a blessed chance I found that there was such a stage in 1860, and I took it from my hotel, instead of going back to Boston and up to Concord as I must have had to do by train. The journey gave me the intimacy of the New England country as I could have had it in no other fashion, and for the first time I saw it in all the summer sweetness which I have often steeped my soul in since. The meadows were newly mown, and the air was fragrant with the grass, stretching in long winrows among the brown bowlders; or capped with canvas in the little haycocks it had been gathered into the day before. I was fresh from the affluent farms of the Western Reserve, and this care of the grass touched me with a rude pity, which I also bestowed on the meagre fields of corn and wheat; but still the land was lovelier than any I had ever seen, with its old farm-houses, and brambled gray stone walls, its stony hillsides, its staggering orchards, its wooded tops, and its thick-brackened valleys. From West to East the difference was as great as I afterwards found it from America to Europe, and my impression of something quaint and strange was no keener when I saw Old England the next year than when I saw New England now. I had imagined the landscape bare of trees, and I was astonished to find it almost as full of them as at home, though they all looked very little, as they well might to eyes used to the primeval forests of Ohio. The road ran through them from time to time, and took their coolness on its smooth hard reaches, and then issued again in the glisten of the open fields.

I made phrases to myself about the scenery as we drove along; and yes, I suppose I made phrases about the young girl who was one of the inside passengers, and who, when the common strangeness had somewhat worn off, began to sing, and sang most of the way to Concord. Perhaps she was not very sage, and I am sure she was not of the caste of Vere de Vere, but she was pretty enough, and she had a voice of a birdlike tunableness, so that I would not have her out of the memory of that pleasant journey if I could. She was long ago an elderly woman, if she lived, and I suppose she would not now point out her fellow-passenger if he strolled in the evening by the house where she had dismounted, upon her arrival in Concord, and laugh and pull another girl away from the window, in the high excitement of the prodigious adventure.

XV.

Her fellow-passenger was in far other excitement; he was to see Hawthorne, and in a manner to meet Priscilla and Zenobia, and Hester Prynne and little Pearl, and Miriam and Hilda, and Hollingsworth and Coverdale, and Chillingworth and Dimmesdale, and Donatello and Kenyon; and he had no heart for any such poor little reality as that, who could not have been got into any story that one could respect, and must have been difficult even in a Heinesque poem.

I wasted that whole evening and the next morning in fond delaying, and it was not until after the indifferent dinner I got at the tavern where I stopped, that I found courage to go and present Lowell's letter to Hawthorne. I would almost have foregone meeting the weird genius only

to have kept that letter, for it said certain infinitely precious things of me with such a sweetness, such a grace as Lowell alone could give his praise. Years afterwards, when Hawthorne was dead, I met Mrs. Hawthorne, and told her of the pang I had in parting with it, and she sent it me, doubly enriched by Hawthorne's keeping. But now if I were to see him at all I must give up my letter, and I carried it in my hand to the door of the cottage he called The Wayside. It was never otherwise than a very modest place, but the modesty was greater then than to-day, and there was already some preliminary carpentry at one end of the cottage, which I saw was to result in an addition to it. I recall pleasant fields across the road before it; behind rose a hill wooded with low pines, such as is made in Septimius Felton the scene of the involuntary duel between Septimius and the young British officer. I have a sense of the woods coming quite down to the house, but if this was so I do not know what to do with a grassy slope which seems to have stretched part way up the hill. As I approached, I looked for the tower which the author was fabled to climb into at sight of the coming guest, and pull the ladder up after him; and I wondered whether he would fly before me in that sort, or imagine some easier means of escaping me.

The door was opened to my ring by a tall handsome boy whom I suppose to have been Mr. Julian Hawthorne; and the next moment I found myself in the presence of the romancer, who entered from some room beyond. He advanced carrying his head with a heavy forward droop, and with a pace for which I decided that the word would be *pondering*. It was the pace of a bulky man of fifty, and his head was that beautiful head we all know from the many pictures of it. But Hawthorne's *look* was different from that of any picture of him that I have seen. It was sombre and brooding, as the look of such a poet should have been; it was the look of a man who had dealt faithfully and therefore sorrowfully with that problem of evil which forever attracted, forever evaded Hawthorne. It was by no means troubled; it was full of a dark repose. Others who knew him better and saw him oftener were familiar with other aspects, and I remember that one night at Longfellow's table, when one

THE GRANARY BURYING-GROUND, BOSTON.

of the guests happened to speak of the photograph of Hawthorne which hung in a corner of the room, Lowell said, after a glance at it, "Yes, it's good; but it hasn't his fine *accipitral* look."

In the face that confronted me, however, there was nothing of keen alertness; but only a sort of quiet, patient intelligence, for which I seek the right word in vain. It was a very regular face, with beautiful eyes; the mustache, still entirely dark, was dense over the fine mouth. Hawthorne was dressed in black, and he had a certain effect which I remember, of seeming to have on a black cravat with no visible collar. He was such a man that if I had ignorantly met him anywhere I should have instantly felt him to be a personage.

I must have given him the letter myself, for I have no recollection of parting with it before, but I only remember his offering me his hand, and making me shyly and tentatively welcome. After a

few moments of the demoralization which followed his hospitable attempts in me, he asked if I would not like to go up on his hill with him and sit there, where he smoked in the afternoon. He offered me a cigar, and when I said that I did not smoke, he lighted it for himself, and we climbed the hill together. At the top, where there was an outlook in the pines over the Concord meadows, we found a log, and he invited me to a place on it beside him, and at intervals of a minute or so he talked while he smoked. Heaven preserved me from the folly of trying to tell him how much his books had been to me, and though we got on rapidly at no time, I think we got on better for this interposition. He asked me about Lowell, I dare say, for I told him of my joy in meeting him and Dr. Holmes, and this seemed greatly to interest him. Perhaps because he was so lately from Europe, where our great men are always seen through the wrong end of the telescope, he appeared surprised at my devotion, and asked me whether I cared as much for meeting them as I should care for meeting the famous English authors. I professed that I cared much more, though whether this was true, I now have my doubts, and I think Hawthorne doubted it at the time. But he said nothing in comment, and went on to speak generally of Europe and America. He was curious as to the West, which he seemed to fancy much more purely American, and said he would like to see some part of the country on which the shadow, or, if I must be precise, the damned shadow, of Europe had not fallen. I told him I thought the West must finally be characterized by the Germans, whom we had in great numbers, and, purely from my zeal for German poetry, I tried to allege some proofs of their present influence, though I could think of none outside of politics, which I thought they affected wholesomely. I knew Hawthorne was a Democrat, and I felt it well to touch politics lightly, but he had no more to say about the fateful

election then pending than Holmes or Lowell had.

With the abrupt transition of his talk throughout, he began somehow to speak of women, and said he had never seen a woman whom he thought quite beautiful. In the same way he spoke of the New England temperament, and suggested that the apparent coldness in it was also real, and that the suppression of emotion for generations would extinguish it at last. Then he questioned me as to my knowledge of Concord, and whether I had seen any of the notable people. I answered that I had met no one but himself, as yet, but I very much wished to see Emerson and Thoreau. I did not think it needful to say that I wished to see Thoreau quite as much because he had suffered in the cause of John Brown as because he had written the books which had taken me; and when he said that Thoreau prided himself on coming nearer the heart of a pine-tree than any other human being, I could say honestly enough that I would rather come near the heart of a man.

This visibly pleased him, and I saw that it did not displease him, when he asked whether I was not going to see his next neighbor Mr. Alcott, and I confessed that I had never heard of him. That surprised as well as pleased him; he remarked, with whatever intention, that there was nothing like recognition to make a man modest; and he entered into some account of the philosopher, whom I suppose I need not be much ashamed of not knowing then, since his influence was of the immediate sort that makes a man important to his townsmen while he is still strange to his countrymen.

Hawthorne descanted a little upon the landscape, and said certain of the pleasant fields below us belonged to him; but he preferred his hill-top, and if he could have his way those arable fields should be grown up to pines too. He smoked fitfully, and

HAWTHORNE.

slowly, and in the hour that we spent together, his whiffs were of the desultory and unfinal character of his words. When we went down, he asked me into his house again, and would have me stay to tea, for which we found the table laid. But there was a great deal of silence in it all, and at times, in spite of his shadowy kindness, I felt my spirits sink. After tea, he showed me a bookcase, where there were a few books toppling about on the half-filled shelves, and said, coldly, "This is my library." I knew that men were his books, and though I myself cared for books so much, I found it fit and fine that he should care so little, or seem to care so little. Some of his own romances were among the volumes on these shelves, and when I put my finger on the Blithedale Romance and said that I preferred that to the others, his face lighted up, and he said that he believed the Germans liked that best too.

LARCH WALK, WAYSIDE.
Trees planted by Hawthorne between Alcott's House and Wayside.

Upon the whole we parted such good friends that when I offered to take leave he asked me how long I was to be in Concord, and not only bade me come to see him again, but said he would give me a card to Emerson, if I liked. I answered, of course, that I should like it beyond all things; and he wrote on the back of his card something which I found, when I got away, to be, "I find this young man worthy." The quaintness, the little stiffness of it, if one pleases to call it so, was amusing to one who was not without his sense of humor, but the kindness filled him to the throat with joy. In fact, I entirely liked Hawthorne. He had been as cordial as so shy a man could show himself; and I perceived, with the repose that nothing else can give, the entire sincerity of his soul.

Nothing could have been farther from the behavior of this very great man than any sort of posing, apparently, or a wish to affect me with a sense of his greatness. I saw that he was as much abashed by our encounter as I was; he was visibly shy to the point of discomfort, but in no ignoble sense was he conscious, and as nearly as he could with one so much his younger he made an absolute equality between us. My memory of him is without alloy one of the finest pleasures of my life. In my heart I paid him the same glad homage that I paid Lowell and Holmes, and he did nothing to make me think that I had overpaid him. This seems perhaps very little to say in his praise, but to my mind it is saying everything, for I have known but few great men, especially of those I met in early life, when I wished to lavish my admiration upon them, whom I have not the impression of having left in my debt. Then, a defect of the Puritan quality, which I have found in many New-Englanders, is that, wittingly or unwittingly, they propose themselves to you as an example, or if not quite this, that they surround themselves with a subtle ether of potential disapprobation, in which, at the first sign of unworthiness in you, they helplessly suffer you to gasp and perish; they have good hearts, and they would probably come to your succor out of humanity, if they knew how, but they do not know how. Hawthorne had nothing of this about him; he was no more tacitly than he was explicitly didactic. I thought him as thoroughly in keeping with his romances as Dr. Holmes had seemed with his essays and poems, and I met him as I had met the Autocrat in the supreme hour of his fame. He had just given the world the last of those incomparable works which it was to have finished from his hand; the Marble Faun had worthily followed, at a somewhat longer interval than usual, the Blithedale Romance, and the House of Seven Gables, and the Scarlet Letter, and had perhaps carried his name higher than all the rest, and certainly farther. Everybody was reading it, and more or less bewailing its indefinite close, but yielding him that full honor and praise which a writer can hope for but once in his life. Nobody dreamed that thereafter only precious fragments, sketches more or less faltering, though all with the divine touch in them, were further to enrich a legacy which in its kind is the finest the race has received from any mind. We are always finding new Hawthornes, but the illusion soon wears away, and then we perceive that they were not Hawthornes at all; that he had some peculiar difference from them, which, by-and-by, we shall no doubt consent must be his difference from all men evermore.

I am painfully aware that I have not summoned before the reader the image of the man as it has always stood in my memory, and I feel a sort of shame for my failure. He was so altogether simple that it seems as if it would be easy to do so; but perhaps a spirit from the other world would be simple too, and yet would no more stand at parle, or consent to be sketched, than Hawthorne. In fact, he was always more or less merging into the shadow, which was in a few years wholly

to close over him; there was nothing uncanny in his presence, there was nothing even unwilling, but he had that apparitional quality of some great minds which kept Shakespeare largely unknown to those who thought themselves his intimates, and has at last left him a sort of doubt. There was nothing teasing or wilfully elusive in Hawthorne's impalpability, such as I afterward felt in Thoreau; if he was not there to your touch, it was no fault of his; it was because your touch was dull, and wanted the use of contact with such natures. The hand passes through the veridical phantom without a sense of its presence, but the phantom is none the less veridical for all that.

XVI.

I kept the evening of the day I met Hawthorne wholly for the thoughts of him, or rather for that reverberation which continues in the young senses and sensibilities after some important encounter. It must have been the next morning that I went to find Thoreau, and I am dimly aware of making one or two failures to find him, if I ever really found him at all.

He is an author who has fallen into that abeyance, awaiting all authors, great or small, at some time or another; but I think that with him, at least in regard to his most important book, it can be only transitory. I have not read the story of his hermitage beside Walden Pond since the year 1858, but I have a fancy that if I should take it up now, I should think it a wiser and truer conception of the world than I thought it then. It was no solution of the problem; men are not going to answer the riddle of the painful earth by building themselves shanties and living upon beans and watching ant-fights; but I do not believe Tolstoy himself has more clearly shown the hollowness, the hopelessness, the unworthiness of the life of the world than Thoreau did in that book. If it were newly written it could not fail of a far vaster acceptance than it had then, when to those who thought and felt seriously it seemed that if slavery could only be controlled, all things else would come right of themselves with us. Slavery has not only been controlled, but it has been destroyed, and yet things have not begun to come right with us; but it was in the order of Providence that chattel slavery should cease before industrial slavery, and the infinitely crueler and stupider vanity and luxury bred of it, should be attacked. If there was then any prevision of the struggle now at hand, the seers averted their eyes, and strove only to cope with the less evil. Thoreau himself, who had so clear a vision of the falsity and folly of society as we still have it, threw himself into the tide that was already, in Kansas and Virginia, reddened with war ; he aided and abetted the John Brown raid, I do not recall how much or in what sort; and he had suffered in prison for his opinions and actions. It was this inevitable heroism of his that, more than his literature even, made me wish to see him and revere him; and I do not believe that I should have found the veneration difficult, when at last I met him in his insufficient person, if he had otherwise been present to my glowing expectation. He came into the room a quaint, stump figure of a man, whose effect of long trunk and short limbs was heightened by his fashionless trousers being let down too low. He had a noble face, with tossed hair, a distraught eye, and a fine aquilinity of profile, which made me think at once of

Don Quixote and of Cervantes; but his nose failed to add that foot to his stature which Lamb says a nose of that shape will always give a man. He tried to place me geographically after he had given me a chair not quite so far off as Ohio, though still across the whole room, for he sat against one wall, and I against the other; but apparently he failed to pull himself out of his revery by the effort, for he remained in a dreamy muse, which all my attempts to say something fit about John Brown and Walden Pond seemed only to deepen upon him. I have not the least doubt that I was needless and valueless about both, and that what I said could not well have prompted an important response; but I did my poor best, and I was terribly disappointed in the result. The truth is that in those days I was a helplessly concrete young person, and all forms of the abstract, the air-drawn, afflicted me like physical discomforts. I do not remember that Thoreau spoke of his books or of himself at all, and when he began to speak of John Brown, it was not the warm, palpable, loving, fearful old man of my conception, but a sort of John Brown type, a John Brown ideal, a

A NEW ENGLAND LANDSCAPE.

THOREAU.

not make out any interval of time between my visit to the disciple and my visit to the master. I think it was Emerson himself who opened his door to me, for I have a vision of the fine old man standing tall on his threshold, with the card in his hand, and looking from it to me with a vague serenity, while I waited a moment on the door-step below him. He would then have been about sixty, but I remember nothing of age in his aspect, though I have called him an old man. His hair, I am sure, was still entirely dark, and his face had a kind of marble youthfulness, chiselled to a delicate intelligence by the highest and noblest thinking that any man has done. There was a strange charm in Emerson's eyes, which I felt then and always, something like that I saw in Lincoln's, but shyer, but sweeter and less sad. His smile was the very sweetest I have ever beheld, and the contour of the mask and the line of the profile were in keeping with this incomparable sweetness of the mouth, at once grave and quaint, though quaint is not quite the word for it either, but subtly, not unkindly arch, which again is not the word.

It was his great fortune to have been mostly misunderstood, and to have reached the dense intelligence of his fellow-men after a whole lifetime of perfectly simple and lucid appeal, and his countenance expressed the patience and forbearance of a wise man content to bide his time. It would be hard to persuade people now that Emerson once represented to the popular mind all that was most hopelessly impossible, and that in a certain sort he was a national joke, the type of the incomprehensible, the byword of the poor paragrapher. He had perhaps disabused the community somewhat by presenting himself here and there as a lecturer, and talking face to face with men in terms which they could not refuse to find as clear as they were wise; he was more and more read, by certain persons, here and there; but we are still so far behind him in the reach of his far-thinking that it need not be matter of wonder that twenty years before his death he was the most misunderstood man in America. Yet in that twilight where he dwelt he loomed large upon the imagination; the minds that could not conceive him were still aware of his greatness. I myself had not read much of him, but I knew the

John Brown principle, which we were somehow (with long pauses between the vague, orphic phrases) to cherish, and to nourish ourselves upon.

It was not merely a defeat of my hopes, it was a rout, and I felt myself so scattered over the field of thought that I could hardly bring my forces together for retreat. I must have made some effort, vain and foolish enough, to rematerialize my old demigod, but when I came away it was with the feeling that there was very little more left of John Brown than there was of me. His body was not mouldering in the grave, neither was his soul marching on; his ideal, his type, his principle alone existed, and I did not know what to do with it. I am not blaming Thoreau; his words were addressed to a far other understanding than mine, and it was my misfortune if I could not profit by them. I think, or I venture to hope, that I could profit better by them now; but in this record I am trying honestly to report their effect with the sort of youth I was then.

XVII.

Such as I was, I rather wonder that I had the courage, after this experiment of Thoreau, to present the card Hawthorne had given me to Emerson. I must have gone to him at once, however, for I can-

essays he was printing in the Atlantic, and I knew certain of his poems, though by no means many; yet I had this sense of him, that he was somehow, beyond and above my ken, a presence of force and beauty and wisdom, uncompanioned in our literature. He had lately stooped from his ethereal heights to take part in the battle of humanity, and I suppose that if the truth were told he was more to my young fervor because he had said that John Brown had made the gallows glorious like the cross, than because he had uttered all those truer and wiser things which will still a hundred years hence be leading the thought of the world.

I do not know in just what sort he made me welcome, but I am aware of sitting with him in his study or library, and of his presently speaking of Hawthorne, whom I probably celebrated as I best could, and whom he praised for his personal excellence, and for his fine qualities as a neighbor. "But his last book," he added, reflectively, "is a mere mush," and I perceived that this great man was no better equipped to judge an artistic fiction than the groundlings who were then crying out upon the indefinite close of the Marble Faun. Apparently he had read it, as they had, for the story, but it seems to me now, if it did not seem to me then, that as far as the problem of evil was involved, the book must leave it where it found it. That is forever insoluble, and it was rather with that than with his more or less shadowy people that the romancer was concerned. Emerson had, in fact, a defective sense as to specific pieces of literature; he praised extravagantly, and in the wrong place, especially among the new things, and he failed to see the worth of much that was fine and precious beside the line of his fancy.

He began to ask me about the West, and about some unknown man in Michigan, who had been sending him poems, and whom he seemed to think very promising, though he has not apparently kept his word to do great things. I did not find what Emerson had to say of my section very accurate or important, though it was kindly enough, and just enough as to what the West ought to do in literature. He thought it a pity that a literary periodical which had lately been started in Cincinnati should be appealing to the East for contributions, instead of relying upon the writers nearer home; and he listened

with what patience he could to my modest opinion that we had not the writers nearer home. I never was of those Westerners who believed that the West was kept out of literature by the jealousy of the East, and I tried to explain why we had not the men to write that magazine full in Ohio. He alleged the man in Michigan as one who alone could do much to fill it worthily, and again I had to say that I had never heard of him.

I felt rather guilty in my ignorance, and I had a notion that it did not commend me, but happily at this moment Mr. Emerson was called to dinner, and he asked me to come with him. After dinner we walked about in his "pleached garden" a little, and then we came again into his library, where I meant to linger only till I could fitly get away. He questioned me about what I had seen of Concord, and

EMERSON.

whom besides Hawthorne I had met, and when I told him only Thoreau, he asked me if I knew the poems of Mr. William Henry Channing. I have known them since, and felt their quality, which I have gladly owned a genuine and original poetry; but I answered then truly that I knew them only from Poe's criticisms:

cruel and spiteful things which I should be ashamed of enjoying as I once did.

"Whose criticisms?" asked Emerson.

"Poe's," I said again.

"Oh," he cried out, after a moment, as if he had returned from a far search for my meaning, "*you mean the jingle-man!*"

I do not know why this should have put me to such confusion, but if I had written the criticisms myself I do not think I could have been more abashed. Perhaps I felt an edge of reproof, of admonition, in a characterization of Poe which the world will hardly agree with; though I do not agree with the world about him, myself, in its admiration. At any rate, it made an end of me for the time, and I remained as if already absent, while Emerson questioned me as to what I had written in the Atlantic Monthly. He had evidently read none of my contributions, for he looked at them, in the bound volume of the magazine which he got down, with the effect of being wholly strange to them, and then gravely affixed my initials to each. He followed me to the door, still speaking of poetry, and as he took a kindly enough leave of me, he said one might very well give a pleasant hour to it now and then.

A pleasant hour to poetry! I was meaning to give all time and all eternity to poetry, and I should by no means have wished to find pleasure in it; I should have thought that a proof of inferior quality in the work; I should have preferred anxiety, anguish even, to pleasure. But if Emerson thought from the glance he gave my verses that I had better not lavish myself upon that kind of thing, unless there was a great deal more of me than I could have made apparent in our meeting, no doubt he was right. I was only too painfully aware of my shortcoming, but I felt that it was shortercoming than it need have been. I had somehow not prospered in my visit to Emerson as I had with Hawthorne, and I came away wondering in what sort I had gone wrong. I was not a forth-putting youth, and I could not blame myself for anything that merited withholding in my approaches; indeed, I made no approaches; but as I must needs blame myself for something, I fell upon the fact that in my confused retreat from Emerson's presence I had failed in a certain slight point of ceremony, and I magnified this into an offence of capital importance. I went home to my hotel, and passed the afternoon in pure misery. I had moments of wild question when I debated whether it would be better to go back and own my error, or whether it would be better to write him a note, and try to set myself right in that way. But in the end I did neither, and I have since survived my mortal shame some thirty-four years or more. But at the time it did not seem possible that I should live through the day with it, and I thought that I ought at least to go and confess it to Hawthorne, and let him disown the wretch who had so poorly repaid the kindness of his introduction by such misbehavior. I did indeed walk down by the Wayside, in the cool of the evening, and there I saw Hawthorne for the last time. He was sitting on one of the timbers beside his cottage, and smoking with an air of friendly calm. I had got on very well with

EMERSON'S HOUSE AT CONCORD.

HAWTHORNE'S COTTAGE—WAYSIDE.

him, and I longed to go in, and tell him how ill I had got on with Emerson; I believed that though he cast me off, he would understand me, and would perhaps see some hope for me in another world, though there could be none in this.

But I had not the courage to speak of the affair to any one but Fields, to whom I unpacked my heart when I got back to Boston, and he asked me about my adventures in Concord. By this time I could see it in a humorous light, and I did not much mind his lying back in his chair and laughing and laughing, till I thought he would roll out of it. He perfectly conceived the situation, and got an amusement from it that I could get only through sympathy with him. But I thought it a favorable moment to propose myself as the assistant editor of the Atlantic Monthly, which I had the belief I could very well become, with advantage to myself if not to the magazine. He seemed to think so too; he said that if the place had not just been filled, I should certainly have had it; and it was to his recollection of this prompt ambition of mine that I suppose I may have owed my succession to a like vacancy some four years later. He was charmingly kind; he entered with the sweetest interest into the story of my economic life, which had been full of changes and chances already. But when I said very seriously that now I was tired of these fortuities, and would like to be settled in something, he asked, with dancing eyes,

"Why, how old are you?"

"I am twenty-three," I answered, and then the laughing fit took him again.

"Well," he said, "you begin young, out there!"

In my heart I did not think that twenty-three was so very young, but perhaps it was; and if any one were to say that I had been portraying here a youth whose aims were certainly beyond his achievements, who was morbidly sensitive, and if not conceited was intolerably conscious, who had met with incredible kindness, and had suffered no more than was good for him, though he might not have merited his pain any more than his joy, I do not know that I should gainsay him, for I am not at all sure that I was not just that kind of youth when I paid my first visit to New England.

THE END.

CAMBRIDGE MEMOIRS

EING the wholly literary
spirit I was when I went
to make my home in
Cambridge, I do not see
how I could well have
been more content if I
had found myself in the Elysian Fields
with an agreeable eternity before me. At
twenty-nine, indeed, one is practically
immortal, and at that age time had for
me the effect of an eternity in which I
had nothing to do but to read books and
dream of writing them, in the overflow of
endless hours from my work with the
manuscripts, critical notices, and proofs
of the *Atlantic Monthly.* As for the social environment, I should have been puzzled, if given my choice among the elect
of all the ages, to find poets and scholars
more to my mind than those still in the
flesh at Cambridge in the early afternoon
of the nineteenth century. They are now
nearly all dead, and I can speak of them
in the freedom which is death's doubtful
favor to the survivor; but if they were
still alive I could say little to their offense, unless their modesty was hurt with
my praise.

One of the first of these friends was
that exquisite intelligence who, in a
world where so many people are grotesquely miscalled, was most fitly named;
for no man ever kept here more perfectly and purely the heart of such as

FRANCIS J. CHILD

the kingdom of heaven is of, than Francis J. Child. He was then in his prime, and I like to recall the outward image which expressed the inner man as happily as his name. He was of low stature and of an inclination which never became stoutness; but what you most saw when you saw him was his face of winning refinement: very regular, with eyes always glassed by gold-rimmed spectacles, a straight, short, most sensitive nose, and a beautiful mouth with the sweetest smile that I ever beheld, and that was as wise and shrewd as it was sweet. In a time when every other man was more or less bearded he was clean-shaven, and of a delightful freshness of coloring, which his thick sunny hair, clustering upon his head in close rings, admirably set off. I believe he never became gray, and the last time I saw him, though he was broken then with years and pain, his face had still the brightness of his inextinguishable youth.

It is well known how great was Professor Child's scholarship in the branches of his Harvard work; and how especially, how uniquely, effective it was in the study of English and Scottish balladry, to which he gave so many years of his life. He was a poet in his nature, and he wrought with passion as well as consummate knowledge in the achievement of as monumental a task as any American has performed. But he might have been indefinitely less than he was in any intellectual wise, and yet been precious to those who knew him for the gentleness and the goodness which in him were protected from misconception by a final dignity as delicate and as inviolable as that of Longfellow himself.

We were still much less than a year from our life in Venice when he came to see us at Cambridge; and in the Italian interest, which then commended us to so many fine spirits among our neighbors, we found ourselves at the beginning of a life-long friendship with him. I was known to him only by my letters from Venice, which afterwards became *Venetian Life,* and by a bit of devotional verse which he had asked to include in a collection he was making, but he immediately gave us the freedom of his heart, which afterwards was never withdrawn. In due time he imagined a home school, to which our little one was asked, and she had her first lessons with his own daughter under his roof. These things drew us closer together, and he was willing to be still nearer to me at any time of trouble. At one such time, when the shadow which must some time darken every door hovered at ours, he had the strength to make me face it and try to realize, while it was still there, that it was not cruel and not evil. It passed, for that time, but the sense of his help remained; and in my own case I can testify of the potent tenderness in him which all who knew him must have known. But in bearing my witness I feel accused, almost as if he were present, by his fastidious reluctance from any recognition of his helpfulness. When this came in the form of gratitude taking credit to itself in a pose which reflected honor upon him as the architect of greatness, he was delightfully impatient of it; and he was most amusingly dramatic in reproducing the pompous consciousness of certain ineffectual alumni who used to overwhelm him at Commencement solemnities with some such an acknowledgment as, "Professor Child, all that I have become, sir, I owe to your influence in my college career."

He did with delicious mockery the old-fashioned intellectual *poseurs* among the students, who used to walk the groves of Harvard with bent head, and the left arm crossing the back, while the other lodged its hand in the breast of the high-buttoned frock-coat; and I could fancy that his classes in college did not form the sunniest exposure for young folly and vanity. I know that he was intolerant of any manner of insincerity, and no flattery could take him off his guard. I have seen him meet this with a cutting phrase of rejection, and no man was more apt at snubbing the patronage that offers itself at times to all men. But mostly he wished to do people pleasure, and he seemed always to be studying how to do it; as for need, I am sure that worthy and unworthy want had alike the way to his heart.

Children were always his friends, and they repaid with adoration the affection which he divided with them and with his flowers. I recall him in no moments so characteristic as those he spent in making the little ones laugh out their hearts at his drolling, some festive evening in his house, and those he gave to sharing with you his joy in his garden. This, I believe, began with violets, and it went on to roses, which he grew in a splendor and profusion impossible to any but a true lover with a genuine gift for them. Like Lowell, he spent his summers in Cambridge, and in the afternoon you could find him digging or pruning among his roses with an ardor which few caprices

W. D. HOWELLS'S HOME, CONCORD AVENUE, CAMBRIDGE

of the weather could interrupt. He would lift himself from their ranks, which he scarcely overtopped, as you came up the footway to his door, and peer purblindly across at you. If he knew you at once, he traversed the nodding and swaying bushes, to give you the hand free of the trowel or knife; or if you got indoors unseen by him, he would come in holding toward you some exquisite blossom that weighed down the tip of its long stem like the finial of Adam Krafft's tabernacle.

He graced with unaffected poetry a life of as hard work and as varied achievement as any I have known or read of; and he played with gifts such as in no greater measure have made reputations. He had a rare and lovely humor, which could amuse itself in Italian verse with such an airy burletta as *Il Pesceballo;* he had a critical sense as sound as it was subtle in all literature; and whatever he wrote he imbued with the charm of a style finely personal to himself. His learning in the line of his Harvard teaching included an Early English scholarship unrivalled in his time, and his researches in ballad literature left no corner of it untouched. I fancy this part of his study was peculiarly pleasant to him; for he loved simple and natural things, and the beauty which he found nearest life. At least he scorned the pedantic affectations of literary superiority; and he used to quote with joyous laughter an Italian critic who proposed to leave the summits of polite learning for a moment with the swelling exclamation: " *Scendiamo fra il po-*

HJALMAR HJÖRTH BOYESEN

polo!" (Let us go down among the people.)

II

Of course it was only so hard-worked a man who could take so much thought and trouble for another. He once took thought for me at a time when it was very important to me, and when he took the trouble to secure for me an engagement to deliver that course of Lowell Lectures in Boston which I have said Lowell had the courage to go in town to hear. I do not remember whether Professor Child was equal to so much, but he would have been if it were necessary; and I rather rejoice now in the belief that he did not seek that martyrdom.

He had done for me, but he had more than enough done only what he was always willing to do for others. In the form of a favor to himself he brought into my life the great happiness of intimately knowing Hjalmar Hjörth Boyesen, whom he had found one summer day among the shelves in the Harvard library, and found to be a poet and an intending novelist. I do not remember now just how this fact imparted itself to the professor, but literature is of easily cultivated confidence in youth, and probably the confession was almost spontaneous. At any rate, as a susceptible young editor, I was asked to meet my potential contributor at the professor's two-o'clock dinner, and when we came to coffee in the study looking out upon the garden, Boyesen took from the pocket nearest his heart a chapter of " Gunnar " and read it to us. A chapter? It may have been two or three, with a judicious selection of passages from yet other chapters ; but it does not matter. To be again in those dear presences, I would gladly listen to the whole novel!

That young romance still remains the most beautiful thing that Boyesen wrote, though he wrote so much and so well in verse, in fiction, and in criticism. He had then already laid the wide foundations of his future scholarship in the Northern European languages and literatures, but his soul was steeped in the aromas of his native poetry and romance, which all his talk breathed out again.

For the rest of this summer I must have had nearly all his talk to myself; of course I wanted "Gunnar" for the magazine, and this brought us constantly and exclusively together. Boyesen afterwards came to know all Cambridge, and when he went back to Europe he celebrated our literary society with such effect that he inspired Tourguénief with the wish to witness it at first hands. The great Russian of course never visited Cambridge, but he affirmed to Boyesen his belief in it as an ideal situation, which could not be matched in his experience of literary centres elsewhere. I do not know whether it was Boyesen's enthusiasm that brought his great compatriot Björnstjerne Jjörnson actually among us; but if it was, it did not suffice, I believe, to realize Tourguénief's ideal to him. He ascertained the Cambridge limitations a little too quickly, a little too keenly, and felt himself cramped in a world where the expansions were upward rather than outward.

However, no alien born more clearly conceived, not only Cambridge, but America, than Boyesen did. His mastery of our character was as extraordinary, as almost miraculous, as his mastery of our language. For full proof of his proficiency in both, he has left his great novel, *The Mammon of Unrighteousness,* which comes within one or two of being the great American novel we shall never have from any single hand. He left other stories of our life which showed how wonderfully well he had conceived it, and he left a volume of poems which testify of the beauty and truth with which he imagined the immeasurable life beyond the nationalities. Poetry, indeed, was what his ardent spirit mainly meditated in that happy hour when I first knew him in Cambridge, before we had either of us grown old and sad, if not wise. He overflowed with it, and he talked as little as he dreamed of anything else in the vast half-summer we spent together. He was constantly at my house, where in an absence of my family I was living bachelor, and where we sat in-doors and talked, or sauntered out-doors and talked, with our heads in a cloud of fancies, not unmixed with the mosquitoes of Cambridge: if I could have back the fancies, I would be willing to have the mosquitoes with them. He read me his things, and I read him mine, and he told me about the Hulder, and the Nixy, and the Midnight Sun, and the Fjords, and the Saeters; and that great movement toward nature and the speech of nature, then beginning among the Norwegian novelists and poets, which has since made their nation great while some other nations have grown big. He looked the poetry he lived: his eyes were the blue of sunlit fjords; his brown silken hair was thick on the crown which it later abandoned to a scholarly baldness; his soft red lips half hid a boyish pout in the youthful beard and mustache. He was short of stature, but of stalwart breadth of frame, and his voice was of a peculiar and endearing quality, indescribably mellow and tender when he read his verse.

I have hardly the right to dwell so long upon him here, for he was only a sojourner in Cambridge, but the memory of that early intimacy is too much for my sense of proportion. Our intimacy was renewed afterwards, when I came to live in New York, where, as long as he was in this *dolce lome,* he hardly let a week go by without passing a long evening with me. Our talk was still of literature and of life, but more of life than of literature, and we seldom spoke of those old times. I still found him true to the ideals which had clarified themselves to both of us as the duty of unswerving fealty to the real thing in whatever we did. This we felt, as we had felt it long before, to be the sole source of beauty and of art, and we warmed ourselves at each other's hearts in our devotion to it, amidst a misunderstanding environment, which we did not characterize by so mild an epithet. Boyesen, indeed, out-realisted me, in the polemics of our æsthetics, and sometimes, when an unbeliever was by, I willingly left to him the affirmation of our faith, not without some quaking at his unsparing strenuousness in disciplining the heretic.

But now that ardent and active soul is Elsewhere, and I have ceased even to expect the ring, which, making itself heard at the late hour of his coming, I knew always to be his and not another's. That mechanical expectation of those who will come no more is something terrible, but when even that ceases we know the irreparability of our loss, and begin to realize how much of ourselves they have taken with them.

III

It was some years before the Boyesen summer, which was the fourth or fifth of our life in Cambridge, that I made the acquaintance of a man very much my senior, who remains one of the vividest personalities of my recollection. I speak of him in this order perhaps because of an obscure association with Boyesen through their religious faith, which was also mine. But Henry James was incomparably more Swedenborgian than either of us: he lived and thought and felt Swedenborg with an entirety and intensity far beyond the mere assent of other men. He did not do this in any stupidly exclusive way, but in the most luminously inclusive way, with a constant reference of these vain mundane shadows to the spiritual realities which project them.

His piety, which sometimes expressed itself in terms of alarming originality and freedom, was too large for any ecclesiastical limits, and one may learn from the books which record it how personal his interpretations of Swedenborg were. Perhaps in that other world whose substantial verity was the inspiration of his life here, the two sages may by this time have met and agreed to differ as to some points in the doctrine of the Seer. In such a case I cannot imagine the apostle giving way, and I do not say he would be wrong to insist, but I think he might now be willing to allow that the exegetic

pages which sentence by sentence were so brilliantly suggestive, had sometimes a collective opacity which the most resolute vision could not penetrate. Yet he put into this dark wisdom a profound and comprehensive faith, and he lighted it up with flashes of the keenest wit and bathed it in the glow of a lambent humor, so that it is truly wonderful to me how it should remain so unintelligible. But I have only tried to read certain of his books, and possibly if I had persisted in the effort I might have found them all as clear at last as the one which seems to me the clearest, and is certainly most encouragingly suggestive: I mean the one called *Society the Redeemed Form of Man.*

James had his whole being in his Belief; it had not only liberated him from the bonds of the Calvinistic theology in which his youth was trammelled, but it had secured him against the conscious ethicism of the prevailing Unitarian doctrine, which supremely worshipped Conduct; and it had colored his vocabulary to such strange effects that he spoke of *moral men* with abhorrence, as more hopelessly lost than sinners. Any one whose sphere tempted him to recognition of the foibles of others, he called the Devil; but in spite of his perception of such diabolism, he was rather fond of yielding to it, for he had a most trenchant tongue. I myself once fell under his condemnation as the Devil, by having too plainly shared his joy in his characterization of certain fellow-men; perhaps a group of Bostonians from whom he had just parted and whose reciprocal pleasure of themselves he dramatically presented in the image of "simmering in their own fat and putting a nice brown on each other."

Swedenborg himself he did not spare as a man. He thought that very likely his life had those lapses in it which some of his followers deny; and he regarded him, on the æsthetical side, as essentially commonplace, and as probably chosen for his prophetic function just because of his imaginative nullity: his tremendous revelations could be the more distinctly and unmistakably inscribed upon an intelligence of that sort, which alone could render again a strictly literal account of them.

As to some other sorts of believers who thought they had a mystical apprehension of the truth, he had no mercy upon them if they betrayed, however innocently, any self-complacency in their possession. I went one evening to call upon him with a dear old Shaker elder, who had the misfortune to say that his people believed themselves to be living the angelic life. James fastened upon him with the suggestion that according to Swedenborg the most celestial angels were unconscious of their own perfection, and that if the Shakers felt they were of angelic condition, they were probably the mock of the hells. I was very glad to get my poor old friend off alive, and to find that he was not even aware of being cut asunder: I did not invite him to shake himself.

With spiritualists James had little or no sympathy; he was not so impatient of them as the Swedenborgians commonly are, and he probably acknowledged a measure of verity in the spiritistic phenomena; but he was rather incurious concerning these, and he must have regarded them as superfluities of naughtiness, mostly; as emanations from the hells. His powerful and penetrating intellect interested itself in all social and civil facts through his religion. He was essentially religious, but he was very consciously a citizen, with most decided opinions upon political questions. My own darkness as to anything like social reform was then so dense that I cannot now be clear as to his feeling in such matters, but I have the impression that it was far more radical than I could understand.

James was of a very merciful mind regarding things often held in pitiless condemnation, but of charity, as it is commonly understood, he had misgivings. He would never have turned away from him that asketh; but he spoke with regret of some of his benefactions in the past, large gifts of money to individuals, which he now thought had done more harm than good.

I never knew him to judge men by the society scale. He was most human in his relations with others, and was in correspondence with all sorts of people seeking light and help; he answered their letters, and tried to instruct them, and none were so low or weak but they could reach him on their own level, though he had his humorous perception of limits. He told of his dining, early in life, next a fellow-man from Cape Cod at the Astor House, where such a man could then seldom have found himself. When they were served with meat, this neighbor asked if he would mind his putting his fat on James's plate: he disliked fat. James said that he considered the request, and seeing no good reason against it, consented.

He could be cruel with his tongue when he fancied insincerity or pretence, and then cruelly sorry for the hurt he gave. He was indeed tremulously sensitive, not only for himself but for others, and would offer atonement far beyond the measure of the offence he supposed himself to have given.

At all times he thought originally in words of delightful originality, which painted a fact with the most graphic vividness, especially a grotesque fact. Of a person who had a nervous twitching of the face, and who wished to call up a friend to them, he said, " He *spasmed* to the fellow across the room, and introduced him." His written style had traits of the same bold adventurousness, but it was his speech which was most captivating.

As I write of him I see him before me: his white-bearded face, with a kindly intensity which at first glance seemed fierce, the mouth humorously shaping the mustache, the eyes vague behind the glasses; his sensitive hand gripping the stick on which he rested his weight to ease it from the artificial limb he wore.

IV

The Goethean face and figure of Louis Agassiz were in those days to be seen in the shady walks of Cambridge, to which for me they lent a Weimarish quality, in the degree that in Weimar itself, a few years ago, I felt a quality of Cambridge. Agassiz, of course, was Swiss and Latin, and not Teutonic, but he was of the Continental European civilization, and was widely different from the other Cambridge men in everything but love of the place. " He is always an *Europaër*," said Lowell one day, in distinguishing concerning him; and for any one who had tasted the flavor of the life beyond the ocean and the Channel, this had its charm. He was of a bland politeness in manner, which he made go far in his encounters with New England character.

It was by his real love for that character, also, that he succeeded so well with it. I have an idea that no one else of his day could have got so much money for science out of the General Court of Massachusetts; and I have heard him speak with the wisest and warmest appreciation of the hard material from which he was able to extract this treasure.

The legislators who voted appropriations for his Museum and his other scientific objects were not mostly lawyers or professional men, with the perspectives of a liberal education, but were hard-fisted farmers, who had a grip of the State's money as if it were their own, and yet gave it with intelligent munificence. They understood that he did not want it for himself, and had no interested aim in getting it; they knew that, as he once said, he had no time to make money, and wished to use it solely for the advancement of learning; and with this understanding they were ready to help him generously. He compared their liberality with that of kings and princes, when these patronized science, and recognized the superior plebeian generosity. It was on the veranda of his summer house at Nahant, while he lay in the hammock, talking of this, when I heard him refer also to the offer that Napoleon III. had made him, inviting him upon certain splendid conditions to come to Paris after he had established himself at Cambridge. But he said that he had not come to America without going over every such possibility in his own mind, and deciding beforehand against it. He was a republican, by nationality and by preference, and I was entirely satisfied with his position and environment in New England.

Outside of his scientific circle in Cambridge he was more friends with Longfellow than with any one else, I believe, and Longfellow told me how, after the doctors had condemned Agassiz to inaction on account of his failing health, he had broken down in his friend's study, and wept like an Europaër, and lamented,

"I shall never finish my work!"

Some papers which he had begun to write for the magazine in contravention of the Darwinian theory (it is well known that Agassiz did not accept this) remained part of the work which he never finished.

After his death, I wished Professor Wyman to write of him in the *Atlantic,* but he excused himself on account of his many labors, and then he voluntarily spoke of Agassiz's methods, which he agreed with rather than his theories, being himself thoroughly Darwinian. I think he said Agassiz was the first to imagine establishing a fact not from a single example, but from examples indefinitely repeated. If it was a question of something about robins, for instance, he would have a hundred robins examined before he would receive an appearance as a fact.

Of course no preconception or prepossession of his own was suffered to bar his way to the final truth he was seeking, and he joyously renounced even a conclusion if he found it mistaken. I do not know whether Mrs. Agassiz has put into her interesting life of him a delightful story which she told me about him. He came to her beaming one day, and demanded,

"You know I have always held such and such an opinion about a certain group of fossil fishes?"

"Yes, yes!"

"Well, I have just been reading ——'s new book, and he has shown me that there isn't the least truth in it," and he burst into a laugh of pleasure, wholly unvexed by having found himself convicted of an error.

I could come in contact with science at Cambridge only on its literary and social side, of course, and my meetings with Agassiz were not many. I recall a dinner at his house to Mr. Bret Harte, when the poet came on from California, and Agassiz approached him over the coffee through their mutual scientific interest in the last meeting of the geological "society upon the Stanislow." He quoted to the author some passages from the poem recording the final proceedings of this body, which had particularly pleased him, and I think Mr. Harte was as much amused at finding himself thus in touch with the savant as Agassiz could ever have been with that delicious poem.

Agassiz lived at one end of Quincy Street, and James almost at the other end, with an interval between them which but poorly typified their difference of temperament. The one was all religious and the other all scientific, and yet toward the close of his life Agassiz may be said to have led that movement toward the new position of science in matters of mystery which is now characteristic of it. He was of the Swiss "Brahminical caste," as so many of his friends in Cambridge were of the Brahminical caste of New England; and perhaps it was the line of ancestral *pasteurs* which at last drew him back, or on, to the affirmation of an unformulated faith of his own. At any rate, before most other savants would consent that they might have souls, he became, by opening a summer school of science with prayer, as consolatory to the unscientific who wished to believe they had souls as Mr. John Fiske himself, though Mr. Fiske, as the arch-apostle of Darwinism, had arrived by such a very different road at a trust which with Agassiz was intuitive.

HENRY JAMES THE ELDER

other Cambridge men of my acquaintance, Dana was very much my senior, and like the rest he recognized my literary promise as cordially as if it were performance, with no suggestion of the condescension which was said to be sometimes his attitude toward his fellow-men. I never saw anything of this, in fact, but I heard much, and I suppose he may have been a blend of those patrician qualities and democratic principles which made Lowell anomalous even to himself. He is part of the anti-slavery history of his time, and he gave to the oppressed his strenuous help both as a man and as a politician; his great gifts and learning in the law were freely at their service. He never lost his interest, either, in those white slaves whose brutal bondage he remembered as bound with them in his *Two Years before the Mast,* and any luckless seaman with a case or cause might count upon his friendship as surely as the black slaves of the South. He was able to temper his indignation for their oppression with a humorous perception of what was droll in its agents and circumstances; and nothing could be more delightful than his talk about sea-etiquette on merchant vessels, where the chief mate might no more speak to the captain at table without being addressed by him than a subject might put a question to his sovereign. He was amusing in his stories of the Pacific trade, in which he said it was very noble to deal in furs from the Northwest, and very ignoble to deal in hides along the Mexican and South American coasts. Every ship's master naturally wished to

V

Mr. Fiske had been our neighbor in our first Cambridge home, and when we went to live at Berkeley Street, he followed with his family and placed himself across the way in a house which I already knew as the home of Richard Henry Dana, the author of *Two Years before the Mast.* Like nearly all the

be in the fur-carrying trade, and in one of Dana's instances two vessels encounter in midocean, and exchange the usual parley as to their respective ports of departure and destination. The final demand comes through the trumpet, "What cargo?" and the captain so challenged yields to temptation and roars back, "*Furs!*" A moment of hesitation elapses, and then the questioner pursues, "Here and there *a horn?*"

There were other distinctions, of which seafaring men of other days were keenly sensible, and Dana dramatized the meeting of a great swelling East Indiaman with a little Atlantic trader which has hailed her. She shouts back through her captain's trumpet that she is from Calcutta, laden with silks, spices, and other Orient treasures, and in her turn she requires like answer from the sail which has presumed to enter into parley with her. "What cargo?" The trader confesses to a mixed cargo for Boston; and to the final question her master replies, in meek apology, "*Only from Liverpool, sir!*" and scuttles down the horizon as swiftly as possible.

Dana was not of the Cambridge men whose calling was in Cambridge. He was a lawyer in active practice, and he went every day to Boston. One was apt to meet him in those horse-cars which formerly tinkled back and forth between the two cities, and which were often so full of one's acquaintance that they had the social elements of an afternoon tea. They were often abusively overcrowded, of course, and one might easily see a prime literary celebrity swaying from a strap,

or hanging uneasily by the hand-rail to the lower steps of the back platform. I do not mean that I ever happened to see the author of *Two Years before the Mast* in either fact, but in his celebrity he had every qualification for the illustration of my point. His book probably carried the American name farther and wider than any American books except those of Irving and Cooper at a day when our writers were very little known, even at home, and our literature was the only infant industry not fostered against foreign ravage, but expressly left to strengthen and harden itself as it best might in neglect at home. The book was delightful, and I strongly remember it, from a reading of thirty years ago, as of the stuff that classics are made of. I venture no conjecture as to its present popularity, but of all books relating to the sea I think it is the best. The author when I knew him was still Richard Henry Dana, Jr., his father, the aged poet, who first established the name in the public recognition, being alive, though past

RICHARD HENRY DANA, JR.

literary activity. It was distinctively a literary race, and in the actual generation it has given proofs of its continued literary vitality in the romance of *Espiritu Santo* by the youngest daughter of the Dana I knew.

VI

There could be no stronger contrast to him in origin, education, and character than a man who lived at the same time in Cambridge, and who produced a book which in its final fidelity to life is not unworthy to be named with *Two Years*

QUINCY STREET, CAMBRIDGE

THE AGASSIZ HOUSE IN BACKGROUND, OBSCURED BY TREES. FORMER LOCATION OF THE JAMES HOUSE IN FOREGROUND

before the Mast. Ralph Keeler wrote the *Vagabond Adventures* which he had lived. I have it on my heart to name him in the presence of our great literary men not only because I had an affection for him, tenderer than I then knew, but because I believe his book is worthier of more remembrance than it seems to enjoy. I was reading it only the other day, and I found it delightful, and much better than I imagined when I accepted for the *Atlantic* the several papers which it is made up of. I am not sure but it belongs to the great literature in that fidelity to life which I have spoken of, and which the author brought himself to practise with such difficulty, and some times under so much stress from his editor. He really wanted to *fake* it, at times, but he was docile at last, and did it so honestly that it tells the history of his strange career in much better terms than it can be reported. He had been, as he claimed, in his early orphanhood " a

cruel uncle's ward," and while yet almost a child he had run away from home, to fulfil his heart's desire of becoming a clog-dancer in a troupe of negro minstrels. But it was first his fate to be cabin-boy and bootblack on a lake steamboat, and meet with many squalid adventures, scarcely to be matched outside of a Spanish picaresque novel. When he did become a dancer (and even a *danseuse*) of the sort he aspired to be, the fruition of his hopes was so little what he had imagined that he was very willing to leave the Floating Palace on the Mississippi in which his troupe voyaged and exhibited, and enter the college of the Jesuit Fathers at Cape Girardeau in Missouri. They were very kind to him, and in their charge he picked up a good deal more Latin, if not less Greek, than another strolling player who also took to literature. From college Keeler went to Europe, and then to California, whence he wrote me that he was coming on to Bos-

JOHN G. PALFREY

ton with the manuscript of a novel which he wished me to read for the magazine. I reported against it to my chief, but nothing could shake Keeler's faith in it, until he had printed it at his own cost, and known it fail instantly and decisively. He had come to Cambridge to see it through the press, and he remained there four or five years, with certain brief absences. Then, during the Cuban insurrection of the early seventies, he accepted the invitation of a New York paper to go to Cuba as its correspondent.

"Don't go, Keeler," I entreated him, when he came to tell me of his intention. "They'll garrote you down there."

"Well," he said, with the air of being pleasantly interested by the coincidence, as he stood on my study hearth with his feet wide apart in a fashion he had, and gayly flirted his hand in the air, "that's what Aldrich says, and he's agreed to write my biography, on condition that I make a last dying speech when they bring me out in the plaza to do it: 'If I had taken the advice of my friend T. B. Al-drich, author of *Marjorie Daw and Other People,* I should not now be in this place.' "

He went, and he did not come back. He was not indeed garroted as his friends had promised, but he was probably assassinated on the steamer by which he sailed from Santiago, for he never arrived in Havana, and was never heard of again. I now realize that I loved him, though I did as little to show it as men commonly do. If I am to meet somewhere else the friends who are no longer here, I should like to meet Ralph Keeler, and I would take some chances of meeting in a happy place a soul which had by no means kept itself unspotted, but which in all its consciousness of error relied cheerfully on the trust that "the Almighty was not going to scoop any of us." The faith worded so grotesquely could not have been more simply or humbly affirmed; few men I think could have been more helplessly sincere.

He had nothing of that false self-respect which forbids a man to own himself wrong promptly and utterly when need is; and in fact he owned to some things in his checkered past which would hardly allow him any sort of self-respect. He had always an essential gayety not to be damped by discipline, and a docility which expressed itself in cheerful compliance. "Why do you use *bias* for opinion?" I demanded in going over a proof with him. "Oh, because I'm such an ass—such a bi-ass."

He had a philosophy of life, which he liked to express with a vivid touch on his listener's shoulder: "Put your finger on the present moment and enjoy it; it's the only one you've got or ever will have." This light and joyous creature could not but be a Pariah among our Brahmins, and I need not say that I never met him in any of the great Cambridge houses. I am not sure that he was a *persona grata* to every one in my own, for Keeler was framed rather for men's liking, and Mr. Aldrich and I had our subtleties as to whether his mind about women was not so Chinese as somewhat to infect his manner. Keeler was too really modest to be of any rebellious mind toward the society which ignored him, and of too sweet a cheerfulness to be greatly vexed by it. He lived on in the house of a suave old actor, who oddly made his home in Cambridge, and he continued of a harmless

bohemianism in his daily walk, which included lunches at Boston restaurants as often as he could get you to let him give them you, if you were of his acquaintance. On a Sunday he would appear coming out of the post-office usually at the hour when all cultivated Cambridge was coming for its letters, and wave a glad hand in air, and shout a blithe salutation to the friend he had marked for his companion in a morning stroll. The stroll was commonly over the flats toward Brighton (I do not know why, except perhaps that it was out of the beat of the better element), and the talk was mainly on literature; in which he was doing less than he meant to do, and which he seemed never able quite to feel was not a branch of the Show Business, and might not be legitimately worked by advertising, though he truly loved and honored it.

I suppose it was not altogether a happy life, and Keeler had his moments of amusing depression, which showed their shadows in his smiling face. He was of a slight figure and low stature, with hands and feet of almost womanish littleness. He was very blond, and his restless eyes were blue; he wore his yellow beard in whiskers only, which he pulled nervously from time to time.

HOME OF RICHARD HENRY DANA, Jr., BERKELEY STREET, CAMBRIDGE

VII

Keeler was a native of Ohio, and there lived at Cambridge when I first came there an Indianian, more accepted by literary society, who was of real quality as a poet. Forceythe Willson, whose poem "The Old Sergeant" Dr. Holmes used to read publicly in the closing year of the Civil War, was of a Western altitude of figure, and of an extraordinary beauty of face in an Oriental sort. He had large, dark eyes with clouded whites; his full, silken beard was of a flashing Persian blackness. He was excessively nervous, to such an extreme that when I first met him at Longfellow's he could not hold himself still in his chair. I think this was an effect of shyness in him, as well as physical, for afterwards when I went to find him in his own house he was much more at ease.

He preferred to receive me in the dim, large hall after opening his door to me himself, and we sat down there and talked, I remember, of supernatural things. He was much interested in spiritualism, and he had several stories to tell of his own experience in such matters. But none was so good as one which I had at second hand from Lowell, who thought it almost the best ghost story he had ever heard. The spirit of Willson's father appeared to him, and stood before him. Willson was accustomed to apparitions, and so he simply said, "Won't you sit down, father?" The phantom put out his hand to lay hold of a chair back as some people do in taking a seat, and his shadowy arm passed through the frame-work. "Ah!" he said,

JOHN HOLMES

"I really forgot that I was not substance." I do not know whether "The Old Sergeant" is ever read now; it has probably passed with other great memories of the great war; and I am afraid none of Willson's other verse is remembered. But he was then a distinct literary figure, and not to be left out of the count of our poets. I did not see him again. Shortly afterwards I heard that he had left Cambridge, with signs of consumption, which must have run a rapid course, for a very little while later came the news of his death.

VIII

The most devoted Cantabrigian, after Lowell, whom I knew would perhaps have contended that if he had staid with us, Willson might have lived; for John Holmes affirmed a faith in the virtues of the place which ascribed almost an aseptic character to its air; and when he once listened to my own complaints of an obstinate cold, he cheered himself, if not me, with the declaration, "Well, one thing, Mr. Howells, Cambridge never let a man keep a cold yet!"

If he had said it was better to live in Cambridge with a cold than elsewhere without one, I should have believed him; as it was, Cambridge bore him out in his assertion, though she took her own time to do it.

Lowell had told me of him before I met him, celebrating his peculiar humor with that affection which was not always so discriminating, and Holmes was one of the first Cambridge men I knew. I knew him first in the charming old Colonial house in which his famous brother and he were born. It was demolished long before I left Cambridge, but in memory it still stands on the ground since occupied by the Hemenway Gymnasium, and shows for me through that bulk a phantom frame of Continental buff in the shadow of elms that are shadows themselves. The *genius loci* was limping about the pleasant mansion with the rheumatism which then expressed itself to his friends in a resolute smile, but which now insists upon being an essential trait of the full-length present to my mind: a short stout figure, helped out with a cane, and a grizzled head with features formed to win the heart rather than the eye of the beholder. In one of his own eyes there was a cast of such winning geniality that it took the liking more than any beauty could have done, and the sweetest shy laugh in the world went with this cast.

I long wished to get him to write something for the magazine, and at last I prevailed with him to review a history of Cambridge which had come out. He did it charmingly, of course, for he loved more to speak of Cambridge than anything else. He held his native town in an idolatry which was not blind, but which was none the less devoted because he was aware of her droll points and weak points. He always celebrated these as so many virtues, and I think it was my passion for her that first commended me to him. I was not her son, but he felt that this was my misfortune more than my fault, and he seemed more and more to forgive it. After we had got upon the terms of editor and contributor, we met oftener than before, though I do not now remember that I ever persuaded him to write again for me. Once he gave me something, and then took it back, with a distrust of it which I could not overcome.

When the Holmes house was taken down, he went to live with an old domestic in a small house on the street amusingly called Appian Way. He had certain rooms of her, and his own table, but he would not allow that he was ever anything but a lodger in the place, where he continued till he died. In the process of time he came so far to trust his experience of me that he formed the habit of giving me an annual supper. Some days before this event he would appear in my study, and with divers delicate approaches, nearly always of the same tenor, he would say that he would like to ask my family to an oyster supper with him. " But you know," he would explain, " I haven't a house of my own to ask you to, and I should like to give you the supper *here*." When I had agreed to this suggestion with due gravity, he would inquire our engagements, and then say, as if a great load were off his mind, " Well, then, I will send up a few oysters to-morrow," or whatever day we had fixed on; and after a little more talk to take the strangeness out of the affair, would go his way. On the day appointed the fishman would come with several gallons of oysters, which he reported Mr. Holmes had asked him to bring, and in the evening the giver of the feast would reappear, with a lank oilcloth bag, sagged by some bottles of wine. There was always a bottle of red wine, and sometimes a bottle of champagne, and he had taken the precaution to send some crackers beforehand, so that the supper would be as entirely of his own giving as possible. He was forced to let us do the cooking and supply the cold-slaw, and perhaps he indemnified himself for putting us to these charges, and for the use of our linen and silver, by the vast superfluity of his oysters, with which we remained inundated for days. He did not care to eat many himself, but seemed content to fancy doing us a pleasure; and I have known few greater ones in life, than in the hospitality that so oddly played the host to us at our own table.

It must have seemed incomprehensible to such a Cantabrigian that we should ever have been willing to leave Cambridge, and in fact I do not well understand it myself. But if he resented it, he never showed his resentment. As often as I happened to meet him after our defection he used me with unabated kindness, and sparkled into some gayety too ethereal for remembrance. The last time I met him was at Lowell's funeral, when I drove home with him and Curtis and Child, and in the revulsion from the stress of that saddest event, had our laugh, as people do in the presence of

death, at something droll we remembered of the friend we mourned.

IX

My nearest literary neighbor, when we
lived in Sacramento Street, was the Rev.
Dr. John G. Palfrey, the historian of
New England, whose chimney-tops
amid the pine-tops I could see from my
study window when the leaves were off
the little grove of oaks between us. He
was one of the first of my acquaintances,
not suffering the great disparity of our
ages to count against me, but tactfully
and sweetly adjusting himself to my
youth in the friendly intercourse which
he invited. He was a most gentle and
kindly old man, with still an interest in
liberal things, which lasted till the infirmities of age secluded him from the
world and all its interests. As is known,
he had been in his prime one of the most
strenuous of the New England antislavery men, and he had fought the good
fight with a heavy heart for a brother
long settled in Louisiana who sided with
the South, and who after the Civil War
found himself disfranchised. In this
temporary disability he came North to
visit Dr. Palfrey upon the doctor's insistence, though at first he would have
nothing to do with him, and refused even
to answer his letters. "Of course," the
doctor said, "I was not going to stand
that from my mother's son, and I simply
kept on writing." So he prevailed, but
the fiery old gentleman from Louisiana
was reconciled to nothing in the North
but his brother, and when he came to return my visit, he quickly touched upon
his cause of quarrel with us. "I can't
vote," he declared, "but my coachman
can, and I don't know how I'm to get the
suffrage, unless my physician paints me
all over with the iodine he's using for my
rheumatic side."

Doctor Palfrey was most distinctly of
the Brahminical caste, and was long an
eminent Unitarian minister, but at the
time I began to know him he had long
quitted the pulpit. He was then so far
a civic or public character as to be post-
master at Boston, but his officiality was
probably so little in keeping with his nature that it was like a return to his truer
self when he ceased to hold the place,
and gave his time altogether to his his-

tory. It is a work which will hardly be
superseded in the interest of those who
value thorough research and temperate
expression. It is very just, and without
endeavor for picture or drama it is to
me very attractive. Much that has to be
recorded of New England lacks charm,
but he gave form and dignity and presence to the memories of the past, and
the finer moments of that great story he
gave with the simplicity that was their
best setting. It seems to me such an
apology (in the old sense) as New England might have written for herself, and
in fact Dr. Palfrey was a personifica-
tion of New England in one of the best
and truest kinds. He was refined in
the essential gentleness of his heart
without being refined away; he kept the
faith of her Puritan tradition though
he no longer kept the Puritan faith; and
his defence of the Puritan severity with
the witches and Quakers was as impartial as it was efficient in positing the
Puritans as of their time, and rather
better and not worse than other people
of the same time. He was himself a
most tolerant man, and his tolerance was
never weak or fond; it stopped well short
of condoning error, which he condemned
when he preferred to leave it to its own
punishment. Personally he was without
any flavor of harshness; his mind was as
gentle as his manner, which was one of
the gentlest I have ever known.

X

Of like gentleness, but of a more pensive temper, with bursts of surprising
lyrical gayety, was the poet Christopher
Pearse Cranch, who came to live in Cambridge rather late in my own life there.
I had already met him in New York at a
house of literary sympathies and affiliations, where he had astonished me by
breaking from his rather melancholy
quiet and singing comic character songs;
but again it was with a mixed emotion,
for which I was not prepared by my former experience, that I heard him at
Longfellow's supper table sing the old
Yankee ballad, "On Springfield Mountain there did dwell." The tragical fate
of the "young man" who was bitten by
a rattlesnake on his native hill took a
quality from the pathetic gravity of the
singer which still affects me as heart-

breakingly funny. It was a delightful piece of art in its way, and Cranch could not only sing and play most amusing songs, but was as much painter as he was poet. I especially liked his pictures of Venice for their simple, unconventionalized, unsentimentalized reality, and I liked and printed many of his poems.

Troubles and sorrows accumulated themselves upon his fine head, which the years had whitened, and gave a droop to the beautiful face which had once been merry. I recall his presence with a tender regard, and I would fain do my part to keep his memory alive, for I think he did things that merit remembrance.

XI

Cambridge, as separable from Boston, was, I think, socially of a wider mind and finer spirit than Boston.

It would be rather hard to prove this, and I must ask the reader to take my word for it, if he wishes to believe it. The great interests in that pleasant world, which I think does not present itself to my memory in a false iridescence, were the intellectual interests, and all other interests were lost in these to such as did not seek them insistently. People held themselves high; they held themselves personally aloof from people not duly assayed; their civilization was still Puritan, though their belief had long ceased to be so. They had weights and measures stamped in an earlier time, a time surer of itself than ours, by which they rated the merit of new-comers, and rejected such as did not bear the test. These standards were their own, and

they were satisfied with them; most Americans have no standards of their own, but these are not satisfied even with other people's, and so our society is in a state of tolerant and tremulous misgiving. Family counted in Cambridge, without doubt, as it counts in New England everywhere, but family alone did not mean position, and the want of family did not mean the want of it. Money still less than family commanded; one could be openly poor in Cambridge without open shame, or shame at all, for no one was very rich there, and no one was proud of his riches. I do not wonder that Tourguénief thought the conditions as Boyesen portrayed them ideal; and I look back at my own life there with wonder at my good fortune. I was sensible, and I still am sensible this had its alloys. I was young and unknown and was making my way, and I had to suffer some of the penalties of these disadvantages; but I do not believe that anywhere else in this ill-contrived economy, where it is vainly imagined that the material struggle forms a high incentive and inspiration, would my penalties have been so light. On the other hand, the good that was done me I could never repay if I lived all over again for others the life that I have so long lived for myself. At times, when I had experienced from those elect spirits with whom I associated some act of friendship, as signal as it was delicate, I used to ask myself, how could I ever do anything unhandsome or ungenerous toward any one again; and I had a bad conscience the next time I did it.

THE SENSE OF NEWPORT

I

NEWPORT, on my finding myself back there, threatened me sharply, quite at first, with that predicament at which I have glanced in another connection or two—the felt condition of having known it too well and loved it too much for description or definition. What was one to say about it except that one *had* been so affected, so distraught, and that discriminations and reasons were buried under the dust of use? There was a chance indeed that the breath of the long years (of the interval of absence, I mean) would have blown away this dust—and that, precisely, was what one was eager to see. To go out, to look about, to recover the sense, was accordingly to put the question, without delay, to the proof—and with the happy consequence, I think, of an escape from a grave discomfiture. The charm was there

again, unmistakably, the little old strange, very simple charm—to be expressed, as a fine proposition, or to be given up; but the answer came in the fact that to have walked about for half an hour was to have felt the question clear away. It cleared away so conveniently, so blissfully, in the light of the benign little truth that nothing had been less possible, even in the early, ingenuous, infatuated days, than to describe or define Newport. It had clearly had nothing about it *to* describe or define, so that one's fondness had fairly rested on this sweet oddity in it. One had only to look back to recognize that it had never condescended to give a scrap of reasoned account of itself (as a favorite of fortune and the haunt of the *raffiné*); it had simply lain there like a little bare, white, open hand, with slightly parted fingers, for the observer with a presumed sense for hands to take or to leave. The observer with a real sense never failed to pay this image the tribute of quite tenderly grasping the hand, and even of raising it, delicately, to his lips; having no less, at the same time, the instinct of not shaking it too hard, and that above all of never putting it to any rough work.

Such had been from the first, under a chastened light and in a purple sea, the dainty isle of Aquidneck; which might have avoided the weak mistake of giving up its pretty native name and of becoming thereby as good as nameless—with an existence as Rhode Island practically monopolized by the State and a Newport identity borrowed at the best and applicable but to a corner. Does not this vagueness of condition, however, fitly symbolize the small virtual promontory, of which, superficially, nothing could be predicated but its sky and its sea and its sunsets? One views it as placed there, by some refinement in the scheme of nature, just as a touchstone of taste—with a beautiful little sense to be read into it by a few persons, and nothing at all to be made of it, as to its essence, by most others. I come back, for its essence, to that figure of the little white hand, with the gracefully spread fingers and the fine grain of skin, even the dimples at the joints and the shell-like delicacy of the pink nails—all the charms, in short, that a little white hand may have. I see all the applications of the image—I see a special truth in each. It is the back of the hand, rising to the swell of the wrist, that is exposed—which is the way, I think, the true lover takes and admires it. He makes out in it, bending over it—or he used to in the old days—innumerable shy and subtle beauties, almost requiring, for justice, a magnifying-glass; and he winces at the sight of certain other obtruded ways of dealing with it. The touchstone of taste was indeed to operate, for the critical, the tender spirit, from the moment the pink palm was turned up on the chance of what might be " in " it. For nine persons out of ten, among its visitors, its purchasers of sites and builders of (in the old parlance) cottages, there had never been anything in it at all—except, of course, an opportunity: an opportunity for escaping the summer heat of other places, for bathing, for boating, for riding and driving, and for many sorts of more or less expensive riot. The pink palm being empty, in other words, to their vision, they had begun, from far back, to put things into it, things of their own, and of all sorts, and of many ugly, and of more and more expensive, sorts; to fill it substantially, that is, with gold, the gold that they have ended by heaping up there to an amount so oddly out of proportion to the scale of nature and of space.

This process, one was immediately to perceive with that renewal of impression, this process of injection and elaboration, of creating the palpable pile, had been going on for years to such a tune that the face of nature was now as much obliterated as possible, and the original shy sweetness as much as possible bedizened and bedevilled: all of which, moreover, might also at present be taken as having led, in turn, to the most unexpected climax, a matter of which I shall presently speak. The original shy sweetness, however, that range of effect which I have referred to as practically too latent and too modest for notation, had meanwhile had its votaries, the fond pedestrian minority, for whom the little white hand (to return for an instant to my figure, with which, as you see, I am charmed) had always been so full of treasures of its own as to discredit, from the point of view of taste, any attempt, from without, to stuff it fuller. Such attempts had, in the nature of the case, and from far back, been condemned to show for violations; violations of taste and discretion, to begin with—violations, more intimately, as the whole business became brisker, of a thousand delicate secret places, dear to the disinterested rambler, small, mild " points " and promontories, far away little lonely, sandy coves, rock-set, lily-sheeted ponds, almost hidden, and shallow Arcadian summer-haunted valleys, with the sea just over some stony shoulder: a whole world that called out to the long afternoons of youth, a world with its scale so measured and intended and happy, its detail so finished and pencilled and stippled (certainly for American detail!) that there comes back to me, across the many years.

THE CASINO

no better analogy for it than that of some fine foreground in an old "line" engraving. There remained always a sense, of course, in which the superimpositions, the multiplied excrescences, were a tribute to the value of the place; where no such liberty was ever taken save exactly *because* (as even the most blundering builder would have claimed) it was all so beautiful, so solitary and so "sympathetic." And that indeed has been, thanks to the "pilers-on" of gold, the fortune, the history of its beauty: that it now bristles with the villas and palaces into which the cottages have all turned, and that these monuments of pecuniary power rise thick and close, precisely, in order that their occupants may constantly remark to each other, from the windows to the "grounds," and from house to house, that it *is* beautiful, it *is* solitary and sympathetic. The thing has been done, it is impossible not to recognize, with the best faith in the world—though not altogether with the best light, which is always so different a matter; and it is with the general consequence only, at the end of the story, that I find myself to-day concerned.

So much concerned I found myself, I profess, after I had taken in this fact of a very distinct general consequence, that the whole interest of the vision was quickened by it; and that when, in particular, on one of the last days of June, among the densely-arrayed villas, I had followed the beautiful "ocean drive" to its uttermost reach and back without meeting either another vehicle or a single rider, let alone a single pedestrian, I recognized matter for the intellectual thrill that attests a social revolution foreseen and completed. The term I use may appear extravagant, but it was a fact, none the less, that I seemed to take full in my face, on this occasion, the cold stir of air produced when the whirligig of time has made one of its liveliest turns. It is always going, the whirligig, but its effect is so to blow up the dust that we must wait for it to stop a moment, as it now and then does with a pant of triumph, in order to see what it has been at. I saw, beyond all doubt, on the spot—and *there* came in, exactly, the thrill: I could remember far back enough to have seen it begin to blow all the artless buyers and builders and blunderers into their places, leaving them there for half a century or so of fond security, and then to see it, of a sudden, blow them quite out again, as with the happy consciousness of some new amusing use for them, some other game still to play with them. This acquaintance, as it practically had been, with the whole rounding of the circle (even though much of it from a distance), was tantamount to the sense of having sat out the drama, the social, the local, that of a real American period, from the rise to the fall of the curtain—always assuming that truth of the reached catastrophe or *dénouement*. *How* this climax or solution had been arrived at—that, clearly, for the spectator, would have been worth taking note of; but what he made of it I shall not glance at till I have shown him as first of all, on the spot, quite modestly giving in to mere primary beguilement. It had been certain, in advance, that he would find the whole picture overpainted, and the question could only be, at the best, of how much of the ancient surface would here and there glimmer through. The ancient surface had been the concern, as I have hinted, of the small fond minority, the comparatively few people for whom the lurking shy charm, all there, but all to be felt rather than published, did in fact constitute a surface. The question, as soon as one arrived, was of whether some ghost of that were recoverable.

II

There was always, to begin with, the Old Town—we used, before we had be-

A MODERN SUMMER RESIDENCE

come Old our-
selves, to
speak of it that
way, in the
manner of an
allusion to Nu-
remberg or to
Carcassonne,
since it had
been leading its
little historic
life for cen-
turies (as we
implied) before
" cottages " and
house-agents
were dreamed
of. It was not
that we had
great illusions
about it or
great preten-
sions for it; we
only thought it,
without inter-
ference, very
"good of its
kind," and we
had as to its *be-
ing* of that kind
no doubt what-
ever. Would
it still be of
that kind, and
what had the
kind itself
been ?—these
questions made
one's heart beat
faster as one
went forth in
search of it.
Distinctly, if it
had been of a
kind it *would*

A Street in the Village of Newport

still be of it; for the kind wouldn't at the
worst or at the best (one scarce knew
how to put it), have been worth changing: so that the question for the restored absentee, who so palpitated with
the sense of it, all hung, absolutely, on
the validity of the past. One might well
hold one's breath if the past, with the
dear little blue distances in it, were
in danger now of being given away. One
might well pause before the possible indication that a cherished impression of

youth had been but a figment of the
mind. Fortunately, however, at Newport, and especially where the antiquities
cluster, distances are short, and the note
of reassurance awaited me almost round
the first corner. One had been a hundred times right—for how *was* one to
think of it all, as one went on, if one
didn't think of it as Old? There played
before one's eyes again, in fine, in that
unmistakable silvery shimmer, a particular property of the local air, the ex-

BEACON ROCK

quisite law of the relative—the application of which, on the spot, is required
to make even such places as Viterbo and
Bagdad not seem new. One may sometimes be tired of the word, but anything
that has succeeded in living long enough
to become conscious of its *note,* is capable on occasion of making that note ef-
fectively sound. It *will* sound, we gather,
if we listen for it, and the small silver
whistle of the past, with its charming
quaver of weak gayety, quite played the
tune I asked of it up and down the tiny,
sunny, empty Newport vistas, perspectives coming to a stop like the very short
walks of very old ladies. What indeed
but little very old ladies did they resemble, the little very old streets? with
the same suggestion of present timidity
and frugality of life, the same implication in their few folds of drab, of mourning, of muslin still mysteriously starched,
the implication of no adventure at any
time, however far back, that mightn't
have been suitable to a lady.

The whole low promontory, in its wider
and remoter measurements, is a region
of jutting tide-troubled "points," but
we had admired the Old Town too for
the emphasis of its peculiar point, *the*

Point; a quarter distinguished, we considered, by a really refined interest. Here
would have been my misadventure, if I
was to have any—that of missing, on the
gray page of to-day, the suggestive passages I remembered; but I was to find,
to my satisfaction, that there was still
no more mistaking their pleasant sense
than there had ever been: a quiet, mild
waterside sense, not that of the bold
bluff outer sea, but one in which shores
and strands and small coast things
played the greater part; with overhanging back verandas, with little private
wooden piers, with painted boat-houses
and boats laid up, with still-water bathing (the very words, with their old slightly prim discrimination, as of ladies and
children jumping up and down, reach
me across the years), with a wide-curving
Bay and dim landward distances that
melted into a mysterious, rich, superior,
but quite disconnected and not at all per-
mittedly patronizing Providence. There
were stories, anciently, for the Point—so
prescribed a feature of it that one made
them up, freely and handsomely, when
they were not otherwise to be come by;
though one was never quite sure if they
ought most to apply to the rather blank-

ly and grimly Colonial houses, fadedly drab at their richest and mainly, as the legend ran, appurtenant to that Quaker race whom Massachusetts and Connecticut had prehistorically cast forth and the great Roger Williams had handsomely welcomed, or to the other habitations, the felicitous cottages, with their galleries on the Bay and toward the sunset, their pleasure-boats at their little wharves, and the supposition, that clung to them, of their harboring the less fashionable of the outer Great, but also the more cultivated and the more artistic. Everything was there still, as I say, and quite as much as anything the prolonged echo of that ingenuous old-time distinction. It was a marvel, no doubt, that the handful of light elements I have named should add up to any total deserving the name of *picture,* and if I must produce an explanation I seek it with a certain confidence in .the sense of the secret enjoyed by that air for bathing or, as one figures, for dipping, the objects it deals with. It takes them uninteresting, but feels immediately what submersion can do for them; tips them in, keeps them down, holds them under, just for the proper length of time: after which they come up, as I say, irradiating vague silver—the reflection of which I have perhaps here been trying to catch even to extravagance.

I did nothing, at any rate, all an autumn morning, but discover again how "good" everything had been—positively better than one had ventured to suppose in one's care to make the allowance for one's young simplicity. Some things indeed, clearly, had been better than one knew, and now seemed to surpass any fair probability: else. why, for instance, should I have been quite awestruck by the ancient State-House that overlooks the ancient Parade, an edifice ample, majestic, archaic, of the finest proportions and full of a certain public Dutch dignity—having brave, broad, high windows, in especial, the distinctness of whose innumerable square white-framed panes is the recall of some street view of Haarlem or Leyden. Here was the charming impression of a treasure of antiquity to the vague image of which, through the years, one hadn't done justice—any more than one had done it, positively, to three or

four of the other old-time ornaments of the Parade (which, with its wide, cobbly, sleepy space, of those years, in the shadow of the State-House, must have been much more of a Van der Heyden, or somebody of that sort than one could have dreamed). There was a treasure of modernity to reckon with, in the form of one of the Commodores Perry (they are somehow much multiplied at Newport, and quite monumentally ubiquitous,) engaged in his great naval act; but this was swept away in the general flood of justice to be done. I continued to do it, all over the place, and I remember doing it next at a certain ample old-time house which used to unite with the still prettier and archaic Vernon, near it, to form an honorable pair. In this mild town-corner, where it was so indicated that the grass should be growing between the primitive paving-stones, and where indeed I honestly think it mainly is, amid whatever remains of them, ancient peace had appeared formerly to reign—though attended by the ghost of ancient war, inasmuch as these had indubitably been the haunts of our auxiliary French officers during the Revolution, and no self-respecting legend could fail to report that it was in the Vernon house Washington would have visited Rochambeau. There had hung about this structure, which is, architecturally speaking, all "rusticated" and indefinable decency, the implication of an inward charm that refined even on its outward, and this was the tantalizing message its clean, serious windows, never yet debased, struck me as still giving. But it was still (something told me,) a question of not putting, anywhere, too many presumptions to the touch; so that my hand quitted the knocker when I was on the point of a tentative tap, and I fell back on the neighbor and mate, as to which there was unforgotten acquaintance to teach me certainty. Here, alas, cold change was installed; the place had become a public office—none of the "artistic" supercivilized, no *raffiné* of them all, among the passing fanciers or collectors, having, strangely enough, marked it for his own. This mental appropriation it is, or it was a few months ago, really impossible not to make, at sight of its delightful hall and almost "grand"

staircase, its charming recessed, cup-
boarded, window-seated parlors, its general panelled amplitude and dignity: the
due taster of such things putting himself straight into possession on the spot,
and, though wondering at the indifference and neglect, breathing thanks for
the absence of positive ravage. For me
there were special ghosts on the staircase, known voices in the brown old
rooms—presences that one would have
liked, however, to call a little to account.
"People don't do those things"; people
didn't let so clear a case—clear for sound
curiosity — go like that; they didn't,
somehow, even if they were only ghosts.
But I thought too, as I turned away, of
all the others of the foolish, or at least
of the responsible, those who for so long
have swarmed in the modern quarter and
who make profession of the finer sense.

This impression had been disturbing,
but it had served its purpose in recon-
stituting, with a touch, a link—in laying
down again every inch of the train of
association with the human, the social,
personal Newport of what I may call
the middle years. To go further afield,
to measure the length of the little old
Avenue and tread again the little old
cliff-walk, to hang over, from above, the
little old white crescent of the principal
bathing-sands, with the big pond, behind them, set in its stone-walled feature-
less fields; to do these things and many
others, every one of them thus accompanied by the admission that all that
had been had been little, was to feel dead
and buried generations push off even the
transparence of their shroud and get
into motion for the peopling of a scene
that a present posterity has outgrown.
The company of the middle years, the
so considerably prolonged formative, tentative, imaginative Newport time, hadn't
outgrown it—this catastrophe was still
to come, as it constitutes, precisely, the
striking dramatic *dénouement* I have already referred to. American society—so
far as that free mixture was to have arrived at cohesion—had for half a century
taken its whole relation with the place
seriously (which was by intention very
gayly); it long remained, for its happiness, quite at one with this most favored
resort of its comparative innocence. In
the attesting presence of all the constant

elements, of natural conditions that have,
after all, persisted more than changed,
a hundred far-away passages of the ex-
tinct life and joy, and of the comparative
innocence, came back to me with an inevitable grace. A glamour as of the
flushed ends of beautiful old summers,
making a quite rich medium, a red sunset haze, as it were, for a processional
throng of charioteers and riders, fortunate folk, fortunate above all in their
untouched good faith, adjourning from
the pleasures of the day to those of the
evening — this benignity in particular
overspread the picture, hanging it there
as the Newport aspect that most lived
again. Those good people all could make
discoveries within the frame itself—beginning of course to push it out, in all
directions, so as sufficiently to enlarge
it, as they fondly fancied, even for the
experience of a sophisticated world.
They danced and they drove and they
rode, they dined and wined and dressed
and flirted and yachted and polo'd and
Casino'd, responding to the subtlest inventions of their age; on the old lawns
and verandas I saw them gather, on the
old shining sands I saw them gallop,
past the low headlands I saw their white
sails verily flash, and through the dusky
old shrubberies came the light and sound
of their feasts.

It had all been in truth a history—
for the imagination that could take it
so; and when once that kindly stage was
offered them it was a wonder how many
figures and faces, how many names and
voices, images and embodiments of youth
mainly, and often of Beauty, and of
felicity and fortune almost always, or
of what then passed for such, pushed,
under my eyes, in blurred gayety, to the
front. Hadn't it been above all, in its
good faith, the Age of Beauties—the
blessed age when it was so easy to *be*,
"on the Avenue," a Beauty, and when it
was so easy, not less, not to doubt of the
unsurpassability of such as appeared
there? It was through the fact that the
whole scheme and opportunity satisfied
them, the fact that the place was, as I
say, good enough for them — it was
through this that, with ingenuities and
audacities and refinements of their own
(some of the more primitive of which
are still touching to think of) they ex-

tended the boundaries of civilization, and fairly taught themselves to believe they were doing it in the interest of nature. Beautiful the time when the Ocean Drive had been hailed at once as a triumph of civilization and as a proof of the possible appeal of Scenery even to the dissipated. It was spoken of as of almost boundless extent—as one of the wonders of the world; as indeed it does turn often, in the gloaming, to purple and gold, and as the small sea-coves then gleam on its edge like barbaric gems on a mantle. Yet if it was a question of waving the wand and of breathing again, till it stirred, on the quaintness of the old manners—I refer to those of the fifties, sixties, seventies, and don't exclude those of the eighties—it was most touching of all to go back to dimmest days, days, such as now appear antediluvian, when ocean-drives, engineered by landscape artists and literally macadamized all the way, were still in the lap of time; when there was only an afternoon for the Fort, and another for the Beach, and another for the "Boathouse"—inconceivable innocence!—and even the shortness of the Avenue seemed very long, and even its narrowness very wide, and even its shabbiness very promising for the future, and when, in fine, chariots and cavaliers took their course, across country, to Bateman's, by inelegant precarious tracks and returned, through the darkling void, with a sense of adventure and fatigue. That, I can't but think, was the *pure* Newport time, the most perfectly guarded by a sense of margin and of mystery.

It was the time of settled possession, and yet furthest removed from these blank days in which margin has been consumed and the palaces, on the sites but the other day beyond price, stare silently seaward, monuments to the *blasé* state of their absent proprietors. Purer still, however, I remind myself, was that stretch of years which I have reasons for thinking sacred, when the custom of seeking hibernation on the spot partly prevailed, when the local winter inherited something of the best social grace (as it liked at least to think) of the splendid summer, and when the strange sight might be seen of a considerable company of Americans, not gathered at a mere

rest-cure, who confessed brazenly to not being in business. Do I grossly exaggerate in saying that this company, candidly, quite excitedly self-conscious, as all companies not commercial, in America, may be pleasantly noted as being, formed, for the time of its persistence, an almost unprecedented small body—unprecedented in American conditions; a collection of the detached, the slightly disenchanted and casually disqualified, and yet of the resigned and contented, of the socially orthodox: a handful of mild, oh delightfully mild, cosmopolites, united by three common circumstances, that of their having for the most part more or less lived in Europe, that of their sacrificing openly to the ivory idol whose name is leisure, and that, not least, of a formed critical habit. These things had been felt as making them excrescences on the American surface, where nobody ever criticised, especially after the grand tour, and where the great black ebony god of business was the only one recognized. So I see them, at all events, in fond memory, lasting as long as they could and finding no successors; and they are most embalmed for me, I confess, in that scented, somewhat tattered, but faintly spiced, wrapper of their various "European" antecedents. I see them move about in the light of these, and I understand how it was this that made them ask what would have become of them, and where in the world, the hard American world, they *could* have hibernated, how they could even, in the Season, have bowed their economic heads and lurked, if it hadn't been for Newport. I think of that question as, in their reduced establishments, over their winter whist, under their private theatricals, and pending, constantly, their loan and their return of the *Revue des Deux-Mondes,* their main conversational note. I find myself in fact tenderly evoking them as special instances of the great—or perhaps I have a right only to say of the small—American complication; the state of one's having been so pierced, betimes, by the sharp outland dart as to be able ever afterwards but to move about, vaguely and helplessly, with the shaft still in one's side.

Their nostalgia, however exquisite,

was, I none the less gather, sterile, for they appear to have left no seed. They must have died, some of them, in order to "go back"—to go back, that is, to Paris. If I make, at all events, too much of them, it is for their propriety as a delicate subjective value matching with the intrinsic Newport delicacy. They must have felt that they, obviously, notably, notoriously, did match—the proof of which was in the fact that to them alone, of the customary thousands, was the beauty of the good walk, over the lovely little land, revealed. The customary thousands, here, as throughout the United States, never set foot to earth—yet this had happened so, of old, to be the particular corner of *their* earth that made that adventure most possible. At Newport, as the phrase was, in autumnal, in vernal hibernation, you *could* walk—failing which, in fact, you failed of impressions the most consolatory; and it is mainly to the far ends of the low, densely shrubbed and perfectly finished little headlands that I see our friends ramble as if to stretch fond arms across the sea. There used to be distant places beyond Bateman's, or better still on the opposite isle of Canonicut, now blighted with ugly uses, where nursing a nostalgia on the sun-warmed rocks was almost as good as having none at all. So it was not only not our friends who had overloaded and overcrowded, but it was they at last, I infer, who gave way before that grossness. How should they have wished to leave seed only to be trampled by the white elephants?

The white elephants, as one may best call them, all cry and no wool, all house and no garden, make now, for three or four miles, a barely interrupted chain, and I dare say I think of them best, and

of the distressful, inevitable waste they represent, as I recall the impression of a divine little drive, roundabout them and pretty well everywhere, taken, for renewal of acquaintance, while November was still mild. I sought another renewal, as I have intimated, in the vacant splendor of June, but the interesting evidence then only refined on that already gathered. The place itself, as man—and often, no doubt, alas, as woman, with her love of the immediate and contiguous—had taken it over, was more than ever, to the fancy, like some dim, simplified ghost of a small Greek island, where the clear walls of some pillared portico or pavilion, perched afar, looked like those of temples of the gods, and where Nature, deprived of that ease in merely massing herself on which "American scenery," as we lump it together, is too apt to depend for its effect, might have shown a piping shepherd on any hillside or attached a mythic image to any point of rocks. What an idea, originally, to have seen this miniature spot of earth, where the sea-nymphs on the curved sands, at the worst, might have chanted back to the shepherds, as a mere breeding-ground for white elephants! They look queer and conscious and lumpish—some of them, as with an air of the brandished proboscis, really grotesque—while their averted owners, roused from a witless dream, wonder what in the world is to be done with them. The answer to which, I think, can only be that there is absolutely nothing to be done; nothing but to let them stand there always, vast and blank, for reminder to those concerned of the prohibited degrees of witlessness, and of the peculiarly awkward vengeances of affronted proportion and discretion.

THE QUEER FOLK OF THE MAINE COAST

OF old, muskets drove the Abnakis off the coast of Maine. Today, money is driving away another race.

Between Kittery Point and Quoddy Head "resorters" have acquired hundreds of headlands and thousands of islands. A phalanx of cottages fronts the sea. More than half the States in the Union are represented in these summer colonies. Cove and cape, the coast is pretty well monopolized by non-residents; "no-trespass" signs are so thickly set that they form a blazed trail. The man from the city resents intrusion. For that matter, the queer squatter people who have been dispossessed find little relish in being stared at as human curiosities. Therefore they have hidden themselves in the deep gashes of the coast cliffs; their little huts are now at the head of crooked coves where pleasure craft do not venture; or they have located on little nubbins of islands that city people do not buy, for these islands may be approached only at flood-tide. And in their retreats the "queer folk"

resent intrusion as heartily as do the rich folk on their reserves.

So the "queer folk" live alone—and it is said that isolation develops eccentricity. The ocean creeps to the doors of their huts, and the winter waves thunder in their ears—and there are those who say that the din of the sea beats curious ideas into the head.

Even the Maine "native" himself, the thrifty farmer who sells his produce to the city "sojourner" or takes summer boarders, does not understand the queer folk of the lonely coves very well. The nooks that they have chosen for hiding-places have no roads leading to them. The islands that they have pre-empted have been "set off" by act of the Legislature from the nearest coast towns, in order that the towns may not have the unfortunates on their hands as paupers. These people who have been abandoned dwell in a sort of "no man's land." They do not pay taxes, they do not vote. Fashion is close to many of them, just over that ridge of coast ledge or down that stretch of water—for fashion has picked most of the choice spots on the Maine coast for its sojourn. But the queer folk are not interested in any display that fashion may make. They are not envious, they do not want to beg. Where penury and pride meet in the cities there are heartburnings. But the man tossing in the battered dory in the swash of the millionaire's yacht neither sighs nor glares, provided he be one of the queer folk. For the queer folk are queer in one respect especially: they dwell content in their own world, which is often a world of illusion—for solitariness and the sea breed strange thoughts.

Ossian Dustin, of Newcastle, would not change places with a millionaire, so he says. Yet Uncle Ossian, at eighty, lives alone in a little hut with a dirt floor, and earns about fifty dollars a year by sawing fire-wood and doing odd jobs. But fifty dollars supply his frugal needs, and he has the most of his time to devote to hunting for Cap'n Kidd's treasure, in the buried existence of which he implicitly believes.

The case of Uncle Ossian illustrates the type of that content that relieves these hidden human tragedies of the Maine coast of some of their pitifulness. During most of his long life, as often as he has found opportunity, Uncle Ossian has hunted and dug along the ragged Lincoln coast. He has toiled nights, for the most part, believing that in the night a treasure-seeker can best circumvent the enchantments laid on buried pirate spoils. He has kept vigil oftenest in the region of Cod Lead Nubble. He searches with a treasure-rod made by his own hands. He has the tip of a cow's horn, plugged with wood and containing various metals. In the wooden plug are stuck parallel strips of whalebone, and he clutches these strips, one in each hand, and walks along, balancing the tip of horn. When he passes over the famous iron pot the tip, thus is his belief, will turn down and point at the buried treasure. There is nothing remarkable in Uncle Ossian's quest, for other men in Maine have hunted for Kidd's treasure. But his radiant courage and his unfailing optimism are striking. He believes that he "is always right on the edge" of finding the gold. He says his spade has struck against the iron pot several times, but that enchantment has whisked away the treasure. He expects that eventually his own charms will prevail over the powers of evil. He believes that the long waiting and the disappointments have been merely a test of his courage and good faith —remarkable philosophy in a man who is eighty years old and has not succeeded. He is reanimated occasionally by the sight of a figure all of shining gold that comes rowing up the reach from the sea, and he is confident that this is a good spirit sent to guide him to the treasure, and that the spirit will sometime prevail over the imps who watch the iron pot.

Uncle Ossian affirms that he has passed as happy a life as any man he knows; he says that the money will

BUSHY ISLAND, WHERE HERMIT TRIPP TOILED AT TREASURE-DIGGING

THE DIVIDED HOUSEHOLD OF LITTLE SPRUCE

"come in handy" in his old age, and that he shall first buy a stone for his mother's grave, and then a house with a floor in it for himself. It can scarcely be said that Uncle Ossian's unfailing cheerfulness springs from any philosophy of life that he has evolved. But after our talk I came out of his dingy hut with the feeling that probably some of the proud folk in the cottages down the bay needed pity more than he.

On Little Spruce island I found three old men, brothers—William, Daniel, and Nehemiah Shanks. They have lived there all their lives in a tumble-down little shelter. They are melancholy old men. They are contented, but the sea has brought to them a strange, brooding, wistful solemnity. William and Daniel never married. Nehemiah has had a poor little romance that broke his heart. When he was young he used to go with his father to Portland to sell their fare of fish. The only woman to whom he had ever spoken was his mother—for no one except the Shanks family has ever lived on Little Spruce. A woman of the water-

side in Portland made him her prey for the sake of his little hoard of savings, married him, induced him to forge his father's name and draw the family savings from the bank—and then deserted him. He went home with his confession of wrong-doing.

"Then you must look out for the boys after I'm dead," said his father, forgiving him. Nehemiah has spent his life "looking out for the boys," who are now infirm old men. "It is my duty in return for my father's pardon of my wrongdoing," he told me, "and I have tried to do my best. I am the youngest, and I am best able to work."

For more than twenty years William has never come out of the hut into the sunshine. He told me that he feared the sun might heat his brains and interfere with his life-work, which is the composition of poetry. There is a blanket hung across one end of the hut. William sits behind this blanket and fixes his eyes on the sunlight that enters through a knothole, and "composes." He states that now he is the author of a thousand pieces of poetry. He has committed nothing to paper. He has memorized all of them, he says.

While William idles, Nehemiah tills the little garden, catches fish, digs clams, and cooks. He is cheerfully the burden-bearer, and with some pride says that he is the head of the family; for when his father imposed the trust on him he did so with a cere-mony truly patri-archal: he gave into Nehemiah's hands the staff on which he had lean-ed for many years, saying that it should be the badge of Nehe-miah's authority. Nehemiah de-scribed the scene to me, tears trick-ling down his wrinkled cheeks. Memory was only a partial spur to this grief.

Daniel, after more than sixty years of obedience, had become a most amazing rebel. He had declared that an-other flood had been prophesied to him in a vision, and that he had been ordered to build an ark on Little Spruce. Little Spruce is owned by a lady in Boston, as part of an extensive holding of islands. The Shanks brothers have been permitted to remain as squatters on condition that they do not disturb the standing timber. Nehemiah gave this promise to the man-ager of the estate.

Daniel, though threescore and ten, took the family axe, hand-saw, and hammer and proceeded to his labors on his ark. Nehemiah stood in front of the lordly spruce that Daniel was about to attack with the axe, and in the name of the Shanks family forbade him to chop. Daniel had the zeal of monomania and insisted. Then Nehemiah brandished the family staff and threatened to chas-tise the disobedient son of their father. Daniel, in a frenzy, made at his brother with the axe, routed him, captured the

HERMIT TRIPP

staff, chopped it up, and then began on the tree. He laid waste quite a section of woodland before Nehemiah got word to the agent. Then in high dudgeon Daniel built a shack of his own. He lives in it and refuses to speak to his brothers. Nehemiah, tall, grave, digni-fied, with the flowing white beard of a patriarch, stood upon a knoll and pointed over to Daniel's hut and told me of the un-fortunate affair, sorrowfully, with-out anger. Dan-iel, realizing that his misdeeds were exposed to a stran-ger, shook his fists from afar and leaped up and down in what was apparently ecstasy of rage. He way-laid me before I had left Little Spruce, and in-formed me that after being bossed by his brother for more than sixty years he proposed to run his own affairs for the rest of his life. Nehemiah came in his turn to the shore after Daniel had trudged away to his hut, cracking his hard little fists above his head in his temper.

"I still hope to be able to meet father at the door of heaven and tell him that I kept the Shanks family together and kept it decent, as he would have liked to have me keep it," said Nehemiah, sadly. "Daniel was always hard to manage; father found him so. But I think he will come back to his home, for I am the only one in the family who can cook things as mother used to cook them."

Bushy Island, to which I came when a poor little human drama was at its climax, is a bare handful of earth without a tree on it. Quarter of a century ago Henry Tripp, after roving along the coast, settled there. He was an old man even then, bent at his hips into almost a right angle. Fourteen years ago a woman, as old as he, came from the main and dwelt with him in his little house. In fourteen years she was off that patch of island only twice.

"Hermit Tripp," as he was called, believed that Kidd had buried his treasure on Bushy. Old and decrepit as he was, he began to dig the island. He wore out shovel after shovel at his task. When he died he had shovelled nearly half the island off into the sea, cleaning the earth down to bed-rock.

He died in August, 1908. On the night of his death a summer gale swept the coast, wrecking cottages and flattening acres of trees on the main near Bushy. When the old woman realized that Tripp was dying she took a big hand-bell and, though so weak and old that she could walk only with difficulty, she went out on the high land of the island and rang the bell with all her strength, hoping that in some lull of the gale the sound would be heard on the main.

NEHEMIAH SHANKS, THE PATRIARCH OF LITTLE SPRUCE

At midnight she went to the hut to minister to the old man, and found him dead. Then she resumed her vigil on the shore, ringing the bell, blinded by the lightning, drenched by the rains, and blown about by the gale.

People heard and came off to the island the next day. But Bushy Island is one of those "set-off" places, a no man's land so far as the law goes. Three towns at first disclaimed responsibility for the burial expenses of a pauper. The old woman stayed alone with her dead a second night. Then came men and dug his grave, a pebble-toss from his hut, and laid him there. Some one read a bit from the tattered old Bible that was found in the house. Those who had buried the old man went away and left the old woman alone. Chance and idle curiosity brought me to Bushy one day. I had supposed that charity had provided a home elsewhere for the lonely tenant. But she was still there. She was ill, she was hungry, she had not

sufficient strength to walk or to build a fire. There is no fresh water on Bushy. She had a scanty supply in a jug.

It is not necessary to go into the details of the measures promptly taken for her relief. At first she concealed her name. We discovered what it was from some old letters that were flying about the little yard. She "had been some one" once on a time. She has a brother living, a worthy and prominent man in an inland town. He came promptly when I communicated with him, and went with me to visit his sister in the hut on Bushy Island. He had not seen her, had not heard from her, for many years. He had sought for her, but she had disappeared. He and she are the only ones left of a well-known family.

One can imagine how fiction would have handled this reunion. But real life has its own grim methods. It was high tide and the launch swung close to the corner of the hut, under which the waves were lapping. The brother hesitated, misery on his countenance.

"Go in first, please!" he implored.

She gave him only a careless glance when he sat down in the unspeakable shelter.

"For God's sake, take me out!" he gasped. "I can't stand this!"

We were not in the place ten seconds. He had not heart or strength to make this forlorn creature know him for what he was. He hurried into the launch and left the island. This is how fact tersely dismissed a situation that fiction would have lingered over.

It is proper in this connection to state that later the brother appointed me his agent and almoner, and before the fall grew late the woman was re-

THE OLD WOMAN OF BUSHY ISLAND

ENTERTAINING THE MISSIONARY—SUNDAY ON MALAGA ISLAND

moved from the island to a comfortable home, where she is now cared for. Her mental faculties that had been impaired by her privations have been regained in a measure, but she has never made any inquiries regarding her family. On our visits to her we find her reading her Bible and, to use her words, "preparing my soul for the great change."

This case also brought to my attention a character who ought to be interesting from a sociological point of view. He is an addition to the varied army of vagrants—he is a water tramp. While search for some honest persons who would take the old woman as a boarder was in progress, those interested in the case carried cooked food each day and plenty of dainties. She declared that she felt perfectly safe to stay alone nights—and, in fact, the hut was too wretched a place to serve as a lodging for any person except the poor old creature who had become accustomed to it.

Now appears a human derelict in a barnacled old dory! He seemed to sniff those food delicacies from afar. He billeted himself on the poor old woman, coming in the edge of the evening, remaining the night, and departing before charity came again with heaped hands.

This especial water tramp has been a peregrinator in Casco waters for many years, a stolid, weather-beaten man, and even the gulls of the bay take more thought as to where they may perch for the night. There are a dozen or more of his ilk scattered alongshore. The city man who comes down to his cottage in the spring and finds a window forced, the left-overs of his larder devoured, and his summer clothes gone, has this gentry of the coast to thank. The water tramp steals only what he can eat and what he can wear. He dwells in a cottage as long as it suits his taste or convenience, or until the crackers, canned goods, and firewood are gone. Then he moves to the next. He is not a good housekeeper, and the cottager who finds his débris in the spring has a bad quarter of an hour and a lively desire for vengeance. If he will keep sharp watch, he will find his old coat on the back of a "dory vagabond." But it doesn't trouble the water tramp if he is sent to jail. He goes up-country stoically, and returns to seek his living in the same old way.

But there is one who stands forth from among these petty thieves with almost the proportions of a modern Viking. He came coasting along from Nova Scotia in a gray and seamed old Hampton boat, leisurely seeking adventures and three

JAKE, GREAT-GRANDSON OF THE PIONEER OF MALAGA

meals a day, and arrived in the Pemaquid region.

He lingered there for some weeks. His name was MacTush, he had the swagger of a border chieftain, and his hair was the hair of a Norseman, and he found favor in the eyes of a wife whose husband was away upon the Grand Banks on a "mack'rel-chancin'" trip. So the stranger stole the wife, four children, and such furniture from the house as could be stowed in the Hampton boat. He sailed back to Nova Scotia.

As time went on the wife regretted. But it was not regret for the abandoned husband. Here once more fact differs from fiction. She was sorry that she had

not been able to take more of her belongings. The Viking's hut in Nova Scotia was but scantily furnished. She kept remembering certain choice things that had been left behind in the hurry of departure and on account of lack of room in the Hampton boat. She urged her new lord to go back and get another load. The story of how she urged came out later in the Lincoln County court. The Viking went back a few months after his first foray. The wife told him that the house would be locked up and the husband away to the Banks once more. The freebooter was removing the rest of the furniture— finding the house untenanted, as the wife had prophesied; but he was apprehended by friends of the absent husband. The judge in imposing sentence stated that a thief who would steal a man's wife, four children, and half his furniture, and then come back after the rest of the household goods, was too much of a rogue to expect mercy, and MacTush is in jail for a number of years.

Louds Island, off the coast of Bristol, occupies perhaps a more anomalous position than any other land along the Atlantic seaboard. It has a considerable population of thrifty fishermen and farmers; they live in good houses and are intelligent. They and their ancestors have dwelt there for more than one hundred and fifty years. But the men of the island have never voted in any election, town or State or national. They have never paid any State, town, or county taxes. They resisted the draft at the time of the Civil War, and drove the officers off the island with clubs and rocks. They say that they do not need the protecting arm of State or national government. They raise money for schools and roads, elect municipal officers to administer affairs, and seem to get along very comfortably as an independent principality. Flattering overtures have been made by Bristol; by coming into the fold the islanders would receive State school money, have an opportunity to vote, and obtain other advantages. But Louds Island will not affiliate. There has never been a crime committed on the island, no one ever locks his door, and almost every one is a relation of some one else.

While Louds Island is genially beckoned into the family by Bristol, Malaga Island is getting the cold shoulder from Phippsburg—the town that contains the site of ancient "Augusta," pioneer of all New England settlements.

As a "no man's land" Malaga has more striking peculiarities than any other island alongshore. There are about fifty persons on it, of all grades of negro blood, and most of them descendants of a runaway slave who came and hid there more years ago than any man about there remembers. These people form a strange clan. They have married and intermarried until the trespass on consanguinity has produced its usual lamentable effects. They are as near to being children of nature as it is possible for people to be who are only a stone's throw from the mainland and civilization. They lack entirely the spirit of thrift and of providing for future emergencies. Winter after winter, through all the years, they have shivered and starved, but never does November find a wood-pile on Malaga, nor a week's supply of food in reserve. To counsel on economy and to preachment on thrift they are as inattentive as little children would be. A coast missionary took in hand one especially improvident family of six—father, mother, and four children well grown. Spurred by him, they fished, dug clams, sold bait to trawlers, and at the end of the summer had saved about seventy dollars among them. Then the missionary went away, confident that at least one Malaga family would reach "March Hill" in comparative comfort. When his back was turned they used for kindlings the shingles that he had given them for the repair of their miserable hut, bought six dogs in order that each member of the family could have his own pet, and spent the rest of the money for sweets, pickles, jellies, and fancy groceries.

Charity, after a few experiences with the "Malagaites," as they are called by their indifferent neighbors on the main, grows a bit discouraged. Donations of money bring more harm to them than otherwise. Old clothes and a doling of something to eat form charity's only resource. A State agent who looks after paupers in unorganized places goes over to Malaga occasionally, thins out the dogs, travels about to see whether medical attendance is required by any one, gives those actually hungry an order on the nearest grocery-store, and does not trouble himself to give good advice; it was discovered a great many years ago that good advice is wasted in Malaga. A while ago the agent took along a notary and had marriages performed between six couples whose naïve ideas of wedlock had not reached out to the fact that a ceremony was necessary.

In summer all the people of the colony work as best they are able, but the scope of what they can do is so limited and the returns in money so small that it is not surprising that winter finds them with hands empty.

Women put on trousers and boots and dig clams with the men. Occasionally farmers on the main hire the women to work in the fields. The men are too lazy. The woman who earns the most money is one who lives in what was once the cabin of a schooner. She takes in washings from the main. As she cannot stand upright in her house, she climbs upon the roof and there toils at her tub.

Certain amateur sociologists have been wondering and planning what to do with Malaga and the Malagaites. Popular subscription has erected a neat little schoolhouse, in which a teacher, paid by the State, began her work in November, 1908. The children will be taught how to read and write, and the women will take lessons in sewing and darning and patching. There have been few needles on Malaga in the past.

The people of the island are singularly

susceptible to religious influence, and most of them row to the main on Sundays to attend church. With the exception that their ideas of the social code of morals are primitive, they are blameless so far as their relations with the world go; they are not vicious, they show none of that sullenness that marks similar strata of society, and they extend the rude hospitality of their island with touching warmth and sincerity.

The rude gashes in the coast of Maine afford good hiding-places for those who desire to leave the world behind. One day a youth dropped off a coaster and looked about a Maine fishing-village. He stayed long enough to fall desperately in love with a girl whose father owned a Grand Banks smack and was accordingly in the upper ranks of village society. The young man, poorly clad and a stranger, was repulsed, naturally. When he undertook to explain that he was a runaway from a wealthy English family he was looked upon with still greater suspicion. He set at work digging clams for a living and feeding his soul on occasional fleeting glimpses of the girl he loved. His story had been scoffed at with so great unanimity that he did not make any more revelations regarding his prospects. But one day he appeared at the office of a lawyer in the shire town of the county, and produced papers just received from England that required only his signature and his oath to yield him $15,000 from an estate in his native country. He got the money, put it into a bank, bought out the general store in the fishing-village, married the girl, and from the butt became the boss of the place. It would be pleasing to state that he remained the boss and lived happy ever after, but again does grim fact tip over fiction's apple-cart—as life is lived in the cracks o' the coast!

That young man was instructed by the lawyer in the use of a check-book, and it did not seem like spending real money when he wrote a check. He bought all the fishing-boats for sale along that part of the coast. Every one who had anything to sell hurried up from cove, island, and far inlet and sold it to this young man, who had become drunken with flattery and adulation after having

been despised so long. Travelling salesmen heard of him, and descended and filled his store to bursting with goods— goods that he tossed out on credit to the throng that hung around him.

When, at the end of eight months or so, he got a notice from the bank stating that he had overdrawn his account he did not understand, and went to the lawyer to have the matter explained. When it was explained he was dazed. He had not thought that fifteen thousand dollars could ever be cleaned out by writing on little slips of paper!

His affairs were so mixed that he was obliged to assign, and it is easy to understand what an assignment would do to a man who did not know that fifteen thousand dollars do not make an inexhaustible treasure. I am afraid that what I have heard is true: that he is digging clams again.

But while he lasted he was the most talked-about young man along a good bit of coast. Even old "Six-fingered Simpson" of the Crumples heard of him —and the Crumples is at the end of the world! Simpson pawed over his scanty possessions, found something to sell, and came up and sold it. He had not been to the mainland before in twenty years. The list of things that Simpson had never seen comprised all of man's inventions between locomotives and phonographs. The new Midas of the coast had a phonograph, and he was willing to amaze Simpson. But Simpson was not amazed. He listened, walked around the contrivance, and declared that some one hidden down-cellar was making the noise that came through the horn. He listened to the parlor organ without comment. But when he rejoined his son, who had been waiting for him at the shore, afraid to venture among those devil gimcracks, he said:

"The most of it didn't amount to much. But you ought to have seen the critter in the. parlor. His woman set down 'side of it, and it showed its teeth to her, and she cuffed along them teeth and trod on its tail, and it growled and whined away savage enough, now, I tell ye!"

So we turned at the Crumples and came home from our exploring, for it is plain that the Crumples is at the end of the world!

OLD SALEM SEA-CAPTAINS

THOSE who may have had occasion, thirty or forty years ago, to visit the custom-houses of the New England coast may remember certain typical figures now vanished—a race of quiet, elderly men, who came and went about their monotonous duties, bearing no trace of stormy and adventurous careers, except a certain slight deference from those around them, and the title of "Captain." The voice that quavered as it slowly read aloud a column of figures had once shouted forth the order to cut away the masts in a hurricane, or to open fire upon a Spanish fort; hands that trembled as they unfolded a manifest had once struck down a Malay pirate with a cutlass, or steered a sinking vessel into an unknown harbor in the Indian Ocean. These men wére the humbler Drakes, the Cavendishes, of their day; they had carried the American flag where it was an unknown ensign; they had voyaged from distant island on to island without chart or light-house; they had made and lost great fortunes—made them commonly for others, lost them for themselves. At twenty they had been ship-masters; at fifty they were stranded hulks. They were like those other seaside products, those floating and homeless jelly-fishes that at first are borne wherever ocean wills, and then change into a fixed, clinging creature that rests in some secluded custom-house in a cleft of rock, thenceforth to move no more.

These were the less fortunate but not less heroic type of Salem sea-captains, the men who could say to their children, as Virgil's Æneas says to Iulus:

"Disce, puer, virtutem ex me, verumque laborem,
Fortunam ex aliis."

There were others who added good fortune to courage and industry; men like Nathaniel Silsbee, who was for years the associate of Daniel Webster in the Senate of the United States, or like the Crown-inshields and Derbys and Grays, who bequeathed large estates to their descendants. These were the conspicuous instances of success; those of financial failure were more frequent. The old sea-captains were more commonly men who, like Dogberry, had had losses, or who, like great inventors, enriched all but themselves. Captain Richard Cleveland left home at twenty-three with $2000 invested, and after twice circumnavigating the globe, returned at thirty with what was then regarded as a comfortable fortune—$70,000. This he naturally invested in the voyages of others; they naturally lost it; and after sacrificing, as he estimates it, $200,000 in all, he brought up in a custom-house at last.

Successful or unsuccessful, the centre and head-quarters of these retired navigators was Salem, Massachusetts. The very seal of that now quiet city drew its proud motto, "Divitis Indiæ usque ad ultimum sinum," from their unwearied labors. There is nothing more brilliant in American history than the brief career of maritime adventure which made the name of Salem synonymous with that of America in many a distant port. The period bridged the interval between two wars: the American Revolution laid its foundation; the later war with England saw its last trophies. Its evolution was very simple. When the chief ports of the colonies were closed and their commerce ruined, the group of ports around Salem became the head-quarters of privateers; and when the Revolutionary war was over, those vessels, being too large for the coasting trade, sought a new outlet, and could not find it short of the Pacific and the southeastern archipelago. By their daring and adventure those who owned

vard College, and Governor of the English colony of Madras—the home-keeping brother suggests that the ex-Governor should make the Massachusetts colony the seat of an Oriental commerce by way of London, and thus enumerates the resources of such a traffic:

HOUSE OF BENJAMIN PICKMAN, BUILT IN 1740.

and sailed these vessels became for a time the heroes of the sea; they competed single-handed with the great chartered companies of European nations; they ventured freely between the giant forces of England and France, both ready to swallow them up. Even when finally crushed between French "decrees" and English "orders in council," they retained vitality enough to lead up to the naval glories of the war of 1812.

Yet long before the Revolution a plan had been vaguely sketched out by which Salem was to obtain something of that share in the India trade which later events brought to her. In an old letter-book containing part of the correspondence that passed in 1669 between Lieutenant-Colonel John Higginson, of Salem, and his brother Nathaniel—graduate of Har-

"All sorts of calicoes, aligers, remwalls, muslin, silks for clothing and linings; all sorts of drugs proper for the apothecaries, and all sorts of spice, are vendible with us, and the prices of them alter much according as they were plenty or scarce. In the late war time all East India goods were extremely dear. Muslins of the best sort, plain, striped, and flowered, were sold for £10 per piece, and some more. Pepper, 3s. per pound; nuts [nutmegs], 10s. per pound; cloves, 20s.; mace, 30s.; but now are abated about a quarter part in value. Some of the china ware, toys, and lacquer ware will sell well, but no great quantity. As for ambergris, we often have it from the West Indies, and it is sold for about 3 per ounce. For musk, pearl, and diamond, I believe some of them may sell well, but I understand not their value."

Thus early, it seems, was the taste for Chinese and Japanese goods—germ of future æstheticism—implanted in the American colonies; but when it comes to pearls and diamonds, the quiet Salem burgher, descendant of three generations of devout clergymen, "understands not their value." Yet he believes that some of them will sell well, even in 1669!

In the early commerce of Salem the whale-fishery took the lead, and this same John Higginson at one time petitioned the General Court (or State Legislature) to recover the value of a whale which was proved to have had a harpoon sticking in it and bearing his mark, but which had afterward been harpooned and brought in by some one else. Later the West India trade flourished, the chief imports being sugar and molasses, and these being very much checked by the arbitrary taxes imposed by the British government. It was on a petition of the Salem collector for a warrant to search after smuggled molasses that James Otis made his celebrated plea against Writs of Assistance. These were among the imports, and they were paid for, first and chiefly, by the historic codfish, the fish whose effigy still adorns the Massachusetts Representatives' Hall, and which the old Salem merchant Benjamin Pickman also commemorated with carving and gilding on each stair of his mansion in Salem—a house built in 1740, and still standing. Like the pious Bishop Willegis, who took for his crest the wheel, his early labors on which were regarded as plebeian by his rivals, so Benjamin Pickman exalted the codfish. Other merchants used for the same purpose the symbolic pineapple, which may be found so frequently carved on old stairways and bureaus; and possibly the scallop-shell which so often appears on colonial furniture or cornices may have had a similar association, and suggested "treasures hid in the sands."

But it took the great stress of the Revolutionary war to evolve the old Salem sea-captain. During that war it is hard to tell how the intercourse between Europe and the colonies would have been kept up—with Boston, Newport, New York, Philadelphia, Charleston, and Savannah successively in the hands of the enemy—but for the merchants and mariners of Salem, Beverly, and Marblehead. Salem alone sent out 158 armed vessels, carrying in all more than 2000 guns, each vessel having twelve or fourteen. They took 445 prizes, 54 out of their own fleet being lost.

The loss of the vessels was to be expected; but the loss from history of all detailed memorial of these daring men is more serious. What is fame that preserves of all that period only the madcap daring of Paul Jones, and forgets the solid heroism of Jonathan Haraden?

Jonathan Haraden was born in Gloucester, but was taken early to Salem in the employ of Richard Cabot, father of the celebrated president of the Hartford Convention. He first went to sea as lieutenant, then as captain of a fourteen-gun sloop built for the State of Massachusetts, and bearing a name that would have delighted Wendell Phillips—the *Tyrannicide*. In her he helped capture a British naval vessel, that was carried in triumph into Salem Harbor. Afterward Haraden was put in command of the *General Pickering*, a Salem privateer of 180 tons, carrying fourteen six-pounders, and a crew of forty-five men and boys. He sailed in 1780 with a cargo of sugar for Bilboa, then a resort for American privateers and prize vessels. On his passage he had a two hours' fight with a British cutter of twenty guns, and beat her off, but on entering the Bay of Biscay found opportunity for an exploit more daring. Running by night alongside a British privateer carrying twenty-two guns and sixty men, he ordered her, through his trumpet, to "surrender to an American frigate or be sunk." The astonished Englishman yielded, and came on board to find himself outgeneralled. A prize crew was put on the captured vessel, and both made sail for Bilboa, when they were met by a king's ship, which, as the captured captain told Haraden with delight, was the *Achilles*, another English privateer, with forty-two guns and 140 men. "I sha'n't run from her," said Haraden, coolly. At once the scene changed; the big Englishman recaptured the little one, then lay alongside Haraden's ship all night to fight her next day. Haraden took a sound night's sleep, and recruited a boatswain and eight sailors from his prisoners in the morning, when they went to work.

The American ship seemed, said an eye-witness, like a long-boat beside a man-of-war; many of the Englishman's shot went over her opponent, while she herself was always hit below the water-line —this modern Achilles, like the ancient, proving vulnerable in the heel. A final broadside of crow-bars from Haraden had great effect, and Achilles fled. The *Pick-ering* gave chase, and Haraden offered a large reward to his gunner if he would carry away a spar, but no such luck occurred, and the Englishman got off. Haraden recaptured his first prize, which had thus changed hands thrice in twenty-four hours, and went into port with her. The battle had lasted three hours, being fought so near the Spanish coast that a hundred thousand spectators, it was said, lined the shores; and it was also said that, before the *Pickering* and her prize had been half an hour at anchor, one could have walked a mile over the water by stepping from boat to boat; and when the captain landed he was borne in triumph through the city on men's shoulders. This is but a sample of this bold sailor's adventures. On another occasion still, in the *Pickering*, he fell in with three armed Englishmen in company, carrying respectively twelve, fourteen, and sixteen guns; and he captured each in succession with his vessel, he carrying just as many guns as the largest of the enemy.

Haraden alone took more than a thousand guns from the British during the war. The Salem ships intercepted the vessels which carried supplies from England or Nova Scotia to the garrisons in New York and Boston; they cruised in

GEORGE CABOT IN YOUTH.
From the painting owned by Mr. H. C. Lodge, Boston.

the Bay of Biscay, and in the English and Irish channels; they raised the insurance on British ships to twenty-three per cent., and obliged a large naval force to be constantly employed in convoying merchantmen; they, moreover, brought munitions of war from the French islands. Some sailed as privateers pure and simple; others under "letters of marque," in voyages whose privateering was incidental, but where the dangers incurred were much the same. Joseph Peabody, for instance, sailed from Salem in the winter of 1781 as second mate of the letter-of-marque *Ranger*, Captain Simmons, carrying seven guns. They took a cargo of salt, sold it at Richmond, Virginia, and at Alexandria loaded with flour for Havana. Part of the cargo, being from General Washington's plantation, was received at Havana at the marked weight; all was sold, and the *Ranger* returned to Alexandria for another freight. Anchoring at the mouth of the Potomac because of headwinds, the officers turned in, but were roused before midnight by the watch, with news that large boats were coming toward the ship from different directions. Simmons and Peabody rushed to the deck, the latter in his night clothes. As they reached it, a volley of musketry met them, and the captain fell wounded. Peabody ran forward, shouting for the crew to

JOSEPH PEABODY.
From the painting in the East India Marine Society, Salem.

ELIAS HASKET DERBY.
From the painting in the East India Marine Society, Salem.

seize the boarding pikes, and he himself attacked some men who were climbing on board. Meantime another strange boat opened fire from another quarter. All was confusion; they knew not who were their assailants or whence; the captain lay helpless, the first officer was serving out ammunition, and Peabody, still conspicuous in his white raiment, had command of the deck. Two boats were already grappled to the *Ranger;* he ordered cold shot to be dropped into them, and frightened one crew so that it cast off; then he ordered his men against the other boat, shouting, " We have sunk one, boys; now let us sink the other!" His men cheered, and presently both boats dropped astern, leaving one of the *Ranger's* crew dead and three wounded. Peabody himself was hurt in three places, not counting the loss of his club of hair, worn in the fashion of those days, which had been shot clean off, and was found on deck the next morning. The enemy proved to be a guerrilla band of Tories, whose rendezvous was at St. George's Island, near where the *Ranger* lay at anchor. There had been sixty men in their boats, while the crew of the *Ranger* numbered twenty; and the same guerrillas had lately captured a brig of seven guns and thirty men by the same tactics, which the promptness of Peabody had foiled.

On such tales as these was the youth of Salem nourished during the bitter period of the American Revolution. That once over, the same bold spirits sought wider adventure. Joseph Peabody himself lived to own, first and last, eighty-three ships, which he freighted himself; he shipped 7000 seamen, and promoted forty-five men to be captains who had first shipped with him as boys. Other merchants, of whom Elias Hasket Derby was the chief, were constantly projecting distant voyages, and taking pains to bring forward enterprising young men, who were given ventures of their own as captain or supercargo. These were often the sons of the ship-owners, and, aided by the excellent public schools of Salem, became officers at an age that seems surprisingly early. Nathaniel Silsbee, the eldest son of a sea-captain, went to sea as captain's clerk at fourteen, his brother William did the same at fifteen, and his brother Zachariah at sixteen. The eldest brother was in command of a vessel before he was nineteen, and the two others before they were twenty. All three retired from the sea when under twenty-nine. Captain Nathaniel Silsbee sailed one East India voyage of nineteen months, at the beginning of which neither he, nor his first mate (Charles Derby), nor his second mate (Richard Cleveland), was twenty years old. My own grandfather, Stephen Higginson—afterward member of the Continental Congress—commanded one of his father's ships at twenty-one. His double-first cousin, George Cabot—afterward the first Secretary of the Navy, and the president of the Hartford Convention—left Harvard College and went to sea at sixteen as cabin-boy under his brother-in-law, Joseph Lee, the traditional opinion expressed in the family being that "Cap'n Joe would put George Cabot's nose to the grindstone," which was doubtless done. At twenty he was himself a captain. In the slower development of the present day there is something amusing in this carnival of youth.

While still too young to vote, these boys were deemed old enough to open new channels of trade, penetrate unknown seas, and risk collision with the great naval nations of Europe. They had to make their own charts, as, for instance, of the coast of Sumatra, where Captain Jonathan Carnes, of Salem, first discovered that pepper grew wild, and then made his way thither on a secret voyage. The private charts of this difficult coast, prepared on "pepper voyages" by Captain Charles M. Endicott and Captain James D. Gillis, were recognized and used by the United States navy as a sufficient guide; and when Commodore Wilkes went on his famous exploring expedition he took with him a Salem sea-captain as pilot, Captain Benjamin Vanderford. But in the earlier voyages there were still greater difficulties than these. Ships were then rarely coppered; mathematical instruments were imperfect, and the rig of vessels was such as is now almost vanished from the seas—as, for instance, that of the old-fashioned cutter, in which the jib was reefed by sliding the whole bowsprit inboard. Bowditch—himself a Salem sea-captain—had not yet prepared his *Practical Navigator*, but the favorite encyclopædia among East India traders was Guthrie's *Geographical Grammar*—a quaint old book, which I remember in my grandfather's library, and which contained the vaguest descriptions of all the remoter countries of the earth.

There exists an impression, not wholly unfounded, that these ship-masters derived some advantage from the fact that, sailing in American vessels, they at least had American crews. This was true, no doubt, when they first left home; but as the voyages lasted for a year or two, and often involved transshipment, or even the sale and purchase of vessels in foreign ports, the more difficult part of the trip was usually made without this advantage. From the manuscripts of a typical Salem sea-captain — Captain Richard J. Cleveland, for which I am indebted to his son, H. W. S. Cleveland, of Minneapolis—it is easy to show with what kind of material these men had to deal. Writing of a voyage from Havre to the Isle of France in 1798, he says:

"It was not till the last hour that I was in Havre (even while the visiting officers were on board) that I finally shipped my crew. Fortunately they were all so much in debt as not to want any time to spend their advance, but were ready at the instant, and with this motley crew (who for aught I knew were robbers or pirates) I put to sea. That you may form some idea of the fatigue and trouble I have had I will attempt to describe them to you.

"At the head of the list is my mate, a Nantucket lad, whom I persuaded the captain of a ship to discharge from before the mast, and who knew little or nothing of navigation, but is now capable of conducting the vessel in case of accident to me. The first of my foremast

hands is a great surly, crabbed, rawboned, ignorant Prussian, who is so timid aloft that the mate has frequently been obliged to do his duty there. I believe him to be more of a soldier than a sailor, though he has often assured me that he has been boatswain's mate of a Dutch Indiaman, which I do not believe, as he hardly knows how to put two ends of a rope together. He speaks enough English to be

NATHANIEL SILSBEE.
From the painting in the Massachusetts Senate Chamber.

tolerably understood. The next in point of consequence is my cook—a good-natured negro and a tolerable cook, so unused to a vessel that in the smoothest weather he cannot walk fore and aft without holding on to something with both hands. This fear proceeds from the fact that he is so tall and slim that, if he should get a cant, it might be fatal to him. I did not think America could furnish such a specimen of the negro race (he is a native of Savannah), nor did I ever see such a perfect simpleton. It is impossible to teach him anything, and notwithstanding the frequency with which we have been obliged to take in and make sail on this long voyage, he can hardly tell the main halyards from the main-stay. He one day took it into his head to learn the compass, and not being permitted to come on the quarter-deck to learn by the one in the binnacle, he took off the cover of the till of his chest, and with his knife cut out something that looked like a cart-wheel, and wanted me to let him nail it on the deck to steer by, insisting that he could 'teer by him better'n tudder one.'

"Next is an English boy of seventeen years old, who, from having lately had the small-pox, is feeble and almost blind—a miserable object, but pity for his misfortunes induces me to make his duty as easy as possible. Finally, I have a little ugly French boy, the very image of a baboon, who, from having served for some time on different privateers, has all the tricks of a veteran man-of-war's man, though only thirteen years old, and by having been in an English prison has learned enough of the language to be a proficient in swearing. To hear all these fellows quarrelling (which from not understanding each other they are very apt to ·do) serves to give one a realizing conception of the confusion of tongues at the tower of Babel. Nobody need envy me my four months' experience with such a set, though they are now far better than when I first took them."

The skill and tact shown by the commanders in handling these motley crews are well illustrated by this extract from the manuscripts of another typical Salem sea-captain, Nathaniel Silsbee. The scene is on board a ship bought by himself at the Isle of France, and on the homeward trip to Salem in 1795. The whole crew except himself and his younger brother—both being then under the age of twenty-three—had been shipped at the Isle of France, and was made up "of all the nations of the earth." The greater part of the voyage having been made in safety, he found himself in this critical position:

"A short time before our arrival at Boston we were for two days in company with and but a few miles from a schooner which we suspected to be a privateer watching for a favorable opportunity to attack us. Having on board the ship six guns and twenty-five men, I was determined to resist, as far as practicable, the attack of any small vessel. On the afternoon of the second day that this vessel had been dogging us she bore down upon us, with an apparent intention of executing what we had supposed to be her purpose, and which we were, as I had imagined, prepared to meet; but on calling our crew to the quarters which had previously been assigned to them, I was informed by one of my officers that there were four or five of the seamen who were unwilling thus to expose themselves, alleging that they had neither engaged nor expected to 'fight.' On hearing this, all hands being on deck, I ordered every passageway which led below-deck, excepting that leading to the cabin, to be securely fastened, then calling to me such of the crew as *had not engaged to fight*, I immediately sent them up the shrouds to repair the ratlines, and to perform other duties which they *had engaged to do*, in the most exposed parts of the ship.

"Finding themselves thus exposed to greater danger than their shipmates, they requested, before the schooner had come within gun-shot of us, to be recalled from their then situation and allowed to participate in the defence of the ship, which request was granted. All our six guns were placed on one side of the ship, and we succeeded, by a simultaneous discharge of the whole of them, as soon as the schooner had approached within the reach of their contents, in causing her to haul off and hasten from us; but whether this was caused by an unexpected resistance on our part, or by any damage caused by that resistance, we could not ascertain. I felt quite as willing to be rid of her, however, as any one of her crew could have been to be rid of us."

But it was not so much in dealing with their own men that the qualities of manhood were tested in these sea-captains as in encountering the insolence of foreign officials, and the attempts of warring nations to crush out these daring invaders. There was as yet no powerful nationality to appeal to, no naval squadron at their back. No other ship within five hundred miles, perhaps, carried the United States flag. They must rely, in order to be respected, on their own address and courage alone. When Captain Nathaniel Silsbee, on his way to India in the ship *Portland*, in 1798, put in at Cadiz, he heard for the first time of the "decrees" of the French government making liable to condemnation any vessel, of whatever nation, having on board any article grown or manufactured in Great Britain or any of its colonies. This greatly enhanced all prices in Mediterranean ports, as well as the risk of capture; and Silsbee at once sold half his cargo, to be delivered, at the risk of the purchaser, at Leghorn or Genoa. He then laid his plans to deliver it, put on shore some English coal he had, and all his English books; erased the name of the English maker from his nautical instruments, and cautioned the crew, if questioned, "to say, what was the truth," that they were not taken on board until after the cargo was put in, and therefore did not know whence it came. He was captured by a French privateer off Malaga, and was carried before the French consul in that city. The consul, before whom the Spanish authorities were utterly prostrate, asked him a dozen questions, and demanded an answer "in five words." Silsbee replied that this was impossible, and called for an immediate and thorough investigation, which, he said, would not take long, and would undoubtedly clear him. The consul said that there were a number of prizes in harbor, and that his case probably would not come on for two months. Silsbee informed him that this was the extreme of injustice, and that he should not leave the consular office, except by force, until his case had been settled. He accordingly sat in his chair, without sleep or food, for more than twenty-four hours, after which the consul, either admiring his pluck or exhausted by his obstinacy, gave him, rather to his astonishment, a free discharge. He learned afterward that the consul, when asked, "Why did you discharge the Yankee so quickly?" had answered, "I found that I must either dismiss him or bury him, and I preferred the former."

The mere accident of keeping a diary is often a preservative of fame, and the best type of these adventurous Salem sailors will always be Captain Richard J. Cleveland, who was just now mentioned. The first instalment of his own reminiscences was given in the *North American Review* for October, 1827, and his *Voyages and Commercial Enterprises* were first published collectively in 1842, and afterward reprinted in 1850. There lies before me a farther collection of manuscript extracts from his diaries and letters, and the same Defoe-like quality runs through them all. He was my father's own cousin, and I remember him well in my childhood, when he had reached the haven of the custom-house, after occupying for a time the temporary retreat, for which every sailor sighs, of a small farm in the country. He was then a serene old man, with a round apple-shaped head, a complexion indelibly sunburnt, and a freshness of look which bore testimony to the abstemiousness of his life; for he asserts that he never had tasted spirituous liquors, or, indeed, anything stronger than tea and coffee, nor had he ever used tobacco. In his mouth a single clove-pink was forever carried. I remember him as habitually silent, yielding admiringly to the superior colloquial powers of a very lively wife, yet easily lured into the most delightful yarns when she happened to be absent. Then he became our Ulysses and our Robinson Crusoe in one. The whole globe had been his home. It could be said of him, as Thoreau says of the sailor brother in a country farmhouse, that he knew only how far it was

to the nearest port, no more distances, all the rest being only seas and distant capes. He had grown to be a perfect, practical philosopher; Epictetus or Seneca could have taught him no farther lessons as to acquiescence in the inevitable; and yet there was an unquenched fire in his quiet eyes that showed him still to have the qualities of his youth. It was easy to fancy him issuing from his sheltered nook to

"point the guns upon the chase
Or bid the deadly cutlass shine,"

as in those adventurous early days.

One of Cleveland's best feats was the performance of a voyage, then unexampled, from Macao to the northwest coast of America and back, for the purchase of furs—a voyage made the more remarkable by the fact that it was achieved in a cutter-sloop of fifty tons, with a crew of the worst description, without any printed chart of the coast, and in the teeth of the monsoon. It was essential to his success to reach his destination before the arrival of certain ships that had been despatched from Boston round Cape Horn;

SANDWICH ISLANDS IDOL, IN THE ESSEX INSTITUTE, SALEM.

RICHARD J. CLEVELAND.

and his plan was to procure a vessel small enough to keep near the coast, sometimes taking advantage of a favorable current, and making a port, although an unknown one, every night. In his letters to his father he frankly says that his plan is pronounced impracticable by all experienced ship-masters at the port; but since nobody has ever tried it, how can it be asserted to be impracticable? They all predicted that he might sail a month without making any progress, and would then return, if at all, with sails and rigging torn to pieces. "I was," he coolly says, "not pleased with such gloomy prospects, but concluded that if I was to meet ruin, it might as well be by being torn to pieces on the China coast as to arrive on the coast of America after the object of my voyage had been secured by other vessels." So he sailed January 30, 1799, with twenty-five on board—two Americans, the rest Irish, Swedes, French, and chiefly English, the last mostly deserters from men-of-war and Botany Bay ships—"a list of as accomplished villains as ever disgraced a country." The work was so hard that the precious crew soon mutinied, and refused one morning to weigh anchor. In preparation for this he had stored all provisions near the cabin, and he coolly informed them that they could

not eat until they worked; and so mounted guard for twenty-four hours, with two or three men, including the black cook. His muskets were flintlocks, and revolvers were not yet introduced; but he had two four-pound cannon loaded with grape. It then occurred to him that if he offered to set them on shore, they would soon have enough of it. They caught at the proposal; but the Chinese would not keep or feed them on land, nor the captain take them on board next day: pointing a cannon, he bade them keep off. He then went to the shore in an armed boat, and offered to take them on board one by one. Several came eagerly; but when it turned out that the boatswain and one other ringleader were not to be taken back on any terms, these two desperadoes presented their knives at the breasts of the others, and swore that they should not stir. Some yielded; others were sullenly indifferent; one lay intoxicated on the beach. It was like one of the mutineering scenes in Stevenson's *Treasure Island*. At last all but six were brought on board, and thenceforth behaved well, having probably coincided by this time with their young captain, who quietly writes to his father, "No grosser miscalculation of character was ever made than by these men in supposing that they could accomplish their object by threats or intimidations."

They kept on their formidable voyage, often finding themselves, after a toilsome day, set back leagues on their way; grazing on rocks, caught in whirlpools, threatened by pirates. The diminished crew proved an advantage, as they had to be put on allowance of provisions at any rate. In thirty days they sighted the north end of Formosa, and had performed that part of the trip deemed impracticable; then they crossed the North Pacific amid constant storms, and anchored in Norfolk Sound on March 30, 1799, after a voyage of two months, and in advance of almost all competing vessels. Even those which had arrived from Boston were at disadvantage, being much larger, and unable to penetrate the innumerable bays and inlets on the northwest coast. Putting up a screen of hides round the deck, and never letting more than one native on board at once, Cleveland concealed the smallness of his crew, and eluded attack, though the Indian canoes were often larger than his little vessel. On one occasion his cutter ran on a rock, and lay there twenty-four hours, at such an angle that no one could stand on deck, the Indians fortunately not discovering his plight. At last the vessel floated with returning tide, and after two months' traffic they reached China, September 15, by way of the Sandwich Islands, laden with a cargo worth $60,000, the sea-otter skins that had been bought at the rate of eight for a musket selling for $36 apiece. His deserters had reached Wampoa before him, and all Cleveland's friends had believed their assertion that he was dead.

The youthfulness of these men gave a flavor of impulse and adventure to the soberest mercantile enterprises. They made up their plans for some voyage round the the oldest of the three not being yet thirty years old. In these days, when every little remote port of the globe has been visited and described in full, its manners sketched, its channels laid down in a chart, and its commercial resources fully known, it is impossible to appreciate the uncertain and vague delights of such an expedition. Every entry into a new harbor might imply a fortune or a prison, for Spain had not yet lost its control of the regions they were to visit, but claimed the right to monopolize the commerce of all. For each port there was some pompous official to be managed or bribed, and in general, where any injustice had been done to them, the pluck and ready wit of the young Americans carried the

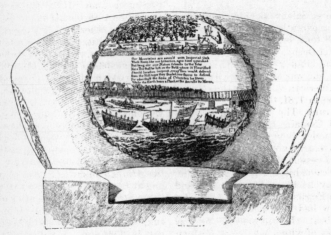

PUNCH-BOWL PRESENTED TO THE EAST INDIA MARINE SOCIETY BY CAPTAIN BENJAMIN HODGES IN 1800, SHOWING SALEM SHIP-YARD.

globe as blithely as if it were a yachting trip. It seemed like commerce on a lark, and yet there was always a keen eye to business. Cleveland and his friend Shaler—whose *Sketches of Algiers* has still a place in the literature of travel—having come together from the Isle of France to Copenhagen, formed the project of a voyage round Cape Horn. They bought at Hamburg an American brig of 175 tons, the *Lelia Byrd*, tossed up a coin to decide which should go as captain and which as supercargo, invited a delightful young Polish nobleman, the Count de Rouissillon, to accompany them, and sailed November 8, 1801, for a two years' voyage, day. More than once, after being actually imprisoned and ordered out of the port, they quietly refused to weigh anchor until their wrongs had been redressed and an apology made. On one occasion, after going on shore with a boat's crew to rescue some of their own men who had been improperly detained, they carried off the Spanish guard also; and then sailed within musket-shot of a fort garrisoned by a hundred men, compelling their prisoners to stand conspicuously by the bulwarks, in order to ward off the fire from the battery. Nevertheless they were under fire for half an hour. One shot struck them just above the water-line, and several cut the sails and rigging. The Spaniards had eight nine-pound guns, the Americans had only three-pounders, but when the latter got within range, the Spanish soldiers fled, and in ten minutes the fight was done. This was at San Diego, California, and we have the testimony of Mr. Richard H. Dana that it was still vividly remembered upon that coast thirty years later. When the *Lelia Byrd* was safe the prisoners were set on shore, and the Americans had soon after a several days' visit from the "jolly padres," as Cleveland calls them, of the old Spanish missions, who took up-roarious satisfaction in the whole affair, and agreed that the Spanish comman-dant, Don Manuel Rodriguez, ought to be sent back to the mother country as a pol-troon.

The pioneer Salem vessel in the Eastern trade was apparently the *Grand Turk*—a ship of 300 tons, built for a privateer by Elias Hasket Derby. She carried twenty-two guns, and took many prizes. The war being over, she was sent by her owner on the first American voyage to the Cape of Good Hope in 1781, the cargo consisting largely of rum. The voyage proved prof-itable, and Captain Jonathan Ingersoll, her commander, bought in the West In-dies on his return enough of Grenada rum to load two vessels, sent home the *Grand Turk*, and came himself in the *Atlantic*. On the way he rescued the captain and mate of an English schooner, the *Amity*, whose crew had mutinied and set them adrift in a boat. By one of those singular coincidences of which maritime life then seemed to yield so many, this very schoon-er was afterward recaptured in Salem Harbor in this way: after their arrival the captain of the *Amity* was sitting with Mr. Derby in his counting-room, and pre-sently saw through the spy-glass his own vessel in the offing. Mr. Derby promptly put two pieces of ordnance on board one of his brigs, and gave the English captain the unlooked-for pleasure of recapturing the *Amity*, whose mutineers had no rea-son to suppose that they should happen upon the precise port into which their victims had been carried.

This was not the only pioneer expedi-tion of the *Grand Turk*, which also made, in 1785-6, the first voyage direct from New England to the Isle of France and China. There exists a picture of this cel-ebrated vessel on a punch-bowl made for Mr. Derby in China, and still preserved in the collections of the East India Ma-rine Society at Salem, side by side with what may be called the official punch-bowl of the society itself, bearing the date of 1800, and adorned with a graphic de-sign representing the ship-building of that period. Another similar design may be found on the quaint certificates of membership of the same society, dated in 1796; and many memorials of the mari-time life of those days are preserved by this honored association itself and by the Essex Institute. Some of these are here reproduced, through the kindness of the officers of this last association, and of the Peabody Academy of Science, to which the remarkable collections of the East In-dia Marine Society are now transferred. For more than half a century the mer-chants and ship-masters of Salem vied with each other in bringing home Ori-ental curiosities for this museum—wea-pons, costumes, musical instruments, car-riages, models of ships, culminating in a great wooden idol that once stood alone in a desert on the Sandwich Islands. This unique collection is now, through the wide munificence of George Peabody, pre-served for all future generations.

Another ship of "King" Derby's, the *Astræa*, was the first to make the direct voyage to Canton, in 1789; and his ship the *Atlantic* first displayed the American flag at Bombay and Calcutta in 1788, and the brig *Sally* first did the same at Batavia in 1796. A Salem captain, James Dever-eux, on a Boston vessel, first visited Ja-pan in 1799, and the Salem ship *Marga-ret* went there two years later, half a cen-tury before the country was freely opened to commerce by Commodore Perry. The schooner *Rajah*, from Salem, first reached Sumatra in 1793. The *Astræa* from Sa-lem entered the port of Manila in 1796, and there exists a manuscript log-book of her voyage, by Nathaniel Bowditch, the mathematician, who was on board. The stars and stripes were first floated at Mocha by Captain Joseph Ropes, of the ship *Recovery*, in 1798. The authorities of the place could not be made to under-stand whence she came, or how many moons she had been sailing, but they readily took their share, perhaps, of the $50,000 which he carried with him in specie to invest in coffee. The trade with the Feejee Islands, Madagascar, and Zanzibar was opened later, and that with Surinam,

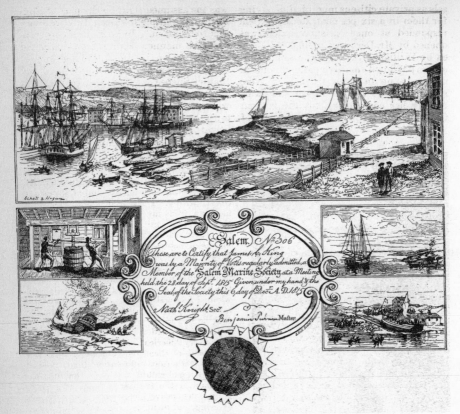

CERTIFICATE OF MEMBERSHIP OF EAST INDIA MARINE SOCIETY, SHOWING SALEM HARBOR, 1797.
From the original in the Essex Institute, Salem.

Cayenne, and other South American ports was carried on during all this period. With Senegal and the west coast of Africa the Salem trade began in 1789, the two schooners *Sally* and *Polly* — seductive creatures — first teaching the poor Africans the taste of rum. It must be remembered that the exportation of cotton had not then begun; it was even imported in small quantities from the West Indies and Demerara; and the cargoes brought from the East Indies were at first chiefly paid for in furs from the northwest coast and in Spanish dollars.

Mr. Derby alone, according to Osgood and Batchelder's *Historical Sketches of Salem*, caused one hundred and twenty-five voyages to be made in fourteen years (1785–99) by thirty-seven different vessels, forty-five of these voyages being to the East Indies or China. He rarely bought or sold on credit, and there were then no banks; so that, while his large ships were on their Oriental voyages, his smaller ones were sent to Gottenburg and St. Petersburg for iron, duck, and hemp; to France, Spain, and Madeira for wine and lead; to the West Indies for spirits; and to New York, Philadelphia, and Richmond for flour, provisions, iron, and tobacco. Accumulating for himself the largest fortune left in this country during the last century — a million dollars — he obtained also the more important memorial of gratitude and affection from the young men whom he trained and encouraged. To him primarily the nation also owed the building of the frigate *Essex*, the pride of the earlier navy. When, in 1798, we were apparently about to engage in a war with France, and had no naval force, Congress authorized President Adams to accept such vessels as private citizens might build, paying for them in a six per cent. stock. Salem responded at once; a subscription was opened by Mr. Derby with $10,000, followed by William Gray with the same sum; others put down smaller amounts, some in money, some in work, till $75,000 were raised, and the frigate *Essex* was built. Among her contractors was the veteran Captain Haraden, who supplied a part of

STEPHEN HIGGINSON.
From the painting by Stuart in possession of George Higginson, Esq., Boston.

the cordage, her large cables being borne in procession to the ship, attended by martial music. She was launched September 30, 1799, carried thirty-two guns, and proved the fastest ship in the navy, as well as one of the cheapest. Captain Edward Preble was her first actual commander, and Farragut served as a midshipman on board. She was credited with taking two millions of dollars in prizes from the enemy during the subsequent war with England, in which she was captured at last, while the stock in which she was paid for fell to fifty cents on the dollar before the war was over, with but few purchasers. In other words, half her value was practically given to the government by the citizens of Salem.

It will be remembered that the prime cause of the war of 1812 against England

was the assumed right on the part of English naval officers to search American vessels for seamen. In how utterly unscrupulous a manner this right was exercised is well shown in the following extract from the manuscript recollections of Nathaniel Silsbee. The narrative makes it also clear with what zeal the Salem men, who had heard the tale of Edward Hulen, must have shipped on board the Salem privateers when it came to open war. The events here described took place in 1796:

"In the course of the few days that I remained at Madras, one of those occurrences took place which more than any and all others led to the late war between the United States and Great Britain. I received a note early one morning from my chief mate, apprising me that one of my sailors (Edward Hulen, a fellow-townsman whom I had known from boyhood) had been impressed and taken on board of a British frigate then lying in port. On receiving this intelligence I immediately went on board my ship, and having there learnt all the facts in the case, proceeded to the frigate, where I found Hulen, and in his presence was informed by the first lieutenant of the frigate that he had taken Hulen from my ship under a peremptory order from his commander 'to visit every American ship in port, and to take from each of them one or more of their seamen.' With that information I returned to the shore, and called upon Captain Cook, who commanded the frigate, and sought, first by all the persuasive means that I was capable of using, and ultimately by threats to appeal to the government of the place, to obtain Hulen's release, but in vain. I then, with the aid of the senior partner of one of the first commercial houses of the place, sought the interference and assistance of the civil authorities of the port, but without success, it being a case in which they said they could not interfere.

"In the course of the day I went again to the frigate, and in the presence of the lieutenant tendered to Hulen the amount of his wages, of which he requested me to give him only ten dollars, and to take the residue to his mother in Salem, on hearing which the lieutenant expressed his perfect conviction that Hulen was an American citizen, accompanied by a strong assurance that if it was in *his* power to release him he should not suffer another moment's detention, adding at the same time that he doubted if this or any other circumstance would induce Captain Cook to permit his return to my ship. It remained for me only to recommend Hulen to that protection of the lieutenant which a good seaman deserves, and to submit to the high-handed insult thus offered to the flag of my country, which I had no means of either preventing or resisting, beyond the expression of my opinion of it to the said Captain Cook, which took place in the presence of

LAUNCH OF THE SHIP "FAME," NEAR CROWNINSHIELD'S WHARF, 1802.
From the painting in Essex Institute, Salem.

other British officers, and in terms dictated by the then excited state of my feelings. After several years' detention in the British navy, and after the peace of Amiens, Hulen returned to Salem, and lived to perform services on board privateers owned in Salem, in the late war between this country and England."

Of the 250 privateers sent out during the war of 1812, Salem furnished forty, Baltimore and New York alone exceeding her. The Salem fleet carried in all 189 cannon. Of these the schooner *Fame*, a mere fishing-boat of thirty tons, with two guns and thirty men, received her commission at noon, sailed in the afternoon, and sent the first prize into Salem. The second prize was sent in by the *Jefferson*, a boat of only fourteen tons, carrying one gun and twenty men. The *America*, belonging to George Crowninshield and Sons, was claimed to be the swiftest vessel afloat during the war—a ship of 350 tons, carrying twenty guns and 150 men, and capturing twenty-six prizes with more than a million dollars. She was commanded successively by Captain Joseph Ropes and Captain Benjamin Chever, Jun. With this war the palmy days of Salem seafaring substantially closed, although this narrative might well be expanded to take in the description of *Cleopatra's Barge*, a pleasure yacht of 197 tons built in 1816 by George Crowninshield, and once sent by him to St. Helena,

with several ladies of the Bonaparte family on board, in the abortive design of rescuing the Emperor Napoleon. She was the first American yacht to cross the Atlantic; and is a curious illustration of the Salem nautical training that the black cook on this yacht, who had sailed under Bowditch, was found as capable of keeping a ship's reckoning as any of the officers.

A type of character so strong as that of the old Salem sea-captains could not well pass away in America without making its final mark on the politics as well as the business of the nation. In the fierce strife between Federalists and Democrats these men not only took the Federalist side as a body, but it was for a time recognized as incarnated in them. A few of them, indeed, were followers of Jefferson, and it is an interesting fact that Captain Richard Cleveland himself, writing to his father from off the Cape of Good Hope, early in 1798, thus indicated the very point of view that led within a few years to the famous embargo for which the New England ship-owners reproached Jefferson so bitterly. "You may perhaps laugh at me," he said, "and call it quixotism, but I believe, if we would keep our ships at home and entirely withhold our supplies, we could be more than a match for these two noisy powers united [England and France]. I see no reason why we can't live for a time without foreign commerce." Again, Nathaniel Silsbee, when first chosen to Congress, was nominated against Timothy Pickering as a Democrat (or, as it was then called, Republican); yet he records in his autobiography that he was opposed in this respect to nearly all his circle of friends; and it is well understood that "Billy" Gray, who was, after Derby, the most important of the Salem merchants, left that town in 1809 to reside in Boston, because of his unpopularity with the Federalists as a supporter of the embargo. Two of the Crowninshield brothers were Secretaries of the Navy under Jefferson and Madison. These were the exceptions that proved the rule. Salem was Federalist, and the head-quarters of Federalism was Salem. The strength of that strong and concentrated party was in the merchants of Essex County, almost all of whom had been ship-masters in their youth. This fact is forever established by the very phrase "Essex Junto." Timothy Pickering says that the first time he heard this phrase was from President John Adams, in 1797, and that the three men whom he named as constituting the clique were George Cabot, Stephen Higginson, and Theophilus Parsons—in other words, two ex-sea-captains and the chief maritime lawyer of his time. The habit of the quarter-deck went all through the Federalist party of Massachusetts; the slave-holders themselves did not more firmly believe that they constituted the nation. To the "Essex Junto" Jefferson himself seemed but a mutineering first mate, and his "rights of man" but the black flag of a rebellious crew. They paid the penalty of their own autocratic habit; they lived to see their cause lost; but they went down with their flags flying, having had the satisfaction—if satisfaction it was—to see most of their cargo of political principles transferred bodily to the hold of their victor.

THE BOSTON SET

SO long ago as 1719, Daniel Neal, an observant traveller, who ought to be held in high esteem by Massachusetts people, wrote of the New England metropolis: "There are five Printing-Presses in Boston, which are generally full of Work, by which it appears that Humanity and the Knowledge of Letters flourish more here than in all the other English Plantations put together, for in the City of New York there is but one Bookseller's Shop, and in the Plantations of Virginia, Maryland, Carolina, Barbadoes, and the Islands, none at all."

Happily humanity and the knowledge of letters are no longer confined to one corner of the country; but notwithstanding the growth of an opinion that Boston and New York are to occupy relatively the positions of Edinburgh and London, the capital of Massachusetts still has a peculiar prestige as the oldest centre of literary culture in the country, causing the eyes of the rest of the Union to turn toward it with a particular interest, a glance compounded of respect and reminiscence with something of insatiable expectancy. The privileged Bostonian, it is true, laughs at Boston in his quiet way. "It is a capital place to live in," said an

eminent publisher who has his dwelling there, "because then you can go to New York. But if you live in New York, where *can* you go?" The *mot* epitomizes the sentiment of many among his townsmen; but if they sometimes join in the alien laugh against their "little city," and recognize a degree of smallness and constraint in its general attitude, they also keenly appreciate the other side. So do some of our friends the New-Yorkers. One of the younger New York poets, on visiting Cambridge for the first time, said to me : "We hear a great deal about the failure of Boston to quite appreciate the mental breadth and energy of New York. But with all the admiration I felt for this region before I came here, I find *I* didn't wholly appreciate *it* : there is such a thing as New York Bostonism."

The city of the Puritans has reached the quarter-millennial anniversary of its settlement, yet is still in its youth. How young we comprehend, when we reflect that the men who have given it a world-wide fame in literature within the present century are still nearly all living. A hundred years later than the time of Neal, clerical influence, which had governed in laws, manners, and literature since the founding of the colony, still prevailed there; but the Liberal Christian or Unitarian movement, which the year 1800 had seen organizing its forces, tended to an active social force, was pervasive in his influence for culture. The upper classes were involved in the passion for a broader intellectual development. La-

THE TICKNOR MANSION, ON PARK STREET.

free minds from the theological traces, and cause them to pass over to new objects of thought. This was what freed imagination, and gave us our poets. In those days Boston village was stirring with new thoughts. Buckminster, the eloquent preacher, gathering by his social grace and conversational power a group of gentlemen who met in his parlors for discussion, was doing for his contemporaries what Emerson as a lecturer did twenty or thirty years later; and the Anthology Club, composed of young liberal ministers, lawyers, and physicians, was so important an affair that ladies did not issue social invitations for the evening when it met, because it eliminated so many bright and desirable men. To this Ralph Waldo Emerson's father, indeed, belonged, with Ware, Thacher, and Kirkland (afterward president of Harvard). Then came Channing, who, though not

dies held fashionable morning drawing classes at their houses; there were also mixed evening parties of young men and women at the house of Miss Nancy Lowell (an aunt of the poet), which were to some extent an innovation. The part that women have played in the advancement of all good interests in Boston, and especially those of the arts, has been an active one. How much has not their pure and humane quality influenced our literature! For us, at this time, it is hard to comprehend how much less was their social sway in the "twenties" than it is now. Even in the forties dinner parties of from fifteen to a score of gentlemen, with only the lady of the house present, were the rule. Quantities of Madeira were drunk. The importance of social contact between men and women was not enough understood, and the gentlemen who met in associations like agricultural or humane societies, and in the venerable Wednesday Evening Century (which still exists), are rumored to have practiced the far from elegant custom of spreading mats about the floors of their drawing-rooms for smokers to spit upon.

In the quickening of thought and the refinement of manners that set in, the smallness and compactness of Boston were advantages. It was a little city; a city of gardens and solid brick houses and stores; cheerful, quiet, unsophisticated; with a fringe of wharves along the bay that supplied the picturesque additions of

whence the occupants, by taking a few steps, could issue forth upon their native or adopted heath of the Common, under the shade of the Great Elm. There still lingers on Beacon Street the fine old house of Harrison Gray Otis, smooth-faced and mellow, deep-roomed, and suffused with a sober ripeness of respectability, which, with that of George Ticknor at the head of Park Street, recalls well the staid aspect of this old Boston. In such a place impressions spread rapidly; theories were infectious; phrenology, Unitarianism, vegetarianism, emancipation, Transcend-

INTERIOR OF TICKNOR'S LIBRARY.

a successful sea-port, and surrounded by villages smaller than itself, of which Cambridge was an important but rather remote one. Two theatres were the most that it could sustain in the line of public amusement, while fashionable life centred upon a dancing hall, imitatively called Almack's, where strictly limited assemblies were held. Within a stone's-throw of each other were the houses of Daniel Webster, Edward Everett, Robert C. Winthrop, George Bancroft, and Rufus Choate, on ground now loaded with merchandise,

entalism, worked their way from street to street like an epidemic. A new course of study or a new thought was as exciting as news of a European war could have been. A lady remembers meeting another on Tremont Street during the full glow of the Emerson lecture epoch, and exclaiming, "Oh, there's a new idea! Have you heard it?"

"Don't talk to me of ideas," retorted her friend; "I'm so full of them now that I can't make room for a single new one."

Perhaps the tendency of the people to

live a great deal by themselves heightened this keen mental appetite. "Everything essential to the most agreeable society exists among them," said an English resident in Boston thirty years since, "with one exception, and that one is the spirit of sociability." The remark is almost as true to-day. "Boston society," one of the most brilliant men in it lately

EDWIN P. WHIPPLE.

said to the present writer, "is a good deal like the Irishman's flea: when you put your finger on it, it isn't there." The substance exists, but one sees it chiefly in mirage. As just hinted, however, the want of gayety or lively intercourse fostered studious habits. Margaret Fuller, for instance, belonged to a family which had expended a good deal of effort on that painful task known as "getting into" the inner circles. The streets of Boston were made narrow and crooked to increase the difficulty of entering good society. This may not be generally known, but it will answer as a good working theory. At all events, the Fullers were to a great extent baffled, and Margaret's father, contenting himself with the most distant social mirage, devoted himself to educating his daughter in the most thorough manner. It was a current saying that the two (who lived in Cambridge) used to walk into town over the West Boston Bridge discussing the higher mathematics. Subsequently Margaret had the ladies of Boston sitting at her feet.

Doubtless there is something touching in the eagerness with which the late descendants of the Pilgrims, having once entered on the field of liberal cultivation, seized upon every fresh atom of æsthetic nutriment. Small beginnings like these appear contemptible or excessively amusing to superficial observers who look back upon them; but there is quite another and a more logical way of measuring them—in the light of what has grown out of them.

With so receptive an audience, a group of young men like the Mercantile Library Association could set going a system of lectures, which brought before the public men to whom they were to look as leaders. Edwin P. Whipple and James T. Fields were active members of this body, which at its anniversary meetings first introduced to fame orators like Edward Everett and Wendell Phillips, and had Daniel Webster, Oliver Wendell Holmes, and George Hillard among its speakers and poets. This was an important factor, for which there is no counterpart in these later days, to the misfortune, be it said, both of the young men and of Boston. It was likewise important and fortunate that as time went on a nervous centre of the growing literary system was situated in the "Old Corner Bookstore," a quaint little red brick building with a sloping roof, very unlike the big publishing establishments since hatched from it, where Mr. Fields played Destiny to the aspirations of authors, and launched the second volume of the *Atlantic*, the first that bore his imprint. Mr. Fields had recommended himself to the rising men of genius as a sympathetic publisher, and when he became a partner at the Old Corner, the authors of the day — Longfellow, Holmes, Lowell, Hawthorne, and George Hillard—made it a literary lounge. Hillard, although like Ticknor he produced little, must be ranked with him as a literary man of note by reason of the aid he gave to the cause of what is called taste. Keenly appreciative of literary form, he

OLD CORNER BOOKSTORE, 1880.

was once the most graceful speaker in the city : no public occasion was complete that was not silvered by his oratory, and his book reviews were of great value in forming the popular judgment. But his prominence did not last. He lived to exchange his early beauty for the aspect of a disappointed and cynical elderly man, no longer figuring in public, but continuing to enjoy his fine library, until stricken with paralysis while editing the life of Ticknor. George Ticknor's activity as a Harvard professor and a counsellor of younger writers, generous with his time and books, has given him a more permanent place in recollection. A foreign recognition of social America, which had not before been bestowed, was the result of his extensive European tour. But at home he accomplished a more important service, and was for a time almost the axis on which the higher culture of Boston turned.

Were he living now, as a young man, he would probably be thought to be posing too much with reference to effect at magnificent distances. You hear him referred to by some as a literary autocrat.

Cold he doubtless was, and conservative in the grain. One day when a young man was telling him of some new philosophical inquiries, he declared, with impatience, "John Locke settled all that for me, sir, years ago." Thackeray, however, made short work of his dignity when, as it is related, on the novelist's dining with him, the historian of Spanish literature fell to musing of love. Ticknor resembled his guest in appearance, even to the latter's oddly shaped nose. "Yes, yes," assented Thackeray, listening to his rather sentimental monologue; "but, after all, what have two broken-nosed old fellows like you and me got to do with love?" Another time, when a young Westerner, who was lecturing in Boston, was asked by Theodore Parker if he had seen Ticknor,

"No," was the reply.

"Well," Parker answered him, "you might as well go to hell without seeing the devil."

This anecdote is calculated to send a shiver through the bones of many dwellers on the trimountain peninsula. It is the sort of thing which may be mention-

STUDY OF T. B. ALDRICH, PONKAPOG.

ed in corners by the privileged, but, when bruited about, it has a damaging effect on that air of historic repose and classic dignity which, by a singular tacit *consensus*, it has been agreed is the proper one for Boston to assume before the rest of the world. This outward appearance must be kept up, even at an occasional expense to truth. The contrast between Parker's intrepid tone and the careful self-adornment and guarded speech of a George Ticknor or an Edward Everett indicates precisely the difference between the Boston atmosphere and that of London or New York. There is a tendency here to make dignity an incumbrance, instead of a natural outgrowth of character strong enough to support a little freedom. Most people, in all places, are sensitive to social opinion; they are to some extent afraid of others. But the Bostonian goes farther than that: he is afraid of himself.

It is only about ten years since Ticknor ceased to walk the streets—a tall, stately figure, instinct with this Boston dignity. The mention of his name should remind us to discriminate somewhat the groups and tendencies of the earlier date to which we have just been reverting. Although,

as has been said, Boston was small and its intellectual enthusiasms spread rapidly, it must not be inferred that it was a unit. The party of thinkers and agitators humorously dubbed "The Jacobins' Club," which about 1840 used to assemble at the Tremont House and George Ripley's house, and once met in the parlors of Miss E. P. Peabody, the enthusiastic educator, the sister-in-law of Hawthorne, and friend of Channing, embraced the most extreme and radical reformers, "come-outers," revolutionists, some of them strong men and afterward useful citizens, but others mere on-lookers attracted by the music of progress, and trying to keep step with the procession, or even to run ahead of it. Between the generality of these theorists and Emerson there was a wide gap; although he, like Hawthorne, if less practically, sympathized with Ripley's Brook Farm experiment. If among the more progressive minds themselves there was division, still greater was the distance at which Ticknor stood, representing in letters the spirit of the wealthy merchant and professional class, who have long made great pretensions to inherited aristocracy. George Bancroft, for his part, was under a ban, stood somewhat apart, because he was a Democratic office-holder; suffering from the same narrow rigor of Massachusetts judgment (a legacy from the seventeenth century) which twice ostracized Sumner, from the most opposite causes, and perhaps escaped doing it again only because he did not live. But Bancroft, from his point of view, sympathized with the intense realistic idealism of Ripley. The lyrists, excepting Whittier, had their eyes cleared by Unitarianism and its successor Transcendentalism; and all of them were abolitionists. They occupied, however, individual grounds. One of the most noticeable things about the whole period, in fact, is the isolation in which the half-dozen men who have shone like a constellation over Boston grew up to power. Because of his shy temperament and his poverty Hawthorne was obscure, and during his Boston custom-house days unknown, his chief distinction to the popular eye, so far as I can learn, having been that he was extremely fond of martial music, and could generally be found— a tall, shapely figure, rendered military by the thick mustache — following any procession headed by a band. Longfellow made his appearance at about this time in Cambridge as the young professor just home from Germany, imbued with

COZY CORNER IN MR. HOWELLS'S HOUSE, ELMWOOD.

the romance of that land, and saying, as we know, a good word to the public for his friend Hawthorne; also settling down to the teaching of under-graduates. Among these last was James Russell Lowell, soon after a youthful lawyer without a practice, somewhat exquisite in matters of dress, and given to penning odes instead of briefs. He also published a novel called *My First Client*—a subject that probably gave free play for the imagination—which has since disappeared from mortal ken. Emerson turned his back on Boston with as much bitterness, perhaps, as we can conceive of in him, for what he considered the city's shams. Holmes was busy with pen and scalpel; man of wit, man of science, keen scholar, writing a good many songs, but not yet known as a brilliant prose author. Meetings and greetings and correspondence took place, of course; but no coterie was formed; the

RALPH WALDO EMERSON.

men were not bound together by a common definition of purpose and mutual criticism, stimulating mutually. These things were reserved for the era of the Saturday Club, which drew together the wise and dazzling circle when they had begun to be famous. It is a pity that this club has had no historian. Among its members, besides those just named, were Felton (professor and president at Harvard, and the friend whose cordiality and humor Dickens so appreciated); Judge Hoar, one of the keenest minds and most pungent after-dinner speakers in the country; E. P. Whipple, the critic; Professor Benjamin Peirce, Rev. James Freeman Clarke; Chief Justice Gray; Agassiz. In the rich reminiscence of his threnody on Agassiz, Lowell has briefly pictured Holmes's "rockets" curving "their long ellipse" at this board so thickly begirt with wonderful men, and has recalled the "face, half rustic, half divine," of Emerson, as he listened,

"Pricked with the cider of the judge's wit."

Agassiz, with his large, generous, and sensitive countenance, suggesting that of an intellectualized god Pan, was the life of the feast. Stored up within him was

that irrepressible merriment which the native New-Englander lacks in himself, but heartily enjoys in others; his voice was the mellow signal of good-fellowship; and he was wont to hail with glee the entrance of the lights which were handed around in a half-mystic ceremony, to furnish the "gloria" for coffee, at the end of dinner. Mr. Fields also tells me that the great naturalist always insisted on having a huge joint of roast mutton served entire, from which he cut his own slice, requiring the meat to be cooked more and more rare as he got on in years. The Saturday met, and continues to meet, every month, at two of the clock on the day its name would indicate, in the mirror-room at Parker's. Its gatherings, rife with wit and sense and high spirits, must have been, until the death of Agassiz, a fine source of cheer and mental stimulus to the members; for they knew how to use conviviality with wisdom, getting the good out of it, and none of the harm.

Possibly their earlier isolation may have assisted in guarding their individuality, just as the smallness and simplicity of the town encouraged that fresh eagerness and sincerity which make the soul of originality. Too much stress can not be laid on this latter influence. Now that the capital has expanded into a large city, and its suburban villages into smaller cities and towns, we see the great difference in the action of the new surroundings on new minds. They are more sophisticated. When the university was called a college, or "the colleges," and that institution was a sort of higher academy, set in a quaint, sleepy village separated from town by the terrors of the "hourly," or omnibus, and bounded on three sides by breezy groves, open country, and huckleberry pastures, the whole atmosphere was—one can imagine what: not Greek, nursing poets terrible as the son of Agamemnon, but yet healthier than it is now. Still, even in these later times, glimpses of old Cambridge when it kept its primitive traits are not wholly wanting. On the northeastern verge of

CHARLES ELIOT NORTON.

the city, in an ample stretch of natural woods, stands Shady Hill, the home of Charles Eliot Norton, where, under the suave hospitality of the scholarly host, amid the treasures of the library, and with original Tintorettos and Titians looking down from the walls, one seems transported to a corner of the fifteenth-century Italy. Within that congenial demesne, in an avenue of tall, rusty-coated pines, a party of four young people (of whom the writer was one) were strolling and sitting one day, a few years since, when Mr. Lowell came down the path, and halted to speak to them. He had in his hand Carlyon's *Early Years and Late Reflections*, which was oddly appropriate to his mood; for he dwelt on the fact of thus encountering a group of the younger generation, saying that it was like coming upon his own vanished youth there in the wood. From this he went on to chat for an hour, telling about the Adirondac expedition recorded in verse by Emerson, and shared in by himself, Judge Hoar, and Mr. W. J. Stillman, who was a genuine Deerslayer with the rifle. He also spoke of poetry; of Browning, Donne, Tennyson, and Morris; quoting from "Pippa Passes" Ottima's lines in the scene with Sebald, where she tells how

> "ever and anon some bright white shaft
> Burnt thro' the pine-tree roof — here burnt and
>   there,
> As if God's messenger through the close wood
>   screen
> Plunged and replunged his weapon at a venture,
> Feeling for guilty thee and me."

"When I read that for the first time," said Mr. Lowell, "I cried out to myself,

T. B. ALDRICH.

'Here is a new poet!'" Yet, somewhat contradictorily, he next branched out into a theory that modern life offered no such intensity of passion for the poet's uses as the world of the Elizabethan age still retained. It would be impossible to reproduce the eloquent glow of his monologue at this distance of time; but the incident is mentioned here to suggest how casually on the Cambridge thoroughfares, or in a little patch of unhistoric woodland like the one referred to, any day or hour may bring the pleasure of unexpected converse with some rare mind—of poet, philosopher, critic, or worker in science. Mr. Lowell's pockets that day were full of proofs. "I'm printing," he explained; and he was, in fact, just preparing his essay on Wordsworth for the *North American Review.* So, in the spacious university town, the routine of life goes on: the students study and the professors profess, the street cars trundle, the hucksters patiently trade, the birds build and sing in the fruit trees, and literature grows up and blossoms under your very eyes. Seeing this, the mind naturally turns back to the time when Longfellow's village smithy really stood under its spreading chestnut in what is now the city of Cambridge (with its improved appliances of a City Hall "Ring"); when the diurnal and nocturnal sights and sounds of their neigh-

borhood passed living into his verse and that of his brother poet at Elmwood, and Harvard fixed upon Parnassus a less myopic and philological eye than at present.

Mr. Longfellow's stately dwelling, Craigie House, occupied, as every one knows, by Washington at the siege of Boston—("This," said the poet, laughingly, to some visitors, "is the head-quarters, and the houses which he occupied during his retreat were the *hind*-quarters") — has yielded more to the prevailing suburban-villa style of its neighbors than Elmwood or Shady Hill. It is fitting enough that it should, since by reason of its distinguished owner's accessibility, his constant and varied hospitality, and his social position, it forms perhaps the strongest connecting link between society and literature in or about Boston. The days follow in something like a continuous levee at this old colonial mansion, whose heavy brass door-knocker is plied (or more often gazed at by a deteriorating generation, in ignorance as to the mode of handling it) by a long stream of pilgrims of high and low degree, drawn by reverence, or curiosity, or the wish for literary advice. But across the street a piece of pasture-land, with some cows munching among the clover and buttercups, and a vista of the sliding Charles and Brighton meadows beyond—upon which the poet can look from behind his magnificent lilacs and lofty elms—still keep the rural aroma in the air he breathes. It may be noticed here that Mr. T. B. Aldrich, who for a time occupied Elmwood, during its owner's absence, and had previously lived in Boston, has gone to Ponkapog, a spot more absolutely removed from human aggregations than the outskirts of Cambridge, or even of Concord. There, in a library as perfect as anything in a French novel, looking out on a landscape that might be a Jacques, he works with loving leisure at his poetry and prose, sallying forth just enough to remind people of what they lose by not oftener enjoying the dry and sparkling wit and drollery of his talk. Mr. Howells, whose ready humor and cordial laugh and singularly modest presence were for a dozen years familiar to Cambridge, has betaken himself to the heights of Belmont, a few miles to the westward. There, in the midst of fields, orchards, and scattered groves, with a cluster of country-seats just below his perch, and a brother of his craft, J. T. Trowbridge, barely half a mile distant, he overlooks the populous plain and hilly amphitheatre, inclosing with wide sweep the city in whose midst the State-House dome— the original "Hub"— shines, gilded into self-respecting, sun-reflecting splendor. Sheltered by a picturesque sloping red roof, the author of *Venetian Life* works with unremitting zeal at his editorial and creative tasks in a white study ceiled with panelled wood, and with a huge fire-place surmounted by hand-carved shelves opposite him. One of several inscriptions in quaint text along the frieze of the room is the Shakspearean line,

"From Venice as far as Belmont."

It may remind us of the long flight his talent and his pen have made since first they became known to us, and of the gain in strength that has resulted from his taking root in American soil, nourished by the same life and scenery which have inspired other writers here. While we are considering the influence of seclusion, we must remember that Whittier has passed most of his life at Amesbury, the village on the Merrimac, and at his present home, Oak Knoll, in Danvers, beyond reach of the madding crowd. Emerson's oftenest-used study has been in Walden woods; and Hawthorne, when his sojournings in the Old Manse and at Lenox and Monte Outo were over, ascended the little thinly wooded hill at his later home, the Wayside—that little hill which came to be known in his household as "the Mount of Vision," where by constant meditative pacings to and fro he wore a narrow trail through the long grass and sweet-fern, which remains to attest his quiet communings with nature.

JAMES T. FIELDS.

Concord is now to Cambridge what that place was to Boston thirty years ago—a village which unites the unaffected and friendly manners of the country with a vigorous cultivation of those things that give life its finer value; an ally of literary Boston, too self-centred to be called a dependency. Its small community is exceedingly democratic, no man's occupation being inevitably a bar to the best companionship if he is fit for that; although certain natural and necessary distinctions are made on the base of fitness or taste, and strictly observed. That strained pitch of intellectual intensity assigned to it in stereotyped caricature— whereof the tale about a small boy digging for the infinite in the front yard is a good example—is unknown to the inhabitants. They are busy folk, but exceedingly fond of recreation, and also fond of study, good reading, and conversation which has some object or point, with opportunities for witty diversion by the way. In a word, they are healthy. Having the good sense to make much of their local patriotic associations, they are the better for doing so. Even Lord Houghton, strange as it may appear, failed to make a convert of Mr. Emerson when, during his visit to this country in 1874, he stood on the field of Concord fight with the author of the famous hymn, and seriously

ed by ladies in issuing social invitations, just as that of the Anthology Club was in Boston seventy years ago. In this Social Circle Ralph Waldo Emerson has been included for many years; and at its meetings the poet, the incisive essayist whom the world knows, encounters his townsmen to talk of affairs probably of no moment to this same inquisitive world, but doubtless of as much worth to him, in

W. D. HOWELLS'S HOUSE AT BELMONT.

tried to persuade him that the revolt of the colonies had been a fatal error, as cutting off all Americans from the glories of the mother-land. And unless one understands what Concord is, and how closely Emerson has been connected with its life, he misses a significant trait of the Massachusetts literary development. There is in particular a club known as the Social Circle, which has kept up its local reunions for more than a hundred years—having grown originally out of the local Committee of Safety in 1775—which brings together in manly and cordial relation citizens of various callings. Farmer, lawyer, judge, merchant, physician, small trader, town-clerk, all meet on an equality at one another's houses through its agency; and the club night is respect-

their place, as the thoughts whose course he has traced for thousands of reverent readers. Formerly, too, there was a pleasant habit, now almost given over, of holding popular receptions at his unpretentious dwelling. The towns-folk in general were heartily welcomed there at a sort of afternoon conversation party; some plain refection was set forth; and it was an excellent custom. Only last summer I saw troops of children from the public schools approaching Mr. Emerson's, one day, and learned that they were going there to be received and entertained by the aged poet and his family.

Such pleasant glimpses as these, and hints of an ideally fraternal commerce between fellow-beings, will be looked for vainly in Boston. There are many de-

Phillips. Sargent. Bartol.   Cranch. Holmes. Weiss. James, Senior.
                                                         Whittier.   Higginson.

RADICAL CLUB MEETING AT MRS. SARGENT'S.

lightful people there, but in general its
society exhibits the organs of social nutri-
tion in a state of arrested development.
Manners are constrained, hospitality is
too reluctant ; and the women, with a
hundred times more information than

their Southern sisters, can not rival these
in conversation.   Among the people best
worth knowing there is a temperate elegance of life which is admirable ; and the
presence of many persons genuinely refined and almost free from the local affec-

EDWARD EVERETT HALE.

points. The social world divides itself into a number of air-tight compartments. If prophets are without honor in their own country, all but a few hundred individuals in Boston should seem to be, socially considered, prophets. Merit is sometimes recognized more quickly here than elsewhere, and sometimes more slowly. Birth as a form of merit is overestimated. Wealth, so far as my observation goes, though it can not open all doors any more than it can in New York, is quite as important, as much worshipped, as in that metropolis, the mercenary tone of which the capital on the Charles affects to despise. In the matter of hospitality it is true that the corporate dignity, already mentioned as a motive to conduct, sometimes leads Bostonians to entertain strangers (especially foreign visitors) with solid cordiality and a consummate grace. But as a rule they show no generous interest in those of their own kith and kin who have done something noteworthy, something which in New York, or Washington, or London, would lead to their being moderately sought for in agreeable circles.

Such interest, at least, arises only after very marked reputation has given these persons a definite conventional value. It follows that between what calls itself by distinction society, and the literary world, there is no intimate relation. "If we only knew how to get at you literary people," said one of the leaders of the fashionable genealogical coterie, to an author whose fame and habits made it far from a laborious task to find him, "we should be running after you all the time." But the persons who cherish this ardent longing continue to defer its gratification. They are proud of the city's fame in literature, and some of them even cherish amateurish ambitions in the line of writing or painting; but the truth is, that they look upon the artistic world a trifle askance, as a region from which intruders should not be admitted with much freedom. A gentleman of undoubtedly meritorious descent and ample fortune, finding it needful on one occasion to call upon a well-known author, announced afterward, with pleased surprise, "Oh, he's a gentleman; a perfect gentleman!" Another member of the class usually recognized as aristocratic, sitting for his portrait to a young artist of great talent, who was not conscious of being a pariah, said to him with a benevo-

tations diffuses an atmosphere of general good taste. But there is no spontaneity, and not much warmth. Bostonians know how to dine exquisitely, but they do it with a half-clandestine air. The purely typical inhabitant, you are convinced, is furnished with an icicle in place of a spine, and he is in terror if he thinks a new person is really going to know him. I have known the invitation, "You must dine with me some day," coming from persons otherwise apparently of good-breeding, to remain in that form for years, without ever ripening into definiteness. An accomplished gentleman, now dead, who had accepted the attentions of some friends in another part of the world, dining, breakfasting, going to parties at their house, which was opened to him as his own—on meeting the lady of that house years afterward in Boston, expressed himself delighted that she had come thither. He might well be, for she was every way his equal, and they had been on terms of the most agreeable and intimate friendship; but, by way of showing his boundless and hospitable cordiality, he invited her to call at his house on a Sunday evening *after* tea. when his wife and himself would go with her to church and give her a place in their pew! This is hardly an extravagant instance. A morbid reserve, a contented selfishness, and distinctions set up with an arbitrariness that is ludicrous, hamper intercourse at all

lence that failed to draw out a responsive gratitude: "You're getting on now to a point where you ought to marry. I should think you'd look around for some young woman *in your own walk of life*, and settle down with her."

But whatever its drawbacks may be, the literary part of Boston has had two any dearth of essayists who are ready to overhaul art, science, philosophy, and theology with improved microscopes, and yet leave something to be discovered. In the conversations that ensue, such men as Dr. Holmes, Edward Everett Hale, and John Fiske sometimes take a share. Dialectics, however, do not prevent lighter

JAMES T. FIELDS'S STUDY.

rallying-points which have formed the centres of many profitable gatherings—the house of Mr. Fields, and that of Mr. John T. Sargent, where the Chestnut Street Club, at one time more widely known as the Radical Club, assembles. Skeptics insist that the instinct of persecution survives in Boston, manifesting itself in the prevalent fondness for making people "read a paper"—or listen to one. But cards to Mrs. Sargent's Mondays are greatly prized, nevertheless, and there is never diversion on occasions, and the 1st of May has often been celebrated in these drawing-rooms with recitation of original verses by ladies and gentlemen, recalling, one might say, the flights of Crescembini's Arcadians, or Lorenzo de' Medici's May-songs. Illustrious company is seen there, for the hostess is untiring in her effort to assemble the best. One memorable occasion I recall, when Whittier, seldom seen in town, had been lured from his shy retirement to aid in honoring the

SOMERSET CLUB HOUSE.

memory of Charles Sumner. Carl Schurz, Longfellow, the late John Weiss, Freeman Clarke, and other famous personages were present. Many eloquent and incisive things were said; but when Dr. Bartol asked the abolitionist poet to add something to the reminiscences of the dead leader, Mr. Whittier replied with a quaintness that made one think of Lincoln. He said that he had no skill in speaking, and that the idea of his saying anything reminded him of the dying petition made by the captain of the Dumfries rifles, "Don't let the awkward squad fire a salute over my grave."

Mr. Fields's house, overlooking the widening of the Charles River known as the Back Bay, is crowded from entrance to attic with artistic objects or literary and historic mementos. On the second floor the library, amazingly rich in autograph copies and full of curious old books, clambers over the walls like a vine, with its ten thousand volumes; and here and there pictures of peculiar interest look down from above the shelves. Among these are portraits of Lady Sunderland, by Sir Peter Lely; of Dickens, painted by

Alexander in 1842; of Pope, the work of Richardson, Sir Joshua's master. Up stairs there is a little bedroom, provided with old furniture, antique engravings, and bric-à-brac, and adjoined by a *cabinet de travail* crammed with more books. In this chamber have reposed at different times, as guests, Dickens, Thackeray, Hawthorne, Trollope, Kingsley, Miss Cushman, Bayard Taylor, and other celebrities; for the graceful hospitality of the owner has been always warmly pressed upon the wandering bards and wise men and women who have passed near the door. The interior of this house is redolent of the positive and work-a-day associations of literature and literary genius as perhaps few other Boston interiors may claim to be; and in its congenial atmosphere a circle of ladies meets from time to time, who read the latest thing they have written; Mrs. Fields, perhaps, contributing a poem, Miss Phelps some chapters from a new story, Mrs. Celia Thaxter one of her sea-pieces, or Miss Preston a critical essay.

There have been, of course, other centres; and when Mrs. Howe was a settled resident of Boston she drew around her, by the force of that magical thing, an instinct for social leadership, the most brilliant people. Her entertainments were informal, but always triumphant in the fine tone of wit, grace, and intellect that pervaded them. Count Gurowski, it is reported, said that Mrs. Howe was the one woman complete both on the side of literature and on that of easy and charming social ability whom he had met in America. For fifteen years, too, the Ladies' Social Club, better known abroad by its satirical title of "Brain Club," flourished as the most remarkable instance, in Boston, at least, of a successful club for mental stimulation and refreshment. It was begun by Mrs. Josiah Quincy, and numbered thirty or forty persons, though the companies assembled were often twice that; and among its active members or readers were Emerson, Professor Rogers, Agassiz, and Whipple. The meetings were at private houses, but membership was gained by many wealthy people, who so increased the variety of entertainment by paid performers and what not, and so overstepped the modest programme of the club as to suppers, that it died naturally two or three years since.

It should be said here that Cambridge, on the other hand, presents a mingling and a balance of elements which form one of the most enjoyable societies in the world. The conventional requirements are simple; the members whose employment is in art, with the university professors, and their families, themselves constitute the upper and fashionable circle, so far as it is fashionable at all; and the receptions, dinners, suppers for gentlemen, and little music parties, with which they entertain each other, are close upon perfection in their tone and in the opportunities given for pleasant intercourse. The only fault is the unevenness of the seasons: some are very dull and others too brilliant.

What Boston, pure and simple, lacks socially, it makes up in clubs. Long ago a public-spirited gentleman, one Captain Keayne, who died in 1656, left money to the town to support "a room for divines, scholars, merchants, shipmen, strangers, and townsmen" to meet in. What has become of the legacy I do not know; but

the spirit of the captain may be excused if, in looking down and beholding the transcendent realization of his kindly forethought by other means, it indulges a thrill of vanity. There are the two chief clubs, the Union and the Somerset; the former frequented by lawyers, judges, merchants, and sometimes by the historian Francis Parkman, by Dr. Holmes, Thomas Gold Appleton (celebrated as a wit and a man of fine æsthetic insight), Fields, and his successor Osgood. The

JOHN BOYLE O'REILLY.

Somerset, being the fashionable club of Boston, embraces some of the Union membership, but is especially a favorite with the old young men and young old men. There are the Temple, the Suffolk, the Central, the Athenian, all carrying houses on their backs; and the Art Club and St. Botolph, in a similar predicament. The Art Club, in fact, is about to put up a new building which will cost fifty thousand dollars. Then there are swarms of small dining clubs, weekly, fortnightly, monthly, for which male Bostonians have a passion. They are limited to some half a dozen or twenty persons each. So powerful is their attraction that members will come miles from the suburbs, through inclement weather, or when no other form of relaxation would draw them, to eat togeth-

er in a hotel or restaurant. The Papyrus
Club is in structure merely one of these
dining companies, gradually enlarged so
as to take in about a hundred gentlemen. Journalists, authors, and painters
originated it, and are conceded a controlling force in its government. A small
admission fee is paid, and each member
may purchase a ticket on the first Saturday of each month, which entitles him to
partake of a dinner, and bring friends with
him, for whom he likewise pays. At these
dinners speeches are made and poems read
after dessert; and some of the most distinguished authors in New England, as well as

tastes in the journalistic direction—an
evening paper founded on the community's desire for literary, artistic, and social
gossip, and edited for eight years by a lady,
the wife of a Boston banker. The Athenian Club is the chief resort of journalists
and theatrical people. But the younger
intellectual elements are even less united
than were the older ones in their prime.
Recently the St. Botolph Club has been
formed, with the hope of bringing together in closer relations artists of all kinds
and those who should be the friends and
supporters of the arts. But the atmosphere
of tradition in Boston is so gelid that a

JULIA WARD HOWE.

from without, have been the club's guests.
The Papyrus, too, holds annually a Ladies'
Night, and it distinguished this occasion
not long since by inviting to it some of
the notable literary women from different
parts of the country. Among its own
members Edwin P. Whipple and the two
Irish-American poets Dr. Joyce and John
Boyle O'Reilly are numbered. The one
last mentioned, by his gifts of imagination and the captivating grace of his social presence, has won a place in local regard, and is certainly the most romantic
figure in literary Boston. Mr. William
A. Hovey, another member of the Papyrus, has become widely known under the
name of "Causeur," and is the editor of the
Transcript, that unique result of Boston

thin crust of ice forms upon the wine of
sympathy as soon as it is poured, and it is
to be feared that a benumbing frost will
creep into even the St. Botolph's house.

The multiplying of clubs, however, is
the sign of an uneasiness which may result in good. They are fissiparous. No
sooner is one formed than it begins to
make another, by subdivision. Men fly
from the clubs they have to others that
they know not of, hoping always to find
one which will yield that generous, pro-
ductive fellowship essential to a healthier
and more joyous life. Perhaps by the
time that Boston's suburbs have extended
so far as to include a White Mountain
school of authors, society itself may have
learned to supply the need.

OLIVER WENDELL HOLMES

IN 1817 Bryant's "Thanatopsis" was
published in the *North American Review.* Richard Henry Dana, the elder,
who was then one of the editors, said that
it could not be an American poem, for
there was no American who could have
written it. But it does not seem to have
produced a remarkable impression upon
the public mind. The planet rose silently and unobserved. Ten years afterward, in 1827, Dana's own "Buccaneer"
was published, and Christopher North, in
Blackwood, saluted it as "by far the
most original and powerful of American
poetical compositions." But it produced
in this country no general effect which
is remembered. Nine years later, in 1836,
Holmes's "Metrical Essay" was delivered
before the Phi Beta Kappa Society at Harvard College, and was as distinct an event
in literary circles as Edward Everett's
oration before the same society in 1824,
or Ralph Waldo Emerson's in 1837, or
Horace Bushnell's in 1848, or Wendell
Phillips's in 1881. Holmes was then
twenty-seven years old, and had just returned from his professional studies in
Europe, where, as in his college days at
Cambridge, where he was born, he had
toyed with many Muses, yet still, with
native Yankee prudence, held fast the
hand of Æsculapius. His poem, like the
address of Emerson in the next year,
showed how completely the modern spirit of refined and exquisite literary cultivation and of free and undaunted thought
had superseded the uncouth literary form
and stern and rigid Calvinism of the Mathers and early Boston.

The melody and grace of Goldsmith's
line, but with a fresh local spirit, have
not been more perfectly reproduced, nor
with a more distinct revelation of a new
spirit, than in this poem. It is retrospective and contemplative, but it is also full
of the buoyancy of youth, of the consciousness of poetic skill, and of blithe
anticipation. Its tender reminiscence and
occasional fond elegiac strain are but
clouds of the morning. Its literary form
is exquisite, and its general impression is
that of bright, elastic, confident power. It
was by no means, however, a first work, nor
was the poet unknown in his own home.
But the "Metrical Essay" introduced

him to a larger public, while the fugitive
pieces already known were the assurance
that the more important poem was not a
happy chance, but the development of a
quality already proved. Seven years before, in 1829, the year he graduated at
Harvard, Holmes began to contribute to
The Collegian, a college magazine. Two
years later, in 1831, appeared the *New
England Magazine,* in which the young
writer, as he might himself say, took the
road with his double team of verse and
prose, holding the ribbons with unsurpassed lightness and grace and skill, now
for two generations guiding those fleet
and well-groomed coursers, which still
show their heels to panting rivals, the
prancing team behind which we have all
driven and are still driving with constant
and undiminished delight.

Mr. F. B. Sanborn, whose tribute to
Holmes on his eightieth birthday shows
how thorough was his research for that
labor of love, tells us that his first contribution to the *New England Magazine*
was published in the third or September
number of the first year, 1831. It was a
copy of verses of an unpromising title—
"To an Insect." But that particular insect, seemingly the creature of a day,
proved to be immortal, for it was the katydid, whose voice is perennial:

> "Thou sayest an undisputed thing
> In such a solemn way."

In the contributions of the young graduate the high spirits of a frolicsome fancy
effervesce and sparkle. But their quality
of a new literary tone and spirit is very
evident. The ease and fun of these bright
prolusions, without impudence or coarseness, the poetic touch and refinement,
were as unmistakable as the brisk pun-
gency of the gibe. The stately and scholarly Boston of Channing, Dana, Everett,
and Ticknor might indeed have looked
askance at the literary claims of such
lines as these "Thoughts in Dejection"
of a poet wondering if the path to Parnassus lay over Charlestown or Chelsea
bridge:

> "What is a poet's fame?
> Sad hints about his reason,
> And sadder praise from gazetteers,
> To be returned in season.

" For him the future holds
    No civic wreath above him;
Nor slated roof nor varnished chair,
    Nor wife nor child to love him.

" Maid of the village inn,
    Who workest woe on satin,
The grass in black, the graves in green,
    The epitaph in Latin,

" Trust not to them who say
    In stanzas they adore thee ;
Oh rather sleep in church-yard clay,
    With maudlin cherubs o'er thee !"

The lines to the katydid, with " L'Inconnue,"

" Is thy name Mary, maiden fair ?"

published in the magazine at about the same time, disclose Holmes's natural melody and his fine instinct for literary form. But his lyrical fervor finds its most jubilant expression at this time in "Old Ironsides," written at the turning-point in the poet's life, when he had renounced the study of the law, and was deciding upon medicine as his profession. The proposal to destroy the frigate *Constitution*, fondly and familiarly known as "Old Ironsides," kindled a patriotic frenzy in the sensitive Boston boy, which burst forth into the noble lyric,

" Ay, tear her tattered ensign down !"

There had been no American poetry with a truer lilt of song than these early verses, and there has been none since. Two years later, in 1833, Holmes went to complete his medical studies in Paris, and the lines to a grisette,

" Ah, Clemence, when I saw thee last
    Trip down the Rue de Seine !"

published upon his return in his first volume of verse, are a charming illustration of his lyrical genius. His limpid line never flowed more clearly than in this poem. It has the pensive tone of all his best poems of the kind, but it is the half-happy sadness of youth.

All these early verses have an assured literary form. The scope and strain were new, but their most significant quality was not melody nor pensive grace, but humor. This was ingrained and genuine. Sometimes it was rollicking, as in "The Height of the Ridiculous" and "The September Gale." Sometimes it was drolly meditative, as in "Evening, by a Tailor." Sometimes it was a tearful smile of the deepest feeling, as in the most charming and perfect of these poems, "The Last

Leaf," in which delicate and searching pathos is exquisitely fused with tender gayety. The haunting music and meaning of the lines,

" The mossy marbles rest
    On the lips that he has pressed
        In their bloom,
And the names he loved to hear
Have been carved for many a year
        On the tomb,"

lingered always in the memory of Lincoln, whose simple sincerity and native melancholy would instinctively have rejected any false note. It is in such melody as that of the "Last Leaf" that we feel how truly the grim old Puritan strength has become sweetness.

To this poetic grace and humor and music, which at that time were unrivalled, although the early notes of a tuneful choir of awakening songsters were already heard, the young Holmes added the brisk and crisp and sparkling charm of his prose. From the beginning his coursers were paired, and with equal pace they have constantly held the road. In the *New England Magazine* for November in the same year, 1831, a short paper was published called the "Autocrat of the Breakfast Table." The tone of placid dogmatism and infallible finality with which the bulls of the domestic pope are delivered is delightfully familiar. This earliest one has perhaps more of the cardinal's preliminary scarlet than of the mature papal white, but in its first note the voice of the Autocrat is unmistakable :

Somebody was rigmarolling the other day about the artificial distinctions of society.
"Madam," said I, "society is the same in all large places. I divide it thus :
"1. People of cultivation who live in large houses.
"2. People of cultivation who live in small houses.
"3. People without cultivation who live in large houses.
"4. People without cultivation who live in small houses.
"5. Scrubs."
An individual at the upper end of the table turned pale and left the room as I finished with the monosyllable.

" 'Tis sixty years since," but that drop is of the same characteristic transparency and sparkle as in the latest Tea-Cup.

The time in which the *New England Magazine* was published, and these firstlings of Holmes's muse appeared, was one of prophetic literary stir in New England.

There were other signs than those in letters of the breaking up of the long Puritan winter. A more striking and extreme reaction from the New England tradition could not well be imagined than that which was offered by Nathaniel Parker Willis, of whom Holmes himself says "that he was at the time something between a remembrance of Count D'Orsay and an anticipation of Oscar Wilde." Willis was a kindly saunterer, the first Boston dandy, who began his literary career with grotesque propriety as a sentimentalizer of Bible stories, a performance which Lowell gayly called inspiration and water. In what now seems a languid, Byronic way, he figured as a Yankee Pelham or Vivian Grey. Yet in his prose and verse there was a tacit protest against the old order, and that it was felt is shown by the bitterness of ridicule and taunt and insult with which, both publicly and privately, this most amiable youth was attacked, who, at that time, had never said an ill-natured word of anybody, and who was always most generous in his treatment of his fellow-authors.

The epoch of Willis and the *New England Magazine* is very notable in the history of American literature. The traditions of that literature were grave and even sombre. Irving, indeed, in his Knickerbocker and Rip Van Winkle and Ichabod Crane, and in the general gayety of his literary touch, had emancipated it from strict allegiance to the solemnity of its precedents, and had lighted it with a smile. He supplied a quality of grace and cheerfulness which it had lacked, and without unduly magnifying his charming genius, it had a natural, fresh, and smiling spirit, which, amid the funereal, theologic gloom, suggests the sweetness and brightness of morning. In its effect it is a breath of Chaucer. When Knickerbocker was published, Joel Barlow's "Hasty-Pudding" was the chief achievement of American literary humor. Mark Twain and Charles Dudley Warner were not yet "the wits of Hartford." Those who bore that name held it by brevet. Indeed, the humor of our early literature is pathetic. In no State was the ecclesiastical dominance more absolute than in Connecticut, and nothing shows more truly how absolute and grim it was than the fact that the performances of the "wits" in that State were regarded — gravely, it must have been—as humor.

For a long time there was no vital response in New England to the chord touched by Irving. Yet Boston was then unquestionably the chief seat of American letters. Dennie had established his *Portfolio* in Philadelphia in 1801, but in 1805 the *Monthly Anthology*, which was subsequently reproduced in the *North American Review*, appeared in Boston, and was the organ or illustration of the most important literary and intellectual life of the country at that time. The opening of the century saw the revolt against the supremacy of the old Puritan Church of New England—a revolt within its own pale. This clerical protest against the austere dogmas of Calvinism in its ancient seat was coincident with the overthrow in the national government of Federalism and the political triumph of Jefferson and his party. Simultaneously also with the religious and political disturbance was felt the new intellectual and literary impulse of which the *Anthology* was the organ. But the religious and literary movements were not in sympathy with the political revolution, although they were all indications of emancipation from the dominance of old traditions, the mental restlessness of a people coming gradually to national consciousness.

Mr. Henry Adams, in remarking upon this situation in his history of Madison's administration, points out that leaders of the religious protest which is known as the Unitarian Secession in New England were also leaders in the intellectual and literary awakening of the time, but had no sympathy with Jefferson or admiration of France. Bryant's father was a Federalist; the club that conducted the *Anthology* and the *North American Review* was composed of Federalists; and the youth whose "Thanatopsis" is the chief distinction of the beginning of that *Review*, and the morning star of American poetry, was, as a boy of thirteen, the author of the "Embargo," a performance in which the valiant Jack gave the giant Jefferson no quarter. The religious secession took its definite form in Dr. Channing's sermon at the ordination of Jared Sparks in Baltimore in 1819, which powerfully arraigned the dominant theology of the time. This was the year in which Irving's *Sketch-Book* was published. Bryant's first volume followed a year or two later, and our distinctive literary epoch opened.

Ten years afterward, when Bryant had

left New England, Dr. Channing was its most dignified and characteristic name in literature. But he was distinctively a preacher, and his serene and sweet genius never unbent into a frolicsome mood. As early as 1820 a volume of Robert Burns's poems fell into Whittier's hands like a spark into tinder, and the flame that has so long illuminated and cheered began to blaze. It was, however, a softened ray, not yet the tongue of lyric fire which it afterward became. But none of the poets smiled as they sang. The Muse of New England was staid and stately—or was she, after all, not a true daughter of Jove, but a tenth Muse, an Anne Bradstreet? The rollicking laugh of Knickerbocker was a solitary sound in the American air until the blithe carol of Holmes returned a kindred echo.

Willis was the sign of the breaking spell. But his light touch could not avail. The Puritan spell could be broken only by Puritan force, and it is the lineal descendants of Puritanism, often the sons of clergymen—Emerson and Holmes and Lowell and Longfellow and Hawthorne and Whittier—who emancipated our literature from its Puritan subjection. In 1829 Willis, as editor of *Peter Parley's Token* and the *American Monthly Magazine*, was aided by Longfellow and Hawthorne and Motley and Hildreth and Mrs. Child and Mrs. Sigourney, and the elder Bishop Doane, Park Benjamin and George B. Cheever, Albert Pike and Rufus Dawes, as contributors. Willis himself was a copious writer, and in the *American Monthly* first appeared the titles of "Inkling of Adventure" and "Pencillings by the Way," which he afterward reproduced for some of his best literary work. The *Monthly* failed, and in 1831, the year that the *New England Magazine* began, it was merged in the New York *Mirror*, of which Willis became associate editor, leaving his native city forever, and never forgiving its injustice toward him. In the heyday of his happy social career in England he wrote to his mother, "the mines of Golconda would not tempt me to return and live in Boston."

This was the literary situation when Holmes was preluding in the magazine. The acknowledged poets in Boston were Dana, Sprague, and Pierpont. Are these names familiar to the readers of this Magazine? How much of their poetry can those readers repeat? No one knows more

surely than he who writes of a living author how hard it is to forecast fame, and how dangerous is prophecy. When Edward Everett saluted Percival's early volume as the harbinger of literary triumphs, and Emerson greeted Walt Whitman at "the opening of a great career," they generalized a strong personal impression. They identified their own preference with the public taste. On the other hand, Hawthorne says truly of himself that he was long the most obscure man of letters in America. Yet he had already published the *Twice Told Tales* and the *Mosses from an Old Manse*, the two series of stories in which the character and quality of his genius are fully disclosed. But although Longfellow hailed the publication of the first collection as the rising of a new star, the tone of his comment is not that of the discoverer of a planet shining for all, but of an individual poetic pleasure. The prescience of fame is very infrequent. The village gazes in wonder at the return of the famous man who was born on the farm under the hill, and whose latent greatness nobody suspected; while the youth who printed verses in the corner of the county paper, and drew the fascinated glances of palpitating maidens in the meeting-house, and seemed to the farmers to have associated himself at once with Shakespeare and Tupper and the great literary or "littery folks," never emerges from the poet's department in the paper in which unconsciously and forever he has been cornered. It would be a grim Puritan jest if that department had been named from the corner of the famous dead in Westminster Abbey.

If the Boston of sixty years ago had ventured to prophesy for itself literary renown, it is easy to see upon what reputations of the time it would have rested its claims. But if the most familiar names of that time are familiar no longer, if Kettell and poems from the *United States Gazette* seem to be cemeteries of departed reputations, the fate of the singers need not be deplored as if Fame had forgotten them. Fame never knew them. Fame does not retain the name of every minstrel who passes singing. But to say that Fame does not know them is not dispraise. They sang for the hearers of their day, as the players played. Is it nothing to please those who listen, because those who are out of hearing do not stop and applaud? If we recall the names most eminent in our literature, whether they were destined for a longer or shorter date, we shall see that they are undeniably illustrations of the survival of the fittest. Turning over the noble volumes of Stedman and Miss Hutchinson, in which, as on a vast plain, the whole line of American literature is drawn up for inspection and review, and marches past like the ghostly midnight columns of Napoleon's grand army, we cannot quarrel with the verdict of time, nor feel that injustice has been done to Thamis or to Cawdor. There are singers of a day, but not less singers because they are of a day. The insect that flashes in the sunbeam does not survive like the elephant. The splendor of the most gorgeous butterfly does not endure with the faint hue of the hills that gives Athens its Pindaric name. And there are singers who do not sing. What says Holmes, with eager sympathy and pity, in one of his most familiar and most beautiful lyrics?

"We count the broken lyres that rest
  Where the sweet waiting singers slumber,
But o'er their silent sister's breast
  The wild flowers who will stoop to number?
A few can touch the magic string,
  And noisy fame is proud to win them;
Alas, for those that never sing,
  And die with all their music in them!"

But as he says also that the capacities of listeners at lectures differ widely, some holding a gallon, others a quart, and others only a pint or a gill, so of the singers who are not voiceless, their voices differ in volume. Some are organs that fill the air with glorious and continuous music; some are trumpets blowing a ringing peal, then sinking into silence; some are harps of melancholy but faint vibration; still others are flutes and pipes, whose sweet or shrill note has a dying fall. Some are heard as the wind or sea is heard; some like the rustle of leaves; some like the chirp of birds. Some are heard long and far away; others across the field; others hardly across the street. Fame is perhaps but the term of a longer or shorter fight with oblivion; but it is the warrior who "drinks delight of battle with his peers," and holds his own in the fray, who finally commands the eye and the heart. There were poets pleasantly singing to our grandfathers whose songs we do not hear, but the unheeded voice of the youngest songster of that time is a voice

we heed to-day. Holmes wrote but two "Autocrat" papers in the *New England Magazine*, one in November, 1831, and the other in February, 1832. The year after the publication of the second paper he went to Paris, where for three years he studied medicine, not as a poet, but as a physician, and he returned in 1836 an admirably trained and highly accomplished professional man. But the Phi Beta Kappa poem of that year, like the tender lyric to Clemence upon leaving Paris, shows not only that the poet was not dead, but that he did not even sleep. The "Metrical Essay" was the serious announcement that the poet was not lost in the man of science, an announcement which was followed by the publication in the same year (1836) of his first volume of poems. This was three years before the publication of Longfellow's first volume of verses, *The Voices of the Night.*

Holmes's devotion to the two Muses of science and letters was uniform and untiring, as it was also to the two literary forms of verse and prose. But although a man of letters, like the other eminent men of letters in New England, he had no trace of the Bohemian. Willis was the only noted literary figure that ever mistook Boston for a seaport in Bohemia, and he early discovered his error. The fraternity which has given to Boston its literary primacy has been always distinguished not only for propriety of life and respectability in its true sense of worthiness and respect, but for the possession of the virtues of fidelity, industry, and good sense, which have carried so far both the influence and the renown of New England. Nowhere has the Bohemian tradition been more happily and completely shattered than in the circle to which Holmes returned from his European studies to take his place. American citizenship in its most attractive aspect has been signally illustrated in that circle, and it is not without reason that the government has so often selected from it our chief American representatives in other countries.

Dr. Holmes, as he was now called, and has continued to be called, practised his profession in Boston; but whether because of some lurking popular doubt of a poet's probable skill as a physician, or from some lack of taste on his part for the details of professional practice, like his kinsman, Wendell Phillips, and innumerable other young beginners, he sometimes awaited a professional call longer than was agreeable. But he wrote medical papers, and was summoned to lecture to the medical school at Dartmouth College in New Hampshire, and later at Pittsfield in Massachusetts, while his unfailing charm as an occasional poet gave him a distinctive name. Holmes's felicity in occasional poems is extraordinary. The "Metrical Essay" was the first and chief of the long series of such verses, among which the songs of '29, the poems addressed year after year to his college classmates of that year, have a delightful and endless grace, tenderness, wit, and point. Pegasus draws well in harness the triumphant chariot of '29, in which the lucky classmates of the poet move to a unique and happy renown.

As a reader, Holmes was the permanent challenge of Mrs. Browning's sighing regret that poets never read their own verses to their worth. Park Benjamin, who heard the Phi Beta Kappa poem, said of its delivery: "A brilliant, airy, and *spirituelle* manner varied with striking flexibility to the changing sentiment of the poem, now deeply impassioned, now gayly joyous and nonchalant, and anon springing up into almost an actual flight of rhapsody, rendered the delivery of this poem a rich, nearly a dramatic entertainment." This was no less true in later years when he read some of his poems in New York at Bishop Potter's, then rector of Grace Church, or of the reading of the poem at the doctors' dinner given to him by the physicians of New York a little later.

Holmes's readings were like improvisations. The poems were expressed and interpreted by the whole personality of the poet. The most subtle touch of thought, the melody of fond regret, the brilliant passage of description, the culmination of latent fun exploding in a keen and resistless jest, all these were vivified in the sensitive play of manner and modulation of tone of the reader, so that a poem by Holmes at the Harvard Commencement dinner was one of the anticipated delights which never failed. This temperament implied an oratorical power which naturally drew the poet into the lecture lyceum when it was in its prime, in the decade between 1850 and 1860. During that time the popular lecture was a distinct and effective public force, and not the least of its services was its part in instructing and

training the public conscience for the great contest of the civil war.

The year 1831, in which Holmes's literary activity began, was also the year on whose first day the first number of Garrison's *Liberator* appeared, and the final period of the slavery controversy opened. But neither this storm of agitation nor the transcendental mist that a few years later overhung intellectual New England greatly affected the poet.

In the first number of the "Autocrat" there is a passage upon puns which, crackling with fun, shows his sensitive scepticism. The "Autocrat" says: "In a case lately decided before Miller, J., Doe presented Roe a subscription paper, and urged the claims of suffering humanity. Roe replied by asking when charity was like a top. It was in evidence that Doe preserved a dignified silence. Roe then said, 'When it begins to hum.'" There are temperaments of a refined suspiciousness to which, when the plea of reform is urged, the claims of suffering humanity at once begin to hum. The very word reform irritates a peculiar kind of sensibility, as a red flag stirs the fury of a bull. A noted party leader said, with inexpressible scorn, 'When Dr. Johnson defined the word patriotism as the last refuge of a scoundrel, he had not learned the infinite possibilities of the word ref-a-a-r-m.'"

The acridity of this jest is wholly unknown to the Autocrat, who has moved always with reform, if not always with reformers, and whose protest against bigotry is as searching as it is sparkling. Not only has his ear been quick to detect the hum of Mr. Honeythunder's loud appeal, but his eye to catch the often ludicrous aspect of honest whimsey. During all the early years of his literary career he flew his flashing darts at all the "isms," and he fell under the doubt and censure of those earnest children of the time whom the gay and clever sceptics derided as apostles of the newness. When Holmes appeared upon the lecture platform it was to discourse of literature or science, or to treat some text of social manners or morals with a crisp Poor Richard sense and mother wit, and a brilliancy of illustration, epigram, and humor that fascinated the most obdurate "come-outer." Holmes's lectures on the English poets at the Lowell Institute were among the most noted of that distinguished platform, and everywhere the poet was one of the most popular of "attractions." There were not wanting those who maintained that his use of the platform was the correct one, and that the orators who, often by happy but incisive indirection, fought the good fight of the hour abused their opportunity.

It was while Holmes was still a professor, but still also touching the lyre and writing scientific essays and charming the great audiences of the lecture lyceum, that in the first number of the *Atlantic Monthly*, in November, 1857, the "Autocrat of the Breakfast Table" remarked, "I was just going to say, when I was interrupted," and resumed the colloquies of the *New England Magazine*. He had been interrupted twenty-two years before. But as he began again it was plain that it was the same voice, yet fuller, stronger, richer, and that we were listening to one of the wisest of wits and sharpest of observers. Emerson warns us that superlatives are to be avoided. But it will not be denied that the "Autocrat" belongs in the highest rank of modern magazine or periodical literature, of which the essays of "Elia" are the type. The form of the "Autocrat"—a semi-dramatic, conversational, descriptive monologue—is not peculiar to Holmes's work, but the treatment of it is absolutely original. The manner is as individual and unmistakable as that of Elia himself. It would be everywhere recognized as the Autocrat's. During the intermission of the papers the more noted Macaulay flowers of literature, as the Autocrat calls them, had bloomed; Carlyle's *Sartor Resartus* and reviews, Christopher North's *Noctes* (now fallen into ancient night), Thackeray's *Roundabout Papers*, Lowell's "Hosea Biglow"—a whole library of magazine and periodical literature of the first importance had appeared. But the Autocrat began again, after a quarter of a century, musical with so rich a chorus, and his voice was clear, penetrating, masterful, and distinctively his own.

The cadet branch of English literature—the familiar colloquial periodical essay, a comment upon men and manners and life—is a delightful branch of the family, and traces itself back to Dick Steele and Addison. Hazlitt, who belonged to it, said that he preferred the *Tatler* to the *Spectator*: and Thackeray, who consorted with it proudly, although he was of the elder branch, restored Sir Richard, whose habits had cost him a great deal of his reputa-

tion, to general favor. The familiar essay is susceptible, as the eighteenth and nineteenth centuries show, of great variety and charm of treatment. What would the Christian Hero, writing to his Prue that he would be with her in a pint of wine's time, have said to "Blakesmoor" and "Oxford in the Vacation"? Yet Lamb and Steele are both consummate masters of the essay, and Holmes, in the "Autocrat," has given it a new charm. The little realm of the Autocrat, his lieges of the table, the persons of the drama, are at once as definitely outlined as Sir Roger's club. Unconsciously and resistlessly we are drawn within the circle; we are admitted *ad eundem*, and become the targets of the wit, the irony, the shrewd and sharp epigram, the airy whim, the sparkling fancy, the curious and recondite thought, the happy allusion, the felicitous analogy, of the sovereign master of the feast.

The index of the *Autocrat* is in itself a unique work. It reveals the whimsical discursiveness of the book; the restless hovering of that brilliant talk over every topic, fancy, feeling, fact; a humming-bird sipping the one honeyed drop from every flower; or a huma, to use its own droll and capital symbol of the lyceum lecturer, the bird that never lights. There are few books that leave more distinctly the impression of a mind teeming with riches of many kinds. It is, in the Yankee phrase, thoroughly wideawake. There is no languor, and it permits none in the reader, who must move along the page warily, lest in the gay profusion of the grove, unwittingly defrauding himself of delight, he miss some flower half hidden, some gem chance-dropped, some darting bird. Howells's *Letters* was called a chamber-window book, a book supplying in solitude the charm of the best society. We could all name a few such in our own literature. Would any of them, or many, take precedence of the *Autocrat of the Breakfast Table*?

It is in this book that the value of the scientific training to the man of letters is illustrated, not only in furnishing noble and strong analogies, but in precision of observation and accuracy of statement. In Holmes's style, the definiteness of form and the clearness of expression are graces and virtues which are due to his exact scientific study, as well as to the daylight quality of his mind.

The delicate apprehension of the finer and tenderer feelings which is disclosed in the little passages of narrative in the record of the Autocrat and of his legitimate brothers, the Professor and the Poet, at the Breakfast Table, gives a grace and a sweetness to the work which naturally flow into the music of the poems with which the diary of a conversation often ends. These traits in the Autocrat suggested that he would yet tell a distinct story, which indeed came while the trilogy of the Breakfast Table was yet proceeding. *Elsie Venner* and the *Guardian Angel*, the two novels of Holmes's, are full of the same briskness and acuteness of observation, the same effusiveness of humor and characteristic Americanism, as the *Autocrat*. Certain aspects of New England life and character are treated in these stories with incomparable vivacity and insight. Holmes's picture is of a later New England than Hawthorne's, but it is its lineal descendant. It is another facet of the Puritan diamond which flashes with different light in the genius of Hawthorne, Emerson, Lowell, Whittier, Longfellow, Holmes, and Judd in *Margaret*. For, with all his lyrical instinct and rollicking humor, Holmes is essentially a New-Englander, and one of the most faithful and shrewd interpreters of New England.

The colloquial habit of the Autocrat is not lost in the stories, and it is so marked generally in Holmes's writings as to be called distinctive. It is a fascinating gift, when it is so restrained by taste and instinctive refinement as not to become what is known as bumptiousness. Thackeray, even in his novels, is apt to drop into this vein, to talk about the persons of his drama with his reader, instead of leaving them to play out their part alone. This trait offends some of Thackeray's audience, to whom it seems like the manager's hand thrust into the box to help out the play of the puppets. They resent not "the damnable faces" of the actors, but the damnable sermonizing of the author, and exhort him to permit the play to begin. Thackeray frankly acknowledged his tendency to preach, as he called it. But it was part of the man. Without the private personal touch of the essayist in his stories they would not be his. This colloquial habit is very winning when governed by a natural delicacy and an exquisite literary instinct. It is the quality of all the authors who are distinctly beloved as persons by their readers, and it is to this class that Holmes especially belongs.

It is not a quality which is easily analyzed, but it blends a power of sympathetic observation and appreciation both of the thing observed and the reader to whom the observation is addressed. The Autocrat, as he converses, brightens with his own clear thought, with the happy quip, the airy fancy. He is sure of your delight, not only in the thought, but in its deft expression. He in turn is delighted with your delight. He warms to the responsive mind and heart, and feels the mutual joy. The personal relation is established, and the Autocrat's audience become his friends, to whom he describes with infinite glee the effect of his remarks upon his lieges at table. No other author takes the reader into his personal confidence more closely than Holmes, and none reveals his personal temperament more clearly. This confidential relation becomes even more simple and intimate as time chastens the eagerness of youth and matures the keen brilliancy of the blossom into the softer bloom of the fruit. The colloquies of the Autocrat under the characteristic title of "Over the Tea-Cups" are full of the same shrewd sense and wise comment and tender thought. The kindly mentor takes the reader by the button or lays his hand upon his shoulder, not with the rude familiarity of the bully or the boor, but with the courtesy of Montaigne, the friendliness of John Aubrey, or the wise cheer of Selden. The reader glows with the pleasure of an individual greeting, and a wide diocese of those whom the Autocrat never saw plume themselves proudly upon his personal acquaintance.

In this discursive talk about one of the American authors who have vindicated the position of American letters in the literature of the language we have not mentioned all his works. It is the quality rather than the quantity with which we are concerned, the upright, honorable, pure quality of the poet, the wit, the scholar, for whom the most devoted reader is called to make no plea, no apology. The versatility of his power is obvious, but scarcely less so the uniformity of his work. It is a power which was early mature. For many a year he has dwelt upon a high table-land where the air is equable and inspiring, yet, as we have hinted, ever softer and sweeter. The lyric of to-day glows with the same ardor as the fervent apostrophe to "Old Ironsides" or the tripping salutation to the remembered and regretted Clemence; it is only less eager. The young Autocrat who remarked that the word "scrub" dismissed from table a fellow-boarder who turned pale, now with the same smiling acuteness remarks the imprudent politeness which tries to assure him that it is no matter if he is a little older. Did anybody say so? The easy agility with which he cleared "the seven-barred gate" has carried him over the eight bars, and we are all in hot pursuit. For just sixty years since his first gay and tender note was heard, Holmes has been fulfilling the promise of his matin song. He has become a patriarch of our literature, and all his countrymen are his lovers.

A NEW ENGLAND COLONY IN NEW YORK

BETWEEN Shinnecock and Peconic bays the Long Island Railroad traverses a very narrow neck of sand. In a document dated December 13, A.D. 1640, it is mentioned as "the place where the Indians hayle over their cannooes out of the north bay to the south side of the island": hence "Canoe Place" to this day. Over this narrow sandy path passed all travel to and from the east end of Long Island, and there has been an inn there for one hundred and fifty years. East of it lie the Shinnecock Hills, bare, barren, sandy. It is to be contended that, whatever laws and maps may say, New York ends at those hills. They themselves are the neutral ground, the *zona libre*, and their eastern line is the western boundary of New England. Witness the introduction to a volume of the ancient records of Southampton, the town in which these hills lie (the pretty *village* being just east of them).

"The conclusion of the first period found our town a part of the colony of Connecticut. This was a union that was a decided benefit, as it placed them under the protection of a power to which they could look for sympathy and assistance in time of danger, and placed them in a position to be helpful in return. Had the wishes of the people been consulted, the union would have still continued, and to-day our delegates to the Legislature would ascend the Connecticut River rather than the Hudson, and we should receive our laws not from Albany but from Hartford. . . . King Charles II. had granted to his brother James, Duke of York and Albany, a patent for a vast extent of territory, of which Long Island formed a part. After the conquest of New Amsterdam the Duke proceeded to organize his colony, and by this decree the island was joined to New York. . . .

"The protest of the people of the eastern towns met with no response. . . .

"But it requires something more than the patent of a king and the order of a governor to change the wishes, the thoughts, and the dispositions of a people, and from that day to the present Southampton has continued to be an integral part of New England, to all intents and purposes, and in all modes of thought and action, as much as any portion of the land of steady habits."

This statement applies with equal force to Easthampton, and as the two towns cover the whole territory from Canoe Place to Montauk Light, here we have our New England colony.

Southampton, as has been often stated, was settled in 1640, by men from Lynn, Massachusetts; Easthampton was settled in 1649, by nine men, of whom six came from that same flourishing town; and in the village of Southampton, when it was two hundred and forty years old, there were living just two Irishmen and one German.

If the people of the United States do not believe that it is a great and glorious thing to have been a Pilgrim Father, or to have descended from Pilgrim Fathers, it can not be because they have not been told so for more than a century by historians, storytellers, orators, and poets. It may be said without prejudice that no people, tribe, or sect ever had abler or more aggressive partisans, and it is not very long since, in New England at least, ostracism awaited the rash man who claimed that the subject was not treated with entire fairness by them; who hinted at *suppressio veri;* or who dragged to light ugly and damaging facts. Yet in these latter days there have arisen scoffers and agnostics who, in defiance of all the speakers at New England Society dinners, have boldly asserted that the ideal Pilgrim Father must go to the realm of fable and join Pocahontas and William Tell.

To no such irreverent people as these should our modern pilgrim join himself. Nevertheless he might invite the attention of those of the strictest sects of the Pharisees—the Cotton Mathers of to-day—to this colony, and ask if they are perfectly satisfied with the fruits there shown of the old Pilgrim seed, the development therein of the pure Pilgrim idea. It was of absolutely unmixed origin. It was planted away from the haunts of the Gentiles, with water on three sides and sand barrens on the fourth. The colonists were stanch and substantial, and they became possessed of broad lands. Ample crops rewarded their tilling, fine grazing nourished their flocks and herds, and game and fish abounded. War and strife touched them but very lightly, and few alien hordes invaded their domain. A charming climate, the purest of air, the most

VILLAGE OF SOUTHAMPTON.

bracing of breezes, the brightest of sunlight, were theirs. Later on, the railroad and telegraph, inevitable even here, met scant welcome, and he who runs may read that the increase of material prosperity in late years, due wholly to the influx of uninvited sojourners from the parts beyond the Shinnecock Hills, is clouded in the minds of some of the people by not a little aversion to its cause. Yet the impartial observer is forced to conclude that this, so to speak, irruption of the Goths and Vandals has been an uncommonly good thing for these descendants of the Pilgrims; has waked them from the sleep of two centuries, and infused into them, in spite of themselves, a portion of the spirit of the nineteenth century.

So, at least, thought one particular modern pilgrim, who pitched his tent in the colony for a summer, and makes some record of what he saw and heard. He avoids subjects treated by able predecessors; he makes no allusion to Lyman Beecher, John Howard Payne, or "Home, sweet home"; and, excepting in one strange and romantic story, he has but to do with the colony of to-day, "the Hamptons" of 1885.

The Southampton village of this year is an altogether charming place. A certain forefather of the hamlet is said to hold a different opinion. He sadly shakes his head and says that it "does not seem like his old home, with all these carriages going up and down the street." Perhaps not; but he ought to find a certain consolation in the fact that land has advanced to $1500 per acre. This "main street," well known in history, has not changed so much, after all, and a walk down it will prove very interesting, especially if one stop, not far from the station, at the pleasant home of Mr. William R. Post (a highly respected and intelligent resident, whose knowledge of the town is as accurate as his memory of the past), and obtain a few data. Just beyond, and where the road from "North Sea" comes in, there is on the west side a grave-yard—not the oldest in the town. Crossing this to "Windmill Lane" and passing through a couple of fields, one comes to an old earth-work, in a very fair state of preservation. This was erected by General Erskine during the British occupation, and is a very respectable Revolutionary relic. Returning to the road, and proceeding southward, we find that two landmarks of the past, the "Pelletreau" and the "Johnes" houses, have disappeared—and more's the pity; but the "Sayre" house, an antique of the best class, still remains. A "Village Improvement Society" (largely, as a matter of course, com-

PECONIC BAY.

posed of Gentiles) has put up pretty and appropriate signs at the corners of the old roads: "Meeting-house Lane" (there you have the genuine old New England preju-

home. Otherwise the architecture is of the Queen Anne style.

"I don't care much," said a venerable visitor, "for these old-fashioned houses.

THE WINDMILL COTTAGE.

dice—no "church" for them), "Job's Lane," "Toylsome Lane," etc. Then by turning to the left and passing through private grounds, one comes to an ancient cemetery, in which Old Mortality would have revelled: 1696 is the oldest date given in previous popular sketches of this region, but 1682 can be seen here. Then there is a substantial estate which, as Mr. Post informs us, *has not once passed by deed since* 1640; and, a little farther on, the house that Captain Barney Green, a splendid old seaman, has built for his boarders, and wherein he has constructed hatches through which, by means of block and tackle, alike the lordly "Saratoga" and the unostentatious portmanteau are hoisted to the upper rooms.

Now appears at the right the Town Pond, or, as it is sometimes called, Lake Agawam. On both sides of it, more especially the western one, appear pretty and commodious modern cottages, and conspicuous among them is as quaint a dwelling as heart could desire, belonging to Mr. C. W. Betts, of New York. He purchased an old windmill at Good Ground, moved it hither, and has converted it into a summer

Just look here; when I want to open the window I have to open half the side of the house. No, sir; new houses are good enough for me."

Beyond the pond, to the south, are seen the *dunes* for which this coast is noted. Just on the hither side of them stands a perfect little gem of an Episcopal church, "St. Andrew's by the Sea," wholly inexpensive and unpretending, but a marvel of good taste. On the farther side are the bathing-houses and the sea; not the summer sea of Newport, nor yet the stern Calvinistic sea north of Boston; but a rough, jolly, hail-fellow-well-met ocean, with a capacity, in certain and frequent lights, of taking on the most exquisite blue that ever delighted the eye. At most times it is a friend and companion; but anon, in its boisterous moods, it pitches the bathers out of the way, and with a great rush bounds over the sand and into the pond.

Over this region lies almost all summer a clear azure sky, and the air is of the purest and the most electric. Witness the testimony of all visitors, with one exception. There once came hither an old, old man, such as he of whom

"They say that in his prime,
Ere the pruning-knife of time
    Cut him down,
Not a better man was found
By the crier on his round
    Through the town."

On one of the exquisite days of summer,
when the atmosphere seemed surcharged
matter from his mind as incomprehensible to the true citizen of the world. Happy indeed is he, pilgrim or resident, cottager or boarder, whose summer lines fall
in such a pleasant place.

But staff in hand, and "with scrip and
sandal shoon," the pilgrim must hie him
eastward. First let him cross the railroad,

GLIMPSE OF WATER MILL.

with a subtle and life-giving ether, he sat
on a pleasant veranda, lugubrious and a
little testy.

"Do you not find this air charming?"
asked an enthusiastic holiday-maker, pausing, lawn-tennis racket in hand, to pay his
respects. The old man raised his lacklustre eyes and surveyed the questioner.
"Sir," he feebly and petulantly said, "I
find it *decidedly debilitating!*"

In summer the place is, socially, a very
pleasant Little Pedlington. In the eyes
of a discreet scribe and pilgrim, the "city
folks" there are all "nice"; the irrepressible conflict between the cottager and the
boarder has a less sanguinary aspect than
at some other sea-side towns; the "dude"
cometh not; and if on the beach or at the
post-office the pilgrim hears rumors of
"cliques" and "sets," he dismisses the
and, taking a steep country road, ascend
"Barrel Hill," chosen of the Coast Survey. The view therefrom is charming.
To the north is Peconic Bay, and across
it the cliff-bound upper shore. To the
west are the Shinnecock Hills, Canoe
Place, and the trees stretching to the horizon. To the south are the village and
the ocean; and to the east a lovely landscape, with a bay, ponds, hills, fertile
farms, and the white spires of Bridge-
hampton.

Were there no other proofs of the New
England origin of this colony, it would be
demonstrated by the existence of sign-
boards, with black letters on a white
ground, and a friendly hand, with index
finger, somewhat out of drawing, pointing
in one direction and another. A jolly
party of pilgrims, on a beautiful morning

DOORWAY, EASTHAMPTON.

near the end of the summer, consulted one of them, and this is what it read: "Bridge-hampton, 6 m.; Easthampton, 12 m.; Sag, 8 m.; Montauk, 30 m.; Sag Harbor, 10 m."

Then, in the bright sunshine and bracing breeze, they proceeded to test its accuracy. Past Water Mill, where is as picturesque a building as ever escaped the attention of an artist, past the head of Mecox Bay, past old windmills and fields of ripe corn and fine houses of the colonial period, they went until the spires and tree-bordered street of Bridgehampton were near. Then, turning from the main turnpike, they wended their way to Sag, or Sagg (formerly Sagaponack), and if there be a place more weird in its preternatural quiet, let it be named. Sag Harbor—known to time-tables of railroads and steamers, and ancient home of the whale-fishery—was but the "harbor of Sag," and is newer than this slumbering hamlet, to which it was once tributary. Let the would-be recluse seek no further. Sag is only "8 m." from Southampton and its gay cottages, but it might be a thousand miles away, and evolved bodily —grass-grown street, old grave-yard, and all—from the seventeenth century. Far-

ther to the eastward Wainscot bears it fitting company, and then, after a glimpse of Georgica Lake, one turns to the northward, then to the eastward, and Easthampton is at hand. As the pilgrims traversed its long, wide, shady main street they passed as usual the southern cemetery, then a small Episcopal church, a substantial brown house, and a little inn; and then one of them, the present scribe, bade them, keeping these landmarks in mind, listen to the following strange and true story, which he called

THE MYSTERY OF EASTHAMPTON.

The time has come when I am at liberty to make public one of the strangest stories ever given to the world—a story so strange and so romantic that if it were not absolutely true it would be pronounced unlikely to the verge of impossibility. Its most minute details have been known to me for more than four years, but for several reasons it has not been permitted me until now to narrate them.

I.

It was April, 1840, forty-five years ago. It was six years before the Mexican war. Where San Francisco, with its 350,000 inhabitants, now stands, was then, and for nine years later, the little Mexican settlement of Yerba Buena, whither a young man who wrote *Two Years before the Mast* went in a Boston ship for hides. Denver, with its 50,000 inhabitants, was founded nineteen years after.

We "make history" so fast in this country that forty-five years with us count for more, indeed, in the world's progress "than a cycle of Cathay." In this sleepy corner of Long Island, however, there has been precious little change for the better, and Easthampton was a more important place than now in this month of April aforesaid. It was perhaps on just such a day as this—the sea as blue, the air as clear, the sails of the old windmills as active—that a high-bred, dignified gentleman, about fifty years of age, walked up to the little inn, followed by an attendant.

In a pleasant voice, and with a Scotch accent, he asked if he could have accommodations. The landlord looked at him with a certain hesitation.

"Is that man your servant?" he asked.

"He is," was the reply.

"Well, he must eat at the same table with you."

"I shall conform to your customs and regulations," was the smiling answer.

For five long years did this courtly gentleman sleep in the cramped chambers, breakfast, dine, and sup at the frugal board, of this humble hostelry. Then he became an inmate—fortunate enough he was to find such good friends—of the home of the Huntington family, and in that substantial house (it is the fourth from the old Presbyterian church, going south) he spent about *twenty-five* years more. He was a man of marked piety and benevolence, of charming manners and address, of extreme culture, of rare social qualities. He had been the friend and associate of Jeffrey and the literary giants of his day. He had ample means, and remittances came to him through a chain of banks, ending in a well-known New York house, who denied any knowledge of his personality or belongings.

He led a blameless, a lovely life, in this quiet town. He was the friend of all, the comforter of the afflicted, the helper of the needy. Books and magazines in large store came to him. He versified the Psalms, and taught Latin to the boys. A blameless and lovely life indeed; but a martyrdom, a living death, one would have said, to a man of his tastes and antecedents. Think of it! He remained, an exile, in this town for nearly *thirty-one* years—from early in his fiftieth to the end of his eighty-first year. In all this time he never saw the face of a relative or an old friend. He went at first on Sundays to the Episcopal church at Sag Harbor, seven miles distant, but he was instrumental in the building of the little one in Easthampton which we just passed; he contributed largely to its support, and he was made a lay reader, and for a long time conducted the services himself. With the exception of this church-going at Sag Harbor, the only time in thirty-one years that this remarkable man passed the limits of the little village was on the occasion of a single trip to Southampton, twelve miles distant. The servant, a Scotch valet, went to the West, and married. He made his appearance at intervals, evidently to extort money from his old master.

During his entire life in Easthampton this man successfully defeated all attempts to discover his identity. When he entered the little inn in April, 1840, the name he gave was John Wallace; John Wallace

he was to the end; and John Wallace is the name which you will find, under a cross and anchor, on the plain white marble slab in that southern cemetery over which the old windmill watches. To the excellent family with whom he lived, and whose kindness to him while on earth and tender regard for his memory are altogether lovely, he, waking or sleeping, stalwart or failing, in the close intimacy of three decades, gave no word. The inhabitants of the village, his neighbors and beneficiaries, accepted his kindness and constructed theories about him. With the perverseness of poor human nature, they constructed them to his detriment. He was a bishop of the English Church—"another good man gone wrong." He was a murderer. He was—Heaven knows what not! As years passed by, and the place was more and more frequented in summer by "city folks," curiosity spread, and grew apace. The most strenuous efforts were made to discover who John Wallace was. One man, bearing an old New York name, and since dead, had the ill grace to threaten him. He told him that the "census marshal" was coming, and that unless he told that functionary just who he was, he would be put in prison. After this interview the late excellent Dr. Huntington found the poor old gentleman in a pitiable state, and learned of the threat just made.

"Give yourself no concern," said he. "The 'census marshal' has been here. He asked your name. I told him, and he has gone." But on the night of the 30th or 31st of December, 1870, there came to the door a census marshal who could not be barred out, a messenger who brought at once a summons and a release. Mr. Wallace raised himself from his peaceful pillow—there was not even time for him, like Colonel Newcome, to say "Adsum" —his head dropped, and his eighty-first year, his lonely life, and the year of our Lord 1870 came to an end together. One can almost fancy that even in the solemn moment when his soul left the weary body there may have come to him a flash of satisfaction that he had baffled all the curious, intrusive disturbers of his peace. In the expressive language of Shakespeare, "he died and made no sign."

Often during his life in the village he would come from the post-office holding a letter in his hand, and remark, "This is from my lady friend in Edinburgh."

When he had passed away, Mrs. Huntington, with rare good taste and pathetic kindness, wrote a letter describing his last moments. She addressed it to "Mr. Wallace's Lady Friend, Edinburgh," and sent it through the chain of banks through which the old man's money had come. In due time a reply arrived—cold, formal, unsympathetic. It was signed, "*Mr. Wallace's Lady Friend.*"

II.

"Who was Mr. Wallace?" I see the question in your eyes. I went to Easthampton in the autumn of 1878, and did my best to find out. I talked with Mrs. Huntington and Miss Cornelia Huntington (author of a charming little monograph anent Easthampton and its ways in days gone by, called "Sea Spray"), and I should count a pilgrimage fruitful which gave me the pleasure of their acquaintance. I found them at the time of my last visit enjoying a green old age, loved and respected by all. They told me much of great interest about Mr. Wallace, and among other things they spoke of finding copies of his accounts (of charities in his native land) with the headings torn off. One had been carelessly torn, and on it I found a name. I sent this name with a mass of notes to my late accomplished friend Robert Mackenzie, Esq., of Dundee, Scotland, author of *A History of the Nineteenth Century*, and other interesting works. In a few weeks he wrote me that he was "on the trail." In a few weeks more he sent me what he properly called "a very tantalizing letter." Said he, "I know the mystery to the very bottom, but—*I may not tell you!*"

Not a little disappointed, I communicated this information to a circle of equally disappointed friends. One of them, a distinguished divine, told me that "it made his flesh creep like one of Wilkie Collins's stories." Then I went to Scotland? No —to Colorado, of all places in the world, and at the foot of Pike's Peak, in the summer of 1879, I found out all about the poor exile. As living persons are concerned in the manner of my discovery, I may not rightly publish the details thereof; but they are among the strangest happenings of any life. Suffice it to say that on my return I held all the clews, proofs, and facts in my hands, and that only now am I permitted to tell the truth about John Wallace.

III.

Perhaps some of you know how distinguished and important a judicial officer is the High Sheriff of a great Scotch county. Such distinguished and important officer was, in 1840, Sheriff W——, resident in Edinburgh. He was a bachelor of fifty years of age. He was famed for his benevolence and his good works. He was the friend of the poor, the widow, and the orphan. His services to the state had earned him a public testimonial. He had "honor, love, obedience, troops of friends." He was a founder and ardent supporter of Sunday-schools. People flocked from cultured Edinburgh homes to hear his weekly addresses to the children.

One day, at the height of his fame, there was made against him the subtle charge of a grave and mysterious crime. At six o'clock in the evening the Lord High Advocate went to a mutual friend.

"Go to Sheriff W—— at once," said he, in sad and measured tones, "and tell him that when I go to my office at ten o'clock to-morrow morning a warrant will issue for his arrest."

That night Sheriff W—— *died out of* Scotland. He had just time to say to a friend that he was not guilty of more than an indiscretion, but that he could not face even the shame of that.

His disappearance is mourned in Edinburgh after all these long years, and tears come to the eyes of old friends when it is mentioned. The man who so patiently bore the long crucifixion of a self-imposed exile, the man who endured the penance of thirty-one years among strangers in a strange land, the man who read the beautiful service in the little Easthampton Church, was no John Wallace. Under the white marble tablet in the old Easthampton cemetery sleeps the scholar, the great jurist, the courtly gentleman, the humble Christian—Sheriff W——

A grim story, is it not? The pilgrims all thought so, and they were still talking about it when they stopped for dinner at the one inn of Amaganset.

Not far from Amaganset the road makes a sharp descent from a bluff, and then comes the five-mile stretch of sand, through which "the chariot wheels drove heavily." Finally, after a sharp climb, one reaches the higher ground. Of the road it would be hard to say a good word. It is inclined at an angle of forty-five degrees, first one way and then the other, and our pilgrims clung anxiously to that side of the wagon which was uppermost for the time being, and dodged the boughs as they traversed the woods. Then, coming out from the trees, they saw the land stretching away to the white tower of the light-house, with little to break the view.

As one looks from the high ground at the edge of the woods he sees some little dots on the greenish-yellow grass five miles away. During part of the intervening distance they are hidden from sight, but at last they loom up as the club-house, cottages, and stable of the "Montauk Association." By the time the pilgrims approached them they were not only fatigued by the long journey, but also impressed

four miles to a railroad, eighteen to a telegraph station, fifteen to a post-office; yet a letter can be sent from New York to Chicago and an answer received in less time than one from Montauk.

The association property is near Great Pond (or Lake Wyandanch), and about four miles west are Fort Pond and Fort Pond Bay. To this bay is to come our old friend the Long Island Railroad; from this bay are to sail large and swift steamers to Milford Haven.

The club-house of the Montauk Association, the hospice of the Long Island St. Bernard, was far too tempting a resting-place for our ascetic pilgrims, and they soon prepared to bid it a grateful farewell, and make for the light-house. Soon they

KING OF THE MONTAUKS.

pressed by the strange loneliness of this unfrequented spot. To them, therefore, this commodious and tasteful club-house was as the hospice of St. Bernard to the Alpine traveller. It is truly a model establishment, containing on the lower floor a large hall and dining-room; on the upper, some exceptionally pleasant and comfortable bedrooms. Around it are grouped some pretty, some elegant cottages. Their inmates all take their meals at the club-house.

This very handsome club-house affords to fortunate guests, as well as the members of the association, more than the comfort of a first-class city hotel. Here are ladies and children, saddle-horses, pony-carriages, lawn-tennis sets. It is twenty-

passed Stratton's, beloved of sportsmen; and here were they tempted to leave the path and visit that unique institution in a New England colony, a genuine monarchy. The pilgrims were nothing if not romantic. Poets and artists had set them an example of throwing a sentimental halo around the relics of past royal greatness, of glorifying the poor remnants of the native race over which Wyandanch ruled, and of which his lineal successor is king to-day. Why should they not cast a scoffing agnosticism to the winds, and seek to trace in the ways of the modern sovereign of the Montauk Indians a glimmer of the poetic greatness of the noble red potentate of antiquity? Alas! it was impossible. With all the good-will in the world, how *can* the most ardent sentimentalist overcome such stubborn statements as were brought out in the following dialogue between a pilgrim and an unemotional summer resident?

"But we want to see the king. Why should you not feel some respect for a genuine monarch? You run after royalty whenever you have a chance. You delight to honor Malagassees, Coreans, what not. Why not exalt this native American king?"

"Well, I'm afraid he is rather a dilapidated monarch. Last year you could hire him and *his* wagon for one dollar per diem. This year prices have advanced. The prince, the heir-apparent, bought an old barouche for thirty dollars at Easthampton, and he charges a dollar and a half."

"I suppose the poor king felt it beneath his dignity to work when all these haughty strangers had arrived. He is one of Dr. Doran's 'monarchs retired from business.'"

"Yes, he *has* retired—into the lock-up at Easthampton."

Shade of Fenimore Cooper! Can these things be so?

In a short time the pilgrimage came to an end. The carriage ceased to roll from side to side, for it could go no farther. It was dusk when the pilgrims ascended the iron stairway of the lonely light-house. An elderly man had just touched the wick with a match, and stood placidly watching the flame creeping around it. On three sides lay the sea; on the fourth, the rolling peninsula. Block Island loomed up to the eastward; on the south, the water reached to the antarctic continent; on the north, one saw the New England which sent our colonists to plant the settlement which New York has claimed.

None have failed, none can fail, to realize the unique character of Montauk Point. One of our pilgrims had read Starr King's graphic description of a night on the summit of Mount Washington, in which he speaks of himself as "in this *foretop* of New England, scudding through space." So he ventured to call Montauk Point the top-gallant forecastle of New York.

People who want an original experience may be confidently recommended to explore this New England colony with some thoroughness, and not to wait for the railroad to visit Montauk Point. May it be the good fortune of some of them to sit on the cliff before dark and look at a fine ship standing well in before she tacks and stands out again! A poet who had "had his hands in the tar bucket," and, as an old captain said, "knew how to tack ship and write poetry too," once described it, and his last three verses will recur to any one who had the good fortune to read them:

"'Let go and haul!' 'tis the last command,
    And the head-sails fill to the blast once more;
Astern and to leeward lies the land,
    With the breakers white on the shingly shore.

"What matters the reef, or the rain, or the squall?
    I steady the helm for the open sea;
The first mate clamors, 'Belay there, all!'
    And the captain's breath once more comes free.

"And so off shore let the good ship fly—
    Little care I how the gusts may blow;
In my fok'sle bunk in a jacket dry,
    Eight bells has struck, and my watch's below."

THE GATEWAY OF BOSTON

WHEN you go to sea from New York, the uninterrupted expanse of the bay is opened to you soon after you leave the wharf, and the channel lies across the middle of it in a nearly straight line. The spaciousness of the harbor is revealed at a glance; the few small islands, like Governor's and Bedloe's, are close to the extremity of the city, and when they are passed the course is clear to the Narrows, where the wooded and villa-dotted shores come so nearly together that a little more stretching would unite them, and make a circular lake with no other outlets to the sea than the East River and Long Island Sound and the Kill von Kull.

The gap in the shores is so narrow, indeed, that any hostile craft would be completely at the mercy of the forts, through the embrasures of which black-nosed cannon can be seen projecting on both sides, and it would not be more than the work of an hour to lay across from side to side such a barrier of torpedoes as would scatter an invader as chaff before the wind, though all the guns should be silent.

From the Narrows you pass down the lower bay, the open expanse of which is also unbroken, except by the two small artificial islands of the quarantine station, and at a little distance from the tropical-looking spit of cedar-tufted white sand which curves out at Sandy Hook the great ship channel debouches in the blue water of the Atlantic.

When you go to sea from Boston, you of course miss the activity of traffic and the picturesque variety of floating things, under steam and sail, which may be seen in New York, for the commerce of Boston is only a trifle compared with that of the metropolis. But you miss more than these the clear, unobstructed reach of water.

Measured by its coast-line, Boston Harbor is probably larger than the upper bay of New York, and the effusive local pride, caring less for accuracy than for the poetical suggestiveness of the comparison, has likened it to that rhetorically serviceable city, Venice.

Writing of it in 1634, the author of *New England Prospects* said of it: "It is a safe and pleasant Harbour within, having but one common and safe entrance, and that not very broad, there scarce being roome for 3 ships to come in board and board at the same time; but being once within, there is anchorage for 500 ships. This Harbour is made by a great company of Ilands, whose high cliffs shoulder out the boisterous seas, yet may easily deceive any unskillfull Pilote; presenting many faire openings and broad sounds, which afford too shallow waters for any ships, though navigable for Boates and small pinnaces."

The islands are not picturesque or interesting, however; had they cliffs, or woods, or cultivated shores, we should not regret the way they deprive Boston Harbor of the splendid unobstructed prospect which New York has. But most of them are arid and treeless and unadorned, except (if these can be regarded as ornaments) by the buildings of the charitable and reformatory institutions of the city, the station of the quarantine officers, and the depot of light-house supplies.

Some of them are low and sloping; others present sandy escarpments, fluted by the washings of the rain, and protected from what Thoreau calls the "nibbling" of the waves only by a low granite seawall. Before the walls were put up the sea had eaten up several without showing any appeasement of appetite, leaving nothing of them undevoured but a shoal like that which has a black sepulchral memorial in the beacon known in local tradition as Nix's Mate.

The beacon marks the sunken ruin of an island upon which pirates were gibbeted in the days when the black flag and the skull and cross-bones were accounted no less among the terrors of the sea than the hurricane. Nix was murdered by his mate, and when the latter was executed he protested his innocence, and prophetically declared that in proof of it the island would disappear.

As we go to sea we wind down past these islands and vestiges of islands through a narrow but deep channel. The craft we see are mostly coasters, of which as many as three hundred are sometimes gathered together waiting for the wind; the transatlantic traffic is represented by the weekly Cunarder and the tremendous Liverpool cattle steamers; a bark alive with walnut-skinned passengers is towed up, inward bound from the Azores, and we may catch the redolence of a Gloucester fishing schooner, with a contented crew busying about her scaly and dripping deck. Large ships are not very frequent, but occasionally an East Indiaman recalls to us that former glory of the harbor when Boston had a large share of the grandest commerce of the world, and her

SPEARING SCULPIN IN BOSTON HARBOR.

wharves were filled with Yankee ships, manned by Yankee crews—officers from Harvard and seamen from the Cape.

Getting farther down the harbor, we catch over the slopes of the islands object in view is Fort Warren, which, with its silent armament and flaming banner, stands at the very edge of the channel. Looking back to the city, we find that it has almost dissolved in a mixture

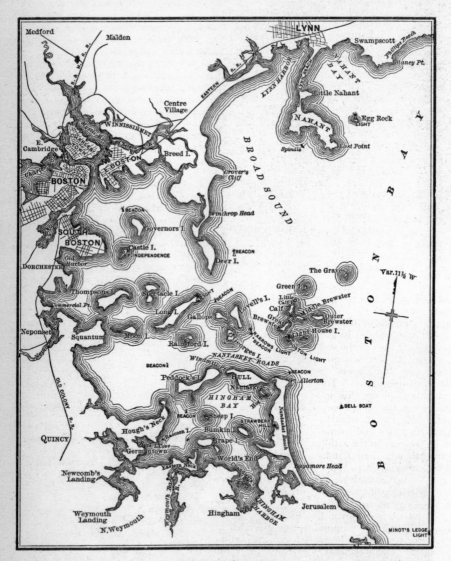

BOSTON BAY AND HARBOR.

glimpses of a southward range of hills steeped in a restful blue haze, and sprinkled with villages; we pass a solitary lobster-man tipping his dory over to the gunwale as he hands in his pots, and the next of purple and gray, through which the gilt on the State-house dome burns like the sun going down in a murky cloud; and now, turning by a squat screw-pile light-house, which looks like an enormous

BUG LIGHT—ENTRANCE TO NARROWS.

tarantula, and is known to mariners as "the Bug," we have a straight course of about a mile to the mouth of the harbor.

Here all disparagement of Boston in comparison with New York must cease.   The entrance to the great ship channel of the latter port is fully twenty-three miles out at sea, and vessels of large draught are exposed to the unchecked force of the Atlantic while they are waiting for the tide.   In Boston the bar is within the harbor, and if any waiting is necessary, it is only in the case of vessels of unusual size, and they can anchor, secure from the storm, under the headlands and within the breakwater which nature has erected across the entrance.

Unlike New York, Boston Harbor has no outer bay; it is an indentation with a narrow mouth in the sweeping curve of Massachusetts Bay, and it has no straggling estuary, so that, once out of it, a ship is at sea, and once within it, she is safe, and Boreas may puff his cheeks till they crack without hurting her.

Sloops and schooners can find their way into the harbor through a northerly passage called Broad Sound, but for larger vessels the only entrance is that of which we have spoken.   It is scarcely more than a mile wide. At one side of it some pale yellow bluffs, deeply grooved by the rain, shoot up perpendicularly to a breezy houseless plateau, the advantages of which were recognized in Revolutionary times, as a series of old redoubts testify.   At the seaward extremity these bluffs terminate in Point Allerton, and on the south they slope easily down to the slab-like crescent of Nantasket Beach, with its reproductions of Coney Island architecture and Coney Island diversions.   At the other side a group of islands form that natural breakwater to which allusion has been made, shouldering out the boisterous seas as described by the

THE HERRING FLEET OFF GREAT BREWSTER.

PAINTING LOBSTER BUOYS.

author of *New England Prospects*, and although the islands within the harbor add little to its attractiveness, these are memorably picturesque in a wild and rugged way. Eight of them are high enough out of the water to be habitable, and the group includes the Shag Rocks and the Graves, which the sea keeps for its own. The largest is the Great Brewster, which is sandy and barren, facing the sea with a yellow escarpment like the bluffs on the opposite shore; the others are masses of rock of irregular outline, which were probably shoved out into their present position by an ancient glacier, and though they have arable surfaces, there are few points in their circumference at which a landing can be effected. These are the Middle Brewster, the Outer Brewster, the Little Brewster, Green Island, Calf Island, and Little Calf Island. The Little Brewster is the site of the graceful white pillar of Boston Light, which marks the entrance of the harbor for inward-bound mariners, and its only occupants are the keepers with their wives and children. The rest of the group are uninhabited during the greater part of the year, except by a few lobster-men, who have yielded nothing of their primitive simplicity to modern influences, and seem to be unconscious of the city which frets and toils so near them, though, if they cared to think of it, a purplish-gray cloud would reveal its proximity by day, and a dome of pale light by night.

Along the coast, both north and south, the summer boarder and the revelling excursionist have full sway; big hotels vying with those at Rockaway and Manhattan Beach have been built for them, and after dark the summer sky is set ablaze by the sheaves of rockets exploded for their amusement. But the Brewsters and their sister islands have been left happily alone. No ferry or telegraph links them with the mainland, and no wharf is there to make landing easy. The only way by which they can be reached is in a private boat, and when the easterly gales are blowing, flinging the surf over the Graves and the Shag Rocks, and dashing the spray as high as the top of the Middle Brewster, nothing can approach or leave them, and the isolation is complete.

The summer brings only three additions to the winter population—a lawyer, a banker, and a marine artist, who are variously benefited or become benefactors through the seclusion. The lawyer is entirely out of the reach of litigious clients, who, if he were accessible to carry out their impulses, would precipitate themselves into actions, from which they refrain after the calmer consideration which his absence allows. He tells how one of these once called at his office to have a deed prepared which, if it had been executed, would have caused a loss of fifty thousand dollars; but instead of being in his office he was down at the Brewsters, drinking in ozone—which, except tea, coffee, and lemonade, is the only thing ever drank there—and before he returned to town his client had abandoned the proposed transaction, having perceived the folly of it. The islands may therefore be said to make a benefactor of the lawyer by keeping him out of the way of reckless clients, and by frustrating unnecessary litigation.

The banker can add nothing to his obnoxious millions while sojourning upon them, and from the point of view of those cheerful philosophers who console themselves for the lack of wealth by stigmatizing it as an evil, he is benefited. But the debt of the marine artist to the islands exceeds that of either of the others, for during the few months he is among them they supply him with more than enough material to occupy him all the rest of the year.

Nature is less variable in her external appearances on land than on the sea, which on a gray day does not seem to be the same element as that which effervesces and sparkles when the sun is shining; the transition from light to shadow affects not merely the color, but the form and substance, and the billows of emerald become with a change of cloud inert ridges of lead.

CANAL, OUTER BREWSTER.

No place could be better than the islands for observing these variations, and very soon after the artist takes possession for the summer the rude boards of the studio walls are hidden under the sketches pinned to them of the sea in all its moods—now broken and ragged, its blackish-green having the sinister effect of some concealed tragedy as sunrise puts a red wedge under

BOSTON LIGHT-HOUSE.

"MUSIC AT THE LIGHT."

the inky clouds which droop along the eastern horizon; now blue and flashing with a jocund brilliancy, the vessels scooping their way through it with a conscious sportiveness; and then pallid and vague, a phantom sea with ghostly ships.

The reference to the rude boards of the studio walls ought, perhaps, to be explained. The isolation of the Brewsters entails upon those who enjoy it the sacrifice of some conveniences, and compels the utilization of many little things which would be disregarded elsewhere. The studio was a cow shed originally, but with a great window cut in its northern side, opening up the Atlantic and the eastern shore as far as Gloucester, it is so well adapted to its new uses that its prosaic antecedents are unthought of.

The life of the summer visitors is as simple as that of the fishermen. The only houses on the islands, except the lawyer's, are fishermen's cottages, one of which is occupied in its primitive condition by the banker, and another by the artist. The lawyer and the banker are bachelors, and may be seen, frying-pan in hand, attending to their own simple wants. But the artist is married, and the feminine presence has expressed itself in refinements which, in contrast with the meagre establishments of the celibates, put the latter on the plane of savages. Her cottage has been transformed by dull red and dark green paint, and the addition of a piazza and hooded dormers, into a cozy little Queen Anne house, and when she comes at the beginning of summer a dory loaded with household luxuries is towed after her. It is usually found, after the difficult landing has been made, that the piano has shipped some water; but when it has been pumped out and oiled it serves well enough to cheer up the evening after the lamps have been lit within, and Boston Light can be seen flashing across the channel, while Minot's Ledge beams steadily out at sea like a star hung in the south.

The piazza of the cottage projects over a nearly perpendicular cliff, and at high water the surf splashes and rattles along the base; but as the tide recedes it reveals a black and chaotic heap of bowlders, bearded by tangles of dark and slippery moss. These are jagged enough to pierce and tear any unfortunate ship driven upon them, but they stretch out to a long bevelled ridge with a sharp edge, which, being higher than they are, would scrape her bottom out before she could reach them. This ridge makes a landing practicable at the Middle Brewster.

The Outer Brewster stands outside the rest of the group, and is more rugged than any of them. It has been so gashed and hacked at by disrupting forces that its scars have become weapons of reprisal, in the manner that a whipped and overdriven mortal himself becomes a scourge when ill treatment obliterates his humanity. More plainly than if she had used any alphabetical language, Nature has written over these cliffs, "No landing here." The bristling rocks vaguely remind us of the regulation position of infantry prepared to receive cavalry, when the foot-soldiers crouch down under their own upright bayonets, which are as a spiked wall to the advancing riders.

But in the northern side of the island there is a cove, and in the hope of making this accessible as a harbor of refuge an attempt was made some years ago to cut through the rocks which barred the entrance. A canal of considerable length was excavated, but the work has never been finished. No ship would dare to steer in a gale for portals so narrow and so beset with snares.

The Outer Brewster is not only the wildest in form, but also the richest in color. Great masses of golden-brown sea-weed droop along the water's edge, and above this tremulous fringe the rocks are of varied shades of red. Higher up they are a grayish-green and purple, and in the places which the surf can not reach grass thrives, adding the brilliance of its verdure to the other colors. Though the largest of the islands contains only twenty-five acres, there are pastoral little hollows in some of them where the sea is out of sight, and for all we can see we might be in some upland valley. Cattle are grazing in the tall grass among the bowlders, and the fishermen have built hanging gardens of vegetables upon the step-ladders of rock. But on the calmest days, in the centremost part of the islands, one can always hear the gurgle of the water in the steep-walled caves; odors are blown from the tangles of kelp and moss which tingle in the nostrils as no land-born breeze ever does, and the whistling-buoy off the Graves is never silent; even when the sea is without a ripple the buoy utters its admonition in a voice of pain, like a tormented spirit murmuring against an irrevocable judgment.

From Telegraph Hill, near the old earthworks on the sandy cliffs which bound the opposite side of the entrance to the

RESCUE OF THE CREW OF THE "FANNY PIKE."

The King of Calf Island

harbor, we can see all the islands at once. It was from this elevation that the villagers of Hull saw the smoke and heard the roar of the cannon in the bloody engagement between the *Chesapeake* and the *Shannon;* and here now, with windows that look far out to sea, is a little signal-box in which a vigilant watcher with a spy-glass telegraphs all arrivals to the city. From this hill the Brewsters seem to be a mere group of bowlders scattered by a giant hand; but they are so distributed that they form a wall across the harbor, and leave, as we have said, only a narrow gateway for ships of large tonnage. The shallow passage called Broad Sound is open to the northward, but it resembles the back door of a gentleman's residence, and is only used by such petty craft as steamers from the provinces and coastwise sloops and schooners, while all the more distinguished visitors come in by the main channel between Telegraph Hill and the Little Brewster, or Lighthouse Island.

The Boston Light is at the very entrance to the channel, and the white shaft towers up from its foundations in the reddish-brown rock of the little island like a saint in the desert. Its rays are visible sixteen miles away—one flash every thirty seconds, and with the twin lights of Thatcher's Island in the northeast and Minot's Ledge to the southward—an American Eddystone, pillared in the sea—it defines the position of the harbor to the approaching mariner.

There has been a light here since 1715, for the "generall benifit to Trade," but the present tower was built in 1783, after the destruction of the original building by the British as they passed out of the harbor. It has been frequently strengthened and altered, and is now in excellent condition. The walls are six feet thick at the base and four feet at the top. The lantern is nearly one hundred feet above the ground, and is nearly ten feet in diameter. In this glass house a man can stand upright, and in the centre of it the illuminating apparatus revolves, emitting its penetrating flashes at intervals of thirty seconds. Under the tower there is a steam fog-horn, which splits the air with stentorian warnings when the weather is thick, and between the harsh trumpetings of this instrument the ear catches the moaning of the whistling-buoy anchored off the Graves, and the tolling of the bell-buoy which floats over the perilous Harding's Ledge.

But the custodians of the light have their Lares and Penates enshrined in the comfortable house which is connected with the tower by a covered passage; and when the curtains are drawn over the windows it is cheerful in there, even though the channel is choked with ice, and the winds blow as if they would rock the pillar with its six-foot walls off its foundations. Music exerts its soothing spell through the medium of an accordion, played by Assistant-keeper Gorham; and sometimes, when the family join voices in "Hold the Fort" or "The Sweet By-and-By," Keeper Bates, carried away with rapture, urgently cries, "B'ar down thar, Edward; b'ar down on that instrument!" as if the accordion were the pump of a sinking ship, and salvation depended on the vigor of the performer.

The keepers occasionally have more exciting work to do than trimming their lamps and rubbing the moisture off the panes of glass in the lantern. Bates is possessor of the Humane Society's medal. He does not wear it on his breast, as bicycle-riders and roller-skaters wear their trophies; it is stowed away somewhere in a drawer, and he does not care to talk about it. It is, however, a memento of the time when the *Fanny Pike*, of Calais, was wrecked on the Shag Rocks, the ledge which extends seaward from the point of the Little Brewster. She struck and went to pieces during a very heavy northeasterly snow-storm, and, reckless of the tremendous sea, Bates put off in a small boat to rescue her crew, all of whom he saved, with the aid of Assistant-keeper Bailey and Charles Pochaska, a young fisherman belonging to the Middle Brewster.

The occupants of the other islands are lobster-men, chief among them being old Turner, who from time immemorial has hauled his pots in the waters surrounding the Brewsters. The islands seem enchained by the buoys which mark the spots where their traps are sunk for the voracious crustacean of the dragonish shape, and no object is seen more frequently than the solitary lobster-man making his rounds in his dory to see what spoils the sea has brought him. He takes with him a basket or a keg filled with sculpin, that hideous and marrowless fish, which is only good for bait, and he has so schooled himself to acquiesce in the unalterable that no curse escapes him when, after laborious hauling, he brings the dripping snare to the surface empty; nor, on the other hand, does he give utterance to any feeling of pleasure when the cage-like pot is seen to be full of prisoners as it is dragged over the tipping gunwale. I do not imagine that old Turner ever smiles; his deep-lined visage is puckered with seriousness, and though he is not talkative, an unexplained pathos speaks out of his eyes, which are screened from the forehead by a bristling pair of brows. He has been so saturated with salt-water for nearly fourscore years that he has a half-pickled appearance, and his beard and the curly locks which still flourish, though bleached by age and exposure, are always wet with brine.

In autumn the surrounding waters are brisk with herring, and for a few weeks the denizens of the islands can find occupation with the motley fleet which comes to catch them. This helps them a little; and now and then they have a chance to earn something more by piloting out of her difficulties some vessel which has been caught in the mazes of the rocks.

Winter smites the Brewsters severely; but we prefer that our parting glance at them should reveal them as they appear on a calm summer evening, when they are masses of purple on a golden sea, and the dying light in the west is reflected so brilliantly in the east that it seems to be a promise of perpetual day.

ON CALF ISLAND.

RECOLLECTIONS OF EMERSON

IT is impossible for those who only knew Emerson through his writings to understand the peculiar love and veneration felt for him by those who knew him personally. Only by intercourse with him could the singular force, sweetness, elevation, originality, and comprehensiveness of his nature be fully appreciated; and the friend or acquaintance, however he might differ from him in opinion, felt the pecul-iar fascination of his character, and revolved around this solar mind in obedience to the law of spiritual gravitation—the spiritual law operating, like the natural law, directly as the mass, and inversely as the square of the distance. The friends nearest to him loved and honored him most; but those who only met him occasionally felt the attraction of his spiritual power, and could not mention him without a tribute of respect. There probably never was another man of the first class, with a general system of thought at variance with accredited opinions, who exercised so much gentle, persuasive power over the minds of his opponents. By declining all temptations to controversy he never raised the ferocious spirit which controversy engenders; he went on, year after year, in affirming certain spiritual facts which had been revealed to him when his soul was on the heights of spiritual contemplation ; and if he differed from other minds, he thought it ridiculous to attempt to convert them to his individual insight and experience by *arguments* against their individual insights and their individual experiences. To his readers in the closet, and his hearers on the lecture platform, he poured lavishly out from his intellectual treasury— from the seemingly exhaustless Fortunatus' purse of his mind—the silver and gold, the pearls, rubies, amethysts, opals, and diamonds of thought. If his readers and his audiences chose to pick them up, they were welcome to them; but if they conceived he was deceiving them with sham jewelry, he would not condescend to explain the laborious processes in the mines of meditation by which he had brought the hidden treasures to light. I never shall forget his curt answer to a superficial auditor of one of his lectures. The critic was the intellectual busybody of the place, dipping into everything, knowing nothing, but contriving by his immense loquacity to lead the opinion of the town. "Now, Mr. Emerson," he said, "I appreciated much of your lecture, but I should like to speak to you of certain things in it which did not command my assent and approbation." Emerson turned to him, gave him one of his piercing looks, and replied, "Mr.——, if anything I have spoken this evening met your mood, it is well; if it did not, I must tell you that I never argue on these high questions ;" and as he thus somewhat haughtily escaped from his would-be querist, he cared little that this gossip and chatterer about philosophy and religion would exert all his influence to prevent Emerson from ever lecturing again in that town.

Indeed, everybody who intimately knew this seer and thinker had the good sense never to intrude into the inward sanctities and privacies of his individual meditations, and vulgarly ask questions as to the doubts and conflicts he had encountered in that utter loneliness of thought, where his individual soul, in direct contact, as he supposed, with the "Oversoul," was trying to solve problems of existence which perplex all thoughtful minds. He would do nothing more than make affirmations regarding the deep things of the spirit, which were to be accepted or rejected as they happened to strike or miss the point of inlet into the other intellects he addressed.

This austere reticence was consistent with the most perfect sincerity. Indeed, Emerson preached sincerity as among the first of virtues. He never hesitated to tell the poets, prose writers, reformers, "fanatics," who were his friends and acquaintances, exactly what he thought of them, and there was never a doubt of his mental and moral honesty in their reception of his criticism. He could afford to be sincere, for everybody felt that there was no taint of envy, jealousy, or malice in his nature. When he frankly told such men as Longfellow, Lowell, Holmes, and Whittier that in a particular poem they did not come up to his high ideal of what a poet should be and do, they assented to the criticism, and never dreamed that his judgment was influenced by the failure of his own poetry to attract that public attention which was righteously due to its vital excellence; for they all cordially agreed in thinking that he was the greatest poet the country had produced. There is not a solitary instance of his hesitating, kindly disapprobation of a writer who ranked among his associates which did not make the writer grateful to Emerson for his criticism, and which did not make him sensible that nothing base or mean could have prompted it. So it was with the ardent reformers. Garrison and Phillips, not to mention others, instinctively felt that Emerson was a man not to be assailed when he differed from them in their method of applying to affairs the moral sentiment of which Emerson was the most eloquent and authoritative spokesman ; not, indeed, a voice crying in the wilderness, but a voice which seemed to utter eternal decrees, coming from the serene communion of the speaker with the very source of moral law.

The native elevation of Emerson's mind and the general loftiness of his thinking have sometimes blinded his admirers to the fact that he was one of the shrewdest of practical observers, and was capable of meeting so-called practical men on the level of the facts and principles which they relied upon for success in life. When I first had the happiness to make his acquaintance I was a clerk in a banking house. I have a faint memory of having written in a penny paper a notice of his first volume of Essays which differed altogether from the notices which appeared in business journals of a higher rank and price. The first thing that struck me was the quaint, keen, homely good sense which was one of the marked characteristics of the volume; and I contrasted the coolness of this transcendentalist, whenever he discussed matters relating to the conduct of life, with the fury of delusion under which merchants of established reputation sometimes seemed to be laboring in their mad attempts to resist the operation of the natural laws of trade. They, I thought, were the transcendentalists, the subjective poets, the Rousseaus and Byrons of business, who in their greed were fiercely "accommodating the shows of things to the desires of the mind," without any practical insight of principles or foresight of consequences. Nothing more amazed me, when I was a clerk, recording transactions in which I incurred no personal responsibility, than the fanaticism of capitalists in venturing their money in wild speculations. The willingness to buy waste and worthless Eastern lands; the madness of the men who sunk their millions in certain railroads; and the manias which occasionally seize upon and passionately possess business men, surpassing in folly those fine frenzies of the imagination which are considered to lead to absurdities belonging to poets alone; all these facts early impressed me with the conviction that a transcendentalist of the type of Emerson was as good a judge of investments on earth as he was of investments in the heavens above the earth.

As far as my memory serves me at this time, I think to me, in my youthful presumption, belongs the dubious honor or dishonor of calling him our "Greek-Yankee—a cross between Plato and Jonathan Slick." I am less certain as to the other statement that he was "a Hindoo-Yankee—a cross between Brahma and Poor Richard"; and there are so many competitors for the distinction of originating these epigrammatic impertinences that I should no more dare to present my claims to priority in inventing them than to re-open the controversy respecting the authorship of "Beautiful Snow," or "Rock me to sleep, mother." But I always wondered that the Franklin side of his opulent and genial nature did not draw to him a host of readers who might be repelled by the dazzling though puzzling sentences in which his ideal philosophy found expression. It is to be supposed that such persons refused to read him because they distrusted his constant tendency to combine beauty with use. The sense of beauty, indeed, was so vital an element in the very constitution of his being that it decorated everything it touched. He was a thorough artist, while inculcating maxims of thrift far beyond those of Poor Richard. His beautiful genius could not be suppressed even when he discoursed of the ugliest sides of a farmer's life; he shed an ideal light over pots and cans, over manure heaps and cattle-raising; and when he announced that maxim of celestial prudence, "Hitch your wagon to a star," the transcendentalist was discovered peeping through the economist, and it became hard to believe that he was in ordinary affairs a really practical man. He should have stuck, the economists said, to the wagon, and left out the star, though the introduction of the star was really the most practical thing in his quaint statement of the vital dependence of individual thrift on directing and all-embracing law.

The raciest testimony that ever came within my knowledge as to the soundness of Emerson in practical matters was delivered by a sturdy, stalwart Vermonter in a car on the Fitchburg Railroad. My journey was to be a tedious one of three hundred miles, and when I took my seat in the car, I felt that my fellow-passengers would give me no such glimpses into their characters as would be afforded by a ride of ten miles in a stage-coach. In a railroad car the passengers are gloomily reticent, as if they expected to be launched into eternity at any moment; in a stage they indulge in all the fury of gossip, and reveal themselves while praising or censuring others. There were two persons in front of me, mighty in bulk, but apparently too much absorbed in their own reflections to speak to each other. The train, as usual, stopped at Concord. Then one of the giants turned to the other, and lazily remarked, "Mr. Emerson, I hear, lives in this town."

"Ya-as," was the drawling rejoinder; "and I understand that, in spite of his odd notions, he is a man of *con-sid-er*-able propity."

This apposite judgment was made when Emerson's essays had been translated into most of the languages of Europe, and when the recognition of his genius was even more cordial abroad than it was among his few thousands of appreciative admirers at home; but the shrewd Yankee who uttered it was more impressed by his thrift than by his thinking. He belonged to the respectable race of *de*scendentalists, and was evidently puzzled to understand how a *trans*cendentalist could acquire "propity."

On one occasion, in my early acquaintance with Emerson, I was hastily summoned to lecture at a country town some five miles from Boston, because Emerson, who had been expected to occupy the desk, had not signified his acceptance of the invitation. He either had neglected to answer the letter of the committee, or his own note in reply had miscarried. About ten minutes before the lecture was to begin, Emerson appeared. Of course I insisted on having the privilege of listening to him, rather than compel the audience to listen to me. He generously declared that as the mistake seemed to have arisen from his own neglect, I had the right to the platform. When I solemnly assured him that no lecture would be heard that evening in that town unless he delivered it, he, still somewhat protesting, unrolled his manuscript, and took his place at the desk. The lecture, though perhaps not one of his best lyceum discourses, was better than the best of any other living lecturer. When it was over, he invited me to take a seat in the chaise which had brought him from Boston. I gladly accepted. The horse was, fortunately for me, one of the slowest beasts which ever had the assurance to pretend to convey faster, by carriage, two persons from one point to another than an ordinary pedestrian could accomplish in a meditative walk. The pace was, I think, about two miles an hour. As soon as we got into the chaise, I began to speak of the lecture, and referring to what he had said of the Puritans, I incidentally alluded to the peculiar felicity of his use of the word "grim," and added that I noticed it was a

favorite word of his in his published essays. "Do you say," he eagerly responded, "that I use the word often ?" "Yes," I replied, "but never without its being applicable to the class of persons you are characterizing." He reflected a minute or two, and then said, as if he had experienced a pang of intellectual remorse, "The word is probably passing with me into a mannerism, and I must hereafter guard against it—must banish it from my dictionary."

By this time we had passed out of the town into the long country road which led to Boston. Emerson was in his happiest mood. He entered into a peculiar kind of conversation with his young companion, in which reverie occasionally emerged into soliloquy, and then again became a real talk between the two, though ever liable to subside into reverie and soliloquy if his interlocutor had tact enough to restrain his own tendency to self-expression. I shall never forget that evening. The moon was nearly at its full, undisturbed by a cloud, and the magical moonlight flooded the landscape and skyscape with its soft, gentle, serene, mystical radiance, making strangely unreal all things which seem so substantial when viewed in the "insolent," revealing glare of the sun. Astronomers tell us that the moon is a dead body, all its central fires burned out, and swinging in space as a lifeless mass of matter, good for nothing except to give us light for about half the nights of every month in the year, or to illustrate the operation of the law of gravitation; but of all the lights in the solar or stellar system it is pre-eminently the idealist and transcendentalist of the tenants of the sky; and I never felt its mystical charm more profoundly than on this ride of two hours with Emerson. The lazy horse seemed to be indulging in the luxury of his own reflections, and was only kept from stopping altogether and setting up as a philosopher on his own account, renouncing his ignominious bondage to harness and bridle, by the occasional idle flap of Emerson's whip on his hide—a stimulant to exertion which was so light that I thought its full force could not have broken the backbone of an ordinary fly. So we "tooled on." The conversation at last drifted to contemporary actors who assumed to personate leading characters in Shakspeare's greatest plays. Had I ever seen an actor who satisfied me when he pretended to be Hamlet or Othello, Lear or Macbeth? Yes, I had seen the elder Booth in these characters. Though not perfect, he approached nearer to perfection than any other actor I knew. Nobody, of course, could really satisfy a student of Shakspeare. Still I thought that the elder Booth had a realizing imagination, that he conceived the nature of the person he embodied in its essential individual qualities, that so firm and true was his imaginative grasp of a character that he preserved the unity of one of Shakspeare's complex natures while giving all the varieties of its manifestation. Macready might be the more popular actor of the two, at least in all " refined" circles; but the trouble with Macready was that, while he was gifted with a good understanding, he was strangely deficient in impassioned imagination, and that he accordingly, by a logical process, inferred the character he wished to impersonate by a patient study of Shakspeare's text, and then played the inference.

"Ah," said Emerson, giving a tender touch of his whip to the indolent horse— an animal who, during the three minutes I consumed in eulogizing Booth, showed a natural disposition to go to sleep—"I see you are one of the happy mortals who are capable of being carried away by an actor of Shakspeare. Now whenever I visit the theatre to witness the performance of one of his dramas, I am carried away by the poet. I went last Tuesday to see Macready in *Hamlet*. I got along very well until he came to the passage:—

'thou, dead corse, again, in cómplete steel,
Revisit'st thus the glimpses of the moon;'

and then actor, theatre, all vanished in view of that solving and dissolving imagination, which could reduce this big globe and all it inherits into mere 'glimpses of the moon.' The play went on, but, absorbed in this one thought of the mighty master, I paid no heed to it."

What specially impressed me, as Emerson was speaking, was his glance at our surroundings as he slowly uttered, "glimpses of the moon"; for here above us was the same moon which must have given birth to Shakspeare's thought, its soft rays of consecrating light insinuating a skeptical doubt of the real existence of the world of matter, which, in the fierce glow of the noontide sun, appears so imperturbably conscious of a solid, incontestable reality.

Afterward, in his lecture on Shakspeare, Emerson made use of the thought suggested in our ride by moonlight. He said: "That imagination which dilates the closet he writes in to the world's dimensions, crowds it with agents in rank and order, as quickly reduces the big reality to be the 'glimpses of the moon.'" It seems to me that his expression of the thought, as it occurred to him when he felt the enchantment of the moonlight palpably present to his eyes and imagination, is better in my version than in the comparatively cold language in which he afterward embodied it. But in the printed lecture there is one sentence declaring the absolute insufficiency of any actor, in any theatre, to fix attention on himself while uttering Shakspeare's words, which seems to me the most exquisite statement ever made of the magical suggestiveness of Shakspeare's expression. I have often quoted it, but it will bear quotation again and again, as the best prose sentence ever written on this side of the Atlantic. "The recitation begins; one golden word leaps out immortal from all this painted pedantry, *and sweetly torments us with invitations to its own inaccessible homes.*"

Emerson's voice had a strange power, which affected me more than any other voice I ever heard on the stage or on the platform. It was pure thought translated into purely intellectual tone, the perfect music of spiritual utterance. It is impossible to read his verses adequately without bearing in mind his peculiar accent and emphasis; and some of the grandest and most uplifting passages in his prose lose much of their effect unless the reader can recall the tones of his voice;—a voice now, alas! silent on earth forever, but worthy of being heard in that celestial company which he, "a spirit of the largest size and divinest mettle," has now exchanged for his earthly companions. There was nothing sensual, nothing even sensuous, nothing weakly melodious, in his utterance; but his voice had the stern, keen, penetrating sweetness which made it a fit organ for his self-centred, commanding mind. Yet though peculiar to himself, it had at the same time an impersonal character, as though a spirit was speaking through him. Thus in his lecture on Swedenborg he began with a compact statement of the opinions of the Swedish sage—opinions which seemed to be wide enough to compel all men, pagans and

Christians, to assent to his dogmatic statements. The exposition was becoming monotonous after the lapse of a quarter of an hour. The audience supposed that he was a convert to the Swedenborgian doctrines. At the conclusion of his exposition he paused for half a minute, and then, in his highest, most piercing tones, he put the question, " *Who is* EMANUEL SWEDENBORG ?" his voice rising as he accented every syllable. The effect was electric. Many persons in the audience who had begun to betray a decided disposition to go to sleep waked up. The lecturer then proceeded to give, in short, flashing sentences, a criticism of the Swedenborgian ideas, which seemed to have bored him as they undoubtedly bored many of his hearers, and everybody present eagerly listened to the objections which rendered it reasonable for them to recognize Swedenborg as a very great representative man, without making it necessary for them to abandon the churches to which they were attached and swell the congregations of those of the New Jerusalem.

Again, after reciting the marvels of Shakspeare's genius, placing him above all other writers, he came to the consideration of the serious side of this greatest of poets. What did he teach ? "He converted the elements, which waited on his command, into entertainments. He was master of the revels to mankind. Is it not as if one should have, through majestic powers of science, the comets given into his hand, or the planets and their moons, and should draw them from their orbits to glare with the municipal fireworks on a holiday night, and advertise in all towns, 'very superior pyrotechny this evening'?" All this was delivered in an intense and penetrating yet somewhat subdued tone, and it is hardly possible to convey by printers' ink and types the gradual rise of his voice as he added: "One remembers again the trumpet text in the Koran, 'The heavens and the earth, and all that is between them, *think ye we have* CREATED THEM IN JEST ?'" It is only by a typographical rise from italics to capitals that the faintest indication can be conveyed of the upward march of his voice as it finally pealed forth in " jest."

In another lecture he had occasion to refer to what Mr. Choate had called "the glittering generalities of the Declaration of Independence." If a printer could put it into the smallest type possible to be read by the aid of the microscope, he could not fitly show the scorn embodied in the first part of the sentence in which Emerson replied; nor could the same printer's largest types suggest an idea of the triumphant tone, shot as from a vocal ten-inch gun, in which he gave the second portion of it: "Glittering generalities!—*rather* BLAZING UBIQUITIES!"

Emerson's generous and thorough appreciation of the genius and character of Henry D. Thoreau was shown in many ways and on many occasions. At my first or second visit to Concord, as a lecturer before its Lyceum, he said to me, in the quaint condensed fashion of speech in which he always sketched an original character: "You should know Thoreau. He became disgusted with our monotonous civilization, and went, self-banished, to our Walden woods. There he lives. He built his own hut, cooks his own food, refuses to pay taxes, reads Æschylus, abjures models, and is a great man." From my first introduction, Thoreau seemed to me a man who had experienced Nature as other men are said to have experienced religion. An unmistakable courage, sincerity, and manliness breathed in every word he uttered. I once met him and Mr. Alcott in State Street, in the busiest hour of the day, while I was hurrying to a bank. They had paused before a saloon to get a glimpse of the crowds of merchants and brokers passing up and down the street. "Ah!" I laughingly said, after shaking hands, "I see it is eleven o'clock, and you are going to take a drink." Mr. Alcott, in his sweetest and most serene tones, replied for both : "No; vulgar and ordinary stimulants are not for us. But if you can show us a place where we can drink Bacchus himself, the soul of the inspiration of the poet and the seer, we shall be your debtors forever." There is hardly any biography recently published more interesting than Mr. Sanborn's life of Thoreau; for Mr. Sanborn knew him so intimately that he gives us an "interior" view of the remarkable person he has taken for his subject. Indeed, what can be more interesting than the spectacle of a man whose independence was so rooted in his nature that he coolly set up his private opinion against the average opinion of the human race, and contrived so to incorporate his opinion into his daily life that he came out in the end a victor in the contest ? And in respect to the sympathy that Nature had for *him*, in return for his sympathy with *her*, one feels that he must have been in Emerson's mind when he celebrated, in "Wood Notes," his "forest seer":

"It seemed as if the breezes brought him;
It seemed as if the sparrows taught him;
As if by secret sight he knew
Where, in far fields, the orchis grew.
Many haps fall in the field,
    Seldom seen by wishful eyes;
But all her shows did Nature yield
    To please and win this pilgrim wise.
He saw the partridge drum in the woods;
    He heard the woodcock's evening hymn;
He found the tawny thrush's broods;
    And the shy hawk did wait for him ;
What others did at distance hear,
    And guessed within the thicket's gloom,
Was showed to this philosopher,
    And at his bidding seemed to come."

Miss Fredrika Bremer, in her book recording her tour in the United States, took unwarrantable liberties in describing the households of those persons whose hospitalities she enjoyed. Emerson was specially annoyed at her chatter about him and his family. What vexed him most, however, was her reference to Samuel Hoar, a man whom Emerson, as well as all other citizens of Concord, held in distinguished honor as the living embodiment of integrity, intelligence, wisdom, piety, and benevolence. Emerson's well-known quatrain, with the simple title "S. H.," is a monument to this good and wise man's memory:

"With beams December's planets dart
    His cold eye truth and conduct scanned ;
July was in his sunny heart,
    October in his liberal hand."

Yet this venerable sage, whose native dignity should have shielded him from the impertinence of even a gossip so incorrigible as Miss Bremer, was represented in that lady's book as a garrulous old gentleman who, at his own table, to which she was an invited guest, had made in lieu of the ordinary grace a prayer which she considered so long as to be tiresome. "As if," said Emerson to me, in his deepest indignant tone—"as if Mr. Hoar was expected to pray for her entertainment!"

He had, from the start, a strong antipathy to "spiritism." When departed spirits, by "knockings" and moving furniture, first began to inform us poor mortals that they were still alive—alive, however, in a world which appeared, on the whole, to be worse than that from which death had released them, the great question of im-

mortality was considered by many pious persons to have obtained new evidences of its truth from these materialistic manifestations. Emerson's feeling was that so exquisitely expressed by Tennyson:

"How pure at heart and sound in head,
    With what divine affections bold,
    Should be the man whose thought would hold
An hour's communion with the dead!

"In vain shalt thou, or any, call
    The spirits from their golden day,
    Except, like them, thou too canst say,
My spirit is at peace with all.

"They haunt the silence of the breast,
    Imaginations calm and fair,
    The memory like a cloudless air,
The conscience as a sea at rest."

Emerson's impatience when the subject came up for discussion in a company of intelligent people was amusing to witness. He was specially indignant at the idea of women adopting spiritism as a profession, and engaging to furnish all people with news of their deceased friends at a shilling a head. The enormous vulgarity of the whole thing impressed him painfully, especially when he was told that some of his own friends paid even the slightest attention to the revelations, as he phrased it, of "those seamstresses turned into sibyls, who charged a pistareen a spasm!" Brougham's well-known remark that the idea of Campbell's writing his life added a new horror to death, was a just anticipation of a terrible fact ; for Campbell did write his life, and made a dreadful wreck of Brougham's reputation. Happily, Emerson's last days were clouded by a failure of memory, or he might have mourned that his spirit would be called by "mediums" from "its golden day" to furnish the public with information detailing his present "gossip about the celestial politics," translated from the terse and beautiful language in which he was accustomed to speak his thoughts on earth into the peculiar dialect which uneducated mediums generally use in their rapt communion with the spirits of such men as Bacon, Milton, Webster, and Channing—spirits who, as far as their style of expression and elevation of thought are concerned, appear to have found their immortality a curse—spirits who have dwindled in mental stature just in proportion as they have ascended into the region of incorporeal existence—spirits not made perfect but decidedly *im*perfect in heaven.

After his return from his second visit to

England, in 1847, I had a natural wish to learn his impressions of the distinguished men he had met. His judgment of Tennyson was this, that he was the most "satisfying" of the men of letters he had seen. He witnessed one of Macaulay's brilliant feats in conversation at a dinner where Hallam was one of the guests. The talk was on the question whether the "additional letters" of Oliver Cromwell, lately published by Carlyle, were spurious or genuine. "For my part," said Emerson, "the suspicious fact about them was this, that they all seemed written to sustain Mr. Carlyle's view of Cromwell's character; but the discussion turned on the external evidences of their being forgeries. Macaulay overcame everybody at the table, including Hallam, by pouring out with victorious volubility instances of the use of words in a different meaning from that they bore in Cromwell's time, or by citing words which were not in use at all until half a century later. A question which might have been settled in a few minutes by the consent of a few men of insight opened a tiresome controversy which lasted during the whole dinner. Macaulay seemed to have the best of it; still, I did not like the arrogance with which he paraded his minute information; but then there was a fire, speed, fury, talent, and effrontery in the fellow which were very taking." When Emerson, on his return, made in his *English Traits* his short, contemptuous criticism on Macaulay as a writer representing the material rather than the spiritual interests of England, it is evident that the verbal bullet hit the object at which it was aimed in the white. "The brilliant Macaulay, who expresses the tone of the English governing classes of the day, explicitly teaches that *good* means good to eat, good to wear, material commodity; that the glory of modern philosophy is its direction or 'fruit'; to yield economical inventions; and that its merit is to avoid ideas and to avoid morals. He thinks it the distinctive merit of the Baconian philosophy, in its triumph over the old Platonic, its disentangling the intellect from theories of the all-Fair and the all-Good, and pinning it down to the making a better sick-chair and a better wine-whey for an invalid; this not ironically, but in good faith; that 'solid advantage,' as he calls it—meaning always sensual benefit—is the only good." This criticism, though keen, is undoubtedly one-sided. Macaulay felt it. In the height of his fame, in January, 1850, he writes in his diary: "Many readers give credit for profundity to whatever is obscure, and call all that is perspicuous shallow. But *coragio!* and think of A.D. 2850. Where will your Emersons be then?" Well, it may be confidently predicted, they will at least march abreast of the Macaulays.

In all Emerson's experience as a lecturer there was only one occasion when he received that tribute to a radical orator's timely eloquence which is expressed in hisses. The passage of the Fugitive Slave Law stirred him into unwonted moral passion and righteous wrath. He accepted an invitation to deliver a lecture in Cambridgeport, called for the purpose of protesting against that infamous anomaly in jurisprudence and insult to justice which had the impudence to call itself a law. Those who sympathized with him were there in force; but a score or two of foolish Harvard students came down from the college to the hall where the lecture was delivered, determined to assert "the rights of the South," and to preserve the threatened Union of the States. They were the rowdiest, noisiest, most brainless set of young gentlemen that ever pretended to be engaged in studying "the humanities" at the chief university of the country. Their only arguments were hisses and groans whenever the most illustrious of American men of letters uttered an opinion which expressed the general opinion of the civilized world. If he quoted Coke, Holt, Blackstone, Mansfield, they hissed all these sages of the law because their judgments came from the illegal lips of Emerson. It was curious to watch him as, at each point he made, he paused to let the storm of hisses subside. The noise was something he had never heard before; there was a queer, quizzical, squirrel-like or bird-like expression in his eye as he calmly looked round to see what strange human animals were present to make such sounds; and when he proceeded to utter another indisputable truth, and it was responded to by another chorus of hisses, he seemed absolutely to enjoy the new sensation he experienced, and waited for these signs of disapprobation to stop altogether before he resumed his discourse. The experience was novel; still there was not the slightest tremor in his voice, not even a trace of the passionate resentment which a speaker under such circumstances and impediments usually feels, and which urges him into the cheap retort about serpents, but a quiet waiting for the time when he should be allowed to go on with the next sentence. During the whole evening he never uttered a word which was not written down in the manuscript from which he read. Many of us at the time urged Emerson to publish the lecture; ten or fifteen years after, when he was selecting material for a new volume of essays, I entreated him to include in it the old lecture at Cambridgeport; but he, after deliberation, refused, feeling probably that being written under the impulse of the passion of the day, it was no fit and fair summary of the characters of the statesmen he assailed. Of one passage in the lecture I preserve a vivid remembrance. After affirming that the eternal law of righteousness, which rules all created things, nullified the enactment of Congress, and after citing the opinions of several magnates of jurisprudence, that immoral laws are void and of no effect, he slowly added, in a scorching and biting irony of tone which no words can describe, "but still a little Episcopalian clergyman assured me yesterday that the Fugitive Slave Law must be obeyed and enforced." After the lapse of thirty years, the immense humor of bringing all the forces of nature, all the principles of religion, and all the decisions of jurists to bear with their Atlas weight on the shoulders of one poor little conceited clergyman to crush him to atoms, and he in his innocence not conscious of it, makes me laugh now as all the audience laughed then, the belligerent Harvard students included.

Emerson's good sense was so strong that it always seemed to be specially awakened in the company of those who were most in sympathy with his loftiest thinking. Thus, when "the radical philosophers" were gathered one evening at his house, the conversation naturally turned on the various schemes of benevolent people to reform the world. Each person present had a panacea to cure all the distempers of society. For hours the talk ran on, and before bed-time came, all the sin and misery of the world had been apparently expelled from it, and our planet was reformed and transformed into an abode of human angels, and virtue and happiness were the lot of each human being. Emerson listened, but was sparing of speech. Probably he felt, with Lamennais, that if facts did not resist thoughts, the earth would in a short time become uninhabitable. At any rate, he closed the *séance* with the remark: "A few of us old codgers meet at the fireside on a pleasant evening, and in thought and hope career, balloon-like, over the whole universe of matter and mind, finding no resistance to our theories, because we have, in the sweet delirium of our thinking, none of those obstructive facts which face the practical reformer the moment he takes a single forward step; then we go to bed; and the pity of it is we wake up in the morning feeling that we are the same poor old imbeciles we were before!"

A transcendentalist is sometimes compelled, by what Cowley calls "the low conveniencies of fate," to subordinate the principles of his system of thought to the practical exigency of the hour. A curious illustration of this fact occurred, some fifteen or twenty years ago, in the early days of the "Saturday Club." After some preliminary skirmishing, Emerson asked Agassiz to give him a short exposition of his leading ideas as a naturalist in respect to what was known of the genesis of things. Agassiz, in his vehement, rapid way, began at the microscopic "cell," beyond which no discovered instrument of investigation could go, and proceeded to show the gradual ascent from this "cell" to the highest forms of animal life. He took about half an hour in making his condensed statement, and then Emerson's turn began. "But, Mr. Agassiz, I see that all your philosophy is under the law of succession; it is genealogical; it is based on the reality of time; but you must know that some of us believe with Kant that time is merely a subjective form of human thought, having no objective existence." Then suddenly taking out his watch, and learning that he had only fifteen minutes to get to the Fitchburg Railroad in order to be in "time" to catch the last train to Concord on that afternoon, he took his hat, swiftly donned his overcoat, and as he almost rushed from the room he assured Agassiz that he would discuss the subject at some other "time," when he was less pressed by his engagements at home. For years afterward, when the transcendentalist met the naturalist at the club, I watched in vain for a recurrence of the controversy. I do not think it was ever re-opened between them.

Many of Emerson's friends and acquaintances thought that his sense of humor was almost as keen as his sense of Beauty and his sense of Right. I do not remember an instance in my conversations with him, when the question came up of his being not understood, or, what is worse, misunderstood by the public, that he did not treat the matter in an exquisitely humorous way, telling the story of his defeats in making himself comprehended by the audience or the readers he addressed as if the misapprehensions of his meaning were properly subjects of mirth, in which he could heartily join. This is the test of the humorist, that he can laugh *with* those who laugh *at* him. For example, on one occasion I recollect saying that of all his college addresses I thought the best was that on "The Method of Nature," delivered before the Society of the Adelphi, in Waterville College, Maine, August 11, 1841. He then gave me a most amusing account of the circumstances under which the oration was delivered. It seems that after conceiving the general idea of the address, he banished himself to Nantasket Beach, secluded himself for a fortnight in a room in the public-house, the windows of which looked out on the ocean, moving from his chamber and writing-desk only to take early morning and late evening walks on the beach; and thought, at the end, he had produced something which was worthy of being listened to even by the Society of the Adelphi. At that time a considerable portion of the journey to Waterville had to be made by stage. He arrived late in the evening, travel-worn and tired out, when almost all the sober inhabitants of Waterville had gone to bed. It appeared that there was some doubt as to the particular citizen's house at which he was to pass the night. "The stage-driver," said Emerson, "stopped at one door; rapped loudly; a window was opened; something in a night-gown asked what he wanted; the stage-driver replied that he had inside a man who *said* he was to deliver the lit-ra-rye oration to-morrow, and thought he was to stop there; but the night-gown disappeared, with the chilling remark that he was not to stay at *his* house. Then we went to another, and still another, dwelling, rapped, saw similar night-gowns and heard similar voices at similar raised windows; and it was only after repeated disturbances of the peace of the place that the right house was hit, where I found a hospitable reception. The next

day I delivered my oration, which was heard with cold, silent, unresponsive attention, in which there seemed to be a continuous unuttered rebuke and protest. The services were closed by prayer, and the good man who prayed, prayed for the orator, but also warned his hearers against heresies and wild notions, which appeared to me of that kind for which I was held responsible. The address was really written in the heat and happiness of what I thought a real inspiration; but all the warmth was extinguished in that lake of iced water." The conversation occurred so long ago that I do not pretend to give Emerson's exact words, but this was the substance of his ludicrous statement of the rapture with which he had written what was so frigidly received. He seemed intensely to enjoy the fun of his material discomforts and his spiritual discomfiture.

Emerson had some strange tastes and some equally strange distastes in regard to poets. Usually his criticism was wonderfully acute and accurate, compressing into a few significant words what other critics would fail to convey in an elaborate analysis. He darted by a combination of insight and instinct to the exact point in a poet's writings where the poetry in him was best embodied and expressed; and his reading of the passages which had most impressed him excelled that of the most accomplished professional elocutionist I ever listened to. But he never could endure Shelley, and declared that if the objections of practical men to poetry rested on such poets as Shelley, he should cordially agree with them. He admitted, of course, the beauty of "The Skylark" and "The Cloud"; but as an apostle of hope and health and cheer, he could not pardon the note of lamentation which runs through Shelley's poetry, and thought that his gifts of imagination and melody, remarkable as they were, were no atonement for his unmanly wailing and sobbing over the ills of existence. A poet, he said, should invigorate, not depress, the soul. It was in vain to tell him that such ethereal powers of imagination and sentiment as Shelley possessed should be considered apart from the direction they happened to take, owing to the unfortunate circumstances of his life. No; he would discard such sick souls from his sympathy, as he would discard all sick bodies. He showed always a comical disgust of sick people generally. Everybody who heard his lecture called "Considerations by the Way," must remember the peculiar force and bitterness with which he described sickness "as a cannibal, which eats up all the life and youth it can lay hold of and absorbs its own sons and daughters. I figure it as a pale, wailing, distracted phantom, absolutely selfish, heedless of what is good and great, attentive to its own sensations, losing its soul, and afflicting other souls with meanness and mopings, and with ministrations to its voracity of trifles. Dr. Johnson severely said, 'Every man is a rascal as soon as he is sick.'" And then he went on to say that we should give the sick every aid, but not give them "ourselves." Then followed a cruelly wise remark, which shocked many in the audience, and the real import of which was taken only by a few. "I once asked a clergyman in a country town who were his companions? what men of ability he saw? He replied that he spent his time with the sick and the dying. I said he seemed to me to need quite other company, and all the more that he had this; for if people were sick and dying to any purpose, we would leave all and go to them, but, as far as I had observed, they were as frivolous as the rest, and sometimes much more frivolous." Every one who has observed how many conscientious clergymen are converted into nerveless moral valetudinarians, losing all power of communicating healthy moral life, by constantly acting as spiritual nurses to the sick, complaining, and ever-dying but never dead members of their parishes, must acknowledge the half-truth in this apparently harsh statement.

The feeling that it is the duty of the teacher of his fellow-men, whether preacher, poet, romancer, or philosopher, to console by cheering and invigorating them, entered into all his criticism. When *The Scarlet Letter*, in many respects the greatest romance of the century, was published, he conceded that it was a work of power; "but," he said to me, with a repulsive shrug of the shoulders as he uttered the word, "it is ghastly." It seemed to me that "ghostly" would be a more truthful characterization of it; but it was impossible to remove from his mind the general impression any book had left on it by arguments. "Ghastly!" he repeated— "ghastly!" He seemed quietly impregnable to any considerations respecting the masterly imaginative analysis which Hawthorne had displayed in depicting the spiritual moods of his guilty hero and heroine, and his keen perception of the outlying spiritual laws which, being violated in their sin, reacted with such terrible force in their punishment. The book left an unpleasant impression on him; that was enough, as it was enough to lead him to condemn Goethe's "Faust."

In judging of works of immensely less importance, which only excited his ridicule, his irony was often delicious. Then there were popular books whose daily sale exceeded that of all his own volumes in ten years; these he spoke of with admirable humor and good-humor. Talking with him once on the character of the first Napoleon, I asked him if he had read the Rev. Mr. Abbott's history of the exploits and objects of the Emperor. "Yes," he dryly answered; "and it has given to me an altogether original idea of that notable man. It seems to teach that the great object of Napoleon in all his wars was to establish in benighted Europe our New England system of Sunday-schools. A book like that is invaluable; it revolutionizes all our notions of historical men."

In such recollections of Emerson as I have here recorded there has been, of course, no attempt to portray his character as a whole, but simply to exhibit some aspects of it. There was a side of his nature, or rather the very centre of his nature—his "heart of heart"—on which I suppose even his intimate friends—with whom I do not presume to rank myself— would speak with a certain reserve. Dr. Bartol, one of these friends, whose beautiful tribute to Emerson has been published, hints of the loneliness of thought in which a large portion of his life was probably passed. The incommunicable elements in Emerson's spiritual experience must, indeed, have exceeded what he felt himself capable of communicating, not to speak of that portion he was indisposed to communicate. In one of his most characteristic essays there is a pregnant sentence in which he declares that, in its highest moods, "the soul gives itself, alone, original, and pure, to the Lonely, Original, and Pure, who, on that condition, gladly inhabits, leads, and speaks through it." This mystic communion of the soul with its source had, with him, a solemnity so sacred that it must needs be secret; it either exalted his mortal nature into a "beatitude past utterance," or depressed it with ominous misgivings and "obstinate questionings" which could find no adequate outlet in words; and though we detect in the noblest passages of his writings traces of this immediate personal communion with the Highest and the Divine, it is doubtful if he ever spoke of it to his nearest relations and friends. In this he differed from most men of profound religious genius, who are sometimes garrulous on those points where he was inexorably mute. He never exclaimed, as other pious souls have exclaimed, "See what the Lord has done for *me!*" His reticence was the modesty of spiritual manliness. What he felt on such high matters he felt to be ineffable and unutterable; but how awful must have been at times his sense of spiritual loneliness, his lips austerely shut even when the closest, dearest, and most trusted companions of his soul delicately hinted their wish he would speak; but he died and made no sign.

Still, at just one remove from the sacred secrecy of his inmost individual consciousness and experience, he is ever found to be the frankest of writers. Matthew Arnold has revived a phrase originally used by Swift in his "Battle of the Books," and made it stand as a mark of the perfection of intellectual character. It is curious that this phrase, "sweetness and light," should have been uttered by the greatest cynical apostle of bitterness and gloom who has left a record of his genius in English literature, and also uttered, as far as the side he took is concerned, in an ignominious literary brawl, in which he was the champion of Temple, Boyle, and Atterbury, against Bentley, the greatest scholar in Europe. Bentley was, of course, victor in the contest, even in the opinion of all candid scholars at first opposed to him.

But "sweetness and light" are precious and inspiring only so far as they express the essential sweetness of the disposition of the thinker, and the essential illuminating power of his intelligence. Emerson's greatness came from his character. Sweetness and light streamed from him because they were *in* him. In everything he thought, wrote, and did we feel the presence of a personality as vigorous and brave as it was sweet, and the particular radical thought he at any time expressed derived its power to animate and illuminate other minds from the might of the manhood which was felt to be within and behind it. To "sweetness and light" he therefore added the prime quality of fearless manliness.

If the force of Emerson's character was thus inextricably blended with the force of all his faculties of intellect and imagination, and the refinement of all his sentiments, we have still to account for the peculiarities of his genius, and to answer the question, why do we instinctively apply the epithet "Emersonian" to every characteristic passage in his writings? We are told that he was the last in a long line of clergymen, his ancestors, and that the modern doctrine of heredity accounts for the impressive emphasis he laid on the moral sentiment; but that does not solve the puzzle why he unmistakably differed in his nature and genius from all other Emersons. An imaginary genealogical chart of descent connecting him with Confucius or Gotama would be more satisfactory. At the time he acquired notoriety but had not yet achieved fame, it was confidently asserted in all Boston circles that his brother Charles, the "calm, chaste scholar" celebrated by Holmes, was greatly his superior in ability, and would, had he not died early, have entirely eclipsed Ralph; Emerson himself, the most generous and loving of brothers, always inclined to this opinion; but there is not an atom of evidence that Charles, had he lived, would have produced works which would be read by a choice company of thinkers and scholars all over the world, which would be translated into all the languages of Europe, and would be prized in London and Edinburgh, in Berlin and Vienna, in Rome and Paris, as warmly as they were in Boston and New York. What distinguishes *the* Emerson was his *exceptional* genius and character, that something in him which separated him from all other Emersons, as it separated him from all other eminent men of letters, and impressed every intelligent reader with the feeling that he was not only "original but aboriginal." Some traits of his mind and character may be traced back to his ancestors, but what doctrine of heredity can give us the genesis of his genius? Indeed, the safest course to pursue is to quote his own words, and despairingly confess that it is the nature of genius "to spring, like the rainbow daughter of Wonder, from the invisible, to abolish the past, and refuse all history."

WILLIAMSTOWN

THE rapidity with which the early settlers of New England spread themselves over a wide reach of territory is somewhat surprising. Few as they were, Eastern Massachusetts was too strait for them, and in less than a score of years they had pushed through the intervening wilderness a hundred miles, and established themselves in the valley of the Connecticut at Windsor, Wethersfield, Hartford, and Springfield. Gradually other settlements were made along that attractive valley, from Saybrook as far as Northfield. "It was not long," says Cotton Mather, "before the Massachuset Colony was become like a hive overstocked with bees, and many of the new inhabitants entertained thoughts of swarming into plantations extended further into the country. . . . . The fame of Connecticut River, a long, fresh, rich river, had made a little Nilus of it, in the expectation of the good people about the Massachuset Bay, whereupon many of the planters, belonging especially to the towns of Cambridge, Dorchester, Watertown, and Roxbury, took up resolutions to travel an hundred miles westward from those towns for a further settlement upon this famous river."

But it was nearly a century before the westward-moving tide reached the next valley, that of the Housatonic and the Hoosac, although by that time there were more than 300,000 people within the settled portions of Massachusetts and Connecticut. Not only was the intervening wilderness a barrier to the further progress of migration toward the West, but there was a dispute between the English and the Dutch as to the boundary between Massachusetts and New York, which served to deter settlers for a long time from venturing to seek homes in this direction. A barrier, however, of a more formidable character was the fear of the Indians.

The early relations of the colonists of New England to the Indians were those of peace and amity. The account of them forms a beautiful chapter in our colonial history. But these amicable relations were soon disturbed. As ship after ship followed the *Mayflower*, and poured its living cargo upon the soil of New England, and the whites spread themselves over their fairest hunting and fishing grounds, the Indians naturally became jealous of those who seemed to be crowding them from their homes. Their lands, though they had been parted with voluntarily, and at a price satisfactory to them at the time, were yet parted with. They saw themselves dispossessed forever. Nor was it pleasant for them to see the threatened predominance of another race, where they had been so long the undisputed lords of the soil. It was an easy thing for the natural feeling of jealousy to be converted into suspicion, and then into hate. And this was made the easier by the incitements furnished by the French colonists of Canada. From the time of the first settlements almost there had been a strife between England and France for the possession of the new continent. As the colonies grew in population and strength, they shared to a large extent the feelings of the parent countries. Taking advantage of the disturbed feeling of the Indians toward the English, the French entered into alliance with them, and stimulated them to open hostility.

There were two natural routes of approach to the English settlements from the direction of Canada. One was by the Connecticut River; the other was down Lake Champlain and the Hudson, until the valley of the Hoosac was reached, then eastward along this valley and that of the Deerfield, which tends in the same direction. By either of these routes it was comparatively easy for the French and Indians to make a descent upon the colonies and harass them. This they did through a long series of years. For nearly a century life on the borders of the English settlements was one of almost constant fear. The stories of sudden attack, of the burning of dwellings, of whole villages, of death by the tomahawk, of death on the march through pathless woods in winter, as the victims of these assaults were taken into captivity, form a large portion of our early history.

On the breaking out of war between England and France in 1744, Massachusetts felt obliged to take additional measures for the defense of her exposed northern and western borders. Accordingly, a new line of forts was built, stretching from the Connecticut, near the boundary of New Hampshire, to the extreme western limit of Massachusetts. The westernmost of these forts, and the strongest, as it needed to be, was erected in the valley of the Hoosac, near where that stream breaks through the lofty mountain barrier which divides Massachusetts and Vermont from New York. Through this gateway which nature had provided, the French and their Indian allies, if unopposed, could make their way, as they had done, to the important towns of Deerfield, Hadley, Northampton, and Westfield on the east, or go southward through the valleys of Berkshire, lately begun to be settled, and threaten all that region, and Connecticut beyond.

The superintendence of the erection and the command of this new line of forts were intrusted to Captain Ephraim Williams, his head-quarters being at the one farthest west, which was named Fort Massachusetts. This fort was located in a beautiful meadow in the valley of the Hoosac, which is here narrowed to a quarter of a mile in width by the towering mass of Saddleback or Graylock on the south, and the Clarksburg and Stamford mountains on the north.

The fort was built of logs, and surrounded with an inclosure of pickets nearly a hundred rods in extent, made of squared posts driven into the ground so as to make an impervious barrier. It was mounted with a few swivels at the best, had a garrison seldom numbering a hundred men, and was defensible against musketry alone.

Captain Williams was young, but had already inspired confidence in his ability. He was of good family, his father having been one of four chosen by the provincial government to settle in Stockbridge when the mission to the Indians in that region was established by Rev. John Sergeant. Williams himself had spent much of his life at sea. He had visited England, Spain, and Holland. He had become familiar with danger in his ocean voyages, while by his wide and varied intercourse with men he had acquired much knowledge, and become accomplished in manners. He was already well known by his repeated engagements as agent at the General Court.

The trust now committed to him he discharged with great fidelity and success. Under his vigorous management scouts were kept continually passing and repassing along the line of forts in order to give prompt notice of the approach of any foe. It was a hazardous service which they had to perform, and as an inducement to engage in it, the provincial government offered a bounty of £30 for every Indian scalp.

A successful attack was made upon Fort Massachusetts in 1746, by a combined force of French and Indians, nearly one thousand strong. The fort was destroyed, but was rebuilt the next year, and its defense was gallantly maintained until the Treaty of Aix-la-Chapelle brought a cessation of hostilities.

At the breaking out of war again in the continued struggle of the French and English for the supremacy, the danger of invasion through the gateway of the

Hoosac was greater than before. When, therefore, news came that the Indians had made an attack upon Dutch Hoosac—a settlement within the jurisdiction of New York, but only ten miles from Fort Massachusetts—and that a small party had even penetrated the colony, and gone as far south as Stockbridge, spreading great alarm along their course, the colonial government saw at once the necessity of taking prompt measures for the protection of the settlers. The forts on the frontier were immediately strengthened, and some new ones built.

Williams, who had successfully defended the frontier during the previous hostilities, was again put in charge, with the rank of major. The next year, however, he was relieved of his command at the fort, and placed at the head of the Hampshire Regiment—part of a force of five thousand men raised by the colonies for the purpose of taking the offensive against the French, and capturing Crown Point, one of the most important fortresses held by them. The attack upon Crown Point was part of a comprehensive plan to make a vigorous assault upon the French at different points. It embraced simultaneous expeditions to Louisburg, Quebec, Crown Point, Niagara, and Fort du Quesne.

The expedition to Crown Point was put in charge of Colonel Johnson. While encamped at the southern extremity of Lake George, waiting for ammunition and transports, Baron Dieskau, with a large force of French, Canadians, and Indians, arrived in that vicinity, with the purpose of attacking Fort Edward, a garrison near by. Johnson, learning of the presence of Dieskau's force, at once sent out a party of one thousand soldiers and two hundred Indians to intercept the enemy. Colonel Williams was appointed to the command. He had proceeded but a little way on his march, however, when he found himself almost surrounded by the French and Indians, who had left Fort Edward on one side, and were advancing upon Johnson's army, and now were lying in ambush awaiting his approach, of which they had doubtless been informed by their scouts. It was a wild wooded region, and Williams's path was through a deep glen. All at once the yells of the savages and volleys of musketry broke upon his ear, and revealed his danger, while the sudden surprise threw his men into confusion. Calm and undaunted

COLONEL WILLIAMS'S MONUMENT, NEAR LAKE GEORGE.

himself, Williams endeavored to get his force out of the glen, upon the higher ground, where they would be less exposed, and could contend with the enemy upon equal terms. As he was doing this, standing upon a rock, or by the side of it, he fell, pierced through the head by a musket-ball.

At his fall Williams was saved from the indignity of the scalping-knife of his Indian foes by the considerate devotion of his comrades in arms, who succeeded in concealing his body from the savages. It was subsequently buried on a height of ground a few rods from the spot where he fell, at the foot of a huge pine-tree near the road. There it lay unmarked by any other monument for nearly a century from the time of his death. Then, moved by the consideration of his great worth and his great benefactions to the country and to the cause of learning, the loving hands of another generation placed a large pyramidal bowlder upon the grave of Williams, inscribed with the initials E. W., and erected also upon the rock which marks the spot where he fell an enduring monument of marble.

But the history of Fort Massachusetts

WEST COLLEGE.

is not yet fully told, and we must turn back to it. Its builder and commander had fallen, but no serious attack was made upon it subsequent to his death. A lasting peace came in three years from the battle near Fort Edward. The French colonies on the north were surrendered to Great Britain. There was no more fear of invasions from Canada. The frontier line of forts no longer needed to be garrisoned for the protection of defenseless settlers. The soldiers could be dismissed to the peaceful industries of life, and the forts themselves be left to fade from sight, as they have done, under the slow decay of time. There is nothing now to mark the site of the old fort except an elm-tree, which a few persons interested in the history of the fort planted not many years ago for the purpose of marking a spot memorable for gallant deeds there wrought, and for its important connection with the history of our country.

At the close of the previous war, in 1748, Williams had retired from his frontier post, and made his home at Hatfield and with a brother at Deerfield. But his long service on the border and in com-mand of the fort had given him a deep interest in that region, and in the soldiers and settlers with whom he had been associated in times of peril. The year after leaving the fort, and mainly at his instigation, it seems, the General Court appointed a committee "to survey and lay out two townships on the Hoosac River, each of the contents of six miles square, in the best of the land, and in as regular form as may be, joining them together; and return a correct plat of said townships; and also to return the course and distance of said towns from Fort Massachusetts."

In 1750, a committee was ordered to lay out the west township of Hoosac into sixty-three contiguous home-lots of from thirteen to fourteen acres, each of these home-lots carrying with it a sixty-third part of the whole township. True to the original custom of the New England colonies, one of these lots was reserved for the first settled minister of the new town, and another as a permanent fund for the support of the ministry. A third lot was set apart for the benefit of schools. The committee were also directed "to grant as many lots to the soldiers of the garrison of Fort Massachusetts as they should think proper." A grant of one hundred and ninety acres in the east township was also made by the General Court to Williams himself, by which he became the owner of the very meadow in which Fort Massachusetts stood.

When the west township was actually laid out, more than half of the lots were taken by the officers and soldiers of the old fort. Williams, among the rest, drew two lots, though these chanced to be of poor quality. The settlement of both townships, under the protection of the fort and one or two block-houses, went on rapidly.

On his way from Deerfield to engage in the expedition against Crown Point, Colonel Williams was once more at Fort Massachusetts, and there met again many of his old comrades, several of whom had become settlers in the new township which he had secured for them four or five years before. Some of these old companions in arms put themselves again under his leadership on the march to Crown Point. Williams seems to have had some foreboding that he was not to return from this expedition, but was looking upon the old fort and the fair fields of the Hoosac around it for the last time. It is said that

as he parted from the garrison he gave some intimation that, in the event of his death, he should leave them some further evidence of his esteem. Being taken ill as his regiment halted for a little at Albany, he was reminded of the uncertainty of life, and that the purpose entertained for some time past of making a final disposition of his property had not been carried out. He proceeded, therefore, at once to make his will. In this instrument, after making some minor bequests to relatives and friends, he declares: "It is my will and pleasure that all of the residue of my real estate, not otherwise disposed of, be sold by my executors, or the survivor of them, within five years after an established peace (which a good God soon grant!), according to their discretion, and that the same be put out at interest on good security, and that the interest money yearly arising therefrom, and the interest arising from my just debts due to me, and not otherwise disposed of, be improved by said executors, and by such as they shall appoint trustees for the charity aforesaid after them, for the support and maintenance of a free school in the township west of Fort Massachusetts (commonly called West Township) forever, provided said township fall within the juris-

EAST COLLEGE AND LIBRARY.

diction of the province of Massachusetts Bay, and continue under that jurisdiction, and provided also the Governor of said province, with the Assembly of said province, shall (when a suitable number of inhabitants are settled there) incorporate the same into a town by the name of Williamstown."

The will then goes on to make other dispositions of the property if these conditions are not complied with.

The will is dated July 22, 1755. Williams fell on the 8th of September following.

The history of Colonel Williams's bequest is interesting as showing what fruit may come from a small seed, and the changed condition of things and of our ideas and estimates since the time that his will was made. The amount of property left by Williams would seem to any one now ridiculously small for the purpose of establishing a school of any sort. Even at the time the bequest was made, it was so inadequate to its purpose that it was only after it had been converted into money and carefully husbanded by the executors, by being allowed to increase at compound interest for thirty years, that they felt warranted in attempting to put the contemplated school in actual operation. At length, in the year 1785, they ventured to apply to the Legislature for an act enabling them to fulfill the intention of the testator. Thereupon an act was passed incorporating Theodore Sedgwick and eight other persons of the highest distinction in Western Massachusetts "trustees of the donation of Ephraim Williams for maintaining a free school in Williamstown."

The trustees, almost all of whom were graduates of Yale College, held their first meeting soon after the act of incorporation was passed. They found the property intrusted to them so insufficient for the purpose for which it was designed that they at once appointed three of their number a committee to procure additional funds. At the same time they voted that the school should be open and free not only to the people of Williamstown, but to "the free citizens of the American States indiscriminately." That they were undertaking to establish something more than an ordinary free school is shown also by a vote, passed at an early stage of their proceedings, that the building for the school should be constructed of bricks,

and should be seventy-two feet in length, forty feet wide, and three stories high. As they went on with their work, however, the ideas of the trustees seem to have expanded, and the building finally erected, and as it stands to-day, is eighty-two feet in length, forty-two in width, and four stories high. It was a notable structure for the place and the time, and compares favorably with many buildings of more pretentious character and more recent date. It is, indeed, a marvel that an edifice so solid and imposing in appearance as it is to-day should have been erected nearly a century ago, and in what was almost literally a wilderness. This is the building now known as West College. The site overlooks the town and a large portion of the adjacent country, the range of vision being limited only by the lofty hills or mountains which lift themselves on every side.

It is another indication of the scarcity of money then, as well as of a change in moral apprehension, that the trustees felt obliged to resort to the help of a lottery in order to secure the funds needful for the erection of their contemplated building. The Legislature, on their application, gave them a grant for a lottery, and the result was an addition of £1037 18s. 2d. to their resources. With this, and a subscription of $2000 by the residents of Williamstown, they were at length enabled to erect their building.

The school was opened October 20, 1791, with the Rev. Ebenezer Fitch, a graduate of Yale College, as preceptor, and Mr. John Lester as assistant. There were two departments—a grammar school, or academy, and an English free school. In the first, the usual college studies of that day were taught; in the second, instruction in the common English studies was given to a company of boys from the higher classes in the common schools of the town.

The school was popular and successful from the beginning. There was no institution so attractive to those ambitious of learning nearer than the colleges at Hanover and New Haven. Young men came to it from the neighboring States, and even from Canada. The popularity of the school was such, indeed, as to lead the trustees to petition the Legislature, the next year after its opening, to erect it into a college. This the Legislature did in 1793, and at the same time made a grant to the new college of $4000. The English free school was now discontinued, but the academy was maintained for several years. Three years later, the Legislature made a further grant of two townships of land in Maine, which was then a part of Massachusetts. These townships were sold for about $10,000, and enabled the trustees, a year or two afterward, to erect another building, known as East College.

The college has had from the beginning an able class of instructors, men of solid rather than showy and superficial qualities, and latterly the instruction has been given wholly by professors, no tutors being employed. A letter of the first president to a friend, as early as 1799, will indicate the character with which the college began. He says: "Things go on well in our infant seminary. Our number is hardly so large as last year. The scarcity of money is one cause of the decline, some leaving through mere poverty. But our ambition is to make good scholars rather than add to our numbers, and in this we mean not to be outdone by any college in New England. Perseverance in the system we have adopted will eventually give reputation to this institution in the view of all who prefer the useful to the showy." An extract from the inaugural address of President Hopkins, nearly forty years later, will show that the college then maintained its early character: "I have no ambition to build up here what would be called a great institution; the wants of the community do not require it. But I do desire, and shall labor, that this may be a *safe* college; that its reputation may be sustained and raised still higher; that the plan of instruction I have indicated may be carried out more fully; that here there may be health, and cheerful study, and kind feelings, and

MISSION PARK MONUMENT.

pure morals; and that, in the memory of future students, college life may be made a still more verdant spot." The prominent characteristics of the college during Dr. Hopkins's long administration, as well as from the beginning, could hardly be better expressed than by those words of his, "health, cheerful study, kind feelings, and pure morals." The situation of the college among the far-famed hills of Berkshire is evidently favorable to health; and all who know anything of it know that during the protracted and distinguished administration to which we have just alluded, the college has had an enviable reputation as a place where the students have been interested in their studies, and in general have been faithful in their work; where the moral tone of life has been high, and where the instructors have sought to blend the offices of teacher and friend, having the true conception of edu-

JACKSON HALL.

One would be safe in saying that in no college is the religious atmosphere more perceptible or more wholesome than at Williams. Free alike from cant and bigotry, from looseness and indifference, the religious tone of the college is pure and healthful as the mountain air which her students breathe. It is, moreover, not the least of the distinctions of this institution that, while a large portion of her students have been persons of avowedly Christian character, the first movement in our country for the Christianization of the heathen world had its origin here. The stranger who visits Williamstown and asks for its most interesting objects will be directed to Mission Park. As he enters its quiet and beautiful seclusion, a marble monument, surmounted by a massive globe—with the continents and the islands of the sea boldly outlined on its surface—emblematic of the worldwide reach of their enterprise, marks the spot where Mills and Richards and Hall and Nott, with their associates, met from time to time, in the early days of the college, to ponder and pray over that divine commission, "Go ye into all the world and preach the gospel to every creature." In those ponderings and prayers originated our great Board of Foreign Missions. And now, among all the gatherings and attractive scenes which mark Commencement week, there is none of more delightful and at the same time profound interest than the assembly around that monument in the park on the Sabbath afternoon, when, for an hour, amid the utterances of prayer and song, and the words of one and another veteran returned from the distant mission fields of the world, the heart is touched with a

cation, as the drawing out—*e-duco*—what is in the pupil, the development of his own powers rather than the endeavor to clothe him with the mantle of another's knowledge or accomplishments.

It speaks well also for the college and the character of its instruction that a larger proportion of the text-books now in general use have been prepared by the professors in this institution than by those of any other college, with the possible exception of Yale and Harvard.

Quality rather than quantity has been the aim of Williams. She has not undertaken to be a university, nor to advertise herself by the numbers that might be drawn to her halls. Calling herself a college, she has aimed to do the appropriate work of a college, but to do that work in the best and most effective manner.

sense of the sublimest work which this earth knows.

Among the special characteristics of the college which grew out of old Fort Massachusetts, whose commander was wont to lament his deficient early education, none is more prominent than its devotion to the study of the natural sciences. Whether owing to the appropriate influence of the peculiar location of the college amid scenery of the most attractive character, or to other causes, it is a fact that it has had in its faculty, from an early date, teachers who have been ardently devoted to the study of nature, and who by their own enthusiasm have kindled a love of this study in many of their pupils. Early in the present century the study of chemistry and natural philosophy was made prominent and attractive in connection with the lectures and illustrative experiments of Professor Dewey. A few years later, lectures on mineralogy, geology, and botany were given by that eminent teacher of these sciences, Professor Amos Eaton, who was a pioneer in these departments of study, and did as much, perhaps, as any one to popularize science in this country. He was an enthusiast. His ardent love of natural science, especially of botany, led him to relinquish the profession of the law, in which he was engaged, and devote himself to the study of nature. He was among the first in this country to teach the sciences, not only in the classroom, but in the open field. He was accustomed to take his classes with him on explorations for the study of the rocks and plants in the homes where nature had placed them.

For several years there existed among the students a society called the "Linnæan Society." This gave way to the "Lyceum of Nat-

THE OBSERVATORY.

ural History," the avowed object of which is "the study of the natural sciences, and the prosecution of antiquarian research." This society has become one of the permanent organizations of the college. It occupies a spacious brick building, erected for its use by the late Nathan Jackson, of New York. Here the society has gathered a large collection of specimens in the various departments of natural history. Here also it holds regular meetings, and in rooms adjoining the museum its members carry on their investigations, and engage in the practical work incidental to their studies. The society has been accustomed also, under the lead often of one or more of the professors in the college, to make explorations, sometimes in quite distant regions, for the purpose of prosecuting its studies and making discoveries. The late Professor Albert Hopkins, brother of President Hopkins, who was an ardent and devout student of nature, often went on such expeditions, both near and remote; and President Chadbourne, when a professor, went with the society to Florida, and on another occasion led an expedition to Greenland. The late Professor

THE OLD COLLEGE CHAPEL, GRIFFIN HALL, AND SOLDIERS' MONUMENT.

Tenney was on his way to the Rocky Mountains, three years ago, with another party, when his sudden death put an end to the expedition.

It is worthy of mention, also, that the first observatory erected in this country for astronomical purposes alone was built here. It was erected through the personal influence, and mainly at the expense, of Professor Hopkins, whose devout and saintly spirit, carrying religion into all the affairs of life, inscribed such texts of Scripture as this over the door of the observatory: "For thus saith the Lord of Hosts, Yet once, it is a little while, and I will shake the heavens, and the earth, and the sea, and the dry land." On the marble base of the sun-dial, which stands by the southern door of the observatory, one reads also, cut in deep letters, this question of our Lord: "How is it that ye do not discern this time?"

The New England Journal of Education has recently published, from data furnished by the secretary of Tufts College, a table showing the proportion of time given to the required studies in ten New England colleges. From this it appears that while Williams gives just about the average time to the ancient and modern languages, 37.5 per cent., she gives to natural history 10.9, the next highest on the list giving only 7.6, and the general average of the ten colleges being only 4.6. In ethics, again, Williams gives 10.8, the next highest being 5.7, and the general average 4.2. In philosophy and history studies, including political economy, Williams gives 29.8, the next highest giving 23.1, and the general average being 17.3.

This table indicates at a glance the fact that while Williams has given the natural sciences an eminent place, it has given to mental and moral science a pre-eminent one. Under the administration of such a man as President Hopkins, it could hardly be otherwise. Indisputably the foremost philosophic thinker of our country since the time of Edwards, and combining with great mental acumen remarkable aptitude as a teacher, it was almost a matter of course that in his hands philosophic studies should have a place of more than usual prominence. Accordingly, during the almost forty years of his presidency over the college, while other studies have not failed to receive due attention, or other sciences proper regard, the Science of Man has had a place which,

MARK HOPKINS.

so far as we know, has nowhere else been accorded to it. In the college curriculum here, while the Senior year has been almost wholly given to this highest science as the fitting crown of a collegiate course, the study of it begins with that course, Dr. Hopkins having been accustomed to give the Freshman Class a series of lectures on physiology and the laws of health. His own early training for the

FRONT AND TRANSEPT OF NEW CHAPEL.

medical profession prepared him to do this with unusual interest and effect. The influence, also, of this early training upon his way of looking at the facts of mental and moral science may have aided him in the construction of a system of philosophy so broad and self-consistent, and so completely in harmony with fact in all departments of knowledge, that it may well be termed a universal philosophy. Dr. Hopkins has not been willing that metaphysics should stand for something intelligible only to the learned few, while inexplicable to the common mind. On the contrary, he has held that the facts of the mind and the laws of its operation, it being nearest of all things to man, may be known by all with as much certainty as the facts and laws of the outward and remoter world. So he has fearlessly taken his students into this realm of study, and accustomed them to be at home with themselves, and while seeing the harmony of all knowledge, to see that the knowledge of themselves is the highest of all, and that

"The proper study of mankind is man."

So far, indeed, has he carried his views of the simplicity and intelligibility of these higher sciences, that he has been accustomed to teach them on the blackboard as one would arithmetic. And his success with this method in the class-room had been such, and his confidence in the system, that he ventured a few years ago to give a popular course of metaphysics before the Lowell Institute, illustrated by diagrams in the same way. The experiment was successful, and the phonographic report of those unwritten lectures now constitutes that remarkable volume, *An Outline Study of Man; or, The Body and Mind in One System*, which has become a text-book in so many of our colleges. It is a small volume in comparison with many which treat of the same subject, but it may be said to condense in itself a complete system of philosophy. Any one who reads it, and considers that such a course of instruction, only greatly expanded, and a similar course in moral science, occupy a large portion of the time during the entire Senior year, will understand how rich that year is to the

CLARK HALL.

and think for themselves, to call no man master, but to seek and welcome the truth as that for which they were made.

It is noticeable that there is a peculiarly warm and deep feeling on the part of the alumni of Williams toward their college, and it seems to us to be explained only by this sense that here their manhood was revealed to them and developed. If our newly chosen President, General Garfield, were to disclose the influences which have given him so honorable a name in the camp, on the

student at Williams. Many a son of Williams looks back to it as the most memorable year of his life. That Senior recitation-room, the throne of the presidency during Dr. Hopkins's long incumbency of the office, and where, although he has laid down the seals of authority, he still presides in a most important sense, and so long as he continues to teach will preside by the regal sway of thought and character which he exercises, makes one think of the old Platonic Academy, or Socrates in friendly converse with his pupils, rather than of the ordinary class-room. The glory of that room has been that there the freest inquiry has been encouraged, and the students taught to see

FLORA'S GLEN.

GOODRICH HALL.

conscious of the value of books and apparatus. "But," said he, "give me a log-cabin in the centre of the State of Ohio, with one room in it, and a bench with Mark Hopkins on one end of it and me on the other, and that would be a college good enough for me."

But Williams is not shut up to the exceptional boast of the President of the nation among her alumni. Her sons are found in full share in the places of honor and power. Of the select company composing the Supreme Court of the country she claims Justice Field. Another of her sons, Judge Betts, long presided over the District Court of New York, while of the judges and chief justices of the State courts, from Vermont to California, her catalogue furnishes a long and worthy roll. In the halls of Congress, and in the professions of law, medicine, and theology, she has been represented by many of national reputation. No college, perhaps, has been oftener or more ably represented in the editorial chair. She has not only well supplied her own offices of instruction, but has furnished professors and presidents to other colleges in this and other lands. Williams presides today at Marietta and in the University of Wisconsin, and no name stands higher in the department of linguistics than that of William D. Whitney, now holding a chair at Yale. As writers on political economy, Professor Perry and Hon. David A. Wells have a reputation that reaches beyond their own country, while in poetry and general literature no name is more honored than that of William Cullen Bryant.

field of battle, and in the councils of the nation, and finally have set him to preside over the nation, he would be ready to say, probably, that when, on receiving the reply from President Hopkins, "If you come here, we will do what we can for you," he placed himself under his helpful instruction, it made him, with his own faithful endeavors, what he is. Indeed, a current story, to say nothing of the public avowals he has made, leaves us in no doubt as to his opinion of Williams College, and especially of his great teacher there. Some years since, as the story goes, a meeting of the alumni of Williams was held in the city of New York, which General Garfield, then a member of Congress, attended. The condition of the college was discussed, and much was said of the pressing need of books and apparatus. The General listened attentively, and when his opinion was asked, expressed himself as

During the administration of President Chadbourne, so well known both as a teacher and for his great executive abili-

MAIN STREET, LOOKING EAST FROM EAST COLLEGE.

ty, new buildings have been erected, and old ones have been made to put on a more attractive appearance, and the college grounds show the results of a more æsthetic care. Graduates of a few years ago would hardly recognize the new chapel with its added transept, its frescoed walls and cushioned seats, and beautiful memorial windows. The student societies have also erected several elegant and tasteful buildings, which have contributed much to the outward appearance of the college and the village of which it forms a part.

Goodrich Hall, the finest of the college buildings at the present time, was a gift to the college, ten years ago, from the Hon. John Z. Goodrich, of Stockbridge. It was intended to contain rooms for the professor of chemistry and physics, and a recitation-room for the mathematical classes, while the upper story, with its high Gothic roof, furnished a most ample and well-provided gymnasium. During the last year Mr. Goodrich has given the college a new building for gymnastic purposes, and the upper story of Goodrich Hall will here-

after be used for meetings of the Alumni, dramatic and oratorical exhibitions, the Commencement dinner, and other college gatherings. Mr. Goodrich has been the largest pecuniary benefactor of the college.

Clark Hall, the gift of Edward Clark, Esq., of New York, designed to contain the archives of the college and the Wilder mineralogical cabinet, which he purchased and gave to the college last year, is now in process of erection. When completed, it will be one of the best of the college buildings. The foundation has just been laid for a new astronomical observatory on the elevated ground a little south of the present college buildings.

The village itself also is greatly changed. By one of the most notable engineering feats of the century, the Hoosac Mountain near by has been pierced by a tunnel, and now more than thirty railway trains go rushing by within sight of the students as they look from their windows, and within a stone's-throw of the old fort out of which the college has grown. The hidden village of the free school is no longer shut in among the hills. The gateways of approach have been opened, and it is accessible to the world. Every morning the palace-car rolls by, which the evening but one before left St. Louis, a city of half a million souls, the very site of which was unknown when Williams made his bequest and endowed the college. Beautiful in its natural site, art and culture have been perfecting the appearance of the village. Noble lines of elms shade and beautify its broad avenue, as it sweeps over one elevation after another for the distance of more than a mile. Within a few years the width of this avenue has been increased by the removal of the fences which formerly bordered it, so that it seems to form one continuous park. The passing traveller expresses surprise at the discovery of such unexpected and unsurpassed beauty, and prolongs his stay, and year by year the denizens of pent-up cities come in increasing numbers to enjoy rest of body and mind in this new-found Arcadia.

It would be difficult to name an institution of learning more favorably situated in point of natural scenery than the college which bears the name of the hero of Fort Massachusetts. If, instead of leaving his property to endow a free school at a spot so far beyond the recognized bounds of civilization that Norton, in his *Redeemed Captive*, says that the French and Indians, in their attack upon the fort, sent some to creep up as near as they could "to observe whether any persons attempted to make their escape, to carry tidings to New England," he had looked forward a hundred years and more, and chosen, out of our now wide and populous territory, a site for a college, he could not have chosen more wisely than he did. In a fertile and silvery valley, threaded by beautiful streams, surrounded by the lofty ranges of the Taghconic and Green mountains, Graylock lifting its hoary summit above every peak in the commonwealth, there is everything in the situation to attract the eye and cultivate the best feelings. Every season, every day and hour, has here its own peculiar charm. There is a perpetual change and variety of scene. Nature never repeats herself, but is constantly turning her kaleidoscopic glass and presenting fresh surprises.

On the college grounds, and within a stone's-throw of the students' windows, is Christmas Lake, with its fringe of evergreens, while less than a mile away is Flora's Glen—a wild and beautiful spot, where tradition says Bryant first brooded over his "Thanatopsis." Going up the glen, if one cares to ascend higher, the summits of Mount Hopkins and Petersburg invite him to points where the eye ranges from the Catskills to the Adirondacks, the Hudson gleaming at intervals almost at his feet. Opposite is the Hopper, with its deep gorges, its massive sweeps of foliage, its wondrous play of light and shade, and its wild wood road to the flank of Graylock and the camping ground where, summer after summer, in its pure ether, and amid its babbling brooks, many find a delightful change of scene and great refreshment both of body and mind.

No more beautiful or healthful surroundings for the student could be found. Shut away from the noise and temptations of city and town life, in the calm seclusion of this, Nature's own retreat, no circumstances could be more favorable for the successful prosecution of the scholar's work. And so, perhaps, the hero of Fort Massachusetts "builded better than he knew" when, in the Free School of West Hoosac, he established another and a better fortress, one not of arms and military enginery, but of moral and intellectual equipment, to guard society from the assaults of ignorance, superstition, and a vain materialism, and to preserve to the nation and the world the best possessions of intelligence and virtue.

A MODEL STATE CAPITAL

HARTFORD is a good place to pass through. It is also a good place to stop at. The two great railroads connecting New York and Boston by way of the Connecticut State capital carry across its corporate bounds perhaps two hundred thousand or a quarter of a million travellers every year; but only a small proportion of the persons on that current stop at this point. Still fewer are those who come to stay. It can not be said that many are called, but the few are certainly chosen, the population, which is not much above fifty thousand, being of an unusually high character. Little poverty, large and energetic thrift, ingenious manufactures, accumulated resources—these are the data one may judge by. The city, in fact, takes its place on statistical tables as proportionally the richest in the United States.*

Set in the black-earthed, fertile Connecticut Valley, encircled by low but picturesque hills over whose violet mass the sunrise and sunset break with peculiar splendor, it is a cheerful and satisfactory place, even to the casual passer, who is struck by

* The assessed valuation is $48,500,000; but counting in establishments situated elsewhere though owned or chiefly represented in Hartford, this would rise to $125,000,000. The city pays one-third of the taxes of Connecticut. The new Capitol, with its land, cost $3,335,000, of which Hartford contributed $1,960,000; that is, nearly two-thirds.

its stately Capitol, near the railroad, and the long line of early French Gothic building farther off that forms one side of the projected quadrangle of Trinity College. The importance of its educational, its benevolent, and protective institutions is at once presented to an observer. In many a village and country by-way had I seen, long before I alighted in Hartford itself, certain unlovely but suggestive tin signs tacked upon the sides of wooden houses indicating by a mystic word or two that those dwellings had been insured with Hartford companies against fire. In like manner the town is a stronghold of life-insurance—a business which, despite its ominous technical phrase describing new policy-holders as "fresh blood," has beneficent results as well as a selfish aim. But I am thinking more particularly of those undertakings meant purely for the relief of the unfortunate. It can not conscientiously be said that it is a cheerful thing, on leaving the station, to find yourself in a thoroughfare which greets you with the name of Asylum Street. A dim suspicion arises that if you follow its lead you will bring up in some place designed for the prompt immurement of strangers; for in old times even temporary residents were not allowed in Hartford except by a vote of town-meeting. This anxiety, however, is dissipated when you learn that the name refers to the American Asylum for the Deaf and Dumb, a most praiseworthy establishment, the first of its kind in the United States. It was founded by a number of gentlemen in 1815, and under the superintendence of the Rev. Mr. Gallaudet it became the inspiration and model of many similar institutions; so that it would hardly be amiss to give the street that devoted teacher's name instead of its present rather doleful one. "Retreat Avenue," painted on the horse-cars, suggests another famous establishment, the Hartford Retreat for the Insane, which likewise antedates all of its class in this country, saving one or two that were publicly endowed. The Retreat was set going by a subscription; and that this was eminently a popular one is manifest in the fact that many of the signers gave but fifty or twenty-five cents, and some only twelve and a half cents. How one charity may aid another I happened to see well exemplified in the case of an insane person who was also a deaf-mute, so that it was necessary for the Retreat to provide an attendant skilled in the manual and sign language—a need which could not easily have been met had it not been for the work of the American Asylum.

But I must hasten to say that the associations called up by street names in Hartford are by no means all of this pensive sort. The horse-cars already mentioned appear to be somewhat browbeaten: they lack the brisk insolence of their species on metropolitan lines; are subject to endless delays at turn-outs and the railroad crossings; are drawn, moreover, by only one horse each, and have not even spirit enough to maintain a conductor; but as they bounce disconsolately along they continue to offer to convey the patient wanderer to Spring Grove and City Garden. There is a fresh rural sound about these names, and others of kindred purport occur, such as Flower Street, Oak Street, Woodland, Laurel, Hawthorn, and Evergreen. The country character reflected in them lingers around Hartford, and enhances its pleasantness. Then we have the historic series, Trumbull, Wolcott, Wadsworth, and the like. Even the early Dutch settlers, so summarily ousted by the English, have returned under the auspices of Colonel Colt (the inventor of the revolver) to haunt Hendricksen and Vredendale avenues; and near Colt's armory likewise are recorded the names of those sachems—Sequassen, Weehassat, and Maseek—who deeded their lands to the colonists. All this reminds us that we are in a city which has an interesting past. The historic impression is deepened if we stray back along Main Street, the single road of the original village, which is wide enough to swallow two or three Broadways without inconvenience, and of about equal proportions with Piccadilly, in London, by St. James's Park. It was where Main Street expands into State-house Square that Washington and Knox met Rochambeau and Admiral Ternay when those leaders of the French allies came from Newport to confer with the commander-in-chief for the first time. A brilliant scene that, and doubtless the most spectacular one in the peaceful annals of the place. On one side were the foreign officers in their royal uniforms adorned with decorations; on the other, Washington and his staff, epauletted with gold, clad in the Continental blue and buff, and attended by Governor Trumbull, with other State worthies, who wore long-skirted

CENTRE CONGREGATIONAL CHURCH.
Photographed by R. S. De Lamater.

drab or crimson coats and embroidered waistcoats. In the American escort was the ancient company known as the Governor's Foot-Guard, resplendent in scarlet and black, which were contrasted with buff breeches and waistcoats, tall bear-skin hats completing what the poets of that period would have called their "horrid front." Then Washington and Rochambeau dismounted, and coming forward into

GEORGE WILLIAMSON SMITH, PRESIDENT OF TRINITY
COLLEGE.
Photographed by R. S. De Lamater.

and protected by a wall with a rusty iron gate, lies the ancient grave-yard, a quaint and melancholy spot containing the tomb stones of early inhabitants, adorned with what appear to be owls' heads, but on consideration must be construed as angels. Under two brown-stone slabs raised on little legs like children's dining-tables the first two pastors are buried, those who led their flock from Cambridge, Massachusetts, to the banks of the Connecticut—Thomas Hoolser, whom Cotton Mather in his *Magnalia* called "the light of the Western churches," and the Rev. Samuel Stone. It was at the wish of the latter, who had been born in Hertford, England, that the plantation was called Hartford; and the Saxon name, meaning "hart's ford," was as applicable here as in the mother country, for doubtless the New World river too had been crossed at this spot by many a herd of wild deer. The epitaph cut upon the stone above his resting-place declares that

"Errors corrupt, by sinewous dispute,
He did oppugne, and clearly them confute.
Above all things he Christ his Lord preferred.
Hartford, thy richest jewel's here interred."

Quite forgotten now is all that "sinewous dispute" which so endeared Mr. Stone to our controversial forefathers, unless by professors in the Congregational Theological Institute up on the hill yonder; but his memory has found a surer foothold in its connection with the municipal name.

the open central space, met and shook hands for the two peoples whom they represented.

Once this same square went by the name of "Meeting-house Yard." The church stood on one side of it, and at other points on its boundary were the scene of the weekly market, the stocks and pillory, the jail, and the slave pen. That was before the pen had been raised *against* slavery, and Mrs. Stowe was not then a resident of Hartford. On the site of the old meeting-house stands to-day its lineal descendant, the Centre Congregational Church—a broad-faced edifice painted a cream-custard tint, and displaying a row of slender pillars in front, which feature seems to have pleased the builders, for they repeated it by putting pillars around the spire quite high up. Behind the church,

To this church the Governor of the State used to repair, after the annual election, at the head of a solemn procession, to begin his term of office with divine service. The next evening occurred the great "election ball," followed on the succeeding Monday by another ball more select in character. The whole week, in fact, was kept as a holiday, and it made a useful vacation and festival-time for peo-

TRINITY COLLEGE.

ple who, swayed by their scruples against everything sanctioned by the Anglican Church, refused to observe Christmas. During this little space everybody was hilarious; families made it an occasion pens, is the site of a tavern where another element of former social life used to centre, namely, the Seven-copper Club, which met there in the Revolutionary period to talk news or gossip and drink a

JOSEPH R. HAWLEY.
Photographed by Parkinson.

for exchanging visits, and kept open house, with "election cake" ready for their callers. In our time the cake appears to precede the election, and takes the form of paid tax bills or some other gentle inducement to the free and unprejudiced citizen to vote for the candidate who favors him; but the old-fashioned plan was for the citizen to vote for the candidate *he* favored, and then eat cake impartially. Almost opposite the church, as it hap-

half-mug of flip, the price of which was exactly seven coppers. Prohibitory legislation was hardly needed, for the landlord, Moses Butler, was a law unto the members: he never allowed them more than one half-mug apiece, and sent them home promptly at nine, with the bluff admonition, "It is time, gentlemen, to go back to your families that are waiting for you."

I do not find that the solid household-

STAIRWAY IN THE CAPITOL.
Photographed by R. S. De Lamater.

ing sort of club has ever taken root very widely in Hartford, but there has been in existence for about a dozen years past a very agreeable club of less than a hundred gentlemen, quite unlike the ancient and humble Seven - copper, I imagine. It borrows its appellation from the city itself; its membership is chiefly commercial and professional, under the presidency of General Joseph R. Hawley, formerly Governor of Connecticut, and it occupies a roomy old mansion on Pleasant Street, which is itself a fine relic of the first post-colonial epoch, for the sidewalks are lined with trees, and behind them the houses rise sedate and prosperous of aspect, with gardens that are not above nurturing a little fruit. The crime of arboricide is of recent development, comparatively, and it is to be hoped will be suppressed. Inside the abode of the Hartford Club one encounters the elegance that is inherent in simplicity and reason-

ableness of arrangement. The rooms bear the stamp of a former squirearchy and a commercial gentry, if one may make the phrase, which were intelligent and refined; all is of the past here, except the convenient contrivances and the quiet Morrisian decoration. In summer the members may pass out at the glass doors of the dining-room to a broad veranda overlooking the garden, and there dinners are served under cover of a roof and an awning curtain. A line of low buildings, the " offices" of the old mansion, runs along one side of the grassy inclosure, for it was a house of some grandeur in its day. Mr. David Watkinson, to whom it last belonged, founded a library, the windows of which look across the yard in neighborly fashion at the club; and connected with this library is the granite bulk of the Wadsworth Athenæum, occupying the spot where formerly stood the house of Daniel Wadsworth, a descendant of the

Charter Oak Wadsworth, Colonel Jeremiah. Washington used to come to that house when he visited Hartford, and the exact room in which be reposed would, if it had not disappeared, be still pointed out, for Washington, like other great historic personages, seems to have been an industrious and ubiquitous sleeper.

aspect, on the contrary, is exceedingly modern. "Meeting-house Yard" and Main Street are now hedged in by lofty insurance buildings, hotels, newspaper offices, "New York Stores," "Boston Bazars," and other shops. A little to the north is a well-devised building of brown stone, with good carving about the doors,

BUST OF SAMUEL CLEMENS, BY KARL GERHARDT.
Photographed by Kurtz.

It should not be understood, however, that these reminiscences of antiquity color the aspect of the city perceptibly; the

a fantastic gargoyle or two at the roof, and a pointed red-tiled tower on one corner—an encouraging example of the pic-

SOLDIERS' AND SAILORS' MONUMENT.
From architect's design.

turesque in a structure wholly designed for business purposes. But the square itself is filled up by the Post-office — a Mullett monstrosity of the tasteless order which we may call the Federal; and there also stands the old State-house, now a City-hall, of no special order, but plentifully supplied with little urns placed upon the cornice balustrades, and the obsolete cupola. The State government has now transferred itself to a more fitting habitation in the new Capitol, built within the bounds of Bushnell Park, and—what is more remarkable—within the appropriation. No suspicion of jobbery tarnishes the brilliant effect of this beautiful piece of architecture. The only bad feature about it is the enormously tall, rather spindling, twelve-sided drum that lifts the gilded dome to a height of two hundred and fifty feet above the ground. Out of the harmonious growth of blue and white marble in the main building, with its pointed windows and slated pavilions, suggesting in a modified way the great municipal halls of the Netherlands and France, this addition lifts a giraffe-like neck toward the sky; and even a large broad dome occupying the middle space, though it would have looked better, must have been out of keeping with the rest. The interior, nevertheless, abounds in good qualities. Convenient, spacious, well-lighted, having the air of ease and spontaneity, it gives numerous good vistas, varied by the great central staircases and the airy columned galleries. The battle flags of Connecticut are ranged in

PORTION OF THE FRIEZE OF THE SOLDIERS'

carven oak cases near one of the great entrances; endless offices open upon the corridors and galleried courts; the State library is ensconced in one huge apartment, and the Supreme Court in another. It is, by-the-way, a curious bit of symbolism that the Supreme Court judges' room has its fire-place surrounded with blue tiles illustrating Scripture subjects, while the tiles in the room devoted to counsel depict scenes from fairy tales. The Representatives are accommodated in a rich and sober chamber with stained-glass windows; it is about as large, but much less stuffy, and to my mind much more beautiful, than the English House of Commons. Near the Speaker's dais is an unobtrusive but huge thermometer, by which, I suppose, the heat of debate may be measured. The Senate of twenty-one has another lordly hall to itself, where there is provided for the President of that body a large chair made out of wood from the Charter Oak, richly carved with leaf and acorn. Both these legislative halls are carried out with an excellent appreciation of what is fittest for their purpose in the resources of art as applied to decoration; the natural grain and color of the woods —oak, ash, and walnut—combine with the subdued tones and good ornament of the walls to make a refreshing environment worthy of republican ideals and much above republican practice.

The exterior walls of the Capitol are haunted by birds, and provided with niches for statues of Connecticut worthies, two of which are already occupied by Oliver Wolcott and Roger Sherman; and between these a marble image of the Charter Oak spreads its branches. Have we not all learned the legend of that venerable tree in our histories at school? It seems almost to require setting down as a distinct species in botanical text-books; but in Hartford it becomes like the ash-tree of Norse mythology, like Ygdrasil, which upheld the whole universe. In spite of historical skeptics, the legend still holds that when Sir Edmund Andros came, in 1687, to reclaim the liberal charter which Charles II. had himself granted, but now wanted to revoke, the lights at the evening council-board were suddenly put out, and that in the darkness Colonel Wadsworth did actually carry off the document and hide it in the hollow oak that stood before Mr. Secretary Wyllys's house. It is not so generally remembered that this tree had been an object of great regard on the part of the Indians before ever the colonists came hither. A deputation of them waited on the white men to ask that no harm be done the oak, since it had long been the guide of their ancestors as to the time for planting corn. "When the leaves," said they, "are of the size of a mouse's ear, then is the time to put the seed in the ground." Time and tempest felled it at last; but it blooms here in marble still; its name is preserved throughout the city as the distinguishing mark of divers stores, shops, and companies; and a pretty marble slab, like a grave-stone, in Charter Oak Place inadequately marks where the original flourished until 1856. In Bushnell Park (named after that eminent theologian, the late Dr. Horace Bushnell, who was the chief promoter of this public pleasure-ground) there is a couple of Charter Oaks junior, sprung from its fruit; and "certified" acorns, possibly taken from these younger trees, but supposed to have grown upon the parent, have been worth their weight in gold at charity fairs. Across the Connecticut, leading to East Hartford, stretches a covered bridge one thousand feet long, and taking up in its construction a corresponding quantity of timber. Mark Twain, showing some friends about, told them that bridge also was built of wood from the Charter Oak.

AND SAILORS' MONUMENT.—From designs by George Keller.

SAMUEL CLEMENS'S HOUSE.
Photographed by R. S. De Lamater.

Not far from the Capitol is the Sóldiers' and Sailors' Monument, which takes the unique form of a memorial arch spanning the southern end of an old stone bridge, which leads into the City Park at the foot of Ford Street. The architect, Mr. George Keller, also designed the Buffalo Soldiers' Monument. The arch is thirty feet wide, and springs from two massive round towers, each of which is sixty-seven feet in circumference and sixty feet high, terminating in a conical roof. Above the archway, about forty feet from the ground, a frieze of sculpture 175 feet in length and 6 feet 6 inches in breadth runs around the monument. "The towers," says the Hartford *Courant*, "seem like two huge sentinels guarding the bridge, or mighty standard-bearers holding aloft a noble banner on which is emblazoned the deeds of the men of Hartford who died for their country on land and sea in the war which kept the Union whole." Circular stairs inside the towers lead to the rampart or gallery at the top of the monument, overlooking the park, and protected by a parapet which has the seal of Hartford carved on its face.

It was about ten years ago that Mr. Clemens—or, as we all now prefer to call him, Mark Twain—came to Hartford to live; and he has built for himself there one of the most delightful of houses, in the pleasantest part of the city, just where it ceases to be visible as city at all, and merges into rolling hill and dale. A large structure, irregular in outline, made of red and brown brick in fantastic courses, it stands on Farmington Avenue, upon a knoll well back from the street, with a grove of beeches and oaks and other trees of good deportment clustering around two sides. The shade and flicker of these trees lend their fascination to a spacious *ombra* at the rear, completely hidden from the thoroughfare, and affording good opportunity for open-air suppers in the evenings of early summer. In-doors and out-doors mingle on the friendliest terms, one may say, throughout the interior. There is no room that has not some charming prospect. The library, which appears to be the favorite of the household, is closed at one end by a conservatory, but one deep-recessed bay-window reveals an exquisite glimpse, through the trees close by, of a little winding stream at the foot of a steep bank. This stream is Park River, which wanders from here down to the Capitol circuitously, and in its wanderings has lost the pretty name which the Puritan colo-

SAMUEL CLEMENS'S LIBRARY.
Photographed by R. S. De Lamater.

CHARLES DUDLEY WARNER'S HOUSE.
Photographed by R. S. De Lamater.

nists gave it. They called it the Riveret. The Riveret is bordered by low meadows on one side, and by the sharp acclivity with its fair woodland on the other. Within this woodland, which is not crossed by either fence or hedge, there are several other villas; among them, not far distant, the picturesque, gabled house of Charles Dudley Warner. The plot of cultivated ground which, in *My Summer in a Garden*, the author so generously annexed to the open common of American humor, was attached to his former home, near by. There also was the hearth from the glow of which came the inspiration for *Back-log Studies*. Before its cheerful light Mr. Warner's friends used to gather of snowy nights, enjoying the crackle of the blazing wood, and the flashes of wit that sparkled there; Mark Twain and their pastor, Rev. Joseph Twichell, and Dr. J. Hammond Trumbull—the only man extant who can read Eliot's Indian Bible—with others not less endeared to the circle because they are not public personages; and perhaps a visiting brother author, Howells from Cambridge, or Stedman from New York, or Sanborn from

Concord, all centring about the quiet, thoughtful-looking host, with his rather pallid face, and his hair and beard strewn with snow that will not melt even before his own geniality.

The new house is charming in all its appointments, and especially rich in bric-à-brac, much of it Oriental, collected by the owner during his several tours in Europe, the East, and Africa. The accompanying illustration represents a corner of one end of the music-room. The sideboard is of mahogany, and over it hangs a painting, "The Martyrdom of Santa Barbara," by Vasquez, a contemporary, perhaps pupil, of Velasquez, painted about 1540 for a convent at Bogota, South America, where it has been until two or three years ago. The picture has a curious heavy frame of ebony, inlaid with masses of tortoise-shell. The mantel-piece is unique. It is made of Saracenic tiles framed in California redwood. Most of the tiles are wall tiles from ancient houses in Damascus and Cairo, one from the Mosque of Omar, in Jerusalem, and some small ones at the side from the pavement of the courts in the Alhambra. The tiles are blues and greens, in arabesques and conventionalized flower patterns, one with a legend in Arabic declaring the unity of God. On top of the mantel-piece stands a large Knight of Malta vase, majolica, probably of Abrazzi make. At Malta it was customary to mould such a jar on the

a study at home, he nevertheless every week-day when he is at home trudges down into the city to the office, a mile and a half away, of the Hartford *Courant* —to get the true local flavor pronounce "currant"—of which he is an editor and part owner. There he enters another

CHARLES DUDLEY WARNER.
From drawing by F. Dielman.

election of a Grand Master of the order. This was made for Adrianolle Vegniancort, elected 1690, and has his portrait on one side and coat-of-arms on the other. Its companion was made for Fra Raimondo Perellos, elected 1697.

Although Mr. Warner of course has

apartment consecrated to the pen; cheerful, sunny, hung with photographs of Old World architecture, but provided with a large writing-table, on which are the paraphernalia of practical newspaper labor, and there, too, he remains for several hours, studying the news of the world,

CORNER OF ONE END OF MUSIC-ROOM IN CHARLES DUDLEY WARNER'S HOUSE.

and writing editorials which surprise even his old associates by their wide range and the familiarity they evince with questions of trade, politics, literature, and foreign affairs. Those who know what writing as a profession really means will understand the kind of ability and industry required to sustain this steady journalistic duty, simultaneously with the production of books and frequent contributions to the magazines, and they will not wonder that Mr. Warner should now and then have to travel for health's sake. But he always brings back from his journeys so much of new acquisition that the literary impulse is quickened into fresh activity.

Near by, in a slate-colored cottage of moderate size, lives the famous author of *Uncle Tom's Cabin.* The atmosphere within-doors is that of literary New England twenty-five years ago: the American Renascence has not yet invaded these rooms, so conspicuously neat and comfortable, yet with a kind of moral rectitude in their comfort. The library is also a sitting-room, where a glowing coal fire burned on the chilly autumn day when I was admitted there; and in the wall spaces between the windows were placed tall panels painted with flowers, and terminating above in points that gave them a half-ecclesiastical air, as if they were tables of the law.

"Is this your study?" I asked.

"I have no particular study," said the authoress, "and I have not written much lately; but if I were to begin, I should be as likely to write here as anywhere."

Thus easily and informally she treats the genius that has given her a world-wide celebrity; indeed, there is nothing about her manner or in her surroundings to indicate a consciousness of the extraordinary power which endowed her first book with an influence that has never been paralleled. A very quiet little lady, plainly attired, and apt during conversation to become abstracted — a life-long habit of reverie which has enabled her to think out her designs and carry on composition in the midst of those interruptions to most writers unbearable—a lady quiet and undemonstrative, with immense determination and character revealed in her face when seen at certain angles, but with an equally natural gentleness and benignity; this is what one sees to-day on meeting Mrs. Stowe. She gives the impression of one who wielded large weapons because Providence put them into her hands to right a great wrong, and not with any joy in the suffering and harm that must come with the good gained. She appears the

sent and militant religion that somehow pervaded the whole spot. The conversation now passed easily to questions of faith, and Mrs. Stowe manifested a strong interest in the old Pilgrim and Puritan qualities of belief. To me it seems regrettable that the physiognomy of a person occupying so remarkable a position should not be carefully recorded in all its stages of development, since a distinctive face increases its sum of meaning with the years; but I learned that Mrs. Stowe had not submitted herself to the arts of the photographer for a long time, and Professor Stowe was firm in the conviction that the portrait painted by Richmond in 1852 was the only one worthy of perpetuation. "That," said he, referring to it, "is the way she will look at the resurrection." I confess that if the resurrection were to preserve the mild womanly maturity of her features as they are at the age of seventy, I should find no fault with its process.

The material aspect of Mrs. Stowe's abode, as perhaps I have hinted, gives little intimation of the part which its occupant has played; but in the small entrance hall stands a plain low cupboard, which, on being opened to the favored visitor, displayed two rows of massive volumes — a dozen on each shelf— containing a petition in favor of the abolition of slavery, signed by half a million women, and offered to Congress as a result of Mrs. Stowe's agitation. In a corner of the parlor, too, there is a closed beaufet well stocked with editions of *Uncle Tom's Cabin*, and others

HARRIET BEECHER STOWE.
From a drawing by J. W. Alexander.

wife, the mother, the grandmother, living in her domestic interests, rather than the woman distinguished in national history and literature. We talked on personal topics, and while this was going forward Professor Stowe came in from a walk, with a tall stick in his hand, which he grasped as a support in the middle. It was like a pilgrim's staff, and completed the suggestion of pre-

of the authoress's works, in several foreign languages: an impressive collection, certainly, and one which has served a secondary purpose, for it has been duplicated in the British Museum, and is there used as the means of curious studies in comparative philology. Since her husband's withdrawal from his professorship at Andover, Mrs. Stowe has spent her time in these simple surroundings, leading a retired life, and going in winter to Florida, where she finds

WILLIAM B. FRANKLIN.
Photographed by R. S. De Lamater.

refuge among her orange groves, in a town which bears the fragrant name of Mandarin. She was drawn to Hartford partly by its general charm, and in part through associations which her sister had given the place by establishing there the Female Seminary. Speaking of the length of her residence here, she said, "I don't remember when I came; I do not live by years." This being repeated to Mark Twain, "I wish," he instantly observed, "the tax-collector would adopt that principle." One most agreeable memory will long remain with me, of an evening spent in Mrs. Stowe's company at the house of Mr. and Mrs. Clemens. Among other things there was after-dinner talk of the days preceding the war, and of the "un-

der-ground railroad" for escaping slaves, and the strange adventures therewith connected. Mrs. Stowe gave her reminiscences of exciting incidents in her life on the Ohio border at that time, and told of the frightful letters she received from the South after publishing her great novel. These anonymous screeds voiced, no doubt, the worst element there, and teemed with threats and abuse that now, happily, would not be offered by even the most wanton survivor of the fire-eaters. To give an idea of the extremes to which these missives proceeded, Mrs. Stowe mentioned that one of them, duly forwarded to her by United States mail, inclosed a negro's ear! It was inevitable that we who listened should meditate upon the marvellous change that had been effected in the condition of our Union within twenty years, and one gentleman who was present said to another, aside, as emphasizing the extent of that change, "To think that I, who can remember when a Boston mob tried to hang William Lloyd Garrison, should have lived to see twenty respectable free negroes asleep at his funeral!" It was a frivolous remark, no doubt, but it was only the light mask of a sincere respect for the prodigious feat so largely prompted by the pen of the demure lady who had just been speaking with us. Extremely interesting, also, was the eager force with which Mrs. Stowe related one or two stories of later date on other themes that had presented themselves to her as deserving literary treatment. It showed that the narrative instinct was deeply ingrained in her, and had not lost its vigor even after so long an exertion as she has given it. Yet her presence, temperament, and conversation confirmed the theory one is likely to form in reading her books, that her imagination acts inseparably with the moral sense.

It is a convenient thing to have the antipodes anchored just around the corner. A few steps only from Mrs. Stowe's brings you to Mr. Clemens's house, and still fewer, if you take the short-cut through the lawns and shrubbery, by which brief transit you pass from old New England to modern America—from the plain quarters of ethical fiction to the luxurious abode of the most Western of humorists. It is not difficult to trace, however, the essential kinship between Sam Lawson of *Oldtown Folks* and the equally quaint and shrewd but more expansive drollery of Mark Twain; and, on the other hand, those who see much of this author in private discover in him a fund of serious reflection and of keen observation upon many subjects that gives him another element in common with his neighbor. The literary group in this neighborhood do not seem to fancy giving names to their houses: they are content with the arithmetical designation. "No, my house has not got any name," said Mr. Clemens, in answer to a question. "It has a number, but I have never been able to remember what it is." No number, in fact, appears on gate or door; but the chances are that if a stranger were to step into any shop on the business streets he could at once obtain an accurate direction to the spot.

And a charming haunt it is, with its wide hall, finished in dark wood under a panelled ceiling, and full of easy-chairs, rugs, cushions, and carved furniture that instantly invite the guest to lounge in front of the big fire-place. But it is a house made for hospitality, and one can not stop at that point. Over the fire-place, through a large plate-glass suggesting Alice's Adventures, a glimpse is had of the drawing-room, luminous with white and silver and pale blue; and on another side, between a broad flight of stairs and a chiselled Ginevra chest drawn against the wall, the always open library door attracts one's steps. There is more dark wood-work in the library, including a very elaborate panel rising above the mantel to the ceiling. This was brought from abroad, and in other portions of the house are other pieces representing the spoils of European tours; one in particular I recall, covered with garlands and with plump cherubs that spring forth in plastic rotundity, and clamber along the edges. But it adds to the pleasurableness of the home that all the cherubs in it are not carved. A genial atmosphere, too, pervades the house, which is warmed by wood fires, a furnace, and the author's immense circulation. One would naturally in such a place expect to find some perfection of a study, a literary work-room, and that has indeed been provided, but the unconventional genius of the author could not reconcile itself to a surrounding the charms of which distracted his attention. The study remains, its deep window giving a seductive outlook above the library, but Mr. Clemens goes elsewhere. Pointing to a large divan extending along the two sides of a right-angled corner, "That was a good idea," he said, "which I got from something I saw in a Syrian monastery; but I found it was much more comfortable to lie there and smoke than to stay at my desk. And then these windows—I was constantly getting up to look at the view; and when one of our beautiful heavy snow-falls came in winter, I couldn't do anything at all except gaze at it." So he has moved still higher upstairs into the billiard-room, and there writes at a table placed in such wise that he can see nothing but the wall in front of him and a couple of shelves of books. Before adopting this expedient he had tried a room which he caused to be fitted up with plain pine sheathing on the upper floor of his stable; but that had serious disadvantages, and even the billiard-room failing to meet the requirements in some emergencies, he has latterly resorted to hiring an office in a commercial building in the heart of the city.

"About four months in the year," said he, "is the time when I expect to do my work, during the summer vacation, when I am off on the farm at Elmira. Yes," he continued, when I expressed surprise, "I can write better in hot weather. And, besides, I must be free from all other interests and occupations. I find it necessary, when I have begun anything, to keep steadily at it, without changing my surroundings. To take up the train of ideas after each day's writing I must be in the same place that I began it in, or else it becomes very difficult."

But nothing, apparently, interrupts the spontaneous flow of his humor in daily life. It is the same in kind with that of his books, though incidental and less elaborate. It is unpremeditated, and always unexpected. He never takes what may be termed the obvious and conventional witty view, yet neither is there any straining for a new form of jest: the novelty comes of itself. Moreover, unlike certain wits whose quality is genuine, but whose reputation becomes a burden to them, he appears to be indifferent whether he ever cracks another joke, and thus lulls his companions into a delusive security, only to take them unawares with some new and telling shot. There is less exaggeration in what he says than in what he writes; but the essence of his fun lies in that same grave assumption of absurdities as solid and reasonable facts with which we are familiar in his works. By a reverse process, when talking to a serious point, or narrating some experience not especially ludicrous in itself, there is a lingering suspicion of humorous possibilities in his manner, which, assisted by the slow, emphatic, natural drawl of his speech, leads one to accept actual facts of a prosaic kind as delicious absurdities. In fine, it is a sort of wizardry that he exercises in conversation, stimulating the hearer by its quick mutations of drolling and earnest.

The life that this Nook Farm literary group have shaped for themselves and their friends is a quiet and retired one. The world does not see much of it, though they see a good deal of the world. The part of Hartford where they live is on the

rolling hill to the west of the railroad, laid out in broad streets, with brick houses embowered in the trees of their lavishly spacious grounds; it is the main district apportioned to residences, in fact, and a very attractive district too. Many of these houses are of the old type—square and bare, with small rectangular cupolas on top, one the counterpart of the other, like boxes containing some mysterious piece of machinery for running the family affairs; but they look eminently comfortable, and at night you see their private gas lamps in porch or veranda, at the end of the driveway, throwing out a cheerful glow. But the new architecture asserts its power over the more recent buildings, and one begins to discern how picturesque even a practical New England city may become in the future. Like Boston, Hartford is accused of having a frigid social atmosphere, but others say that it is very warm and encouraging: a thing like this is as difficult to define as the New England climate. At all events, the inhabitants are, I believe, fond of the usual gayeties of society; and although there is so much accumulated wealth among them, it is said that money has very little to do with the standing of persons in any of the various circles of the local world. A commendable sentiment of democracy seems to prevail, and there is little tendency to ostentation. That particular circle which takes the Nook Farm group within its compass has a fondness for amusement clubs—the Surprise Party and the As You Like It, two of these organizations have been named—consisting of about twenty members, that meet fortnightly at each other's houses, and bring guests to about twice their own number. There is also a large theatre in the city, where most of the notable actors playing in New York and Boston give performances in passing.

On the evening of my arrival, as it chanced, I was taken to the Monday Club, to which Warner and Mark Twain both belong; so, too, does their friend General Hawley, who, after being a lawyer, a journalist, a military leader, a Governor, is now a Senator of the United States, and continues his editorial connection. Of him it is related that, when the war broke out and the first call was issued for volunteers, he made several attempts to write an adequate editorial sustaining the call; then suddenly throwing down his pen, he exclaimed to his associates, "Boys, I'm going to do the fighting for this office; you must run the paper." Forthwith he went out and enlisted, and now enjoys the honor of having been the first volunteer from Connecticut. At the Monday Club was present another distinguished officer, General William B. Franklin, who commanded a corps in the Army of the Potomac. We had, besides, an ex-mayor of Hartford, a professor of Trinity College, two Congregational ministers, a second journalist, the State Attorney, and two other members. I am particular in this enumeration because the whole thing was so significant. Here were these gentlemen, busy citizens of a small city, representatives of what Matthew Arnold calls "the great middle-class public of America," coming together quite informally to exchange views—on what subject? Of all things the least likely to occur to an uninformed observer like Mr. Arnold, the subject was England in Egypt. There was no regular debate, but each person spoke in order, setting forth his opinions in few words or many, with occasional breaks of dialogue as the mood prompted. Two or three had been in Egypt, and had made observation for themselves. The rest had read and thought. What was interesting was the amount of careful knowledge and reflection developed in the course of an hour and a half; the Eastern question and possible policies affecting it were treated as comprehensively as if they had been matter of home politics, instead of something as remote from our own affairs as could well be chosen. To an American this is not a startling phenomenon. Why should it be? But it is a good illustration of what goes on in those smaller cities and towns concerning which there has of late been discussion with foreigners who insist upon knowing all about them by intuition.

Alert intelligence and varied activity have always characterized Hartford, and a local vein of literature is traceable from the close of the Revolution down. Here that group of writers assembled who made a reputation under the name of the Hartford Wits: John Trumbull, author of "McFingal," the ponderous mock-heroic poem of the war of Independence; Timothy Dwight, who produced an epic on "The Conquest of Canaan"; and Joel Barlow, whose "Columbiad" has successfully resisted the author's attempt to install it among the world's classics. Lesser lights, who co-operated with these in satirical effusions that had a political value, were Lemuel Hopkins, David Humphreys, and Richard Alsop. The house of Mrs. Sigourney is still standing, and her bust may be seen in the rooms of the Historical Society; it has a serene expression, as if the original had never suffered from that infliction which her poems imposed on the rest of the world. Here, too, Noah Webster lived, thought out his impossible etymologies, and compiled his dictionary. S. G. Goodrich, who employed Hawthorne in his early days to write the "Peter Parley" geography, and then published it as his own, was a resident of Hartford; so was the disappointed poet James Percival. Edmund Clarence Stedman, who so immortally sang John Brown, and has given us the best book of criticism upon the Victorian poets, came from Hartford; and one of its later representatives in current literature is Mr. Bishop, the new novelist. The town is plentifully supplied with arsenals for future authors in its several libraries, which have made a sort of treaty with one another to follow out special lines, in order not to conflict. The Hartford is a popular subscription concern, which supplies the reading immediately in demand; the State library at the Capitol is chiefly devoted to law, in which its collections are peculiarly complete, including many rarities. At Trinity College the library is especially strong in classics; the Theological Institute embraces religious and archæological works; and the Watkinson gives its attention more to general literature of a standard sort. The Historical Society, too, has a special accumulation of its own. Together, they contain something over a hundred thousand volumes. In artistic development the city has not been so forward. The Wadsworth Athenæum (in the same building with which are the Hartford, the Watkinson, and the Historical libraries) contains a few old pictures; among them some interesting landscapes by Thomas Cole, and a portrait of Benjamin West by Sir Joshua; but the institution appears to be lifeless. A branch of the Decorative Art Society, however, has lately been established; and Hartford has produced several painters who have gained a good standing: Gedney Bunce, the colorist, who treats Venetian fishing-boats with strong poetic feeling; Gordon Trumbull, who is called one of the best American fish painters; and the great landscape painter, F. E. Church.

When one reflects upon the literary associations of Hartford, and the number of things in which it has shown excellence or commendable energy—on one side its humane establishments, including that where the deaf-mute children lead with so much good cheer their life of silent imagery, and on the other its hum of factories, producing all manner of things, from paper, pins, paper barrels, to machinery, revolvers, and Gatling guns (the invention of a Hartford citizen) — one is led to ask what is the cause of it all. Perhaps the character of the place is in part explained by the fact that of Rev. Mr. Hooker's company "many were persons of figure, who had lived in England in honor, affluence, and delicacy," but likewise did not shrink from the hardship of their journey hither on foot through the wilderness. They knew how to build up the centre of a commonwealth with force and enterprise, as well as with refinement; and their spirit has survived. But be the causes what they may, Hartford offers perhaps our best example of what an American city may become, when it is not too large for good government, when it avoids stagnation, preserves the true sentiment of a democracy, cares well for education and literature, and has had two centuries and a half of free and favorable growth.

A NEW ENGLAND VAGABOND

THERE may usually be found in the best-regulated minds some concealed liking for a vagabond, the relic of days when we thought it would be a very pleasant thing to run away with a circus or to sleep under a hay-stack. And even apart from this, it is certain that the lives of vagabonds often afford the very best historical materials. We have in copious profusion the letters and public documents of the able and upright men who organized and carried through the great revolt of the American colonies against the crown; but many events of that epoch are still imperfectly understood for want of adequate memorials of the scoundrels. Points of the greatest historical importance, such as the difficulties encountered by Washington in organizing the army at Cambridge, the frequent depletion of that army through desertion, the depreciation of the Continental currency, the startling outbreak of Shays's rebellion, can never be understood except by studying the revelations of the reprobates. Such confessions are very rare: there is, so far as I know, but one book which fully and frankly proclaims them; of that book I know but one copy, now in my possession, and this

condition of things furnishes ample reason for bringing to light once more the wholly disreputable and therefore most instructive career of Henry Tufts.

He was a man whose virtues might doubtless have been very useful to us, had he possessed any, but whose great historical value lies, strange as it may seem, in his vices. His dingy little book derives its worth from the very badness of the society into which it brings us; it reveals the existence, behind all that was decent and moral in that period, of a desperate and lawless minority.

Henry Tufts was born at Newmarket, New Hampshire, June 24, 1748, and he not only belonged to the true race of vagabonds, but was indeed the first thorough and unimpeachable member of that fraternity recorded amid our staid New England society. Previous examples, such as Morton of Merry Mount, and Sir Christopher Gardiner, Knight, were mere exotics, the consummate flower of an elder civilization. Our interest in them is to see how they bore the transplantation, and indeed how the transplantation bore them. But Henry Tufts was indigenous; purely a home product. Indeed, he belonged distinctly to what Dr. Holmes once called the Brahmin blood of New England, for his grandfather was a clergyman, and graduated at Harvard College in 1701. But if of clerical blood, the grandson came also of the breed of Autolycus, and his autobiography belongs essentially to what has been called the "picaresque" literature—that which includes Gil Blas, Guzman d'Alfarache, and Meriton Latroon. It is indeed unsurpassed in that department, for it contains a smaller proportion of anything but vagabondism than any similar work known to me in any language. His whole book records hardly a trace of honest industry, unless we include his service in the Revolutionary army, and even there his labors seem to have been strictly in the line of those afterward performed by Sherman's bummers. All else is unmitigated but not unvaried rascality. In some lives theft is an incident; with him it was the stated means of support. Whatever he had he stole. He can hardly be said to have invariably stolen his lodgings, for he often slept in haymows, and one night in a family tomb; but for all else—food, drink, and clothing—he relied upon what he graphically calls the rule of thumb. He would have fulfilled Falstaff's longing, "O for a fine young thief!" It was needless to inquire of him, as Charles Lamb asked of his Australian correspondents, what he did when he was not stealing. He was thieving all the time, unless we separate the periods when he was running away with his booty, or being taken to prison, or breaking out of it, which he did again and again.

He began his career in the usual manner of country boys who take to bad courses, by robbing orchards and henroosts. At fourteen he planned with two companions to steal bread, cheese, and cucumbers, and hide them in the woods. The others provided the bread and cheese, and he the cucumbers, stripping a whole patch. Being dissatisfied with the provision the others had made, he resolved to frighten them out of their share, so he raised an alarm so that they all took fright, after which he came back and carried off all the supplies. Not content with this, he informed his companions that the farmer they had robbed had captured him, and had exacted of him three days' labor, so that each of the other boys gave him a day's work on his father's farm as their share of the imaginary penalty. This early incident gives the key to his whole life, which was spent in first defrauding others and then his accomplices. When he was twenty-one he began the more public practice of his profession by stealing his father's horse and selling it for thirty dollars.

In the active practice of his profession he travelled habitually between Canada and Virginia, having a line of confederates, like a trapper's line of traps, through the whole route. His system of living reached a singular perfection. When he needed food he took it, wherever he found it, not confining himself to the necessaries of the table, but adding the luxuries, as when he stole a beehive and carried it some distance, on which occasion he must have discounted, so to speak, the stings of remorse. When he needed a pair of boots, he looked out for a shoemaker's shop, and contrived to be near it at nightfall. In respect to linen, for him the land seemed as covered with clothes-lines as now with telegraphic wires, and once when he needed smallclothes he spied through the window of a church a suitable pulpit cushion, stole it, sold the feathers, and made a pair of breeches of the green plush.

It is needless to say that in him horse-stealing—which has been in all ages, as Scott says of treason, "the crime of a gentleman"—rose to the dignity of a fine art. Some fifty separate thefts of this kind are recorded in his book. He asserts that he could go into a stable at night and select a particular horse by his way of eating his hay. He could so disguise a horse by paint that his former owner, riding by his side, did not know him. He would steal a horse, ride him twenty miles, and exchange him for another, and make two more exchanges before reaching one of his homes again; for he had almost as many homes as horses. In one case he took a neighbor's horse, sold it for fifty-one dollars, and on being detected, guided the neighbor to the place where it was sold, hoping to find it and steal it back again. Not finding it, they each stole another horse, were caught, and were punished with thirty-five lashes each from a cat-o'-nine-tails. In another case a man boasted that his horse had a special guard every night, and could not be stolen. Tufts accepted the challenge, gave the guards rum and opium, and rode the horse away. Nor was this talent limited to horses. While travelling up the Merrimac River he stole a valuable dog, sold it at Newbury for ten shillings, and then crossed the ferry. The dog swam the river and rejoined him. Aided by this happy suggestion, Tufts sold him twice more, at Newburyport for six shillings and at Bradford for a dollar, the dog each time swimming the river and rejoining his unwearied salesman.

His whole life was spent either in eluding pursuers or giving them reason to pursue him anew. He was so constantly suspected that he was often arrested when he had done nothing. The shop of Mr. Jacob Sheafe, in Portsmouth, had been robbed, and Tufts was stated to have been seen carrying a bundle through the streets in the evening. That was enough, and he was confined in Exeter jail some days, and then released. The same winter he was arrested under a similar suspicion in Newmarket, went to Exeter jail again for a week, and was again discharged. For the first of these detentions he was paid by Mr. Sheafe at the rate of a dollar per day. The jail thus became not only his lodging, his restaurant, his shelter from the cold, but the source of a moderate income, the most innocent perhaps that he ever enjoyed. The dollar a day was a sort of retaining fee for not thieving. It is observable that these unjust detentions happened always in the winter, and that he never complained of them; it was only when he deserved to be in jail that he repined under it.

It is said that hypocrisy is the homage that vice renders to virtue, and that counterfeit money vindicates the true. It therefore throws no discredit on two learned professions when I point out the obvious fact that medicine and theology always prove attractive to vagabonds. Tufts tried both. He says of himself, in his usual Micawber strain, "Destitute of a single shilling in the world, it was requisite to levy contributions on the public [*Il faut vivre, monsieur!*], so that I might elude 'haggard poverty's cruel grasp.' In some places, therefore, I practised physic, in others told fortunes, and in others again I discharged the sacerdotal office. I could turn my hand with equal facility to either of these scientific branches, and acquired some celebrity in them all." Accordingly, like another New England vagabond, Stephen Burroughs, Tufts combined preaching with his other

pursuits. "Having a mind to view the country and try my skill as a preacher, I purchased me a new suit of black, a large Scotch plaid gown, and cocked-up beaver." This was therefore the clerical costume in 1777, and the sect to which he proposed to minister was known as New Lights. It is a good instance of what is called feminine intuition that the only person who ever found him out in this character was a young girl. He being at Little Falls, Maine, was invited because of this clerical dress to speak at a weekday meeting, and the officiating clergyman declared that he had preached such a sermon as to prove him "an incarnate saint, if ever there was one upon the footstool." Upon this, Tufts says, a young woman named Peggy Cotton, a churchmember, rose and said: "He a saint? So is the devil incarnate. For my own part, I have no belief in his pretended sanctity, let him profess what he will." Being severely taken to task, the plain-spoken young woman proceeded to explain that on his first entrance into the meeting this gentleman of clerical appearance had surveyed her from head to foot in such a carnal manner that she "perceived that he had the devil in his heart." Great was the confusion; the speaker was severely rebuked by the officiating clergyman, followed by Tufts himself, who says, "As two against one are odds at tennis, so poor Peggy, finding her ground untenable against both, presently withdrew." Tufts, triumphant against her, became the clergyman's guest, and preached daily through his whole tour, undisturbed by the fear of man or woman.

His medical practice was really impaired by the same drawback with his preaching, for in one case a young girl whom he had brought back almost from the grave fell in love with him, and insisted on his eloping with her, which indeed required no great persuasion. He had a little more preparation, however, for medicine than for theology, taking the latter only by what is now called "heredity" from his grandfather, while to the former he devoted three years of exceedingly irregular study among the Indians. He was fond of all athletic feats, and having injured himself severely when about twenty-four, was advised by Captain Josiah Miles, "the great Indian fighter," to visit the aborigines at Sudbury, in Canada, who would cure him if any one could. Thither he went, therefore, by way of Pigwacket, in Maine, a region famous in the Indian wars, this being about fifty miles from the place of his stay among the savages. For three years (1772–5) he remained with them, and at first was visited daily by Molly Orcut, whose name is still preserved in memory as the most noted of Indian doctresses. He observed her methods, took her medicines, and received her bounty, for patients came to her from far and near, and she always had a considerable sum of money in her house. Besides her there were other renowned doctors, such as "Sabattus" and "old Philips"; and Tufts took great pains to study what he calls "Indian botany and physic," and thus gained a knowledge of simples, on which he frequently traded for the rest of his life. He added an Indian wife to the two or three others whom he had already accumulated, and he has left in his autobiography a very clear and compact account of the whole way of living among these people in Canada a hundred years ago—their mode of hunting, their habits in winter, their sleeping on the snow before a fire, their annual church pilgrimages to Montreal, their torturing punishment of their own criminals by putting thongs through the tendons of their arms and legs and stringing them up between two saplings to die.

On his return from Canada he found the country plunged in a war, and now begins what is historically the most valuable part of his record. In him we have the reverse side of the Revolutionary soldier; he shows vividly the worst part of that material out of which Washington had to make an army—the two months' men. Tufts enlisted, he tells us, because he thought it an easy life and more honorable than thieving; "though," as he justly remarked, and proceeded to exemplify, "a soldier may be a thief." He enlisted first under a Captain Clark, marched to Portsmouth, New Hampshire, worked at building barracks, serving, as he tells us with admiration, "through the whole term of his enlistment without desertion." Here he met General Sullivan and Colonel Cilley. Later he enlisted with one Captain Benbo for two months, and was marched to Winter Hill, near Boston. "Here," he says, "our troops fared at times so slenderly that we had to atone for the dearth of allowance by stealing pigs, poultry, and such articles."

Then follows a series of descriptions of thefts and cajoleries, all aided and abetted by the captain, who, if any one came to him with a complaint, allowed his troops to drive the complainant out of camp with snowballs. Then Tufts went home, staid awhile, and re-enlisted for a third term of two months, being first quartered at Winter Hill, then at Harvard College, and helping to build forts at Lechmere Point, now East Cambridge. The troops had half allowance of food, and had to spend their pay to eke it out, while Tufts's peculiar genius took the form of cheating the commissary and getting a double share of pork. "As our wants had been pressing, the officers of the company were by no means offended at my successful stratagem. Justly concluding that we should want a moderate quantity of rum while devouring this acquisition, I told them I would undertake to provide this desideratum likewise." He accordingly found an ignorant man, took an old summons for debt—of which he doubtless had many about him—and gave it to this man as a four-dollar bill, telling him to go to the sutler, buy rum, and bring back the change. He sent somebody else to fetch the rum before the cheat was discovered, and says that they "regaled themselves like lords," soldiers, officers, and all, apparently, while he "received the applause of every guest as well for my [his] zeal as ingenious contrivance." It was, no doubt, after dealing with some such company as this that Washington wrote those expressions of despair which have been so often quoted about his troops at Cambridge.

At a later time Tufts was arrested by mistake for a namesake who had enlisted "for the Ohio" as a soldier, but he was discharged. Then he went on a stolen horse to visit his brother, near West Point, at a place called "Soldier's Fortune." He carried to his brother, who was apparently a soldier, two shirts, doubtless from somebody's clothes-line; the brother accepted one only, having already a supply, and probably asking, like the little boy who had but one, "Do you suppose a man needs a thousand shirts?" But the other shirt brought Tufts into trouble, as he sold it to Sergeant Hodgdon for seventeen cartridges and a quarter-pound of powder. Buying or selling soldier's powder was then a capital offence, and he was presently brought before one Colonel Reid, who had the long-roll beaten and four com-panics of foot paraded under arms. Luckily every man proved to have his allowance of ammunition; so Tufts was dismissed. Then he made his way homeward among such a variety of French deserters, and other men who were hunting deserters and murderous Tory tavern-keepers, that it seems like a chapter out of Cooper's *Spy*. Later he enlisted for three years, under Captain True, for the regiment of Colonel Crane, at West Point, and was four weeks with three hundred others at the Castle in Boston Harbor, now Fort Independence. Then they went to Watertown, where he deserted; then he was captured and sent to Exeter jail, his old retreat. He escaped, was again captured, again escaped, and though closely followed, showing, as he says, the great need of soldiers in those days, he never again rejoined the army. In 1781, to be sure, he was taken as a deserter and carried nearly to West Point, but the whole party contrived to escape, and he made his way home on stolen horses, as usual.

It was while he was a deserter from the army, in the year 1780, that an event occurred which throws much light from below, as I may say, on the whole history of the Continental currency. He had rambled from West Point to Vermont, when the whim took him, he says, to visit "in rotation"—a good name for his mode of life—the town of Charlemont, in order to gain sight of Sally Judd, whom he had married when he had another wife living. He there put up at Spencer's tavern. A stranger rode to the door, a genteel, well-looking man, who dismounted to refresh himself, but declined to stay longer. On being pressed by Tufts, who liked his company, he said that his money was almost out, and he must be getting home. Tufts, who describes himself as being always generous when flush of money, offered to pay his bill. So he staid all night, and they shared the same room. In the darkness of the night the stranger made a confession. His name was Whiting, "and he had long been an agent for the British, who had engaged him for an emissary to explore the country and circulate counterfeit money." "As Congress had issued a paper medium to raise armies and pay off their troops, it imported their adversaries to discredit the currency as much as possible. And as such large quantities of paper had been issued already, the speediest way to effect the entire dissolution of

the system was to inundate the country with counterfeit bills." It accordingly proved that this genteel stranger, who had not enough good money to pay his landlord, had fifty thousand dollars of counterfeit Continental money in his pocket, and one thousand of this he gladly transferred to Tufts in exchange for "a little silver to discharge bills in particular places." Mr. Whiting rode away after breakfast, having had a distinction which belonged to few men, of teaching to Henry Tufts a wholly new line of roguery.

It is of historical interest to know how this fresh branch of industry succeeded. To all appearance, admirably. He says: "On the same day of my receiving the spurious bills, curiosity prompted me to make experiment of their currency. On trial, I found not the slightest difficulty in passing them. Indeed, my bills were such an exact imitation of the genuine ones that a man must have had more penetration than ordinary to have discerned the slightest difference." Accordingly, as the currency daily depreciated, he made haste to invest his hoard in something permanent; "bought a good horse, a new outfit of clothes, and materials for a complete suit of female apparel," which last he sent as a present to the yet unseen Sally Judd, intending it as a kind of atonement for the damage her character had suffered through his acquaintance. It is interesting to know that it brought Sally to an immediate interview, though a stormy one, which closed with a farther atonement in the shape of fifty counterfeit dollars, which she accepted, though without yielding her wrath. He then departed, and says: "I had not travelled many miles before I had the address to traffic away my horse for money and goods, which articles I transported, like an honest man, to my own family." Even Henry Tufts, it seems, had his standard of what constituted an honest man.

In the spring of 1793 Tufts got into serious difficulty. He bought, as he says, a silver table-spoon and five teaspoons, which turned out to have been stolen; for this he was tried for burglary, then a capital offence. The trial took place in 1793, James Sullivan being the prosecuting attorney. Tufts applied to the celebrated Theophilus Parsons to defend him; but he declining, Messrs. Sewall and Dana undertook the case—probably James Sewall, then of Marblehead, afterward a member of Congress, and

Francis Dana, afterward Chief-Justice, and father of the poet. Twice the jury disagreed and were sent out again; but they finally brought a verdict of guilty, and Tufts was sentenced to death. After several attempts to escape, he resigned himself to his fate, and his cell at Ipswich was cheered by visits from a man who offered him seventy dollars for authority to write his life, and from another who bid two guineas for his skeleton. He was to be hanged August 13, 1795. Great efforts were made for his reprieve, and the Harvard students signed a petition for it; but it was not till the very hour of execution had arrived that the order came from Governor Samuel Adams. Tufts says: "The people, who had collected to the number (it was said) of 3000, dispersed in the same manner as they came; but seeing their gathering had been but little gratifying to my feelings, I was far from regretting their departure."

Governor Adams afterward, at the petition of his nominal wife, Nabby, commuted his sentence to imprisonment for life, and he was sent to the Castle in Boston Harbor. I do not know that we have any other inside view of the Castle when used as a jail. There were then thirty pieces of artillery, and what he calls a company of soldiers. There were fifty prisoners—French, English, Dutch, Spanish, Irish, and American—giving an impression of greater variety than we would have supposed.

He was five years in this imprisonment, and when in 1798 (June 23d) the Castle was turned over to the United States government, he was transferred to Salem jail, where the jailer apparently had no wish to be troubled with him, and remarked, he says, that "the room was in a slender predicament, wherefore I must behave peaceably if I intended to stay long." He took the hint, got out within half an hour, and walked away, "musing upon the versatility of human affairs." Resolving to turn over a new leaf, "forswear sack and live cleanly," he debated for some time with which of his wives—the old Lydia or the new Abigail—he should carry out these virtuous purposes. Deciding on the old one, he followed her to the State of Maine, whither she had removed, first writing a high-sounding letter to Abigail, whose years of fidelity he thus repaid. Thenceforward he lived in Maine, "marching to and fro in the qual-ity of an Indian doctor," and thenceforward never, as he declares, although tradition does not confirm this, "taking clandestinely from man, woman, or child to the value of a single pin." This did not, however, prevent his stealing from a farmer his daughter—who was not worth "a row of pins," at any rate, by his account—and wandering into the wilderness in his old way; but they were captured. He himself returned to the long-suffering Lydia, and seems to have passed his declining years as decently as his nature and habits permitted. He died, it is said, at Limerick, Maine, January 31, 1831, in the eighty-third year of an uncommonly misspent life.

"At length," he says, in the preface to his book—"at length have my crimes and misdemeanors become antiquated, and the effects of them by lapse of time been done away. I no longer dread the scourge of future punishment, for on me has been exhausted its almost every species." "The major part of the following account was digested from the storehouse of memory, where long it lay quiescent in dormancy." This preface was dated at Limington, Maine, which he calls Lemington, in 1807, but the book was published at Dover, New Hampshire. The title-page reads: "A Narrative of the Life, Adventures, Travels, and Sufferings of Henry Tufts, now residing at Lemington, in the District of Maine. In substance as compiled from his own lips. *Ab ovo usque ad mala.*—Ovid. *Meliora video, proboque, deteriora sequor.*—Idem."

As has been already made obvious, the style of the book, whoever wrote it, is to the last degree high-flown and amusing. "Now had the more vertical rays of propitious Phœbus subdued the rigors of the inclement year, and transformed the truly hiemal blasts into pleasing zephyrous gales. Already had he renewed the beauties of the vernal bloom, and restored to the animate world the festive joys of a mild atmosphere." As my friend Mr. Charles Francis Adams, Jun., would no doubt remark, he who wrote this had studied Latin. He accordingly speaks of Virgil and Cicero, also of Milton and Dr. Cullen and Corporal Trim. He has peculiar names for places—names which have a geographical interest. "Number Four" for Charlestown, New Hampshire, and the "Lily Mountains" for the White Mountains. He has slang phrases now vanished: "hot-foot," "tanquam," "troynovant," "the rule of thumb" for thieving, and "to dance Sallinger's round" for immoral indulgences. He gives a very interesting catalogue of some seventy words in the thieves' jargon, or "flash language," which is thus shown to have come to this country in the last century. About half these words reappear in the similar catalogue of Captain Matsell, of the New York police, printed in 1859; the rest I have not yet identified. One phrase, "You're spotted," which he defines "You are likely to be found out," is now familiar, but is wrongly stated by Bartlett, in his *Dictionary of Americanisms*, to be of very recent origin. If this singular book were not interesting as the record of reprehensible actions, it would have a certain philological value as fixing the date of many reprehensible words.

I hope to have made it plain that it is not solely for the love of bad company that I have rescued from oblivion this irreclaimable old sinner. The historical value of the book is manifest. His whole picture exhibits to us at a most interesting period a wholly distinct and almost undescribed phase of New England society. If by a transformation scene the Continental Congress, with all its members sitting in tie-wigs, were to vanish from view and to disclose a scene from the *Black Crook*, the change would hardly be greater than to turn, let us say, from Washington's correspondence to Henry Tufts's autobiography. The latter discloses to us the underworld of the Revolutionary period—a world of sharpers and whippingposts, of drunken tavern-keepers and loose women. Tufts found an old acquaintance, always a scoundrel, in every piece of woods, and obtained without the least difficulty a mistress in every town. Drunken Barnaby's ride to London hardly brought him into more objectionable companionship. The whole book is like a Kirmesse of Rubens or Teniers, and many passages will not bear quotation. Tufts seems rarely to have been given to liquor—perhaps he found, like Bret Harte's gamblers, that it interfered with business —but his taste for all loose company was inexhaustible; and after he was fifty or more, and had, by his own account, utterly given up stealing, he was still at the mercy of every disreputable female that came along; and they often came, and sometimes in the form of respectable farmers' daughters and women on their way to prayer-meeting. Of course it is easy to say that he lied; that probability must steadily be kept in view at every page. The general atmosphere of a book is unmistakable, and here the coarse verisimilitude is very great. No one can read these pages and not recognize that there must have been throughout a large part of rural New England a stratum of society like that still found in some isolated and degraded settlements among the mountains—hamlets whose wandering inhabitants are habitually called gypsies, although without gypsy blood.

SALEM

IN those devout days of Salem, during
the seventeenth century, if a man
possessed a somewhat personal opinion or conviction, it behooved him to get
rid of it suddenly and unostentatiously,
without losing any time. He was wise
in not thinking at all, except within his
own home at night, with the doors securely bolted, and preferably in bed when
the lights were extinguished and his head
lay buried beneath the blankets.

For if one may believe the early annals
of Salem, a New England Christian community in 1640 was not a healthy or
agreeable place of residence for one who
was troubled with mental activity. Your
God-fearing Puritan of this period, with
its peculiar atmosphere and pressure,
was so earnest in his desire to serve his
God that he did things to his brother
who did not happen to share his views,
that were extremely original but dis-
agreeable—to the brother, of course—
and usually hurt, and not infrequently
disfigured, him.

In his religious zeal he would pounce
on his neighbor, and after beating him
unmercifully, would slit and sear his
nostrils, and send him through the streets,
condemned to wear a halter visibly about
his neck for life. Or during this eruption
the Salemite might have the good fortune to fall in with some unhappy Friend
whom old associations had lured back to
Salem after banishment from Massachusetts; and though firmly believing that
the latter was created in God's image,
this did not prevent him from slightly
remodelling him by the simple process of
peeling one of his ears off as he would
skin an orange. There was a thoroughness about the work of the early Salemite
which commands attention.

If the Friend returned, his Puritan
brother showed himself a man with a keen
sense of the symmetrical—and removed
his other ear. If the Quaker was hardy
enough to venture back a third time, the
man to whom godly attainments were as
food and drink still had his trump card
to play; for the Court of Assistants enacted "that they [Friends] shall have
their tongues bored through with a hot
iron, and be employed in the house
of correction till sent away at their
own cost."

The extraordinary courage and enterprise that lifted Salem on a tidal wave
of prosperity in the first half of the nineteenth century, when, in the romantic
East India days, a fleet of one hundred
and ninety-eight vessels flying the Salem
signal opened commerce with every civilized and barbaric market on the globe,
have left not a little of their fibre in the
present generation. They reveal themselves
in the Salem gamin, whom you at first
barely notice as he strolls casually along in
your wake, intent on your every movement.
When, fifteen minutes after his advent,
he is still to be seen circling abstractedly
about you, his diminutive presence becomes slightly oppressive. But after you
have selected a comfortable post at the
Custom House, and settled exquisitely
and drowsily back to evoke with each
breath of the soft sea air the deep wooden
drumming of the calking-hammers that
once sounded along these empty quays
in mellow reverberations, you begin to
realize that the small boy of Salem is
about to become an obsession, as he pops
out at you again from behind an adjoining column, bringing you out of the early
forties with an unpleasant start.

Facing the same predicament in New
York, I should know from experience
how to act; for the New York urchin
is merely interested in the price the
artist is receiving for his work. I should
therefore take him aside and state the
modest sum; he would reply, "Aw, say—
quit yer kiddin'," and I should be at
liberty to move down the street in peace.
In Virginia, the boy who follows you
patiently for blocks has designs on your

A BIT OF LOWER SALEM
Etched by C. H. White

cigar stub, and will make overtures for its possession when the propitious moment arrives. I anticipate his move; present the stub; make a valuable friend, and avoid future trouble by smoking a pipe. In Boston, when the small boy appears with monotonous regularity at each new street corner, eying me narrowly, I take pains to make his acquaintance, and explain kindly that I am not looking for trouble; that the thing I carry as unostentatiously as possible under my arm is not a club, but a three-legged sketching-stool. Then I open the thing, to show him the mechanism, and request him to sit on it for a minute or two to see how it feels. He invariably accepts my invitation, with the result that I am as a monarch in his eyes, while he becomes my faithful chamberlain, who, with insistent devotion, stands beside me while I work, squashing the flies as they light on the imperial body, or skilfully removing the insects as they ascend my trouser leg.

But with the Salem boy one's previous experience is of little avail, and I hastened helplessly down the steps of the Custom House with a subconscious feeling that something was following me, and with a premonition that it would soon overtake me. It appeared no larger than the little speck that seems to float persistently in the retina when one is bilious, but it was equally irritating. I quickened my steps and tried to put the thing out of my mind; but the distinct pattering of diminutive feet made this an impossibility; and as I hurried on I could feel a gimletlike eye boring its way into my back and through my pockets, making a careful inventory of my belongings.

By darting rapidly into one of the narrow streets intersecting my course I succeeded in giving him the slip, and followed up my advantage by diving into what appeared to be a short cut to Essex Street. Here I breathed freely again, until hasty reconnoitring revealed this to be a blind alley. It was while I stood deliberating upon the advisability of remaining quietly where I was until he should have passed on down the street, that I realized that I was a marked man, and that he had pocketed me.

Through the only exit open to me an extremely small boy was rapidly approaching. It was my first opportunity to look him over carefully. His cap, tilted far back on his head, revealed a shock of hair the color of bleached straw, that emphasized the deep sunburnt skin mottled with large freckles. The *ensemble* formed a quaint mask, through which peeped out two keen gray eyes that never left me. In a moment we were face to face.

"Where are you going, mister?" he asked.

"Down the street."

"What are you going to do there?"

"Nothing."

"Who are you looking for?"

"Nobody."

I felt I had him in ruins—utterly

CLASSIC PORTICOS OF SILVER WHITE

Etched by C. H. White

crushed by my brevity. But at that time I was unfamiliar with the resources of the Salem boy; he is irresistible. Stepping back for a moment to settle his hat more firmly on his head, he closed in and spoke briskly without a comma or a period.

"Say—mister," he began, "come on and let me show you the House of the Seven Gables the place where Hawthorne was married his sweetheart's house the place where he lost his job."

He paused for a moment to catch his breath, and proceeded: "Fer ten cents I'll show you the whole business and let you see the funny things in the Old Burial Ground."

He is the same boy who, in the golden days of Salem's maritime supremacy, knew the characteristics of every ship in Salem's great merchant fleet, from figurehead to each particular patch in the canvas; the same wide-awake urchin who was to be found in his idle moments on some deserted wind-swept promontory scanning the horizon; who noted the distant speck of white heading for port, observed the trim of her sail, and having compared it with the ships due in Salem on his schedule of arrivals, raced wildly across-country for the town to notify the captain's wife and receive the customary fee of one dollar.

As you enter Derby Street on your way to the Custom House, where, in more prosperous times, the main current of the commercial life of the city ebbed and flowed, making the streets ring with the cheerful din of business activity, and reach the deserted quays, you feel not unlike a stranger who has wandered into an abandoned theatre and walks alone across the stage, picking his way gingerly through the tattered scenery, long after generations of actors who made the place echo with their laughter have departed.

Here one is continually stumbling across eloquent reminders of past splendor in the numerous old mansions of former Salem merchants, still marshalled in broken line, looking seaward, with their graceful porticos tufted with ivy, fluttering in the clear sunlight; and you have an irresistible desire to sneak up the narrow path and give the heavy knocker a resounding thump on the massive door just to hear the echoes roll through the house with a deep, gloomy resonance.

I seldom passed this way without catching a fleeting glimpse of the white, almost transparent, faces of extreme old age framed in the neat little Colonial window panes of the Aged Women's Home, gazing wistfully through lacklustre eyes upon the crumbling wharves below, where, as young women, many of them had stood with blanched cheeks in an agony of suspense during the intensely dramatic moment when every woman tasted the bitter sorrows of widowhood, and stood crushed with a premonition of impending disaster, looking out to where the great merchantman, after a two-year absence, loomed up in her distorted imagination as a mammoth coffin, as she stood on her last tack for Derby wharf with her flag at half mast.

Where formerly the broad quays swarmed with "lumpers," or longshoremen, busily unloading the cargo of silk and ivory or heaping the wharf with dates and coffee, there rise now pyramids of dilapidated hogsheads and rusty iron rails. The hoarse orders of the landing have given place to a silence broken only by the distant humming of the looms in the great cotton factory across the water, punctuated at times by the tremolo of a motor boat threading its way through the channel, and filling the air, once redolent with foreign spices, with the stench of gasoline and bilge-water.

A few Greeks repairing hogsheads, a solitary fisherman asleep over his line, a white-haired, sunbaked derelict who saw the thing accomplished, are all that remain to link one with the days when on one voyage a ship paid in duties the neat sum of ninety-two thousand three hundred and ninety dollars and ninety-four cents!

If one did not wander through the neighborhood of the docks, one would never suspect that the old town had ever suffered reverses. It is one of the best fed, the most prosperous looking towns in New England to-day. The streets, spanned by titanic elms, become cathedral naves; and through the lofty arch of whispering foliage steal at infrequent intervals into the cool depths below shafts of limpid sunlight, sifting across the splendid rows of Colonial mansions, dipping in restless golden blots into the privacy of some sombre interior, to fan

An Old Corner

Etched by C. H. White

to life again the rich crimson smouldering in rare mahogany.

The masts that once served in half forgotten ships plying between Salem and the Orient are to be found to-day in their supreme metamorphosis, serving as doorposts or columns in the classic porticos of silver white, overlooking the well groomed lawns like ghosts of a time when good taste in America was hereditary. Each immaculate porch one passes in a day's idling and every brightly polished door-knocker of the most humble cottage gives one a sense of Dutch cleanliness, evoking visions of well stocked larders and kitchen floors scrubbed white with holystone.

Evidence of that thrift which contributed its share in making Salem the prosperous little city it is to-day smote me unawares the first day I ventured into one of the numerous "antique" stores.

The shop's exterior was tempting, and I entered, to find some indifferent mahogany littered about a severe maiden lady who stood framed in an extremely interesting interior. I noted the disposition of things, and was preparing to leave, having just replaced something on the shelf where it belonged, when the lady said, " That will be ten cents."

" Thank you; I really couldn't use it," I replied, edging away for the door.

" But the *charge* is ten cents," she added, coldly, moving nearer.

" So I understand," said I, skilfully manœuvring for a hurried but dignified exit.

" The admission to the store is ten cents," she put in here, with chilly distinctness, outflanking me.

For anything savoring of novelty in this *fin de siècle* business world let us be truly thankful! The shopkeeper who charges you a fee for the privilege of entering her store does not lose in dignity by the proceeding. She insists upon the disbursement with such an air of divine right that for the moment you feel strangely like the recipient of a favor, and wander down the street a prey to vague fears that possibly you may owe her money.

What extraordinary enterprise and daring did to bring Salem into prominence in · the early thirties and forties, the civic spirit displayed by her citizens to-day is doing in a measure to make Salem unique, by her possession of two museums—in the Essex Institute and the East India Marine Society—without parallel in America, and with few prototypes in Europe.

In Salem one finds the curious anomaly of an American city whose entire population possesses a Gallic concern for the preservation of every atom of evidence that may serve to shed light on graceful traditions or obsolete customs. Fortunately nothing was deemed too unimportant by the voluntary contributors, and to-day nothing is lacking. You may sit before the fire in a Colonial kitchen, complete with all the utensils, or—here let me whisper it—turn to the less known corner where reposes the quaint collection of the dainty French garters affected by Colonial belles, quaintly inscribed with an appropriate *chanson d'amour* of Béranger that mingled with the white mist of lingerie.

The public spirit that has contributed to make these museums what they are to-day I found later in its full bloom at the Major's elm; and only realized then the latent significance of sundry corners we idlers pass thoughtlessly by in our rambles when seen through the retrospective eye of an old resident. Now I know that if I were carelessly to toss a brick into the crowded section of Essex Street, I could not fail to hit some member of the last generation who could claim kinship with those sturdy pioneers whose untiring efforts brought order and beauty out of chaos and turned the prim formality of the streets into Dantesque avenues of elms.

In this particular corner I have in mind there is a doorstep so secluded that one may work for hours at a time in the shade without being disturbed, watching the light and shade play over the leviathan elm that occupies the centre of the little square before you, dwarfing everything in the vicinity. Nestling comfortably beneath an almost impenetrable cloud of foliage is a sombre porch surrounded by a Palladian window. It is from this house, half veiled in perpetual twilight, that I noticed an extremely well preserved old gentleman emerging one morning. This was the Major, and a few steps brought him opposite me.

" I hope that you will pardon my intruding on your privacy," he began; " but I could not resist the temptation of asking whether you are going to include the tree in your sketch?"

" It is my principal motive," I replied, exhibiting the embryonic etching.

" I am particularly interested in that old tree, as my father planted it," he continued, thoughtfully. " Of course I was too young to recall the incident." We chatted for a time, and then he left me, with an invitation to drop in on him when I had finished.

I sat for some. time pondering over this occurrence, when a well modulated feminine voice awakened me from my reverie, and said, " I suppose as the others have looked, I may?"

She was a matronly woman of sixty years, whose clear, transparent, luminous skin and heavy tresses of pure white hair lent a sunny brightness to her smile.

Her clear, gray eyes met mine with engaging frankness.

"I am particularly interested in that tree," she mused, as she compared my work with the original before her. "In fact, we seldom look at it without a feeling of proprietorship. You see, my father planted it, about eighty years ago."

"I have heard rumors," I put in gently, "that the Major's father was the man who claimed that honor."

At this she was seized with an uncontrollable fit of mirth.

"Well, we'll let it go at that," she replied, trying her best to regain her composure. Then, in a tone more confidential, she whispered, "His father may have been present when father planted it; but I doubt it."

It was precisely midday when a shadow stole over my copperplate, and I looked up to find in the old gentleman who cast it a type such as one instinctively connects with the period when cross-country rides, roaring wood fires, and good ale were part of the day's routine. He was a lovable, distinguished figure in his neat old-fashioned clothes. After bowing with extreme urbanity, and expressing the hope that he was not disturbing me, he remarked that the tree interested him.

"It's a wonderful old tree—wonderful!" He lifted his eyes to the network of soaring, twisted branches above us. "A suitable subject—very. If my father could have only known—" he resumed, reflectively. "Ah yes, if he could only have realized that the result of his industry should have become the inspiration for another."

"You mean—?" I asked.

"Planted that elm. Yes, sir. I can see him now as I stand here, digging away with his little shovel. I recall distinctly, as if it were yesterday, the sharp slap he gave me for wandering near that well."

Then suddenly recollecting that there was no well where he indicated, he added: "Of course they've filled it in. It used to stand before the house; that was a long time ago."

"What a curious coincidence!" I exclaimed; "for only a moment ago I must have been speaking to your sister. She was explaining to me how her father had planted the elm."

"Is it possible?" he exclaimed, much interested. "It is true I have a married sister in Salem."

"Lives across the street?" I queried, indicating the house.

"Ah no . . . I'm afraid it cannot have been she. Her residence is at the other end of the town."

Then searching his memory for a moment, his eyes brightened as he muttered: "Who would have dreamt it? Did I understand you to say that the lady intimated that—"

"Her father planted it," I completed the sentence. "Do you know her?"

"Oh, perfectly," he replied, still puzzled; "a charming woman—worthy people,—but at the time to which I allude I doubt very much whether their family had moved to Salem."

"And the Major—?" I asked. "I have heard that his father is credited with—er—the business to which you alluded." I was afraid to come right out with it.

"Dear me! What an amazing development!" He gasped. "I knew his father well. Knew the Major—capital fellows —both of them. But, my *dear* sir . . ." His explanation was cut short by an explosion of innocent merriment. When he had recovered himself sufficiently he added, whimsically, "But do not let me disillusion you," and soon was lost to view in the bend of the street.

It is true that an aged ship-carpenter, who appeared just as I had bundled my things together to depart, did frankly admit that he was in no way implicated in the planting of the tree; but our subsequent conversation soon developed that he hailed from Essex. He exonerated himself still further by offering to produce evidence to prove that the elm in question had never been planted, but had stood there long before the houses. I pass him by without comment, for my duty is plain to me in the midst of these conflicting statements; it is the Major's story that I gladly accept unconditionally: he saw me first.

THE REPUBLIC OF VERMONT

WITHIN the domain of the United States on the North-American continent there have been divers independent republics, the very name of three of which is known to but a few, while the record of two others, though memorable, is fast fading. How many Americans of to-day have heard, for example, of the Commonwealth of Watauga, which in 1772 was organized as an independent community by North-Carolinians who had crossed the Alleghenies, and, descending into the basin of the Tennessee, had made themselves homes in the valley of the Watauga River? How many remember the Commonwealth of Transylvania, which was organized in the eastern part of what is now Kentucky in 1775, and which sent to the Continental Congress a delegate, —who, however, was not admitted? How many have heard of the short-lived State of Franklin, or Frankland, which at a somewhat later period was self-created

out of certain western counties of North Carolina? Of the present generation of schoolboys at the North, not many are familiar with the early history of Texas, which declared its independence of Mexico in 1836, and which for some nine years remained an autonomous republic, entering into treaties with foreign countries, including the United States. Again, but little attention is now paid to that part of the annals of Vermont which deals with the fourteen years during which the territory bearing that name was an independent republic, unadmitted to the union of the American colonies, although it disclaimed allegiance to the British crown, rejected the overtures of British generals, and bore a conspicuous and useful part in the war of the Revolution. It is worth while to review the circumstances under which Vermont assumed a position so anomalous and so calculated to test the stuff of which her patriots were made.

Although the region which we call Vermont was made known to Europeans by Samuel Champlain as early as 1609, and although during the next century and a half the lake named after that explorer was a thoroughfare for military expeditions in Indian and colonial wars, and although strategic points within the area of the present State were occupied by French and English military posts, the first permanent settlement was made as lately as 1724, at Fort Dummer, within the limits of the town of Brattleboro. Even in 1760 Vermont did not contain more than 300 inhabitants, and these were scattered along the western bank of the Connecticut River, within fifty miles of the southern border of the present State. The truth is that, aside from the danger to which English settlers would be exposed at the hands of the French and the Indians, there was no provincial authority which could give an undisputed title to the lands lying between the Connecticut and Lake Champlain. New Hampshire claimed that, under a royal grant, it extended as far west as did Massachusetts. Massachusetts claimed a strip of Vermont lying between the Connecticut River and Lake Champlain and immediately north of the present boundary of the old Bay State. New York, on the other hand, claimed that, under the grant made by Charles II. to his brother, the Duke of York, her territory stretched as far east as the Connecticut River. Ultimately, in 1764, the boundary controversy was determined by the British crown in favor of New York; but meanwhile Wentworth, the royal Governor of New Hampshire, had chartered 138 towns in the disputed territory, and the settlers declined to recognize the New York provincial authorities. The determination of New York to enforce its jurisdiction would, no doubt, have led to bloodshed had not the attention of the colonists been diverted from local disputes by the controversies with the mother country which preceded the Revolutionary war. It is worth while to note the grounds on which the British Board of Trade, which at first regarded the boundary controversy with indifference, was ultimately persuaded to confirm New York's claim to the land between the Connecticut River and Lake Champlain. Weight was attached by the Board of Trade to the argument put forward by Lieutenant-Governor Colden of New York, who pointed out that the New England governments were all formed on republican principles, and that those principles were zealously inculcated in the minds of their youth. The government of the province of New York, on the other hand, was framed, he said, as nearly as might be, after the model of the English Constitution. It would be bad policy, therefore, for British statesmen to contract the frontiers of New York and enlarge the power and influence of New-Englanders.

MAJOR-GENERAL ARTHUR ST. CLAIR

The Green Mountain Boys, as the occupants of the New Hampshire Grants west of the Connecticut River were called, had, perhaps, stronger reasons than any other American colonists for rebelling against the British crown. They had at stake not only the political liberties which were threatened by Parliament's assumption of a right to tax the colonies, but also the title to the homes which they had created in the wilderness;

GENERAL RICHARD MONTGOMERY

for the provincial government of New York, which, as we have seen, had procured a confirmation of its jurisdiction from the Board of Trade, had made grants amounting in the aggregate to nearly two million five hundred thousand acres, and covering much of the same territory previously conveyed by the Governor of New Hampshire. If the colonies should proclaim and achieve their independence, it was extremely improbable that New York's claim to jurisdiction over the tract between Lake Champlain and the Connecticut could be enforced, while, on the other hand, should the colonies remain subject to the British crown, it would only be a question of time when British troops would be called upon to make good the decision of the Board of Trade and to oust the

Green Mountain Boys from their farms. Indeed, a beginning in that direction had already been made, and the first victims in the contest between the colonists and the King fell, not at Lexington, but in Vermont. Early in 1775 orders had been given to open the Court of Common Pleas under the royal judges, in what was called by the New York authorities the county of Cumberland, at Westminster in the New Hampshire Grants, on the eastern side of the Green Mountains,— which bisect, it will be remembered, the State of Vermont from the northeast to the southwest. To prevent this assertion of the King's authority and of New York's jurisdiction a body of young men from the neighboring farms took possession of the court-house on March 13 of the year named. The royal sheriff, who, against the wish of the judges, had raised sixty men armed with guns and bludgeons, demanded possession of the building, and, after reading the riot act and refusing to concede terms, late in the night ordered his party to fire. In this way he made his entry by force, having mortally wounded two of the occupants of the court-house. The act put an end to the supremacy of King George III. and of New York to the east of Lake Champlain. Armed men poured in from towns in the grants, and from the borders of New Hampshire and Massachusetts; they instituted a jury of inquest, and the royalists implicated in the attack were sent to jail in Massachusetts for trial.

Even before this shedding of blood at Westminster, Ethan Allen, one of the

THE CONSTITUTION OF THE REPUBLIC OF VERMONT
Facsimile (somewhat reduced) of the title-page as first printed

most influential settlers in the disputed territory, foreseeing war with Great Britain, had sent assurances to Oliver Wolcott, of Connecticut, that a regiment of Green Mountain Boys would assist their American brethren. On March 29, 1775, John Brown, of Pittsfield, who had passed through the district on his way to Montreal, wrote to Samuel Adams and Joseph Warren at Boston that "should hostilities be committed by the King's troops, the people of the New Hampshire Grants would seize the fort at Ticonderoga." He added that they were the proper persons for the job. So, indeed, they proved. The great deed which supplied the patriots with the cannon and the ammunition indispensable for the relief of Boston was planned, it is true, in Connecticut, but it was mainly executed by Vermonters. Parsons of Connecticut, on his way to Hartford, meeting Benedict Arnold, who was bound for Massachusetts, obtained from him an account of the state of the fortress at Ticonderoga, and learned how large a number of brass cannon had been collected there. At Hartford, on April 27, 1775, Parsons, with the assistance of five others, projected the capture of the fort, and without formally consulting the Assembly or the Governor and Council, obtained on their own receipts the necessary money from the public treasury. On May 1 a party of sixteen Connecticut men left Salisbury, having meanwhile urged Ethan Allen, by an express messenger, to raise recruits for the projected expedition in the New Hampshire Grants. Having been joined at Pittsfield in Massachusetts by Colonel James Easton and some volunteers from Berkshire, the Connecticut men pushed forward, and at Bennington found Ethan Allen, who had sent the alarm throughout the hills and valleys of Vermont. On Sunday, the 7th of May, about a hundred Green Mountain Boys and nearly fifty soldiers from Massachusetts had assembled at Castleton. Just then arrived Benedict Arnold with only one attendant, but bringing a commission from the Massachusetts Committee of Safety. The commission was disregarded, so was Colonel Easton's superior rank, and the men unanimously elected Ethan Allen their chief.

According to Bancroft's narrative, on May 9 the party arrived at Orwell on Lake Champlain. With the utmost difficulty a few boats were brought together, and eighty-three men, crossing the lake with Allen, landed near Ticonderoga. The boats were sent back for the rearguard, but, if they were to be waited for, the fort could not be taken by surprise. The eighty-three men were, therefore, at once drawn up in three ranks, and as the sun rose Allen addressed them. Then placing himself at the head of the centre file he marched to the gate. The sentry snapped a gun at him, but the Americans rushed into the fortress, darted

upon the guards, and raising the Indian war-whoop, formed on the parade-ground in a hollow square, so as to face each of the barracks. The British commander came out, undressed, with his breeches in his hand. "Deliver to me the fort instantly," said Allen. "By what authority?" asked the commander. "In the name of the great Jehovah and the Continental Congress," answered Allen. Thus Ticonderoga, which had cost the British nation forty million dollars, a succession of campaigns, and many lives, was won in ten minutes by a few undisciplined Green Mountain Boys without any loss of life or limb. With the fortress the Americans acquired a 13-inch mortar and more than a hundred pieces of cannon, besides swivels, small arms, and military stores. To a detachment under Seth Warner the neighboring fortress of Crown Point surrendered upon the first summons. Another detachment took possession of Skenesboro, now known as Whitehall.

The capture of Ticonderoga was not by any means the only service rendered to the Revolutionary cause by the inhabitants of the New Hampshire Grants. In September, 1775, General Montgomery, who commanded the expedition against Montreal, was joined by Seth Warner's regiment of Green Mountain Boys. Ethan Allen, who was detached with Warner to the banks of the St. Lawrence, was taken prisoner in a desperate attempt to take Montreal by surprise. He experienced very hard usage, being carried to England in irons on the ground that he was a leader of banditti rather than a prisoner of war. Again, in the summer of 1777, when the British under Burgoyne moved southward and overtook the rearguard of St. Clair,—who, much to Washington's regret, had abandoned Ticonderoga,—one of the American regiments fled disgracefully, but the other two regiments, one of which was commanded by Seth Warner, made a stout resistance, until they were overpowered by numbers. Warner, however, with some ninety men, came up with St. Clair at Rutland two days after the battle. Again, it is well known that Burgoyne was fatally weakened by the loss of nearly eight hundred men at Bennington, where, although Stark of New Hampshire commanded, a great part of the work was done by Warner's regiment of Green Mountain Boys.

It might be supposed that such a record of sturdy patriotism would have induced the American colonies to fulfil the wishes of the Vermonters for territorial autonomy. Such, however, was not the case. On January 15, 1777, the inhabitants of what is now Vermont had organized themselves into an independent State, had applied to Congress for admission to the Union, and had adopted a Constitution. As we have seen, a Continental regiment had been raised and officered in Vermont, of which Warner had been commissioned colonel. Nevertheless, the Continental Congress, through the influence of New York, disclaimed any intention of countenancing the pretensions of Vermont to independence, and the Vermont petition for admission into the Union was dismissed with some asperity. From that moment until the close of the war the British officials in Canada spared no effort to court the good-will of the Green Mountain Boys, and to persuade them to renew allegiance to the British crown. Burgoyne, for instance, issued a proclamation for a convention of ten deputies from each township in the New Hampshire Grants, who were to assemble at Castleton and to take measures for the re-establishment of the royal authority. The failure of this first attempt to take advantage of the repellent attitude assumed by the American Congress toward the Vermonters did not discourage Carle-

THOMAS CHITTENDEN
Elected Governor of the Republic of Vermont in
March. 1778

ton, the Governor of Canada, for he continued to make similar overtures until nearly the end of the contest.

Now let us trace, as briefly as possible, the civil history of the New Hampshire Grants during the period of their existence as an independent republic. Undaunted by the rejection of their application for admission into the Union, they organized themselves under a Constitution, and in March, 1778, elected Thomas Chittenden as Governor. There is no doubt that Chittenden was a man of decided ability; but such was the simplicity of manners in the New Hampshire Grants that, though Governor of a new State, to which office he continued to be annually re-elected for many years, he still retained his former occupation of farmer and innkeeper. In colonial times, to keep an inn had not been looked upon as a mean occupation. No fewer than three American generals, Putnam, Weedon, and Sumner, besides numerous inferior officers, had been drawn from that calling.

Having been kept out of the Union by New York, and having some ground for the belief that New Hampshire also had looked unfavorably on her request for admission to the Union, the Republic of Vermont struck back. In June, 1778, sixteen of the newly settled townships on the east bank of the Connecticut, desiring to escape from the heavy taxes which the progress of the war had made needful in New Hampshire, sought annexation to Vermont. After some hesitation, the applicants were adopted into the new State; but as the Continental Congress disapproved of the proceeding, and sent a committee to inquire into it, the connection with the New Hampshire towns was presently dissolved. In June, 1779, an ineffectual attempt was made by the towns on both banks of the river to secede from New Hampshire on the one hand and from Vermont on the other, and to constitute themselves into an independent commonwealth by the name of New Connecticut. New Hampshire, assuming that the movement had been fomented by Green Mountain Boys, revived her old claim to the territory of Vermont. Thereupon Massachusetts, suspecting connivance between New Hampshire and New York for the purpose of dividing the land west of the Connecticut between them, reasserted her old claim to the southern part of Vermont, averring that her northwestern boundary was a line drawn due west from the junction of the two principal branches of the Merrimac. Meanwhile, collisions having taken place between the authorities of Vermont and the adherents of New York, who formed a considerable minority in the southwestern townships, the Continental Congress recommended that all the claimants should refer their pretensions to her decision. In September, 1780, New York and New Hampshire consented to do so; but Massachusetts, sincerely anxious for the independence of Vermont, refused to take part in the reference, fearing that it might end in the partition of the new State between the other two claimants. As at the date named the Articles of Confederation still remained unratified, Congress had as yet no compulsory powers in the matter.

Resenting her treatment at the hands of her western and eastern neighbors, Vermont again recurred to the offensive. Not only were the New Hampshire towns on the east bank of the Connecticut readmitted in February, 1781, as a part of the new republic, but along with them in May of the same year all the townships of New York recently created east of the Hudson and north of the Massachusetts line. Simultaneously, negotiations, the management and, indeed, the knowledge of which were confined to Chittenden and a few others, were entered into with the British authorities in Canada, with the double object of guarding against invasion from that quarter and of operating on the fears of Congress. Alarmed at these negotiations, which became known through intercepted letters, Congress, later in 1781, consented to a conference between a committee of that body and certain agents of Vermont, and the result of the conference was a resolution of Congress which indirectly but virtually promised that if Vermont would relinquish her late encroachments on New Hampshire and New York, she should be recognized as an independent State and admitted into the Union. Vermont at first declined to accede to this proposal, but subsequently, influenced by the prospect of civil war, and especially by a letter which Washington addressed to Governor Chittenden, the Legislature of Vermont dissolved connection with the annexed townships and retired within the original limits of the New Hampshire Grants.

Having thus complied with the conditions prescribed by Congress, Vermont, in February, 1782, claimed the promised admission into the Union. Peace with Great Britain, however, was now regarded as certain, and the fear of Vermont's adhesion to Canada being over, the influence of New York again became predominant in the councils of the Confederation. The application of Vermont to Congress was not acted upon; on the contrary, she was called upon to make restitution to the banished partisans of New York,—a demand accompanied with threats, which Congress, however, had no means of carrying into execution. Henceforward until 1791 Vermont remained an independent republic. Nor, indeed, until the more efficient government established by the Constitution went into operation in 1789, was she much tempted to join the Confederation. Free from the burden of the Continental debt, and from the perpetual calls of Congress for money, and safeguarded by the rapid increase and hardy character of her population from any attempt at coercion on the part of New York, Vermont for a number of years after the peace of 1783 evinced little anxiety for admission into the Union. The opposition of New York to her admission was strongly supported by the four Southern States, which, as experience had shown, through the creation of the commonwealths of Watauga, Transylvania, and Frankland, had good reason to dread the effect of Vermont's example upon their own backwoodsmen. Pennsylvania also was alarmed by some movements toward independence on the part of the settlers in her territory west of the Alleghenies, and she went so far as to impose the penalties of treason upon any attempts to set up an independent government within her limits. On the Vermont question, therefore, Pennsylvania went with New York and the South.

In order to learn what kind of republic it was that the Green Mountain Boys set up we must glance at its organic law. The Constitution originally adopted in 1777 was slightly altered in 1785. Most of its provisions seem to have been copied from the first Constitution of Pennsylvania, with some modifications borrowed from Connecticut. When we call to mind how many of the United States had at the time property qualifications for the franchise, we shall appreciate the fact that the Green Mountain Boys gave the right of suffrage to every man twenty-one years old, of peaceable behavior, and a resident of the State for one year preceding the election. These liberal conditions had undoubtedly much to do with the rapid inpour of settlers into Vermont from adjoining States. The executive power was vested in a Governor, or, in case of his death or disability, a Lieutenant-Governor, and twelve counsellors annually chosen on a general ticket. The legislative power was confided to a single Assembly, of which the members were annually elected by the towns—each town to have one representative and no more, irrespective of its population. Remarkable were the provisions for consulting public opinion. No bill could be passed by the Legislature until after it had been printed for the consideration of the people; nor until it had been laid before the Governor and Council, who had the right to suggest amendments; nor, except in cases of urgent necessity, until it had lain over for one session. By the revision of 1785, however, this delay could only be imposed at the will of the Governor and Council

in the event of the non-adoption of such amendments as they might have proposed. The judicial power was vested in a supreme court of five judges, county courts, and probate courts. Here again it is surprising to find Vermont providing at that early date that all judges of all the courts, as well as sheriffs and justices of the peace, should be elected annually by the Assembly. Unique, so far as we know, in modern times, was the provision, seemingly borrowed from the practice of the Roman Republic,—the provision, namely, that a Council of Censors, thirteen in number, should be chosen by the people on a general ticket once in seven years, to inquire if the Constitution had been violated, and to suggest amendments to it for the consideration of a convention which the censors were authorized to call by a two-thirds vote. The proposed amendments, however, must be published six months beforehand for the consideration of the people.

Still more creditable to the Republic of Vermont was the first article of the Bill of Rights, which declared that "no male person born in this country, or brought from over sea, ought to be bound by law to serve any person as a servant, slave, or apprentice after he arrives at the age of twenty-one years—nor female, in like manner, after she arrives at the age of twenty-one years—unless they are bound by their own consent, after they arrive at such age, or are bound by law for the payment of debts, damages, fines, costs, or the like." Inasmuch as this provision is contained in the Constitution of 1777, it is certain that neither to Massachusetts nor to Pennsylvania, but to the backwoodsmen of Vermont, belongs the honor of having been the first American commonwealth to abolish and prohibit slavery.

From one point of view the first Constitution of Vermont did not outshine the organic laws originally framed for some of the American colonies. In respect of toleration, it exhibited a compromise between the spirit of religious freedom and the spirit of religious bigotry. It is true that the right of freedom of worship according to the dictates of every man's understanding and every man's conscience was asserted; but this conscience and this understanding were "to be regulated by the word of God"; nor could any man sit as a member of Assembly who did not sign a declaration of his belief in a God, the Creator and Governor of the universe, the rewarder of the good and the punisher of the wicked; with an acknowledgment of the inspiration of the Old and New Testaments, and a profession of the Protestant faith. It has often been pointed out that these tests, which were principally copied from the Constitution of Pennsylvania, would, in either State, have excluded from the Assembly a very distinguished citizen, to wit, Franklin in Pennsylvania and Ethan Allen in Vermont. It is to be noted, however, that by the revision of 1785 Vermont struck out the requirement of Protestantism, and another revision in 1793, still following the example of Pennsylvania, released the members of Assembly from any religious subscription.

Although the occupants of the New Hampshire Grants were long stigmatized as backwoodsmen, the importance of education was as keenly appreciated by them as by the inhabitants of the oldest and most densely peopled parts of New England. The support of schools in every town at the public expense was made a constitutional provision, and the establishment of county grammar-schools and a university was recommended. In the townships originally granted by the royal Governor of New Hampshire, tracts of land of 340 acres each had been reserved for the use of schools, and others for the British Society for the Propagation of the Gospel in Foreign Parts, which latter, by an act of the Legislature in 1794, were also appropriated for the use of schools. In the townships granted by the State of Vermont, one land right was reserved for town schools and another for county grammar - schools. The University of Vermont, established at Burlington in 1791, was endowed by private subscriptions to the amount of $33,333, nearly half of which was contributed by Ira Allen, who was a younger brother of Ethan Allen, and who, like him, was conspicuous in the affairs of the State. The Legislature added a donation of land amounting to nearly 50,000 acres. It should be added that while the use of a single legislative assembly, originally introduced by Pennsylvania

and Georgia, was quickly abandoned by them, Vermont persisted in it until 1836, when she modified her Constitution so as to adopt a Senate of thirty members as a part of her Legislature, and to abolish the Executive Council.

The independent existence of the Republic of Vermont came to an end in 1791, or about two years after the Federal government created by the Constitution had become operative. The rapid increase of her population having destroyed all hope on the part of New York of re-establishing her jurisdiction over the region occupied by the Green Mountain Boys, the holders of the New York Grants were ready to accept an indemnity. Political considerations had also tended to change the attitude of Congress. The Northern States perceived that the vote of Vermont might aid to fix the seat of the Federal government at New York, and in any event Vermont would serve to counterbalance Kentucky, the speedy admission of which was foreseen. Already in July, 1789, the Assembly of New York had appointed commissioners with full powers to acknowledge the independence of Vermont, and to arrange a settlement of all matters in controversy. Terms of adjustment were soon agreed upon. For an indemnity of thirty thousand dollars to the New York grantees, New York on October 7, 1790, renounced all claim of jurisdiction, consented to the admission of Vermont into the Union, and assented to the boundary previously claimed: the western line of the westernmost townships granted by New Hampshire and the middle channel of Lake Champlain. Three weeks later the agreement was ratified by the Vermont Legislature. A convention which met at the beginning of 1791 voted to ratify the Federal Constitution and to ask admission into the Union. Commissioners were soon after appointed by the Assembly to wait upon Congress, and in February, within fourteen days after the passage of the bill for the prospective admission of Kentucky, an act was passed admitting Vermont at the termination of that session of Congress. For sixteen years the Green Mountain Boys had been practically independent, and for fourteen years they had been organized in an autonomous republic.

WILLIAM DEAN HOWELLS

IS it true that the sun of a man's mentality touches noon at forty and then begins to wane toward setting? Dr. Osler is charged with saying so. Maybe he said it, maybe he didn't; I don't know which it is. But if he said it, and if it is true, I can point him to a case which proves his rule. Proves it by being an exception to it. To this place I nominate Mr. Howells.

I read his *Venetian Days* about forty years ago. I compare it with his paper on Machiavelli in a late number of *Harper,* and I cannot find that his English has suffered any impairment. For forty years his English has been to me a continual delight and astonishment. In the sustained exhibition of certain great qualities—clearness, compression, verbal exactness, and unforced and seemingly unconscious felicity of phrasing—he is, in my belief, without his peer in the English-writing world. *Sustained.* I intrench myself behind that protecting word. There are others who exhibit those great qualities as greatly as does he, but only by intervalled distributions of rich moonlight, with stretches of veiled and dimmer landscape between; whereas Howells's moon sails cloudless skies all night and all the nights.

In the matter of verbal exactness Mr. Howells has no superior, I suppose. He seems to be almost always able to find that elusive and shifty grain of gold, the *right word.* Others have to put up with approximations, more or less frequently; he has better luck. To me, the others are miners working with the gold-pan — of necessity some of the gold washes over and escapes; whereas, in my fancy, he is quicksilver raiding down a riffle—no grain of the metal stands much chance of eluding him. A powerful agent is the right word: it lights the reader's way and makes it plain; a close approximation to it will answer, and much travelling is done in a well-enough

fashion by its help, but we do not welcome it and applaud it and rejoice in it as we do when *the* right one blazes out on us. Whenever we come upon one of those intensely right words in a book or a newspaper the resulting effect is physical as well as spiritual, and electrically prompt: it tingles exquisitely around through the walls of the mouth and tastes as tart and crisp and good as the autumn - butter that creams the sumac-berry. One has no time to examine the word and vote upon its rank and standing, the automatic recognition of its supremacy is so immediate. There is a plenty of acceptable literature which deals largely in approximations, but it may be likened to a fine landscape seen through the rain; the right word would dismiss the rain, then you would see it better. It doesn't rain when Howells is at work.

And where does he get the easy and effortless flow of his speech? and its cadenced and undulating rhythm? and its architectural felicities of construction, its graces of expression, its pemmican quality of compression, and all that? Born to him, no doubt. All in shining good order in the beginning, all extraordinary; and all just as shining, just as extraordinary to-day, after forty years of diligent wear and tear and use. He passed his fortieth year long and long ago; but I think his English of to-day —his perfect English, I wish to say —can throw down the glove before his English of that antique time and not be afraid.

I will go back to the paper on Machiavelli now, and ask the reader to examine this passage from it which I append. I do not mean, examine it in a bird's-eye way; I mean search it, study it. And, of course, read it aloud. I may be wrong, still it is my conviction that one cannot get out of finely wrought literature all that is in it by reading it mutely:

Mr. Dyer is rather of the opinion, first luminously suggested by Macaulay, that Machiavelli was in earnest, but must not be judged as a political moralist of our time and race would be judged. He thinks that Machiavelli was in earnest, as none but an idealist can be, and he is the first to imagine him an idealist immersed in realities, who involuntarily transmutes the events under his eye into something like the visionary issues of reverie. The Machiavelli whom he depicts does not cease to be politically a republican and socially a just man because he holds up an atrocious despot like Cæsar Borgia as a mirror for rulers. What Machiavelli beheld round him in Italy was a civic disorder in which there was oppression without statecraft, and revolt without patriotism. When a miscreant like Borgia appeared upon the scene and reduced both tyrants and rebels to an apparent quiescence, he might very well seem to such a dreamer the savior of society whom a certain sort of dreamers are always looking for. Machiavelli was no less honest when he honored the diabolical force of Cæsar Borgia than Carlyle was when at different times he extolled the strong man who destroys liberty in creating order. But Carlyle has only just ceased to be mistaken for a reformer, while it is still Machiavelli's hard fate to be so trammelled in his material that his name stands for whatever is most malevolent and perfidious in human nature.

You see how easy and flowing it is; how unvexed by ruggednesses, clumsinesses, broken metres; how simple and—so far as you or I can make out—unstudied; how clear, how limpid, how understandable, how unconfused by cross-currents, eddies, undertows; how seemingly unadorned, yet is all adornment, like the lily-of-the-valley; and how compressed, how compact, without a complacency-signal hung out anywhere to call attention to it.

There are thirty-four lines in the quoted passage. After reading it several times aloud, one perceives that a good deal of matter is crowded into that small space. I think it is a model of compactness. When I take its materials apart and work them over and put them together in my way I find I cannot crowd the result back into the same hole, there not being room enough. I find it a case of a woman packing a man's trunk: he can get the things out, but he can't ever get them back again.

The proffered paragraph is a just and fair sample; the rest of the article is as compact as it is; there are no waste words. The sample is just in other ways: limpid, fluent, graceful, and rhythmical as it is, it holds no superiority in these respects over the rest of the essay. Also, the choice phrasing noticeable in the sample is not lonely; there is a plenty of its kin distributed through the other paragraphs. This is claiming much when that kin must face the challenge of a phrase like the one in the middle sentence: "an idealist immersed in realities, who involuntarily transmutes the events under his eye into something like the visionary issues of reverie." With a hundred words to do it with, the literary artisan could catch that airy thought and tie it down and reduce it to a concrete condition, visible, substantial, understandable and all right, like a cabbage; but the artist does it with twenty, and the result is a flower.

The quoted phrase, like a thousand others that have come from the same source, has the quality of certain scraps of verse which take hold of us and stay in our memories, we do not understand why, at first: all the words being the right words, none of them is conspicuous, and so they all seem inconspicuous, therefore we wonder what it is about them that makes their message take hold.

> The mossy marbles rest
>   On the lips that he has prest
>   In their bloom,
> And the names he loved to hear
> Have been carved for many a year
>   On the tomb.

It is like a dreamy strain of moving music, with no sharp notes in it. The words are all "right" words, and all the same size. We do not notice it at first. We get the effect, it goes straight home to us, but we do not know why. It is when the right words are conspicuous that they thunder—

> The glory that was Greece and the grandeur
>   that was Rome!

When I go back from Howells old to Howells young I find him arranging and clustering English words well, but not any better than now. He is not more felicitous in concreting abstractions now.

than he was in translating, then, the visions of the eye of flesh into words that reproduced their forms and colors:

In Venetian streets they give the fallen snow no rest. It is at once shovelled into the canals by hundreds of half-naked *facchini;* and now in St. Mark's Place the music of innumerable shovels smote upon my ear; and I saw the shivering legion of poverty as it engaged the elements in a struggle for the possession of the Piazza. But the snow continued to fall, and through the twilight of the descending flakes all this toil and encounter looked like that weary kind of effort in dreams, when the most determined industry seems only to renew the task. The lofty crest of the bell-tower was hidden in the folds of falling snow, and I could no longer see the golden angel upon its summit. But looked at across the Piazza, the beautiful outline of St. Mark's Church was perfectly pencilled in the air, and the shifting threads of the snowfall were woven into a spell of novel enchantment around the structure that always seemed to me too exquisite in its fantastic loveliness to be anything but the creation of magic. The tender snow had compassionated the beautiful edifice for all the wrongs of time, and so hid the stains and ugliness of decay that it looked as if just from the hand of the builder—or, better said, just from the brain of the architect. There was marvellous freshness in the colors of the mosaics in the great arches of the façade, and all that gracious harmony into which the temple rises, of marble scrolls and leafy exuberance airily supporting the statues of the saints, was a hundred times etherealized by the purity and whiteness of the drifting flakes. The snow lay lightly on the golden globes that tremble like peacock-crests above the vast domes, and plumed them with softest white; it robed the saints in ermine; and it danced over all its work, as if exulting in its beauty—beauty which filled me with subtle, selfish yearning to keep such evanescent loveliness for the little-while-longer of my whole life, and with despair to think that even the poor lifeless shadow of it could never be fairly reflected in picture or poem.

Through the wavering snowfall, the Saint Theodore upon one of the granite pillars of the Piazzetta did not show so grim as his wont is, and the winged lion on the other might have been a winged lamb, so gentle and mild he looked by the tender light of the storm. The towers of the island churches loomed faint and far away in the dimness; the sailors in the rigging of the ships that lay in the Basin wrought like phantoms

among the shrouds; the gondolas stole in and out of the opaque distance more noiselessly and dreamily than ever; and a silence, almost palpable, lay upon the mutest city in the world.

The spirit of Venice is there: of a city where Age and Decay, fagged with distributing damage and repulsiveness among the other cities of the planet in accordance with the policy and business of their profession, come for rest and play between seasons, and treat themselves to the luxury and relaxation of sinking the shop and inventing and squandering charms all about, instead of abolishing such as they find, as is their habit when not on vacation.

In the working season they do business in Boston sometimes, and a character in *The Undiscovered Country* takes accurate note of pathetic effects wrought by them upon the aspects of a street of once dignified and elegant homes whose occupants have moved away and left them a prey to neglect and gradual ruin and progressive degradation; a descent which reaches bottom at last, when the street becomes a roost for humble professionals of the faith-cure and fortune-telling sort.

What a queer, melancholy house, what a queer, melancholy street! I don't think I was ever in a street before where quite so many professional ladies, with English surnames, preferred Madam to Mrs. on their door-plates. And the poor old place has such a desperately conscious air of going to the deuce. Every house seems to wince as you go by, and button itself up to the chin for fear you should find out it had no shirt on,—so to speak. I don't know what's the reason, but these material tokens of a social decay afflict me terribly: a tipsy woman isn't dreadfuler than a haggard old house, that's once been a home, in a street like this.

Mr. Howells's pictures are not mere stiff, hard, accurate photographs; they are photographs with feeling in them, and sentiment, photographs taken in a dream, one might say.

As concerns his humor, I will not try to say anything, yet I would try if I had the words that might approximately reach up to its high place. I do not think any one else can play with humorous fancies so gracefully and delicately and deliciously as he does, nor has so many to play with, nor can come so near making them look as if they were doing the playing themselves and he was not aware that they were at it. For they are unobtrusive, and quiet in their ways, and well conducted. His is a humor which flows softly all around about and over and through the mesh of the page, pervasive, refreshing, health-giving, and makes no more show and no more noise than does the circulation of the blood.

There is another thing which is contentingly noticeable in Mr. Howells's books. That is his "stage directions"—those artifices which authors employ to throw a kind of human naturalness around a scene and a conversation, and help the reader to see the one and get at meanings in the other which might not be perceived if intrusted unexplained to the bare words of the talk. Some authors overdo the stage directions, they elaborate them quite beyond necessity; they spend so much time and take up so much room in telling us how a person said a thing and how he looked and acted when he said it that we get tired and vexed and wish he hadn't said it at all. Other authors' directions are brief enough, but it is seldom that the brevity contains either wit or information. Writers of this school go in rags, in the matter of stage directions; the majority of them have nothing in stock but a cigar, a laugh, a blush, and a bursting into tears. In their poverty they work these sorry things to the bone. They say:

". . . . replied Alfred, flipping the ash from his cigar." (This explains nothing; it only wastes space.)

". . . . responded Richard, with a laugh." (There was nothing to laugh about; there never is. The writer puts it in from habit—automatically; he is paying no attention to his work, or he would see that there is nothing to laugh at; often, when a remark is unusually and poignantly flat and silly, he tries to deceive the reader by enlarging the stage direction and making Richard break into "frenzies of uncontrollable laughter." This makes the reader sad.)

". . . . murmured Gladys, blushing." This poor old shop-worn blush is a tiresome thing. We get so we would rather Gladys would fall out of the book and break her neck than do it again. She is always doing it, and usually irrelevantly. Whenever it is her turn to murmur she hangs out her blush; it is the only thing she's got. In a little while we hate her, just as we do Richard.

". . . . repeated Evelyn, bursting into tears." This kind keep a book damp all the time. They can't say a thing without crying. They cry so much about nothing that by and by when they have something to cry *about* they have gone dry; they sob, and fetch nothing; we are not moved. We are only glad.

They gravel me, these stale and overworked stage directions, these carbon films that got burnt out long ago and cannot now carry any faintest thread of light. It would be well if they could be relieved from duty and flung out in the literary back yard to rot and disappear along with the discarded and forgotten "steeds" and "halidomes" and similar stage-properties once so dear to our grandfathers. But I am friendly to Mr. Howells's stage directions; more friendly to them than to any one else's, I think. They are done with a competent and discriminating art, and are faithful to the requirements of a stage direction's proper and lawful office, which is to inform. Sometimes they convey a scene and its conditions so well that I believe I could see the scene and get the spirit and meaning of the accompanying dialogue if some one would read merely the stage directions to me and leave out the talk. For instance, a scene like this, from *The Undiscovered Country*:

". . . . and she laid her arms with a beseeching gesture on her father's shoulder."

". . . . she answered, following his gesture with a glance."

". . . . she said, laughing nervously."

". . . . she asked, turning swiftly upon him that strange, searching glance."

". . . . she answered, vaguely."

". . . . she reluctantly admitted."

". . . . but her voice died wearily away, and she stood looking into his face with puzzled entreaty."

Mr. Howells does not repeat his forms, and does not need to; he can invent fresh ones without limit. It is mainly the repetition over and over again, by the third-rates, of worn and commonplace and juiceless forms that makes their novels such a weariness and vexation to us, I think. We do not mind one or two deliveries of their wares, but as we turn the pages over and keep on meeting them we presently get tired of them and wish they would do other things for a change:

".... replied Alfred, flipping the ash from his cigar."

".... responded Richard, with a laugh."

".... murmured Gladys, blushing."

".... repeated Evelyn, bursting into tears."

".... replied the Earl, flipping the ash from his cigar."

".... responded the undertaker, with a laugh."

".... murmured the chambermaid, blushing."

".... repeated the burglar, bursting into tears."

".... replied the conductor, flipping the ash from his cigar."

".... responded Arkwright, with a laugh."

".... murmured the chief of police, blushing."

".... repeated the housecat, bursting into tears."

And so on and so on; till at last it ceases to excite. I always notice stage directions, because they fret me and keep me trying to get out of their way, just as the automobiles do. At first; then by and by they become monotonous and I get run over.

Mr. Howells has done much work, and the spirit of it is as beautiful as the make of it. I have held him in admiration and affection so many years that I know by the number of those years that he is old now; but his heart isn't, nor his pen; and years do not count. Let him have plenty of them: there is profit in them for us.

EARLY NEW ENGLAND ARTISTS

ACCORDING to Governor Bradford, the *Mayflower* brought over in her hold the goods and chattels of about one hundred English settlers; according to their descendants, she brought over enough to stock the whole of New England. But nowhere in his history do we find any mention of pictures.

This omission from her cargo was due partly to the want of room, but largely, no doubt, to the disapproval with which our pious forefathers viewed all works of art, especially those religious masterpieces in which the great artists of the Old World had excelled.

To those first settlers life was too stern and hard to permit even the thought of anything not required by strict necessity. And to the thrifty housewife the bunches of dried herbs and onions and the ears of red and yellow corn that decorated her walls gave more genuine satisfaction than any picture could have given.

Notwithstanding these adverse conditions, the love of art, the desire to create some form of beauty, still survived.

In the dawn of the eighteenth century, when the first stress of hardship and poverty had passed, when Boston had become a thriving little city, when the plain Puritan dress had given place to furbelows and flounces, pictures of home manufacture began to make a place for themselves. Among the quaintest productions of this time are the cut paper pictures, one of which is reproduced in the diary of Anna Green Winslow, recently edited by Mrs. Alice Morse Earle, the original of which was kept between 1770 and 1773.

This paper-cutting was taught in private schools under the dignified name of papyrotamia, and when the dainty misses of Boston went to their afternoon tea parties, they often took with them a sheet of paper and a pair of tiny scissors, and as they gossiped over the small news of the day they snipped away the bits of paper, until there grew under their nimble fingers pictures wonderful to behold. A whole village, including an inn with swinging sign, cart-horses, cattle and men, an old-fashioned well, a hay-maker carrying his scythe over his shoulder, a man with a wheelbarrow, a shepherdess with her sheep, a bridge with full-rigged ships sailing under it, fences, winding roads, and trees so full of little birds that one would think an aviary had been let loose—all these are to be seen in one single quaint old picture that is preserved in the Trott family of Niagara Falls.

Another quaint style of imitation flowers was made of raised paper, and as we look at an odd specimen still remaining we can easily imagine the maker, Miss Abby Buckingham, at her artistic labors, as she draws or perhaps traces the flowers on a heavy piece of card-board, and then, after cutting almost around a rose petal, inserts her pen-knife under one thickness of the paper and carefully lifts the petal from the surface, until her rose, two or three petals deep, rises from its paper background in nature's true similitude.

The painting of artificial flowers was carried on in the large cities, and in Brooks's *Curious Advertisements* we find, taken from the Boston *Gazette* of October 19, 1767, this advertisement:

TO THE YOUNG LADIES OF BOSTON.

Elizabeth Courtney, as several Ladies has signified of having a desire to learn that most ingenious art of Painting on Gauze and Catgut, proposes to open a School, and that her business may be a public good, designs to teach the making of all sorts of French Trimmings, Flowers, and Feather Tippets. And as these Arts above mentioned, (the Flowers excepted,) are entirely unknown on the Continent, she flatters herself to meet with all due encouragement; and more so as every Lady may have a power of serving herself of what she is now obliged to send to England for, as the whole process is attended with little or no expence. The Conditions are Five Dollars at entrance; to be confined to no particular hours or time: and if they apply Constant may be Compleat in six weeks. And when she has fifty subscribers school will be opened.

"RIDICULOUS TASTE, OR, THE LADIES' ABSURDITY"
(Example of the quaint painted prints)

It is to be supposed that this

"CYBELE AND CUPID"
(Painted by Miss Betsy Rockwell)

school was opened and good use made of its advantages, for painted flowers appear often in the hair, the stomacher, and the hats of the well-to-do Bostonian dames.

To this time belong also the quaint painted prints, in imitation of painted glass. In making these, the print, generally of English origin, was stuck on to the back of a plate of glass, with a varnish that rendered it partly transparent, and then the artist colored it from the back in gorgeous daubs of red, blue, and yellow.

Many of these painted prints are still in existence. The Connecticut Historical Society has one of unusual interest, entitled, "Ridiculous Taste, or, The Ladies' Absurdity." The subject is a grand lady seated in a barber's chair, while the hair-dresser, a prim little man, climbs on a stepladder to finish the top of her ladyship's tower of powdered hair.

In the private dame schools were taught not only plain sewing, but "All kinds of Needlework, viz: point, Brussles, Dresden, Gold, Silver, and Silk Embroidery of every kind. Tambour, Feather, Indian and Darning. Sprigings with a Variety of Openwork to each.

Tapestry plain, lines & drawn. Catgut, black & white, with a number of beautiful Stitches. Diaper and Plain Darnings."

The young ladies' finishing schools of fifty years later kept up the teaching of embroidery, and one of the most pleasing pictures of the time is "The Departure of Coriolanus," a really charming piece of color, with its delicate pink sky, its tender blues, and soft olive-greens.

This picture, now owned in East Windsor Hill, Connecticut, by descendants of Governor Wolcott, was made by Miss Ursula Wolcott—"Suley," as her father calls her in his endorsement on the tuition bill—at Mrs. Royse's finishing school at Hartford.

From this famous school came also an interesting collection which now hangs on the wall of one of the oldest houses of Windsor, Connecticut. This consists of water-colors done by Miss Betsy Rockwell, under Mrs. Royse's supervision.

The most striking feature of the collection is Cybele, clad in silver armor, and riding in a golden, crimson-lined chariot. Cupid is her charioteer, and the steeds ne drives are two great lions, whose grin is frightful to behold, and whose bared teeth indicate a fierceness somewhat at variance with their gentle amble. The magnificence of Cybele is shown not only by the gorgeousness of her chariot and armor, but by the fact that her very toe-nails are of silver.

There is in one old house in Litchfield a fine blue satin petticoat that danced with Washington, and that has in its quilting the whole story of the Garden of Eden. Up the front grows the tree of the knowledge of good and evil, dividing at the top, and spreading its branches in each direction; on one side is Adam, on the other is Eve, with the fatal apple in her hand, while around the bottom of the petticoat prance all the animals of creation. We hardly realize, in these days of cheap picture reproduction, when the humblest school may have its copies of the fine old masters, and the Sistine Madonna is familiar to even the street urchins, how absolutely void of anything that could be called art were the farmhouses and the smaller villages in the New World. Search the inventories of the probate courts in the early colonial days, and it will be rare indeed that you find any picture mentioned. Enter the old houses of a little

AN OLD CLOCK PANEL
(Painted by Amy Lewis)

Our grandmothers knew how to apply their art to household purposes as well as do their present-day daughters, and they were not sparing of that knowledge. One pin-cushion has on it a wonderful robin, large as life; his breast is red, his head and tail blue, and he is shaded with green. Each feather is carefully painted, and well separated from its neighbor. But the quaintest bit of his anatomy is his great eye, set well back of the middle of his head, and gazing at us with stiff severity.

later date, and you may find a funeral wreath, an ornamented marriage certificate—and that is all. Yet the children of long ago had the same love of nature and of beauty that we find in our own little ones, but they died not knowing it. To be sure, there were Benjamin Wests among them, in whom the genius for art was so strong that it must out, even by way of the cat's tail; and there were Copley and Smybert and Trumbull. But the influence of even the greatest of these had but a small radius.

Then to some of the quiet Connecticut villages, to some of these farmers' daughters, came a chance to break away a little from the treadmill of farm and household labor, to go a few steps into an unknown land of pictures, color, art. The open door was the clock-shop.

The kindly emancipator who was bringing a new glow into their lives was the good old deacon who presided, with more business shrewdness than artistic skill, over the painting of the dials and panels; and the masterpieces which were produced were those prim and decorous landscapes, those pillared mansions, those prancing horses, and those grass-green trees so familiar to old-furniture hunters. We smile at them, but to the humble artists it was an open gate, leading out of the daily drudgery and the soul-benumbing monotony of life. To draw, to paint, to linger lovingly over the dainty curves, to lay on the rich warm color and watch the pictures grow under their hands; to create! Think what it must have been to those starved souls!

In the clock-shops were two grades of painters: those who stencilled on the figures and ornamented the dials, who were called the face-painters, and were looked down upon by their more advanced sisters; and the panel-painters, the real makers of pictures. I can see them now, those fresh-faced farmer lasses, in their quaint, short-waisted gowns, sitting on their benches at the long, well-lighted tables, each with her tools beside her, her paint saucers, or dry powder colors, her brushes, and her paper stencil patterns.

Their work was by no means wholly mechanical. There were patterns, to be sure, small papers with the design cut through in outline, or to be traced by means of red transfer-paper. These patterns were of single objects: a house, always after the Mount Vernon model, well-rounded trees, spirited horses, wondrous shrubbery, baskets of sum-mer fruit, and men and women dressed in the latest fashion. These were but the elements of the design; from these same stately mansions, green trees, men and women, picture after picture was evolved, all alike, and yet all different. Sometimes the house was in the middle, with the tall elm on the right and the willow on the left; sometimes it was on one side, with a thicket of shrubbery on the other; sometimes the fiery steeds pranced through leafy avenues, and sometimes stood before the door; the man and maid might wander side by side through the landscape, or take their separate ways. The patterns must be followed in the separate figures, but there was room for fancy in the composition.

And when the complete picture was outlined in black, then the colors were laid on, the intricate foliage of the trees in vivid greens, the house always of white, with gay-colored windows, the horses brown, and the ladies' gowns in a fine bravery of color.

But even here the modern spirit of rebellion crept in, for there is still told the story of Polly B——, who, boldly defying all the canons of art and nature, painted her hero's horse a brilliant blue,

" ARMENIA "

and to the good deacon's remonstrance replied that she was sick and tired of always painting horses brown. "Well, let it go so this time," answered the patient man, "but the next horse must be the usual color."

The great centre of clock-manufacture was then in Thomaston and Bristol, Connecticut, where are still some of the largest clock-factories. And here clock pictures abound. In every old attic lingers some evidence of ancient skill. Almost every one's great-grandmother painted, and the great-grandmother of one family, the fair Amy Lewis, was not only a highly prized clock-painter, one who could draw her own designs, but an artist in her own right.

As a business she painted clock panels, and for pleasure she painted all the rest of the world.

There must have been a touch of romantic sentiment in her nature, for one of the largest pictures, one on which much labor has evidently been bestowed, is that of the fair Armenia carving on the tree trunk the name of her Tancred. And patriotism is there too, in a large piece in which a young man and two young women approach, weeping, or at least with handkerchiefs, the tomb sacred to the memory of George Washington and his consort. I have seen at least twenty paintings known to be the work of Amy Lewis, including one valuable roll which was snatched from a bonfire after the death of an aged aunt to whom it had been presented.

Her tools are still tucked away in a drawer: the "paint saucers," the powders with their quaint old names, and the tiny brush that worked those wonders. I have copied some of the pictures in order to discover the technique of those times, and find that a small brush will do it all, from the broad shaded washes to the delicate outlines, and even the foliage on the trees. This last, after repeated experiments, I find to be made by holding the brush in a vertical position and dabbing at the paper until the surface is covered. Nor did she despise the tricks of the trade; for upon close examination the sheep that repose by Armenia's side are found to be pricked through with a pin from the back, giving the fleece a truly woolly look.

The picture of two strolling damsels in red and yellow gowns, taken "direct from the latest Paris fashions," is most instructive as to the dress of that period, for, even to the hairs on the great fur tippet and the points on the artificial rose, it is given with careful accuracy.

Some of the great houses boasted a few fine pictures, possibly painted in America, but more probably brought from abroad. Miss Betsey Jaquelin Ambler, a visitor at Washington's house in 1799, writes to her dear friend Mildred Smith: "Everything within-doors is neat and elegant, but nothing re-

DESIGN FROM COVER OF PIN-CUSHION

markable except the paintings of different artists. I think there are five portraits of the General, some done in Europe, and some in America. There are other specimens of the fine arts from various parts of the world that are admirably executed and furnish pleasant conversation."

The Bible seems to be a principal source of material, since we find "Joseph Interpreting," "Pharaoh's Cup Found," the "Prodigal Son," and many similar titles. The "Ruth and Naomi" of Betsy Rockwell may have been copied from such an original. Says one dear old lady, whose memory goes back almost to the beginning of the century: "We had a beautiful picture on our walls. It was about the prodigal son; I wish I had it now. My mother did not think it was quite proper, because one of the women with whom he had wasted his substance in riotous living had her foot in the prodigal's lap. Mother wanted it taken down, but father—he was a deacon in the church—he liked it, so it stayed."

One piece of amateur art which is even older than the Amy Lewis pictures has in it much of human interest, for it is evidently in celebration of our peace with England. In it a tall and gracious maiden, somewhat long in the legs and swelled in the ankles, but with a face beaming with good-will to all the world, comes forward from the clouds of war, indicated by dark smoke and hostile ships. Clad in clinging robes of pale yellow and shrimp-pink, with a blue scarf

" PEACE BETWEEN AMERICA AND ENGLAND "
(Painted about 1785)

floating from her shoulders, she comes bearing in one hand the symbolic olive branch, and in the other a flaming torch, with which she is about to destroy all the weapons of war, together with the prostrate union-jack of England. In the background two doves of snowy whiteness are billing and cooing in a very amiable manner, and at her feet spring the flowers of peace. The picture is very pleasing in its color, for the delicate figure of the maiden is brought out by the dark background of smoke, and around the whole scene is thrown a frame of Indian red.

But even more interesting than allegorical or sentimental pictures are the few—and they are very few—that were drawn directly from life. It is the sense of contact with the actual, homely, everyday life that gives the charm to Amy

A VIEW IN FOURTH STREET, TROY

Lewis's sketch from her own front window of "J. Goodell's Bakery, Mrs. Phelps's School, Mr. Williams's and Mr. Reed's, on Fourth Street, Troy."

This is a real place, and these are real people. Possibly the bakery with its green shutters and half-door still stands. At least the trees are there, and we look with Amy Lewis from her window and watch the townspeople pass by, the women with calashes and beaver hats, the girls in pantalets, and one unhatted and carrying a parasol, as in the present day. We half identify the blue-shawled lady with Miss Phelps herself, and feel a thrill of fear for the small boy into whose dinner-pail that huge mastiff is looking.

The question of framing these many amateur pictures opened a new field for the exercise of artistic talent. A few of the pictures, like the "Washington's Tomb" of Amy Lewis, were taken to the city and put into showy gilt frames, bearing the name of the artist. But all could not be so fortunate, and so the girls enclosed their pictures in frames that were only less wonderful than the pictures. Some of the more elaborate of these frames were made from pine cones, the cones being pulled to pieces, and the separate scales then sewed on in fantastic patterns. The greatest favorite seems to

have been the rose pattern, which appears with variations in nearly all.

Such frames were made not only for the small water-color paintings, but for life-size oil paintings, and in a few old houses they still grace the walls in their tattered elegance.

In my attic researches one day I came upon a box of yellow paper leaf-patterns, each carefully cut out, and labelled with the name of its tree—maple, laurel, or oak. I was at a loss to guess their use. But later on there was pulled out from under the eaves a huge frame, to whose sides a mass of leather leaves still adhered, brown, withered, and curled, a leaf from every tree in the forest. In its day it must have been a wonderful creation.

Mirrors furnished another opportunity for the same brilliant decoration that was applied to clock panels. Many of the stilted landscapes and bright-colored mansions closely resembled the mechanical country scenes already described. In the picture prefixed to this article, of Fortune filling the sails of a merchant navy with prosperous wind, there is much more of freedom and vitality, although the work was done on the back of the glass. This picture was apparently painted freehand, with considerable skill.

THE ENGLISH IN NEW ENGLAND

WHEN a modern American makes a pilgrimage, as I have done, to the English village church at whose altars his ancestors once ministered, he brings away a feeling of renewed wonder at the depth of conviction which led the Puritan clergy to forsake their early homes. The exquisitely peaceful features of the English rural landscape—the old Norman church, half ruined, and in this particular case restored by aid of the American descendants of that high-minded emigrant; the old burial-ground that surrounds it, a haunt of such peace as to make death seem doubly restful; the ancestral oaks; the rooks that soar above them; the flocks of sheep drifting noiselessly among the ancient grave-stones—all speak of such tranquillity as the eager American must cross the Atlantic to obtain. No Englishman feels these things as the American feels them; the antiquity, as Hawthorne says, is our novelty. But beyond all the charm of the associations this thought always recurs—what love of their convictions, what devotion to their own faith, must have been needed to drive the educated Puritan clergymen from such delicious retreats to encounter the ocean, the forest, and the Indians!

Yet there was in the early emigration to every American colony quite another admixture than that of learning and refinement; a sturdy yeoman element, led by the desire to better its condition and create a new religious world around it; and an adventurous element, wishing for new excitements. The popular opinion of that period did not leave these elements out of sight, as may be seen by this London street ballad of 1640, describing the emigration:

"Our company we feare not, there goes my Cosen Hanna,
And Ruben doe perswade to goe his sister faire Susanna,
Wᵗʰ Abigall and Lidia, and Ruth noe doubt comes after,
And Sara kinde will not stay behinde my Cosen Constance dafter—
Then for the truth's sake goe.

"Nay Tom Tyler is p'pared, and ye Smith as black as a cole,
And Ralph Cobbler too wᵗʰ us will goe for he regards his soale,
And the weaver honest Lyman, wᵗʰ Prudence Jacobs daughter,
And Agatha and Barrbarra professeth to come after—
Then for the truth's sake goe."

There were also traces, in the emigration, of that love of wandering, of athletic sports and woodcraft, that still sends young men of English race to the far corners of the earth. In the Virginia colonization this element was large, but it also entered into the composition of the Northern colonies. The sister of Governor Winthrop wrote from England in 1637 of her son, afterward Sir George Downing, that the boy was anxious to go to New England, and she spoke of the hazard that he was in "by reson of both his father's and his owne strange inclination to the plantation sports." Upham accordingly describes this same youth in Harvard College, where he graduated in 1642, as shooting birds in the wild woods of Salem, and setting duck-decoys in the ponds. Life in the earlier days of the emigration was essentially a border life, a forest life, a frontier life—differing from such life in Australia or Canada mainly in one wild dream which certainly added to its romance—the dream that Satan still ruled the forest, and that the Indians were his agents.

Whatever else may be said of the Puritan emigration, it represented socially and intellectually much of what was best in the mother country. Men whose life in England would have been that of the higher class of gentry might have been seen in New England taking with their own hands from the barrel their last measure of corn, and perhaps interrupted by the sight of a vessel arriving in the harbor with supplies. These men, who ploughed their own fields and shot their own venison, were men who had paced the halls of Emanuel College at Cambridge, who quoted Seneca in their journals of travel, and who brought with them books of classic literature among their works of theology. The library bequeathed by Rev. John Harvard to the infant college at Cambridge included Homer, Pliny, Sallust, Terence, Juvenal, and Horace. The library bought by the commissioners from Rev. Mr. Welde, for Rev. Mr. Eliot, had in it Plutarch's Morals and the plays of Aristophanes. In its early poverty the colony voted £400 to found Harvard College, and that institution had for its second president a man so learned, after the fashion of those days, that he had the Hebrew Bible read to the students in the morning, and the Greek Testament in the afternoon, commenting on both extemporaneously in Latin. The curriculum of the institution was undoubtedly devised rather with a view to making learned theologians than elegant men of letters—thus much may be conceded to Mr. Matthew Arnold—but this was quite as much the case, as Mr. Mullinger has shown, in the English Cambridge of the seventeenth century.

The year 1650 may be roughly taken as closing the first generation of the American colonists. Virginia had then been settled forty-three years, New York thirty-six, Plymouth thirty, Massachusetts Bay twenty-two, Maryland nineteen, Connecticut seventeen, Rhode Island fourteen, New Haven twelve, and Delaware twelve. A variety of industries had already been introduced, especially in the New England colonies. Boat-building had there begun, according to Colonel C. D. Wright, in 1624; brick-making, tanning, and windmills were introduced in 1629; shoemaking and saw-mills in 1635; cloth mills in 1638; printing the year after; and iron foundries in 1644. In Virginia the colony had come near to extinction in 1624, and had revived under wholly new leadership. In New England, Brewster, Winthrop, Higginson, Skelton, Shepard, and Hooker had all died; Bradford, Endicott, Standish, Winslow, Eliot, and Roger Williams were still living, but past their prime. Church and state were already beginning to be possessed by a younger race, who had either been born in America or been brought as young children to its shores. In this coming race, also, the traditions of learning prevailed; the reading of Cotton Mather, for instance, was as marvellous as his powers of memory. When he entered Harvard College, at eleven, he had read Cicero, Terence, Ovid, Virgil, and the Greek Testament; wrote Latin with ease; was reading Homer, and had begun the Hebrew grammar. But the influences around these men were stern and even gloomy, though tempered by scholarship, by the sweet charities of home, and by some semblance of relaxation. We can hardly say that there was nothing but sternness when we find Rev. Peter Thacher at Barnstable, Massachusetts — a man of high standing in the churches—mitigating the care of souls, in 1679, by the erection of a private nine-pin alley on his own premises. Still there was for a time a distinct deepening of shadow around the lives of the Puritans, whether in the Northern or Southern colonies, after they were left wholly to themselves upon the soil of the New World. The persecutions and the delusions belong generally to this later epoch. In the earlier colonial period there would have been no time for them, and hardly inclination. In the later or provincial period society was undergoing a change, and wealth and aristocratic ways of living were being introduced. But it was in the intermediate time that religious rigor had its height.

Modern men habitually exaggerate the difference between themselves and the Puritans. The points of difference are so great and so picturesque, we forget that the points of resemblance must necessarily outweigh them. We seem more remote from them than is really the case, because we dwell too much on secondary matters —a garment, a phrase, a form of service. Theologian and historian are alike overcome by this; as soon as they touch the Puritans all is sombre, there is no sunshine, no bird sings. Yet the birds filled the woods with their music then as now; children played; mothers talked pretty nonsense to their babies; Governor Winthrop wrote tender messages to his third wife in a way that could only have come of long and reiterated practice. We can not associate a gloomy temperament with Miles Standish's doughty defiances, or with Francis Higginson's assertion that "a draught of New England air is better than a flagon of Old English ale." Their

lives, like all lives, were tempered and moulded by much that was quite apart from theology—hard work in the woods, fights with the Indians, and less perilous field-sports. They were unlike modern men when they were at church, but not so unlike when they went on a bear-hunt.

In order to understand the course of Puritan life in America we must bear in mind that the first-comers in the most strictly Puritan colonies were more and not less liberal than their immediate descendants. The Plymouth colony was more tolerant than the later colony of Massachusetts Bay, and the first church of the Massachusetts Bay colony was freer than those which followed it. The covenant drawn up for this Salem church in 1629 has seldom been surpassed in benignant comprehensiveness; it is thought that the following words constituted the whole of it: "We covenant with the Lord and one with another, and do bind ourselves in the presence of God, to walk together in all His ways, according as He is pleased to reveal Himself to us in His blessed word of truth." This was drawn up, according to Mather, by the first minister of Salem; and even when this covenant was enlarged into a confession of faith by his son and successor, some years later, it nevertheless remained more liberal than most later documents of the same kind. The trouble was that the tendency was to narrow instead of to widen. The isolation and severity of the colonial life produced its just effect, and this tendency grew as the new generation developed.

But it must be noticed that this greater early liberality never went so far as to lay down any high-sounding general principles of religious liberty, or to announce that as the corner-stone of the new enterprise. Here it is that the great and constant injustice comes in—to attribute to these Puritans a principle of toleration which they never set up, and then to reproach them with being false to it. Even Mr. Francis Parkman, who seems to me to be, within his own domain, unquestionably the first of American historians, loses his habit of justice when he quits his Frenchmen and his Indians and deals with the Puritans. "At the outset," he says, in his *Pioneers of France*, "New England was unfaithful to the principles of her existence. Seldom has religious toleration assumed a form more oppressive than among the Puritan exiles. New England Protestantism appealed to liberty; then closed the doors against her. On a stock of freedom she grafted a scion of despotism." Surely this is the old misstatement often made, often refuted. When were those colonists unfaithful to their own principle? When did they appeal to liberty? They appealed to truth. It would have been far better and nobler had they aimed at both, but in this imperfect world we have often to praise and venerate men for a single virtue. Anything but the largest toleration would have been inconsistency in Roger Williams, or perhaps—for this is less clearly established—in Lord Baltimore; but in order to show that the Puritans were false to religious liberty it must be shown that they had proclaimed it. On the contrary, what they sought to proclaim was religious truth. They lost the expansive influence of freedom, but they gained the propelling force of a high though gloomy faith. They lost the variety that exists in a liberal community where each man has his own opinion, but they gained the concentrated power of a homogeneous and well-ordered people.

There are but two of the early colonies of which the claim can be seriously made that they were founded on any principle of religious freedom. These two are Rhode Island and Maryland. It was said of the first by Roger Williams, its spiritual founder, that "a permission of the most paganish, Jewish, Turkish, or anti-Christian conscience" should be there granted "to all men of all nations and countries." Accordingly, the colony spread such shelter on a very wide scale. It received Anne Hutchinson after she had set the state as well as church in a turmoil at Boston, and had made popular elections turn on her opinions. It not only sheltered but gave birth to Jemima Wilkinson, prophetess of the "Cumberland Zealots," who might under the stimulus of a less tolerant community have expanded into a Joanna Southcote or a Mother Ann Lee. It protected Samuel Gorton, a man of the Savonarola temperament, of whom his last surviving disciple said, in 1771, "My master wrote in heaven, and none can understand his writings but those who live in heaven while on earth." It cost such an effort to assimilate these exciting ingredients that Roger Williams described Gorton in 1640 as "bewitching and bemadding poor Providence," and the Grand Jury of that city

was compelled to indict him as a nuisance in the same year, on this count, among others, "that Samuel Gorton contumeliously reproached the magistrates, calling them Just-asses." Nevertheless, all these, and such as these, were at last disarmed and made harmless by the wise policy of Rhode Island, guided by Roger Williams, after he had outgrown the superfluous antagonisms of his youth, and learned to be conciliatory in action as well as comprehensive in doctrine. Yet even he had so much to undergo in keeping the peace with all these heterogeneous materials that he recoiled at last from "such an infinite liberty of conscience," and declared that in the case of Quakers "a due and moderate restraint and punishment of these incivilities" was not only no persecution, but was "a duty and command of God."

Maryland has shared with Rhode Island the honor of having established religious freedom, and this claim is largely based upon the noble decree passed by its General Assembly in 1649:

"No person whatsoever in this province professing to believe in Jesus Christ shall from henceforth be any way troubled or molested for his or her religion, or in the free exercise thereof, or any way compelled to the belief or exercise of any other religion against his or her consent."

But it is never hard to evade a statute that seems to secure religious liberty, and this decree did not prevent the Maryland colony from afterward enacting that if any person should deny the Holy Trinity he should first be bored through the tongue and fined or imprisoned; then, for the second offense, should be branded as a blasphemer, the letter "B" being stamped on his forehead; and for the third offense should die. This was certainly a very limited toleration; and granting that it has a partial value, it remains an interesting question who secured it. Cardinal Manning and others have claimed this measure of toleration as due to the Roman Catholics, but Mr. E. D. Neill has conclusively shown that the Roman Catholic element was originally much smaller than was supposed, that the "two hundred Catholic gentlemen" usually claimed as founding the colony were really some twenty gentlemen and three hundred laboring-men; that of the latter twelve died on shipboard, of whom only two confessed to the priests, thus giving a clew to the proba-

A QUAKER EXHORTER IN NEW ENGLAND.

ble opinions of the rest; and that of the Assembly which passed the resolutions the majority were Protestants, and even Puritans. But granting to Maryland a place next to Rhode Island in religious freedom, she paid, like that other colony, what was then the penalty of freedom, and I must dwell a moment on this.

In those days religious liberty brought a heterogeneous and often reckless population; it usually involved the absence of a highly educated ministry; and this implied the want of a settled system of education, and of an elevated standard of public duty. These deficiencies left both in Rhode Island and in Maryland certain results which are apparent to this day. There is nothing more extraordinary in the Massachusetts and Connecticut colonies than the promptness with which they entered on the work of popular education. These little communities, just struggling for existence, marked out an educational system which had then no parallel in the European world. In the Massachusetts Bay colony, Salem had a free school in 1640, Boston in 1642, or earlier, Cambridge about the same time, and the state, in 1647, marked out an elaborate system of common and grammar schools for every township—a system then without a precedent, so far as I know, in Europe. Thus run the essential sentences of this noble document, held up to the admiration of all England by Lord Macaulay in Parliament:

.... "Y^t learning may not be buried in ye grave of o^r fath^{rs} in ye church and comonwealth, the Lord assisting o^r endeavors—It is therefore ord^{r}ed, y^t ev^{r}y township in this iurisdiction, aft^r y^e Lord heth increased y^m to y^e number of 50 household^{rs}, shall then forthwth appoint one wthin their towne to teach all such children as shall resort to him to write and reade; * $\overset{*}{\overset{}{?}}$ * * and it is furth^r ordered, y^t where any towne shall increase to y^e numb^r of 100 families or houshould^s, they shall set up a gramer schoole, y^e m^r thereof being able to instruct youth so farr as they may be fited for y^e university."

The printing-press came with these schools, or before them, and was actively employed, and it is impossible not to recognize the contrast between such institutions and the spirit of that Governor of Virginia (Berkeley) who said, a quarter of a century later, "We have no free schools nor printing, and I hope shall not have these hundred years." In Maryland, convicts and indented servants were sometimes advertised for sale as teachers at an early day, and there was no public system until 1728. In Rhode Island, Newport had a public school in 1640, but it apparently lasted but a year or two, nor was there a general system till the year 1800. These contrasts are mentioned for one sole purpose: to show that no single community unites all virtues, and that it was at that period very hard for religious liberality and a good school system to exist together.

There was a similar disproportion among the colonies in the number of university-trained men. Professor F. B. Dexter has shown that no less than sixty such men joined the Massachusetts Bay colony within ten years of its origin, while after seventeen years of separate existence the Virginia colony held but two university men, Rev. Hant Wyatt and Dr. Pott; and Rhode Island had also but two in its early days, Roger Williams and the recluse William Blaxton. No one has more fully recognized the "heavy price paid" for this "great cup of liberty" in Rhode Island than her ablest scholar, Professor Diman, who employs precisely these phrases to describe it in his Bristol address; and who fearlessly points out how much that state lost, even while she gained something, by the absence of that rigorous sway and that lofty public standard which were associated with the stern rule of the Puritan clergy.

In all the early colonies, unless we except Rhode Island, the Puritan spirit made itself distinctly felt, and religious persecution widely prevailed. Even in Maryland, as has been shown, the laws imposed branding and boring through the tongue as a penalty for certain opinions. In Virginia those who refused to attend the Established Church must pay 200 pounds of tobacco for the first offense, 500 for the second, and incur banishment for the third. A fine of 5000 pounds of tobacco was placed upon unauthorized religious meetings. Quakers and Baptists were whipped or pilloried, and any ship-master conveying Nonconformists was fined. Even so late as 1741, after persecution had virtually ceased in New England, severe laws were passed against Presbyterians in Virginia; and the above-named laws of Maryland were re-enacted in 1723. At an earlier period, however, the New England laws, if not severer, were no doubt more rigorously executed. In some cases, to be sure, the so-called laws were a deliberate fabrication, as in the case of the Connecticut "Blue Laws," a code reprinted to this day in the newspapers, but which existed only in the active and malicious imagination of the Tory Dr. Peters.

The spirit of persecution was strongest in the New England colonies, and chiefly in Massachusetts, because of the greater intensity with which men there followed out their convictions. It was less manifest in the banishment of Roger Williams —which was, after all, not so much a religious as a political transaction—than in the Quaker persecutions which took place between 1656 and 1660. Even these, it must be remembered, were never persecutions in the sense which had become familiar in Europe—that is, of forbidding heretics to leave the realm, and then tormenting them if they staid. Not a Quaker ever suffered except for voluntary action; that is, for choosing to stay, or return after banishment. To demand that they should consent to be banished seems to us so unreasonable as to be an outrage; but it seemed quite otherwise, we must remember, to those who had already banished themselves to secure a spot where they could worship in their own way. Cotton Mather says, with some force:

"It was also thought that the very Quakers themselves would say that if they had got into a Corner of the World, and with an immense Toyl and Charge made a Wilderness habitable, on purpose there to be undisturbed in the Exercises of their Worship, they would never bear to have New-Englanders come among them and interrupt their Publick Worship, endeavor to seduce their Children from it, yea, and repeat such Endeavors after mild Entreaties first, and then just Banishments, to oblige their departure."

We now see that this place they occupied was not a mere corner of the world, and that it was even then an essential part of the British dominions, and subject to British laws. We can therefore see that this was not the whole of the argument, but as an *argumentum ad hominem* it was very strong. Had the Quakers, like the Moravians, made settlements and cleared the forests for themselves, this argument would have been quite disarmed; and had those settlements been interfered with by the Puritans, the injustice would have been far more glaring; nor is it probable that the Puritans would have molested such settlements—unless they happened to be too near.

It must be remembered, too, that the Puritans did not view Quakers and other zealots as heretics merely, but as dangerous social outlaws. There was among the colonists a genuine and natural fear that if the tide of extravagant fanaticism once set in, it might culminate in such atrocities as had shocked all Europe while the Anabaptists, under John of Leyden were in power at Münster. In the frenzies and naked exhibitions of the Quakers, or rather Ranters, they saw tendencies which might end in uprooting all the social order for which they were striving,

and ultimately in the revocation of their charter. I differ with the greatest unwillingness from my old friend Mr. John G. Whittier in his explanation of a part of these excesses. He thinks that these naked exhibitions came chiefly from those who were maddened by seeing the partial exposures of Quakers whipped through the streets. This view seems to me to overlook the highly wrought condition of mind among these enthusiasts, and the fact that they regarded everything as a symbol. When, on February 13, 1658, Sarah Gibbins and Dorothy Waugh broke two empty bottles over Rev. John Norton as "a sign of his emptiness," they deemed it right to sacrifice all propriety for the sake of a symbolic act; and in just the same spirit we find the Quaker writers of that period defending these personal exposures, not by Mr. Whittier's reasons, but as a figurative act. In Southey's *Commonplace-Book* there is a long extract, to precisely this effect, from the life of Thomas Story, an English Friend who had travelled in America. He seems to have been a moderate man, and to have condemned some of the extravagances of the Ranters, but gravely argues that the Quakers might really have been commanded by God to exhibit this nakedness "as a sign."

But whatever provocation the Friends may have given, their persecution is the darkest blot upon the history of the time —darker than witchcraft, which was a disease of supernatural terror. And like the belief in witchcraft, the spirit of persecution could only be palliated by the general delusion of the age, by the cruelty of the English legislation against the Jesuits, which the Puritan Legislature closely followed as regarded Quakers; and in general by the attempt to unite church and state, and to take the Old Testament for a literal modern statute-book. It must be remembered that our horror at this intolerance is also stimulated from time to time by certain extravagant fabrications which still appear as genuine in the newspapers; as that imaginary letter said to have been addressed by Cotton Mather to a Salem clergyman in 1682, and proposing that a colony of Quakers be arrested and sold as slaves. This absurd forgery appeared first in some Pennsylvania newspaper, accompanied by the assertion that this letter was in possession of the Massachusetts Historical Society. No such paper was ever known to that

SAMUEL SEWALL.
From the collections of the Massachusetts Historical Society

are executed daily." In a single Swedish village threescore and ten witches were discovered, most of whom, including fifteen children, were executed, besides thirty children who were compelled to "run the gauntlet" and be lashed on their hands once a week for a year. The eminent English judge Sir Matthew Hale, giving his charge at the trial for witchcraft of Rose Cullender and Anne Duny in 1668—a trial which had great weight with the American judges—said that he "made no doubt there were such Creatures as Witches, for the Scriptures affirmed it, and the Wisdom of all Nations had provided Laws against such Persons." The devout Bishop Hall wrote in England: "Satan's prevalency in this Age is most clear, in the marvellous numbers of Witches abiding in all places. Now hundreds are discovered in one Shire." It shows that there was, on the whole, a healthy influence exerted on Puritanism by American life when we consider that the witchcraft excitement was here so limited and so short-lived.

The first recorded case of execution for this offense in the colonies is mentioned in Winthrop's journal, March, 1646-7, as occurring at Hartford, Connecticut, where another occurred in 1648, there being also one in Boston that same year. Nine more took place in Boston and in Connecticut before the great outbreak at Salem. A curious one occurs in the Maryland records of 1654 as having happened on the high seas upon a vessel bound to Baltimore, where a woman was hanged by the seamen upon this charge, the case being afterward investigated by the Governor and Council. A woman was tried and acquitted in Pennsylvania in 1683, one was hanged in Maryland for this alleged crime by due sentence of court in 1685, and one or two cases occurred at New York. The excitement finally came to a head in 1692 at Salem, Massachusetts, where nineteen persons were hanged, and one "pressed to death" for refusing to testify—this being the regularly ordained punishment for such refusal. The excitement being thus relieved, a reaction followed. Brave old Samuel Sewall won for himself honor in all coming time by rising in his place in the congregation, and causing to be read an expression of regret for the part he had taken in the trials. The reaction did not at once reach the Southern colonies. Grace

society; Cotton Mather was, at the time alleged, but nineteen years old, and the Quaker persecution had substantially ceased twenty years before. But when did such contradictions ever have any effect on the vitality of a lie?

The dark and intense convictions of Puritanism were seen at their highest in the witchcraft trials—events which took place in almost every colony at different times. The wonder is that they showed themselves so much less in America than in most European nations at the same period. To see the delusion in its most frightful form we must go beyond the Atlantic and far beyond the limits of English Puritanism. During its course 30,000 victims were put to death in Great Britain, 75,000 in France, 100,000 in Germany, besides those executed in Italy, Switzerland, and Sweden, many of them being burned. Compared with this vast estimate—which I take from that careful historian Mr. W. F. Poole—how trivial seem the few dozen cases to be found in our early colonies; and yet, as he justly remarks, these few have attracted more attention from the world than all the rest. Howells, the letter-writer, says, under date of February 22, 1647: "Within the compass of two years near upon 300 witches were arraigned, and the larger part of them executed, in Essex and Suffolk [England] only. Scotland swarms with them more and more, and persons of good quality

Sherwood was legally ducked for witchcraft in Virginia in 1705, and there was an indictment, followed by acquittal, in Maryland as late as 1712.

any such emotion. "If a drop of innocent blood should be shed in the prosecution of the witchcrafts among us, how unhappy are we!" wrote Cotton Mather.

ARRESTING A WITCH.

That the delusion reached this point was due to no hardened inhumanity of feeling; on the contrary, those who participated in it prayed to be delivered from

Accordingly Mr. Poole has shown that this eminent clergyman, popularly identified beyond any one else with the witchcraft delusion, yet tried to have it met by united prayer rather than by the courts; would never attend any of the witchcraft trials; cautioned the magistrates against credulity, and kept secret to his dying day the names of many persons privately inculpated by the witnesses with whom he conversed. It was with anguish of spirit and the conscientious fidelity of the Anglo-Saxon temperament that these men entered upon the work. Happy would they have been could they have taken such supposed visitations lightly, as the Frenchmen on this continent have taken them. Champlain fully believed that there was a devil inhabiting a certain island in the St. Lawrence, under the name of the Gougou; but he merely crossed himself, carolled a French song, and sailed by. Yet even in France, as has been seen, the delusion raged enormously; and to men of English descent, at any rate, it was no such light thing that Satan dwelt visibly in the midst of them. Was this to be the end of all their labors, their sacrifices? They had crossed the ocean, fought off the Indians, cleared the forest, built their quaint little houses in the clearing, extirpated all open vice, and lo! Satan was still there in concealment, like the fabled ghost which migrated with the family, being packed among the beds. There is no mistaking the intensity of their lament. See with what depth of emotion Cotton Mather utters it:

" 'Tis a dark time, yea a black night indeed, now the Ty-dogs of the Pit are abroad among us, but *it is through the wrath of the Lord of Hosts!*......Blessed Lord! Are all the other Instruments of thy Vengeance too good for the chastisement of such Transgressors as we are? Must the very *Devils* be sent *out of their own place* to be our troublers?......They are not swarthy Indians, but they are sooty Devils that are let loose upon us."

Thus wrote Cotton Mather, he who had sat beside the bedside of the "bewitched" Margaret Rule and had distinctly smelled sulphur.

While the English of the second generation were thus passing through a phase of Puritanism more intense than any they brought with them, the colonies were steadily increasing in population, and were modifying in structure toward their later shape. Delaware had passed from Swedish under Dutch control, Governor Stuyvesant having taken possession of the colony in 1655 with small resistance. Then the whole Dutch territory, thus enlarged, was transferred to English dominion, quite against the will of the same headstrong Governor, known as "Hardkoppig Piet." The Dutch had thriven, in spite of their patroons and their slaves and their semblance of aristocratic government; they had built forts in Connecticut, claimed Cape Cod for a boundary, and even stretched their demands as far as Maine. All their claims and possessions were at last surrendered without striking a blow. When the British fleet appeared off Long Island, the whole organized Dutch force included only some two hundred men fit for duty, scattered from Albany to Delaware; the inhabitants of New Amsterdam refused to take up arms, although Governor Stuyvesant would fain have had them, and he was so enraged that he tore to pieces the letter from Nicolls, the English commander, to avoid showing it. "The surrender," he said, "would be reproved in the fatherland." But the people utterly refused to stand by him, and he was thus compelled, sorely against his will, to surrender. The English entered into complete occupation; New Netherlands became New York; all the Dutch local names were abolished, although destined to be restored during the later Dutch occupation, which again ceased in 1674. Yet the impress of that nationality remains to this day on the names, the architecture, and the customs of that region, and has indeed tinged those of the whole country; and the Dutch had securely founded what was from its early days the most cosmopolitan city of America.

Their fall left the English in absolute possession of a line of colonies that stretched from Maine southward. This now included some new settlements made during the period just described. Carolina, as it had been called a hundred years before by Jean Ribault and his French Protestants, was granted in 1663 by King Charles II. to eight proprietors, who brought with them a plan of government framed for them by the celebrated John Locke—probably the most absurd scheme of government ever proposed for a new colony by a philosopher, and fortunately set aside from the very beginning by the common-sense of the colonists. Being the most southern colony, it was drawn into vexatious wars with the Spaniards, the French, and the Indians; but it was many years before it was divided by the King into two parts, and before Georgia was set-

PETER STUYVESANT TEARING THE LETTER DEMANDING THE SURRENDER OF NEW YORK.

tled. Another grant by Charles II. was more wisely planned, when in 1681 William Penn sent out some emigrants, guided by no philosopher except Penn himself, who came the following year. A great tract of country was granted to him as a sort of equivalent for a debt owed by the King to his father, Admiral Penn; the annual rent was to be two beaverskins. Everything seemed to throw around the coming of William Penn the aspect of a lofty enterprise: his ship was named "*The Welcome*"; his new city was to be called "Brotherly Love," or "Philadelphia." With the opportunity of su-

preme control, Penn ordained for his people entire self-government; and he directed them from the beginning to a policy of peace, contentment, and wise comprehensiveness. His harmonious relations with the Indians have been the wonder of later times, though it must be remembered that he had to do with no such fierce tribes as had devastated the other colonies. Peace prevailed with sectarian zealots, and even toward those charged with witchcraft. Yet even Philadelphia did not escape the evil habits of the age, and established the whipping-post, the pillory, and the stocks —some of which Delaware, long a part of

Pennsylvania, still retains. But there is no such scene of contentment in our pioneer history as that which the early annals of "Penn's Woods" (Pennsylvania) record.

Other great changes were meanwhile taking place. New Hampshire and New Jersey came to be recognized as colonies by themselves; the union of the New England colonies was dissolved; Plymouth was merged in Massachusetts, New Haven in Connecticut, Delaware temporarily in Pennsylvania. At the close of the period which I have called the second generation (1700) there were ten distinct English colonies along the coast—New Hampshire, Massachusetts, Rhode Island, Connecticut, New York, New Jersey, Pennsylvania, Maryland, Virginia, Carolina.

It is a matter of profound interest to observe that whatever may be the variations among these early settlements, we find everywhere the distinct traces of the old English village communities, which again are traced by Freeman and others to a Swiss or German origin. The founders of the first New England towns did not simply settle themselves upon the principle of "squatter sovereignty," each for himself; but they founded municipal organizations, based on a common control of the land. So systematically was this carried out that in an old town like Cambridge, Massachusetts, for instance, it would be easy at this day, were all the early tax lists missing, to determine the comparative worldly condition of the different settlers simply by comparing the proportion which each had to maintain of the great "pallysadoe" or paling which surrounded the little settlement. These amounts varied from seventy rods, in case of the richest, to two rods, in case of the poorest; and so well was the work done that the traces of the "fosse" about the paling still remain in the willow-trees on the play-ground of the Harvard students. These early settlers simply reproduced, with a few necessary modifications, those local institutions which had come to them from remote ancestors. The town paling, the town meeting, the town common, the town pound, the fence-viewers, the field-

drivers, the militia muster, even the tipstaves of the constables, are "survivals" of institutions older than the Norman conquest of England. Even the most matter-of-fact transactions of their daily life, as the transfer of land by giving a piece of turf, an instance of which occurred at Salem, Massachusetts, in 1696, sometimes carry us back to usages absolutely mediæval—in this case to the transfer "by turf and twig" so familiar to historians. All that the New England settlers added to their traditional institutions—and it was a great addition—was the system of common schools. Beyond New England the analogies with inherited custom are, according to Professor Freeman, less clear and unmistakable; but Professor Herbert B. Adams has lately shown that the Southern "parish" and "county," the South Carolina "court-greens" and "common pastures," as well as the Maryland "manors" and "court-leets," all represent the same inherited principle of communal sovereignty. All these traditional institutions are now being carefully studied, with promise of the most interesting results, by a rising school of historical students in the United States.

The period which I have assigned to the second generation in America may be considered to have lasted from 1650 to 1700. Even during this period there took place collisions of purpose and interest between the home government and the colonies. The contest for the charters, for instance, and the short-lived power of Sir Edmund Andros, occurred within the time which has here been treated, but they were the forerunners of a later contest, and will be included in another paper. It will then be necessary to describe the gradual transformation which made colonies into provinces, and out of a varied emigration developed a homogeneous and cohering people; which taught the English ministry to distrust the Americans, and caused the Americans to be unconsciously weaned from England; so that the tie which at first had expressed only affection became at last a hated yoke, soon to be thrown aside forever.

MEMOIRS OF WENDELL PHILLIPS

I AM indebted to a broadcloth mob for my first acquaintance with Wendell Phillips. It was he who gave that name to the riotous assemblages of the respectability of Boston which, from time to time during the long antislavery struggle preceding the war, used to break up antislavery meetings and mob antislavery orators. How long ago it all seems! I imagine that the younger generation which has grown up since the war may have some difficulty in realizing the state of things which then existed. The difficulty would perhaps be greater and not less if the inner history of that period were better known than it is. It was not and could not have been widely known at the time. It has had no historian since, nor is it a history which I shall attempt to write, but only the story of an incident or two which may serve as illustrations of those singular days. I confine myself to what I heard and saw.

My connection with the Abolitionists began in the winter of 1860. I had been four years at the bar, and I was a Whig—again a word which takes us a long way back—a Whig by family tradition and relationship, junior law partner to a Whig uncle, and hardly knew anybody who was not of that political faith, which was also a social faith or a social shibboleth. The Whig of those days had an academic partiality for freedom as against slavery. Circumstances sometimes converted it into an active policy; sometimes stifled it, or the expression of it, altogether. Cotton was still King. Webster's apostasy had not cost him the admiring allegiance of his own State. He had dragged her down with him. As Lowell sang:

"Massachusetts, God forgive her!
She's a-kneelin' with the rest."

Webster and his party had made Massachusetts and the other Northern States the slave-hunters of the South, and the South took care to find work for them. The Fugitive Slave Law had been passed in 1850. The 7th of the March of that year, the date of Webster's speech in the Senate in favor of that infamous act, proved an epoch-making date. Two years later came the surrender of Sims. Four years later came the surrender of Anthony Burns. The trial, the Court-house in chains, the meeting in Faneuil Hall, the midnight attack on the Court-house, the killing of Batchelder, the decree of the United States Commissioner, Edward Greely Loring, which gave Burns back to his master, and finally that ever-memorable day when, under a guard of United States marines and artillery, with the streets of Boston kept by Massachusetts militia, the shameful procession took its way down State Street, amid the groans and humiliation of the people of the proud old city, and delivered Burns on board a revenue-cutter to go back to the slave plantation in Virginia;—that long yet rapid series of events reconverted in a measure the old Bay State to the faith of the Pilgrim Fathers, and to her ancient hatred of the slave-owner and the slave-hunter. The weapon which Webster had forged turned in his dead hand. From 1850 to 1861 Massachusetts went through a process of re-education. The lesson of freedom which she had unlearned from Webster she learned again from Garrison, from Phillips, from Charles Sumner, from John A. Andrew, from Emerson, from Lowell, finally from John Brown at Harper's Ferry.

The two names which connect themselves more closely than any others with the history of that gloomy winter of 1860-61 in Boston are those of John Brown and Wendell Phillips; and for this reason: The starting-point of the agitation which shook the city during those months was a meeting in Tremont Temple, called in commemoration of the death of John Brown. It was captured by the pro-slavery party under the leadership of Richard S. Fay. The "gentlemen" of Boston got possession of the Tremont Temple by force and stealth, turned out those who had hired it, and passed resolutions of their own. The expelled Abolitionists held another meeting the same evening in a little hall in, I think, Belknap Street. This last I attended, and under the influence of the events of the day and of what I heard in the evening, I wrote a letter to Phillips, whom I did not know, saying how strongly I sympathized with him, and offering to do anything I could for what seemed the cause of free speech and of freedom. This was not entirely the impulse of the moment. I had often heard him on the platform, and of course admired him as an orator, and respected the policy he pursued with reference to slavery, though I did not agree with him. Even his enemies—and at that time almost everybody was his enemy—admired his gallantry, and not even the respectable dailies of Boston questioned his unselfish sincerity. His answer to my letter came in the unexpected shape of a visit from the orator himself. My law office was in State Street, and when the door opened my first thought was of a client, not then a very frequent apparition. He came in with that air of keen scrutiny which was, in a way, natural to him, but had grown keener under the pressure of events, and was presently, as dangers thickened about him, to become still more marked. It was the air of a man who did not mean to be taken by surprise. He embraced everything at a glance—me, the office, the books, the furniture, the view out of the window, like a general giving to himself an account of a country seen for the first time. This alertness did not impair the charm of his manner, nor his distinction; —this last I never knew him to lose, and I was to see him tried in many difficult circumstances. He wore the light gray soft felt hat and the pale brown overcoat so well known in the streets of Boston. As I stepped forward he said:

"You wrote me a letter?"

"Yes."

"I want to talk to you, but not now. Will you come to my house at nine this evening?"

Again I said yes. He held out his hand, and was gone without another word. At nine I was at the little house in Essex Street, and was shown at once into the drawing-room on the first floor. I pass over most of the conversation, and most of what I have to say about Phillips personally, in order to find room for matter which touches closely on the history of that eventful time. The beauty and kindliness of his manner would have fascinated an enemy, much more did they one who was already devoted to him. The talk very soon took a practical turn. I knew Phillips was in some danger, and asked him if he knew it. He said he had been threatened, and had heard stories of violence, but that he had heard much the same thing for many years past, "and, after all, you know nothing has happened." He was aware, nevertheless, that times had changed, and that a desperate spirit was abroad. He admitted that the police had warned him that his house might be attacked.

"Then why not defend it?"

"That is the business of the police," he answered.

"But you must have friends who would help?"

He turned rather suddenly, his eyes fixed on me, and asked,

"Will you help?"

It was the beginning of a singular experience which was to last some months, and of a friendship which was to last forever. I put myself at his disposal, and he gave me the names of a few men who could be relied on; young Abolitionists all of them, and at least one, Hinton, who had served an antislavery apprenticeship in Kansas under John Brown, and had some share, or was to have had, in the Harper's Ferry expedition. The others were Le Barnes, Hoyt (who had also been in Kansas), Heywood, Edward L. Pierce, the biographer of Sumner, and Frank Sanborn.

This little group came, or some of them came, night after night while the danger lasted, and then at intervals later as fresh crises arose. Essex Street was watched by the police, who had reasons of their own for thinking that an attack was likely to be made on the house. A small police reserve was stationed not far off. The Deputy Chief of Police, Mr. Ham, had charge of the outside arrangements, as he did subsequently when the danger was transferred to the streets. He was not an Abolitionist; but then neither was he a border ruffian. He was simply an excellent officer, who did his duty without fear or favor. Those of us who were inside had the best of it. We camped out in the little red drawing-room; one at a time kept watch; the rest slept on sofas and chairs. A supper was always provided. We had to keep very quiet. Mrs. Phillips, then as always an invalid, slept in the room above, and woke at the slightest noise. We were, of course, well armed, and some of us were accustomed to the use of one weapon or another. Certain pikes with which John Brown had armed his men formed part of our equipment. They might not have been very useful, but they added to the enthusiasm. Hinton had seen some fighting in Kansas, and had military ideas.

He used to draw up plans of campaign, and decide how the door was to be defended, and how the steep and narrow staircase should be held if our friends once got inside. Each of us had his station; but as the attendance was irregular, these plans might have gone wrong at an awkward moment. The awkward moment, however, never came. It must have been known that the house was garrisoned, and the police preparations were visible, and intended to be visible. In the earlier days, and at times afterwards, mischief was clearly meant. In the intervals the enemy, I think, slept.

All this time Phillips was lecturing here and there about the country, and opportunities were not wanting to resolute men who meant business. On some of these excursions I went with him; more often he went alone. He was about the streets of Boston at all times, day and night. Nothing would induce him to be prudent. He had the fearlessness of a high nature, and also a certain contempt for his foes, and the feeling of him who said, "Better be killed once than die every day from fear." He carried a revolver, and was perfectly ready to use it should the occasion arise. I said to him once that some of the baser sort might try to insult him in the street. "They never shall," he answered. "I keep my eyes open, and I can see a man who comes from behind before he can reach me. I would shoot him sooner than endure an outrage." He knew the use of a revolver, had practised with it, and could shoot quick. The next summer, at Milton, the danger then all over, we used to practise together, and he was more than an average shot.

Phillips was under engagement to speak once a month of a Sunday morning at the Music Hall, to the Twenty-eighth Congregational Society—Theodore Parker's—during the winter of 1860-61, and he did speak. The first critical occasion came not long after the John Brown meeting had been broken up, when he delivered the discourse now reprinted in a volume of speeches, under the title "Mobs and Education." He was warned publicly and privately that he would not be allowed to speak. Some of the respectable dailies of Boston protested against his being heard. They wanted to silence every voice hostile to what they called compromise and we called surrender.

Some of his friends urged him to give way. It was not in his nature to give way. He said, in that easy manner which was so engaging, as we sat with him at home, "I suppose some of you will stand by me; but in any case I must go." We found out, moreover, that the police had no notion of allowing a Sunday congregation to be broken up, or what was in effect a religious service interfered with. If Phillips or anybody else was to be gagged, it must be upon some pretext, and here there was none. The police were allowed by the Mayor to make their own preparations, and they were ample, though, as the event showed, there was not much to spare. His friends made their own arrangements independently of the police. We had possession of the platform, about twenty men in all, most of whom were as steel.

The hall, which held nearly 3000 people, was crowded. The discourse was in every sense of the word a Phillipic. The orator was determined at all risks to free his mind about the cotton clerks and State Street merchants who composed and captained the mob which had wrecked the John Brown meeting a fortnight before. As a piece of invective, it ranks high. Phillips knew all these men, and the history of them and of their families, and he so used his knowledge that the sentences stung. Disorder began early. There were cries and yells. More than once the police, of whom two bodies were held in readiness out of sight, proposed to enter the hall, but were dissuaded. We thought Phillips would hold his audience to the end, and he did. But the place was hot with rage. A few men in such circumstances can create a great disturbance, and of the whole audience we judged that perhaps a third were hostile. Word was brought that a crowd was collecting outside, which could have but one meaning. When Phillips ended there was a storm, both of applause, and of groans and angry shouts, from the audience. I went to the police officer in charge. He met me with a beaming face and the remark, "Well, you see it has passed off all right." "It has not yet begun," I said. I begged him to take possession with all his force of the long, narrow, open-air passage leading from the Music Hall to Winter Street, and I told him the message that had come in from our own men. He stared, but replied it could do no harm, and marched his two companies off. They were just in time. The mob were already pouring into the passage, which, from its narrowness and length, was only too well suited to their purpose. The police formed in front of the doorway. When the officer saw what he had to deal with, he sent off for re-enforcements. "Tell Mr. Ham we want every man he can spare." Mr. Ham did better than send all he could spare, he came himself. He was an officer who knew his duty, and did it; clear-headed, prompt, resolute, courageous, and a tactician. The passage from the hall enters Winter Street at a point about equidistant from either end. To reach Washington Street, the direct road to Essex Street, you turned out of the passage to the left. Winter Street was already packed from end to end with a mob. The deputy chief sent a body of his men in, formed them to the right across the whole breadth, and cut the mob in two. As Phillips came out of the door his friends closed in, and we started down the passage. There were cries, "There he is," "Down with him," "Kill him," and a rush which came to naught. The police held steadily on, and we reached Winter Street, which there had been no time to clear, nor was the force adequate. Turning the corner was a delicate business, but once in the street the police soon made room for themselves, the different sections of the force united, and the march to Essex Street began. The distance is from a third of a mile to a half. It took us an hour to make the journey. The mob was numbered by thousands. The pressure and crush were very great. But for the police our little company would have been swept away at once, and Phillips with them.

It was just past noon, a brilliant morning, the sun shining, the air clear and cold, and never before had the Sabbath been celebrated in this way in this Puritan capital of a Puritan commonwealth. The morning services in the churches were over, the church bells were silent, prayers had been duly offered up in the commercial spirit then prevalent in the churches, and you heard the echo of them in the curses and murderous threats which filled the air outside. Phillips listened to them, and watched the throng struggling to get at him. We walked together, his arm was in mine, and the

pressure of it was light and steady. His eyes burned, and he was evidently ready for whatever might befall, but, on the whole, his bearing was that of an interested observer of events. Washington Street, the main business thoroughfare of Boston, was packed as tight with human beings, mostly in a state of anger, as Winter Street. Once there, I thought the worst over. The solid ranks of the stalwart policemen had never been broken, though often shaken, and we moved a little faster. The mob could not be kept out of Essex Street, but the entrance to the house, which looked down Harrison Avenue, was finally cleared; Phillips, with half a dozen friends, went safely in, the police remained on guard, and the baffled mob had nothing to do but disperse.

It was still only December of 1860, and the winter was before us. There were few days which did not bring some incident or adventure. There was another Sunday at the Music Hall, another uncompromising discourse, and another disturbance, less serious, however, than the first. Close upon that came the meeting of the Massachusetts Antislavery Society, January 21, 1861—one of the critical incidents which preceded the war. Few men, I imagine, who were not then in Boston are aware how high the anti-antislavery feeling ran, or what violent and even criminal measures the party of submission to the South was at that time ready to adopt. It was my fortune to have a foot in both camps. Of the Abolitionists, I knew hardly anybody except Phillips, but Phillips gave me his confidence and told me everything he knew. My Whig friends had not cast me off. They were good enough to look on my connection with Phillips as only a temporary aberration. It was known there would be trouble at Tremont Temple. The respectable classes had been protesting for weeks that the meeting should not be held. The Mayor of Boston, himself none too respectable, was on their side; perhaps not much more than their tool. No doubt public opinion, then more bitterly than ever, was against the society, against Phillips, against Garrison, against everybody who was not willing to see slavery the dominant force in the republic. But among the Abolitionists there was not one, so far as I know, who faltered or flinched. They went on with their preparations for the annual meeting just as steadily as if no opposition existed. The programme of speakers, resolutions, business, and the rest was settled. The defence of the platform was organized. The platform was high, and ran along nearly the whole of the east side of the hall, with stairs at either end. It was expected that an attempt would be made to storm it, and to take possession of the meeting, as had been done before. That had to be provided against. Men were chosen to defend it, their positions assigned them, and officers appointed. We were not strong enough to do more, and no attempt was made to hold either the floor of the hall or the deep gallery at the end opposite the platform. An application was addressed, for form's sake, to the police, but nobody relied on them, except perhaps the rioters. Phillips always said he had no blame for the police, or for their officers. They acted under the orders of the Mayor; some of them, as we knew, reluctantly. When allowed, they had behaved extremely well, and once at least Phillips probably owed his life to them. But as we talked matters over before this memorable day, Phillips put his trust elsewhere. "Whoever is Mayor of Boston," said he, "John A. Andrew is Governor of Massachusetts, and we are safe in his hands."

That wintry morning of the 21st of January, 1861, broke gray and cold. The meeting was called for ten o'clock. An hour before that those of us who were on duty had collected in the committee-room. But the mob were earlier than we. Whether by connivance of the hall-keepers or not, they had found their way in long before the hour fixed for opening the doors, and had taken possession of the gallery, and were yelling and singing when we came; stamping also, perhaps to keep their feet warm. Few or none were in the body of the hall, and none on the platform, which we were suffered to occupy without hinderance. It was evident from the first that if we on our side were organized, so were the mob, and that their plan of operations was to be different from what we had imagined. We knew afterwards that their leaders had determined to reserve their main effort for the evening. During the morning they devoted themselves chiefly to turning Tremont Temple into

a pandemonium. The business of the Antislavery Society was transacted for the most part in dumb-show. The gallery would allow nobody to be heard. They perceived ladies on the floor, and one of the amusements of the forces in the pay of State Street was to throw cushions at them. They were primed for much rougher work. Free drinks were the order of the day, and at least one barroom was open all the morning where brandy and rum were to be had for the asking. In the body of the hall sat some of the foremost men of Boston—it would be cruel at this late day to mention their names — men who certainly had never before been seen at an antislavery meeting, and who were there as ringleaders of the mob; silent leaders thus far, but looking on at the riot with evident approval and delight. For it had speedily become a riot. The din and tumult were overwhelming, and presently some of the occupants of the gallery began to come down on the floor and press slowly forward toward the platform. We expected a rush, and were ready, but that was not part of the morning programme. Presently Phillips, a past master in the art of dealing with mobs, rose to speak. A roar greeted him, of hatred and defiance. I have seen him often in presence of a hostile audience. He never was finer than on that morning. The gallery was resolved to silence him, and he was equally resolved that he would not be silenced. He wasted no strength, nor made the least effort to be heard while the rioters were trying their lungs. When they were out of breath he would get in a sentence; then the uproar recommenced. As a rule he wore out his opponents in these contests. Often they were so keen to hear what he said that they forgot for a time to interrupt. He was a master of "chaff," of irony, of invective, and sent his winged shafts into the depths of the throng, which had seldom any articulate answer in its stolid rage. So it went on. Toward the end there came a message from outside, which was handed up to Phillips, who read it. There was a certain commotion at the door of the hall, and people turned to look. "You may well look," said the orator, in those softly penetrating, smooth tones audible to the furthest corner. "I hear that the State House is awake at last, and that State troops will be here shortly to sweep that gallery where it belongs—into the calaboose." That quieted them for a moment, and they looked anxious, and I think even the roughs from the North End, who half filled the place, felt and admired the serene courage of the man who faced them. There was, I suppose, no moment all that morning when they were not masters of the meeting had they chosen. On the platform we were not fifty. We were armed ; but what were fifty against two thousand? It soon appeared that the alarm of troops was a false one, and the uproar grew wilder than ever. Phillips turned away, his speech half unmade, and much of it unheard. "We have but one chance," he said; "come with me at once." I could not conceive what he meant to do, nor why we should leave the hall and our comrades, but I obeyed, and going down the steps and out by a private door, we were soon in the street. Phillips said, "We are going to the State House to see Governor Andrew."

We found Governor Andrew in his private room on the south of the great hall, on the second floor. Andrew and Phillips were old friends, coworkers, though by different methods, in a common cause; each with a deep respect for the other, and a real personal regard. Phillips, though he would have no part in politics, had rejoiced in Andrew's election as Governor of the great Commonwealth, and had high hopes of his future. I knew Governor Andrew but slightly, and had asked Phillips if it were not better he should see him alone. "No," he said; "I don't wish to see him alone. I want an aide-de-camp and a witness." So we went in together.

The Governor sat at a table with the green blinds behind him closed, the light from the other windows, for it was a corner room, falling full on his face. He welcomed us rather gravely, as if he knew on what errand we had come. In those days—it may still be so—the Governor of Massachusetts was a great man because he was Governor; because he was the successor of a long line of men who to us of Massachusetts were illustrious, and will, I hope, remain illustrious to the men of Massachusetts for all time. Andrew's great fame as a War Governor was, of course, yet to come. We knew him as a successful lawyer, an orator, the head of a party, and a man whose name was

stainless. I have often thought since that there was a certain resemblance between him and Gambetta. It was outwardly more a bodily resemblance than anything else. Both were men whose bulk and girth were out of proportion to their height ; unwieldy, undignified in movement, wanting in delicacy and in distinction. But both had the stamp of power, of authority; something in the manner, something in the look, which denoted a strong nature; and both were men of extraordinary intellectual energy. Both also were tribunes of the people, and looked to the people as the true source of their position and influence. They were men of large and overflowing sympathies, and they were, the one a consummate, the other an extremely able, politician. One was a great War Minister, the other a great War Governor, and each did services to his country which will not be forgotten so long as either has a country to remember him, and to do honor to his memory. Gambetta looked the Italian he was—dark, dark-eyed, dark-haired, with an olive-tinted skin, beneath which flowed and flamed the hot red blood of his Genoese race. Andrew was pure Saxon, a blond deepening into red, the auburn hair clustering in curls over a broad low Greek brow, with as much fire as the Italian in his deep blue eyes, and plenty of firmness in the chiselled chin with its deep dent; the mouth and lips with as many curves as a Cupid's. I used to go to him sometimes before this in the interest of needy clients. There never was a kinder heart; and he would squander hours that meant much in the effort to help people who had no claim on him.

Phillips went, as his habit was, straight to the point:

"Governor Andrew, we come to you from the Massachusetts Antislavery Society to ask the protection of the State for our meeting. The Mayor is with the mob. The police cannot act without orders, which he refuses to give. We cannot protect ourselves, and we appeal to you as Governor of the Commonwealth to vindicate the rights of public meeting and of free speech, for the sake of which the Commonwealth was founded."

"What would you have me do, Mr. Phillips?"

"Call out the troops and suppress the riot the police encourage; send them to Tremont Temple."

On the table behind which Governor
Andrew sat was a copy of the Revised
Statutes. He laid his hand on the book,
looked straight at Phillips, and said:

"Show me my authority. Tell me what
law of the State of Massachusetts you ask
me to enforce."

Phillips answered, the color beginning
to come into his face,

"Governor Andrew, it is your business
to know the law, not mine."

The Governor opened the volume, turned it, spread it out before us, and repeated,
"Show me the statute."

"I think," said Phillips, "you misun-
derstand me and my errand. This is not
a court of law, and we are not here to split
hairs about acts of the Legislature. We
are here as citizens to ask you as Govern-
or to see that our rights as citizens are
preserved to us. You ask for a statute?
I send you to the Bill of Rights. You
ask for authority? I answer, you are the
Executive of Massachusetts. You have
taken an oath to the Commonwealth.
You are responsible to the State and to
God. In the last resort, you are the
guardian of public order and peace, and
of the rights of every citizen. You know
what they are as well as I do, and I tell
you that if you refuse to do your duty
now, they exist no longer."

"Gentlemen," replied the Governor,
"you both know me, and you know on
which side are my private sympathies
and feelings and wishes. But you come
to me as Governor. You ask me to take
a very serious step. The very request for
it implies that it may involve bloodshed."

"Not at all," broke in Phillips; "the
mob will disperse at the first sight of a
musket."

"If you were in my place, under my
responsibilities, you might not be quite so
sure. But I repeat, you come to me as
Governor. My duties and powers as Governor are strictly defined by law. Every
one of them is a creation by statute, and
I say to you again, show me the statute."

It was impossible to move him from
that position. Phillips pleaded and ar-
gued, to no purpose, till it became plain
to him that Governor Andrew was inexorable. The interview lasted perhaps half
an hour, and at moments was a little
stormy. The end was abrupt. "We are
wasting time," said Phillips to me, bowed
to the Governor, and so departed. As we
walked down stairs I saw that his face was
pale with anger, and in his eyes burned a
deeper fire than the mob had managed to
call into them. "I will never again speak
to Andrew as long as I live," he said. I
am not sure whether he ever did.

On thinking the matter over a good
while after, I came to the conclusion that
Governor Andrew had a reason which he
did not care to disclose. Matters were
not yet ripe for a conflict. Passions were
running high, and on the wrong side. It
was nearly three months before the first
rebel shot at Fort Sumter. The North
did not know its real mind, and few
guessed how deep was the feeling for the
flag and for the Union, or with what enthusiasm States which had so long bent
the knee to the South would spring to
their feet in defence of both. A false
step might have spoiled all. The use of
the State troops might have divided the
State against herself, might have strengthened the cause of secession, might have
given its Northern friends the pretext they
wanted, might have altered the course of
events for the worse. Governor Andrew
had the statesman's instinct. He calculated forces, and looked ahead. I never
doubted that, if he had yielded to his own
impulses, he would have called out the
militia. I don't think it is quite certain
they would have come. Later, Phillips
must have seen that there were two sides
to the question—two right sides, if you
like, which sometimes happens. Be that
as it may, it is impossible to doubt that
Governor Andrew, then, as ever, acted
from honorable convictions of duty.

None the less was the disappointment
of the hour bitter. It was the more bitter because of the friendship between the
two men whom the exigency of this crisis
parted, and for Phillips's public and recent testimony to Andrew, who had said
in a letter written after his election as
Governor: "The right to think, to know,
and to utter, as John Milton said, is the
dearest of all liberties. Without this
right there can be no liberty to any
people; with it there can be no slavery."
And in the same letter he had declared
that this right of free speech must first
be secure before free society can be said
to stand on any foundation. "Thank
God for such a Governor!" had been
Phillips's exclamation in his Music Hall
speech only a month before. And now
free speech was at the mercy of the or-

ganized ruffians who had stolen Tremont Temple, and the Governor for whom the orator had thanked God would not stir in defence of the right which he had described as the foundation of free society.

We went back to the Temple to find the meeting adjourned, and there was nothing to do but return to Essex Street. It was evident the business was not over, and the question was, What next? The afternoon brought the answer. One of my friends from the other side came to see me, and began by saying he had something to tell in confidence about the meeting to be held in the evening. I said I would listen to nothing which I might not communicate to my friends. "But it concerns your safety and theirs." "The more reason they should know of it." I saw he was anxious, troubled, and bent on telling, but I would give no promise. Presently, out it came. The leaders of the mob were resolved, it appeared, to do something more than prevent the Abolitionists from being heard. They had conceived the idea of offering up a sacrifice to propitiate their Southern deities. They were going to the Tremont Temple that evening armed, they would be in overwhelming force, and if they were resisted the platform was to be cleared with their revolvers. I said I did not believe they would do anything of the kind; that if they did, we were armed as well as they, and the shooting would not be all on one side. He grew agitated. "What you say is sheer madness. They are ten to your one. If you don't believe what I tell you, I can only say you know my position, you know I am in the confidence of these men, I am betraying it for your sake, and I pledge you my word of honor that what I tell you is true." It was impossible to doubt him. I asked, "What do you want me to do?" "Stay away from the meeting." "You know I cannot. I must go with Mr. Phillips." "Then tell him and keep him out of harm's way." "You don't know Phillips, and I do. He will go to the meeting if a meeting is held." He still urged me. "Say anything you like, only don't use my name. Get the meeting adjourned on some pretext. It is the only chance to save your friends." I thanked him heartily, as he deserved, but could make no promise except that his name should not be mentioned.

What had happened at the Temple in the afternoon gave only too much color of probability to this warning for the evening. The mob had been more violent than in the morning. The Mayor had appeared, said a few words about protecting property, been received with a roar of derision, and had fled with a white face. A rush to the platform had been attempted while Phillips was again speaking, and spectators on the platform had seen in the gathering dusk the gleam of knives in the hands of the leaders. It may be hard to carry the mind back to those days, or to form to one's self a notion of the savage spirit that prevailed. But it did prevail. When the afternoon meeting came to an end the mob lay in wait for Phillips, and when the little guard of friends who had surrounded him on the platform were seen emerging, the mob surged down upon them. They never got very near, and Phillips, meantime, with his usual cool carelessness of danger, was walking home alone. I found him in Essex Street, and told him my friend's story. "Do you believe it?" was his first question. I said I believed in the good faith of the man, and I thought he must know. He was in a position to know what was afoot. "Well, we shall have to face it," was his only comment. All day long, as was the custom at these meetings, there had been ladies on the platform. They at least must be kept away, I suggested. "If you think you can prevent their going, you are welcome to try," was the answer, with a humorous smile. I did try, vainly. I asked Phillips to use his authority. He would not admit that he had any authority in such a matter. Two of them started with us, and we arrived only to find the hall doors shut and a notice posted that the Mayor, in the interest of public order, had closed the Temple. Had he, too, heard of the programme on which his friends had resolved? We never knew. He was aware, of course, that violence was to be expected, and as he would not protect the meeting or the Abolitionists, the next best thing was to close the hall. It was the resource of a weak man. It was a capitulation. But as Mayor Wightman had not the courage nor the wish to do his duty as Mayor, and to defend a particular form of public meeting which happened to be unpopular, it was perhaps well that he should adopt a course which at least saved some imperilled lives.

Twice or three times before April, Phillips gave discourses in the Music Hall, one section of the mob dancing attendance outside, and another inside interrupting and hooting. There came at last the Sunday which followed Fort Sumter, when he had to decide what attitude he would take to the war for that Union which all his life he had assailed. He had preached Disunion all the winter in terms, and it was no light matter to recall or recant his doctrine. True, the Union now meant Freedom and not Slavery, and the North had all at once flung off its chains, but Phillips had never been a man to follow because others showed the way. It was to him a struggle, the story of which I may tell fully some day. Now I wish only to put side by side the scene of December and the scene of April. The audience which assembled in the Music Hall on the morning of Sunday, April 21, 1861, found the platform and desk and walls and galleries hung with the American flag. It was Charles Follen who had conceived this idea, and Phillips, on being asked whether he objected, answered: "As many flags as you like. I am going to speak for the flag." The papers announced that he was to retract his opinions. "No, not one of them," said Phillips in almost his first sentence. "I need them all, every word I have spoken this winter, every act of twenty-five years of my life, to make the welcome I give this war hearty and hot. Civil war is a momentous evil. It needs the soundest, the most solemn justification. I rejoice before God to-day for every word I have spoken counselling peace. But I rejoice more profoundly still that now, for the first time in my antislavery life, I speak beneath the Stars and Stripes, and welcome the tread of Massachusetts men marshalled for war."

It was Sunday morning, but the vast audience rose to their feet and cheered long. The Sixth Massachusetts Regiment, only two days before, had fought its way through Baltimore. That is enough to explain everything. Phillips, the most hated man in the State, became the idol of the hour. The Music Hall rang with cheers that morning, not once, nor twice, but almost every moment while his speech lasted. It was a scene possible only in such a crisis, at the first great uprising of a great people, in the presence of an orator capable of expressing in words of unmatched eloquence the feeling which burned in every heart.

"No matter what the past has been or said, to-day the slave asks God for a sight of this banner, and counts it the pledge of his redemption."

The slave, too, had become an idol, and Freedom, long forgotten, all at once was accepted as a religion. "Massachusetts has been sleeping on her arms since '83, but the first cannon-shot brings her to her feet with the war-cry of the Revolution on her lips." Washington was in danger. "Rather than surrender that capital, cover every square foot of it with a living body; crowd it with a million of men, and empty every bank vault in the North to pay the cost." These heroic accents must stir every American heart, but no man who did not hear them can form to himself a notion of the passion of patriotism they kindled as they were uttered.

The hall and its approaches and the adjacent streets were filled with the same multitudes, of whom no small part, four months earlier, had done their best to tear the orator in pieces. These were the men who now cheered him. They came to him when his speech ended. They grasped his hand. They owned themselves enemies who had become friends. They offered him their homage. They surrounded him as he left the hall. They attended him as he made his way through the throng outside, almost as slowly as before. The streets were thronged now as then, and thronged with the men who would have burned him then and adored him now. Perhaps never had any man passed more suddenly through a more marvellous change of position and of popular feeling. His return from the Music Hall to Essex Street was a triumphal march. It was the atonement which Boston offered to the great citizen whom she had so long misunderstood and reviled. It was the crown of Phillips's antislavery life. The nation and the government had come round to him. The Boston he loved learned to love him also. They were often at variance afterwards, but the memory of that day of reconciliation will outlive all others. All others, or all save that still more solemn day, twenty-three years later, when the body of the golden-lipped orator lay in state in Faneuil Hall, and Boston passed in mute procession by the mortal remains of her immortal apostle of freedom.

LITERARY BOSTON

I.

AMONG my fellow-passengers on the train from New York to Boston, when I went to begin my work there in 1866, as the assistant editor of the Atlantic Monthly, was the late Samuel Bowles, of the Springfield Republican, who created in a subordinate city a journal of metropolitan importance. I had met him in Venice several years earlier, when he was suffering from the cruel insomnia which had followed his overwork on that newspaper, and when he told me that he was sleeping scarcely more than one hour out of the twenty-four. His worn face attested the misery which this must have been, and which lasted in some measure while he lived, though I believe that rest and travel relieved him in his later years. He was always a man of cordial friendliness, and he now expressed a most gratifying interest when I told him what I was going to do in Boston. He gave himself the pleasure of descanting upon the dramatic quality of the fact that a young newspaper man from Ohio was

about to share in the destinies of the great literary periodical of New England.

I do not think that such a fact would now move the fancy of the liveliest newspaper man, so much has the West since returned upon the East in a refluent wave of authorship. But then the West was almost an unknown quantity in our literary problem; and in fact there was scarcely any literature outside of New England. Even this was of New England origin, for it was almost wholly the work of New England men and women in the "splendid exile" of New York. The Atlantic Monthly, which was distinctively literary, was distinctively a New England magazine, though from the first it had been characterized by what was more national, what was more universal, in the New England temperament. Its chief contributors for nearly twenty years were Longfellow, Lowell, Holmes, Whittier, Emerson, Dr. Hale, Col. Higginson, Mrs. Stowe, Whipple, Rose Terry Cooke, Mrs. Julia Ward Howe, Mrs. Prescott Spofford, Mrs. Phelps Ward, and other New Eng-

SAMUEL BOWLES.

land writers who still lived in New England, and largely in the region of Boston. Occasionally there came a poem from Bryant, at New York, from Mr. Stedman, from Mr. Stoddard and Mrs. Stoddard, from Mr. Aldrich, and from Bayard Taylor. But all these, except the last, were not only of New England race, but of New England birth. I think there was no contributor from the South but Mr. M. D. Conway, and as yet the West scarcely counted, though four young poets from Ohio, who were not immediately or remotely of Puritan origin, had appeared in

early numbers; Alice Cary, living with her sister in New York, had written now and then from the beginning. Mr. John Hay solely represented Illinois by a single paper, and he was of Rhode Island stock. It was after my settlement at Boston that Mark Twain, of Missouri, became a figure of world-wide fame at Hartford; and longer after, that Mr. Bret Harte made that progress Eastward from California which was telegraphed almost from hour to hour, as if it were the progress of a prince. Miss Constance F. Woolson had not yet begun to write. Mr. James Whitcomb Riley, Mr. Maurice Thompson, Miss Edith Thomas, Octave Thanet, Mr. Charles Warren Stoddard, Mr. H. B. Fuller, Mrs. Catherwood, Mr. Hamlin Garland, whom I name at random among other Western writers, were then as unknown as Mr. Cable, Miss Murfree, Mrs. Rives Chanler, Miss Grace King, Mr. Joel Chandler Harris, Mr. Thomas Nelson Page, in the South, which they by no means fully represent.

The editors of the Atlantic had been eager from the beginning to discover any outlying literature; but, as I have said, there was in those days very little good writing done beyond the borders of New England. If the case is now different, and the best known among living American writers are no longer New-Englanders, still I do not think the South and West have yet trimmed the balance; and though perhaps the new writers now more commonly appear in those quarters,

THE WATER-SIDE AT BEVERLY.

I should not be so very sure that they are not still characterized by New England ideals and examples. On the other hand, I am very sure that in my early day we were characterized by them, and wished to be so; we even felt that we failed in so far as we expressed something native quite in our own way. The literary theories we accepted were New England theories, the criticism we valued was New England criticism, or, more strictly speaking, Boston theories, Boston criticism.

II.

Of those more constant contributors to the Atlantic whom I have mentioned, it is of course known that Longfellow and Lowell lived in Cambridge, Emerson at Concord, and Whittier at Amesbury. Colonel Higginson was still and for many years afterwards at Newport; Mrs. Stowe was then at Andover; Miss Prescott of Newburyport had become Mrs. Spofford, and was presently in Boston, where her husband was a member of the General Court; Mrs. Phelps Ward, as Miss Elizabeth Stuart Phelps, dwelt in her father's house at Andover. The Bostonians were Mrs. Julia Ward Howe, Dr. Holmes, and Dr. Hale. Yet Boston stood for the whole Massachusetts group, and Massachusetts, in the literary impulse, meant New England. I suppose we must all allow, whether we like to do so or not, that the impulse seems now to have pretty well spent itself. Certainly the city of Boston has distinctly waned in literature, though it has waxed in wealth and population. I do not think there are in Boston to-day even so many talents with a literary coloring in law, science, theology, and journalism as there were formerly; though I have no belief that the Boston talents are fewer or feebler than before. I arrived in Boston, however, when all talents had more or less a literary coloring, and when the greatest talents were literary. These expressed with ripened fulness a civilization conceived in faith and brought forth in good works; but that moment of maturity was the beginning of a decadence which could only show itself much later. New England has ceased to be a nation in itself, and it will perhaps never again have anything like a national literature; but that was something like a national literature; and it will probably be centuries yet before the life of the whole country, the American life as distinguished

JAMES R. OSGOOD.

from the New England life, shall have anything so like a national literature. It will be long before our larger life interprets itself in such imagination as Hawthorne's, such wisdom as Emerson's, such poetry as Longfellow's, such prophecy as Whittier's, such wit and grace as Holmes's, such humor and humanity as Lowell's.

The literature of those great men was, if I may suffer myself the figure, the Socinian graft of a Calvinist stock. Their faith, in its varied shades and colors, was Unitarian, but their art was Puritan. So far as it was imperfect—and great and beautiful as it was, I think it had its imperfections—it was marred by the intense ethicism that pervaded the New England mind for two hundred years, and that still characterizes it. They or their fathers had broken away from orthodoxy in the great schism at the beginning of the century, but, as if their heterodoxy were conscience-stricken, they still helplessly pointed the moral in all they did; some pointed it more directly, some less directly; but they all pointed it. I should be far from blaming them for their ethical intention, though I think they felt their vocation as prophets too much for their good as poets. Sometimes they sacrificed the song to the sermon, though not always, nor nearly always. It was in poetry and in romance that they excelled; in the novel, so far as they attempted it, they failed. I say this with the names of all the Bostonian group, and those they influenced, in mind, and with a full sense of their greatness. It may be ungracious to say that they have left no heirs to their peculiar greatness; but it would be foolish to say that they had left an estate where they had none to bequeath. One cannot take account of such a fantasy as Judd's Margaret. The only New-Englander who has attempted the novel on a scale proportioned to the work of the New-Englanders in philosophy, in poetry, in romance, is Mr. De Forest, who is of New Haven, and not of Boston. I do not forget the fictions of Dr. Holmes, or the vivid inventions of Dr. Hale, but I do not call them novels; and I do not forget the exquisitely realistic art of Miss Jewett or Miss Wilkins, which is free from the ethicism of the great New England group, but which has hardly the novelist's scope. New England, in Hawthorne's work, achieved perfection in romance; but the romance is always an allegory, and the novel is a picture in which the truth to life is suffered to do its unsermonized office for conduct; and New England yet lacks her novelist, because it was her instinct and her conscience to be true to an ideal of life rather than to life itself.

Even when we come to the exception that proves the rule, even to such a signal exception as Uncle Tom's Cabin, I think that what I say holds true. That is by far the greatest work of imagination that we have produced in prose, and it is the work of a New England woman, writing from all the inspirations and traditions of New England. It is like begging the question to say that I do not call it a novel, however; but really, is it a novel, in the sense that War and Peace is a novel, or Madame Flaubert, or L'Assommoir, or Phineas Finn, or Doña Perfecta, or Esther Waters, or Marta y María, or The Return of the Native, or Virgin

PARK STREET CHURCH, BOSTON.

Soil, or David Grieve? In a certain way it is greater than any of these except the first; but its chief virtue, or its prime virtue, is in its address to the conscience, and not its address to the taste; to the ethical sense, not the æsthetical sense.

This does not quite say the thing, but it suggests it, and I should be sorry if it conveyed to any reader a sense of slight; for I believe no one has felt more deeply than myself the value of New England in literature. The comparison of the literary situation at Boston to the literary situation at Edinburgh in the times of the reviewers has never seemed to me accurate or adequate, and it holds chiefly in the fact that both seem to be of the past. Certainly New York is yet no London in literature, and I think Boston was once vastly more than Edinburgh ever was, at least in quality. The Scotch literature of the palmy days was not wholly Scotch, and even when it was rooted in Scotch soil it flowered in the air of an alien speech. But the New England literature of the great day was the blossom of a New England root; and the language which the Bostonians wrote was the native English of scholars fitly the heirs of those who had brought the learning of the universities to Massachusetts Bay two hundred years before, and was of as pure a lineage as the English of the mother-country.

III.

The literary situation which confronted me when I came to Boston was, then, as native as could well be; and whatever value I may be able to give a personal study of it will be from the effect it made upon me as one strange in everything but sympathy. I will not pretend that I saw it in its entirety, and I have no hope of presenting anything like a kinetoscopic impression of it. What I

THOMAS BAILEY ALDRICH.

can do is to give here and there a glimpse of it; and I shall wish the reader to keep in mind the fact that it was in a "state of transition," as everything is always and everywhere. It was no sooner recognizably native than it ceased to be fully so; and I became a witness of it after the change had begun. The publishing house which so long embodied New England literature was already attempting enterprises out of the line of its traditions, and one of these had brought Mr. T. B. Aldrich from New York, a few weeks before I arrived upon the scene in that dramatic quality which I think never impressed any one but Mr. Bowles. He was the editor of Every Saturday when I came to be assistant editor of the Atlantic Monthly. We were of the same age, with a shifting semester between us which neither cares now to claim, but he had a distinct and distinguished priority of reputation, insomuch that in my Western remoteness I had always ranged him with such elders and betters of mine as

J. T. TROWBRIDGE.

is but an instrument at the best; but there is no mistouch in the hand that lays itself upon the reader's heart with the pulse of the poet's heart quick and true in it. There are sonnets of his, grave, and simple, and lofty, which I think of with the glow and thrill possible only from very beautiful poetry, and which impart such an emotion as we can feel only

"When a great thought strikes along the brain
And flushes all the cheek."

When I had the fortune to meet him first, I suppose that in the employ of the kindly house we were both so eager to serve, our dignities were about the same; for if the Atlantic Monthly was a somewhat prouder affair than an eclectic weekly like Every Saturday, he was supreme in his place, and I was subordinate in mine. The house was careful, in the attitude of its senior partner, not to distinguish between us, and we were not slow to perceive the tact used in managing us; we had our own joke of it; we compared notes to find whether we were equally used in

Holmes and Lowell, and never imagined him the blond, slight youth I found him, with every imaginable charm of contemporaneity. It is no part of the office which I have intended for these slight and sufficiently wandering glimpses of the past to show any writer in his final place; and above all I do not presume to assign any living man his rank or station. But I should be false to my own grateful sense of beauty in the work of this poet if I did not at all times recognize his constancy to an ideal which his name stands for. He is known in many kinds, but to my thinking he is best in a certain nobler kind of poetry; a serious sort in which the thought holds him above the scrupulosities of the art he loves and honors so much. Sometimes the file slips in his hold, as the file must and will; it

LUCY LARCOM.

this thing or that; and we promptly shared the fun of our discovery with Fields himself.

We had another impartial friend (no less a friend of joy in the life which seems to have been pretty nearly all joy, as I look back upon it) in the partner who became afterwards the head of the house,

American house were to continue at Boston, it must be hospitable to the talents of the whole country. He founded his future upon those generous lines; but he wanted the qualities as well as the resources for rearing the superstructure. Changes began to follow each other rapidly after he came into control of the house.

THE OLD CEMETERY NEXT THE PARK STREET CHURCH.

and who forecast in his bold enterprises the change from a New England to an American literary situation. In the end James R. Osgood failed, though all his enterprises succeeded. The anomaly is sad, but it is not infrequent. They were greater than his powers and his means, and before they could reach their full fruition, they had to be enlarged to men of longer purse and longer patience. He was singularly fitted both by instinct and by education to become a great publisher; and he early perceived that if a leading

Misfortune reduced the size and number of its periodicals. The Young Folks was sold outright, and the North American Review (long before Mr. Rice bought it and carried it to New York) was cut down one-half, so that Aldrich said, It looked as if Destiny had sat upon it. His own periodical, Every Saturday, was first enlarged to a stately quarto and illustrated; and then, under stress of the calamities following the great Boston Fire, it collapsed to its former size. Then both the Atlantic Monthly and Every Saturday were sold away from their old ownership, and Every Saturday was suppressed altogether, and we two ceased to be of the same employ. There was some sort of evening rite (more funereal than festive) the day after they were sold, and we followed Osgood away from it, under the lamps. We all knew that it was his necessity that had caused him to part with the periodicals; but he

CELIA THAXTER.

professed that it was his pleasure, and he said, He had not felt so light-hearted since he was a boy. We asked him, How could he feel gay when he was no longer paying us our salaries, and how could he justify it to his conscience? He liked our mocking, and limped away from us with a rheumatic easing of his weight from one foot to another: a figure pathetic now that it has gone the way to dusty death, and dear to memory through benefactions unalloyed by one unkindness.

IV.

But when I came to Boston early in 1866, the Atlantic Monthly and Harper's then divided our magazine world between them; the North American Review, in the

control of Lowell and Professor Norton, had entered upon a new life; Every Saturday was an instant success in the charge of Mr. Aldrich, who was by taste and training one of the best editors; and Our Young Folks had the field of juvenile periodical literature to itself.

It was under the direction of Miss Lucy Larcom and of Mr. J. T. Trowbridge, who had come from western New York, where he was born, and must be noted as one of the first returners from the setting to the rising sun. He naturalized himself in Boston in his later boyhood, and he still breathes Boston air, where he dwells in the street called Pleasant, on the shore of Spy Pond, at Arlington, and still weaves the magic web of his satisfying stories for boys. He merges in their popularity the fame of a poet which I do not think will always suffer that eclipse, for his poems show him to have looked deeply into the heart of common humanity with a true and tender sense of it.

Miss Larcom scarcely seemed to change from date to date in the generation that elapsed between the time I first saw her and the time I saw her last, a year or two before her death. A goodness looked out of her comely face, which always made me think of the Madonna's in Titian's Assumption, and her whole aspect expressed a mild and friendly spirit which I find it hard to put in words. She was never of the fine world of literature; she dwelt where she was born, in that unfashionable Beverly which is not Beverly Farms, and was of a simple, sea-faring, God-fearing race, as she has told in one of the loveliest autobiographies I know, A New England Girlhood. She was the author of many poems, whose number she constantly enlarged, but she was chiefly, and will be most lastingly, famed for the one poem, Hannah Binding Shoes, which years before my days in Boston had made her so widely known. She never again struck so deep or so true a note; but if one has lodged such a note in the ear of time, it is enough; and if we are to speak of eter-

WHITE ISLAND LIGHT, ISLES OF SHOALS, EARLY HOME OF MRS. THAXTER.

nity, one might very well hold up one's head in the fields of asphodel, if one could say to the great others there, "I wrote Hannah Binding Shoes." Her poem is very, very sad, as all who have read it will remember; but Miss Larcom herself was above everything cheerful, and she had a laugh of mellow richness which willingly made itself heard. She was not only of true New England stock, and a Boston author by right of birth, but she came up to that city every winter from her native place.

By the same right and on the same terms, another New England poetess, whom I met those first days in Boston, was a Boston author. Celia Thaxter is so lately dead that one must speak of her with something of the hush of the house of mourning, even when one has nothing but praise to speak. When I saw her she was just beginning to make her effect with those poems and sketches which the sea sings and flashes through as it sings and flashes around the Isles of

Shoals, her summer home, where her girlhood had been passed in a freedom as wild as the curlew's. She was a most beautiful creature, still very young, with a slender figure, and an exquisite perfection of feature; she was in presence what her work was: fine, frank, finished. I do not know whether other witnesses of our literary history feel that the public has failed to keep her as fully in mind as her work merited; but I do not think there can be any doubt but our literature would be very sensibly the poorer without her work, which had qualities of keenest pathos, vivid fancy, humorous reality, and constant beauty. It is interesting to remember how closely she kept to her native field, and it is wonderful to consider how richly she made those sea-beaten rocks to blossom. Something strangely full and bright came to her verse from the mystical environment of the ocean, like the luxury of leaf and tint that it gave the narrow flower-plots of her native isles. Her gift, indeed, could not satisfy itself with the terms of one art alone, however varied, and she learned to express in color the thoughts and feelings impatient of the pallor of words.

She remains in my memories of that far Boston a distinct and vivid personality; as the authoress of Amber Gods, and In a Cellar, and Circumstance, and those other wild romantic tales, remains the gentle and somewhat evanescent presence I found her. Miss Prescott was now Mrs. Spofford, and her husband was a rising young politician of the day. It was his duties as member of the General Court that had brought them up from Newburyport to Boston for that first winter; and I remember that the evening when we met he was talking of their some time going to Italy that she might study for imaginative literature certain Italian cities he named. I have long since ceased to own those cities, but at the moment I felt a pang of expropriation which I concealed as well as I could; and now I heartily wish she could have fulfilled that purpose if it was a purpose, or realized that dream if it was only a dream. Perhaps, however, that sumptu-

ous and glowing fancy of hers, which had taken the fancy of the young readers of that day, needed the cold New England background to bring out all its intensities of tint, all its splendors of light. Its effects were such as could not last, or could not be farther evolved; they were the expression of youth musing away from its environment and smitten with the glories of a world afar and beyond, the great world, the fine world, the impurpled world of romantic motives and passions. But for what they were, I can never think them other than what they appeared: the emanations of a rarely gifted and singularly poetic mind. I feel better than I can say how necessarily they were the emanations of a New England mind, and how to the subtler sense they must impart the pathos of revolt from the colorless rigidities which are the long result of puritanism in the physiognomy of New England life.

Their author afterwards gave herself to the stricter study of this life in many tales and sketches which showed an increasing mastery; but they could not have the flush, the surprise, the delight of a young talent trying itself in a kind native and, so far as I know, peculiar to it. From time to time I still come upon a poem of hers which recalls that earlier strain of music, of color, and I am content to trust it for my abiding faith in the charm of things I have not read for thirty years.

V.

I speak of this one and that, as it happens, and with no thought of giving a complete prospect of literary Boston thirty years ago. I am aware that it will seem sparsely peopled in the effect I impart, and I would have the reader always keep in mind the great fames at Cambridge and at Concord, which formed so large a part of the celebrity of Boston. I would also like him to think of it as still a great town, merely, where every one knew every one else, and whose metropolitan liberation from neighborhood was just begun.

Most distinctly of that yet

E. P. WHIPPLE.

uncitified Boston was the critic
Edwin P. Whipple, whose sympathies were indefinitely wider
than his traditions. He was a
most generous lover of all that
was excellent in literature; and
though I suppose we should
call him an old-fashioned critic
now, I suspect it would be with
no distinct sense of what is
newer fashioned. He was certainly as friendly to what
promised well in the younger
men as he was to what was
done well in their elders; and
there was no one writing in his
day whose virtues failed of his
recognition, though it might
happen that his foibles would
escape Whipple's censure. He
wrote strenuously and of course
conscientiously ; his point of
view was solely and always
that which enabled him best
to discern qualities. I doubt
if he had any theory of criticism except to find out what
was good in an author and
praise it; and he rather blamed
what was ethically bad than
what was æsthetically bad. In

HARRIET PRESCOTT SPOFFORD.

this he was strictly of New England, and
he was of New England in a certain
general intelligence, which constantly
grew with an interrogative habit of
mind.

He liked to talk to you of what he had
found characteristic in your work, to analyze you to yourself; and the very modesty of the man, which made such a study
impersonal as far as he was concerned,
sometimes rendered him insensible to the
sufferings of his subject. He had a keen
perception of humor in others, but he had
very little humor; he had a love of the
beautiful in literature which was perhaps
sometimes greater than his sense of it.

I write from a cursory acquaintance
with his work, not recently renewed. Of
the presence of the man I have a vivider
remembrance: a slight, short, ecclesiasti-
cized figure in black, with a white neck-
cloth and a silk hat of strict decorum,
and between the two a square face with
square features, intensified in their regard
by a pair of very large glasses, and the
prominent, myopic eyes staring through
them. He was a type of out-dated New
England scholarship in these aspects, but

in the hospitable qualities of his mind and
heart, the sort of man to be kept fondly
in the memory of all who ever knew
him.

Out of the vague of that far-off time
another face and figure, as essentially
New England as this, and yet so different,
relieve themselves. Charles F. Browne,
whose drollery wafted his pseudonym as
far as the English speech could carry
laughter, was a Westernized Yankee. He
added an Ohio habit of talking to the
Maine habit of thinking, and he so became
a literary product of a rarer and stranger
sort than our literature has otherwise
known. He had gone from Cleveland to
London, with intervals of New York and
the lecture platform, four or five years
before I saw him in Boston, shortly after
I went there. We had met in Ohio, and
he had personally explained to me the
ducatless well-meaning of Vanity Fair in
New York; but many men had since
shaken the weary hand of Artemus Ward
before I grasped it one day in front of the
Tremont Temple. He did not recognize
me, but he gave me at once a greeting of
great impersonal cordiality, with "How

do you do? When did you come?" and other questions that had no concern in them, till I began to dawn upon him through a cloud of other half-remembered faces. Then he seized my hand and wrung it all over again, and repeated his

GEORGE TICKNOR.

friendly demands with an intonation that was now "Why, *how* are you,—how *are* you?" for me alone. It was a bit of comedy, which had the fit pathetic relief of his impending doom: this was already stamped upon his wasted face, and his gay eyes had the death-look. His large, loose mouth was drawn, for all its laughter at the fact which he owned; his profile, which burlesqued an eagle's, was the profile of a drooping eagle; his lank length of limb trembled away with him when we parted. I did not see him again; I scarcely heard of him till I heard of his death, and this pathetic image remains with me of the humorist who first gave the world a taste of the humor which characterizes the whole American people.

VI.

I was meeting all kinds of distinguished persons, in my relation to the magazine, and early that winter I met one who remains in my mind above all others a person of distinction. He was scarcely a celebrity, but he embodied certain social traits which were so characteristic of literary Boston that it could not be approached without their recognition. The Muses have often been acknowledged to be very nice young persons, but in Boston they were really ladies; in Boston literature was of good family and good society in a measure it has never been elsewhere. It might be said even that reform was of good family in Boston; and literature and reform equally shared the regard of Edmund Quincy, whose race was one of the most aristocratic in New England. I had known him by his novel of Wensley (it came so near being a first-rate novel), and by his Life of Josiah Quincy, then a new book, but still better by his Boston letters to the New York Tribune. These dealt frankly, in the old antislavery days between 1850 and 1860, with other persons of distinction in Boston, who did not see the right so clearly as Quincy did, or who at least let their interests darken them to the ugliness of slavery. Their fault was all the more comical because it was the error of men otherwise so correct, of characters so stainless, of natures so upright; and the Quincy letters got out of it all the fun there was in it. Quincy himself affected me as the finest patrician type I had ever met. He was charmingly handsome, with a nose of most fit aquilinity, smooth-shaven lips, "educated whiskers," and perfect glasses; his manner was beautiful, his voice delightful, when at our first meeting he made me his reproaches in terms of lovely kindness for having used in my Venetian Life, the Briticism *directly* for *as soon as.*

Lowell once told me that Quincy had never had any calling or profession, because when he found himself in the enjoyment of a moderate income on leaving college, he decided to be simply a gentleman. He was too much of a man to be merely that, and he was an abolitionist, a journalist, and for conscience' sake a satirist. Of that political mood of society which he satirized was an eminent man whom it was also my good fortune to meet in my early days in Boston; and if his great sweetness and kindness had not instantly won my liking, I should still have been glad of the glimpse of the older and statelier Boston which my slight acquaintance with George Ticknor gave me. The historian of Spanish literature, the friend and biographer of Prescott, and a leading figure of the intellectual society of an epoch already closed, dwelt in the fine old square brick mansion which yet stands at the corner of Park Street and Beacon, though sunk now to a variety

JULIA WARD HOWE.

of business uses, and lamentably changed in aspect. The interior was noble, and there was an air of scholarly quiet and

THE TICKNOR MANSION.

ARLINGTON SPY POND.

of lettered elegance in the library, where the host received his guests, which seemed to pervade the whole house, and which made its appeal to the imagination of one of them most potently. It seemed to me that to be master of such circumstance and keeping would be enough of life in a certain way; and it all lingers in my memory yet, as if it were one with the gentle courtesy which welcomed me.

Among my fellow-guests one night was George S. Hillard, now a faded reputation, and even then a life defeated of the high expectation of its youth. I do not know whether his Six Months in Italy still keeps itself in print; but it was a book once very well known; and he was perhaps the more gracious to me, as our host was, because of our common Italian background. He was of the old Silver-gray Whig society too, and I suppose that order of things imparted its tone to what I felt and saw in that place. The war had come and gone, and that order accepted the result if not with faith, then with patience. There were two young English noblemen there that night, who had been travelling in the South, and whose stories of the wretched conditions they had seen moved our host to some open misgiving. But the Englishmen had no question; in spite of all, they defended the accomplished fact, and when I ventured to say that now at least there could be a hope of better things, while the old order was only the perpetuation of despair, he mildly assented, with a gesture of the hand that pathetically waived the point, and a deeply sighed, "Perhaps; perhaps."

He was a presence of great dignity, which seemed to recall the past with a steadfast allegiance, and yet to relax itself toward the present in the wisdom of the accumulated years. His whole life had been passed in devotion to polite literature and in the society of the polite world; and he was a type of scholar such as only the circumstances of Boston could form. Those circumstances could alone form such another type as Quincy; and I wish I could have felt then as I do now the advantage of meeting them so contemporaneously.

VII.

The historian of Spanish literature was an old man nearer eighty than seventy when I saw him, and I recall of him personally his dark tint, and the scholarly refinement of his clean-shaven face, which seemed to me rather English than American in character. He was quite exterior to the Atlantic group of writers, and had no interest in me as one of it. Literary Boston of that day was not a solidarity, as I soon perceived; and I understood that it was only in my quality of stranger that I saw the different phases of it. I should not be just to a vivid phase if I failed to speak of Mrs. Julia Ward Howe and the impulse of reform which she personified. I did not sympathize with this then so much as I do now, but I could appreciate it on the intellectual side. Once, many years later, I heard Mrs. Howe speak in public, and it seemed to me that she made one of the best speeches I had ever heard. It gave me for the first time a notion of what women might do in that sort if they entered public life; but when we met in those earlier days I was interested in her as perhaps our chief poetess. I believe she did not care much to speak of literature; she was alert for other meanings in life, and I remember how she once brought to book a youthful matron who had perhaps unduly lamented the hardships of housekeeping, with the sharp demand, " Child, where is your *religion ?*" After the many years of an acquaintance which had not nearly so many meetings as years, it was pleasant to find her, not long ago, as strenuous as ever for the faith of works, and as eager to aid Stepniak as John Brown. In her beautiful old age she survives a certain literary impulse of Boston, but a still higher impulse of Boston she will not survive, for that will last while the city endures.

THE WHITE MOUNTAINS

PART I.

NEW HAMPSHIRE is a State reclining with its head pillowed on high mountains and its feet washed by the ocean. These elevated summits are the White Mountains.

Enthusiastic tourists long ago gave to this beautiful mountain region the name, a trifle grandiose, of the "Switzerland of America." For beauty and general attractiveness it is believed nothing in our own land can pretend to rival it. There are, it is true, higher mountains, deeper valleys, broader lakes, more stupendous

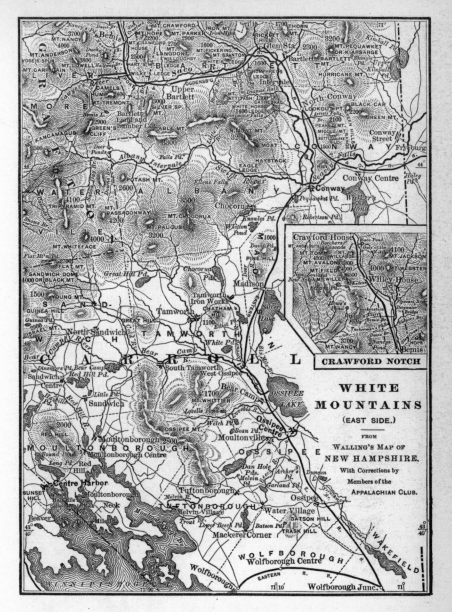

ravines; yet for that rare and exquisite combination of all the most salient and picturesque types of mountain scenery, the travelled and the untravelled alike award to the White Mountains an incontestable superiority.

This is saying a great deal. In order to put it to the test how far this eulogium is deserved, I wish my readers to make with me a veritable tour of the mountains, laying everything under contribution, as their lofty peaks do passing clouds.

With this object we will first journey leisurely along its eastern skirts, into the heart of the mountain region. Supposing ourselves now on board an Eastern Rail-

LAKE WINNIPISEOGEE,
FROM RED HILL.

way train, let us, while rapidly leaving the glittering leagues of sea-coast behind, sketch with equal rapidity an outline to be filled in by the fireside at home.

The Indians, it is known, inhabited these mountains long before the settlement of any portion of New England by whites. But their villages were chiefly situated upon the skirts, where the hunting and fishing were good, and the ground favorable to their primitive mode of cultivating it. His infallible eye for the best sites is sufficiently evident, since we find the Indian's uncouth wigwam invariably succeeded by the most important settlements of the English.

Otherwise, the mountains were for the American Indian, as for the natural man in all ages, a sealed book. He regarded them not only as an image, but as the actual dwelling - place, of Omnipotence. His dreaded Manitou, whose voice was the thunder, whose anger the lightning, and on whose face no mortal could look and live, was the counterpart of the terrible Thor, the Icelandic god, throned in a palace of ice, among frozen and inaccessible peaks. So far, then, as he was concerned, the mountain remained inviolate, inviolable, as a kind of hell filled with the despairing shrieks of those who in an evil hour transgressed the limits sacred to immortals.

The first mention I have met with of the Indian name for these mountains is in the narrative of Captain John Gyles, printed in Boston in 1736, saying that "the White Hills called the Teddon [Katahdin], at the head of Penobscot River, are by the Indians said to be much higher than those called Agiockochook, above Saco." The probable signification of this Indian word is, according to the best living authority, "the mountains on that side," or "over yonder," to distinguish them from the mountains of the Penobscot.

It is not precisely known when or how these granite peaks first took the name of White Mountains. We find them so designated in 1672 by Josselyn, who himself performed the feat of ascending the highest summit, of which a brief record is found in his *New England's Rarities*. One can not help saying of this book that either the author was a liar of the first magnitude, or else we have to regret the degeneracy of nature, exhausted by her long travail; for this writer gravely tells us of frogs that were as big as a child a year old, and of poisonous serpents which the Indians caught with their bare hands, and ate alive with great gusto. These are rarities indeed!

The name is traced, not, as in the case of Mont Blanc, to the fact that their peaks are covered with perpetual snows, for this is true of only half the year, but from the circumstance that the bare granite of which the highest are composed transmits a white light when observed from a distance. Mariners approaching from the open sea descried what seemed a cloud-bank rising from the landward horizon when twenty leagues from the nearest coast, and before any other land was visible.

But we are at length, not at the end of our history, but at Wolfborough Junction, and here we are transferred by a short branch railroad to Wolfborough, a very charming village on the shore of Lake Winnipiseogee, where we take steamer for a voyage to Centre Harbor, at the head of the lake. The change comes gratefully to relieve the lassitude we were beginning to feel, the air is so pure, the breezes so refreshing. As the boat glides out of the land-locked inlet, at the bottom of which Wolfborough is situated, one of those pictures forever ineffaceable is presented. All the conditions of a beautiful picture are realized.

Here is the shining expanse of the lake, stretching away in the distance, and finally lost among tufted islets and interlocking promontories. To the right, dark, vigorously outlined, and wooded to their summits, are the Ossipee Mountains; to the left, more distant, are the double-domed Belknap peaks; in front, and closing the view, the imposing Sandwich summits dominate the scene. All these mountains seem advancing into the lake.

Having taken in the grander features, the eye is occupied with the details. We see the lake quivering in sunshine. From bold summit to beautiful water, the shores are clothed in most vivid green. The islands are almost tropical in the luxuriance and richness of their vegetation, and in the deep shadows they fling down into the lake the image of each is reflected, like that of Narcissus lost in the contemplation of his own beauty. Here and there the glimmer of water through the trees denotes secluded little havens. Boats float idly on the calm surface of the lake, water-fowl rise and beat the glassy dark water with startled wings, white tents appear, and handkerchiefs flutter on the jutting points. Over all tower the mountains.

As we advance up the lake, new and rare vistas succeed each other. After passing Long Island an opening appears, through which, blue as lapis lazuli, a chaplet of clouds crowning his imperial front, Mount Washington bursts upon the view. Slowly, majestically, he marches by, and now Chocorua scowls upon us. A murmur of admiration runs from group to group as these monumental figures, the two grandest types these mountains inclose, are thus displayed in the full splendor of noonday.

The low, athletic mountain now gliding into the gap through which we looked at the panorama of moving mountains is Red Hill. Its position at the head of the

PASSACONAWAY, FROM BEAR-CAMP RIVER.

lake, overlooking its whole extent, assures us that we shall find an incomparable view from its summit. Let us therefore ascend, as we may easily do before the close of the day, and from its heights behold 'the gorgeous spectacle of sunset on the lake.

From this point the Sandwich Mountains obtain far greater interest and character. No two summits are precisely alike in form or outline. Higher and more distant peaks peer curiously over their brawny shoulders from their lairs in the Pemigewasset Valley; but more remarkable, more weird, than all, is the gigantic monolith topping the rock-ribbed pile of Chocorua. As the sun glides down the west, a ruddy glow tinges its pinnacle ; while the shadows lurking in the ravines, stealing darkly up the mountain-side, crouch for a final spring upon the summit. Little by little twilight flows over the valley, and a thin haze rises from its surface.

Glowing in sunset splendor, streaked with all the hues of the rainbow, the lake is indeed magnificent. In vain the eye roves hither and thither, seeking some foil for this peerless beauty. Everywhere the same unrivalled picture leads its captive over the long leagues of gleaming water, up the graceful curves of the mountains, to rest at last among crimson clouds floating in rosy vapor over their notched summits.

To attempt to describe this ravishing spectacle is like a profanation. Paradise seems to have opened wide its gates to our enraptured gaze; or have we, indeed, surprised the secrets of the unknown world ? We stand spell-bound, with a strange, exquisite feeling at the heart; we feel a thrill of pain when a voice breaks the solemn stillness alone befitting this almost supernatural vision. Vanquished by the incomparable scene, the mind, turning away from earth, runs over the most sublime or touching incidents of Scripture—the Temptation, the Sermon on the Mount, the Transfiguration—and memory brings to our aid these words, so simple, so tender, yet so expressive, " And He went up into the mountain apart to pray."

Let us now vary the journey by taking the stage for Tamworth. Let us now go and pay a visit to this strangely fascinating, this Mephistopheles of mountains, gaunt Chocorua. Let us now, sitting at his feet, imbibe the fullness of that grandeur which the mountain in its moments of benevolence vouchsafes.

For very obvious reasons, an outside seat, being preferable, is always a bone of contention, affording quite too often a display of that impudent selfishness which is seen when a dozen or more travellers eral competitors of her own sex, to say nothing of the men. She beamed. As I made room for her, she said, with a toss of the head, "I guess I haven't been through Lake George for nothing."

Our route lay through the villages of Moultonborough Corner and Sandwich,

"ALONE WITH ALL THOSE MEN."

are all struggling for precedence. Even before the steamboat is securely made fast, travellers rush pell-mell up the wharf, surround the stage, and begin, women as well as men, a promiscuous scramble for the two or three unoccupied seats at the top.

On one occasion, when I was an amused spectator, two men and one woman succeeded in obtaining the prizes. The woman interested me by the intense triumph that sparkled in her black eyes and glowed on her cheeks at having distanced sev- that is to say, through the depression seen from the summit of Red Hill, which is the natural outlet between the upper lake region and the highlands of Maine. Sometimes we were in a thick forest, sometimes on a broad, sunny glade; now threading our way through groves of pitch-pine, now winding along the course of the swift and foaming Bear-camp River. But the landscape is not all that may be seen to advantage from the top of a stage-coach.

CHOCORUA.

From time to time, as something provoked an exclamation of surprise or pleasure, certain of the inside travellers manifested a good deal of impatience. They were losing something, when they had expected to see everything. While the horses were being changed, one of the insides—I need not say it was a woman—thrust her head out of the window, and addressed the young person, perched like a bird upon the highest seat. Her voice was soft and persuasive.

"Miss."

"Madam."

"I'm so afraid you find it too cold up there! Sha'n't I change seats with you?"

The little one gave her voice a droll inflection as she briskly replied, "Oh dear no, thank you; I'm very comfortable indeed."

"But," urged the other, "you don't look strong. Indeed, dear, you don't. Aren't you very, *very* tired sitting so long without any support for your back?"

"Thanks, no; my spine is the strongest part of me."

"But," still persisted the inside, changing her voice to a loud whisper, "to be sitting alone, with all those men!"

"They mind their business, and I mind mine," said the little one, reddening. "Besides," she quickly added, "you proposed changing places, I believe."

"Oh!" returned the other, with an accent impossible to convey in words, "if you like it—"

"I tell you what, ma'am," snapped the one in possession, "I've been all over Europe alone, and was never once insulted except by persons of my own sex." This home thrust ended the colloquy.

The view of the ranges which on either side elevate two immense walls of green is kept for nearly the whole distance. We pass in review all those eminences forming the Sandwich chain, which throw a Titanic arm around the head of the lakes Winnipiseogee and Squam. As the afternoon wears away, these mountains grow more and more interesting. Cloud-shadows chase each other up and down the steeps, or flit slowly across the valley. On one side all is light; on the other, all gloom. In the cool of the evening we roll over the sandy plains, and up the last stony hill into Tamworth, with Chocorua heaved high above us in the northern sky.

I can not call Chocorua a beautiful mountain, yet of all the White Mountain peaks it is the most individual. Nothing can be more striking than the way it presents itself here. Fast locked in the embrace of encircling hills, a lovely little lake voluptuously reposes at the foot of the mountain. Patriarchal pines, lofty and dignified, advance into it from the yellow shores. Its charming seclusion, its rare combination of laughing water and impassive old mountains, above all, the striking contrast between its chaste beauty and the weird, huge-ribbed thing rising above, awaken a variety of sensations. The mountain attracts and at the same time repels you. It is passing strange. Two sentiments struggle here for mastery—admiration and repulsion. For the first time in his life the spectator feels an antipathy for a creation of inanimate nature. Chocorua suggests some fabled prodigy of the old mythology—a headless Centaur sprung from the foul womb of earth. The lake seems another Andromeda exposed to a monster.

The mountain, as seen from Tamworth, shows a long undulating ridge of white rising over a green one, both extending toward the east, and opening between them a deep ravine by which a path ascends to the summit. But this path affords no views until the summit is close at hand. Above the humpbacked ridge of Chocorua, the tip of the southern peak of Moat Mountain peers over like a mountain standing on tiptoe.

When reconnoitring the pinnacle of Chocorua through your glass, at a distance of five miles, you will say to scale it would be difficult; when you have climbed close underneath, you will say it is impossible. After surveying it from the bare ledges of Bald Mountain, first of the four swells forming the green ridge, I asked my guide where we could ascend. He pointed out a long crack, or crevice, toward the left, in which a few bushes were growing. It is narrow, almost perpendicular, and seemingly impracticable. It is, however, there or nowhere you must ascend.

The whole upper zone of the mountain seems smitten by palsy. Except in the hollows between the inferior summits nothing grew, nothing relieved the widespread desolation. Beyond us, scarred and riven by lightning, rose the enormous conical crag which gives to Chocorua its highly distinctive character. Many years ago this region was devastated by fire. In the night old Chocorua lighted his fiery torch, and stood in the midst of his own funeral pyre. The red glare, overspreading the sky, put out the stars. A brilliant circle of light, twenty miles in extent, surrounded the mountain like a halo; while, underneath, an immense tongue of forked flame licked the red summit with devouring haste. In the morning, a few charred trunks, still erect, were all that remained of the original forest.

Crossing a bare ledge, as steep as a roof, smoothly polished by ice, we proceeded to drag ourselves up the gully by the aid of bushes, or such protruding rocks as

MOUNT WASHINGTON, FROM SACO RIVER, NORTH CONWAY—WINTER SCENE.

LOVEWELL'S POND, FRYEBURG.

offered a hold. After a breathless scramble, we came to a sort of shelf, on which was a ruined hut, and from which the view is varied and extensive. We then hastened to complete the ascent, in order to enjoy in all its perfection the prospect that awaited us.

Like Goethe's Wilhelm Meister, it is among mountains that my knowledge of them has been obtained. I have little hesitation, then, in pronouncing the view from Chocorua one of the noblest that can reward the adventurous climber; for notwithstanding it is not a high peak, and can not therefore unfold the whole mountain system at a single glance, it yet affords an unsurpassed view-point from which one sees the surrounding mountains, rising on all sides in all their majesty, and clothed in all their terrors. The arc of the circle of vision extends from the Penobscot to the Piscataqua, looking toward the sea-coast. The day being one of a thousand, I distinctly saw the ocean with the naked eye, not merely as a white blur on the horizon's edge, but actual blue water, over which smoke was curling. This magnificent *coup d'œil* embraces the scattered villages of Conway, Fryeburg, Madison, Eaton, Ossipee, with their numerous lakes and streams. I counted seventeen of the former flashing in the sun. Turning now to the mountains, one is lost in the contemplation of the great peaks crowded in irredeemable confusion before him.

But we can merely taste the pleasure, and must hasten onward to that *ultima thule* of pleasure-seekers, North Conway, which deserves, like Lorenzo de' Medici, to be called "the Magnificent."

But first let us make a *détour* to historic Fryeburg, leaving the cars at Conway, which in former times enjoyed a happy pre-eminence as the centre upon which the old stage routes converged, and where passengers going or returning always passed the night. But those old travellers have mostly gone where the name of Chatigee, as both drivers and travellers liked to call Conway, is going: only for the name there is fortunately no resurrection. No one knows its origin, none will mourn its decease.

It is here at Conway, or Conway Corner if you like, that first enrapturing view of the White Mountains rising over the Saco meadows bursts upon the traveller like a splendid vision. But we shall see it again on our return from Fryeburg.

Fryeburg stands on a dry and sandy plain elevated above the Saco River. It is behind the mountain range, which, terminating in Conway, compels this river to make a right angle. With one grand sweep to the east it takes leave of the mountains, flows awhile through the lowlands of Maine, and in two or three infuriated plunges reaches the sea. Chocorua and Kearsarge are the two prominent objects in the landscape.

The village street is most beautifully shaded by elms of great size, which form an arcade of foliage through which we look up and down. At one end justice is dispensed in the Oxford House, an inn with a pedigree; at the other, learning is diffused in the academy, where Webster once taught and disciplined the rising generation. On our way to the remarkable rock, emerging from the plain like a walrus from the sea, we linger in the village grave-yard to read the inscription on the monument of General Joseph

Frye, a veteran of the old wars, and founder of the town which bears his name. Ascending now the rock to which we just referred, called the Jockey Cap, we are lifted high above the plain, and have the dark sheet of Lovewell's Pond stretched at our feet.

Here, on the shores of this pond, was fought one of the bloodiest and most obstinately contested battles that can be found in the annals of war: so terrible, indeed, that the story was repeated from fireside to fireside, and from generation to generation, as worthy a niche beside that of Leonidas and his band of heroes.

In April, 1725, a picked corps of rangers, led by Captain John Lovewell, encountered here the entire tribe of Pigwackets, and fought them from early in the morning until night-fall put an end to the sanguinary conflict. While this long combat was proceeding, one of the rangers, going to the lake to cleanse his gun, descried an Indian washing his own. This Indian was Paugus, the greatest warrior of his nation. Both began to charge their guns at the same instant. The affair was to be decided by seconds.

"Me kill you," said Paugus, forcing his ball down the barrel with a nervous arm.

"The chief lies," retorted the ranger, striking the breech of his piece to the ground with such force that it primed itself. An instant after, Paugus fell, shot through the heart.

"I said I should kill you," muttered the ranger, striding over the dead body of his enemy, and plunging into the thickest of the fight.

The rangers lost their commander, and were cut to pieces. A remnant retreated under cover of the night. The Indians sustained such losses that they abandoned in terror the graves of their fathers, and fled farther into the wilderness.

The entrance to North Conway is, without doubt, the most beautiful and imposing introduction to the White Mountains. Nature has formed here a vast antechamber, into which you are ushered through a gateway of mountains upon the numerous inner courts, galleries, and cloisters of her most secluded retreats. An involuntary exclamation of delighted surprise escapes even the most apathetic traveller. And why should it not? This is the moment when every one feels the inadequacy of his own conceptions.

Here the mountains fall back before the impetuous flood of the Saco, which comes pouring down from the summit of the great notch, white and panting with the haste of its flight. Here the river gives rendezvous to several of its larger affluents—the East Branch, the Ellis, the Swift —and like an army taking the field, their united streams sweeping grandly around the last mountain range, emerge into the open country. Here the valley, contracted at its extremity between the gentle slopes of Kearsarge and the abrupt declivities of Moat, incloses a verdant and fertile ellipse of land, ravishing to behold, skirted on one side by thick woods, behind which precipices a thousand feet high rise black and threatening; overlooked on the other by a high terrace, along which the village stretches itself indolently in the sun. The superb silvergray crest of Kearsarge is seen rising in a regular pyramid behind the right shoulder of its inferior summit. Ordinarily the house perched on the granite pinnacle is as distinctly seen as those in the village. It is the last in the village.

Looking up through this verdant mountain park, at a distance of twenty miles, the imposing masses of the great summits seem scaling the skies. Then, heavily massed on the right, comes the Carter range, divided by the cup-shaped dip of the Carter Notch; then the truncated cone of Double Head. The mountain in front, looking up the village street, is Thorn Mountain, on the other side of which is Jackson, and the way up the Ellis Valley to the Glen House, Gorham, and the Androscoggin.

The traveller, who is ushered upon this splendid scene with the rapidity of steam, perceives that he is at last among real mountains, and quickly yields to the indefinable charm which from this moment surrounds and leads him a willing captive.

Looking across the meadow, the eye is stopped by an isolated ridge, with bare overhanging precipices. It is thrust out into the valley from Moat Mountain, of which it forms part, presenting two singular and regularly arching cliffs toward the village. The green forest below contrasts vividly with the lustrous black of these precipitous walls, which glisten brightly in the sun where they are wet by tiny streams flowing down. On the nearest is a very curious resemblance to a white horse in the act of rearing, occasioned by

THE LEDGES, NORTH CONWAY.

the intrusion of white rock in the face of the cliff. This accident gives it the name of White-horse Ledge. All marriageable ladies, maiden or widow, run out to look at it, in consequence of the superstition, current in New England, that if after seeing a white horse you count a hundred, the first gentleman you meet will be your future husband. Underneath this cliff a charming little lake lies hid. The next is called the Cathedral Ledge, from the curious rock cavity it contains.

But now from these masses of hard rock let us turn once more to the valley where the rich intervales spread an exhaustless feast for the eye. If autumn be the season, the vase-like elms, the stacks of yellow corn, the golden pumpkins, the cloth of green and gold, damasked with purple gorse and coppice, give the idea of an immense table groaning beneath its luxurious weight of fruit and flowers.

Our first visit will naturally be to the ledges. I will not ask the reader to wade the river, as I once did, but taking one of the light mountain wagons in vogue here, we pass it by a bridge, hearing the Saco resounding below in its bed of pebbles, and catching, up and down its tumultuous course, the loveliest vistas imaginable through the frame-work of elm-trees.

As we approach nearer, the ledges are full of grim recesses, rude rock niches, and traversed by perpendicular cracks from brow to base. Take care! there is a huge piece of the cliff just ready to fall. In some places the rock is sheer and smooth; in others it is broken regularly down for

half its whole height to where it is joined by rude buttresses of massive granite. The maples climb up the steepest ravines, but can not pass the waste of sheer rock stretching between them and the firs, which look down from the brink of the precipice. The prevailing color is a rusted purple, marked with scattered blotches of white like the drip oozing from limestone.

Hovering under the precipices which lie heavily shadowed on its glossy surface are gathered the waters flowing from the little rills, the rivulets, the cascades leaping from the airy heights above. The tremendous shadow which the cliff flings down seems lying deep in the bosom of the lake, as if perpetually imprinted there. Slender birches, green and gold leafage, are daintily etched upon the surface, like arabesques on polished steel. The water is perfectly transparent and without a ripple. Indeed, the breezes playing around the summit, or humming in the tree-tops, seem forbidden to enter this haunt of Dryads. The lake laps the yellow strand with a light, fluttering movement. The place is dedicated to silence itself.

A small cannon is loaded and fired to destroy our illusion. The echo comes sharp and angry. The after-effect is like knocking at half a dozen doors at once. And the silence which follows seems all the deeper.

Following a woodland path, skirting the base of the cliffs, we stand at the entrance to the Devil's Den, formed by a huge piece of the cliff falling upon other detached fragments in such a way as to leave

KEARSARGE IN WINTER.

an aperture large enough to admit fifty persons at once. A ponderous mass divides the cavern into two chambers, one of which is light, airy, and spacious, the other dark, gloomy, and contracted—a mere hole. This might well have been the lair of the bears or panthers which formerly roamed the woods unmolested.

The Cathedral is a recess higher up in the same cliff, hollowed out by the cleaving off of the lower rock, leaving the upper portion of the precipice overhanging. The top of the roof is as high as a tall tree. Some maples that have grown here since the outer portion of the rock fell, assist with their straight-limbed, columnar trunks the resemblance to a chancel. A little way off, this cavity has really the appearance of a gigantic shell, like those fossils seen imbedded in subterranean rocks. We must not miss here the delicious glimpses of Kearsarge, and of the mountains across the valley. The shadows fall here early in the afternoon, filling the groves with coolness, while through the fringe of foliage sunlight still brightens all that side, as if the light had been turned off here to give greater effect there.

Still farther on, we come upon a fine cascade falling down a long irregular staircase of broken rock. One of these steps extends, a solid mass of granite, for more than a hundred feet across the bed of the stream, and is twenty feet high. Unless the brook is full, it is not a single sheet we see, but twenty, fifty crystal streams gushing or spirting from the grooves they have channelled in the hard granite, and falling into basins they have hollowed out beneath. It is these curious stone cavities, out of which the freshest and cleanest water constantly flows, that give to the cascade the name of Diana's Baths. The water never dashes itself noisily down, but slips like oil from the rocks, with a pleasant, purling sound we know not how to describe.

This is quite enough for one day. We therefore reserve for another our visit to Artists' Falls, and our ramble in the Cathedral Woods among the fragrant pines. The falls are on Artists' Brook, which comes from the Green Hills, on the east side of the village. I found the walks along this brook, following its picturesque windings, more remunerative than the falls themselves. The brook, flowing first over a smooth granite ledge, collects in a little pool below, out of which the pure water filters through bowlders and among glittering pebbles, to a gorge between two rocks, down which it plunges. The beauty of this fall consists in its waywardness. Now it is a thin sheet flowing demurely along, now it breaks out in a succession of cascades, and at length, as if tired of this sport, darts like an arrow down the rocky fissure, and is a mountain brook again.

The ascent of Kearsarge or of Moat fittingly crowns the series of excursions which are the most attractive feature of out-of-door life at North Conway. The northern peak of Moat is the one most frequently climbed, but the southern affords equally admirable views of the Saco, the Ellis, and the Swift river valleys, with the mountain chains inclosing them. The high ridge is an arid and desolate heap of summits, stripped bare of vegetation by fire. When this fire occurred, twenty odd years ago, it drove the bears and rattlesnakes from their forest homes, so that they fell an easy prey to their destroyers. We can not stop to describe the view, but content ourselves with saying that all the great summits are finely visible, in a clear day, from the massive and firmly crested Moats. For a wide region they divide with Chocorua the honors of the landscape.

In the winter of 1876, finding myself at North Conway, I determined to make the ascent of Kearsarge. Ordinarily this is only fatiguing. The mountain has an elevation of only 3250 feet above the sea, but its position is a most commanding one, with reference to all the summits lying east of the great chain. This, with the extraordinary purity of the air at this season, was my sole inducement. The mercury stood at three degrees below zero when I set out on foot from the village.

After a laborious upward march through snow, I emerged from the woods to find the bare ledges sheeted in ice, over which you might go as you pleased, but certainly not in an erect posture. I therefore approached the summit like a pious Moslem the tomb of the Prophet—on my knees, and shedding tears. But at last I did reach it; and standing in the midst of a most exquisite garden of frost-work, surrounded by a death-like silence, confronted by a vast expanse, below, all dead white, above, all steely-hard blue, felt stirred as never before on a mountain-top, and triumphed in the thought of having thus stolen a march upon the mountain. But this triumph was short-lived. It was necessary to descend, as I had quite forgotten, so fully absorbed was I in the surpassing extent of this glorious winter landscape. I therefore prepared to descend, for the cold was intense, the wind cut to the bone.

I say prepared to descend, for the thing at once so easily said, yet so difficult of performance, presented a really perplexing problem to be solved. But it must be solved. Go down I must. But how? Inspired by the crisis, I suddenly recollected that Bourrienne relates in his memoirs how Bonaparte was forced to slide down the Great St. Bernard *seated*, while making his famous passage of the Alps. Yes, the great Bonaparte advanced to the conquest of Italy in this undignified posture. But never did great example find more unworthy imitator. Seating myself as the Little Corporal had done, using my stick for a rudder, and steering for protruding rocks, in order to check the force of the descent, I slid down the peak with a celerity the very recollection of which makes my head swim, arriving safely at the snow patch, but breathless, much astonished, and white as a miller.

But we must leave the village, with all its enticements, behind us—enticements which nobody has ever succeeded in analyzing; for North Conway, when parched by drought, is dry, dusty, and hot. Why will people put the knife into their pleasures to see of what they are composed? If I am happy, shall I make myself miserable trying to find out the why and the wherefore? Not if I know it.

The road up the valley first skirts a wood. This wood has always been a fa-

In a little inclosure of rough stone, on the Bigelow place, lie the remains of the ill-fated Willey family, who were destroyed by the memorable slide of 1826. The inscription closes thus metaphorically:

" We gaze around, we read their monument.
We sigh, and when we sigh we sink."

Proceeding onward to where the high terrace, making one grand sweep to the

À LA BONAPARTE.

vorite retreat during the heat of the day or the cool of the evening. Tall, athletic pines, that bend in the breeze like whalebone, lift their immense clusters of impenetrable foliage on high. The sighs of lovers are softly echoed in their green tops. Voices and laughter issue from it. We, too, will swing our hammock here, and breathe the healing fragrance.

right, again unveils the same superb view of the great summits seen from the village, but wholly unobstructed by houses or groves, we are before a picture unrivalled in these mountains, not surpassed, perhaps, upon earth. Its leading features have already been mentioned, but here, in their very midst, nature seems to have snatched a garden spot from the mount-

BARTLETT BOWLDER.

ains, arrested in their advance by the command, "Thus far, and no farther." The vale regards the stormy summits around in perfect security. It rests you to look at it.

Again we scan the great peaks which on clear days come boldly down and stand at your very doors, but on hazy ones remove to a vast distance, and keep vaguely aloof day in and day out. They are by turns graciously condescending, or tantalizingly incomprehensible. Nevertheless, we enjoy this constant espionage from a distance, this exchange of preliminary civilities, before invading the heart of the mountains.

But we can no longer delay our departure for the Notch. The locomotive takes us as far as Bartlett, which indicates the limit of progress in this direction. Near Glen Station is the remarkable Bartlett Bowlder. While on its travels through the mountains it was left, poised upon four smaller stones, in the position seen in the illustration. All who can should pass over the remaining thirteen or fourteen miles on foot. Thoroughly imbued with the spirit of the mountains, the traveller now regards distances with indifference, fatigue with disdain. He learns to make

his toilet by the running stream, and his bed in groves. Truly the brown face that peers at him as he bends over some pine-bowered pool is not that he has been accustomed to seeing; but having solved the problem of man's true existence, having returned like the Prodigal Son to creative nature, he only laughs at his tawny countenance while shouldering his pack and tightening his belt.

At Bartlett we enter an ellipse of fertile land inclosed by mountain walls, through which a river murmurs unseen. Kearsarge looks up and Carrigain looks down the valley. One gives his adieu, the other his welcome. One is the perfection of symmetry, of grace; the other simply demands our homage. These two mountains are the presiding genii of this charming nook.

Step out into the village street, and take the road with me on a crisp October morning, sharp air and cutting wind acting like whip and spur. Only, for the moment, I must be the narrator.

I retain a vivid recollection of this morning. Soft as three-piled velvet, the green turf left no trace of our quick tread. The sky was of a dazzling blue, and frescoed with light clouds, transparent as gauze, pure as the snow glistening on the high summits. On both sides of us audacious mountains braced their feet in the valley, while others mounted over their brawny shoulders as if to scale the heavens.

NANCY IN THE SNOW.

But what shall I say of the grand harlequinade of nature which the valley now presented to our view? I can not employ Victor Hugo's odd simile of a peacock's tail; that is more of a witticism than a description. The death of the year seemed to prefigure the surpassing changes of color in a dying dolphin, putting on unparalleled beauty at the moment of dissolution, and so going out in a blaze of glory.

From the meagre summits enfiladed by the north wind, and where a solitary pine or cedar intensified the desolation, to the upper forests, the mountains bristled with a scanty growth of dead or dying trees. Those scattered birches, high up the mountain-side, looked like quills on a porcupine's back; that group, glistening in the morning sun, like the pipes of an immense organ. From this line of death, which vegetation crossed at its peril, the eye now dropped down over a limitless forest of dark evergreens spotted with yellow. The effect of sunlight upon this foliage was magical. Myriad flambeaux, illuminating the deep gloom, doubled the intensity of the sun.

This splendid light, which the heavy masses of orange seemed to absorb, gave a velvety softness to all the lower ridges and spurs, covering their hard angular

lines with a magnificent drapery. The lower forests, the valley itself, were one vast sea of color. Here the bewildering *mélange* of green and gold, orange and crimson, purple and russet, produced the effect of an immense Turkish rug. This quality, the blending of a thousand tints, the dreamy grace, the sumptuous profusion, the inexpressible tenderness, intoxicated the senses. Earth seemed no longer earth. We had entered a garden of the gods.

Four miles above Bartlett we crossed Sawyer's River, which comes from the defiles of Mount Carrigain, and leads the way to it. Then to a second intervale, in which was a deserted farm-house, a little grave-yard, and an orchard. Here we left the highway for the railway embankment, which from this point affords superior views. The road now turned abruptly to the north, skirting the base of the Nancy range. We were at the door of the second chamber in this remarkable gallery of nature. Before crossing its threshold, it is expedient to allude to the incident which gives a name, not only to the mountain, but to the torrent we see tearing its way down from the upper forests. The story of Nancy's Brook is as follows:

In the latter part of the last century, a maiden, whose Christian name of Nancy is all that has come down to us, was living in the little hamlet of Jefferson. She loved and was betrothed to a young man of the farm. The wedding day was fixed, and the young couple were on the eve of setting out for Portsmouth, where their happiness was to be consummated at the altar. In her simple trustfulness, the young girl confided the small sum which constituted all her marriage portion to her lover. This man repaid her with the basest treachery. Seizing his opportunity, he left the hamlet, without a word of explanation or adieu.

The deserted girl was one of those natures which can not sit quietly down under calamity. She resolved to pursue her faithless lover. She was young, vigorous, intrepid. In vain her friends tried to turn her from her purpose. At night-fall she set out.

A hundred years ago the route taken by this brave girl was not, as to-day, a thoroughfare which one may follow with his eyes shut. It was only an obscure path, little travelled by day, deserted by night. For thirty miles there was not a human habitation. It was midwinter. The forests were filled with wild beasts. But nothing could daunt the heroic spirit which animated poor Nancy.

The girl's hope was to overtake her lover at the usual camping-place in the Notch. She found the camp deserted, and the embers extinguished. Spurred on by hope or despair, she pushed on down the tremendous defile, fording the turbulent and frozen Saco, toiling through snow-drifts, and over rocks and fallen trees, until she sank exhausted on the margin of the brook, which seems perpetually bemoaning her sad fate.

Here, cold and rigid as marble, under a canopy of evergreen, which the snow tenderly drooped over, they found her. She was wrapped in her cloak, and in the same attitude of repose as when she fell asleep on her nuptial couch of snow.

It was not quite noon when we entered the beautiful and romantic glen under the shadow of Mount Crawford. Upon our left, a little in advance, a solidly built English country house, gabled and chimneyed, stood on a terrace well above the

ABEL CRAWFORD.

valley. At our right, and below, was the old Mount Crawford tavern; one of the most ancient of mountain hostels. Upon the opposite side of the vale arose the enormous mass of Mount Crawford; and near where we stood, a humble mound, overgrown with bushes, incloses the remains of Abel Crawford, the hardy pioneer whose monument is the mountain.

Abel was six feet four, Erastus, the oldest son, was six feet six, and Ethan was still taller, being nearly seven feet. In fact, not one of the sons was less than six feet, so that it may be imagined what sort of family group it was when "his boys," as Abel loved to call them, were all at home. It is a pity, but with these athletes the race of guides has disappeared. The very sight of one of those giants inspired the timid with confidence. Ethan was a man of iron frame and will. Fear and he were strangers. He would take up an exhausted traveller in his sinewy arms and carry him as you would a baby, until his strength or his courage returned.

We now had a fine view of the Giant's Stairs, which, from the valley, really look like two enormous steps cut in the granite heights of the opposite ridge. No name could be more appropriate, though each of the degrees of this colossal staircase demands a giant not of our days, for they are respectively three hundred and fifty and four hundred and fifty feet in height.

A mile or more from the Crawford Glen we emerged from behind a projecting spur of the mountain, which hid the upper valley, when, by a common impulse, we stopped, fairly stupefied with admiration and surprise.

Thrust out before us, athwart the pass, a black and castellated pile of precipices shot upward to a dizzy height, and broke off abruptly against the sky. Its bulging sides and regular outlines strongly resembled the clustered towers and frowning battlements of some antique fortress built to command the pass. Gashed, splintered, defaced, it seemed to have withstood for ages the artillery of heaven and the assaults of time. With what solitary grandeur it lifted its iron front above the forest, and regarded even the mountains with disdain!

This was Frankenstein. We at once accord it a place as the most suggestive of cliffs. It has a black gorge for a moat, so deep that the head swims when crossing it; and to-day, as we creep over the cat's-cradle of a bridge thrown across for the railway, and listen to the growling of the torrent far down beneath, the whole frail structure seems trembling under our weight. We feel a sense of relief when our feet are again planted on the solid earth.

But what a contrast! Heaped at the foot of this grisly precipice, clothing it with almost superhuman beauty, was a plantation of maples and birches, all resplendent in crimson and gold. Such masses of color! such a background! Below, all was light and splendor; above, all darkness and gloom. Here, the eye fairly recoiled in terror; there, it revelled in beauty. The cliff was a naked and swarthy Ethiopian up to his knees in roses.

Another turn of the road ushered us upon a scene deserving to be remembered as one of the marvels of this glorious picture-gallery. This is the surpassingly fine view of the great summits seen looking up through the valley of Mount Washington River, which is driven deep into the heart of the great range. Through this valley, cutting the sapphire sky with their silver silhouette, the great mountains, surmounted by the splendid white dome of Washington himself, once more greeted us.

The perfection and magnificence of this truly regal picture, the gigantic scale on which it is presented, without the least blemish to disturb its exquisite harmony, or to mar the impression of one grand whole, is a revelation to the least susceptible nature in the world. We feel that we are before one of nature's masterpieces. We can no longer combat the subtle influence that surrounds us, but surrender at discretion. Overwhelmed, humiliated, as we are, we are also uplifted, and inwardly singing the praises of nature, until every nerve and every fibre of our being is in accord with her sublime harmony, her sublime discord even, as when pointing out some haggard and dying peak we see imprinted on its perishing yet indomitable front, in heroic characters, the lofty resolution to die as becomes an emperor, erect to the last.

Turning now our faces toward the north, we beheld the immense bulk and superb crest of Mount Willey. On the other side of the valley was the long battlement of Mount Webster. We were at the entrance to the great Notch.

The valley, which had continually contracted since leaving Bartlett, now appeared fast shut between these two mountains, but on turning the tremendous support which Mount Willey flings down, we were in presence of the amazing defile cloven through the midst, and giving entrance to the heart of the White Hills.

These gigantic mountains divided to the right and left, like the Red Sea before the Israelites. Through the immense trough over which their crests hang suspended in mid-air, the highway creeps, and the river steals away. The road is only seen at intervals through the forest. A low murmur, like the hum of bees, announces the river.

I have no conception of the man who can approach this stupendous chasm without a sensation of fear. The idea of imminent annihilation is everywhere, is

MOUNT WILLEY AND THE NOTCH.

overwhelming. The mind refuses to fix itself except upon a single point: what if the
same power that commanded these awful mountains
to remove should hurl them back to ever-during fix-
edness? Should? The gulf seemed contracting
under our very eyes, the great mountains toppling
to their fall. With an eagerness excited by high
expectation, we had pressed on; but now we hesitated. Below, it was all
admiration and surprise; here, all amazement and fear. We moved on,
looking with all our eyes, absorbed, silent, almost worshipping.

The wide split of the Notch, which we had now entered, has on one side Mount
Willey, drawn up to his full height, and on the other Mount Webster, striped with

ELEPHANT'S HEAD, WHITE MOUNTAIN NOTCH—WINTER.

dull red on dingy yellow, like an old tiger's skin. Willey is the highest, Webster the most remarkable. Willey has a conical spire, Webster a long, irregular battlement. Willey is a mountain, Webster a huge block of granite.

For two miles the gorge winds between these mountains, to where it is apparently sealed up by a mass of purple precipices lodged full in its throat. This is Mount Willard. The vast chasm glowed with the gorgeous hues of the foliage even when passing clouds obscured the sun. These general observations made, we cast our eyes down into the vale reposing at our feet.

Five hundred feet below us was a little clearing, containing a hamlet of two or three houses. From this hamlet to the storm-crushed crags glistening on the summit of Mount Willey the track of an ancient avalanche was still distinguishable, though the birches and alders rooted among the débris threatened to obliterate it at no distant day.

We descended to the houses at the mountain's foot by this still plain path. One and the other are associated with the most tragic event connected with the history of the great Notch.

Since quite early in the century, the smaller house, the walls of which were scribbled over by curious pilgrims, was kept as an inn, and for a long time it was the

CASCADES ON MOUNT WEBSTER, FROM MOUNT WILLARD.

only stopping-place between Abel Crawford's below and Captain Rosebrook's above, a distance of thirteen miles. Its situation at the entrance to the Notch was advantageous to the public, but attended with a danger which seems not to have been sufficiently regarded, if, indeed, it caused successive inmates particular concern. This fatal security had a lamentable sequel.

In 1826 this house was occupied by Samuel Willey, his wife, five children, and two hired men. During the summer a drought of unusual severity dried the streams and parched the thin soil of the mountains. On the 28th of August, at dusk, a storm burst upon the mountains, and

MOUNT WILLARD, FROM LEDGE OF WILLEY BROOK.

raged with indescribable fury throughout the night. The rain fell in sheets. Innumerable torrents suddenly broke forth on all sides, deluging the narrow valley, and bearing with them forests that had covered the mountains for ages. The turbid and swollen Saco rose over its banks, flooding the intervales, and spreading destruction in its course.

Two days afterward a traveller succeeded in forcing his way through the Notch. He found the Willey house standing uninjured in the midst of woful desolation. A land-slide descending from Mount Willey had buried the little vale beneath its ruins. The traveller reported at the nearest house what he had seen. Assistance was dispatched to the scene of disaster. The rescuers came too late to render aid to the living, but they found, and buried on the spot, the bodies of Mr. and Mrs. Willey and the two hired men. The children were never found.

We passed by the beautiful brook Kedron, flung down from the utmost heights of Willey, between banks mottled with color. Then, high up on our right, two airy water-falls hung, suspended from the summit of Mount Webster. These dancing sprites, called respectively the Silver Cascade and the Flume, withdrew our attention from every other object, until a sharp turn to the right brought the overhanging precipices of Mount Willard full upon us. Here the railway seems fairly stopped, but with a graceful sweep it eludes the mountain, and glides around its massive shoulder, giving, as it does so, a hand to the high-road, which comes straggling up the sharp ascent.

Now and here we entered a close dark defile hewn down between cliffs ascending on the right in regular terraces, on the left in ruptured masses. For a few rods this narrow cleft continues, then, on a sudden, the rocks, which lift themselves on either side, shut together. An enormous mass has tumbled from its ancient location on the left side, and taking a position within twenty feet of the opposite precipice, forms the natural gate of the Notch, through which a way was made for the common road with great labor, through which the river frays a passage, but where no one would imagine there was room for either. Passing now the crag which so curiously resembles an elephant's head and trunk, all three emerge from the gloom of the pass into the cheerful sunshine of a little prairie, at the extremity of which are seen the white walls of a hotel.

The whole route we have traversed is full of contrasts, full of surprises, but this sudden transition is the most picturesque, the most startling of all. We seemed to have reached the end of the world.

CARTER NOTCH, FROM THORN HILL.

THE WHITE MOUNTAINS.

PART II.

IT is Petrarch who says, "A journey on foot hath most pleasant commodities: a man may go at his pleasure; none shall stay him; none shall carry him beyond his wish; none shall trouble him; he hath but one labor, the labor of nature, to go." Here is a creed every true pedestrian may embrace with enthusiasm; and should he, too, chance to have his Laura, he will see her somewhere, or everywhere, I promise him.

Our first journey terminated at the summit of the great White Mountain Notch. A second and equally romantic tour leads us through a region into which railways have not yet penetrated, and where, even now, there are solitudes as inviolate as were ever the abiding-place of the silences of ages. From North Conway, then, we once more turn our faces to the north. It is our purpose to ascend slowly the valleys conducting to the summit of the Carter and the Pinkham passes, pushing investigation into and beyond these interesting defiles, which distribute with impartial hand the melted snows arrested in their swift descent from the mountain-tops.

GIANT'S STAIRS, FROM THORN HILL.

The walk over Thorn Hill gives ravishing backward glimpses, opening gradually to a full and broad panorama of the Saco meadows. Then, advancing to the summit, full upon the charmed eye comes that glorious vision of the great mountains elevated to an immense height, and seeming, in their benevolence, to say, "Approach, mortals."

Underneath us, at the bottom of a deep vale, with mountains all around, we look down upon a handful of white houses huddled about one little church spire, like a congregation sitting at their pastor's feet. So completely is this vale shut in that you perceive neither entrance nor exit. The streams that make two veins of silver in its green floor seem vainly seeking a way out. Nature, one would think, had locked the door and thrown away the key. This is the village of Jackson. This is the valley of the Ellis.

What traveller can pass beyond the crest of Thorn Hill without paying his tribute of silent admiration to the splendid pageant of mountains visible from this charmed spot? But admiration gives way to astonishment when he sees this immense wall pierced through its centre by the deep hollow of the Carter Notch. Right before him the mighty rampart, bristling with its countless towers, is breached as cleanly as if a cannon-ball had just crashed through it. It is an enormous hole. It is the cavity, appar-

ently, from which one of those great iron teeth has just been extracted. Only it does not disfigure the landscape: it really exalts the surrounding mountains. They are immensely aggrandized by it.

One of the streams we see is the Ellis, the other the Wildcat, which unites with it at the edge of the village. The Wildcat cuts the village in two. It is a perfect highwayman of a stream. The very air is tremulous with its rush and roar. Halting on the bridge that spans it, and looking down the long pathway it makes, we enjoy a fine retrospect of the Moats, and looking up, see the torrent come bounding toward us. Here it makes a swift descent over granite ledges, clean and fresh from constant scrubbing as the face of a country urchin, and as freckled. Every rod of its course is beset by huge humpbacked bowlders: a river in fetters! Every step it takes is a headlong rush: a tempest of waters! For half a mile the ledges forming its bed look as if an earthquake had ripped them up, not to make a channel, but to waylay, entrap, and cut the stream hopelessly in pieces.

Conspicuous from the village rise in the north the two massive steps of the Giant's Stairs, which we have already seen from the Saco Valley.

This little river, tumbling step by step down its broken ledges into Jackson, comes direct from the Notch, and its stream is the thread which conducts through the labyrinth of thick woods.

I dearly love the companionship of these mountain streams. They are the voices of the wilderness singing high or low, softly humming a melodious refrain to your thoughts, or joining innumerable cascades in one grand chorus, they salute the ear with a gush of sound that robs the forest of its loneliness and awe. But that is not all the river signifies. It has a deeper meaning.

" Stranger, if thou hast learned a truth which needs
No school of long experience, that the world
Is full of guilt and misery, and hast seen
Enough of all its sorrows, crimes, and cares
To tire thee of it, enter this wild wood,
And view the haunts of nature."

For five miles the road skirts the western slopes of the Wildcat Valley, which grows continually deeper, narrower, and higher. We catch for a moment the snowy cupola of Washington and the slender peak of Adams. Then they vanish. Before us the grand downward curves of Carter Notch open wider and wider.

We pick up *en route* the guide of the locality, who lives on the side of the mountain near where the road is left for the woods. While he is strapping on his knapsack we have leisure to observe the manner of man he is.

The guide, whose Christian name is Jonathan, is known to all the country round as " Jock" Davis. He is a medium-sized, muscular man, whiskered like a Cossack, with a pair of bare arms the color of unglazed earthenware, and a step like a panther. Having built a cabin there, cut a path to it, and having conducted in and out about all who have ever visited it, this decidedly queer but singularly alert figure, leaning on an alpenstock before us, is entitled to be considered the tutelary genius of the Notch. When not engaged as a guide, he hunts, traps, and " gums" for a living—a scanty and precarious one, it must be confessed, and full of hardship; but sympathy may well be spared when the man himself laughs or shrugs his broad shoulders at the word "hardship" as a thing to be expected, and as a matter of course overcome. This Davis reminds me of a boy in a strange house. He has been on top of everything.

Seeing me ready, Davis whistled to his dog, and we entered the path in Indian file. In ten steps the forest closed over our heads. A brisk pace brought us in a short time to the edge of an ancient clearing, now badly overgrown with bramble and coppice, and showing how easily nature obliterates the mark of civilization when left alone. In this clearing an old cellar told its sad story but too plainly. Those pioneers who first struck the axe into the noble pines here are all gone. They abandoned in consternation the effort to wring a scanty subsistence from this inhospitable and unfruitful region. Even the poor farms I had seen encroaching upon the skirts of this wilderness seemed fighting in retreat.

We quickly came to a second clearing, where the axe of God had smote the forest even more ruthlessly than that of man. The ground was encumbered with half-burned trees, among which the gaudy fire-weed grew rank and tall. Divining my thought, the guide explained, in his quaint, sententious way, "Fire went through it; then the wind harricaned it down." A comprehensive sweep of his staff indicated the area traversed by the whirlwind of fire and the tornado. This opening disclosed at our left the gray cliffs and yawning aperture of the Notch —by far the most satisfactory view yet obtained, and the nearest.

An hour and a half of pretty rapid walking found us at the bottom of a steep rise. We were at length come to close quarters with the formidable outworks of Wildcat Mountain. The brook has for some distance poured a stream of the purest water over moss of the richest green, but it now most mysteriously vanishes from sight. From this point the singular rock called the Pulpit is seen overhanging the upper crags of Carter Dome. We had now attained an altitude of 2250 feet above the village of Jackson; we were then a thousand higher than the renowned Crawford Notch.

On every side the ground was loaded down with huge gray bowlders, so ponderous that it seemed as if the solid earth must give way under them. Some looked as if the merest touch would send them crashing down the mountain. Undermined by the slow action of time, these fragments have fallen one by one from the high cliffs, and accumulated at the base. Among these the path serpentined for half a mile more, bringing us at last to the summit of the spur we had been climbing, and to the broad entrance of the Notch. We passed quickly over the level ground we were now upon, stopped by the

MOAT MOUNTAIN, FROM THE WILDCAT, NEAR JACKSON.

side of a well-built cabin of bark, threw off
our loads, and then, fascinated by the exceeding strangeness of everything I saw
around me, I advanced to the edge of the
scrubby growth in front of the camp, in
order to command an unobstructed view.

Shall I live long enough to forget this
sublime tragedy of nature, enacted Heaven knows when or how? How still it
was! I seemed to have arrived at the instant a death-like silence succeeds the catastrophe. I saw only the bare walls of

a temple of which some Samson had just
overthrown the columns — walls overgrown with a forest, ruins overspread
with the tokens of a mighty struggle.

Imagine the light of a mid-day sun
brightening the tops of the mountains,
while within a sepulchral gloom rendered all objects—rocks, trees, cliffs—all the
more weird and fantastic. I was between
two high mountains whose gaunt walls
inclose the pass. Overhanging it, fifteen
hundred feet at least, the sunburned crags

of the dome towered above the highest precipices of the mountain behind me. Impossible to conceive anything more enduring than this imperishable rock. So long as the world stands, these mountains will stand. They look so strong, so incapable of change.

But what, then, is this dusky gray mass, stretching huge and irregular across the chasm from mountain to mountain, completely filling the space between, and so effectually blockading the entrance that we were compelled to pick our way up the steep side of the mountain in order to turn it?

Picture to yourself acres upon acres of naked granite split and splintered in every conceivable form, of enormous size and weight, yet pitched, piled, and tumbled about like playthings, tilted or so poised and balanced as to open numberless caves which sprinkled the whole area with a thousand shadows—figure this, I repeat, to yourself, and the mind will then but faintly grasp the idea of this colossal barricade, seemingly built by the giants of old to guard their last stronghold from all intrusion.

Whence came this colossal débris? I had at first the idea that the great arch springing from peak to peak, supported on the Atlantean shoulders of the two mountains, had fallen into ruins. I even tried to imagine the terrific crash with which heaven and earth came together in the fall. Easy to realize here Schiller's graphic description of the Jungfrau: "One walks there between life and death. Two threatening peaks shut in the solitary way. Pass over this place of terror without noise; dread lest you awake the sleeping avalanche."

It is evident, however, as soon as the eye attaches itself to the side of the dome, that one of its loftiest precipices, originally measuring an altitude as great as any yet remaining, has precipitated itself in a crushed and broken mass into the abyss. The track of the convulsion is easily traced. From top to bottom the side of the mountain is hollowed out, exposing a shallow ravine in which nothing but dwarf spruces will grow, and in which the erratic rocks, arrested here and there in their fall, seem endeavoring to regain their ancient position on the summit. There is no trace whatever of the rubbish ordinarily accompanying a slide; only these rocks.

But besides all this wreck and ruin, which is so astounding when first seen, nature plays here one of those pranks constituting the really remarkable episode of the spectacle before us, and diverting the mind from the somewhat depressing influences of such irremediable chaos—a chaos which seems to prefigure the death of the mountain, and of which we are unable to divine the object. From a flat rock pushed above the mass of the barricade we saw two little lakes lying beneath us in the hollow opening between this natural intrenchment and the little mountain constituting the head, and true summit, of the Notch.

No incident of the whole excursion is more curiously inexplicable than the total disappearance of the brook at the mountain's foot. Notice that it was last seen gushing from the side we ascended, half a mile below the camp. Whence does it come? When we are on top of the bowlders, looking down into the black water of the little lakes, we ask ourselves in wonder, "Where does it go? how does it get out?" The mystery is, however, solved by the certainty that their waters flow out underneath the barrier; but notwithstanding one or the other of us was continually dropping out of sight into the caverns with which it is filled, we could neither hear nor see anything to indicate the route by which the stream contrives its escape. It is buried out of sight and sound.

Descending the spur upon which the hut is situated, we were in a few moments at the bottom of the deep cavity between the Giant's Barricade and the little mountain forming the northern portal. We had now taken a position between the lakes. Looking backward, the barricade lifted a black and frowning wall a hundred and fifty feet over our heads. Looking down, the water of the lakes seemed "an image of the Dead Sea at the foot of Jerusalem destroyed."

Here I parted from my guide, and after threading the woods two hours longer, came out into the stony pastures above the Glen House.

The Glen House is one of the last strongholds of the old ways of mountain travel. The nearest railway station is eight miles off, at Gorham. The nearest steam-whistle is there. So much for its seclusion.

Situated at the base of Carter Mountain, on a terrace rising above the Peabody River, which it overlooks, it has only the valley of this stream—a half-mile of level meadow here—between it and the base of Mount Washington. The carriage-road to the summit, which in 1861 superseded the old bridle-path, is seen crossing this meadow. The road occupied six years in building, and is eight miles long.

Respecting the appearance of Mount Washington from the Glen House itself, it is a received truth that neither the height nor the proportions of a high mountain are properly appreciated when the spectator is placed exactly at the base. The same is true here of Mount Washington, which is too much foreshortened for a favorable estimate of its grandeur or its elevation. The dome looks flat, elongated, obese. But it is only a step to more eligible posts of observation in the immediate vicinity.

Still, Mount Washington is surveyed with more astonishment, perhaps, from this point than from any other. The lower zone is covered with a dense forest, out of which rise the successive and stupendous undulations, culminating at last in the absolutely barren summit, which the nearer swells almost conceal. The true peak stands well to the left, indicated by a white building when the sun is shining, and a dark one when it is not. Seen from this spot, the peculiar conformation of the mountain gives the impression strongly of a semi-fluid mass, first cooled to hardness, then receiving successive additions, which, although eternally united with its bulk, have left the point of contact visible forever. When the first mass cooled, it received a second, afterward a third, and then a fourth. One believes certain intervals to have elapsed in the process of solidifying these masses, which seem, to me at least, not risen out of the earth, but poured down upon it.

It is related that an Englishman, seated on the balcony of his hotel at Chamouni, after having conscientiously followed the peripatetics of a sunset, remarked, "Very fine, very fine indeed! but it is a pity Mont Blanc hides the view." In this sense Mount Washington hides the view to the west. No peak dares show his head in this direction.

But we are still a long way from comprehending what is before us until we look down the valley, open throughout nearly its whole length, and fully expos-ing the magnificent sweep of the great northern peaks, here bending majestically round to the northeast, exhibiting their titanic props, deep hollows, soaring peaks, to the admiring scrutiny of every wayfarer. It is impossible to appreciate this view all at once. No one can pretend to analyze the sensations produced by looking at high mountains. The bare thought of them creates a flutter of enthusiasm wherever we may be. At such moments one lays down the pen to revel in the recollection.

Go with me now up to the summit of the Pinkham Pass in order to gain some knowledge, not so much of what it shows as of what it hides from the traveller.

The four miles of highway back through the Pinkham forest deserve to be called the Avenue of Cascades. Not less than four drop from the mountain-tops or leap down the confined gorges. Two miles from the hotel we meet a sprightly and vigorous brook coming down from Wildcat Mountain to swell the Peabody. A short walk up this stream brings us to Thompson's Falls, which are several pretty cascades slipping down a bed of granite. The ledges over which they glide afford a practicable road to the top of the falls, from which is a most full and interesting view of Tuckerman's Ravine and of the summit of Mount Washington.

Near these falls a well-trod path leads from the road to the Emerald Pool, which Bierstadt's painting has rendered famous. At first one sees only a deep hollow, with a glassy pool at the bottom, and a cool light coming down through the high tree-tops. Two large rocks tightly compress the stream which fills it, so that the water gushes out with sufficient force to whiten a little without disturbing the placid repose of the still basin. This gives the effect of milk poured upon ink. Above these rocks we look up the stony bed of the frantic stream, and meet the humid blue of a distant mountain. Large rocks are picturesquely posed about the margin. Upon one side a birch leans out over the pool, which reflects brilliantly from its polished surface the white light of the satin bark. One sees the print of foliage on this black water like that of ferns and grasses upon coal, or rather like the most beautiful Italian mosaics—black marble inlaid with arabesques of color.

Just beyond here—for we are now back in the road, and keenly alert lest something may escape us—comes that remarkable view of Tuckerman's Ravine, which is the chief glory of the walk thus far. From this spot the summit is also finely visible. At the third mile a guide-board announces the Crystal Cascade and the way into the ravine. We do not turn aside here, for Glen Ellis is our present destination. We now cross the summit of the pass.

The road is gloomy enough, edging its way always through a dense wood around a spur of Mount Washington, which it closely hugs. A signboard now shows

TO TUCKERMAN'S RAVINE.

where to leave the highway, but the noise of the fall coming clearer and clearer is an even surer guide. The sense of seclusion is perfect. Stately pines, funereal cedars, sombre hemlocks, throng the banks, as if come to refresh themselves with the fine spray ascending from the cataract. This spray sparkles in the sun like diamond-dust. Through the thickset, clean-limbed tree trunks jets of foam can be seen in mad riot along the rocky gorge. Backward up the stream, downward beyond the fall, we see the same tumult of waters in the midst of this statuesque immobility; we hear the roar of the fall echoing in the tops of the pines; we feel the dull earth throb with the superabundant energy of the wild river.

Descending slippery stairs to the pool beneath the fall, I saw, eighty feet above me, the whole stream force its way through a narrow cleft, and stand in one unbroken column, superbly erect, upon the level surface of the pool. The sheet was as white as marble, the pool as green as malachite. As if stunned by the fall, it turns slowly round; then, recovering, precipitates itself down the rocky gorge with greater passion than ever.

On its upper edge the curling sheet of the fall was shot with sunlight, and shone with enchanting brilliancy. All below was one white feathery mass, gliding down with the swift and noiseless movement of an avalanche of fresh snow. No sound until the moment of contact with the submerged rocks beneath; then it finds a voice that shakes the hoary forest to its centre. How this exquisite white thing fascinates! One has almost to tear himself from the spot. From the tender dalliance of a sunbeam with the glittering mists constantly ascending is born a pale Iris. Exquisitely its floating scarf of green, crimson, and gold decorates the virgin drapery of the fall.

Our plan includes a trip in and out of Tuckerman's Ravine: in by the old Thompson Path, out by the Crystal Cascade.

Before the Mountain Club smoothed the way this was no holiday promenade, but a rude encounter with nature in arms. One day myself and a companion, a veteran of many hard-fought fields among mountains, resolved, if the thing were possible, to force our way into the ravine. For two miles our plain way led up the summit road, but at this point we turned aside and plunged into the forest.

I recall no mountain path that is so richly diversified with all the wildest forms of mountain beauty. At first our progress through primitive groves of pine, hemlock, and birch was not seriously impeded, but we advanced to find the way continually and effectually barred by giant trees, fallen from sheer old age, or uprooted by storms while still in the prime of a vigorous growth. These exasperating windfalls, and their thick abatis of branches, forced us alternately to go down on our hands and knees, creeping underneath, and to mount and dismount, like recruits on the wooden horse of a cavalry school.

But the woods, those countless gray and black and white trunks and outspread frames of branches, supported a canopy of thick foliage filled with voices innumerable. Something stirred in the top of a dead pine, and then, like an alguazil on a watch-tower, a crow, apparent sentinel of all the feathered colony, rose clumsily on his talons, flapped two sable wings, and thrice hoarsely challenged, "Caw! caw! caw!" What clamor! what a Lilliputian Babel ensued! Our ears fairly tingled with the calls, outcries, and objurgations apparently flung down at us by the multitudinous populace overhead. Hark to the woodpecker's rat-tat-tat, the partridge's muffled drum! List to the bugle-note of the wood-thrush, sweet and clear. Now sounds the cat-bird's shrill alarm, the owl's hoot of indignant surprise. Then the squirrels, those little monkeys of our Northern woods, grated their teeth sharply at us, and let fall nuts on our heads as we passed underneath.

We now began to thread a region where the forest was more open. The moss we trampled under foot, and which here replaces the grass of the valleys, was beating the tallest trees in the race for the mountain-top. It was the old story of tortoise and hare over again. But these mosses, enveloping rocks, trees, roots, everything, in one universal decoration, have you ever looked at them before your heel bruised the perfumed flowers springing from their velvet? Here are tufts daintily brilliant with coral lichens; here the violet and anemone nestle lovingly together; here it has crept by stealth up the gray trunks, and there it covers the bared roots, so that they look like huge fingers of a gloved hand. Tread softly. This is the abode of elves and fairies. Step lightly. You expect to hear the crushed flowers cry out with pain.

From here the ground rose rapidly for half a mile more, when we suddenly came out of the low firs full upon the Lion's Head crag, rising above Hermit Lake. To be thus unexpectedly confronted by this wall of imperishable rock stirs one very deeply. For the moment it dominates *us* even as it dominates the little pool so unconsciously slumbering at its feet. It is horribly gashed and defaced. Its sides are thickly sowed with stunted trees that bury their roots in its cracks with a gripe of iron. Crouched underneath, by the shores of the lake, is a matted forest of firs and spruces dwindled to half their usual size, grizzled with long lichens, and

post of observation, though we had yet rough work to do. We saw the whole magnificent sweep of the ravine, to where it terminates in a semicircle of stupendous cliffs that seem hewn perpendicularly a thousand feet down. Lying against the western wall we distinguished patches of snow, but they appeared of trifling extent. Great wooded mountain-slopes stretched away from the depths of the gorge on either side, making the iron lineaments of

HERMIT LAKE.

occupying, as if by stealth, the debatable ground between life and death. It is, in fact, more dead than alive.

Deeply sunk beneath is the lake. Its solitary state, its waters green and profound, and the thick shades by which it is surrounded, seem strangely at variance with the intense activity of the foaming torrents we had seen and could still hear rushing down the mountain. It was too small for a lake, or else it was dwarfed by the immense mass of overshadowing rock towering above it, whose reflected light streamed across its still and glossy surface.

We had now gained a commanding

the giant cliffs seem harder by their own softness and delicacy. Here and there these exquisite draperies were torn in long rents by land-slides. In the west arose the shattered peak of Monroe, a mass of splintered granite, conspicuous at every point for its irreclaimable deformity. Everywhere was a Dantesque grandeur and solemnity.

We watched the bellying sails of a stray cloud which intercepted our view of the great summit; but it soon floated away, discovering the whitish-gray ledges to the very cap-stone of the dome itself. We then pushed on into the ravine.

UNDER THE SNOW ARCH IN TUCKERMAN'S RAVINE.

From Hermit Lake the only practicable way was by clambering up the bed of the mountain brook that falls through the ravine. The whole expanse that stretched on either side was a chaos of shattered granite, pitched about in awful confusion. Path there was none. No matter what way we turned, "no thoroughfare" was carved in stolid stone. We tried to force a passage through the stunted cedars that are mistaken a mile away for patches of grass, but were beaten back, torn and bleeding, to the brook. We then turned to the great bowlders, to be equally buffeted and abused, and finally repulsed upon the brook, which seemed all the while mocking our efforts. Once, while forcing a route inch by inch through the scrub, I was caught and held suspended over a deep crevice, until extricated by my companion. At another time he disappeared suddenly in a hole, from which I drew him like a blade from its scabbard. At this moment we were actually unable either to advance or retreat. The dwarf trees squeezed us like a vise. Who would have thought there was so much life in them? At our wits' end, we looked first at our bleeding hands, then at each other. The brook was the only clew to such a labyrinth, and to it, as from Scylla to Charybdis, we turned as soon as we recovered breath. But to reach it was no easy matter; we had literally to cut our way out of the jungle.

After this rude initiation into the mysteries of the ravine, we advanced directly up the bed of the brook. But the brook is for half a mile nothing but a succession of leaps and plunges, its course choked with bowlders. We, however, toiled on from rock to rock, first boosting, then hoisting, each other up; one moment splashing in a pool, the next halting dismayed under a cascade which we must either mount like a chamois or ascend like a trout. At length the stream grew narrower, suddenly divided, and we stood at the mouth of the Snow Arch, confronted by the vertical upper wall of the ravine.

We were within an arena "more majestic than the circus of a Titus or a Vespasian." The scene was one of awful desolation. A little way below us the gorge was heaped with the ruins of some unrecorded convul-

CRYSTAL CASCADE.

IMP MOUNTAIN.

sion by which the precipice had been cloven from base to summit, and the enormous fragments heaved into the chasm with a force the imagination is powerless to conceive. In the interstices among these blocks rose thickets of dwarf cedars as stiff and unyielding as the livid rock itself. It was truly an arena which might have witnessed the gladiatorial combats of immortals.

We did not at first look at the Snow Arch. The eye was irresistibly fascinated by the tremendous mass of the precipice above. From top to bottom its tawny front was streaked with countless little streams that clung to its polished wall without once quitting their hold. Twining and twisting in their downward course like a brood of young serpents escaping from their lair, the cliff resembled the ghastly head of a Gorgon clothed with tresses of serpents. A poetic imagination has named this tangled mass of mountain rills "The Fall of a Thousand Streams." At the foot of the cliff the scattered waters unite before entering the Snow Arch in a single stream. Turning now to the right, the narrowing gorge, ascending by a steep slope as high as the upper edge of the precipice, points out the only practicable route to the summit of Mount Washington in this direction.

This forgotten fragment of winter, the Snow Arch, had never been seen to greater advantage. We estimated its width at above two hundred feet, where it threw a solid bridge of ice over the stream, and not far from three hundred in its greatest length, where it lay along the slope of the gorge. Summer and winter met on this neutral ground. Entering the Arch was joining January and May with a single step. Flowers blossomed at the threshold, icicles hung from the roof. We caught water as it dripped ice-cold from the vaulted ceiling, and pledged old Winter in his own cellarage. The brook foamed at our feet. Looking up, there was a pretty picture of a water-fall pouring in at the upper end, and out at the ragged portal of the grotto. But I think we were most charmed with the remarkable sculpture of the roof, which was a groined arch, fashioned as featly as was ever done by human hands. What the stream had begun in secret the warm vapors of returning spring had chiselled with a bolder hand, but not altered. As it was formed, so it remained, a veritable chapel of the hills, the brook droning its low monotonous chant and the dripping roof telling its beads unceasingly. Thus under a cold exterior is nourished the principle of undying love, which the aged mountain yields in order that earth may forever renew her fairest youth.

The Crystal Cascade is formed where the mountain torrent flowing out of Tuckerman's Ravine makes its début at the summit of the Pinkham Notch. It divides with Glen Ellis the honor of being the most beautiful cascade of the White Mountains. In fact, they are as unlike as two human countenances. Every one is astonished at the changes effected by simple combinations of rocks, trees, and water. I have attempted a description of Glen Ellis, but one should possess the language of a Ruskin, the imagination of a Dumas, the poetry of a Longfellow or a Tennyson, the pencil of a Turner or a Church, to do justice to this pre-eminently beautiful of cascades.

Look around. On the right bank of the stream, where a tall birch leans out over the pool below, a jutting rock embraces in one glance the greater part of the fall. The cliffs rising upon either side make a most wild and impressive setting. The trees which shade or partially screen it exclude the light. The sides of the mountains, receding into impenetrable shades, seem set with innumerable dusky columns. All this combines to produce the effect of standing under the vault of some old, dimly lighted cathedral—a subdued, a softened feeling. A voice seems whispering, ''God is here.''

Through the sombre shades the cascade comes like a gleam of light. It redeems the solitude. High up, hundreds of feet up the mountain-side, it boils and foams. It can hardly be said to run. How it turns and tosses and writhes on its hard bed! The green leaves quiver at its struggles. Birds fly silently by. Down, down, and still down over its shattered stairs falls the doomed flood, until, beaten and broken into a mere feathery cloud, it reaches a narrow gorge between abrupt cliffs of granite. A little pellucid basin, half white, half black water, receives it in full career. It then flows out by a pretty water-fall of twenty feet more. But here again the sharp, wedge-shaped cliff, advancing from the opposite side, compresses its whole volume within a deep and narrow trough, through which it flies with the rapidity of light, makes a right angle, and goes down the mountain uttering loud complaints. Behind the keen-edged, jagged cliff is a rock perfectly black, and smooth as polished ebony, over which the surplus water of the fall spreads a web of antique lace.

We will now proceed awhile down the valley in the direction of Gorham, turning our backs upon the Glen House for the purpose. In three miles we cross the Peabody by a bridge, and arrive in front of the old Copp farm-house, snugly ensconced at the foot of Mount Madison. The reader has now to make a singular acquaintance. Without further ceremony or preamble, I present him to the Imp.

Directly opposite the farm-house the inclined ridge of the mountain range is broken down perpendicularly some two hundred feet, leaving a ragged cliff resembling an immense step facing up the valley. Upon this cliff, or this step, is the distorted human profile which gives the mountain its name of Imp Mountain. A strong, clear light behind it is necessary to bring all the features, the mouth especially, into bold relief against the sky, when the expression is certainly almost diabolical. One imagines that some goblin, imprisoned for ages within the mountain, like the malignant genii of the *Thousand and One Nights*, and suddenly liberated by an earthquake, thus exhibits his hideous face, still wearing the same look it wore at the moment it was entombed in the granite. The forenoon is the best time, and the road, a few rods back from the house, the best point from which to see this natural curiosity. The coal-black countenance is then in shadow.

The Copps have lived here about half a century, and the house, as we see by Mistress Dolly Copp's register, has been known to many generations of tourists. The picture of the old weather-stained roof nestling among the sleeping giants around it

MOUNT WASHINGTON, FROM SHELBURNE.

revives in fullest vigor our preconceived idea of life in the mountains, already shaken by the balls, routs, and grand toilets of the hotels. One is dropped here into the easy-going, methodical, and uneventful ways of the primitive inhabitants, and is astonished to observe how little the bustle and excitements borne past its door on the current of pleasure-travel from year to year have affected the absolute tranquillity of the old farm-house, or disturbed the fixed habits of its occupants. We all agree, I think, that there is something strangely inconsistent in the appearance of a huge white barrack of a hotel in the midst of our mountains. We would not have it there. But when we see one of these dingy red cottages, and hear the bleating of sheep up the mountain-side, instead of experiencing the feeling of discordance, we at once brighten up, and say: "This is right; this belongs here. It has not bought or pushed its way among these old grandees, but lies in humble dependence and trustfulness at their feet. It might always have been there."

Within two miles of Gorham we again cross the river, and ascending the hill above it, see the village before us, with the long slopes of Mount Hayes meeting in a regular pyramid behind it. Against the dusky wall of this mountain one white spire is cut in sharp relief. At our right is a cluster of saw-mills, sheds, and shanties; beyond, an irregular line of forest conceals the village, all except the steeple; beyond that is the mountain. As we enter the skirts the shrill scream of a locomotive pierces the still air, and, like the horn of Ernani, breaks our dream of forgetfulness with its fatal blast. We cross the line of the Grand Trunk Railway. Adieu, illusory dreams; we are once more manacled with the city.

Dismissing the village, which contains little of interest, but is beautifully placed on the shores of the swift Androscoggin, abandoning the idea even of a *résumé* of its surroundings, which are highly interesting and attractive, we may appropriately epitomize the whole by taking a rapid *coup d'œil* from one of the favorable points of observation a few miles down the river valley. For whether we go up or down this valley, it is always the same objects, under different aspects, that we see.

Some enticing views may be had from the Shelburne intervales, embracing Washington on the left and Madison on the right. It is therefore permitted to steal an occasional look back until we reach the Lead Mine Bridge, so called, and stand over the middle of the flashing Androscoggin.

The dimpled river, broad here, and showing tufts of foliage on its satin surface, recedes between wooded banks to the middle distance, where it disappears. Swaying to and fro, without noise, the lithe and slender willows on the margin continually dip their budding twigs in the stream, as if to show its clear transparency while letting fall drop by drop its crystal globules. They gently nod their green heads, keeping time to the music of the river.

Beyond the river, over gently meeting slopes of the valley, two magnificent shapes, Washington and Madison, rise grandly. These truly regal peaks still wear their winter ermine. They are drawn so widely apart as to exhibit the familiar summits of Mount Clay protruding between. It is hardly possible to imagine a more beautiful picture of mountain scenery. Noble river, hoary summits, blanched precipices, over which a little color is beginning to steal, eloquently appeal to every perception of the beautiful and the sublime.

We loiter along the river road, hoping, as the sky is clear, to see the sun go down on the great summits. Nor are we disappointed. Soon the highest precipices of Mount Moriah are kindled with a ruddy glow, while a wonderful white light rests like a halo on the august brow of the monarch. Of a sudden the crest of Moriah pales, then grows dark. Night rises from the black glen, twilight falls from the dusky heavens. For an instant the bold humps of Clay redden in the after-glow. Then the light goes out, and we see only the towering forms of the giant mountains dimly traced upon the sky. A star falls. At this signal the great dome sparkles with myriad lights. Night has ascended her mountain throne.

Having served our apprenticeship, and having observed, as it were, all those formalities which the royal state of the monarch demands of all who approach his presence, and which are indispensable to a proper appreciation of his greatness, we will now venture to ascend the steps of the throne itself. But before being announced, it is proper and expedient to consult a friend who has already gone through with the ceremony of presentation.

The first days of May, 1877, found me again at the Glen House, prepared to put in execution the long-deferred purpose of ascending Mount Washington in early spring. Before separating for the night,

my young Jehu, who drove me from Gorham in an hour, said, with a grin, "You are going where they cut their butter with a chisel, and their meat with a handsaw."

"What do you mean?"

"Oh, you will learn to-morrow."

"Till to-morrow, then."

"Good-night."

"Good-night."

At six in the morning I stood in the road in front of the Glen House. The morning was glorious. Everything announced a beautiful day. In ten minutes I was alone in the forest with the squirrels, the partridges, the woodpeckers, and my own thoughts.

A steady tramp of four miles through the forest—long and weary ones if you are on foot, desirable to get over with all possible expedition—brought me to the Half-way House, built nearly upon the line of demarkation between forest and naked rock. It is only when emerging upon the bare crags above this spot that the wonders of the ascent begin, and the succession of views, dimly visible to our eyes, challenges the attention at every step.

Years ago it was no uncommon thing for a bear to be seen along this road, but the war of extermination waged against poor Bruin now renders a visit from him to these parts an extremely rare thing.

One of the old drivers once related to me that while going up this road with a heavy load, his horses suddenly stopped, showing unmistakable signs of terror. The place was a dangerous one, where the road had been wholly excavated from the steep side of the mountain; so, keeping one eye upon his fractious team, he threw quick glances right and left with the other, while the passengers, alarmed by the sudden stop, the driver's shouts to his animals, and the still more alarming backward movement of the coach, thrust their heads out of the windows, and with white faces demanded what was the matter.

"What was it?"

"A big black bear, would weigh six hunderd, all huddled up in a bunch, a-takin' his mornin' observations on the scenery from the top of a dead sycamore clost to the road."

"What did you do?"

"Dew?" echoed the driver, laughing—"dew?" he repeated. "Why, them crazy

MOUNT ADAMS AND GREAT GULF.

loons, when they
found Mr. Bear
couldn't get at
them, just picked
up loose rocks and hove them at
the old cuss. When one hit him a
crack, Lord! how he'd growl and shake
his head! But, you see, he couldn't get
at 'em; so they whanged away until Bruin
couldn't stan' it no longer, an' slid right down

the tree as slick as grease, an' mad as Old Nick. It tickled me so to see him a-makin' tooth-picks fly from that ar tree."

The high sun poured down with dazzling brilliancy upon the ghastly white ledges, which, rising like a wall above the solitary cabin before me, thrust out their jagged edges as if to forbid further progress. Out of this glittering precipice dead trees stretched huge antlers. This formless mass, overhanging the Half-way House, is one of the most terrific sights of the march.

But what a frightful silence! Not a murmur, not a rustling leaf, but all as still as death. I was half afraid.

At my feet yawned the measureless void of the Great Gulf, torn from the entrails of the mountain by Titanic hands. Crevassed with wide splits, encompassed round by lofty mountain walls, the gorge was at once fascinating and forbidding, grand yet terrible. The high encircling steeps of Clay and Jefferson, Adams and Madison, inclosing the ravine in one mighty sweep, ascended out of its depths, and stretched along the sky, which really seemed receding before their daring advance. Peering over into the abyss, where the tallest pines were shrubs, and the stark trunks needles, the earth seemed split to its centre, and the feet of these mountains rooted in the midst. Above my head, forming the nearer wall of the gulf, leaped up the endless pile of the great dome.

From my next halting-place I perceived that I had been traversing a promontory of the mountain, jutting out into the Great Gulf; and on looking down over the parapet wall, a mile or more of the road uncoiled its huge folds, turning hither and thither, doubling upon itself like a bewildered serpent, but always gaining a little upon the mountain. This is one of the strangest sights of this strange journey; but in order to appreciate it at its full value, one should be descending by the stagecoach, when the danger, more apparent than real, is intensified by the swift descent of the mountain into the gulf below, over which the traveller sees himself suspended, with feelings more poignant than agreeable. But, as one of the most experienced drivers said to me before the lamentable accident of last year, "there should be no fooling, no chaffing, and no drinking on that road."

Thus far I had encountered little snow, though the rocks were crusted with ice from the time I stepped out of the forest upon the waste of granite, into a colder region. But now a sudden turning brought me full upon an enormous bank, completely blocking the roadway, which here skirted the edge of a high precipice. Had a sentinel suddenly barred my way with his bayonet, I could not have been more astonished. I was brought to a dead stand.

I looked over the parapet, then at the snow-bank, then at the mountain against which it had lodged, and which here was only a continuation of the precipice, bent slightly back from the perpendicular, and ascending several hundred feet higher. The first look made me shudder; the second made me thoughtful; the third gave me the headache.

When a thing is to be done, the best way is to do it. I therefore tried the snow, and finding a solid foot-hold, resolved to venture. Had it been soft, I should not have dared. Using my umbrella as an alpenstock, I crossed the parapet where the declivity was the least, without accident, but slowly and breathlessly until near the opposite side, when I passed the intervening space in two bounds, alighting in the road with the blood tingling to my finger-ends.

A sharp turn around a ledge, and the southeast wall of Tuckerman's Ravine rose up like a wraith out of the forest. Here is a most enchanting view of the valleys of the Ellis and the Saco. Turning now my back upon these familiar scenes, the way led in the opposite direction, and I began to look over the depression between Clay and Jefferson into the world of blue peaks beyond. From here the striking spectacle of the four great northern peaks, their naked summits, their sides ploughed by old and new crevasses, and flecked with snow, towering above the ravine, confronted me. The terrible rents in the side of Clay; the blasted firs leaning over the abyss, and clutching the rocks with a death-gripe; the rocks themselves, tormented, formidable, impending—astound by their vivid portrayal of the formless, their suggestions of the agony in which these mountains were brought forth.

I was now fairly upon the broad grass-grown slope at the foot of the pinnacle. The low peak of black rocks rising upon its limits is a monument to the fatal temerity of a traveller who, having climbed, as he supposed, to the top of the mountain, died from hunger or exposure, or both,

SIGNAL SERVICE STATION, MOUNT WASHINGTON.

at this inhospitable spot. A skeleton in rags was found at the end of a year huddled under some rocks. Farther down, Dr. Ball, of Boston, was rescued, after having passed two nights upon the mountain without food, shelter, or fire, and after as many days of fruitless wandering up and down. More dead than alive, he was supported down the mountain as far as the Ledge. His re-appearance at the Glen House had the effect of one risen from the dead. In reality, the rescuing party took up with them materials for a rude bier, expecting to find a dead body stiffening in the snow.

While traversing the plateau, with the Summit House in full view, my eye caught, far above me, the figure of a man pacing up and down before the building, like a sentinel on his post. I swung my hat—again—but he did not see me. Nevertheless, I experienced a thrill of pleasure at seeing this man, so acutely had the feeling of loneliness come over me in these awful solitudes.

In half an hour I crossed the last rise, when the solitary pedestrian, making an about-face at the end of his beat, suddenly discovered a strange form and figure emerging from the rocks before him. He stopped short, took the pipe from his teeth, and then, as I continued to approach, he hastened toward me, met me half way, and between rapid questions and answers led the way into the signal station.

While I was resting, my host bustled about the two or three apartments constituting this swallow's nest. He put the kettle on the stove, gave the fire a stir, spread a cloth upon the table, took some plates, cups, and saucers from a locker, some canned meats from a cupboard, I, meanwhile, following all these movements with an interest easily imagined. His preparations completed, my host first ran his eye over them approvingly, then, with perfect politeness, begged me to draw my chair to the table and fall to. I did not refuse. While he poured out the tea, I asked, "Whom have I the pleasure of addressing?"

And he modestly replied: "Private Doyle, sir, of the United States Signal Service. Have another bit of deviled ham? No? Try these peaches."

"Thank you. At least Uncle Sam renders your exile tolerable. Is this your ordinary fare?"

"Oh! as to that, you should see us in the dead of winter, chopping our frozen meat with a hatchet, and our lard with a chisel."

This, then, was what my young Jehu had meant. Where was I? I glanced out of the window. Nothing but sky;

nothing but rocks. Immensity and desolation. I disposed my ideas to hear my companion ask, "What is the news from the other world?"

After the repast we walked out upon the narrow platform behind the house. According to every appearance I had reached Ultima Thule.

All seemed chaos. On every side the great mountains fell away like mists of the morning, dispersing, receding to an endless distance, diminishing, growing more and more vague, and finally vanishing in a limitless horizon, neither earth nor sky. Never before had such a spectacle offered itself to my gaze. The first idea was of standing upon the threshold of another planet, looking down upon this world of ours outspread beneath. For an instant, thinking of eternity, the imagination recoiled in terror.

INTERIOR OF SIGNAL SERVICE STATION DURING A STORM.

LAKE OF THE CLOUDS AND PEAK OF MONROE.

But by degrees order came out of this chaos. The bewildering throng of mountains arranged itself in chains, clusters, or families. Hills drew apart, valleys opened, streams twinkled in the sun, towns and villages clung to the skirts of the mountains or dotted the rich meadows; but all was mysterious, all as yet unreal.

Comprehending at last that all New England was under my feet, I began to search out certain landmarks. But this investigation is fatiguing. Besides, it conducts to nothing, absolutely nothing. Pointing to a scrap of blue haze in the west, my companion observed, "That is Mount Mansfield," and I mechanically repeated, "Ah, is that Mount Mansfield ?" It sufficed for me, God knows, to be admitted near the person of the great autocrat of New England, while under skies so fair and radiant he gave audience to his imposing and splendid retinue of mountains.

I consider this first introduction to what the peak of Mount Washington looks down upon an epoch in any man's life. I saw the whole noble company of mountains from highest to lowest. I saw the deep depressions through which the Connecticut, the Merrimac, the Saco, and the Androscoggin wind toward the lowlands. I saw the lakes which nurse the infant tributaries of these streams. I saw the great Northern forests, the notched wall of the Green Mountains, the wide expanse of level land, flat and heavy like the ocean, and finally the ocean itself. And all this was mingled in one mighty scene.

While looking down from this eagle's nest upon the southern peaks to where the bridle-path could be distinctly traced across the plateau, and still winding on around the peaked crest of Monroe, my eye caught the sparkle of water underneath this mountain.

What a sight for the rock-wearied eye was this little alpine tarn, this Lake of the Clouds, cuddled close to the hairy breast of the granite peak! On the instant the prevailing gloom was lighted, as if by magic, by this dainty nursling of the clouds, which seemed innocently smiling in the face of the hideous mountain. And the stooping monster seemed to regard the little waif, lying there in its rocky cradle, with astonishment, and to forego his first impulse to strangle it where it lay. Lion and lamb were lying down together.

Noticing that the sides of the summit were strewed with boards, beams, and débris of all sorts, my guide explained that what I saw was the result of the great January gale, which had demolished the large shed used as an engine-house, scattering the loose fragments far and wide. I begged him to give me his recollection of it.

"During the forenoon preceding the gale we observed nothing very unusual; but the clouds kept sinking and sinking until the summit was quite above them. Late in the afternoon my comrade, Sergeant M——, came to where I was lying abed sick, and said, 'There is going to be the devil to pay, so I guess I'll make everything snug.'

"By nine in the evening the wind had increased to one hundred miles an hour, with heavy sleet. At midnight the velocity of the storm was one hundred and twenty miles, and the exposed thermometer recorded twenty-four degrees below zero. With the stove red, we could hardly get it above freezing inside the house. Water froze within three feet of the fire— in fact, where you are now sitting.

"At this time the noise outside was deafening. About one o'clock the wind rose to one hundred and fifty miles. It was now blowing a hurricane. The wind, gathering up all the loose ice of the mountain, dashed it against the house with one continued roar. I lay wondering how long the building would stand this, when all at once came a crash. M—— shouted to me to get up; but I had tumbled out in a hurry on hearing the glass go. You see, I was dressed, to keep myself warm, in bed.

"Our united efforts were hardly equal to closing the storm shutters from the inside, but we finally succeeded, though the lights went out when the wind came in, and we worked in the dark."

He rose to show me how the shutters, of thick oak, were first secured by an iron bar, and secondly by strong wooden buttons firmly screwed in the window-frame.

"We had scarcely done this," resumed Doyle, "and were shivering over the fire, when a heavy grist of wind again burst open the shutters, as easily as if they had never been fastened at all. We sprang to our feet. After a hard tussle we again secured the windows, by nailing a cleat to the floor, against which one end of a board was fixed, using the other end as a lever. You understand ?" I nodded. "Well, even then it was all we could do to force the shutters back into place. But we did it. We had to do it.

"The rest of the night was passed in momentary expectation that the building would be blown into Tuckerman's, and we with it. At four in the morning the wind registered one hundred and eighty-six miles. It had shifted then from east to northeast. From this time it steadily fell to ten miles, at nine o'clock. This was the biggest blow ever experienced on the mountain."

"Suppose the house had gone, and the hotel stood fast, could you have effected an entrance into the hotel?" I asked.

"We could not have faced the gale."

"Not for a hundred feet? not in a matter of life and death?"

"Impossible. The wind would have lifted us from our feet like bags of wool. We would have been dashed against the rocks, and smashed like egg-shells," was the quiet reply.

"And so for some hours you expected to be swept into eternity?"

"We did what we could. Each wrapped himself in blankets and quilts, binding these tightly around him with ropes, to which were attached bars of iron, so that if the house went by the board, we might stand a chance—a slim one—of anchoring somewhere, somehow."

Somewhere, indeed!

When, on the following morning, I busied myself getting ready to go down the mountain, I heard a profound sigh, followed by some half-audible words, proceeding from the adjoining room. These words rang in my ears all that day:

"Ah, this horrible solitude!"

THE WHITE MOUNTAINS.

PART III.

A SON of Erin is said to have exclaimed, on seeing the White Mountains for the first time, "Bedad, there is, then, so much waste land in America that they have to stack it!" Could these mountains be levelled, and the materials they contain be spread out, a vast area would be gained, at the price of reducing New England to a desert. We are therefore content that there is not enough faith in the world, at least since the day of the apostles, to say unto these mountains, "Remove!"

In the language of the great French poet, and without more ceremony, once more,

"Levons les yeux vers les saintes montagnes."

Plymouth, in New Hampshire, lies at the entrance to the Pemigewasset Valley like an encampment pitched to dispute its passage. At present its design is to facilitate the ingress of tourists. A single glance at the map will suffice to show its strategic importance.

Perhaps it is scarcely remembered that Nathaniel Hawthorne breathed his last in this village on the night of May 18, 1864. He who was born in sight of these mountains had come among them to die.

At three in the afternoon I set out for Campton, seven miles up the valley, which the carriage road soon enters upon, and which, by a few unregarded turnings, is presently as fast shut up as if its mountain gates had in reality swung noiselessly together behind you. Hardly had I recovered from the effect of the deception produced by seeing the same mountain first upon one side, then upon the other, when I saw, spanned by a high bridge, the river in violent commotion below me. The Pemigewasset, confined here between narrow banks, has cut for itself two deep channels through its craggy and cavernous bed; but one of these being dammed for the purpose of deepening the other, the general picturesqueness of the

BLACK AND TRIPYRAMID MOUNTAINS,
FROM CAMPTON.

fall is greatly diminished. Still, it is a pretty and engaging sight, this cataract, especially if the river be full, although you think of a mettled Arabian harnessed in a tread-mill when you look at it. Livermore Fall, as it is called, is but two miles from Plymouth, the white houses of which look hot in the same brilliant sunlight that falls so gently upon the luxuriant green of the valley. Half a mile below the little village of West Campton, the road crossed the point of a spur thrust well out into the valley from the mountain. It is here that the circlet of mountains inclosing it on all sides like a gigantic palisade is first seen. Dimmed by distance, surrounded by an atmosphere deliciously tender, clothed with poetic feeling, we now see the great clump of granite spires, the family of grand peaks, dividing with Mount Washington and his distinguished compeers the honor of keeping watch and ward over New England. We salute these venerable towers from afar, before beginning a last pilgrimage

FRANCONIA NOTCH, FROM THORNTON.

into the domain exclusively their own.

The vista of mountains on the east side becomes every moment more and more extended and more and more interesting. The beautiful valley is now open throughout its whole extent. Green as a carpet, level as a floor, the valley, adorned with clumps of elms, groves of maples, strips of tilled land of a rich chocolate brown, makes altogether a picture which sets the eye fairly dancing. Even the daisies, the clover so plentifully spangling the green meadows, the buttercups gleaming like patches of sunshine, seem far brighter and sweeter in this atmosphere, and nod a playful welcome as we pass them by. It is not clothed with a feeling of overpowering grandeur, this valley, but it is beautiful. It is not terrible, but bewitching.

In one place, far away to the north, the

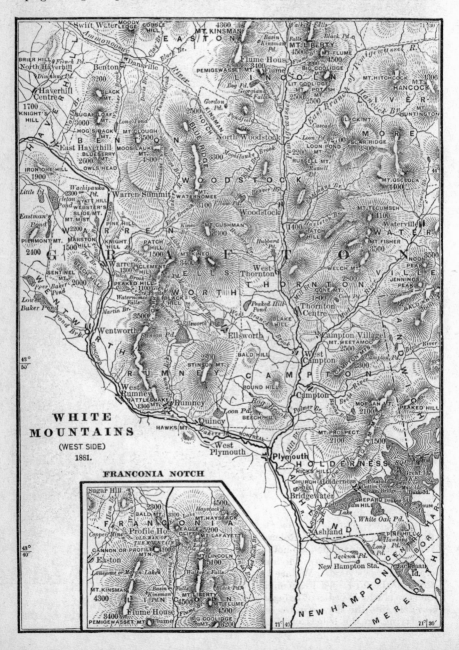

WHITE MOUNTAINS

(WEST SIDE)
1881.

FRANCONIA NOTCH

wall of mountains
is shattered down
to its centre, like
the famous Breach of Roland, and
through this enormous loop-hole we see
golden mists rising above the undiscovered country beyond.   We are looking
through the far-famed Franconia Notch.   On one
side the clustered peaks of Lafayette lift themselves
serenely into the sky.   On the left, a silvery light
is playing on the ledges of Mount Cannon, soft-

WELCH MOUNTAIN, FROM MAD RIVER,
COMPTON.

ening all the asperities of this stern-visaged mountain. The two great groups stand fully and finely exposed, though the lower and nearer summits are blended with the higher by distance. Remark the difference of outline. A series of humps distinguishes the crest line of the group, culminating in the oblique wall of Cannon or Profile Mountain. On the contrary, that on the right, culminating in Lafayette, presents two beautiful and regular pyramids, older than Cheops, which sometimes in early morning exactly resemble two monuments springing alert and vigorous as the day which gilds them. This exquisite landscape seldom fails of producing a rapturous outburst from those who are making the journey for the first time.

Looking now across the valley, we distinguish the deep trough through which Mad River descends from the mountains of Waterville. Peering over the nearer elevations, surmounting its valley, the huge blue-black mass of Black Mountain flings two splendid peaks aloft.

Having dedicated one day to an exploration of the Mad River Valley, I can pronounce it well worth any tourist's while to tarry long enough in the vicinity for the purpose. Fording the river, and ascending the opposite slopes, we come at once upon one of those villages that seem retreating from civilization rather than illustrating its advance. Campton Village completely fills the artistic sense. The environment of mountains is so perfect that one might pass and repass the Pemigewasset Valley a hundred times without once suspecting its existence. The colossal mass of Black Mountain, a veritable black giant, with a nipple, a pyramid, and a flattened mound protruding from its summit, and greedily absorbing the sunlight, towers above us four thousand feet. For nearly ten miles its unbroken wall forms one side of the valley of Mad River, which is there far down below us, although we do not see it. Between this mountain and the next a rough and broken pass communicates with Sandwich and the upper lake region. In fact, this is the mountain which Professor Arnold Guyot calls Sandwich Dome.

The end of the valley was reached in two hours of very leisurely driving. The road now abruptly terminates among a handful of houses scattered about the bottom of a deep and narrow vale. This glen, known to comparatively few by the name of Greeley's, is surrounded by peaks that for boldness, savage freedom, and power of statuesque expression challenge any that we can remember. They threaten while maintaining an attitude of lofty scorn for the saucy and intruding hamlet planted upon their big feet. Noon Peak—we are at length at the end of the almost endless Black Mountain—nods familiarly from the south. Tecumseh—a noble mountain—and Osceola rise to the north.

Our space is inadequate to further delineation of this little visited but most enticing mountain nook. To sum up the whole experience, the Mad River drive is a delightful episode. In the way of mountain valley there is nothing like it. Bold crag, lonely cabin, blue peak, deep hollows choked up with the densest foliage, and resounding with the roar of an unchained torrent, constitute its varied and ever-changing features.

The remainder of the route up the Pemigewasset Valley is more and more a revelation of the august summits that have so constantly met us since entering this lovely vestibule of the Franconia Mountains. Emerging one by one from the mass, they present themselves at every mile in new combinations. Through Thornton and Woodstock the view is scarcely interrupted. Gradually the finely pointed peaks of the Lafayette group deploy and advance toward us. Now they pitch sharply down into the valley of the East Branch; now the great shafts of stone are crusted with silvery light, or sprayed with the cataract; now the sun gilds the slides that furrow but do not deface them. Stay a moment at this rapid brook that comes from the west. It is an envoy from yonder great billowy mountain that lords it so proudly over

"many a nameless slide-scarred crest
And pine-dark gorge between."

That is Moosehillock, or Moosilauke, wrapped in imperturbable repose. Facing again the north, the road is soon swallowed up by the forest, and the forest by the mountains. A few poor cottages skirt the route. Still ascending, the miles grow longer and less interesting, until the white house, first seen from far below, suddenly stands uncovered at the left. We are at the Flume House, and before the gates of the Franconia Notch.

The Flume House is the proper tarrying-place for an investigation of the mountain gorge from which it derives both its custom and its name. It is also the hardest marble with sand and water. Cliffs, traversed and cicatrized by cracks and rents, rise a hundred feet higher. The water is a glossy and lustrous sea-

THE BASIN.

green, and of such marvellous transparency that you see the brilliant and variegated pebbles with which the bottom is paved, respond, as in the turn of a kaleidoscope, to the waves of light constantly moving across the surface,

placed *vis-à-vis* the Pool, another of the natural wonders with which the pass is crowded, and which tempt us at every step to turn aside from the travelled road.

This Pool is a caprice of the river, here hemmed in between steep-sided mountains. Imagine a cistern deeply sunk in granite receiving at one end a weary cascade which seems craving a moment's respite before hurrying on down the rocky pass. In the mystery and seclusion of ages, and with only the rude implements picked up by the way—a stray bowlder and a little sand—the river has hollowed a basin a hundred feet wide and forty deep out of the stubborn rock. Without doubt nature thus first taught us how to cut

gently agitated by the cascade. Overtopping trees lean timidly out, and peer down into the Pool, which coldly repulses their shadows. Only the colorless hue of the rocks is reflected, and the stranger, seeing an old man with a gray beard standing erect in a boat, has no other idea than that he has arrived on the borders and is to be accosted by the ferryman of Hades.

The Flume is a remarkable rock gallery driven several hundred feet into the heart of the mountain, through which an ice-cold brook rushes. The miracle of Moses seems repeated here sublimely. You approach over broad ledges of freckled granite, polished by the constant flow of a thin, pellucid sheet of water to slippery smoothness. Proceeding a short distance up this natural esplanade, you enter a damp and gloomy fissure between perpendicular walls, rising seventy feet above the stream, and on lifting your eyes, suddenly espy an enormous bowlder tightly wedged between the cliffs. Now try to imagine a force capable of grasping the solid rock, and dividing it in halves as easily as you would an apple with your two hands!

At sight of the suspended bowlder, which seems like Paul Pry to have "just dropped in," I believe every visitor has not omit to find a moral in this curiosity, which really looks to be on the eve of dropping, with a loud splash, into the torrent beneath. On top of the cliffs I picked up a visiting-card, on which some one with a poetic turn had written, "Does not this bowlder remind you of the sword of Damocles?" To a civil question, civil reply: No; to me it looks like a nut in a cracker.

Over the gorge bends an arcade of interlaced foliage, shot through and through with sunlight; underneath, the swollen torrent storms along, dashing itself against

THE OLD MAN OF THE MOUNTAIN.

his moment of hesitation, which he usually ends by passing underneath, paying as he goes with a tremor of the nerves, more or less, for his temerity. But there is no danger. It is seen that the deep crevice, into which the rock seems jammed with the special purpose of holding it asunder, hugs the intruder like a vise—so closely, indeed, that, according to every appearance, it must stay where it is until Doomsday, unless released by some passing earthquake. Sentimental tourists do protruding bowlders, or else passing them with a curl of disdain. The cold granite walls are constantly wet with tiny streams that do not run but glide unperceived down, furnishing sustenance to ferns, trailing vines, mosses, delicate flowers, that cling or droop along the craggy way. Nothing could be more cunning than to see these hardy little waifs thus extorting a subsistence from the rocks which nourish them in spite of themselves. The sight of the gorge with the torrent foaming far below, the glitter of falling waters through the trees, the splendid light in the midst of deepest gloom, the solemn pines, the odorous forest, the wildness, and the coolness—impart an indescribable charm. Ladies ascend to the head of the gorge, and perform the feat of crossing on a fallen tree that makes a crazy bridge from cliff to cliff. One, I noticed, had left her pocket-handkerchief, with the scent fresh upon it, and her initials in a corner. I picked it up, and out hopped a toad.

I left the Flume House in company with a young-old man whom I met there, and in whom I hoped to find another and surer pair of eyes, for were he to have as many as Argus, the sight-seer would find employment for them all.

While gayly threading the greenwood, we came upon a miniature edition of the Pool, situated close to the highway, called the Basin. A basin, in fact, it is, and a bath fit for the gods. A cascade falls into it with hollow roar. It has been worn by the rotary motion of large pebbles, which the little cascade, pouring down into it from above, set and kept actively whirling and grinding, until what was at first a mere depression became as we now see it. Long and constant attrition only could have scooped this cavity out of the granite, which is here so clean, smooth, and white, and filled to the brim with a grayish emerald water, light, limpid, and incessantly replenished by the effervescent cascade. But the really curious feature of the Basin is a strip of granite projecting into it, which closely resembles a human leg and foot luxuriously cooling itself in the stream.

We are still advancing in this region of wonders. In our front soars an insuperable mass of forest-tufted rock. Behind it rises the absolutely regal Lafayette. Our footsteps are stayed by the glimmer of water through the trees. We have reached the summit of the pass.

Six miles of continual ascent have brought us to Profile Lake. Although a pretty enough piece of water, it is not for itself this lake is resorted to by the thousand, or for the trout which you take for the reflection of birds on its burnished surface, but for the mountain rising high above, whose wooded slopes it so faithfully mirrors. Now lift the eyes to the bare summit. It is difficult to believe the evidence of the senses. Upon the high cliffs of this mountain is the remarkable and celebrated natural rock-sculpture of a human head, which, from a height twelve hundred feet above the lake, has for uncounted ages looked with the same stony stare down the pass upon the windings of the river through its incomparable valley. The profile itself measures about forty feet from the tip of the chin to the flattened crown, which imparts to it such a peculiarly antique appearance. It is perfect, except that the forehead is concealed by something like the visor of a helmet. And all this illusion is produced by several projecting crags. It might be said to have been begotten by a thunder-bolt.

Taking a seat within a rustic arbor on the high shore of the lake, one is at liberty to peruse at leisure what, I dare say, is the most extraordinary sight of a lifetime. A slight change of position varies more or less the character of the expression, which is, after all, the marked peculiarity of this monstrous alto-relievo; for, let the spectator turn his gaze vacantly upon the more familiar objects at hand, as he inevitably will, to assure himself that he is not the victim of some strange hallucination, a fascination born neither of admiration nor horror, but strongly partaking of both emotions, draws him irresistibly back to the Dantesque head stuck like a felon's on the highest battlements of the pass. The more you may have seen, the more your feelings are disciplined, the greater the confusion of ideas. The moment is come to acknowledge yourself vanquished. This is not merely a face, it is a portrait. That is not the work of some cunning chisel, but a cast from a living head. You feel and will always maintain that those features have had a living and breathing counterpart. Nothing more, nothing less.

But where and what was the original prototype? Not man; since ages before he was created the chisel of the Almighty wrought this sculpture upon the rock above us. No, not man; the face is too majestic, too nobly grand, for anything of mortal mould. One of the antique gods may, perhaps, have sat for this archetype of the coming man. And yet not man, we think, for the head will surely hold the same strange converse with futurity when man shall have vanished from the face of the earth.

Had Byron visited this place of awe and mystery, his "Manfred," the scene of which is laid among the mountains of

ON THE PROFILE ROAD.

the Bernese Alps, would doubtless have had a deeper, perhaps
a more sinister, impulse; but
even among those eternal realms
of ice the poet never beheld an
object that could so arouse the
gloomy exaltation he has breathed into that tragedy. His line,

"Bound to earth, he lifts his eye to heaven,"

becomes descriptive here.

This gigantic silhouette, which has
been christened the Old Man of the

Mountain, is unquestionably the greatest curiosity of this or any other mountain region. It is unique. But it is not merely curious; nor is it more marvellous for the wonderful accuracy of outline than for the almost superhuman expression of frozen terror it eternally fixes on the vague and shadowy distance—a far-away look, an intense and

MOUNT CANNON, FROM EAGLE CLIFF.

speechless amazement, such as sometimes settles upon the faces of the dying, untranslatable into words, but seeming to declare the presence of some unutterable

CLOUD EFFECT ON MOUNT LAFAYETTE,
FROM BRIDLE-PATH.

vision too bright and dazzling for mortal eyes to behold. The face puts the whole world behind it. It does everything but speak—nay, you are ready to swear that it is going to speak. And so this chance jumbling together of a few stones has produced a sculpture before which Art hangs her head.

I renounce in dismay the idea of reproducing on the reader's mind the effect which this prodigy produced on my own. Impressions more pronounced, yet at the same time more inexplicable, have never so effectually overcome that habitual self-command derived from many experiences of travel among strange and unaccustomed scenes. The face is so amazing that I have often tried to imagine the sensations of him who first discovered it peering from the mountain-top with such absorbed, open-mouthed wonder. Again, I see the tired Indian hunter, pausing to slake his thirst by the lake-side, start as his gaze suddenly encounters this terrific apparition. I fancy the half-uttered exclamation sticking in his throat. I behold him standing there, with bated breath, not daring to stir either hand or foot, his white lips parted, his scared eyes dilated, until his own swarthy features exactly reflect that unearthly, that intense amazement, stamped large and vivid upon the livid rock. And in this immovable human figure I see the living counterpart of the great stone face.

The novelist Hawthorne makes this Sphinx of the White Mountains the interpreter of a noble life. For him the Titanic countenance is radiant with majestic benignity. He endows it with a soul, surrounds the colossal brow with the halo of spiritual grandeur, and marshalling his train of phantoms, proceeds to pass inexorable judgment upon them one by one.

At noon we reached the spacious and inviting Profile House, which is hid away in a deep and narrow glen nearly two thousand feet above the sea. No situation could be more sequestered or more charming. The place seems stolen from the unkempt wilderness that shuts it in. An oval grassy plain, not extensive, but bright and smiling, spreads its green between a grisly precipice and a shaggy mountain. And there, if you will believe me, in front of the long white-columned hotel, like a Turkish rug on a carpet, was a pretty flower garden. Like those flowers, on the lawn were beauties sauntering up and down in exquisite morning toilets, coquetting with their bright-colored parasols, and now and then glancing up at the grim old mountains with that air of elegant disdain which is so redoubtable a weapon even in the mountains. Little children fluttered about the grass like beautiful butterflies, and as unmindful of the terrors that hovered over them so threateningly. Nurses in their stiff grenadier caps and white aprons,

lackeys in livery, cadets in uniform, elegant equipages, blooded horses, dainty shapes on horseback, cavaliers, and last, but not least, the resolute pedestrian or the gentlemen strollers up and down the shady road, made up a scene which, being where it is, first strikes us as odd in the extreme, but which we soon adapt ourselves to and are reconciled with, because we see that for each in his way it is good to be here. The rich man may enter the White Mountains.

Peals of laughter startle the solemn old woods. You hear them high up the mountain-side. There go a pair of lovers, the gentleman with his book, whose most telling passages he has carefully conned, the lady with some trifle of embroidery, over which she bends lower as he reads on. Ah, happy days! What is this youth which, having it, we are so eager to escape, and when it is gone we look back upon with such infinite longing?

The lofty crag opposite the hotel is Eagle Cliff—a name at once legitimate and satisfying, although it is no longer tenanted by the eagles formerly making their home in the security of its precipitous rocks. In simple parlance it is an advanced spur of Mount Lafayette. The high curving wall of this cliff incloses on one side the glen, while Mount Cannon forms the other. Bald Mountain is seen to the north. The precipices tower so far above the glen that large trees look like shrubs. Here and there, among thick-set evergreen trees, beech and birch and maples spread a drapery of rich green, and mottle it with softness. The purple rock bulges daringly out, forming a parapet of adamant. The black giant distends his enormous chest until we see the iron ribs, huge and gaunt, protruding.

The turf underneath the cliff was most beautifully and profusely spangled with the delicate pink anemone, the *fleur des fées*, that pale darling of our New England woods to which the arbutus resigns the sceptre of spring. It is a moving sight to see these little drooping flowerets, so shy and modest, yet so meek and trustful, growing at the foot of a bare and sterile rock. The face hardened looking up, grew soft looking down. "Don't tread on us! May not a flower look up at a mountain?" they seem to plead. Lightly fall the night dews upon your upturned faces, dear little flowers! Soft be the sunshine and gentle the winds that kiss

ECHO LAKE AND EAGLE CLIFF.

those sky-tinted cheeks! In thy sweet purity and innocence I see faces that are beneath the sod, flowers that have blossomed in paradise.

We see, also, from the hotel, the singular rock that occasioned the change of name from Profile to Cannon mountain. It really resembles a piece of artillery protruding threateningly from the parapet of a fortress.

Taking one of the well-worn paths conducting to the water-side—for another lovely mountain tarn is hidden by yonder fringe of trees—a short walk finds us standing by the shore of Echo Lake, with Eagle Cliff now rising grandly on our right.

Nowhere among the White Hills is there a fuller realization of a mountain lakelet. The high peak of Lafayette, covered with snow, looked down into it with freezing stare. Cannon Mountain now showed his retreating wall on the right. The huge castellated rampart of Eagle Cliff lifted on its borders precipices dripping with moisture, glistening in the sun like aerial casements. Light flaws frosted the lake with silver. Sharp keels

cut it as diamonds cut glass. The water is so transparent that you see fishes swimming or floating indolently about. Without the lake the whole aspect would be irredeemably savage and forbidding—a blind landscape; now it is instinct with a buoyant and vigorous life. In fact, it is like an eye of piercing brilliancy set deep and overhung by bushy, frowning brows. But it is not alone the eye, it is the soul of the landscape. It is dull or spirited, languid or vivacious, stern or mild, according to the varying moods of nature.

The echo adds its feats of ventriloquism. The marvel of the phonograph is but a mimicry of nature, the universal teacher. Now the man blows a strong clear blast upon a long Alpine horn, and like a bugle-call flying from camp to camp the martial signal is repeated, not once, but again and again, in waves of bewitching sweetness, and with the exquisite modulations of the wood-thrush's note. From covert to covert, now here, now there, it chants its rapturous melody. Once again it glides upon the entranced ear, and still we lean in breathless eagerness to catch the last faint cadence sighing itself away upon the palpitating air.

A cannon was then fired. The report and echo came with the flash. In a moment more a deep and hollow rumbling sound, as if the mountains were splitting their huge sides with suppressed laughter, startled us.

The ascent of Mount Lafayette fittingly crowns the series of excursions through which we have passed since leaving Plymouth. This mountain, whose splendid crest is concealed from us at the Profile House, dominates the valleys north and south with undisputed sway. It is the King of Franconia.

The climber will not fail to notice the remarkable natural causeway connecting Eagle Cliff with the mountain itself, nor omit to observe the little lakes reposing between the principal and subordinate peaks. Even those who have little inclination for the long climb to the top of the mountain ought not to miss the first, for I do not recall anything like it on this side of the great Sierras so finely typical of a mountain defile. But to do justice to this ascension I should have a chapter, and I have only a penful of ink. The fascination of being on a mountaintop has yet to be explained. Perhaps, after all, it is not susceptible of explanation.

As we come down the long three-mile descent from Echo Lake to the village of Franconia, to the level of the valley, and to the northern base of the Notch Mountains, an eminence rises to the left. This is Sugar Hill. Half way up there is a hotel, occupying a well-chosen site, and on the high ridge another commands not only this valley, but those water-courses lying to the west. Opposite to us rise the green heights of Bethlehem, Mount Agassiz conspicuous by the observatory on its summit. Between these walls the long ellipse of fertile land beckons us to descend.

Distinguished by the beautiful groves of sugar-maple that adorn it, Sugar Hill is destined to grow more and more in popular esteem. It is certainly one of the finest sites among the mountains that I have seen. No traveller should pass it by. It is so admirably placed to command all the highest mountains in one magnificent *coup d'œil*. The days are not so breathless or so stifling as they are down in the valley, because it is lifted into sun and air by an eleva-

tion sufficient to reach the cooler upper currents. You look deep into the Franconia Notch, and watch the evening shadows creep up the great east wall. Extending beyond these nearer mountains the scarcely inferior Twin summits pose themselves like gigantic athletes. But better than all, grander than all, is that kingly coronet of great mountains set on the lustrous green cushion at the head of the valley. Nowhere, I venture to predict, will the felicity of the title, "Crown of New England," receive more unanimous acceptance than from this favored spot. Especially when a canopy of clouds overspreading permits the pointed peaks to reflect the illuminated fires of sunset does the crown seem blazing with jewels and precious stones.

The Bridal Veil Fall, discovered on the northern slope of Mount Kinsman, will by-and-by attract many visitors. At present access is difficult. The height of the fall is given at seventy-six feet, and the surroundings are said to be of the most romantic and picturesque character. The name is certainly entitled to respectful consideration from its long service in connection with water-falls and cascades the world over.

The reader who has thus far followed us patiently from point to point may now form some estimate of the relative attractions of the two principal groups with which most of the subordinate mountain chains are allied. Both have their admirers, their adherents even, who grow warm in praise of the locality of their predilection. The reason why this preference can not be explained is that there is no real difference at all.

From Littleton we will first make a rapid retrograde movement to the western border of the mountains, having now again reached the railway line by which we might have come directly from Plymouth, had we not, in a fortunate moment, decided in favor of first exploring the Pemigewasset Valley. The configuration of the country is such that this railway is compelled to make a long detour. We will now, therefore, run down the rail as far as Wells River. Here we behold that most noble and interesting entrance formed by the meeting of the Ammonoosuc with the Connecticut.

But we can not linger here, though tempted to do so. We proceed on our way up the Ammonoosuc Valley, which

MOUNT LAFAYETTE, FROM BETHLEHEM.

so abounds in picturesque details—farms, hamlets, herds, groups of pines, maples, torrents, roads feeling their way up the heights—to that anomaly of mountain towns, Bethlehem.

Bethlehem is ranged high up along the side of a mountain, like the best china in a cupboard. Mount Agassiz rises behind it. Below the village the ground descends rather abruptly to the Ammonoosuc, which winds through matted woods its way out of the mountains.

But there are here none of those eye-catching gleams of water which so agreeably diversify these interminable leagues of forest and mountain land.

In the valley of the Aar, at the head of the Aar Glacier, in Switzerland, is a peak named for Agassiz, who thus has two enduring monuments, one in his native, one in his adopted, land.

Bethlehem has arisen, almost by magic, at the point where the old highway up

VIEW FROM ETHAN CRAWFORD'S, JEFFERSON.

the Ammonoosuc is intersected by that coming from Plymouth. In time a small road-side hamlet clustered about the spot. Dr. Timothy Dwight, one of the earliest as well as one of the most observant travellers here, speaks of the appearance of Bethlehem in 1803. "There is," he says, "nothing in Bethlehem which merits notice except the patience, enterprise, and hardihood of the settlers, which have induced them to stay upon so forbidding a spot, a magnificent prospect of the White Mountains, and a splendid collection of other mountains in their neighborhood, particularly in the southwest." It was then reached by one wretched road, passing the Ammonoosuc by a dangerous ford. The few scattered habitations were mere log-cabins, rough and rude. The few planting fields were still covered with dead trees, stark and forbidding, which the settlers, unable to fell with the axe, killed by girdling, as the Indians did.

From this historical picture of Bethlehem in the past we turn to the Bethlehem of to-day. It is turning from the post-rider to the locomotive. Not a single feature is recognizable except the splendid prospect of the White Mountains and the magnificent collection of other mountains in the neighborhood. Fortunate geographical position, salubrity, fine scenery —these features, and these alone, are the legitimate cause of what may be termed the rise and progress of Bethlehem. All that the original settlers seem to have accomplished is to clear away the forests which intercepted, and to make the road conducting to, the view.

It does seem at first almost incredible that the two or three houses, the store, the solitary meeting-house, of those days should suddenly become the most populous and most frequented of mountain resorts. This newness, which you at first resent, besides introducing here and there some attempt at architectural adornment, contrasts very agreeably with the ill-built, rambling, and slipshod appearance of the older village centres. They are invaria-

CASTELLATED RIDGE, MOUNT
JEFFERSON.

bly most picturesque from a distance.   But here there
is an evident effort to render the place itself attractive
by rendering it beautiful.   Good taste generally prevails.   I suspect, however, that the era of good taste,
beginning with the incoming of a more refined and intelligent
class of travellers, communicated its spirit to two or three enterprising and sagacious men, who saw in what nature had done an
incentive to their own efforts.   We walk here in a broad, well-
built thoroughfare, skirted on both sides with modern cottages,
in which four or five thousand sojourners annually take refuge.   All this has grown
from the one small hotel of a dozen years ago.   An immense horizon is visible from
these houses.   The landscape swarms with mountains, although neither of the great
ranges is in sight from the thickly settled district called "The Street."   One is hid
by the curvature of the mountain, which also intercepts the view of the other.

Even the sultriest summer days are rendered tolerable here by the light airs set in motion by the oppressive heats of the valley. The hottest season is therefore no bar to out-of-door exercise for persons of average health. But in the evening all these houses are emptied of their occupants. The whole village is out-of-doors enjoying the coolness, or the panorama, with all the zest unconstrained gratification always brings. The multitudes of well-dressed promenaders surprise every new-comer, who immediately thinks of Saratoga or Newport, and their social characteristics, *minus* their so-called "style" and fussy consequentialness. These people really seem to be enjoying themselves; you are left in doubt as to the others. Bethlehem, we think, should be the ideal of those who would carry city—or at least suburban—life among the mountains, who do not care a fig for solitude, but prefer to find their pleasures still closely associated with their home life. They are seeing life and seeing nature at one and the same time. Between this and that aspect of life among mountains and what is to be derived from it there is the same difference that exists between a well-conducted picnic, where the ladies wear their prettiest dresses, and everything is perfectly *comme il faut*, and the abandon and unconstraint of camp life, where the ladies wear blue flannels, which the men think so becoming. One class of travellers takes its world along with its trunks, the other is bent on discovering a new one. Which is nearer Eden? *Chacun à son goût.*

A strikingly large and beautiful prospect opens as we come to the Belleview. Here the road, making its exit from the village, descends to the Ammonoosuc. Six hundred feet below us the bottom of the valley exhibits its rich savannas, interspersed with cottages and groves. The valley broadens and deepens, exposing to view all the town of Littleton, picturesquely scattered about the distant hillsides. Above this deep hollow, the Green Mountains glimmer in the far west. "Ah!" you say, "we will stop here."

A second ramble to the top of the mountain by the old road to Franconia reveals in the most striking manner possible the grandeur of those mountains through which we have just come. A third is altogether indispensable before we can say we know Bethlehem. We continue along the high plateau to the eastern skirt of the village. No envious hill now obstructs the truly "magnificent view." Through the open valley the lordly mountains again inthrall us with the might of an overpowering majesty. This locality has taken the name of the great hotel erected here by Isaac Cruft, whose hand is everywhere visible in Bethlehem. It is known as the Maplewood, in distinction to the more central portion clustered around the Sinclair House.

Bethlehem is emphatically the place of sunsets. In this respect no other mountain haunt can pretend to rival it. From no other village are so many mountains visible at once; at no other has the landscape such length and breadth for giving full effect to these truly wonderful displays. I have seen some here that may never be repeated, certainly never excelled, while the sun, the heavens, and the mountains shall last.

Like Bethlehem, Jefferson lies reposing in mid-ascent of a mountain. Here the resemblance ends. The mountain above it is higher, the valley beneath more open, permitting an unimpeded view up and down. The hill-side, upon which the clump of hotels is situated, makes no steep plunge into the valley, but inclines gently down to the banks of the river. Instead of crowding upon and jostling each other, the mountains forming opposite sides of this valley remain tranquilly in the alignment they were commanded not to overstep. The confusion there is reduced to admirable order here. The smooth slopes, the clean lines, the ample views, the roominess, so to speak, of the landscape, indicate that everything has been done without haste, with precision, and without deviation from the original plan, which contemplated a paradise upon earth.

On the north side Starr King Mountain rises 2400 feet above the valley, and 3800 feet above the sea. On the south side Cherry Mountain lifts itself 3670 feet higher than tide-level. The village lies on the southern slope of the former mountain. These two summits form the broad basin through which Israel's River flows for more than half its length, after issuing from the wasted side of Mount Adams. Here again, and as at Bethlehem, only arranged in a strikingly different and unique order, at the head of the valley,

MOUNT WASHINGTON RAILWAY.

we have the great range.   Madison now stands
a little thrown back on the right, Adams next
erects his sharp lance, Jefferson his shining crescent, Washington his broad buckler, and Monroe his twin crags against the
sky.   Jefferson, as the nearest, stands boldly forward, showing its tremendous ravines and long supporting ridges with great distinctness.
Washington loses something of his grandeur here.   From Madison to Lafayette, our two rallying-points, the distance can hardly be less than forty miles
as the eye travels; the entire circuit can not fall short of seventy or eighty miles.